W9-BUT-945

American
Foreign Policy
Since World War II

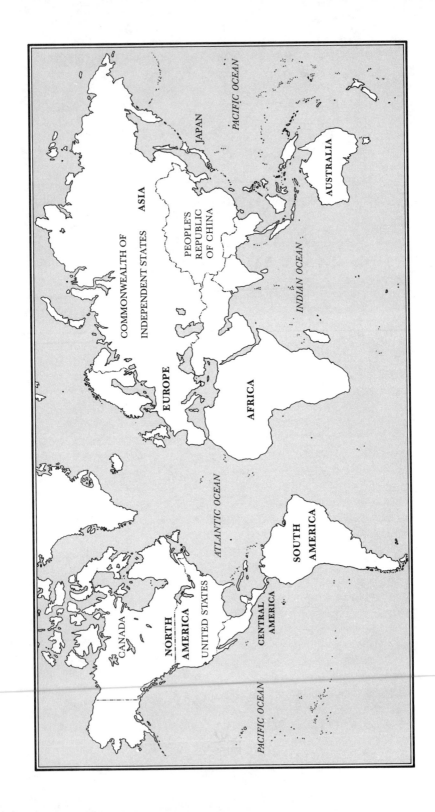

American
Foreign Policy
Since World War II

Twelfth Edition, Revised

John Spanier
University of Florida

A Division of Congressional Quarterly Inc.

Copyright © 1992 Congressional Quarterly Inc.
1414 22nd Street, N.W., Washington, D.C. 20037

Printed in the United States of America

Original cartography by Bill Clipson.

Cover design by Carol Crosby Black

Second Printing

Library of Congress Cataloging-in-Publication Data

Spanier, John W.
   American foreign policy since World War II / John Spanier. -- 12th ed., rev.
      p.   cm.
   Includes bibliographical references and index.
   ISBN 0-87187-727-9
   1. United States--Foreign relations--1945-1989. 2. United States-
-Foreign relations--1989- I. Title.
E744.S8   1992
327.73--dc20   92-7848
                                                         CIP

For David and Lisa

Love, all alike, no season knows, or clime,
Nor hours, days, months, which are the rags of time.

—John Donne, *The Sun Rising*

Contents

Maps

Preface

The first edition of this book was published in 1960 at the height of the cold war. Thirty-two years later this revised twelfth edition appears as the cold war has ended, the Soviet Union has collapsed and disappeared, and the United States, with an army larger than the forces that liberated Western Europe in 1944, has fought a short victorious war against Iraq, which had invaded and annexed the tiny city-state of Kuwait. It is because of the astounding events in what is now the former Soviet Union and the unexpected but challenging events in the Persian Gulf that this edition, which appeared in January 1991, has been updated. All this has taken place on the very heels of the profound changes that already had taken place in Eastern Europe and the Soviet Union. The political and economic transformations that began there in 1989, and that ended one of the most protracted great power conflicts in history, have been nothing less than revolutionary.

Had any Western leader, or for that matter the leaders of the Soviet Union, been asked early in 1989 what the world would look like a year hence, none of them could have predicted what did in fact occur: the disintegration of the Soviet empire in Eastern Europe. One country after another rejected Soviet-imposed regimes, repudiated the Communist party's leading role, and arranged for free elections in 1990. No leader could have predicted the collapse in 1989 of both the Berlin Wall and the East German economy, followed by the collapse of the new East German government's authority and the increasingly rapid acceleration toward German unification in October 1990. Although the Soviet economy long had shown signs of great strain, things got even worse as the economy stagnated further, ethnic strife increased as more violence erupted, and outright demands for independence were voiced more assertively than ever before, especially in the Baltic republics (Estonia, Latvia, and Lithuania).

But perhaps most astounding of all was the abortive coup against Mikhail

Gorbachev in August 1991. This event was followed by the rapid disintegration of the Soviet Union itself. The Baltic republics regained their independence as nations, and the other republics, asserting their nationalism while also expressing their fear of the dominance of the huge Russian republic, the successor state to the Soviet Union, sought their independence from Moscow's central government. The Soviet Union, plus the Communist party that had in 1917 created that state and governed it so harshly for more than seven decades, disappeared in the late summer of 1991, to be replaced by the Commonwealth of Independent States, composed of eleven of the former republics. By removing the principal obstacle to more radical political and economic reforms, the commonwealth presented the proponents of democracy and the free market an opportunity to transform the system. Whether a country with no democratic tradition or experience with a market economy could seize that opportunity remains to be demonstrated.

It is amid these truly momentous events that this revised edition appears. This book still endeavors to discuss American foreign policy from the closing days of World War II up through the present, which in this edition will take us through the first three years of the Bush administration. My focus is, as before, on the superpower rivalry, which has dominated postwar international politics, although this focus neither excludes events in other regions nor ignores problems such as the role of terrorism or the plight of developing countries and their relations with the industrialized world. But this book is not a diplomatic history—a detailed presentation of American action in the world since 1945. Rather, it is an interpretation of the roles the United States has played on the world stage over nearly five decades. The assumption is that the present cannot be understood without a historical context. As Germany again became a single state, for example, and the "German question" arises once more, the manner in which policy makers dealt with Germany following World War II, and the reasons they did so, provides us with a much-needed perspective on today's news. As the Soviet threat declines, attention is once more focusing on Germany.

The thesis of the book continues to be what I call the "American style" in foreign policy, a style unlike that of any other major nation in its distaste for "power politics." The United States has historically preferred an isolationist course. If it cannot avoid power politics, however, the United States will launch moral crusades against its enemies. The constancy of this style in the making of foreign policy since World War II has been remarkable. Richard Nixon, much influenced by Henry Kissinger, has perhaps been the only postwar U.S. president not to adopt it. I have balanced this emphasis on the American "style" of the making of foreign policy with a section on the Soviet Union's style, which, until Gorbachev's advent, was a composite of czarist Russian and Soviet historical experiences and perceptions. This presentation is included partly to show how antithetical the two styles were and partly to provide a better explanation and understanding of Soviet behavior during World War II and immediately after, when the alliance forged during the war fell apart and the cold war began.

This book also has placed a strong emphasis on the international, or "state," system in explaining the origins and conduct of the cold war. That is to say, the environment in which states exist is the primary influence on their behavior. By placing the U.S.-Soviet rivalry within the context of twentieth century geopolitics, I am able to stress the similarities between the two wars that pitted Germany, a land power, against Great Britain, a maritime power, and the cold war conflict between the Soviet Union and the United States.

This edition continues to place great emphasis on international economics. There is ample discussion of the Organization of Petroleum Exporting Countries (OPEC) and its manipulation of oil prices and also of the plight of the developing countries and their debt problems. Greater weight is assigned, however, to the difficulties being experienced by the U.S. economy and its growing uncompetitiveness in an increasingly interdependent world economy. In my judgment, the implications of this development are profound.

The United States may have won the cold war as the collapse of the Soviet economy made it necessary for Gorbachev to call for an end to the conflict to focus on the Soviet Union's domestic problems. But it may not be wrong to add that the United States simply outlasted the Soviet Union. Reagan left the country with a huge trade deficit and an even bigger federal deficit; the United States is the world's largest debtor nation. With a labor force poorly prepared by an educational system that placed American students in math and science among the lowest in the industrial world, with insufficient nonmilitary research and development, and corporate managers and financiers focusing on quarterly returns rather than long-term development of commercial products, the United States was losing its technological edge to Japan and other Pacific Rim countries. In the 1990s it will also be faced with a Europe moving toward greater unity and economic efficiency. The trade deficit, while narrowing to some degree, stubbornly resisted elimination. The United States too needed time off from the cold war to concentrate on its own *perestroika*.

The swiftness with which the world changes is truly astounding. It provides the impetus to incorporate unfolding events into the patterns of foreign policy analysis. Revising this text has been a major task given the number of momentous developments since the publication of the last edition. My burden has been lightened by a number of helpful individuals. I wish to thank the reviewers, with whom I did not always agree but whose observations put matters in a new perspective. I also thank David Tarr, Nancy Lammers, Carolyn Goldinger, and Kathryn Suárez for making my working relationship with CQ Press so pleasant and rewarding.

U.S. Administrations Since World War II

Dates	President	Secretary of State	Secretary of Defense	National Security Adviser
1945-1952	Harry Truman	Edward Stettinius James Byrnes George Marshall Dean Acheson	James Forrestal Louis Johnson Robert Lovett George Marshall	
1953-1960	Dwight Eisenhower	John Dulles Christian Herter	Charles Wilson Neil McElroy Thomas Gates	
1961-1963	John Kennedy	Dean Rusk	Robert McNamara	McGeorge Bundy
1963-1968	Lyndon Johnson	Dean Rusk	Robert McNamara Clark Clifford	McGeorge Bundy W. W. Rostow
1969-1974	Richard Nixon	William Rogers Henry Kissinger	Melvin Laird Elliot Richardson James Schlesinger	Henry Kissinger
1974-1976	Gerald Ford	Henry Kissinger	James Schlesinger Donald Rumsfeld	Henry Kissinger Brent Scowcroft
1977-1980	Jimmy Carter	Cyrus Vance Edward Muskie	Harold Brown	Zbigniew Brzezinski
1981-1988	Ronald Reagan	Alexander Haig George Shultz	Caspar Weinberger Frank Carlucci	Richard Allen William Clark Robert McFarlane John Poindexter Frank Carlucci Colin Powell
1989-	George Bush	James Baker	Richard Cheney	Brent Scowcroft

The American Approach
to Foreign Policy

N<small>ATIONS</small>, like individuals, face the world differently. How nations see the world, their place in it, and how they act in the international arena depend in large measure on their geography, historical backgrounds, and experiences. These national styles, as we shall call them, vary considerably. The perceptions and behavior of most states are heavily influenced, if not primarily influenced, according to some observers, by the environment or state system in which they coexist. States quickly learn "the rules of the game" or what they must do to ensure their survival and to achieve a measure of security. They ignore or disregard these rules at their peril.

Because for most of its existence the United States had isolated itself from the European state system, its national style was molded to a far greater extent than that of other states by its domestic experiences and democratic values and outlook. Not schooled by continuous involvement in international politics, as were the Europeans, the Americans approached foreign policy in a way that was not only peculiarly theirs, but also significantly different from that of other great powers. The contrast was particularly strong between the American experience and that of the Soviet Union, which emerged after World War II as the United States' chief adversary. The United States felt absolutely secure in the Western Hemisphere, but czarist Russia (later Soviet Russia) could never feel secure because of its proximity to other great powers who, over the centuries, had their own problems and ambitions.[1] During the postwar decades of conflict with the Soviet Union, the United States learned

---

1. John Spanier, *Games Nations Play,* 7th ed. (Washington, D.C.: CQ Press, 1990), esp. 92-117.

1

to play the international game with increasing skill, but its distinctive national style exerted a strong influence for most of that period.

The State System

American foreign policy since World War II is the story of the interaction and tension between the state system and the American style of dealing with other countries. In the state system, each member—especially the great powers, its principal actors—tends to feel a high degree of insecurity. In the absence of a world government that could safeguard it, each state knows that it can depend only on itself for its preservation and safety. Self-protection is the only protection in an essentially anarchical system; understandably, states tend to regard one another as potential adversaries, menaces to one another's territorial integrity and political independence. In short, the very nature of the state system breeds feelings of insecurity, distrust, suspicion, and fear.

This atmosphere produces a constant scramble for power. To reduce its insecurity, each state seeks to enhance its power relative to that of a possible foe. If a state perceives its neighbor as a potential enemy, it tries to deter an attack or political coercion by becoming a little stronger than its neighbor. The neighbor, in turn, also fears attack or political intimidation. It understands that its best interests lie in increasing its strength to forestall either contingency or if necessary, in winning a war, should matters go that far.

It is not the alleged aggressive instinct of humans as "naked apes" or their presumed desire for acquiring ever greater power that accounts for what is popularly called "power politics." Rather, power politics stems from each state's continuous concern with its security, which is the prerequisite for each for the enjoyment of its particular way of life. Because the external environment is seen as menacing to their security, states react fearfully against what they believe to be threats. In such a context it does not take much for one state to arouse another's apprehensions and to stimulate reciprocal images of hostility that each finds easy to substantiate by its opponent's behavior. Indeed, in most instances this enmity is maintained despite contradictory evidence and even avowedly friendly acts. Conciliatory behavior is likely to be seen as an indicator of weakness and may invite exploitation. Or it may be regarded as a trick to persuade a state to relax its guard.

It is easy to understand why in these circumstances a balance of power is what keeps the state system from breaking down. A balance or equilibrium makes victory in a war less probable and more costly. Therefore, a balance is presumed to be that distribution of power most likely to deter an attack. By contrast, possession of disproportionate power might tempt a state to undertake aggression by making it far less costly to gain a predominant position and impose its will upon other states. In other words, the fundamental assumption underlying the state system is that its members cannot be trusted with power because they will be tempted to abuse it. Unrestrained power in the system constitutes a threat to all states; power is, therefore, the best antidote to power. As one close observer of international politics, Arnold Wolfers, has noted:

> Under these conditions [of anarchy] the expectation of violence and even of annihilation is ever-present. To forget this and thus fail in the concern for enhanced power spells the doom of a state. This does not mean open constant warfare; expansion of power at the expense of others will not take place if there is enough counterpower to deter or to stop states from undertaking it. Although no state is interested in a mere balance of power, the efforts of all states to maximize power may lead to equilibrium. If and when that happens, there is "peace" or, more exactly, a condition of stalemate or truce. Under the conditions described here, this balancing of power process is the only available "peace" strategy.[2]

Power thus elicits countervailing power. The basic rule of the "international game" is to resist attempts by any state to expand and seek a predominant position in the international system. Therefore, when the balance is disturbed, equilibrium tends to be restored by the emergence of counterpower. States ignore at their peril the rule to maintain the balance of power.

The Balance of Power and the End of U.S. Isolationism

What all this means is that any state's behavior can be explained to a very significant degree in terms of the ever-changing distribution of power. As that distribution changes, so does a state's behavior or foreign policy. For example, the impact of a shift in the distribution of power is evident in U.S. participation in the two world wars of this century. During most of the nineteenth century and early twentieth century, the United States was able to preserve its historical isolation from power politics and enjoy an unprecedented degree of security because the balance of power on the European continent was maintained by Britain.

Germany's unification in 1870 and its subsequent rapid industrialization eventually forced the United States to end its isolation. The immediate impact of Germany's growing strength was the relative decline of British power. The early years of World War I showed clearly that even when British power was thrown in on the side of France and Russia, the three allies could barely contain Germany. With the collapse of czarist Russia in 1915 and the transfer of almost 2 million German soldiers from the Russian front to the western front, a German victory became a distinct possibility. The United States would then have faced a Germany astride an entire continent, dominating

---

2. Arnold Wolfers, *Discord and Collaboration* (Baltimore: Johns Hopkins University Press, 1965), 83.

European Russia and, in alliance with Austria-Hungary, the Ottoman Empire, extending German influence into the Balkans and the Middle East as far as the Persian Gulf. It was at that point that Germany's unrestricted submarine warfare, which included attacks on American shipping, led to a U.S. declaration of war. America's entry into the war was what made it possible to contain the German spring offensive of 1918, leading to Germany's defeat.

After its victory, the United States retreated into its customary isolationism. American bankers, with the tacit approval of the government, maintained ties to Europe, playing an important role in its economic recovery and stabilization during the 1920s. Their primary motive, however, was to recover money loaned to the European allies during World War I. Although the U.S. economy rivaled that of all of Europe and the United States exercised some economic influence, it refused to define for itself a political and military role consistent with its economic power. U.S. military power had been decisive in Germany's defeat, but the United States wanted nothing to do with international politics. It began to play a political role again only when the balance of European power was upset once more by the eruption of World War II in 1939 and the unexpected defeat of France in 1940. The United States faced the possibility of Britain's defeat and the control of Eurasia by Germany, Italy, and Japan, all antidemocratic states. To prevent this, President Franklin Roosevelt undertook a number of measures to help Britain withstand any Nazi assault. He sent fifty old destroyers to defend the English Channel, and he set up the lend-lease program that provided munitions, food, and other material support. This commitment to Britain was necessary, even though such actions increased the risk of war with Germany. In fact, by the time of the bombing of Pearl Harbor in December 1941, the United States was already engaged in an undeclared naval war with Germany in the Atlantic, and full-scale war was merely a matter of time.

The U.S. Definition of Security

Two points deserve emphasis. First, the defense of U.S. security has always involved more than physical security. The German threat during World War I was not the likelihood of an immediate invasion; nor was invasion the main threat even after the defeat of France early in World War II. Then why should the United States twice have forsaken its isolationism? Surely, the width of the Atlantic and Pacific oceans would protect the United States.

American security was threatened because any state, especially a state that was undemocratic as well as antidemocratic, that controlled all the resources—human, natural, and industrial—of Eurasia, the Middle East, and Africa, and that organized these resources and transformed them into military power, might some day be able to attack North America. This would be particularly true had Britain been defeated and the British navy no longer guarded the sea highway to the Western Hemisphere. Even if Britain sank its navy rather than see it joined with the fleets of Germany and its allies (Italy in World War II) and defeated nations (like France in World War II), the German navy might come to dominate the Atlantic approaches to the Western Hemisphere. This would certainly be true if Germany absorbed the British fleet. Such circumstances would require the United States to mobilize its resources fully and be on constant alert for a possible attack by an opponent with more people and superior resources. Most probably, the only way the United States could match this dominant Eurasian power would be by transforming itself into a "garrison state," a disciplined, militarized state, which, in the name of security, would have to sacrifice democracy and individual liberty as ideological excess baggage.

The more immediate reason for U.S. intervention was that the security of a democratic America was inextricably interwoven with the survival of other democracies, especially France and Britain. After France collapsed in 1940, Roosevelt explained to the American public why the United States had to assist Britain: the United States could not survive as a lone democratic island surrounded by totalitarian seas. Democracy in America could not flourish unless democratic values prospered in other societies. There might be no physical threat to the nation, but the aim of American foreign policy has never been just the security of the United States as a piece of real estate; the purpose has been to defend the security of a democratic America. A democratic America required democratic values to flourish internationally.

The other point to be emphasized is that, despite the U.S. concern with security in Europe, the timing of the interventions in 1917 and 1941 were not rational decisions made by Washington. It was Berlin's decision in 1917 to launch unrestricted submarine warfare against all shipping to England that brought the United States into the war; and it was Tokyo's decision to sink the U.S. fleet at anchor in Hawaii that led to the American declaration of war against Japan. But for Hitler's reckless declaration of war against the United States—a country he held in great contempt—U.S. power would have been directed only against Japan, and Germany, the far stronger power, would have faced only Britain and Russia, both already reeling from German blows. But for German and Japanese mistakes, the United States would *not* have entered the two world wars. At the very least, the timing would have been different. The decisions to go to war were not made by the United States even though the balances of power in Europe and Asia were imperiled and American security was at stake. The United States was saved from itself by its enemies.

Great powers usually do not leave decisions about their security to their adversaries. The strategy of the major states in the state system is—or should be—to oppose any state that seeks predominance because this constitutes a grave threat to its own security. Power is the best antidote to power, and a balance of power provides the best protection for all members of the state system. The failure of the United States twice to act according to the logic dictated by the balance of power is due largely to its particular national style. Each nation is the product of its geography, historical experiences, economic resources, and political values and organization; each tends to see the world and its role in it differently. Each nation has a unique history from which, correctly or incorrectly, it draws certain lessons. Each therefore develops a specific personality and behavior patterns that are its national style.

The American National Style

The particular style reflected in the American response to war in Europe and later to the cold war was the product of domestic experience. The priority of internal political and economic tasks, a characteristic of the United States since its beginning, demonstrated that the United States had successfully isolated itself from European power politics. As a nation with nonthreatening neighbors to the north and south, and fish to the east and west, the United States could take security for granted. Free from external threat, it could focus on its development as a democratic society.

The American Sense of Destiny

The ability of the United States to live in isolation during the nineteenth century and the first decade of the twentieth century cannot be attributed *only* to the nation's distance from Europe, or to Europe's preoccupation with industrialization and class conflict at home and colonialism abroad, or to the strength of the Royal Navy. The nature of democracy must also be considered. The United States saw itself as more than just the world's first "new nation"; it was also the world's first democracy and, as such, the first country in history with the desire to improve the lot of ordinary people, to grant them the opportunity to enrich and ennoble their lives. ("Give me your tired, your poor, your huddled masses yearning to breathe free," reads the inscription on the Statue of Liberty.) The more perfect union was to be an egalitarian society. European concepts of social hierarchy, nobility and titles, and bitter class struggles were not to be planted in its democratic soil.

From the very beginning of their national life, Americans professed a strong belief in what they considered their destiny—to spread, *by example,* freedom and social justice to all and to lead humankind away from its wicked ways to the New Jerusalem on earth. The massive immigration of the nineteenth century—particularly after 1865—was to reinforce this sense of destiny. "Repudiation of Europe," John Dos Passos once said, "is, after all, America's main excuse for being." Europe stood for war, poverty, and exploitation; America, for peace, opportunity, and democracy. But the United States was not merely to be a beacon of a superior democratic domestic way of life. It was also to be an example of a morally superior democratic pattern of international behavior. The United States would voluntarily reject power politics as unfit for the conduct of its foreign policy. Democratic theory posits that people are rational and moral and that differences among them can be settled by rational persuasion and moral exhortation. Indeed, granted this assumption, the only differences that could arise would simply be misunderstandings, and, since people are endowed with reason and a moral sense, what quarrels could not be settled, given the necessary good will? Peace—the result of harmony among people—was considered the natural or normal state.

Conversely, conflict was considered a deviation caused primarily by wicked leaders whose morality and reason had been corrupted by their exercise of uncontrolled authority. Power politics was an instrument of selfish and autocratic rulers—that is, leaders unrestrained by democratic public opinion—who love to wield it for personal advantage. To them, war was a grand game. They could remain in their palatial homes, continuing to eat well and to enjoy the luxuries of life. They suffered none of the hardships of war. These fell upon the ordinary people, who had to leave their families to fight, to endure the higher taxes to pay for the war, and possibly to see their homes and families destroyed. The conclusion was clear: undemocratic states were inherently warlike and evil; democratic nations, in which the people controlled and regularly changed their leaders, were peaceful and moral.

The American experience seemed to support this conclusion: the United States was a democracy, and it was at peace. Furthermore, peace seemed to be the normal state of affairs. It was logical that democracy and peaceful behavior and intentions should be thought of as synonymous. Americans never asked themselves whether democracy was responsible for the peace they enjoyed, or whether peace was the product of other forces. The constant wars of Europe appeared to provide the answer: European politics was power politics, and this was because of the undemocratic nature of European regimes. Americans had cut themselves off from Europe and its class conflicts and power politics after the Revolutionary War. America had to guard its democratic purity and abstain from any involvement in the affairs of Europe lest it be soiled and corrupted. Nonalignment or isolationism, therefore, was the morally correct policy, for it allowed the United States to quarantine itself from Europe's hierarchical social structures and immoral international habits.

By confusing the results of geography and Europe's focus on Asia, the Middle East, and Africa with the virtues of American democracy, Americans could smugly enjoy their self-conferred moral superiority as the world's first democracy. It was the Monroe Doctrine, proclaimed in 1823, that first stressed, officially and explicitly, this ideological difference between the New World and the Old World. It declared specifically that the American political system was "essentially different" from that of Europe, whose nations were constantly engaged in warfare. The implication was very clear: democratic government equals peace, and aristocratic government—which was identified with despotism—means war.

The Depreciation of Power in International Politics

But this association of peace with democracy was not the only reason for the American depreciation of power politics. Another was that the United States was overwhelmingly a one-class society, in which most shared belief in a common set of middle-class, capitalistic, and democratic values. America was unique among nations in this respect. The European countries were, by contrast, three-class societies. In addition to the middle class, they contained in their bodies politic an aristocratic class, whose energies were devoted either to maintaining itself in power or to recapturing power and returning to the glorious days of a feudal past. Moreover, European urbanization and industrialization during the nineteenth century had given birth to a proletariat, which, because it felt it did not receive a fair share of the national income, became a revolutionary class. The nations of the Old World were a composite of these three elements: a reactionary aristocracy, a democratic middle class, and a revolutionary proletariat. These nations had, in an intellectual as well as a political sense, a right, a center, and a left.

The United States had only a center, both intellectually and politically. It had never experienced a feudal past and therefore possessed no large, powerful aristocratic class on the right. Because it was, by and large, an egalitarian society, it also lacked a genuine left-wing movement of protest, such as socialism and communism. America was, as Alexis de Tocqueville had said, "born free" as a middle-class, individualist, capitalistic, and democratic society. It was not divided by the kind of deep ideological conflicts that in France, for instance, set one class of people against another. No one class was ever so afraid of another that it preferred national defeat to domestic revolution—as in France in the late 1930s, when the *haute bourgeoisie* was so apprehensive of a proletarian upheaval that its slogan became "Better Hitler than Blum" (Leon Blum, the French Socialist leader).

This overwhelming agreement on the fundamental values of American society and Europe's intense class struggles reinforced the American misunderstanding of the nature and functions of power on the international scene. Dissatisfied groups never developed a revolutionary ideology because the growing prosperity spread to them before they could translate their grievances against the capitalist system into political action. (Black Americans were the exception because they never shared this wealth or political power.) With the exception of the Civil War, America—politically secure, socially cohesive, and economically prosperous—was able to resolve most of its differences peacefully. Living in isolation, this country could believe in an evolutionary, democratic, economically prosperous historical process; revolution and radicalism were considered bad. In sharp contrast, because of their internal class struggles and external conflicts among themselves, the nations of Europe fully appreciated that social conflict is natural and that power plays a role in resolving conflict.

Americans in the past have been so in accord on basic values that whenever the nation has been threatened externally it has also become fearful of internal disloyalty. It is one of the great ironies of American society that, while Americans possess this unity of shared beliefs to a greater degree than any other people, their apprehension of external danger has repeatedly led them, first, to insist upon a general and somewhat dogmatic reaffirmation of loyalty to the "American way of life," and then to hunt for internal groups that might betray this way of life. Disagreement tended to become suspect as disloyalty; people were accused of "un-American" thinking and behavior and labeled "loyalty or security risks." Perhaps only a society so overwhelmingly committed to one set of values could have been so sensitive to internal subversion and so fearful of internal betrayal. Perhaps only a society in which two or more ideologies have long since learned to live together can genuinely tolerate diverse opinions: Who has ever heard of "un-British" or "un-French" activities? The United States has often been called a "melting pot" because of the many different nationality groups it comprises, but, before each generation of immigrants has been fully accepted into American society, it has had to be "Americanized." Few Americans have ever accepted diversity as a value. American society has, in fact, taken great pride in destroying diversity through assimilation.

Politics did not, in any event, seem very important to Americans. The United States matured during the nineteenth century, the era of laissez-faire capitalism, the basic assumption of which was that people were economically motivated. Self-interest governed behavior. It might be referred to as "enlightened self-interest," but it was self-interest nevertheless. Individuals, seeking to maximize their wealth, responded to the demand of the free market. In an effort to increase profits, they produced what the consumers wanted. The laws of supply and demand therefore transformed each person's economic selfishness into socially beneficial results. In this way, the entire society would prosper. The free market was considered the central institution that provided "the greatest good for the greatest number." Politics mattered little in this self-adjusting economic system based upon individuals whose combined efforts resulted in the general welfare. The best government was the government that governed least. Arbitrary political interference with the economic laws of the market only upset the results these laws were intended to produce. Private property, profit, and the free market were the keys to ensuring the happiness of people by providing them with abundance. Capitalism, in short, reflected the materialism of the age of industrialization.

To state the issue even more bluntly: economics was good and politics was bad. This simple dichotomy came naturally to the capitalist middle class.

Were the benefits of economic freedom not as "self-evident" as the truths stated in the Declaration of Independence? And had this economic freedom not been gained only by a long and bitter struggle of the European middle class to cut down the authority of the powerful monarchical state, and finally to overthrow it by revolution in France? The middle class, as it had grown more prosperous and numerous, had become increasingly resentful of paying taxes from which the aristocracy was usually exempt, of the restrictions placed upon trade and industry, of the absence of institutions in which middle-class economic and political interests were represented, of the class barriers to the social status that came with careers in the army and in the bureaucracy, and of the general lack of freedom of thought and expression. Because the middle class identified the power of the state with its own lack of freedom, its aim was to restrict this power. Only by placing restraints upon the authority of the state could it gain the individual liberty as well as the right to private enterprise it sought. Democratic philosophy stated these claims in terms of the individual's "natural rights." The exercise of political authority was equated with the abuse of that authority and the suppression of personal freedoms. The power of the state had to be restricted to the minimum to ensure the individual's maximum political and economic liberties. It was with this purpose in mind that the American Constitution divided authority between the states and the federal government, and, within the latter, among the executive, legislative, and judicial branches. Federalism and the separation of powers were deliberately designed to keep all governments—and especially the national government—weak. Secular problems would be resolved, not by the state's political actions, but by the individual's own economic actions in society in peacetime.

The American experience reflected this philosophy; millions came to the United States from other lands to seek a better way of life. America was the earthly paradise where everyone could earn a respectable living. A virgin land, America presented magnificent opportunities for individual enterprise. First, there was the Western frontier with its rich soil; later, during the Industrial Revolution, the country's bountiful natural resources. The environment, technology, individual enterprise, and helpful governmental policies enabled the American people to become the "people of plenty." But to earn money was not only economically necessary to attain a comfortable standard of living; it was also psychologically necessary to gain social status and to earn the respect of one's fellow citizens.

It follows logically that, if material gain confers social respect and position, everyone will pursue the "almighty dollar." If people in an egalitarian society are judged primarily by their economic achievements, they will concentrate on getting ahead. It is not surprising, therefore, that money comes closer to being the common standard of value in the United States than in any other country. Money is the symbol of power and prestige; it is the sign of success, just as failure to earn enough money is a token of personal failure.

It has been said, not without some justice, that the American male prefers two cars to two mistresses.

It was hardly surprising that in these circumstances the solution to international problems should be considered a matter of economics rather than politics. Economics was identified with social harmony and the welfare of all peoples; politics was equated with conflict, war, and death. Just as the "good society" was to be the product of free competition, so the peaceful international society would be created by free trade. An international laissez-faire policy would benefit all states just as a national laissez-faire policy benefited each individual within these states. Consequently, people all over the world had a vested interest in peace in order to carry on their economic relations. Trade and war were incompatible. Trade depended upon mutual prosperity (the poor do not buy much from one another). War impoverishes and destroys and creates ill will among nations. Commerce benefits all the participating states; the more trade, the greater the number of individual interests involved. Commerce created a vested interest in peace; war was economically unprofitable and therefore obsolete. Free trade and peace, in short, were one and the same cause.

The Penchant for Crusading

One result of this American depreciation of power politics was that the United States historically has drawn a clear-cut distinction between war and peace in its approach to foreign policy. Peace, on the one hand, was characterized by a state of harmony among nations; power politics, on the other, was considered abnormal and war a crime. In peacetime, one needed to pay little or no attention to foreign problems; indeed, to do so would have diverted people from their individual, materialistic concerns and upset the whole scale of social values. The effect of this attitude was clear: Americans turned their attention toward the outside world with reluctance and usually only when provoked—that is, when the foreign menace had become so clear that it could no longer be ignored. Or, to state it somewhat differently, the United States rarely initiated policy; the stimuli responsible for the formulation of American foreign policy came from beyond America's frontiers.

Once Americans were provoked and the United States had to resort to force, the employment of this force was justified in terms of the moral principles with which the United States, as a democratic country, identified itself. War could be justified only by presuming noble purposes and completely destroying the immoral enemy who threatened the integrity, if not the existence, of these principles. American power had to be "righteous" power; only its full exercise could ensure salvation or the absolution of sin. A second result of the depreciation of power politics was, therefore, that the national aversion to violence became transformed on occasion into a national glorification of violence, and wars became ideological crusades to destroy the enemy state and then send its people to democratic reform school. Making the world safe for democracy—the stated objective during World War I—was to be achieved by democratizing the populace of the offending nation, making its new rulers responsible to the people they governed and thereby converting the formerly authoritarian or totalitarian state into a peaceful democratic state and banishing power politics for all time. Once that aim had been achieved, the United States could again withdraw into itself, secure in the knowledge that American works had again proved to be "good works." In this context, foreign affairs were an annoying diversion from more important domestic matters. But such a diversion was only temporary because maximum force was applied to the aggressor as punishment and as instruction that aggression was immoral and would not be rewarded. As a result, American wars were total wars to end war itself, and once the wars were over, the United States would once more withdraw from international politics. Normalcy having been restored, the pendulum would swing back.

This is the pattern of American foreign policy: from isolationism to interventionism, from withdrawal to crusading and back again. As a self-proclaimed morally and politically superior country, the United States could remain uncontaminated only by abstaining from involvement in a corrupt world or, if the world would not leave it alone, destroying the source of evil. In short, both the isolationist and the crusading impulses sprang from the same moralism. These swings tended, moreover, to be accompanied by radical shifts of mood: from one of optimism, which sprang from the belief that America was going to reform the world, to one of disillusionment as the grandiose objectives the United States had set for itself proved beyond its capacity to reach. Feeling too good for this world, which clearly did not want to be reformed but preferred its old corrupt habits, the nation retreated into isolationism to perfect and protect its way of life. Having expected too much from the use of its power, the United States then also tended to feel guilty and ashamed about having used its power at all.

The third result of the depreciation of power politics was that Americans divorced force from diplomacy. In peacetime, diplomacy unsupported by force was supposed to preserve the harmony among states. But, in time of war, political considerations were subordinated to force. Once the diplomats had failed to keep the peace with appeals to morality and reason, military considerations became primary, and the soldier was placed in charge.

The United States, then, has traditionally rejected the concept of war as a political instrument and Carl von Clausewitz's definition of war as the continuation of politics by other means.[3] Instead, it has regarded war as a

---

3. This phrase sums up the essence of Clausewitz's famous book, *On War*. First published in 1832, it remains the most outstanding effort in Western history to understand war's internal dynamics and its relationship to political policy and goals. The best modern translation and editing is by Michael Howard and Peter Paret, *On War* (Princeton: Princeton University Press, 1976).

politically neutral operation that should be guided by its own professional rules and imperatives. The military officer was a nonpolitical man who conducted his campaign in a strictly military, technically efficient manner. And war was a purely military instrument whose sole aim was the destruction of the enemy's forces and despotic regime. Policy and strategy were unrelated; strategy began where policy ended. After the Japanese attack on Pearl Harbor, the secretary of state turned to the secretary of war (as he was then called) and said the situation was now out of his hands; it was all up to the War Department. As the war in Europe was coming to a close, the British asked General George C. Marshall, architect of the Western allies' victory, to send U.S. forces to liberate Prague and as much of Czechoslovakia as possible before the Soviet army arrived. Marshall responded that he would not risk American lives for "purely political purposes"—a commendable sentiment, but what is war about if not the achievement of political purposes?

War was a means employed to abolish power politics; war was conducted to end all wars. This same moralistic attitude, which was responsible for the Americans' all-or-nothing approach to war, also militated against the use of diplomacy in its classical sense: to compromise interests, to conciliate differences, and to moderate and isolate conflicts. Although Americans regarded diplomacy as a rational process for straightening out misunderstandings between nations, they were also extremely suspicious of it. If the United States was by definition moral, it obviously could not compromise; for a nation endowed with a moral mission could hardly violate its own principles. That constituted appeasement and national humiliation. The nation's principles would be transgressed, the nation's interests improperly defended, the national honor stained. To compromise with the immoral enemy was to be contaminated with evil. Moreover, to reach a settlement with enemies, rather than wiping them out in order to safeguard those principles, would be to acknowledge American weakness. This attitude toward diplomacy, which, in effect, made its use as an instrument of compromise difficult, reinforced the predilection for violence as a means of settling international problems. War allowed the nation to destroy its evil opponent, but permitted it to keep its moral mission intact and unsullied by any compromises.

The Contrast Between the United States and Traditional Great Powers

On the eve of the cold war, then, the American approach to foreign policy contrasted sharply in a number of important respects with the conduct of states long immersed in international politics. As a highly secure state, it needed neither a large army nor navy to protect it. The military and its values were basically despised because they were believed to be contrary to those of a democracy, and it was the building of democracy that the nation considered its first task. The result has been the pattern just described: a swing from an isolationist position in which the country served as an example of social justice on earth to a posture of massive and violent intervention. Consistent continuous participation in the international system has not been the norm.

Furthermore, the American perception of an international harmony of interests stood in stark contrast to the state system's emphasis on the inevitability of conflict and differences of interests among states. The former view regarded conflict as an abnormal condition; the latter perceived harmony as an illusion. The United States, long isolated from Europe and therefore not socialized by the state system, did not accept the reality and permanence of conflicts among its members. Differences between states were considered unnatural; certainly such differences should not be deep or long-lasting. Rather, they were attributed to wicked leaders (who could be eliminated), authoritarian political systems (which could be reformed), or misunderstandings (which could be straightened out if the adversaries approached each other with sincerity and empathy). Once these obstacles had been removed, peace, harmony, and good will would reign supreme.

Because the United States considered itself a morally and politically superior society, its attitude toward the use of power internationally was dominated by the belief that the struggle for power did not exist or could be avoided by isolating the country from it or could be eliminated by crusading against those countries indulging in power politics. Moralism in foreign policy proscribed the use of power in peacetime; power could be employed only in confrontations with unambiguous aggression, transformed then into an obligation to fight on behalf of righteous causes. In short, power could be legitimated only by democratic purposes; otherwise, its exercise would be evil and would necessarily arouse guilt feelings.

The great American compulsion to feel moral about the nation's behavior reinforced the cyclical swings from isolationism to crusading and back again. The perception of power as simply the raw material of international politics—its use as an instrument of compromise, conciliation, and moderation in interstate politics, its discriminating application toward achievement of specific and less-than-total objectives—was clearly antithetical to the American understanding of power. The term *power politics* was itself kind of "dirty," an anathema, a reminder of a way of doing things that the New World hoped it had left behind, and a potential threat to its virtue if the nation were to indulge in that kind of immoral Old World behavior.

One of the most telling symptoms of America's national style in conducting foreign policy is that after every major war the reasons for the country's participation in struggle and bloodshed have been reinterpreted. These revisionist histories have certain common themes: the conflicts in which the nation had become entangled did not in fact threaten its security interests; it became involved because the politicians saw a menace where none existed, and this illusion had been promoted by propagandists who aroused and manipulated public opinion, by soldiers with bureaucratic motives, and, above all else, by bankers and industrialists—the "merchants of death" of the 1930s, the "military-industrial complex" of the 1960s—whose economic interests benefited from the struggle. America's engagements in the two world wars of this century (as in the cold war later) were mistakes; they were really unnecessary or immoral, if not both. The enemy identified yesterday as the aggressor and *provocateur* apparently did not represent a threat to American security at all; to the contrary, the threat turns out to have come from within. But for certain *domestic forces* the United States could have continued to isolate itself from international politics. Note also that these internal groups propelling the nation into war were said, in characteristic American fashion, to be motivated by profit.

The fundamental revisionist assumption, then, has been that the nation had a choice whether it wanted to employ power politics. Conversely, revisionism rejected the idea that the distribution of power in the state system left the United States—or any other country, for that matter—with a choice only of whether it would help maintain the balance of power. Power was equated with its abuse. Abstention from its use and the creation of a truly just society at home were considered wiser and more moral policies. Crusading, allegedly for the reform of the world, risked corrupting America's very soul because it diverted attention and resources from reform at home to military preparation and war. Revisionism, then, was essentially an argument for continued isolation from power politics. International involvements, especially wars, were aberrations from the norm of harmony.

But if one could no longer avoid power politics or abolish it, there was yet another solution: to escape from it, to flee the troublesome and divisive world of power into the more peaceful and united world of economics. The belief that political conflict among states could be transformed into cooperation among nations when they focused on what was truly important—the improvement of humanity's material and social life—was another major characteristic of American style. If power politics and concern for security led to conflict and war, economics with its concern for raising everyone's standard of living bound all people together, regardless of nationality or race. They had to cooperate for their common good. The revulsion against the concept of maintaining the balance of power and a renewed emphasis on "interdependence" that followed the Vietnam War was hardly novel. Even while the republic was still young there were already those who felt that

> The [national political] barriers that existed seemed artificial and ephemeral in comparison with the fine net by which the merchants tied the individuals of the different nations together like "threads of silk.". . . [T]he merchants—whether they are English, Dutch, Russian, or Chinese—do not serve a single nation; they serve everyone and are citizens of the whole world. Commerce was believed to bind the nations together and to create not only a community of interests but also a distribution of labor among

them—a new comprehensive principle placing the isolated sovereign nations in a higher political unit. In the eighteenth century, writers were likely to say that the various nations belonged to "one society"; it was stated that all states together formed "a family of nations," and the whole globe a "general and unbreakable confederation." [4]

The United States after World War II, therefore, faced the world with attitudes and behavior patterns formed by its long period of isolationism from Europe. More specifically, the nation confronted the Soviet Union, a state with long experience in power politics.

The Soviet Style

The Russian Background

Russia was not blessed by geography. Unprotected by natural barriers such as oceans or mountains, it suffered frequent invasions. During the thirteenth and fourteenth centuries, Russia was ruled by the Mongols from the East. By the middle of the fifteenth century Mongol domination had been repelled, and Moscow emerged as the capital of a Russian state that was the equivalent of the European and Great Russian-speaking part of the contemporary Soviet Union. In more modern times, Napoleon's armies invaded and captured Moscow in 1812; British and French armies landed in the Crimea in 1854-1856; Japan attacked and defeated Russia in 1904-1905. Germany twice invaded Russia during the twentieth century, defeating it in 1917—which led to the collapse of the monarchy and brought the Bolsheviks to power—and almost defeating it again within a few months after the attack in June 1941. In between, the Western allies intervened on the anti-Bolshevik side, and the Poles in 1920 almost defeated a Russia exhausted by civil war. Historically, therefore, Russia could not take its security for granted or give priority to domestic affairs. Not surprisingly in these circumstances, political power became centralized in the state, and the possession of large standing military forces was thought to be a necessity. Indeed, Russia's experiences led its leaders to believe that there was no such thing as too much military power, and their forces have been considerably larger than those of the other European great powers, although this numerical superiority has not prevented their defeat.

Historian Richard Pipes has remarked, however, that Russia no more became the world's largest territorial state by repelling repeated invasions than a man becomes rich by being robbed. As the map (page 371) shows, Russia spans Eurasia. Its people, 285 million in 1989 (compared to 245 million for the United States), composed of just over 100 nationalities, occupy almost 9 million square miles, spread over 11 time zones, and speak

---

4. Felix Gilbert, *To the Farewell Address: Ideas of Early American Foreign Policy* (Princeton: Princeton University Press, 1961), 57.

130 languages. Occupying Eurasia's heartland, Russia borders on Europe, the Middle East, and Asia, the regions that together possess most of the world's population and resources. The same lack of natural frontiers that fails to protect Russia from invasion also allows Russian power to extend outward all around its frontier, which is precisely the course Russia has followed since the fourteenth century. Sustained territorial expansion has been called the "Russian way." President Jimmy Carter's national security adviser, Zbigniew Brzezinski, said that any list of aggressions against Russia in the last two centuries would be dwarfed by Russian expansionist moves against its neighbors.[5]

Historically, whether Russian motives were defensive or offensive, the result has been a pattern of expansionism. To the degree that Russian rulers have feared attacks, they have pushed outward to keep the enemy as far away as possible. Territorial extension became a partial substitute for the lack of wide rivers or mountains that might have afforded a degree of natural protection. Individual rulers' ambitions, such as Peter the Great's determination to have access to the sea, also resulted in territorial conquest and defeat of the power blocking that aim (in this instance, Sweden). This pattern of insecurity and appetite set up a vicious cycle. Expansion might momentarily satisfy Russian ambitions and relieve Russian fears, but it intensified its neighbors' insecurities, leading to new conflicts; this, in turn, stimulated Russian insecurity once more, leading to another round of expansion. Even before the Bolsheviks seized power in 1917 authoritarianism, militarism, and expansionism characterized the Russian state; being good neighbors was an alien concept. The basic "rules" of the state system—the emphasis on national interests, distrust of other states, expectation of conflict, self-reliance, and the possession of enough power, especially military power—were deeply ingrained in Russia's leaders.

The Soviet Ingredient

These attitudes were strengthened by the outlook of the new regime after 1917. Russia was a state; Soviet Russia was also a church. The new leaders' ideological outlook did not tell them what to do in a specific foreign policy situation, but it gave them a broad framework for perceiving and understanding the world. Theirs was essentially a revolutionary perspective. History was the history of the class struggle between the rich and privileged, who owned the means of production, be it slaves, land, or factories, and those who worked for them. Why were most human beings poor, illiterate, and unhealthy? Why did states fight wars? The answer was that a small minority of capitalists,

---

5. Zbigniew Brzezinski, "The Soviet Union: The Aims, Problems, and Challenges to the West" in *The Conduct of East-West Relations in the 1980s*, Adelphi Paper No. 189, Part I (London: International Institute for Strategic Studies, 1984), 4.

who controlled both the wealth and power in capitalist states, exploited those who worked in their factories to maximize profits. To keep wages down, they kept food prices low so that agricultural labor also lived in destitution. Wars were the result of these capitalists' constant search for profits not only domestically but also internationally. One result was conflict over dividing up the non-European colonial world. If human beings were ever to live in freedom and enjoy a decent standard of living in peace and fraternity with other countries, capitalism would have to be replaced by communism. This line of thinking made the domestic order of other states *the* key issue for the Soviet leaders.

Ideology then was more than a way of viewing the world; it also gave the Soviet leaders a mission. Their perspective that capitalism was the chief obstacle to humanity's liberation meant that from the moment the Soviets seized power they defined capitalist states as enemies. Soviet leaders considered the American and West European governments as enemies because of what they were—capitalist. Believing the West to be hostile, the Soviets interpreted all Western actions that way. Sooner or later, a state that considers other states as enemies and acts accordingly will be proven correct as other states reciprocate. Whereas in the traditional state system, states had no permanent friends and enemies, changing allies as the distribution of power changed, Soviet ideology clearly discriminated friend from foe on a permanent basis. Because the Soviet Union defined the capitalist states as foes, and because the Soviet mission internationally was to export its revolution and create a new postcapitalist international order, the relationship between it and the latter would be marked by conflict until the victory of what the Soviets call *socialism* and the defeat of capitalism. Soviet leaders, moreover, took it for granted that the capitalist states were equally hostile to them and equally determined to eliminate the Soviet Union, if only to avoid their own demise. Although the fervor of their mission faded over the decades following 1917 and the impact of ideology declined, the Soviet leaders' continued to see the capitalist states as enemies and the Soviet relationship with them as one of constant struggle.

The overall effect was to accentuate historic Russian suspicions of foreigners and feelings of insecurity so strong they might be described as paranoia. The Soviet leaders believed that the state system, composed of capitalist states, was a very hostile environment. They were unwilling to accept the latter's professions of good will and peaceful intentions, regarding them as duplicitous, and they committed the Soviet Union to the "inevitable and irreconcilable struggle" against these states. They fostered a strong emphasis on self-reliance and an equally intense concern with the Soviet Union's relative power. They were convinced that when an enemy makes concessions in negotiations or becomes more accommodating, it is not because the enemy wants a friendlier relationship but because it is *forced* to do so by the Soviet Union's growing strength—a viewpoint that obviously leads to a self-sustaining rationale for ever more military power. Before Mikhail Gorbachev, who faced a bankrupt economy when he acquired power, there was no such thing as too much military power for Soviet leaders, even more than for their czarist predecessors.

These attitudes reinforced the traditional Russian tendency toward expansionism: fear of capitalist states demands that they be kept away from Soviet frontiers. But, as the physical embodiment of a cause, the Soviet Union's task was also to wage an unrelenting struggle to liberate humanity from the chains of capitalist exploitation and oppression. Russian history stood as a warning to Soviet leaders that peace was but a preparation for the next war; their ideological perceptions strengthened the view that peace is but the continuation of the last war by other means. The Soviet mentality, in short, reinforced the historically repetitive cycles that have always resulted in a further expansion of power. Even if it were to be granted that insecurity drives this expansion, rather than any historical mission, the result for neighboring states remains the same—they are endangered. A drive to achieve absolute security in a system in which no state can achieve that aim short of total domination, leaves other states very insecure. In short, the contrast between American culture and national style, which emphasizes peace as normal and conflict as abnormal, and that of the Soviet Union, which stresses precisely the opposite view, could not be more striking.

The Beginning of the Cold War

BEFORE the 1945 Quebec conference between Prime Minister Winston Churchill and President Franklin Roosevelt, a U.S. War Department memorandum forecasting the Soviet Union's postwar position concluded that the Soviet Union would be the dominant power on the continent of Europe:

> With Germany crushed, there is no power in Europe to oppose her tremendous military forces.... The conclusions from the foregoing are obvious. Since Russia is the decisive factor in the war, she must be given every assistance, and every effort must be made to obtain her friendship. Likewise, since without question she will dominate Europe on the defeat of the Axis, it is even more essential to develop and maintain the most friendly relations with Russia.[1]

The importance of this assessment lies less in its prediction of the Soviet Union's postwar position—which was, after all, fairly obvious—than in its reflection of American expectations about future Soviet-American relations. American policy makers apparently accepted without any major misgivings the prospect of the Soviets as the new dominant power in Europe; they did not conceive of its replacing Nazi Germany as a grave threat to the European and global balance of power. The United States twice in the twentieth century had been propelled into Europe's wars at exactly those moments when Germany became so powerful that it almost destroyed this balance. The lessons of history—specifically, the impact upon American security of any nation's domination of Europe—had not yet been absorbed. Roosevelt and the American government did not aim at reestablishing a balance of power in Europe to safeguard the United States; they expected this security to stem

---

1. Quoted in Robert E. Sherwood, *Roosevelt and Hopkins,* vol. 2 (New York: Bantam Books), 363-364.

from mutual Soviet-American good will, unsupported by considerations of power. This reliance upon mere good will and mutual esteem was to prove foolish at best and, at worst, might have been fatal.

American Wartime Illusions

The expectation of a postwar "era of good feeling" between the Soviet Union and the United States was characteristic of the unsuspecting and utopian nature of American wartime thinking, which held that war was an interruption of the normal state of harmony among nations, that military force was an instrument for punishing the aggressor or war criminals, that those who cooperated with their country in its ideological crusade were equally moral and peace-loving, and that, once the war was finished, the natural harmony would be restored and the struggle for power ended. The implication was clear: the United States need take no precautionary steps against its noble wartime allies in anticipation of a possible disintegration of the alliance and potential hostility among its partners. Instead, it was hoped that the friendly relations and mutual respect that American leaders believed had matured during war would preserve the common outlook and goals and guarantee an enduring peace.

These optimistic expectations of future Soviet-American relations made it necessary, however, to explain away continuing signs of Soviet suspicion of American and British intentions and hostility toward its two Western allies. This was particularly true with regard to the Western delay in opening up a second front. When the front was postponed from 1942 to 1943 to 1944, Joseph Stalin, dictator of the Soviet Union, became very bitter. He brusquely rejected Allied explanations that they were not yet properly equipped for such an enormous undertaking, and he especially denounced Churchill for declaring that there would be no invasion until the Germans were so weakened that Allied forces would not have to suffer forbiddingly high losses. To Stalin, this was no explanation, for the Soviets accepted huge losses of men as a matter of course. "When we come to a minefield," Marshal G. K. Zhukov explained to General Dwight Eisenhower after the war, "our infantry attacks exactly as if it were not there. The losses we get from personnel mines we consider only equal to those we would have gotten from machine guns and artillery if the Germans had chosen to defend that particular area with strong bodies of troops instead of with minefields." [2]

It was no wonder, then, that the Soviets should dismiss Allied explanations and fasten instead upon what was for them a more reasonable interpretation of American and British behavior. From the Marxist view-

2. Quoted in Dwight Eisenhower, *Crusade in Europe* (New York: Doubleday, 1948), 514.

point, the Allies were doing exactly what they should be doing—namely, postponing the second front until the Soviet Union and Germany had exhausted each other. Then the two Western powers could land in France, march into Germany without heavy losses, and dictate the peace to Germany and the Soviet Union. The Western delay was seen as a deliberate attempt by the world's two leading capitalist powers to destroy their two major ideological opponents at one and the same time. Throughout the war, the Russians displayed again and again this almost paranoid fear of hostile Western intentions.

American leaders, however, found a ready explanation for these repeated indications of Soviet suspicion. They thought of Soviet foreign policy not in terms of the internal dynamics of the regime and its ideological enmity toward all non-Communist nations, but solely in terms of Soviet reactions to Western policies; new to international politics, they had little knowledge of Russian history and, therefore, of Russia's historical goals under czarist and Soviet rule. The few experts the State Department had were ignored; in fact, Roosevelt never took the secretary of state along to any of the wartime conferences with Churchill and Stalin. Soviet distrust of the West was viewed by the president against the pattern of prewar anti-Soviet Western acts: the Allied intervention in Russia at the end of World War I aimed at overthrowing the Soviet regime and, after the failure of that attempt, the establishment of the *cordon sanitaire* in Eastern Europe to keep the Soviet virus from spreading; the West's rejection of Soviet offers in the mid- and late 1930s to build an alliance against Hitler; and especially, the Munich agreement in 1938, which, by destroying Czechoslovakia, opened Hitler's gateway to the East. Western efforts to ostracize and ultimately destroy the Soviet Union, as well as attempts to turn Adolf Hitler's threat away from the West and toward Russia, were considered the primary reasons for the existence of Soviet hostility.

To overcome this attitude, American leaders thought they had only to demonstrate good intentions and prove their friendliness. The question was not whether Soviet cooperation could be won for the postwar world, but how it could be gained. And if these efforts bore fruit and created good will, what conflicts of interest could not be settled peacefully in the future? Various Soviet policies and acts during the war—the disbanding of the Comintern (the instrument of international communism), the toning down of Communist ideology and placing new emphasis on Soviet nationalism, the relaxation of restrictions upon the church and, above all, the statement of Soviet war aims in the same language of peace, democracy, and freedom used by the West—all seemed to prove that if the Western powers demonstrated their friendship they could convert the Soviets into friends.

Roosevelt's efforts to gain this cooperation focused on Stalin. In that respect Roosevelt's instincts were correct: if he could gain Stalin's trust, postwar Soviet-American relations would be peaceful. "To win a friend is to be a friend" is, after all, a deeply felt American belief. But in another respect his instincts were poor. Roosevelt's political experience was in the domestic arena. He had dealt successfully with all sorts of politicians and managed to resolve differences by finding compromise solutions. As a result he had great confidence in his ability to win Stalin's friendship. He would talk to Stalin as "one politician to another." In short, Roosevelt saw Stalin as a Russian version of himself, who, as a fellow politician, could be won over by a mixture of concessions and good will. It did not occur to Roosevelt that all of his considerable skills and charm might not suffice. At home, these qualities were enough because he and his opponents agreed on goals; differences were over the means. But between the United States and the Soviet Union the differences were over the ends, the kind of world each expected to see when the war was over.

Roosevelt and his advisers believed that they had firmly established amicable and lasting relations with the Soviet Union at the Yalta Conference of the Big Three—Roosevelt, Stalin, and Churchill—in February 1945. Stalin had made concessions on a number of vital issues and promised good will for the future. He had accepted the United Nations on the basis of the American formula that the veto in the Security Council should be applied only to enforcement action, and not to peaceful attempts at the settlement of disputes. Moreover, in the "Declaration of Liberated Europe," he had promised to support self-government and allow free elections in Eastern Europe. He also had responded to the wishes of the American military and promised to enter the war against Japan. Finally, he had repeatedly expressed his hope for fifty years of peace and "big power" cooperation.

At the end of the conference the American delegation felt a mood of "supreme exaltation." The new era of good will was to be embodied in the United Nations. Here the peoples of the world could exercise vigilance over their national leaders. The United Nations was regarded as democracy working on an international scale: just as citizens within democratic states could constantly watch their representatives and prevent them from effecting compromises injurious to their interests, so the people of all countries would now be able to keep an eye on their leaders, making it impossible for them to arrange any secret deals that would betray the people's interests and shatter the peace of the world. Peace-loving world public opinion, expressing itself across national boundaries, would maintain a constant guard over the diplomats and hold them accountable. Covenants were to be open, and "openly arrived at," as President Woodrow Wilson had once expressed it.

Power politics would be banned once and for all. In the words of Secretary of State Cordell Hull: "There will no longer be need for spheres of influence, for alliances, balance of power, or any other of the special arrangements through which, in the unhappy past, the nations strove to safeguard their security or promote their interests." [3] Reliance would instead be placed on sound principles and good fellowship. In almost identical words, but more pointedly, the president upon his return from Yalta told Congress and the American people that his recent conference with Stalin and Churchill "ought to spell the end of the system of unilateral action, the exclusive alliances, the spheres of influence, the balances of power, and all the other expedients that have been tried for centuries—and have always failed." Instead, "We propose to substitute for all these, a universal organization in which all peace-loving nations will fully have a chance to join." [4] The Advisory Commission on Postwar Foreign Policy to the State Department had been even more emphatic on the subordination of power politics to principles. Its Subcommittee on Territorial Problems specifically stated that "the vital interests of the United States lay in following a 'diplomacy of principle'—of moral disinterestedness instead of power politics." [5] No comment could have summed up more aptly the American habit of viewing international politics in terms of abstract moral principles instead of clashes of interest and power. And no institution could have embodied more fully the immediate postwar hope for a return to "normalcy," the desire for minimum international involvement, and the expectation that the wartime cooperation with the Soviet Union would continue, than the United Nations, which was essentially seen as a *substitute* for the vigorous, self-reliant, national conduct of foreign policy.

Soviet Postwar Expansion

The American dream of postwar peace and Big Three cooperation was shattered as the Red Army, having finally halted the Nazi armies and decisively defeated the Germans at Stalingrad in late 1942, began slowly to drive the enemy out of the Soviet Union and then relentlessly pursued the retreating Germans to Berlin. The Soviet Union, which in 1940 had annexed the three Baltic states (Latvia, Lithuania, and Estonia) after signing the Nazi-Soviet Pact, thus expanded into Eastern and central Europe and began to impose its control on Poland, Hungary, Bulgaria, Romania, and Albania even before the end of the war. (Yugoslavia was by then under the Communist control of Marshal Tito, the Yugoslav partisan leader who had fought bravely against the German occupation, and Czechoslovakia was under the threat of the Red Army.)

---

3. Quoted in Herbert Feis, *Churchill, Roosevelt, Stalin: The War They Waged and the Peace They Sought* (Princeton: Princeton University Press, 1957), 238.
4. Quoted in James MacGregor Burns, *Roosevelt, The Soldier of Freedom* (New York: Harcourt, Brace, Jovanovich, 1970), 582.
5. Quoted in Feis, *Churchill, Roosevelt, Stalin*, 207.

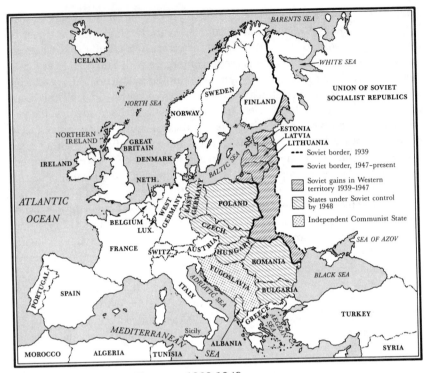

Soviet Expansion in Europe, 1939-1948

In each of the nations of Eastern Europe where the Soviets had their troops, they unilaterally established pro-Soviet coalition governments. The key posts in these regimes—the ministries of the interior, which usually controlled the police, and defense, which controlled the army—were in the hands of the Communists. With this decisive lever of power in their grasp, it was an easy matter to extend their domination and subvert the independence of these countries. As the war drew to a close, it became clear that the words of the Yalta Declaration, in which the Soviets had committed themselves to free elections and democratic governments in Eastern Europe, meant quite different things to the Soviets and to the Americans. For the Soviet Union, control of Eastern Europe, and especially Poland, was essential. This area constituted a vital link in its security belt. After suffering two German invasions in less than thirty years, it was perhaps inevitable that the Soviet Union would try to establish "friendly" governments throughout the area. To the Soviets, democratic governments meant Communist governments, and free elections meant elections from which parties not favorable to the Communists were barred. The peace treaties with the former German satellite states (Hungary, Bulgaria, Romania), which were painfully negotiated by the victors in a series of foreign ministers' conferences during 1945 and 1946, could not therefore loosen the tight Soviet grip on what were by now Soviet satellite states.

In terms of the state system, this Soviet behavior is understandable. Each state must act as its own guardian against potential adversaries in a system characterized by conflict among states and a sense of insecurity and fear on the part of its members. As the alliance against the common enemy came to an end, the Soviet Union predictably would strengthen itself against the power most likely to be its new opponent. As czarist Russia, with a long history of invasions from the East and West, it had learned the basic rules of the international game through bitter experience; as *Soviet* Russia, its sense of peril and mistrust had been intensified by an ideology that posited capitalist states as implacable enemies. In the war, it had suffered over 20 million casualties, soldiers and civilians, and saw the establishment of non-Communist regimes in Eastern Europe as unacceptable. The American insistence upon free elections was seen as an attempt to push the Soviet Union out of Europe. The assumption was that a non-Communist government would be an anti-Communist one.

U.S.-USSR Differences

No issue could have reflected more accurately the differences between the Soviet Union and the United States. Roosevelt acted precisely on the assumption that non-Communist did not have to mean anti-Soviet. During the war, he had been all too aware of the consequences of a possible Soviet-American clash in the wake of Germany's defeat. He therefore single-mindedly pursued a policy of friendship toward the Soviet Union. Roosevelt, however, did not view free elections in that area in terms of the creation of a new anti-Soviet belt. For him, free elections, non-Communist coalition governments in which Communists might participate if they gained a sizable vote, and a friendly attitude toward West *and* East were quite compatible.

The model he had in mind was Czechoslovakia. As the only democracy in that area, Czechoslovakia had maintained close ties with the West since its birth after World War I. But because France and Britain had failed to defend Czechoslovakia at Munich in 1938, and betrayed it by appeasing Hitler, it had also become friendly with the Soviet Union. After 1945 Czechoslovakia, like the other East European states, knew that it lay in the Soviet sphere of influence and that its security depended upon getting along with, not irritating, its powerful neighbor. Czech leaders expressed only amicable feelings for the Soviet Union and signed a security treaty with it; and, in one of the rare free elections the Soviets allowed in Eastern Europe, the Communist party received the largest vote of any party and therefore the key posts in the government. To share power in a coalition government, however, was to share power with class enemies. A "friendly" state, to the Soviets, was one totally controlled by the Communist party. Soviet security therefore required ideological homogeneity in

Eastern Europe and total Soviet domination. A "friendly" state, in Roosevelt's eyes, was sensitive to Soviet security interests but retained its domestic autonomy. A Communist party monopoly of power was not a necessary prerequisite for the states of Eastern Europe to adopt a pro-Soviet foreign policy. Great powers historically have created spheres of influence on their borders, and the neighboring states have usually accommodated themselves to this fact because they have recognized the wisdom of doing so.

During the war, the heroic Soviet war effort and sacrifices had created an enormous "reservoir of good will" in the West. Had the Soviets acted with greater restraint after the war and accepted states that, regardless of their governments' composition, would have adjusted to their great-power neighbor, Stalin could have had the security he was seeking. But Stalin did not trust Roosevelt. No matter how personable the president was, no matter how sincere his statements of good will and postwar friendship, Stalin saw him as the leader of a capitalist nation: as a "tool of Wall Street," Roosevelt could not be sincere in his peaceful professions. To Stalin, Roosevelt was an American version of himself, a man who was fully aware of the impending postwar Soviet-American struggle and equally determined to weaken his adversary and gain the advantage for his nation. In Eastern Europe Soviet bayonets enforced Stalin's will. The Soviet style ensured that the wartime alliance would break up and that eventually the Western allies would return Stalin's hostility, thus proving to him that he had been right all along about Western enmity!

Ignoring a Lesson of History

The power vacuum created by Germany's defeat was virtually a replay of the situation that existed after the end of the war against Napoleon. The czar's troops entered Paris, and his alliance with Prussia and control over what then constituted Poland presented his allies—Austria-Hungary and England—with the possibility of Russian continental hegemony. These two states plus their former enemy, France, signed a secret agreement pledging to go to war with Russia if the czar refused a peace treaty that distributed power so that all the principal states could feel reasonably secure. When the news of this secret arrangement was leaked, the czar became more compliant.

The United States did not follow this strategy. Churchill, concerned about Stalin's behavior in Eastern Europe, urged the United States to send forces to capture the symbolically important German capital of Berlin instead of rounding up the remnants of Germany's defeated army; to advance the U.S. armies as far east as possible, including farther into Czechoslovakia; not to pull back U.S. forces to their agreed-upon occupation zones in Germany until Stalin observed his agreements in Eastern Europe; and until then not to shift the bulk of American military power from Europe to the Far East for the final offensive against Japan. Washington declined all these suggestions. Roosevelt had assured Stalin that all American troops would be withdrawn within two years after the war. Why then should Stalin worry about American opposition to his efforts to control Eastern Europe? Stalin exercised caution when he encountered opposition, but he ignored diplomatic notes of protest. Carefully waiting to see what the United States would do, Stalin allowed free elections in Czechoslovakia and Hungary, the two states nearest to American power. But continued U.S.—and British—verbal protests, unsupported by action, did not impress Stalin.

Consequently, Hungary's freedom was soon destroyed by the Soviets; finally in 1948, even the Czech government, in which the Communist party had the largest plurality, was overthrown by the Soviets in a coup d'état. Contrary to Roosevelt's earlier expectations, not even a Communist-controlled coalition government was acceptable to Stalin. Indeed, as the Soviet satellization of Eastern Europe was to show, the failure of the United States was not the failure of efforts to accommodate Soviet interests in Eastern Europe, but the failure to resist Stalin earlier. Because Stalin apparently saw no limits to Soviet expansion and his conception of Soviet security left little, if any, security for his neighbors, that limit had to be defined by the two Western powers, of whom the United States was, at the end of the war, by far the stronger. Setting that limit first occurred on the Soviet Union's southern perimeter.

The Soviet Push to the South

As in the two world wars, in which Britain had led the effort to contain Germany, it was London—not Washington—that took the first steps in opposing the Soviet Union after 1945. Indeed, the United States at first tried to play the role of mediator between the Soviet Union and Britain! At Yalta, Roosevelt had made it a point not to meet with Churchill before seeing Stalin; he did not wish to appear to be "ganging up" with Britain's leader against Stalin. Similarly, Truman did not stop in London on the way to or from Potsdam, the first postwar conference, lest it appear he was colluding with Britain against our Soviet ally. Only when British power proved to be insufficient did the United States take over the task of balancing Soviet power. American initiative evolved gradually in the 1946-1947 period and was precipitated by Stalin's attempt to extend Soviet influence beyond Eastern Europe. The United States had accommodated itself to Soviet control over Eastern Europe, especially Poland, the corridor through which Germany had attacked Russia twice in a quarter-century. Moscow's security interests were understandable, and Washington, despite its disappointment over the Soviet failure to fulfill its Yalta obligations in Poland, quickly recognized the new Polish government as well as the other Soviet-installed regimes in Eastern Europe. The United States tried to convince Stalin that it was not hostile, understood Soviet security concerns, and wished to get along with the Soviet Union in peace.

But then the Soviets began moving toward the Persian Gulf and into the Mediterranean. Iran, Turkey, and Greece were the first to feel Communist pressure. If Soviet behavior in Eastern Europe could be explained in defensive terms, this was less true for the area south of the Soviet Union, the line that runs from Turkey to India. Long before Stalin, the czars had sought access to the Mediterranean via the Dardanelles; simultaneously, they had tried to expand to the south to bring Russian power closer to the Middle East and the Persian Gulf.

The pressure on Iran began in 1946, when the Soviets refused to withdraw their troops from that country. These troops had been there since late 1941, when the Soviet Union and Britain had invaded Iran to forestall increased Nazi influence and to use Iran as a corridor through which the West could ship military aid to the Soviet Union. The Soviets had occupied northern Iran, the British the central and southern sections. When the British withdrew, the Soviets sought to convert Iran into a Soviet satellite. The Iranian prime minister's willingness to offer oil concessions to get the Soviets to withdraw was rebuffed. Moscow's goal was nothing less than detaching the northern area of Azerbaijan and then by various means pressuring Iran into a servile status.

During this period, the Soviet Union also exerted pressure on Turkey. Indeed, the Soviets had begun to do this as early as June 1945, when they made several demands: the cession of several Turkish districts lying on the Turkish-Soviet frontier, the revision of the Montreux Convention governing the Dardanelles Straits in favor of a joint Soviet-Turkish administration, the severance of Turkey's ties with Britain and the conclusion of a treaty with the Soviet Union similar to those that the Soviet Union had concluded with its Balkan satellites, and finally, the leasing to the Soviet Union of bases for naval and land forces in the Dardanelles for its "joint defense." Moscow rejected a compromise proposal that would have given the Soviet Union a veto over any non-Black Sea powers' warships seeking passage through the straits. This suggested that the Soviet motive was not primarily defensive. (In fact, after Stalin's death in 1953, Moscow renounced its claims on Turkey.) In August 1946 the Soviet Union, in a note to the United States and Britain, renewed its demand for a new administration of the straits. By now, the United States was convinced that the Soviet goal was nothing less than domination of Turkey and fulfillment of the historic Russian/Soviet ambition to control Constantinople and gain access to the Mediterranean. Control of Turkey, of course, would have left Moscow in a better position to intimidate Iran and Greece.

In Greece, Communist pressure was exerted on the government through wide-scale guerrilla warfare, which began in the fall of 1946. Civil war in Greece was nothing new; the Communist and anti-Communist guerrillas had spent much of their energy battling each other instead of the Germans. When the British landed in Greece and the Germans withdrew, the Communists had attempted to take over Athens. Only after several weeks of bitter street fighting and the landing of British reinforcements was the Communist control of Athens dislodged; a truce was signed in January 1945. Just over a year later—in March 1946—the Greeks held a general election in which right-wing forces captured the majority of votes.

The Greek situation did not improve, however. The country was exhausted from the Italian and German invasions, the four years of occupation, and the Germans' scorched-earth policy as they retreated. Moreover, Greece had always depended on imports that were paid for by exports; now its traditional market in Central Europe was closed. While the masses lived at a bare subsistence level, the black market flourished. The inability of any government to deal with this situation aroused a good deal of social discontent. And the 100,000-man army that Greece needed to protect itself from its Communist neighbors (Albania, Yugoslavia, and Bulgaria) had brought the country to near-bankruptcy. If Britain had not helped finance, train, and equip the army and kept troops in the country, Greece probably would have collapsed. In August 1946 the Communist forces renewed the war in the north, where the Soviet satellites could keep the guerrillas well supplied. A victory for these forces would have been another way for the Soviets to reach the Mediterranean and Turkey.

In all these situations, the American government was once more confronted with the need to support Britain, the traditional guardian of this area. In the case of Iran, the United States and Britain delivered firm statements that strongly implied that they would use force to defend Iran and took the issue to the United Nations for a public airing. The Soviet response, in late March 1946, was the announcement that the Red Army would be withdrawn during the next five to six weeks. In the case of Turkey, the United States sent a naval task force into the Mediterranean immediately after the Soviets made their demand over the Dardanelles. Twelve days later, the United States formally replied to the Soviets by rejecting their demand to share responsibility for the defense of the straits with Turkey. Britain sent a similar reply. The Greek situation had not yet come to a head, and the need for American action could have been postponed for a while longer.

But it should be pointed out that President Harry Truman's actions in support of Iranian and Turkish political independence and territorial integrity were merely swift reactions to immediate crises. They were not the product of an overall American strategy. Such a coherent strategy came only after a new assessment of Soviet foreign policy had been made.

Toward the Strategy of Containment

Eighteen months passed before the United States undertook that reassessment—from the surrender of Japan on September 2, 1945, until the announcement of the Truman Doctrine on March 12, 1947. Perhaps such a reevaluation could not have been made any more quickly. Public opinion in a democratic country does not normally shift drastically overnight. It would have been too much to expect the American public to change suddenly from an attitude of friendliness toward the Soviet Union—inspired largely by the picture of Soviet wartime bravery and endurance and by hopes for peaceful postwar cooperation—to hostility. The United States wished only to be left alone to occupy itself once more with domestic affairs. The end of the war signaled the end of power politics and the restoration of normal peacetime harmony among nations.

In response to this expectation, the public demanded a speedy demobilization. In May 1945, at the end of the war with Germany, the United States had an army of 3.5 million organized into 68 divisions in Europe, supported by 149 air groups. By March 1946, only ten months later, the United States had only 400,000 troops left, mainly new recruits; the homeland reserve was six battalions. The army made further reductions, as did the air force and navy. This deliberate reduction of military strength, as a symptom of America's psychological demobilization, no doubt encouraged Soviet intransigence in Europe and attempts to extend their influence. American diplomacy and force retained their traditional separation. America's large and powerful armed forces and its enormous industrial strength, which could have provided the basis for serious negotiations about Eastern Europe, were respectively dismantled and converted back to the production of consumer goods. American policy, unsupported by sufficient conventional military power, was impotent. And "atomic diplomacy," despite what later revisionists have written, was not used either in the immediate postwar period. Or, if it was used, as was claimed, it certainly did not frighten Stalin or deter him from strengthening his grip on Eastern Europe or trying to expand Soviet power into new areas.

A Change in Direction

These Soviet efforts finally provoked the United States and led to a reevaluation of American policy. Three positions became clear during this period. At one extreme stood that old realist Winston Churchill. At the end of the European war, he had counseled against the withdrawal of American troops. He had insisted that they stay, together with British troops, to force the Soviet Union to live up to its Yalta obligations regarding free elections in Eastern Europe and the withdrawal of the Red Army from eastern Germany. The United States had rejected Churchill's plea. In March 1946, at Fulton, Missouri, Churchill took his case directly to the American public. The Soviet Union, he asserted, was an expansionist state:

> From Stettin in the Baltic to Trieste in the Adriatic, an iron curtain has descended across the continent. Behind that line lie all the capitals of the ancient states of Central and Eastern Europe. Warsaw, Berlin, Prague,

Vienna, Budapest, Belgrade, Bucharest, and Sofia, all the famous cities and populations around them lie in the Soviet sphere and all are subject in one form or another, not only to Soviet influence but to a very high and increasing measure of control from Moscow.

Churchill did not believe that the Soviets wanted war: "What they desire is the fruits of war and the indefinite expansion of their power and doctrines." This could be prevented only by the opposing power of the British Commonwealth and the United States. Churchill, in short, said bluntly that the cold war had begun, that Americans must recognize this fact and give up their dreams of Big Three unity in the United Nations. International organization was no substitute for the balance of power. "Our difficulties and dangers will not be removed by closing our eyes to them. They will not be removed by mere waiting to see what happens; nor will they be relieved by a policy of appeasement." [6] An alliance of the English-speaking peoples was the prerequisite for American and British security and world peace.

At the other extreme stood Secretary of Commerce Henry Wallace, who felt it was precisely the kind of aggressive attitude expressed by Churchill that was to blame for Soviet hostility. The United States and Britain, he said, had no more business in Eastern Europe than had the Soviet Union in Latin America; to each, the respective area was vital for national security. Western interference in nations bordering on the Soviet Union was bound to arouse Soviet suspicion, just as Soviet intervention in countries neighboring on the United States would. "We may not like what Russia does in Eastern Europe," said Wallace. "Her type of land reform, industrial expropriation, and suspension of basic liberties offend the great majority of the people of the United States. But whether we like it or not, the Russians will try to socialize their sphere of influence just as we try to democratize our sphere of influence (including Japan and Western Germany)." The tough attitude that Churchill and other "reactionaries" at home and abroad demanded was precisely the wrong policy; it would only increase international tension. "We must not let British balance-of-power manipulations determine whether and when the United States gets into a war ... 'getting tough' never bought anything real and lasting—whether for schoolyard bullies or world powers. The tougher we get, the tougher the Russians will get." [7] Only mutual trust would allow the United States and the Soviet Union to live together peacefully, and such trust could not be created by an unfriendly American attitude and policy.

The American government and public wavered between these two positions. The administration recognized that Big Three cooperation had ended, and it realized that the time had passed when the United States needed to demonstrate good will toward the Soviet Union to overcome its suspicions. The United States would make no further concessions to preserve the

6. *Vital Speeches,* March 25, 1946, 329-332.
7. Ibid., October 1, 1946, 738-741.

appearance of friendship with the Soviet Union. America had tried to gain Soviet amity by being a friend; it was now up to Soviet leaders to demonstrate a friendly attitude toward America as well. Paper agreements, written in such general terms that they actually hid divergent purposes, were regarded as having little value. Something more than paper agreements was needed: Soviet words would have to be matched by Soviet deeds.

The American secretary of state, James Byrnes, called this new line the "policy of firmness and patience." This phrase meant that the United States would take a firm position whenever the Soviet Union became intransigent and that it would not compromise simply to reach a quick agreement. This change in the official American attitude toward the Soviet Union was not, however, a fundamental one. A firm line was to be followed only on specific issues. The assumption was that if the United States took a tougher bargaining position and no longer seemed in a hurry to resolve particular points of tension, the Soviet rulers would see the pointlessness of their obduracy and agree to fair compromise solutions of their differences with the United States and the West. In short, American firmness would make the Soviets "reasonable." But there was no suggestion in this call for a tactical shift in how to negotiate with Moscow that the United States needed to organize international opposition to the Soviet Union. The new American position, as one political analysis has aptly summed it up, "meant to most of its exponents that the Soviet Union had to be induced by firmness to play the game in the American way. There was no consistent official suggestion that the United States should begin to play a different game." [8] The prerequisite for such a suggestion was that American policy makers recognize that the Soviet Union was no longer just a difficult ally but an enemy.

Kennan and the New American Policy

George Kennan, the Foreign Service's foremost expert on the Soviet Union, in 1946 first presented the basis of what was to be a new American policy that recognized the hostile character of the Soviet regime. In a long telegram, sent from the U.S. embassy in Moscow (later reprinted in the famous "X" article in the July *Foreign Affairs* issue of 1947), Kennan analyzed the Communist outlook on world affairs. [9] In the Soviet leaders' pattern of thought, he said, the Soviet Union had no community of interest with the capitalist states; indeed, they saw their relationship with the Western powers in terms of an innate antagonism. Communist ideology had taught them "that the outside world was hostile and that it was their duty eventually

---

8. William Reitzel, Morton A. Kaplan, and Constance G. Coblenz, *United States Foreign Policy, 1945-1955* (Washington, D.C.: Brookings Institution, 1956), 89.
9. This telegram is reproduced in George F. Kennan, *American Diplomacy, 1900-1950*, 107-128.

to overthrow the political forces beyond their borders. The powerful hands of Russian history and tradition reached up to sustain them in this feeling. Finally, their own aggressive intransigence with respect to the outside world began to find its own reaction. . . . It is an undeniable privilege for every man to prove himself right in the thesis that the world is his enemy; for if he reiterates it frequently enough and makes it the background for his conduct, he is bound to be right." [10] According to Kennan, this Soviet hostility was a constant factor; it would continue until the capitalist world had been destroyed: "Basically, the antagonism remains. It is postulated. And from it flow many of the phenomena which we find disturbing in the Kremlin's conduct of foreign policy: the secretiveness, the lack of frankness, the duplicity, the war suspiciousness, and the basic unfriendliness of purpose. . . . These characteristics of the Soviet policy, like the postulates from which they flow, are basic to the *internal* nature of Soviet power, and will be with us . . . until the nature of Soviet power is changed [italics added]." [11] Until that moment, he said, Soviet strategy and objectives would remain the same.

The American-Soviet struggle would thus be a long one, but Kennan stressed that Soviet hostility did not mean that the Soviets would embark upon a do-or-die program to overthrow capitalism by a fixed date. They had no timetable for conquest. In a brilliant passage, Kennan outlined the Soviet concept of the struggle:

> The Kremlin is under no ideological compulsion to accomplish its purposes in a hurry. Like the Church, it is dealing in ideological concepts which are of a long-term validity, and it can afford to be patient. It has no right to risk the existing achievements of the revolution for the sake of vain baubles of the future. The very teachings of Lenin himself require great caution and flexibility in the pursuit of Communist purposes. Again, these precepts are fortified by the lessons of Russian history: of centuries of obscure battles between nomadic forces over the stretches of a vast unfortified plain. Here caution, circumspection, flexibility, and deception are the valuable qualities; and their value finds natural appreciation in the Russian, or the Oriental mind. Thus the Kremlin has no compunction about retreating in the face of superior force. And being under the compulsion of no timetable, it does not get panicky under the necessity of such a retreat. Its political action is a fluid stream which moves constantly, wherever it is permitted to move, toward a given goal. Its main concern is to make sure that it has filled every nook and cranny available to it in the basin of world power. But if it finds unassailable barriers in its path, it accepts these philosophically and accommodates itself to them. The main thing is that there should always be pressure, increasing constant pressure, toward the desired goal. There is no trace of any feeling in Soviet psychology that the goal must be reached at any given time. [12]

How could the United States counter such a policy—a policy that was always pushing, seeking weak spots, attempting to fill power vacuums?

---

10. Ibid., 111-112.
11. Ibid., 115.
12. Ibid., 118.

Kennan's answer was that American policy would have to be one of "long-term, patient, but firm and vigilant containment." The United States would find Soviet diplomacy both easier and more difficult to deal with than that of dictatorships:

> On the one hand, it [Soviet policy] is more sensitive to contrary force, more ready to yield on individual sectors of the diplomatic front when that force is felt to be too strong, and thus more rational in the logic and rhetoric of power. On the other hand, it cannot be easily defeated or discouraged by a single victory on the part of its opponents. And the patient persistence by which it is animated means that it can be effectively countered not by sporadic acts which represent the momentary whims of democratic opinion, but only intelligent long-range policies on the part of Russia's adversaries—policies no less steady in their purpose, and no less variegated and resourceful in their application, than those of the Soviet Union itself.

Kennan viewed containment as a test of American democracy to conduct an effective, responsible foreign policy *and* contribute to changes within the Soviet Union that ultimately would bring about a moderation of its revolutionary aims. The United States, he emphasized in a passage that was to take on great meaning forty years later,

> has it in its power to increase enormously the strains under which Soviet policy must operate, to force upon the Kremlin a far greater degree of moderation and circumspection than it has had to observe in recent years, and in this way to promote tendencies which must eventually find their outlet in either the breakup or the gradual mellowing of Soviet power. For no mystical, messianic movement—and particularly not that of the Kremlin—can face frustration indefinitely without eventually adjusting itself in one way or another to the logic of that state of affairs.

Why was the United States so favorably positioned for a long-term struggle with the Soviet Union? The reason, Kennan argued, was that industry was the key ingredient of power and the United States controlled most of the centers of industry. There were five such centers in the world: the United States, Britain, West Germany, Japan, and the Soviet Union. The United States and its future allies possessed four of these centers, the Soviet Union just one. Containment meant confining the Soviet Union to that one. The question, Kennan said, was not whether the United States had sufficient power to contain the Soviet Union but whether it had the patience and wisdom to do so.

Alternatives to Containment

The policy of containment implicitly rejected two other courses of action. The first one was a retreat into historic isolationism. That became clear when, on the afternoon of February 21, 1947, the first secretary of the British embassy in Washington visited the State Department and handed American officials two notes from His Majesty's government. One concerned Greece, the other

Turkey, but, in effect, they said the same thing: Britain could no longer meet its traditional responsibilities in those two countries. Because both were on the verge of collapse, the meaning of the British notes was clear: a Soviet breakthrough could be prevented only by an all-out American commitment.

February 21 was a turning point for the West. Great Britain, the only remaining power in Europe, acknowledged its exhaustion. It had fought Philip II of Spain, Louis XIV and Napoleon of France, Kaiser Wilhelm II and Adolf Hitler of Germany. It had preserved the balance of power that had protected the United States for so long that it seemed almost natural for it to continue to do so. But its ability to protect that balance had steadily declined in the twentieth century. Twice it had needed American help. Each time, however, Britain had fought the longer battle; the United States had entered the wars when it was clear that Germany and its allies were too strong for Great Britain and that America would have to help safeguard its own security. Now there was no power to protect the United States but the United States itself; no one stood between it and the present threat to its security. All the other major powers of the world had collapsed—except the Soviet Union. A bipolar or two-power world suddenly faced the United States. That was also the difference between Britain in the two world wars and the United States: Britain could fall back on American power, but the United States had no one to back it up.

The immediate crisis was in the eastern Mediterranean. Iran and Turkey had so far successfully resisted direct Soviet pressure, but Greece's northern Communist neighbors, Yugoslavia and Bulgaria, were helping the Communists in the Greek civil war, while Stalin watched to see what would happen. If Greece should fall, as Washington feared, it would be only a matter of time until Turkey and Iran also fell. But the collapse of Greece would not only affect its neighbors to the east and inject Soviet power into the Mediterranean and Persian Gulf; it would also lead to an increase of Communist pressure on Italy because Italy would then have two Communist states to its east—Yugoslavia and Greece—as well as the largest Communist party in Western Europe within its borders. To the northwest of Italy lay France, with the second-largest Communist party in the West. If the security of all of Western Europe were endangered, a policy of isolationism would not protect the United States.

The other course rejected in the adoption of the strategy of containment was a preventive war. The United States had an atomic monopoly until late 1949. (By 1950 the United States had fifty bombs plus the means to deliver them, and the Soviet Union had only tested an atomic device.) For a short time, then, the United States had possessed the opportunity of establishing a *Pax Americana,* or world domination. Certainly, if that had been the U.S. intention, it could have built up its atomic stockpile and means of delivery. But exploiting this atomic monopoly was never seriously considered. Quite apart from the relatively small size of the stockpile, launching an atomic "Pearl Harbor" on the Soviet Union was contrary to American tradition and morality. Indeed, after Hiroshima, the conviction grew that atomic weapons were too horrible to use and that in a future war there would be no winners. The bomb signaled a significant change: historically, the principal task of the military had been to win wars; from now on its main purpose was to deter them. Atomic weapons could have no other rationale. By the mid-1950s, after both superpowers had tested nuclear devices and had confronted one another in a number of crises, and after the range of destruction had taken a quantum leap from kilotons (thousands of tons of TNT) to megatons (millions of tons of TNT), this conviction grew to absolute certainty. Such weapons could not defend a nation; rather, their use would destroy it.

The consequences of the potentially suicidal nature of nuclear warfare were profound: the United States was committed to a long struggle, and this struggle was to be carried on in a new way. Conflicts between great powers— between Athens and Sparta for the control of ancient Greece, between Rome and Carthage for control of the Mediterranean, or, in more modern times, between Germany and England for control of Europe, if not Eurasia—had been settled on the battlefield. Such a solution was no longer feasible. This required the United States, a country that, when provoked by an enemy, had usually set out to destroy and punish its enemy by force of arms, to conduct a *protracted conflict* alien to its style. The term frequently given to this conflict—cold war—was apt indeed. *War* signified that the U.S.-Soviet rivalry was serious; *cold* referred to the fact that nuclear weapons were so utterly destructive that war could not be waged with "hot" (nuclear) weapons, but only with "cold" weapons (which included the use of limited conventional force but not nuclear force). But for the existence of nuclear weapons, the superpower conflict at some point might well have escalated into a shooting war, as had already happened twice in the twentieth century.

The nonuse of force meant the continuation of that conflict. The resulting cold war may therefore be defined as a relationship characterized by long-term hostility *and* by a mutual determination not to resort to war— nuclear war—to decide who is the winner. As it took over Britain's role as the keeper of the balance of power, the United States had to learn power politics; but, in protecting itself, it also had to learn how to conduct a protracted conflict in peacetime, a completely new experience and one at odds with its historic ways of dealing with an enemy state.

The Changing of the Guard: Sea Power Versus Land Power

The U.S. role, then, was historically similar to Britain's: primarily a naval power, it was to contain the outward thrust of a land power from the Eurasian "heartland." After World War I, a British geographer, Halford MacKinder, interested in the relationship of geographic position to international politics (referred to as *geopolitics*), stated the following axiom: "Who rules East Europe commands the Heartland [Eurasia]; Who rules the Heartland commands the World-Island [Eurasia and Africa, which, on the map, look like a centrally located island]; Who rules the World-Island commands the World." Some years later, an American geopolitician, Nicholas Spykman, coined a reply to MacKinder: "Who controls the Rimland [the peripheral areas around Eurasia] controls Eurasia; who rules Eurasia controls the destinies of the world." Although these axioms may be considered too simplistic, and there is some danger in accepting geography as too deterministic a factor in explaining the behavior of states, they explain rather well the essence of the British-German and the U.S.-Soviet conflicts. As the heartland power sought domination over Eurasia, if not the World-Island, which would have made it the dominant global power, the "off-shore" naval power sought control of the Eurasian rimlands in order to deny that domination to the heartland power and thereby contain it.

Indeed, before World War I, before the German threat received Britain's primary attention, it had been *czarist* Russia—then incorporating Finland, the three Baltic states, and Poland—that had been London's concern. Russian power was spreading eastward to the Pacific, southward from Siberia into Manchuria and into northern China, southward from the Caucasus to Turkey and into Iran toward the Persian Gulf, and southeasterly toward the frontier of British India, the area of today's Afghanistan and Pakistan. British power along the rim running from Turkey to India guarded the perimeter around Russia. When Russia pushed into Korea toward Japan, Japan attacked and defeated Russia, thereby also limiting the spread of Russian influence in northern China. After that, Russia focused on the Balkans, where it came into conflict with Austria-Hungary, the ally of Germany, which had become the Continent's most powerful country. Germany became the great threat to British interests, and Britain twice went to war with Germany which, in each conflict, invaded Russia. A victorious Germany would have controlled the heartland—indeed, in World War II, victory would have given Germany control from the Atlantic to the Pacific— plus the Middle East, the area linking Europe, Asia, and Africa.

After Germany's second defeat in 1945, the Russian threat reemerged. Already the heartland power, Russia extended its power into the center of Europe, reclaimed its dominant position in northern China, and sought to exploit weaknesses along its southern border from Turkey to Pakistan. Thus, one reason for the postwar conflict was *geopolitical:* Russian land power expanded but was countered by the countervailing power exerted by a maritime nation. These clashes occurred along the perimeter from Turkey to Iran and then in Western Europe.

It is important to understand the location of the initial conflicts because revisionists argue that whatever the Soviet Union's intentions were, its lack of a large fleet and intercontinental air power meant that it represented no threat to the United States. They point out, moreover, that the United States held an atomic monopoly. Thus, the demobilization from a military force of 12.1 million to 1.6 million and the reduction from a budget of more than $80 billion to approximately $13 billion counted for little. In fact, the United States was a hegemon, that is, the dominant power in the system and there really was no Soviet threat. Only one part of this argument is correct: the Soviet Union did not represent a direct threat to the security of the United States in the Western hemisphere. But the Soviet army, even after substantial demobilization, remained a formidable force of 175 divisions, certainly one that was able to pressure Soviet neighbors to the south and threaten the western rimlands of Eurasia and hold America's friends and potential allies hostage. That is why the governments of Iran, Turkey, Greece, and Western Europe feared a revival of American isolationism and sought U.S. countervailing support. To be sure, the small U.S. atomic arsenal could have wreaked great damage on Russian cities but it could not have stopped the Soviet army from overrunning Western Europe.

The balance that emerged after the war was one in which the United States was favored by an enormously productive economy that had not been damaged by the war; its atomic monopoly, although the number of bombs and bombers to deliver them remained small in the first years after the war; and the appeal of its democratic political system. Conversely, the Soviet Union was favored by its powerful conventional forces; its geographical position at the center of Eurasia; and, at a time when democracy was still widely identified with the failed capitalism of the 1930s and the Soviet Union with its heroic resistance to the Nazis, its Communist ideology. The ideology had appeal to the working classes in nations like France and Italy, as well as political movements that sought power in countries like China. Thus American political leaders after 1945 not only did not conclude that the United States was a hegemonic power but, to the contrary, were anxious about a balance that to them appeared very precarious.[13]

What was also important about the emerging bipolar balance was that America's opponent was *Soviet* Russia. By Soviet definition (as noted in Chapter 1), the United States was its primary enemy, the object of permanent hostility. Indeed, the Soviet leadership's legitimacy was tied to its claim that it was waging this conflict for the liberation of humanity; to relax from the struggle against world capitalism would be a betrayal of its Marxist-Leninist legacy. Whether the leadership believed in Communist ideology was beside the point; it needed it to justify its rule and monopoly of power. Unable to rule by divine right, as the czars had, and unwilling to submit to democratic elections despite its claim to govern on behalf of the people, it legitimated its hold on political power by its self-acclaimed historical duty to create a better life not only for the people of Russia but also for the people of the world. The

---

13. Joseph S. Nye, Jr., *Bound to Lead* (New York: Basic Books, 1990), 70-72.

struggle to bring about a postcapitalist socialist international order became a rationale for both dictatorial and eternal power. Asserting that the Soviet Union was besieged by enemies, the regime asserted that it must retain its grip on power and maintain its vigilance against external threats and internal subversion and dissension. The Soviet leadership, in brief, not only required a foreign enemy, but the ideology that legitimated its power also conveniently defined that enemy. If the changing distribution of power was one cause for the cold war, the character of the Soviet state was the second one. Indeed, former Soviet foreign minister Maxim Litvinov said after the war that the "root cause" of the cold war was Moscow's ideological preconception that conflict between capitalism and communism was "inevitable." When asked if Western compliance with Stalin's demands would have created goodwill and an end to U.S.-Soviet tensions, he replied that after a short time it would have led to the United States being faced with the next set of Stalin's demands.[14]

The U.S. Declaration of (Cold) War

On March 12, 1947, President Harry Truman went before a joint session of Congress to deliver one of the most important speeches in American history. After outlining the situation in Greece, he spelled out what was to become known as the Truman Doctrine. The United States, he said, could survive only in a world in which freedom flourished. And it would not realize this objective

> unless we are willing to help free peoples to maintain their institutions and their national integrity against aggressive movements that seek to impose upon them totalitarian regimes. *This is no more than a frank recognition that totalitarian regimes imposed on free peoples, by direct or indirect aggression, undermine the foundations of international peace and hence the security of the United States....*
>
> At the present moment in world history nearly every nation must choose between alternative ways of life. The choice is often not a free one.
>
> One way of life is based upon the will of the majority, and is distinguished by free institutions, representative government, free elections, guarantees of individual liberty, freedom of speech and religion, and freedom from political oppression.
>
> The second way of life is based upon the will of a minority forcibly imposed upon the majority. It relies upon terror and oppression, a controlled press and radio, fixed elections, and the suppression of personal freedoms.
>
> I believe it must be the policy of the United States to support free peoples who are resisting attempted subjugations by armed minorities or by outside pressure.

---

14. Quoted in William Taubman, *Stalin's American Policy* (New York: W. W. Norton, 1982), 133.

I believe that we must assist free peoples to work out their own destinies in their own way.

I believe that our help should be primarily through economic and financial aid which is essential to economic stability and orderly political processes.[15]

The president asked Congress to appropriate $400 million for economic aid and military supplies for Greece and Turkey and to authorize the dispatch of American personnel to assist with reconstruction and to provide their armies with appropriate instruction and training. The United States thus began the policy of containment.

A number of points about what was to be called the Truman Doctrine need special emphasis because of its universal nature and call for a new anti-Communist crusade. First, Soviet expansionist efforts left the United States little choice but to adopt a countervailing policy. With the war over, the United States would have much preferred to concentrate on domestic affairs, as the massive postwar demobilization clearly demonstrated. Americans were about to unleash their pent-up and postponed demands for consumer goods as U.S. industry converted from wartime to peacetime production. Not dependent upon exports for economic growth, the United States did not need extensive foreign markets; the domestic market sufficed and the United States within a decade became the "affluent society." The change from isolationism to internationalism was the product of the postwar bipolar distribution of power in which a gain of power and security by one tends to be seen as a loss of power and security for the other. As one side pushes, the opponent pushes back.

Second, anticommunism was not the major ingredient of American policy during and immediately after World War II. During the war, the United States had sought to overcome the Kremlin's suspicions of the West to lay the foundation for postwar harmony and peace. At the end of the war, the principal concern of American policy makers was not to eliminate the self-proclaimed bastion of world revolution and enemy of Western capitalism, nor to push the Soviet Union out of Eastern Europe, but to forestall a complete return to the historic position of isolationism. The public mood was all too evident in the hasty military demobilization, the riots of some overseas units that felt that their demobilization was not rapid enough, and the cries of America's children heard by both Congress and the White House: "We want our daddies." For the United States to have pursued the assertive foreign policy complete with atomic threats that the revisionists have claimed it did would have required a dictatorial disregard for the widespread demands of public opinion.

It was not until a year and a half after World War II ended that the Truman Doctrine was enunciated. Containment was launched after further

---

15. Italics added. The drama of this period and Truman's speech to Congress are still best captured in Joseph M. Jones, *The Fifteen Weeks* (New York: Viking Press, 1955), 17-23.

attempts to reconcile differences with Moscow failed and after continued Soviet pressure, denunciations, and vilifications. Hostile Soviet behavior and words were the reasons for the gradual shift of American policy and public opinion from amity to enmity. American policy was not the product of a virulent and preexisting anti-Communist ideology; rather, it was activated by the same concern for preventing a major nation from achieving dominance in Europe that had twice in the twentieth century led the United States into war. American policy after 1945 was consistent with U.S. behavior in 1917 and 1940-1941; in both cases, the nation had gone to war to prevent such an outcome. This was not fundamentally an ideological issue. In the two world wars, the enemy was Germany; in the initial engagement, Germany was led by a conservative monarchy, in the second, by an extreme right-wing fascist regime. In the cold war, the adversary was Soviet Russia, a radical left-wing regime. American action, however, remained the same, regardless of the ideological nature of the opponent.

Third, the role of anticommunism in American policy was essentially to mobilize congressional and public support for the policy once it had been decided upon. A nation that had historically condemned power politics as immoral and as a corruption of the democratic ideal needed a moral basis for its new use of power. For a people weary after four years of war, who identified the termination of war with the end of power politics, who were used to isolation from Europe's wicked affairs, and who were preoccupied with the pursuit of happiness, success, and the dollar at home, anticommunism was like the cavalry's bugle call to charge; it fitted neatly into the traditional American dichotomy of the world into extremes of good and evil, thereby arousing the nation for yet another foreign policy mission. Truman was conscious (as were Eisenhower and Kennedy later) of the U.S. desire to retreat into isolationism after a war, and he was unsure the American public was ready to commit itself to a potential conflict. He recognized the need to "sell" the public on the United States' new role in foreign policy by exaggerating the threat the nation faced.

The Truman Doctrine, with its dichotomy between the free world and communism and the United States' universal mission, served this purpose well. In 1950, following the first Soviet atomic test in 1949, years before it had been expected, the National Security Council, composed of the president's main foreign policy advisers, issued a famous report—NSC 68—depicting the all-encompassing character of the Soviet threat and the possibility of a possible Soviet atomic strike against the United States by 1954. The Soviet Union, it said, was "unlike previous aspirants to hegemony . . . animated by a fanatical faith, antithetical to our own, and seeks to impose its absolute authority over the rest of the world." [16] Since the United States stood in the way

---

16. Quoted in Samuel F. Wells, Jr., "Sounding the Tocsin: NSC 68 and the Soviet Threat," *International Security* (Fall 1979): 116-158.

of realizing this goal, the Soviet Union had to destroy or subvert this country. The report was intended to arouse the foreign policy bureaucracy and alert it to the need for military rearmament to block Soviet designs. Until the Vietnam War undermined this anti-Communist consensus, it served the policy makers' purposes; the policy of containment received widespread public and congressional support from both Democrats and Republicans. (Asian policy was to be the major exception to this rule, as we shall see.)

Fourth, despite the universalism of the Truman Doctrine, its application was intended to be specific and limited, not global. American policy makers were well aware that the United States, although a great power, was not omnipotent; therefore, national priorities—which interests were vital and which were not—had to be decided carefully and power applied discriminately. American responses would depend, then, both on where the external challenges occurred and on how Washington defined the relation of such challenges to the nation's security. Containment was to be implemented only where the Soviet state appeared to be expanding its power. The priority given to balance-of-power considerations was evident from the very beginning. Despite the democratic purposes stated by the Truman Doctrine, its first application was to Greece and Turkey, neither of which was democratic. Their strategic location was considered more important than their domestic nature.

In Western Europe, of course, America's strategic and power considerations were compatible with its democratic values. The containment of the Soviet Union could be equated with the defense of democracy. But outside of Western Europe, strategy and values were often incompatible with one another. The United States confronted a classic dilemma: protecting strategically located but undemocratic nations, such as Iran, Turkey, and Greece, might make the containment of Soviet power possible, but it also risked America's reputation and weakened the credibility of its policy—the defense of the free world. However, to align itself only with democratic states, of which there were all too few, might make it impossible for the United States to carry out the containment policy. The purity of the cause might be preserved, but the security of democracy would be weakened. This dilemma was to plague U.S. policy throughout the cold war.

The fifth point, and perhaps the most important, is the contrasting nature of American and Soviet expansion. The Soviet Union, which had already annexed the Baltic states, imposed Communist regimes on its neighbors and stationed Soviet forces there to ensure the loyalty of these states. None of these governments could have survived without the presence of Soviet troops. By contrast, Iran, Turkey, and Greece invited American assistance because they feared Soviet pressure and intimidation. *Soviet expansion meant their loss of independence; America's expansion guaranteed it.* If ever there was a defensively motivated expansion, it was the U.S. commitment in the eastern Mediterranean, which was followed by an even larger commitment to first revive and then defend the nations of Western Europe. All shared the U.S. perception of the Soviet Union as a threat to their political independence and territorial integrity and urged Washington to redress the post-1945 imbalance. Their concern was not U.S. expansion, but U.S. isolationism.

If the state system and the character of the Soviet state were fundamental in precipitating the cold war, what was America's responsibility? By comparison to the Soviet contribution, which was one of commission, that of the United States was basically one of omission. Perhaps the United States could have done no more than protest Soviet satellization of Eastern Europe. It was also true that the American people, like the British, enormously admired the heroic efforts of the Red Army in stopping and driving back the Nazi forces. Moreover, the staggering Soviet losses, compared to the relatively light losses of the Allies, who until 1944 fought the Germans only in North Africa and Italy, made Western leaders and publics feel guilty. In these circumstances, the hope for good postwar relations with the Soviet Union was understandable, and that this would feed the desire to believe the best of the Russians, to find explanations and excuses for their continued suspicions of and hostility toward their Western allies, and minimize the problems among the Big Three was very natural.

But could Roosevelt, whose optimistic assessments of the future were largely responsible for America's expectations, not have prepared the public better for what was to happen after the war? National self-determination was, after all, the fundamental Western principle underlying the war effort. On that basis, the president was quite willing to push a reluctant Churchill to give national independence to British colonies: self-determination was not to be limited to the conquered nations of Europe. Yet, could Roosevelt not have rallied the nation around this principle as Stalin's conquest of Eastern Europe proceeded and deflated America's exaggerated wartime hopes for future U.S.-Soviet harmony? World War II had started over the independence of Poland; it ended with Poland under Soviet domination. By contrast, the United States proceeded with its hasty demobilization, encouraging Stalin to expand Soviet power. Not content with surrounding his country with subservient states, Stalin appeared to have no limit to his ambitions. Where did Soviet security interests end? Did they include control of all of Germany so that the states of Western Europe would then accommodate themselves to Soviet supremacy? Could Soviet security interests be met without creating insecurity problems for all states beyond the Soviet Union's new sphere of dominance? The answer clearly was no, and the threatened states took the initiative in asking the United States to exert countervailing power. The United States finally took the necessary measures to oppose Stalin and draw the lines beyond which Soviet expansion would not be tolerated. Stalin, incapable of defining the limits of his ambitions, now found that the United States would do it for him.

Containment
in Europe

IT WOULD probably not be amiss to label American foreign policy just after 1945 as revolutionary as well. Later, critics looked back at the long years of containment and condemned it for its lack of adaptability to a changing world and its lack of sensitivity to Soviet postwar concerns. But the title of former secretary of state Dean Acheson's book *Present at the Creation* says it best. After more than a century of isolationism, the collapse of all the great powers of Western Europe, leaving the Soviet Union as the only great power in Eurasia, led the United States to accept its role as counterbalancer and assume leadership of the West. This period was perhaps the most imaginative of U.S. postwar policy. During these years President Harry Truman together with his first secretary of state, George Marshall—who during the war had been General Marshall, America's top soldier and the architect of victory in Europe and the Pacific—and then with his second secretary of state, Acheson, reconstructed a prosperous and democratic Western Europe, edged its nations away from their past rivalries toward cooperation and unity, created West Germany and admitted it into the Western community, and provided Europe with security. This alliance of Western Europe and the United States has survived more than four decades and has been a key reason for the avoidance of nuclear war.

Western Europe's Collapse

The commitment to Greece and Turkey had been only the first act under the new American policy of containing Soviet expansion. The war in Europe had devastated the economies of all the countries, winners and losers alike. The deepest fear was that Moscow would be able to exploit Europe's postwar economic and psychological vulnerability. Britain's state of near collapse was symptomatic of the situation throughout Europe. Basically, Britain's crisis was economic. An island nation, Britain depended on international trade for its livelihood. The Industrial Revolution of the nineteenth century had almost completely urbanized England, and less than 5 percent of the population was engaged in agriculture. This meant that Britain had to import much of its food and, except for coal, almost all the raw materials needed by its industries.

Before 1939 Britain had paid for food and raw materials three ways: services such as shipping, income from foreign investments, and manufactured exports. But the war had crippled its merchant marine, liquidated most of its investments, and destroyed many of its factories. With the first two means of financing its imports all but gone, Britain had to increase its exports; just to maintain the 1939 standard of living it had to raise its exports by 75 percent. By December 1946, despite an American loan and a severe austerity program that included the rationing of bread, Britain had reached only its prewar level of production. It was in these circumstances that nature delivered what proved to be almost a knockout blow. In the winter of 1946-1947, Europe suffered one of its severest cold periods in history; temperatures went below 0° Fahrenheit. The British transportation system came to a virtual standstill. Industries could not be supplied with the fuel to keep them running, and factories were closed. By February 1947 more than half of Britain's factories lay idle. Coal was not mined, and gas and electricity were in short supply. When the thaw finally arrived, Britain was beset by floods.

The export drive came to a halt, and Britain was at the end of its rope. The financial editor of Reuters saw the true measure of the winter disaster: "This is not the story of a couple of snowstorms. It is the story of the awful debility in which a couple of snowstorms could have such effects." The future looked bleak and ominous: millions of Britons were unemployed, cold, and hungry—worn out by the long years of war and the determined postwar efforts to recover. Despite all the sacrifices they had made, their efforts had come to nothing. Britain's fate could have been worse only if the war had been lost.

Postwar conditions in Germany were also dreadful. The war had been carried into the heart of Germany, and few cities or towns had escaped Allied bombing, street fighting, or willful destruction by the Nazis as they retreated. To make matters worse, 10 million additional Germans came into these ruins from former German territory annexed by Poland. Millions of people were without food, shelter, or work. There was only one word to describe Germany in 1945—chaos.

One indication of Germany's financial devastation was that the cigarette replaced money as the prevailing unit of exchange. Cigarettes could buy almost anything, and the black market flourished. Even as late as 1947, a package of cigarettes was equivalent to a working man's monthly wages. Most people did not receive the Allied target ration of 1550 calories per day, which was hardly sufficient to sustain a healthy human being. Everywhere people were hungry. There was no fuel for heating. Three-quarters of the factories still standing in the American and British zones of occupation were closed. In January 1947 production fell to 31 percent of the 1936 level, Germany's best year; by February it had declined to 29 percent. Even before this industrial shutdown German steel production during 1946 had reached only 2 million tons—approximately one-third of Allied authorization.

Allied policy was not designed to alleviate this situation. The Allies were primarily engaged with Germany's disarmament and demilitarization, and with the elimination of all industries whose output could be used for military production. The United States and Britain were not particularly eager to rebuild Germany's industrial power; after all, it had taken the combined efforts of three world powers to bring the Nazi war machine to a halt and defeat it. Nor were the Allies especially concerned with the lot of the German people during the immediate postwar days. After six years of brutal warfare, such concern could hardly have been expected. The revelations of Nazi atrocities and crimes, of wanton destruction, and of millions of innocent people slaughtered in concentration camps were too recent to be dismissed. The hatred the Nazis had engendered could not be erased overnight, and the Allies were unlikely to display much forgiveness and compassion toward them.

The French, above all others, were not likely to forget the Nazis. Although the French economy had been badly damaged during the war, by late 1946 they had made a remarkable recovery. But iron and steel production had reached only half the prewar total. Here, too, coal was the key factor because the iron and steel industries were dependent on imported coal. But European coal production was still well below the pre-1939 annual average. German production was low, and Britain needed for itself all the coal it mined. Scarce dollars had to be spent for high-cost American coal. The result was a vivid demonstration of the division of labor between the industrial and agricultural sectors of a modern economy. France's industry was unable to produce sufficient goods for its sizable farm population to buy. Farmers withdrew fields from crop cultivation and used them for grazing. They kept more food for their families and fed more grain to their livestock. Meanwhile, the urban population was short of food, and the government had to spend its few remaining dollars—which it needed for reconstruction—to buy food from abroad. Matters grew even worse during the winter of 1946-1947 when an estimated 3 to 4 million acres of wheat were destroyed by frost.

This situation was made to order for the large, well-organized French Communist party. One-quarter of France's electorate—practically the entire working class—voted for the Communists. (In Italy, the figure was one-third of the electorate.) The reason for this was simple: French and Italian capitalism had alienated these voters. The workers were, in effect, internal émigrés who voted Communist to protest a system they felt had long mistreated them; unlike workers in Britain and the United States, they had suffered all the hardships of capitalism while enjoying few of its benefits, such as good wages and social opportunities. As a result, the Communist party in France enjoyed a powerful position in politics and trade unions. The party was the largest in France and could prevent any reforms from being adopted, thereby preserving its raison d'être. The party also controlled the largest French trade union, which had a membership of 80 percent of the workers during the immediate postwar years. In 1947, as U.S.-Soviet tensions increased, the party used this control to initiate or exploit strikes to paralyze the entire economy and bring France to its knees.

With Europe on the verge of not only economic ruin but also a complete political and social breakdown, everything seemed to force it into dependence on America. Most of the items needed for reconstruction—wheat, cotton, sulphur, sugar, machinery, trucks, and coal—could be obtained in sufficient quantities only from the United States. Short of food and fuel, and with its cities and factories destroyed, Europe could not earn the dollars to pay for these goods. Moreover, the United States was so well supplied with everything that it did not have to buy much from abroad. The countries of Europe, therefore, were unable to earn enough dollars for the purchase of the commodities required for their recovery. The result was the ominous *dollar gap*—a term that frightened the Europeans as much as *cold war* because it denoted Europe's economic collapse and its complete dependence on the United States, which would have to supply the dollars with which Europe could buy what it needed for its economic and political recovery.

The Marshall Plan

Europe's collapse posed once again the fundamental question whether Europe was vital to U.S. security. America's two previous interventions suggest that the answer was obvious. But both times the United States had been drawn in by Germany. The wars were crusades for democracy; the public had never been made to understand the relationship between U.S. security and the European balance of power. At the end of each conflict the United States had tried to regain its isolationism. For the first time the United States was forced to clarify its relationship with Europe because this time it alone had the resources to take the initiative. Europe's vital importance became starkly clear in the emerging bipolar world. It ranked second only to the United States in its potential power: in industry, productivity, skilled manpower, scientists, and engineers. If these assets shifted toward the Soviet side, the military balance would swing so sharply that U.S. security would be endangered. Given its enormous potential and its geographic position, Europe's security was indeed inseparable from U.S. security.

Because the United States could not permit the Soviet Union to control the western approaches to the Atlantic, it had to find a way to help Europe recover. The prescribed cure was a massive injection of dollars. Only a tremendous program of economic aid could restore Europe's economy, enable it to surpass its prewar agricultural and industrial production, close the dollar gap, and lead Europe to the recovery of its *élan vital,* political stability, and economic prosperity. If these measures succeeded, France and Italy might reintegrate their working classes into their bodies politic.

American aid was made conditional, however, on economic cooperation among the European states. In this respect, the United States clearly held itself up as a model. The Economic Cooperation Act of 1948 called specifically for European economic integration. America, it stated, was "mindful of the advantage which the United States has enjoyed through the existence of a large-scale domestic market with no internal trade barriers and [believed] that similar advantages can accrue to the countries of Europe." In official American opinion, integration became the prerequisite for Europe's recovery and the necessary basis for long-range prosperity.

It is not difficult to see why American policy makers, with their belief in low-cost mass production, should have felt that Europe's economic recovery and health were dependent on the creation of a mass market. The European nations, living together on a continent one-fourth the size of the United States, had shut their markets off from one another with tariff walls, quota systems, and import and export licenses. By this means, manufacturers assured themselves of the lion's share of their national markets. Sheltered from external competition, they had little incentive to modernize their equipment or techniques, for they minimized domestic competition by dividing their relatively small domestic markets among themselves. The American aim was to modernize this machinery, to overcome the cartelization of industry and the inefficiency of small family enterprises (as in France), and to erase national divisions. Europe's industries were expected to enlarge and become competitive by the creation of a United States of Europe.

Secretary of State Marshall first stressed the economic cooperation required by the United States; he called upon the European states to devise a plan for their *common* needs and *common* recovery. The United States would furnish the funds, but the Europeans had to assume the initiative and do the planning. The result was the Organization for European Economic Cooperation (OEEC). Its estimate of the cost of Europe's recovery over a four-year period was $33 billion. The president asked for $17 billion, which Congress cut to $13 billion. The amount actually used by the Economic Cooperation Administration (ECA) between 1948 and the end of 1951, when the program ended, was just over $12 billion. Britain, France, and West Germany together received more than half of this amount.

Europe's Split into East and West

The original invitation by the United States to the nations of Europe to plan their joint recovery was deliberately extended to *all* European countries, including the Soviet Union and the nations of Eastern Europe. If the United States had invited only the nations of Western Europe, it would have placed itself in a politically disadvantageous position in which it would have been blamed for the division of Europe and the intensification of the cold war. Actually, had the Soviets participated, Congress probably would not have supported the Marshall Plan for two reasons: first, the costs would have risen astronomically as a result of the very heavy damage suffered by the Soviet Union during the war; and second, anti-Soviet feeling was growing. The risk had to be accepted, however; it had to be the Soviets, who, by their rejection of Marshall Plan aid, would be responsible for the division of Europe.

The likelihood that the Soviets would do precisely that was very strong. European cooperation would mean that the Soviet Union would have to disclose full information about its economy and allow the United States to have some control in its economic planning, as well as in that of its satellites. This was unthinkable to a totalitarian state; a Communist state could hardly permit capitalists to have a voice in its economic development. Soviet participation would also have required the Soviet Union and its satellites to contribute toward Europe's recovery with food and raw materials in return for the help they were receiving from the United States. The Soviets would actually be helping to stabilize Europe. But if they did not participate, preferring to exploit Europe's misery, they would be blamed for continuing and aggravating the cold war. In either case, the United States could not lose by invoking Karl Marx's slogan, "From each according to his ability, to each according to his need." When Soviet foreign minister V. M. Molotov came to Paris with a large delegation of experts, he gave American policy makers a scare—but only for a moment. Molotov denounced the plan as an attempt to interfere with Soviet sovereignty and withdrew. Western Europe could now plan the use of America's dollars for its recovery.

Was the Marshall Plan a success? The results tell their own story. By 1950, when the Korean War broke out, Europe was already exceeding its prewar production by 25 percent; two years later, this figure was 200 percent higher. British exports were doing well, French inflation was slowing, and German production had reached its 1936 level. The dollar gap had been reduced from $12 billion to $2 billion. In human terms, Europe's cities were being rebuilt, its factories were busy, the stores restocked, and its farmers productive. The Marshall Plan was a huge success, and at a cost that represented only a tiny fraction of the U.S. national income over the same four-year period. Indeed, it was smaller than America's liquor bill for the same years! These were the State Department's best years as it took the lead in organizing U.S. foreign policy, which reflected some of the best characteristics of the country: its self-confidence and generosity, energy and imagination. These were years of excitement as the United States emerged as a great power and as young men and women from government, business, finance, and academia flocked to Washington and Western Europe to ensure the success of the Marshall Plan. Winston Churchill called it "the most unsordid act in history."

The U.S. Commitment to Europe's Defense

Soon after the Marshall Plan was launched, however, it became clear that the plan by itself would not suffice. In February 1948 the Soviets engineered a coup d'état in Prague, and—ten years after Munich and Hitler's subsequent seizure of that betrayed nation—Czechoslovakia disappeared behind the iron curtain. A few months later, in June, the Soviets imposed a blockade on Berlin in an effort to dislodge the Western powers. It is not surprising that the Europeans felt extremely jittery at these overt signs of Soviet hostility and aggressive intent. In this atmosphere of tension and insecurity, in which comparisons of Joseph Stalin's Russia with Hitler's Germany seemed all too valid, it became obvious that Europe's economic recovery was impossible. People do not make the necessary sacrifices and work hard to recuperate today if they feel that tomorrow they will be conquered and that their efforts will all have been in vain. In short, it suddenly became crystal clear that a prerequisite for Europe's recovery was military security.

The Europeans had already made some moves in this direction. In March 1947 France and Britain had signed the Treaty of Dunkirk to provide for their mutual defense against a threat to their security. Exactly a year later, Great Britain, France, the Netherlands, Belgium, and Luxembourg signed the Brussels Pact of collective self-defense. The pact was established as a military counterpart to the OEEC. Just as the OEEC was dedicated to economic cooperation, the pact was committed to military cooperation. And just as the vitality of the OEEC had depended on the influx of American capital for its success, the pact members expected their alliance to attract American military support.

The Formation of NATO

They were not disappointed. In April 1949 Belgium, Canada, Denmark, France, Great Britain, Iceland, Italy, Luxembourg, the Netherlands, Norway, Portugal, and the United States created the North Atlantic Treaty Organization (NATO). For the United States, the NATO commitment set a precedent: for the first time in its history, the country had committed itself to an alliance in peacetime. Europe had become "our first line of defense." It was precisely the knowledge that the United States would fight to preserve Europe's freedom that was supposed to prevent a Soviet attack. American participation in two world wars had proved Europe's vital importance to American security. Instead of again allowing the balance of power to be upset and once more becoming drawn into a war after it had started, the United States now expected to prevent this by committing itself to the preservation of the European balance in peacetime. The presumption was that the fear of meeting American resistance and fighting an all-out war with the United States would deter a potential aggressor.

The policy of deterrence relied almost exclusively on American strategic air power—that is, upon the ability of the Strategic Air Command (SAC) to completely destroy the Soviet Union with atomic bombs. This strategy was based on two assumptions: first, that a future war would be a total war that would be precipitated by a direct Soviet attack on the United States or Western Europe; and second, that deterrence could be achieved by air power and its ability to inflict such heavy damage that an enemy would, in effect, be committing suicide if it launched an attack.

Two events were to change this reliance on air power alone to deter or destroy the enemy. The first was the explosion of the first Soviet atomic bomb in late 1949. This foreshadowed a time when the Soviet Union, too, would possess a stockpile of nuclear weapons and the means to deliver them. The American monopoly would then no longer be able to restrain the superior Soviet conventional forces. The second event was the North Korean attack on South Korea in June 1950. Because it was presumed that such an attack could not have occurred without Soviet permission, the North Korean aggression suggested a change in Soviet intentions. Perhaps Moscow would risk another Berlin crisis, permit East Germany to attack West Germany, or even launch an invasion of Western Europe itself. The Western response to the contingencies was large-scale rearmament.

This involved three tasks for NATO: the establishment of a command structure, the formulation of a strategy by which to defend Europe on the ground, and the rebuilding of its ground forces. These efforts began with the appointment of General Dwight Eisenhower to serve as Supreme Allied Commander in Europe.

The 'Forward Strategy'

The strategy NATO adopted was known as the "forward strategy"— that is, Europe's defense was to be established at the line between East Germany and West Germany, the so-called intra-German border. Politically, the Europeans wanted no part of a strategy that called for a withdrawal that would bring the Soviet army to their borders, if not into their countries. They had no desire to be a battlefield again. And liberation in a war in which atomic bombs would be dropped was no liberation at all: one could not liberate a corpse. From a political standpoint, Allied forces could not retreat.

Such a defense required troops and proper logistical support. When Eisenhower arrived in Europe, he found, including the American troops, only twelve divisions—none of which was at full strength, properly trained, or fully equipped with the latest weapons. Nor were there any effective reserves to back them up. Perhaps neither of these facts was surprising: the European powers had greater needs and more important priorities in the immediate postwar days than to maintain or rebuild sizable military forces. In addition, because of America's atomic monopoly, it seemed quite safe to rely solely on SAC for deterrence and to use the troops in Germany mainly for occupation duties.

But Eisenhower needed more ground forces for two purposes. First, they would act as a "tripwire." In case the Soviets harbored doubts that the United States would defend Western Europe, the tripwire troops were to make the U.S. commitment credible. An attack by the Red Army would cost American lives; this would ensure American retaliation against the Soviet Union. Second, the NATO army was to act as a "shield" by holding the Soviet army at the point of attack while SAC destroyed the Soviet Union. Military planners believed that such shield forces would have to be quite large because of the size of the Soviet army.

But the need for an ample number of divisions presented the European states with a painful dilemma. They were still in the midst of economic recovery and were not able to devote too large a share of national budgets to rearmament. The American answer was the rearmament of Germany. If France and Britain could not supply the necessary troops, Germany would have to. This decision seemed eminently correct because the forward strategy required that NATO would try to hold West Germany. It was only fitting that the Germans should contribute to their own defense. In turn, of course, German rearmament reinforced the need for a forward strategy. The West Germans could hardly be persuaded to rearm if they could not be assured that West Germany would not be turned into a battlefield and that German troops would not be used merely for the defense of France and Britain. Thus, the question of Germany once more raised its head. It was not a new question, but this time it received new answers.

The Revival of Germany

Germany has held the key to the European balance of power since at least 1870 when Prussia defeated France, Europe's preeminent land power, and established a united Germany. This was true of Germany even in defeat in 1945. Almost from the cessation of hostilities, the Soviet Union and the United States began their contest over Germany. East Germany was in Soviet hands; the Western powers occupied West Germany. Actually, the Allies were lucky, for West Germany contained the great majority of Germany's population and the heart of its industrial power. West Germany, in short, was the chief prize in Europe.

During the war Joseph Stalin, Winston Churchill, and Franklin Roosevelt had decided to govern Germany through a four-power Allied

Control Commission (with France as the fourth power), which would administer the entire country as a single economic unit. In practice, this task proved impossible. The Soviet Union, Britain, and France, as well as the smaller European nations, had been promised reparations payments in compensation for the widespread destruction the Germans had caused. The Soviets were to receive all the industrial equipment in the Soviet zone, plus one-quarter of the far greater industrial complex in West Germany (it was somehow assumed during the war that Germany's industrial power would be intact at the end of the war). But—and these were the decisive points—the United States and Great Britain had insisted upon two restrictions on these reparations payments. First, Germany was to be left enough of its nonmilitary industries to maintain its standard of living at the same level as the rest of Europe (but definitely not higher); and second, no reparations were to be paid out of current production until Germany had earned enough money with its exports to pay for the imports it needed. Germany was to support itself. The Allies had no desire to spend their money supporting their former enemy.

The Soviets quickly began demolishing the industry in their zone without informing the Western powers how much they were taking. The Soviets also cut off the regular food supply from East Germany, which traditionally had been Germany's breadbasket; under the original agreement, the Soviets were to furnish this food in return for the three-fifths of capital equipment they were allowed to remove from the Western zones. These Soviet actions led to trouble. Almost exactly a year after V-E Day (May 7, 1945), the United States announced that it was suspending all further West German reparations payments to the Soviet Union. They were not to be resumed until the Soviet Union operated its zone under the original terms of agreement. The reason for the American action was clear: if East Germany no longer furnished the food that West Germany needed, West Germany would have to increase its exports to buy food from abroad; and if it had to increase exports, it had to increase production. The British agreed. The wartime agreement to hold German industrial production down for fear that Germany would again use its heavy industry in a secret rearmament program—as it had during the years between the two world wars—was abrogated. The American and British purpose was to make Germany pay for its own needs.

But the two powers had a more important aim in mind: as Europe's economic collapse became clearer and the cold war began, it became necessary to lift Germany out of its economic stagnation and make its industry contribute to the general economic recovery of Europe. In July 1946 the United States offered to merge its zone with those of Britain and France; Germany was to be decompartmentalized to speed up its industrial recovery. The French, fearing Germany's reviving strength, at first refused to partici- pate, but later joined. But this fusion would not by itself achieve Germany's economic recovery; it needed the willing cooperation of the Germans, too. The

United States and Britain decided to let the Germans begin to take a more active part in running their own country; this, in effect, foreshadowed the eventual establishment of a West German government.

The Soviets reacted to this event by blockading West Berlin in 1948. Berlin, like Germany, was supposed to be administered by the four occupying powers, but the growing cold war divided the city just as it did Germany. Lying deep in East German territory, surrounded by Soviet divisions, the Western half of the city was an easy and vulnerable spot for the Soviets to apply pressure on the Western powers. The issue at stake was more than the Western presence in Berlin: it was Germany itself. Berlin, as the old capital of Germany, was the symbol of the conflict. The Soviets did not want to see West Germany become a partner of the West. Germany and Russia had fought two wars in forty years. Germany had beaten Russia the first time and almost defeated it on the second occasion.

The Soviet Union's fear of Germany, however, was not completely responsible for its actions in Berlin. If Soviet fear of Germany was so deep, the Soviets would have accepted an American proposal, offered by Secretary of State James Byrnes, of an alliance of twenty-five or even forty years to neutralize Germany. Moreover, although the Soviet Union had been much weaker than Germany before World War II, it emerged from that conflict far stronger—a superpower, in fact—while Germany, in spite of its potential strength, was now only a second-class power. The Soviet-German balance of power had shifted decisively in the Soviet Union's favor, and another German attack on the Soviet Union was unlikely. In any war, whether it acted unilaterally or as an ally of the United States, Germany would be the battlefield and therefore the first country to be destroyed. Fear of this consequence was a sufficient deterrent.

But Soviet concerns were also offensive because, once the power of a revived Germany was added to that of the United States and its NATO allies, the American position in Europe obviously would be greatly strengthened. This, in turn, stood in the way of two Soviet objectives: one, the withdrawal of American forces and the neutralization of Western Europe (hence the rejection of a German neutrality treaty that kept America involved in Europe);[1] and two, Germany's participation in a subservient partnership. Germany's recovery, in short, would block the Soviet aims of excluding the United States from Europe and becoming the dominant power in Europe. The Soviet aim was therefore to inflict a diplomatic defeat on the United States to destroy its credibility as Europe's protector.

To forestall West Germany's revival, therefore, the Soviets resorted to a test of strength. If the Allies could be forced out of Berlin, German confidence in the United States would be undermined. The

---

1. One suspects that Moscow today would eagerly embrace such a solution in preference to a reunited Germany within NATO.

Germans would not attach themselves to a friend too weak or too fearful to protect them. Indeed, if American willpower crumbled under Soviet pressure, France and Britain would also lose confidence in the United States. Had it not been met, the Berlin crisis would have destroyed the evolving American commitment in Europe (NATO was still in the future) and nullified U.S. efforts to rebuild Western Europe as a partner in the struggle against the Soviet Union. The United States had to defend its position in West Berlin because the consequences for failure were so enormous.

The method of conflict was decided at the outset by the unwillingness of either the United States or the Soviet Union to risk a total war. The Western powers ruled out any attempt to reopen the corridor to Berlin by challenging the Soviet army with troops and tanks. Instead, they decided on an airlift to supply the city with all its needs. The Soviets did not challenge this effort, for they were aware that in doing so they would leave the West no alternative but to fight a total war. Rather, the Soviets waited to see if the Western powers could take care of Berlin's 2.5 million citizens. It would take a minimum of 4,000 tons of food and fuel daily—an enormous amount of tonnage to ship in by air. After 324 days the Soviets were convinced that the Americans and the British were more than equal to the task. Although the total supplies did not immediately attain the 4,000-ton target, Western planes eventually flew in as much as 13,000 tons daily. Planes landing at three-minute intervals flew in 60 percent more than the 8,000 tons that had previously been sent each day by ground transport. By the spring of 1949, West Berliners were eating better than at the beginning of the blockade—and considerably better than the East Berliners! Faced with this colossal Allied achievement, the Soviets called off the blockade in May.

The U.S. determination to hold Western Europe and not to allow further Soviet expansion had been demonstrated. The West Germans clearly saw that they could count on America to protect them. Just as NATO had been the prerequisite for Europe's economic recovery, the Berlin airlift was the final American act that led to Germany's resurgence. The United States had laid the basis for Germany's economic recovery through Marshall Plan funds; in NATO, it had given Germany the sense of military security without which its economic reconstruction could not have been completed. For the time being, the Soviet efforts to "decouple" Western Europe from the United States ended.

Europe Moves Toward Unification

Ironically, it was renewed fear of Germany's rising strength that stimulated further efforts toward European integration. The specter of a fully revived Germany struck fear into most of Germany's neighbors. The French, with their memories of 1870, 1914, and 1940, were particularly alarmed. Germany's recovery, stimulated by America's response to the cold war, posed a serious problem for Germany's partners: How could they hold Germany in check when it was potentially the strongest nation in Europe outside of the Soviet Union? Ever since Germany's unification, France had dealt with the inherently greater strength of its aggressive and militaristic neighbor by forming alliances that could balance Germany's power. Because Britain had usually preferred to retain a free hand, and because British interests were also at times opposed to those of France, the French had relied primarily on Continental allies. Before World War I, they discovered such an ally in Russia, and between the two wars they found partners in Poland, Czechoslovakia, Romania, and Yugoslavia. None of these alliances had saved France, however. In both world wars, British and American power (aided by the Soviets in World War II) had been the decisive factor in defeating Germany. After the war and despite the extension of Soviet power into the heart of Europe, France still saw Germany as the enemy, and in December 1944 the French signed a mutual assistance treaty with the Soviets, making an alliance they considered necessary for their security. Soviet hostility soon disillusioned the French and deprived the treaty of any meaning, however. In fact, this hostility made it necessary to add Germany's power to that of the West.

The failure of a traditional balance-of-power technique, by which an inferior power sought to balance a stronger nation, led France to seek a new way of exerting some control over Germany's growing power. French leaders found an imaginative means in European integration. It was through the creation of a supranational community, to which Germany could transfer certain sovereign rights, that German power could be controlled. Instead of serving national purposes, German power would serve Europe's collective purposes.

France's Initiative and Aims

France made its first move in the direction of a united Europe in May 1950, when Foreign Minister Robert Schuman proposed the European Coal and Steel Community (ECSC) composed of "Little Europe" (France, Germany, Italy, and the Benelux countries of Belgium, the Netherlands, and Luxembourg). The aim of the Schuman Plan, as it was also known, was to interweave German and French heavy industry to such an extent that it would be impossible ever to separate them. Germany would never again be able to use its coal and steel industries for nationalistic and militaristic purposes. War between Germany and France would become not only unthinkable but also impossible.

But the new French technique of restraining Germany was more than an incorporation of Germany's superior strength, thereby subjecting Germa-

European Coal and Steel Community

ny's power to a certain degree of French control. "Europeanization" was also a means for France to achieve a balance with Germany. The combination of the French and German coal and steel industries would strengthen French heavy industry and create a Franco-German equilibrium within the ECSC. Economic integration would allow France to overcome its inferior industrial strength, due primarily to its lack of energy sources. In Lorraine, France possessed Europe's largest iron ore deposits—resources that during Germany's annexation of Alsace-Lorraine from 1871 to 1918 had helped make Germany the greatest industrial power in Europe before 1914. But even when it had regained Alsace-Lorraine after World War I, France still lacked the coal to heat the furnaces. Europe's largest coal deposits lay in the Ruhr and to a lesser extent in the Saar—that is, in Germany.

The Schuman Plan, in effect, held out a bargain to West Germany. France was to receive coal from Germany at the same price paid by German manufacturers, not at the previously higher prices that had made French products more expensive than German products. In return, France was to abandon its opposition to raising German production and prevail upon Britain and the United States to lift *all* controls from Germany's heavy industry. This would mean that Germany could compete again in the international market. Even more important for Germany, entry into the ECSC would be the first step toward nationhood. Despite its moral shame, recovering its sovereignty and strengthening its ties with its former Western enemies meant that eventually Germany could join NATO. Thus, the Schuman Plan had both an economic and a political appeal for the Germans as well as the French.

The French plan, however, was not devised only to control Germany's resurgent power or to give France greater strength relative to Germany. It had a third and more ambitious goal in mind: a united Europe under French leadership. France alone was too weak to pursue an active part in a world dominated by two superpowers. Even in the Western coalition, the most influential European nation was not France, but Britain. With Germany's recovery, it was very likely that Bonn's voice and opinions would also outweigh those of Paris in Washington. By itself, France would remain dependent on its American protector, powerless to affect major Western policy decisions. A united Europe, with Franco-German unity at its core, was therefore France's alternative to remaining subservient to the United States and without major influence either in NATO or on the world stage. Through a united Europe France could gain an equal voice with what Charles de Gaulle was later to call the "Anglo-Saxons" in NATO, and possibly even exert independent pressure upon the Soviet Union.

These, then, were the benefits the French expected to gain from the Schuman Plan. They saw clearly that the nucleus of a united Europe would have to be a Franco-German union. The antagonism between these two states, born of their traditional enmity, would first have to be healed. Moreover, the French scheme did more than just evoke the dream of a united Europe, hoping that its vision would so fire people's imagination that they would suddenly discard their narrow nationalistic loyalties for a wider European allegiance. The new Europe could not be created by sentiment alone; the French were determined to build it on a solid foundation. They knew they would have to tie together the interests of politically powerful and economically important groups in the various nations *across* national boundaries. The removal of all trade barriers in the coal and steel sector would encourage the modernization of mines and plants, as well as the elimination of mines and plants that continued to operate inefficiently. Once producers had adjusted to the wider market and witnessed its opportunities, they would want to remove national barriers in other areas. Further, as production increased, Europe's standard of living would rise, and, as French and Italian workers received more of what they believed to be their share, labor would see that its goal of a welfare state could be achieved only at the European level.

The French showed great political astuteness in their selection of heavy industry as the first to be integrated because coal and steel form the basis of the entire industrial structure and represent a sector that cannot possibly be separated from the overall economy. The French expected that, as the benefits of the pooling of heavy industry became clear, other sectors of the economy would follow suit, eventually leading to the creation of a United States of Europe with a huge market and a mass-production system. In brief, this approach stressed supranational cooperation and institutions within a limited sphere and the creation of common interests within that particular area of activity before extending it to other fields.

German Rearmament and Solving the German Problem

The ECSC institutions, then, were the embryo of a united Europe. They were soon applied to a new area: the military forces of the different countries. The French originated this idea, too, in response to American insistence on German rearmament. To the French, the rearmament of their old enemy was distasteful and dangerous, but unavoidable because France could not supply more troops. But the French remained determined that the world would never see another *German* army, *German* general staff, *German* war ministry, or *German* ministry of armaments. The French proposed the formation of a European Defense Community (EDC). A European army, composed of army corps in which no more than two divisions could be of one nationality, would be an instrument for checking Germany's rising military power while using it for Europe's defense. The EDC treaty was signed in May 1952. NATO, of course, remained the supreme command and maintained a formal link to the EDC. Because all EDC members except Germany were members of NATO, this link ensured that Germany was obligated to come to NATO's defense and vice versa. It also made it clear that NATO had a double purpose: contain Soviet power as well as control German power.

For Germany, entry into the EDC was another step toward regaining full equality with the other Western powers and asserting its political prestige. Most important, in return for providing the EDC with 500,000 men organized into twelve divisions, Germany recovered its sovereignty, with certain limitations. The allies reserved their authority to protect the security of their forces in Germany (not only against external aggression but also against possible attempts by the extreme left or right to subvert West Germany from within), to govern Berlin, and—to prevent any Soviet-German deal—to preserve their exclusive right to negotiate with the Soviet Union on the question of German reunification. The kind of Germany they would have liked to achieve was a unified Germany enjoying a democratic constitution—like that of the new Federal Republic, as West Germany came to be called—and integrated into the European community.

The likelihood of attaining this objective, however, was small. Western proposals to unite Germany constantly included terms that the Soviet Union could not possibly accept. These terms included reunification via free elections in both halves of Germany and insistence on allowing the government of this reunified Germany freedom to conduct its own foreign policy. The first part of the proposal would have meant the end of the Soviet-imposed Communist regime in East Germany, ironically called the German Democratic Republic; and the second part would have allied a unified Germany, probably headed by the pro-Western government of Konrad Adenauer, with the West. As this would bring NATO to the Polish frontier and the Eastern satellite belt, the Soviets were hardly likely to accept.

Allied terms, in short, ensured a continuation of a divided Germany, which was precisely what the Western Europeans wanted. France did not want to integrate with a united Germany, which the French feared would be too strong. Symptomatic of this concern was the cynical remark made by a French novelist that "I love Germany so much that I want there to be two of them." France, therefore, opposed Germany's reunification; although it, together with the United States, paid lip service to this goal to keep the West German government of Chancellor Adenauer in power. For the German people, reunification was a vital concern; at least, there were constant reaffirmations of it as a declaratory goal. Among other things, it allowed Adenauer to claim that through West Germany's alliance with the Western powers the country would some day be able to negotiate the Soviet Union's exit from East Germany.

But it is doubtful that Adenauer preferred a reunited Germany, which would have to be neutralized to satisfy Moscow, to a divided Germany whose western part would be tightly integrated into a democratic Western Europe. For it ought to be noted that West Germany is a Germany without Prussia, the state whose authoritarianism and militarism in 1870 had unified Germany, which reflected these values and twice plunged the world into war in the twentieth century. The southern part of Germany had been hostile to Protestant Prussia, and the Rhineland has been much influenced historically by Western (especially French) democratic thought. A reunified Germany might have stimulated a movement to resurrect Prussia, which had finally been destroyed by the war. It might therefore be said that, if Germany had to be divided, the postwar division, which cuts Prussia off from the Western part of Germany, could not have been more aptly drawn.

This division of Germany solved the German problem for Moscow as well because it brought Soviet power to West Germany's doorstep, reminding it of the dangers of any further military adventures, and legitimated the presence of the Soviet army in Eastern Europe. In short, the division of Germany served both adversaries' purposes and—except for a short but dangerous period in the late 1950s and early 1960s when the Soviets tested the status quo—served as the basis for the longest peace Europe has known in the twentieth century. A divided Germany might not have been just according to the principle of national self-determination, but it was part of a clearly split Europe in which both Moscow and Washington knew where the lines, or "frontiers," were between their respective spheres of influence and what the danger was of crossing this line at any point.

It seems a cruel twist of fate that the success of American foreign policy in fortifying Western Europe should have brought about a shift in the focus of Soviet pressure from Europe to Asia, a shift that in June 1950 led to the outbreak of the Korean War. The Truman Doctrine had prevented a Soviet breakthrough into the Middle East, the Mediterranean, and the Persian Gulf. The Marshall Plan had set Europe on the path to economic recovery and health. NATO had guaranteed Europe its security. The lessons of two world wars had been absorbed, and the NATO commitment was the proof of this.

The United States had transformed a position of great weakness and vulnerability into one of relative strength. It had drawn a clear line between the American and Soviet spheres of influence and had demonstrated, in Turkey, Greece, and Berlin, that it was in Europe to stay. (The Greek crisis had passed when Yugoslavia was ejected from the Soviet bloc in 1948; the Yugoslavs no longer provided aid to the Greek guerrillas.) What all this meant was that Europe was no longer a profitable field for guerrilla warfare, coups d'état, subversive attempts, or military intimidation. Instead, it had become a barrier to the extension of Soviet influence. To cross the line drawn by the United States was to risk total war, and the Soviet Union was not willing to assume this risk while the United States held atomic superiority. The Soviet leaders, as George Kennan had said, did not believe in pursuing an "adventuristic" policy that gambled with the very existence of the Soviet state.

They turned their attention instead to the Far East. Here was a much more attractive field for political and military exploitation. Most countries in this area had only recently emerged from Western colonialism, and their nationalistic and anti-Western feelings were very strong. Nationalist China's collapse and the establishment of a Communist government on the mainland in late 1949 had further weakened the American position in Asia, for it had shifted the balance of power in the Far East against the United States. The United States no longer confronted only the Soviet Union; it was now faced with the challenge of the combined strength of the Sino-Soviet bloc. In addition, pressure in Europe united the Western powers, but pressure in Asia divided them, because they were split over the character and nature of the new Chinese regime. And finally, no expansionist move in the Far East would entail the risk of total war. In the American pattern of defense, Europe held strategic priority; Asia was of secondary interest. Europe was so vital to American security that any Soviet move in Western Europe ran the risk of an all-out clash with the United States; no single area in Asia was worth the cost of total war. The recovery of Europe and China's collapse, then, created a vacuum in the East and turned Soviet pressure toward Asia. It was here that the dramatic clashes of the cold war occurred during the next four years. These clashes led to a reaction within the United States against its foreign policy.

Containment
in the Far East

SUCCESS in Europe was followed by disaster in Asia. The collapse of Nationalist China, upon whose postwar support the United States had counted, was followed by the Korean War, the first limited war in U.S. experience in the twentieth century. As the war dragged on without the victory American arms traditionally had won, President Harry Truman and his administration lost popularity. These problems in Asia had serious domestic consequences. Charges of conspiracy and betrayal limited the administration's diplomatic freedom, pressured it into a policy of global anticommunism, and resulted in more than twenty years of confrontation with the new Communist China. The failure to establish normal relations with China was a strategic error of the first dimension: it helped to provoke Chinese intervention in the Korean War; prevented Washington from exploiting Sino-Soviet differences when they first surfaced; and was one cause of the tragic U.S. involvement in Indochina. Indeed, the events in Asia in the late 1940s and early 1950s were to have a profound impact on American foreign policy for the next two decades.

The Fall of Nationalist China

During World War II the United States had a twofold purpose in the Pacific: to defeat Japan and to create a powerful and friendly China in its place. It was hoped that a strong and democratic China would play a leading role in protecting the postwar peace in the Far East. The United States took several actions to confer upon China the status of a great power. It renounced its extraterritorial rights in China, repealed the Chinese exclusion laws, established an annual Chinese immigration quota, and made it possible for legally admitted Chinese to become American citizens. At Cairo in 1943, together with Great Britain, the United States promised to return "all the territories Japan had stolen from the Chinese, such as Manchuria, Formosa, and the Pescadores." It also awarded China one of the five permanent seats on the United Nations Security Council; China was granted equal status with the Soviet Union, Great Britain, France, and the United States.

The conviction of President Franklin Roosevelt and his advisers that the mere pronouncement of China as a great power could actually convert it into one was typically American: one need only believe strongly enough in the desirability of an event for it to happen. Perhaps American policy makers also hoped that if China were considered a great power, it would behave like one. But American faith without Chinese cooperation was insufficient to accomplish the task. It would have taken a miracle to do that, and, although national leaders at times delude themselves into thinking that they can perform miracles, such things happen only in storybooks.

The first obstacle to creating a strong China was the sharp division within the country. Quite apart from the Japanese occupation of large areas of the country during the war, the Chinese were deeply split among themselves. There was not one China, but two—a Communist China and a Nationalist China. The Communists were not scattered throughout the whole population, as they were in Europe. Already in control of large segments of northwest China, the Communists extended their sphere during the war by infiltrating north-central China. In this region the Japanese held the cities and the major lines of communication and the Communists organized the countryside. By 1945 they controlled 116 million people, one-fifth of China's entire population, within an area that constituted 15 percent of China's territory exclusive of Manchuria. Communist China was, in short, a nation within a nation, and the two were engaged in a bitter civil war.

If the United States wanted to create a united China, it would have to end the civil war. The American aim was to establish a coalition government in which all parties would be represented. The desirability of such a government was not questioned. What possible harm could there be in uniting the Nationalists and the Communists? The United States and the Soviet Union were cooperating against the common enemy, and most leaders and officials of the American government looked forward to friendly postwar relations. If these two nations, each representing a totally different way of life, could overcome past differences and get along together, why should the two Chinese parties not be able to settle their conflict? The United States had another, more immediate reason to end China's division as quickly as possible. A China torn apart by internal strife could not make an effective contribution to fighting the Japanese. After Pearl Harbor, the Nationalists and the Communists assumed that the United States would defeat Japan; therefore, they were fighting for control of China after the war. But the American attitude is that, once war breaks out, the total effort must be directed toward the single goal of military victory; any diversion of strength—particularly for "extraneous" political purposes—is considered unjustifiable. The war had to be won in the quickest possible time and with the minimum number of casualties. This attitude reinforced the American desire to establish a coalition government in China.

All efforts aimed at achieving this goal, both during the war and afterward, were in vain. Neither side trusted the other. Both sought a monopoly of power, and both were aware of the important role their armies played in the struggle for power: the Nationalists recognized that they would have to gain control of the Communist army to ensure their own survival; the Communists knew that they needed their army to defeat Chiang Kai-shek. Control of the army of a coalition government was a key obstacle to unifying the nation. At the end of the war, each side—particularly the Nationalists—believed they could defeat their opponent; compromise was thought to be unnecessary.

China's pro-American Nationalist government, however, was losing popular support and disintegrating. Perhaps the Nationalists were the victims of fate. Except for the two years from 1929 to 1931, the government was constantly engaged in fighting for its very survival—against the Japanese (who attacked Manchuria in 1931 and China in 1932 [Shanghai] and 1937), as well as the Communists. Faced with both external and internal danger, Chiang had neither the time nor the resources to formulate and implement the political, social, and economic reforms China needed. His principal concerns were military: to stem the Japanese advance and maintain himself in power. The problem of modernizing China—above all, of meeting peasant aspirations—was strictly secondary. Moreover, Japanese successes during the war cut off an important source of Chiang's support and thereby rendered any agrarian reform impossible. By 1939 the Japanese had occupied the entire coastal area of China and had driven the Nationalists inland. This meant that Chiang's Kuomintang party, which controlled the government, had lost the main pillar of its support, the progressive commercial and financial interests in the coastal cities. Instead, it was forced to rely on the conservative landlord class.

A government whose principal social and economic support came from the landlords was unlikely to carry out land reforms the peasants sought. That the peasants constituted four-fifths of China's population also meant that they provided most of the conscripts for the Nationalist army. The able-bodied and eligible sons of the rich avoided military service because their families bribed corrupt officials. In the same way, the rich tended to avoid paying taxes. Chiang, in short, seemed to be doing his best to alienate the peasants, the vast majority of China's population. The Nationalist position deteriorated even further because of China's unchecked inflation, which had a devastating effect on low-level government officials. It provided them with a massive incentive for corruption because their salaries were wholly inadequate.

As Chiang's government lost popularity, it began to resort increasingly to force to hold its position. The resulting police and military measures further alienated the people. The American commander in China during the war, General Albert Wedemeyer, described this situation: "Secret police operate widely, very much as they do in Russia and as they did in Germany. People disappear. . . . No trials and no sentences. . . . Everyone lives with a feeling of fear and loses confidence in the government." This was particularly true of the intellectuals, who, together with the peasantry, have been the traditional supporters of China's governments. Professors were dismissed, even arrested, when they began to criticize the government for its policies. Students similarly inclined were also thrown into jail.

The result, not surprisingly, was that the majority of Chinese simply disengaged themselves from the Nationalists and became indifferent to the outcome of the civil war. They did not rise up against the government in a "popular revolution." The Communists won the civil war—and the military conflict played the decisive role in determining this issue—and they did so because most Chinese were willing to give the Communists the benefit of the doubt and allow them to demonstrate that they could give China a more effective government.

The Communist Strategy for Victory

One reason for the lack of hostility and suspicion toward the Communists, then, was that they were not the Nationalists. A more positive reason was the favorable picture the Communists presented to the Chinese population. In the areas they controlled, the Communists did not destroy the traditional tenure system or eliminate the landlords. Rather, they reduced the rents to a fixed maximum. They permitted private enterprise and allowed all factions to participate in local government. Although they assured Communist control by retaining the power to approve all candidates, their activities nevertheless seemed to support their claim that they stood for democracy, freedom, and individual liberty. Certainly, their economic and political practices demonstrated little Marxist bias. They appeared, instead, as genuine democrats, and their pose as agrarian reformers was widely accepted— precisely because they actually carried out reforms. This was, of course, a tactical device. But the point remains that it was effective and achieved its purposes: it attracted minority support among the various strata of China's population disaffected by Nationalist policies, and it gained acquiescence among the rest of the population.

The Communist position for the final military struggle was further strengthened when, near the end of the Pacific war, the Soviet army marched into Manchuria. Once established, the Soviets did two things that hurt the Nationalists. First, they dismantled Manchuria's industry and transported the machinery back to the Soviet Union to help restore their own badly damaged industry. As a result, Manchuria, China's industrial heartland, was unable to contribute to the country's economic recovery. Second, the Soviets allowed the Chinese Communists to infiltrate the countryside and handed them large stocks of Japanese arms and ammunition. Conversely, the Soviets delayed the return of Nationalist troops, who had to launch a major offensive to establish their control over Manchuria. The government forces captured the cities, but the Communists remained in control of the countryside. The Soviet invasion of Manchuria dealt a serious blow to the Nationalists.

The U.S. Role in China's Fall

The blame for these events has often been attributed to President Franklin Roosevelt and the Yalta "betrayal," which granted the Soviet Union, among other things, a continuation of the status quo (that is, Soviet control) in Mongolia; a restoration of the rights Russia had held in Manchuria before its defeat by Japan in 1904-1905; the lease of Port Arthur as a Soviet naval base; the internationalization of the commercial port of Talien, which, unlike the Soviet Union's own Siberian port of Vladivostok, was not icebound part of the year; and the joint Sino-Soviet operation of the Chinese-Eastern and South-Manchurian railroads, which served these three cities. Joseph Stalin, in short, was seeking to regain Russia's preeminent influence, which the czarist government had lost, in Manchuria and northern China along the Chinese-Soviet frontier.

To take the charge of betrayal seriously, however, one has to deny certain clear facts of wartime military strategy: namely, that the American military was unsure the atomic bomb would be a success; that they believed an invasion of Japan would be necessary to bring about Japan's surrender; that they expected to suffer large numbers of casualties and feared even more if the Japanese reinforced the home-island garrison with troops from Manchuria and northern China; and that, therefore, they wanted the Red Army to tackle these mainland forces before the U.S. invasion. The American government was willing to reward the Soviets if this would help save the lives of American soldiers. Moreover, the Americans were certain that the Soviets planned to restore the czarist position in Manchuria anyway by declaring war on Japan at the moment the United States seemed to be on the verge of victory. The Soviet takeover would then be a practically bloodless operation, with a minimal contribution to Japan's defeat. American officials wanted the Soviet Union to pay at least some kind of price for what it could actually take for nothing. Moreover, as noted earlier, U.S. wartime policy aimed to satisfy the Soviet Union's traditional security interests (as in Eastern Europe) and great power interests (as in northern China). The assumption was that once the Soviet Union achieved its principal goals, it would not seek further expansion and jeopardize the postwar peace.

Finally, the Americans wanted to secure a promise from the Soviets that they would sign a treaty of alliance and friendship with the Nationalist government. The purpose of this treaty was to secure the Soviet Union's support for Chiang and to isolate his Communist opponents; this would enable Chiang to consolidate his grip on China and perhaps allow him to defeat his domestic enemy. Chiang encouraged the United States in this effort because he knew how vulnerable he was domestically and he did not want Moscow to support the Chinese Communists after the war. The Soviets, in fact, signed such a treaty with the Nationalists but then violated it by aiding their Chinese comrades. Stalin apparently did not believe, however, that this help strengthened the Chinese Communists sufficiently to defeat the Nationalists. He is reported to have counseled Mao Zedong to join Chiang in a coalition government, to accept Chiang's supremacy, and "bore from within." China was thought to be in America's sphere of influence (except where Soviet power had established itself), and for this reason Mao had to be very cautious. Mao is said to have nodded his assent to Stalin's advice and then to have disregarded it; he was more confident than Stalin of a final victory.

The Nationalists' Defeat

Throughout 1946 and 1947 the Chinese Communists limited their combat operations largely to raiding supply depots and communications lines, ambushing Nationalist forces, engaging in small-scale skirmishes, and attacking isolated garrisons. These local tactical successes heightened the Communist forces' confidence and morale just as they added to their opponents' demoralization. By 1948 the Communists had so increased the strength of their forces and firepower that they no longer had to rely solely on hit-and-run tactics; they attacked the Nationalists at will, completely overwhelming them with superior masses of troops. By February 1, 1949, they controlled all of Manchuria.

Nationalist strength by then had declined to 1.5 million men. Up until mid-September 1948, the Nationalists had been able to replace their combat losses and maintain their army at 2.7 million. In other words, in only four and a half months, the Nationalists had lost 45 percent of their troops. Meanwhile, Communist strength had risen to 1.6 million regular troops—including defectors from the Nationalist armies. Eighty percent of the American equipment furnished to the government forces during and after the war had been lost, with an estimated 75 percent of it falling into Communist hands. General David Barr, head of the American military mission in China, summed up the situation succinctly: "No battle has been lost since my arrival due to lack of ammunition or equipment. Their [the Nationalists'] military debacle, in my opinion, can all be attributed to the world's worst leadership and many other morale-destroying factors that led to a complete loss of the will to fight." [1] Nowhere was this more clearly demonstrated than in Chiang's failure, after his loss of northern China, even to attempt a defense of south China by making a stand along the Yangtze River. Chiang thereby forfeited the mainland. He withdrew to Taiwan (in those days also called Formosa), an island lying 100 miles off China's coast. In the fall of 1949 Mao proclaimed the People's Republic of China.

One question about Nationalist China's defeat remains: could the United States have prevented it? The answer is "perhaps"—*if* American officers had taken over the command of the Nationalist armies, *if* the United States had been willing to commit large-scale land, air, and sea forces, and *if* the United States had been willing to commit even greater financial aid than the approximately $2 billion it had already given since V-J Day. But these conditions could not have been met. America's rapid demobilization left it with insufficient forces either for supplying the officers for the direction of the Nationalist forces or for intervention in China. The United States had only a small standing army at home. Nor were the American people in any mood to rearm and remobilize in 1947-1948, particularly to fight a war in China.

The problem of extending further economic aid to Chiang was equally vexing. His corrupt, inefficient, and reactionary government did not provide a politically effective instrument through which to carry out the social and economic reforms China needed. Aiding Chiang seemed to be "pouring money down the drain." In contrast, U.S. economic aid to Europe, the area considered most vital to American security, had a good chance of achieving its objective—the political and economic recovery of Britain and the Continent. It probably would have been unwise in these circumstances to divert a large slice of the government's not unlimited funds to attempt to restore a government that had lost the confidence of its own people. The power and wealth of the United States was, after all, not infinite; it would have to be applied selectively. Hence, those areas of vital interest in which its use would be most effective were to be the prime focus. As Dean Acheson stated it:

> Nothing that this country did or could have done within the reasonable limits of its capabilities could have changed that result; nothing that was left undone by this country has contributed to it. It was the product of internal Chinese forces, forces which this country tried to influence but could not. A decision was arrived at within China, if only a decision by default. [2]

Reevaluation of U.S. Far East Policy

Despite Chiang Kai-shek's debacle and the disintegration of the Far Eastern balance of power, the U.S. government took an optimistic view of

1. Department of State, *United States Relations with China* (Washington, D.C.: Government Printing Office, 1949), 358.
2. Ibid, xvi.

developments. Shortly after the Nationalist collapse, Acheson expressed his belief that, despite the common ideological points of view of the Chinese and Soviet regimes, they would eventually clash with one another. Acheson predicted that Russia's appetite for a sphere of influence in Manchuria and northern China would arouse Chinese nationalism. The implications of this point of view are clear. The first is that if the Chinese Communists were genuinely concerned with the preservation of China's national interest, they would resist Soviet penetration. Mao might be an independent Communist leader like Tito. If Mao proved subservient to the Soviet Union, however, he would lose the support of the Chinese people. His regime would be identified with foreign rule because he would appear to serve the interests of another power, not of China. Given time, Acheson declared, the Chinese people would throw off this "foreign yoke." Whichever of these two developments occurred, the United States could only gain from the antithesis between communism and Chinese nationalism.

This analysis of Sino-Soviet relations indicated that the United States first had to disentangle itself from Chiang. Without this disassociation, the Chinese would link the United States with the government they had rejected. This connection would foster the growth of anti-American sentiment in China, which was just what the administration hoped to prevent. The attention of the Chinese people must remain on the Soviet Union's actions. Under no circumstances, Acheson emphasized, must America "seize the unenviable position which the Russians have carved out for themselves. We must not undertake to deflect from the Russians to ourselves the righteous anger, and the wrath, and the hatred of the Chinese population which must develop." [3] Only by disengaging itself from Chiang Kai-shek could the United States exploit the alleged clash of interests between China and the Soviet Union.

Truman's first step to implement this policy was the release of a White Paper that argued that the Nationalists had lost control of the mainland despite adequate American economic and military aid. The clear implication was that Chiang was no longer worthy of U.S. support and that American recognition of his government as the official government of China should be withdrawn. Conversely, it argued that the Communists should be recognized as the official government of China. A second act was an announcement that American military forces would not be used to defend Taiwan, and that the administration would no longer provide the Nationalists with military aid or advice: "The United States Government will not pursue a course which will lead to involvement in the civil conflict in China." This opened the way for the Chinese Communists to take Taiwan—an event that was expected before the end of 1950. The Communist government would then be the only claimant to represent China, and the United States could extend it recogni-

---

3. "Crisis in Asia—An Examination of United States Policy," *Department of State Bulletin,* January 23, 1950, 115.

tion. Chiang, through whom containment had been impossible because he had been not a container but a sieve, would have been eliminated; containment of the Soviet Union could then be implemented through the Chinese Communists. In short, the Truman administration wanted to do in 1950 what Richard Nixon finally did in 1972. But before this could happen, war had broken out in another area in the Far East—Korea—with the unfortunate result of a bitter twenty-two year gulf between the United States and the new China.

Korea: The Limited War Before Vietnam

Korea had been a divided nation since the end of World War II; Soviet forces had entered Korea two days after Japan surrendered. The nearest American troops at the time were in Okinawa, 600 miles away, and in the Philippines, 1,500 miles away. Consequently, the two powers decided to divide the country temporarily at the thirty-eighth parallel. The Soviets would disarm the Japanese above the parallel, the United States below. With the beginning of the cold war, this division became permanent. All American attempts to negotiate an end to the division and establish a democratic and united Korea failed.

The United States took the problem to the United Nations in late 1947, calling upon that organization to sponsor a free election throughout Korea. The General Assembly established a temporary commission and charged it with the responsibility of holding and supervising such an election. The Soviets, however, refused to grant the commission access to North Korea, which had been transformed into a dictatorship, and the election was limited to South Korea. Following the election, the United States recognized South Korea as the official republic and the government of Syngman Rhee as its legitimate representative. The American government also extended to Rhee economic, technical, and military aid to bolster his non-Communist government and to help Korea establish a reasonably open society despite Rhee's increasingly arbitrary rule. Although South Korea was not an ally of the United States, there could be little doubt that the young republic was America's protégé.

In the North, the Soviets had established "their" Korea. Both the South and North Korean regimes regarded themselves as the legitimate representative for Korean nationalism, and each was dedicated to the reunification of the peninsula under its control. In that sense, the war that broke out when North Korea attacked South Korea on June 25, 1950—after protracted border fighting—was a civil war between two regimes determined to eliminate the other. But it was also an international war. For events in Korea since 1945 had largely reflected the cold war rivalry and conflict between the Soviet Union and the United States. North Korea's invasion of the south could not have occurred without Stalin's acquiescence, if not approval (which,

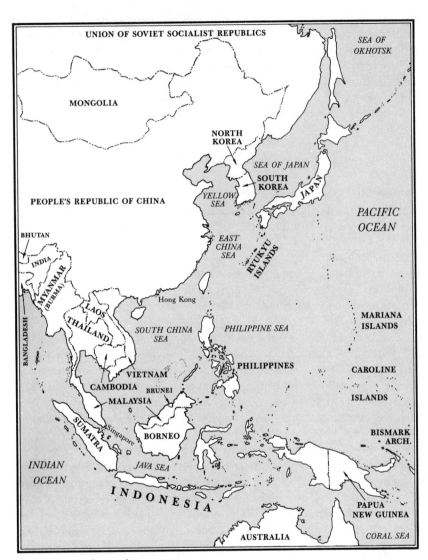

Far East and Southeast Asia

according to Stalin's successor, was given in March 1949), and considerable Soviet military aid. By contrast, the Americans had worried Rhee might go north and thus withheld the type of military equipment, such as heavy tanks, that would be needed for such a thrust. The South Korean army was not, therefore, sufficiently armed to resist an invasion. The Americans, in any case, were taken by surprise by the attack.

But the main reason for the shock was that American policy makers had thought only in terms of all-out war. It was precisely this single-minded

American preoccupation with total war that had accounted for Korea's being left outside the American Pacific defense perimeter, which ran from the Aleutians to Japan, through the Ryukyus (Okinawa) to the Philippines. This had made Korea militarily dispensable within the pattern of American security, for in a global war its fate would be decided in other theaters of war. The Korean Peninsula itself would be neutralized by American air and sea power. American troops indeed had been withdrawn from Korea because in a major war they would be vulnerable to Soviet land power and would probably be trapped. The absence of a clear American commitment turned South Korea into a vacuum for Communist expansion. Not expecting the United States to intervene in these circumstances, Stalin assented to the North Korean army attack.

South Korea's Political Importance

But overnight the survival of South Korea became identified with the security interests of the United States itself. North Korea's aggression, which in Washington's opinion could not have been launched without Soviet encouragement and support, altered the basis upon which Korea's strategic significance had been calculated. Korea's value could no longer be assessed in terms of its relative unimportance during a total war. The cold war focused attention upon the wider political and military implications for the containment policy of a North Korean military victory. If the principal purpose of containment was to prevent further Soviet expansion, American inaction in the face of Soviet aggression could only encourage future aggressive acts. The appetites of dictators were believed to be insatiable. At the very least, it had to protect South Korea.

And if containment was possible only through an alignment of U.S. power with that of allies, then failure to respond to South Korea's pleas for help must result in the disintegration of the alliance system and the isolation of the United States. If the United States stood by while South Korea fell, it would demonstrate to the world that the United States was either afraid of Soviet power or unconcerned with the safety of its friends or allies. American guarantees to help preserve their national integrity and political independence would thereafter be regarded as valueless, and this would leave nations whose security depended on U.S. willingness to live up to its commitments with no alternative but to turn to neutralism for protection and seek some form of accommodation with the Soviet Union.

This reasoning applied particularly to Japan. With the demise of Nationalist China and the disintegration of the Far Eastern balance of power, the United States was about to turn Japan into an ally in an effort to recreate some semblance of strength in the Pacific. Japan had long regarded South Korea as critical to its security. At the turn of the century, as Russian power had penetrated first Manchuria and then Korea, Japan had proposed that

Russia and Japan divide Korea at the thirty-eighth parallel. The czarist government rejected the offer, and Japan attacked Russia in 1904. The United States, as the occupying power after Japan's defeat in World War II, and responsible for Japan's security, faced a similar situation in 1950 when North Korea, close to Soviet Russia, invaded across that same parallel. Not to defend South Korea would mean that Japan would remain neutral (Stalin probably saw this as the major benefit of a North Korean victory). The same security rationale would apply in Western Europe if the United States demonstrated that it would not come to the aid of a stricken friend. The North Atlantic Treaty Organization (NATO) countries, having just signed the treaty, all recalled the U.S. retreat to isolationism after World War I. If the United States did not rescue South Korea, the likely result would be the neutralization of Western Europe as its nations would feel that, despite its NATO pledge of protection, the United States could not be counted on to keep its word. The stakes in Korea were therefore enormous: inaction would shift the Eurasian balance toward the Soviet Union and leave the United States strategically isolated. Consequently, Washington believed it had no choice but to oppose force with force.

The aggression in Korea, however, did not fit American strategic doctrine, which was based on its ability to strike an enemy with atomic bombs. The Soviets had cleverly confronted the United States with the dilemma of either risking a total war for a limited objective or taking no action and surrendering South Korea. American policy was prepared to deal only with an all-out Soviet surprise attack on the United States or Western Europe; such an attack would be met by the power of the Strategic Air Command. But American strategy was completely unprepared to deal with the kind of less-than-total challenge the Soviets posed in Asia. The North Korean aggression, in effect, meant that massive retaliation outside of Europe was not an effective policy because the deterrent effect of U.S. retaliatory power depended on whether an enemy believed that the country would actually "unleash" this power in the face of aggression. The limited attack in Korea demonstrated that the Soviet leaders were not deterred by the policy of massive retaliation, despite America's far greater atomic stockpile and ability to deliver it. They did not believe that the United States would risk all-out war to save Korea. This type of challenge could be met only by local response and primarily through the commitment of American ground forces. Containment depended not just on the capacity to deter total war with strategic air power; it required, in addition, an army to meet precisely this kind of limited incursion.

But the administration had been cutting the armed forces since the end of World War II. General George C. Marshall recalled in 1951 that the army was so small in the years preceding the Korean War that there were only one and one-third divisions in the United States. The Chiefs of Staff had so few troops at their command that they worried about obtaining enough men to guard airstrips at Fairbanks, Alaska. According to Marshall, "We had literally almost no military forces outside of our Navy and outside of an effective but not too large Air Force, except the occupation garrisons, and . . . even in Japan they were only at about 60 percent strength." [4]

For two days, June 27 and 28, the United States tried to stem the North Korean advance with air and sea forces alone. But on June 29, General Douglas MacArthur, the commander-in-chief in the Far East, reported that Korea would be lost unless ground forces were employed to halt the enemy army. The United States sent its occupation divisions from Japan to Korea, but under the aegis of the United Nations. This was done for two reasons. First, by virtue of the free election it had sponsored in South Korea, the United Nations had been intimately concerned with the birth of the young state. Second, one of the aims of American foreign policy was to associate its cold war policies with the symbolic, humanitarian values of the United Nations. Although it is traditional for nations to justify their policies in moral terms, the United States has shown a marked propensity for doing so. American depreciation of power and reluctance to recognize it as a factor in human affairs make it psychologically necessary to rationalize actions in the international arena in terms of ideological objectives and universal moral principles. American power must be "righteous" power used, not for purposes of power politics and selfish national advantage, but for the peace and welfare of all mankind. In fact, the war was an American effort, not controlled by the United Nations.

After initial setbacks, the war went well for a while. In a daring operation on September 15, MacArthur, now UN supreme commander, landed an army at the west coast port of Inchon, 150 miles behind the North Korean lines. These forces then drove northward, trapping more than half the enemy army. The rest of the shattered Communist army was in flight. On September 30, the UN forces reached the thirty-eighth parallel. The question confronting the United States was whether to cross it. The political aims of the war were all compatible with the restoration of South Korea; this implied a return to the status quo. This goal was now abandoned. The military situation favored the fulfillment of an American goal of several years' standing: the unification of the whole of Korea. The U.S. government shifted its emphasis from containing the expansion of Soviet power to the forceful liberation of a Soviet satellite. The victory at Inchon, in short, transformed the whole character of the war. It also taught the United States the foolishness of changing political goals in the middle of a war in response to battlefield successes.

The Chinese Communists React

Stricken with what the Japanese, reflecting on their experience in World War II, had called the "victory disease," the U.S. government believed that it

---

4. Quoted in John Spanier, *The Truman-MacArthur Controversy and the Korean War* (Cambridge: Belknap, 1959), 18.

was politically safe to cross the parallel and unify Korea. The administration did not think the Chinese Communist leaders would consider the UN advance a threat to their security, because they were Chinese first and Communists second. Mao and his colleagues were already thought to be so involved in their struggle with the Soviet Union over the detachment of northern China, Manchuria, and Sinkiang that their eyes were fixed on their own northern provinces rather than on North Korea. "I should think it would be sheer madness on the part of the Chinese Communists to do that [interfere]," Acheson had said a few days before Inchon. He repeated that in northern China "a great cloud from the north, Russian penetration, is operating." And he continued:

> Now I give the people in Peiping [Beijing] credit for being intelligent enough to see what is happening to them. Why should they want to further their own dismemberment and destruction by getting at cross purposes with all the free nations of the world who are inherently their friends and have always been friends of the Chinese against this imperialism coming down from the Soviet Union I cannot see.[5]

In short, there was nothing to fear. The new objective of a militarily united Korea was sanctioned by a UN resolution on October 7.

But American policy makers miscalculated. The Chinese, who were reportedly only told of the original plan for the invasion of South Korea, indeed viewed the American march to their border as threatening, just as Washington had perceived the North Korean march southward toward Japan as threatening. So Beijing sent its armies into North Korea under the guise of "volunteers," and in late November it launched a major offensive that drove the UN forces back below the thirty-eighth parallel. Throughout December 1950 and early January 1951, there was no certainty that UN troops could hold the peninsula, but they rallied and turned back the Chinese offensives. By March they had once more advanced to the thirty-eighth parallel. The administration was again faced with a decision: whether to seek a militarily unified Korea or accept a divided Korea.

There was no doubt about what MacArthur wanted to do. War, he said, indicated that "you have exhausted all other potentialities of bringing the disagreements to an end," and once engaged, "there is no alternative than to apply every available means to bring it to a swift end. War's very objective is victory—not prolonged indecision. In war there is no substitute for victory." The very term *resisting aggression* indicated "that you can destroy the potentialities of the aggressor to continually hit you" and not "go on indefinitely, neither to win or lose." One cannot fight a "half war." The administration's policy was based on the assumption that "when you use force, you can limit that force." This introduced a "new concept into military operations—the concept of appeasement." [6] MacArthur recommended a

---

5. "Crisis in Asia," 115.
6. Quoted in Spanier, *Truman-MacArthur Controversy*, 222.

naval blockade of the Chinese coast; air bombardment of China's industrial complex, communication network, supply depots, and troop assembly points; reinforcement of his forces with Chinese Nationalist troops; and "diversionary action possibly leading to counter-invasion" by Chiang against the mainland.

The Truman-MacArthur Conflict

The Truman administration rejected MacArthur's proposals because they were considered too risky. It was feared that bombing China and defeating the Soviet Union's principal ally would lead to another global war. The Sino-Soviet treaty of February 1950 bound the Soviet Union to come to the aid of China if it were attacked by Japan "or any other state which should unite with Japan" (an obvious reference to the United States). Even without this treaty, China was the Soviet Union's largest and most important ally. Soviet self-interest in the Far East and the necessity for maintaining Soviet prestige in the Communist sphere would make it difficult for the Soviet Union to ignore a direct attack upon the Chinese mainland.

But even if the Soviet Union remained a spectator, the United States could not extend the war. A "war of attrition" waged by Chinese soldiers in Korea would "bleed America dry" and make it impossible to build a strong military defense in Europe. A large-scale diversion of U.S. power to Asia would expose Europe to Soviet armies and might very well incite an attack at a moment of maximum American weakness on the Continent. The United States had to conserve its strength to check its principal enemy, the Soviet Union; the country could not afford to dissipate its power in a peripheral area against a secondary enemy. MacArthur's strategy, in the opinion of General Omar Bradley, chairman of the Joint Chiefs of Staff, would involve the United States in the wrong war, at the wrong place, at the wrong time, and with the wrong enemy.

This view was shared by Britain and France. America's chief allies were naturally reluctant to see American power diverted to the Far East before Europe was secure against Soviet attack; and they had no desire to risk such an early outbreak of World War III for an area that was of minor strategic significance to them. If the United States decided to carry the war to China, it would have to act unilaterally. But the objective of balancing Soviet might and deterring a total war was predicated on NATO's unity and combined strength.

Finally, the Joint Chiefs of Staff rejected MacArthur's proposals because they were judged militarily ineffective. All of China's essential supplies came overland from the Soviet Union. The United States decided to concentrate its air power on the 200 miles of supply line in North Korea to interdict the Chinese logistical system. The employment of Nationalist troops was rejected because they had already demonstrated their ineffectiveness in China. Moreover, the Chinese people were unlikely to welcome Chiang back.

Inherent in the administration's rejection of MacArthur's recommendations—and his dismissal when he continued to push them—was the abandonment of its objective of a militarily unified Korea and a reassertion of the original aim of the war, the defense of South Korea. This goal remained compatible with the other political reasons for which the United States had gone to war: the defense of Japan and the preservation of the NATO alliance—that is, the protection of the eastern and western rims of Eurasia. Indeed, by the time the war ended in 1953, Japan had become a U.S. ally, and NATO had not only been preserved but also strengthened by its own rearmament and the stationing of four American divisions in Europe. The wisest course was therefore to end the war where it had begun.

From Anti-Sovietism to Anticommunism

The collapse of Nationalist China and the Korean War changed U.S. foreign policy from anti-Soviet to anti-Communist. These two events constrained the flexibility of American policy and turned Washington to a more crusading and interventionist policy. It was the "loss of China" that initiated this change. Americans had regarded China as their special ward since just before the turn of the century. The original interest in China was not political but commercial—China was a potentially huge market for American products. But U.S. policy toward China had also contained a strong missionary element—a genuine interest in the welfare and Christian salvation of the Chinese people. In fact, the United States had long regarded itself as the protector of China from foreign exploitation and invasion. Through the 1899 Open Door policy—aimed at preventing Great Britain, France, Russia, Germany, and Japan from shutting American commerce out of China and at obtaining an equal opportunity to sell on the Chinese market—the United States had become politically committed to preserving the territorial integrity and political independence of China.

Because the American people had never been prepared to fight for this objective, however, the United States had failed to protect China from external pressures and invasions. The Russians had established a sphere of influence in Manchuria by about 1900, and the Japanese had replaced them after the Russo-Japanese War. During and after World War I, Japan had expanded its influence and control over China, and in 1931 had begun another war to further its ambition to turn China into a Japanese vassal or colony. The Open Door policy, then, had been largely verbal. Indeed, the United States had never been prepared to support this policy militarily; it was one in which diplomacy was divorced from force, and what it meant was that the United States usually disregarded its commitment whenever Russia or Japan challenged it. Even though this suggested that in reality the United States regarded its stakes in China as low, Americans, even in those days, believed that words were a substitute for an effective policy. The result was the illusion that the United States had long been China's friend, extending to the Chinese people the bountiful benefits of Western civilization and coming to their rescue during World War II.

Americans were therefore shocked by the collapse in 1949 of Chiang, who during the war had been lauded as a Chinese George Washington, and the establishment of Communist control of the Chinese mainland. Certainly, they were totally unprepared for, and deeply resentful of, the propaganda emanating from Beijing accusing the United States of being "the Chinese people's implacable enemy . . . a corrupt imperialistic nation, the world center of reaction and decadence . . . a paper tiger and entirely vulnerable to defeat." They had expected that a "loyal" and fundamentally democratic China, grateful to America for protection and help, would emerge from World War II as a strong friend and powerful and reliable ally. The failure of these expectations in late 1949 came as a blow. Suddenly, the relative security achieved by the containment policies in Europe—the Truman Doctrine, the Marshall Plan, the Berlin airlift, and NATO—seemed to have disintegrated. It appeared that the United States had stemmed the Communist menace in Europe only to allow it to achieve a breakthrough in Asia.

The resulting insecurity and anxiety were further heightened by two other events occurring at about the same time. The first was the explosion of the Soviet Union's first atomic bomb, which shattered the American monopoly of the weapon widely regarded as the principal deterrent to a Soviet attack. The second was the conviction in early 1950 of Alger Hiss for perjury in connection with charges that he had delivered documents to the Soviet government in the 1930s. The Hiss case was followed shortly by the confession of British scientist Klaus Fuchs that he had passed atomic secrets to the Soviets, clearly pointing to Soviet espionage in high places. The outbreak of the Korean War and Communist China's subsequent intervention compounded the West's sense of betrayal and anxiety.

The Erosion of Bipartisan Support for Foreign Policy

At the time all this was occurring, bipartisan support for U.S. policy was ending. The congressionally dominant conservative wing of the Republican party had long been restless; the party, led by liberal Republicans, had lost the presidential elections of 1940, 1944, and 1948. They wanted to win with a conservative leader in 1952. But they could not win the presidency on the Republican record on domestic issues. The Republicans were the party of President Herbert Hoover and the Great Depression. The Democrats, who had won every presidential election since 1932, were the party of Roosevelt and the New Deal. Conservative Republicans therefore needed a foreign policy issue with which to beat the Democrats, even though liberal and moderate Republicans, led by Senator Arthur Vandenberg, a former isolationist, had supported the internationalist policy of the Truman administration. But Vandenberg was dying, and, after China fell to the Communists, bipartisanship on the Far East was eroding. Foreign policy became a partisan issue as the Republicans decided to exploit the public's frustrations with the perceived failures under Democratic administrations.

Whenever the United States had been drawn into the international arena in the past, its actions had met with quick success. It had beaten the British, the Mexicans, the Spaniards, the Germans, and the Japanese. America had never been invaded, defeated, or occupied, as most other nations had been; it had, to be sure, made mistakes, but with its great power it had always been able to rectify them. To a nation in which one popular slogan expressed confidence in doing "the difficult today, the impossible tomorrow," failure was a new experience. America's history had been a witness to victories only; its unbroken string of successes seemed evidence of national omnipotence.

It was this unquestioned assumption that the United States was omnipotent that suggested to the Republicans the reason for America's failures: treason within its own government! If America was all-powerful, its setbacks must have been the result of its own policies. Ostensibly, the reason China fell was that the "pro-Communist" administrations of Franklin Roosevelt and Harry Truman either deliberately or unwittingly had "sold China down the river." This conspiracy charge articulated by Senator Joseph McCarthy, supported by senators Robert Taft and Richard Nixon, was simplicity itself: America's China policy had ended in Communist control of the mainland; the administration leaders and the State Department were responsible for the formulation and execution of foreign policy; therefore, the government must be filled with Communists and Communist sympathizers who "tailored" American policy to advance the global aims of the Soviet Union. Low morale among the Nationalists, administrative and military ineptness, and repressive policies that had alienated mass support had nothing to do with it; nor did the superior Communist organization, direction, morale, and ability to identify with popular aspirations.

The State Department bore the brunt of the onslaught. Calls for Acheson's resignation and congressional efforts to cut funding of the department—including eliminating Acheson's salary—failed but carried symbolic weight. With the attacks coming faster than they could be refuted, morale plummeted. Old China hands were forced out, although they were cleared of all charges against them. Those foreign service officers who stayed learned a lesson they would not forget: make no controversial recommendations because in the future they might be held against you. A report analyzing the weakness of the Nationalist government, forecasting its possible demise if it failed to reform, and recommending opening contacts with the Communists as the likely successor regime, would be read by a witch-hunting committee as a hostile attitude toward a friendly government, a desire to see it fail, and an attempt to turn China over to the Communists. It is no wonder that when

Washington was considering intervention in Vietnam that few foreign service officers were willing to report on the South Vietnamese government's weaknesses and its possible defeat by the Viet Cong. Honest reporting and analysis might later condemn them as security risks and cost them their jobs and, worse, their reputations.

The political atmosphere during the 1950s, in short, often bordered on hysteria. The accusations, usually in the press, were not directed only to the State Department or government officials. Academics and others were also charged as "security risks" or "un-American." Many such individuals were fired, and others were blacklisted. For example, the Hollywood studios stopped hiring actors and writers who had been associated with radical causes during the depression years. So-called controversial books and authors were banned. (One library took *Robin Hood* off the shelf because the hero robbed the rich to give to the poor, an obvious Communist or sympathizer!) The United States Information Agency even burned some books to avoid any accusations of left-wing disposition by eager congressional hunters for un-American activities, and a West Point debating team had to cancel a debate on the wisdom of recognizing the new China.

One significant result was to shift U.S. foreign policy from a stricter anti-Soviet orientation to a broader anti-Communist crusade. To be sure, U.S. actions in the Eastern Mediterranean and in Western Europe had been taken in the name of anticommunism, but operationally these actions had been limited to countering Soviet moves. Washington had not hesitated to support Communist Yugoslavia after its break with Moscow and for a brief moment it had even predicted the likelihood of conflict between Communist China and the Soviet Union. But the Republican attacks on the Democrats, the charges of appeasement, of being soft on communism, of losing China, and of treason, placed the Democrats in a vulnerable position. When the Korean War began, the Republicans demanded protection of the Nationalist government on Taiwan as the price for support of the war. To avoid political division, Truman sent the fleet into the Taiwan Straits, reinserting the United States into the Chinese civil war. Once U.S. troops had reached the thirty-eighth parallel in Korea, the Republicans charged that not to advance north and defeat the North Koreans would constitute appeasement. This assault on the administration probably played a part in the decision to exploit MacArthur's military victory at Inchon. After UN forces had recovered from China's intervention and driven back to the thirty-eighth, incessant Republican attacks made it impossible for Truman to end the war at that point. (Truman's successor, Dwight Eisenhower, would end the war in 1953 on virtually the same terms after considerably more casualties.) In this highly charged emotional atmosphere, it was impossible to extend official recognition to the government of mainland China.

Indeed, the aim of U.S. policy became anticommunism: the expansion of any member of the Sino-Soviet bloc, as it came to be called, was to be prevented. All Communist states were now considered enemies, regardless of whether they were large or small, strategically located or not, tied to Moscow as satellites or nationalist Communist states, which, like Yugoslavia and Communist China, were likely to pursue their own interests, even in conflict with the Soviet Union. Distinctions between America's vital and secondary interests, the importance of concentrating on the main adversary and not getting bogged down and wasting resources in conflicts with secondary enemies, and the ability to distinguish Communist regimes that represent a threat to American interests and those that do not—all were lost in the crusading spirit. Future Democratic administrations, trying to avoid Republican accusations of having lost some country or being soft on communism, were particularly disposed to anticommunist interventions. The Republican charges had hurt the Democrats in 1952; they lost that presidential election and were kept out of power for eight years.

Sino-American Enmity

Anticommunism also intensified the deep rift between the United States and China. In 1950 Beijing saw that the United States not only did not recognize it but also continued its intervention in the Chinese civil war, protecting the rival Nationalist regime; that the United States increasingly assisted the French fighting in Indochina; that it was strengthening its alliance with Japan, China's recent enemy; and that U.S. troops were marching to China's border with North Korea, despite Chinese warnings not to do so. Fearing that U.S. forces might cross the border, the Chinese government, perceiving the United States through Marxist-Leninist glasses and therefore defining it as an enemy, intervened in Korea.

From Washington's perspective, the Chinese intervention was unwarranted because the United States had repeatedly reassured Beijing that the border was safe. But the heavy fighting in the winter of 1950-1951, the loss of lives, and length of the war embittered Sino-American relations. The friendly relationship the United States once thought it had with China turned into hatred. That the United States had once been China's protector and benefactor may have been an illusion, but it was widely held, and the betrayal of friendship, alleged or real, always leaves a sense of frustration and anger. The Sino-American relationship had an emotional intensity that did not characterize the relationship between the United States and the Soviet Union. China, now seen as aggressive and militantly anti-American, was commonly called "Red China."

One can only speculate how events might have turned out during the Korean War if the United States had recognized the new Chinese government and had diplomatic representatives in Beijing. Diplomats might have alerted Washington that the Chinese were alarmed at the U.S. advance in North Korea and that the warnings to stop American forces short of China's frontier ought to be taken seriously. The American government received similar warnings from the Indian ambassador but, believing the ambassador to be pro-Chinese, the United States rejected the warnings. It would have had less reason to be suspicious of its own representatives and might not have blundered up to China's border subsequently.

The United States paid a heavy price for the breakdown of bipartisanship, for McCarthy's charges of treason, and for the crusading style that Nationalist China's collapse unleashed. But the even greater folly may have been that U.S. policy, now applying containment to the Sino-Soviet bloc, no longer considered the possibility that Mao Zedong might become a second Tito, that Mao, like Tito, drew his power from control of his party and military, not from the Soviet Union. Nor, therefore, did Washington any longer entertain the possibility that Communist China might be used to contain Soviet power. Instead, for more than two decades the United States and China were bitter enemies, and the United States felt compelled to contain not only Soviet power but Chinese power as well.

c h a p t e r   f i v e

The Strategy of 'Frontiersmanship'

T̲HE PRINCIPAL achievement of President Dwight Eisenhower's two terms was the completion of the walls of containment around the Sino-Soviet bloc spanning Eurasia. This was done primarily by organizing two multilateral alliances—one in the Middle East, the other in Southeast Asia—and backing them up against Soviet and Chinese encroachment with the growing nuclear capability of the Strategic Air Command (SAC). These alliances proved to be weak barriers, however, for the application of containment outside of Europe could not be superimposed on regional rivalries, civil wars, and the powerful forces of nationalism. Moreover, America's nuclear arsenal, while deterring all-out war with Moscow and Beijing, could not prevent lesser challenges, although it helped to prevent their escalation.

It is ironic that Eisenhower's reputation soared after America's involvement in Vietnam concluded in the 1970s. That misadventure made a president whose record was basically negative look good: he ended the war in Korea; he did not go to war in Indochina; he kept the United States out of the Suez war; he did not get the United States involved in war with Communist China in its civil war with Nationalist China; and he avoided a showdown over Berlin. Democratic presidents immediately before him and after him were activists and interventionists. Paradoxically, it was liberal Democrats, once the chief advocates of an energetic containment policy, who praised the Republican Eisenhower during the 1970s and 1980s for his caution and avoidance of a hasty resort to military power. Although he threatened its use on several occasions, he avoided direct military interventions, except in Lebanon. At the time, however, the Democrats were highly critical of the administration's strong ideological anticommunism and rhetoric and what were seen as its inept policies. Toward the end of Eisenhower's second term, as the Soviets achieved spectacular space shots and missile tests, critics saw him presiding over a self-satisfied nation, which, while basking in affluence, was losing dynamism and its primacy to the Soviet Union. The nation turned subsequently to a younger, more dynamic president and new generation "to get the country moving again."

Eisenhower's Promise of Liberation

During the presidential election campaign of 1952, the Republicans cleverly exploited the public's frustration with containment—a frustration grounded in the popular illusion of national omnipotence. America's great insecurity and its present involvement in the Korean War, they asserted, were the result of the "tragic blunders" that Franklin Roosevelt and Harry Truman had committed at the Tehran, Yalta, and Potsdam conferences with the Soviets. The Democratic leaders had deliberately and stealthily paved the way for communism's postwar expansion by selling out Eastern Europe and betraying Chiang Kai-shek. The two presidents, according to the Republican party platform, had

> flouted our peace-assuring pledges such as the Atlantic Charter, and [they] did so in favor of despots, who, it was well known, consider that murder, terror, slavery, concentration camps, and the ruthless and brutal denial of human rights are legitimate means to their desired ends. Tehran, Yalta, and Potsdam were the scenes of those tragic blunders with others to follow. The leaders of the administration acted without the knowledge or consent of Congress or the American people. They traded our overwhelming victory for a new enemy and for new oppressions and new wars which were quick to come.

In other words, America's wounds were self-inflicted.

The Republicans charged that Truman's postwar foreign policy was self-defeating. It underwrote the false premise that American power was limited and committed the United States to continued coexistence and constant involvement in foreign policy. As John Foster Dulles, a lawyer and Republican activist who had long shown an interest in foreign affairs and was now the chief Republican spokesman on foreign policy, put it: "We are not working, sacrificing, and spending in order to be able to live *without* this peril—but to be able to live *with* it, presumably forever." The administration's policies were "treadmill policies, which, at best, might perhaps keep us in the same place until we drop exhausted." The failures of containment were many: it was a negative policy; it surrendered the initiative to the enemy; it merely reacted to counter the Communist danger wherever and whenever the latter chose to attack; it was so costly that it would bankrupt the country; and it aimed only at preserving the status quo. In short, Dulles condemned the policy of containment as "negative, futile, and immoral." [1]

---

1. John Foster Dulles, "A Policy of Boldness," *Life*, May 19, 1952, 146.

The aim of American foreign policy, Dulles stressed, should not be to coexist indefinitely with the Communist menace; it should be a rollback of Soviet power. The United States had only to proclaim its stand for freedom and announce that it would never be a party to any "deal" that confirmed Soviet despotism. Such a declaration would preserve the courage and hope of those living in Soviet satellites and prevent them from accepting the Soviet regime. In Dulles's words, the United States "should make it publicly known that it wants and expects liberation to occur. The mere statement of that wish and expectation would change, in an electrifying way, the mood of the captive peoples. It would probably put heavy new burdens on the jailers and create new opportunities for liberation." [2]

Never had the illusion of American omnipotence received a greater tribute. America's cause was righteous, and to be victorious it need only publicize this cause by launching a moral crusade. Right would then again prevail over might. The Republican program of action apparently envisaged Dulles, the future secretary of state, like the Old Testament Joshua, marching around the walls of the Kremlin empire, sounding the call of freedom upon his trumpet. The walls would tumble down, the enslaved peoples would be liberated, and Soviet power forced to retreat, leaving the world once more safe for democracy.

The Republicans not only promised an end to the cold war—but they also pledged it at less cost. They claimed that the Democrats' foreign policy of indefinite coexistence, with its vast outlay for armaments and economic aid, undermined the nation's economy. The Republicans asserted that it was the Soviet Union's aim to destroy the United States by forcing it to spend itself into bankruptcy—an aim furthered by Democratic policy. America's defense had to be provided with a healthy economic foundation. This required a sharp cut in foreign aid and military expenditures. The Republicans promised the nation at one and the same time an offensive strategy, a balanced budget, and reduction of taxes. They pledged a curtailment of Soviet power and a simultaneous cut in the appropriations for America's defense.

The Republican Rollback to Containment

Such goals were not only incompatible; they were unattainable. The enunciation of the doctrine of liberation would not free any Soviet satellite; good intentions, unsupported by concrete political and military policies, are notoriously impotent on the international scene. But perhaps this did not really matter, because the policy of liberation was devised primarily to roll back the Democrats in the United States, not the Red Army in Eastern Europe. And for this domestic purpose, liberation was a highly effective strategy.

---

2. Ibid., 154.

The country desperately wanted a more vigorous and forthright anti-Communist policy that promised an end to the cold war. At the same time, it was unprepared to take the risks involved. And a policy that actively sought the liberation of the satellite states would have to accept the very definite risk of all-out war with the Soviet Union. In these circumstances, the only kind of dynamism the country could afford was a verbal dynamism. And this was all the people seemed to want. It allowed them to delude themselves that the United States once again pursued a vigorous and forthright policy that would defeat its opponent. Liberation was the Republican party's therapy for a public that refused to accept the facts of America's limited power in the world and rejected any changes in its traditional approach to foreign policy.

That this policy of liberation was meant only to impress the American people was clearly demonstrated at the time of the anti-Communist revolt in East Berlin and other East German cities in June 1953, and during the national uprising in Hungary in late 1956. The Eisenhower administration failed to act—except to condemn the Soviet Union for its suppression of Germans and Hungarians and to express its sympathy for the victims. In Berlin, it substituted food packages to the East Berliners for liberation, and in Hungary, it even reassured the Soviet Union that it had no intention of intervening. The status quo was thereby reaffirmed. Liberation had returned to the "womb" of containment.

The Globalization of Containment and Massive Retaliation

The administration, however, carried out its promises of military and economic retrenchment. This involved three measures. The first was to end the Korean War, which allowed the administration to cut the size of the army and avoid the cost of maintaining large standing ground forces. The second was to draw a clear line of containment, or "frontier," around the entire Sino-Soviet bloc. The Democrats had already drawn such a frontier from Norway to Turkey; the Republicans expected to strengthen and extend it to the Middle East and Far East. The third measure was to preserve this global boundary around the Communist world with the deterrent power of SAC. The Soviets and Chinese could cross the line only at the risk of total war with the United States; the fear of total destruction was expected to deter them. For Moscow had only a minimum capability to reach the United States; Beijing had none. SAC's bomber force was to reach 2,000 in the 1950s.

The reliance on strategic air power was also expected to appeal to the American public. "Massive retaliation" sounded more dynamic than containment and made possible a reduction of overall military expenditures. It was obviously cheaper to concentrate military spending on a one-weapon system than to build up and maintain large balanced forces to meet any contingency. Large armies with all their equipment were expensive to maintain; so were the navies to transport and supply them. But bombers and, later, missiles were cheaper in the long run. Deterrence enforced by all the services would require huge annual defense budgets and higher taxes; deterrence by airpower could provide containment "on the cheap." Another appealing feature of massive retaliation was that it rejected the concept of limited war, or "half war," and reasserted the old American doctrine of either abstaining from or fighting an all-out war. This return to the more traditional American approach to war was natural in 1952. The Republicans had been elected largely because of the deep popular revulsion against the Korean War; it was clear that the American people wanted no more such wars. Nor did much of the military leadership, which formed a "Never Again Club."

Basically, then, Eisenhower's policy was not very different from Truman's: containing communism but extending containment beyond Europe by drawing a frontier around the Sino-Soviet periphery and supporting that frontier with nuclear air power. But in one essential aspect the new administration's policy was different—and this difference was crucial. Truman and Dean Acheson had relied on atomic striking power to deter an attack on either the United States or America's "first line of defense" in Europe. But in Asia, once the Communists had faced them with a limited aggression, the Truman administration had met this challenge with ground troops. The Eisenhower administration also expected to deter an all-out war with the threat of massive retaliation and declared that it would not fight local ground wars. Presumably this meant that it planned to deter any future limited attacks by threatening to retaliate against the Soviet Union or China.

This basic policy decision reflected Dulles's strong conviction that the only effective means of stopping a prospective aggressor was to give fair warning of what constituted aggression and to make clear that the punishment for an attack would far outweigh any possible military gains. Dulles believed that Korea would never have been invaded had the Communists known their attack would be met with retaliatory air strikes on Moscow. It was the absence of such a warning that had led the Communists to miscalculate. The Eisenhower administration did not intend to repeat this mistake. It meant to draw the line so clearly that the enemy could be left in no doubt of the consequences of crossing the line. The expectation was that by going to the "brink of war," the United States would be able to deter future Koreas. This policy, which later became known as "brinkmanship," was to be applied first in an attempt to bring about a cease-fire in Korea.

Ending the Korean War

Truce talks in Korea had begun in the summer of 1951, but the negotiations dragged on fruitlessly until they reached a deadlock. The war was a drain on the United States: it had to be ended. When the Eisenhower administration took office in January 1953, it decided that if its efforts to gain an armistice failed, it would bomb Chinese bases and supply sources in Manchuria and China, blockade the mainland coast, and possibly use atomic weapons. The administration later claimed that its willingness to use these weapons and to not confine future hostilities to the Korean Peninsula were conveyed by Dulles to Prime Minister Jawaharlal Nehru of India in May 1953. The assumption was that Nehru would pass the message on to the Chinese Communists.

In early June the deadlocked negotiations resumed, and in late July the armistice was signed. Whether the administration's threats were primarily responsible for the Chinese Communists' willingness to conclude the war remains dubious. Probably other factors were more critical. Chief among these was that Joseph Stalin had died in March, and his successors were proclaiming their belief in "peaceful coexistence" and trying hard to convince the non-Communist world that they wanted to relax international tensions. Agreement on an armistice and an end to the war would provide evidence of their earnestness. More important, they could not afford to risk increased international tensions and an enlarged war at a time when they were engaged in a struggle among themselves to succeed the late dictator. Right after his funeral, the Chinese made the key concessions holding up a truce agreement. Moreover, Dulles, according to his own account of his visit to India, never mentioned atomic weapons, only the possibility of stronger U.S. action. Nevertheless, Dulles later thought he had threatened to unleash American air power against China and had induced the Chinese Communists to end the fighting; in turn, this reinforced his faith in the utility of the advance warning coupled with the threat of heavy punishment.

The Korean War ended just where it had begun—on the thirty-eighth parallel. It had taken three years of fighting to decide that this line was to become part of the global dividing line between the Communist bloc and the non-Communist bloc. In August 1953 the United States signed a mutual security pact with South Korea designed to deter another attack from the north. This alliance had already been preceded by a declaration, signed by the fifteen nations that had fought in Korea, warning the Chinese Communists that, in the event of renewed aggression, it would probably be impossible to confine hostilities to Korea. They added this significant warning: the armistice must not "result in jeopardizing the restoration or the safeguarding of peace in any other part of Asia." Events in Indochina were soon to prove the meaninglessness of this statement.

The First Indochina War

After World War II, colonies that had long been ruled by European powers renewed their demands for independence. The British complied in

India, Burma, and Ceylon, but the French in Indochina did not. Returning there after its years of Japanese occupation, the French refused to grant any meaningful concessions to the government, which, under Ho Chi Minh, had proclaimed Vietnam's independence. The French, determined to reestablish sovereignty over their colony, recognized Ho's "Democratic Republic of Vietnam" as a free state within the French Union. As a part of the agreement, the French would be allowed to maintain garrisons in Vietnam for five years. Within less than a year, the Vietminh accused the French of violating the agreement. The Vietminh, or Revolutionary League for the Independence of Vietnam, was organized by Ho during World War II to convert Vietnam from a feudal society to a classless Communist society. After the war it emphasized nationalism rather than communism to win independence for Vietnam. Open conflict developed and soon escalated into the first Indochina war.

When France established an "independent" state of Vietnam in 1949 under Emperor Bao Dai, the Vietminh became, in effect, "rebels," but with the important difference that they were rebels identified as fighting for the independence of Vietnam. By contrast, Bao Dai, who spent much of his time on the French Riviera, was seen as a French puppet; in fact, he could not have survived one day in office without the support of French arms. Like Mao Zedong in China, Ho conducted guerrilla warfare and met with considerable success. The French, who generally held the cities, were at a disadvantage from the beginning, for in the absence of genuine independence, the Vietnamese identified themselves with the Vietminh and saw the French as colonial rulers. In the long run, France paid a high price for the war in lost manpower, materiel, and morale.

The Escalating U.S. Involvement

During the first years of the war, American public opinion was unsympathetic to France's attempt to reestablish its colonial control over Indochina. Three events led to U.S. involvement in this conflict. The first was the defeat of Chiang Kai-shek. This was seen as a blow to France, because it meant that the Chinese Communists could now provide assistance to the Vietminh. The second event was the outbreak of the Korean War, with the resulting shift of containment to Asia. The third event was the change in the political climate in the United States to anticommunism. The French, who earlier were seen as trying to hold onto the vestiges of their colonial empire, now were regarded as fighters in the common struggle against communism.

The Eisenhower administration began to provide France with economic and military aid. By 1954 the United States was paying about 75 percent of the costs of the war. The French position continued to deteriorate, however, especially once the Korean armistice was signed. Despite American warnings,

Communist China shifted its pressure from Korea to Indochina and increased its assistance to the Vietminh. On March 13, 1954, Vietminh forces launched an assault on the French fortress at Dienbienphu. The French position in northern Vietnam seemed close to collapse. It became painfully clear that the French could not hold on without American intervention. What was the United States to do?

Eisenhower had already declared that the fall of Indochina "would be of a most terrible significance to the United States of America," and he had termed Southeast Asia of "transcendent importance" to American security. If Indochina fell, Thailand, Burma, Malaysia, and Indonesia were expected to collapse like a set of dominoes. The secretary of state had issued several statements that rather strongly suggested that the United States would not stand idly by while this occurred. He had warned the Chinese Communists in the same terms he had used after the armistice in Korea: any aggression—that is, open aggression—would incur "grave consequences which might not be confined to Indochina." This warning also applied to any indirect Chinese intervention, such as assistance in the form of military advisers, equipment, and training for the Vietminh forces. The strategic significance of Indochina was seen as important, not what course the Chinese chose.

Dienbienphu was the moment of decision for the administration. Eisenhower and Dulles had declared Indochina to be of strategic importance to American security and had cautioned China against direct or indirect intervention by threatening it with massive retaliation. The Chinese ignored these warnings, and the U.S. government had to "put up or shut up." It shut up; its threats turned out to be only bluffs.

The Refusal to Intervene Militarily

The reason for this inaction is fairly clear: American public opinion might be strongly anti-Communist, but Eisenhower had withdrawn from Korea because the nation had tired of the war. He was unwilling to involve the United States in another such war. Furthermore, the administration was already cutting the size of the army, and the army Chief of Staff counseled against intervention because of a lack of available troops. The administration considered two courses of action. The first was to rescue the French by attacking the Communist positions with air power alone, but this was rejected because air strikes by themselves could not halt the Communist ground advance. Air power had failed to stop the North Korean army during the opening days of that war, and this failure had necessitated the commitment of U.S. troops.

The alternative strategy was to retaliate massively against China. That would have been consistent with the administration's announced policy, but in Indochina the administration did not follow its policy. The reason is simple: it is one thing to deliver a threat of massive retaliation to an opponent, and quite another to have the opponent believe it. The Soviets had not believed it before Korea, nor did the Chinese in Indochina. Indeed, an atomic threat against China was never delivered; the possible use of nuclear weapons was discussed—and rejected—only within the inner sanctums of the administration. Admittedly, the administration's declared policy was one of massive retaliation. Both Communist powers, however, apparently rejected the notion that the United States would risk a total war for anything less than an attack on the United States or Europe. Because the Eisenhower administration shared with the Truman administration the fear that an attack on China would precipitate Soviet intervention, the United States was faced again with the terrible dilemma of doing nothing or risking all-out war.

Truman's experience with Korea had clearly shown that containment could not be successful without the willingness and capability to fight a limited war. Reliance on strategic air power was not a credible strategy for deterring or winning "Koreas." The United States' ability to drop atom bombs on Moscow or Beijing was less than useless when the problem was a "little" war. Ground forces were absolutely necessary if the United States were to escape either defeat or involvement in a total conflict. (Indochina should also have demonstrated—as Americans were to learn a decade later—that a limited war against guerrilla forces also required political, social, and economic measures to alleviate the popular grievances on which the guerrillas feed.) The Eisenhower administration ignored these lessons of the Korean War. It persuaded itself that Korea had happened only because the enemy had not received a previous warning that an attack on South Korea would bring retaliatory strikes. Although such warnings were certainly desirable to prevent enemy miscalculation, Indochina proved that warnings alone were not enough. It showed that containment was incompatible with heavy budget cutting.

The result of American inaction was the French government's decision to make the best of the situation by negotiating with the Communists directly for an end to the war. The French people were as weary of the fighting as the American public had been of Korea. Just as the Americans had elected Eisenhower to end the war, the French National Assembly had elected Pierre Mendès-France to end the Indochina hostilities. Concerned that Washington might yet intervene—and perhaps use nuclear weapons—the Soviets and Chinese agreed to a division of the country at the seventeenth parallel. The Communists kept control of northern Indochina, but it seemed only a matter of time until they took the rest of the country because the collapse of the southern rump state seemed imminent. The United States, however, prevented such a takeover by supporting the new government of Ngo Dinh Diem, a staunch anti-Communist nationalist appointed by Bao Dai after Dienbienphu (Diem later ousted Bao Dai). The

Eisenhower administration gave Diem economic and military aid to stabilize the situation in Vietnam, and the danger of collapse temporarily receded.

SEATO's Founding

The seventeenth parallel, like the thirty-eighth parallel in Korea, became part of the international frontier separating the Communist and non-Communist worlds. To protect this frontier, the United States, Britain, France, Australia, New Zealand, the Philippines, Pakistan, and Thailand in September 1954 signed a treaty forming the Southeast Asia Treaty Organization (SEATO) to defend the area of the South Pacific, with the exception of Hong Kong and Taiwan. A protocol to the treaty extended SEATO's protection to Vietnam, Laos, and Cambodia. It also provided for joint action to meet aggression; an attack on any of its members would be considered a threat to all, and each would then act to meet the common danger in accordance with its constitutional processes. In case of subversion, the parties agreed to consult one another immediately and agree on common measures to meet this threat.

SEATO, unlike the NATO alliance, had no unified command or joint forces. Its principal force was American sea and air power. The crucial element—land power—would have to be supplied by the member nations if the occasion arose. Moreover—and again unlike NATO—SEATO did not include most of the nations in the areas it planned to protect. India, Burma, Sri Lanka, and Indonesia did not join. They had just emerged from Western colonialism and were unwilling to be tied again to the West through a military alliance. They preferred to remain neutral in the struggle between the Western powers and the Sino-Soviet bloc. The Philippines was willing to join because of its traditional ties to the United States, and Pakistan because it wished to acquire a source for arms against India. Only Thailand was genuinely concerned with Communist China's expansion. Australia and New Zealand were not really Asian powers.

SEATO was mainly a non-Asian alliance formed for the defense of an Asian area, a weakness that was to plague the alliance. The absence of regional concern about Communist China's expansion ensured SEATO's eventual failure. French and British membership did not prevent that result. France was unlikely to defend an area from which it had been forced to withdraw in humiliation. Britain, which had opposed U.S. intervention, saw the alliance as a means of restraining a similar act in the future. SEATO was, in reality, a U.S. guarantee for the defense of South Vietnam; it would provide a legal basis for a unilateral intervention to preserve the dividing line between the two Vietnams. Like West Germany and South Korea, South Vietnam had become part of the Free World, that is, the American sphere of influence.

The Taiwan Straits and the Offshore Islands

Sino-American relations had turned increasingly bitter and confrontational after the United States intervened in the Chinese civil war and China intervened in Korea. Soon after the Korean War ended, China's interest turned back to eliminating its rival on the other side of the Taiwan Straits. During the summer of 1954, the Chinese Communists openly proclaimed their intention of taking Taiwan and began shelling the Nationalist-held offshore islands. Quemoy is only nine miles outside the Xiamen harbor; Matsu lies almost as close, blocking the harbor of Fuzhou; and airplanes attacked the Tachen Islands, 200 miles north of Taiwan. In December the United States and the Nationalists signed a treaty of mutual defense in which the United States guaranteed the security of Taiwan and the nearby Pescadores. The Nationalists pledged not to attack the mainland or to reinforce their offshore garrisons without the consent of the United States.

The offshore islands were not specifically included under the terms of the treaty. However, as the situation in the straits grew more tense in January 1955, the president requested and received from Congress the authority to employ American armed forces to protect Taiwan and the Pescadores. This authority extended to the protection of "such related positions and territories" as the president judged necessary. Although this did not specifically clarify whether the United States would defend Quemoy and Matsu, the Communists certainly thought that it might, and they abstained from any invasion attempts of these islands within artillery range from the mainland. (Meanwhile, the United States had encouraged the Nationalists to evacuate the Tachens.)

Three years later, in August 1958, any ambiguities about the American position became clear when the Communists again began to shell the offshore islands. The Seventh Fleet—with orders to retaliate if fired upon—escorted Nationalist supply ships to within three miles of the beleaguered islands and helped them break a blockade. The Nationalist air force, equipped by the United States with air-to-air missiles, defeated the Communist air force's attempt to establish air supremacy in the sky between the mainland and Quemoy.

The line remained where it had been before the two Taiwan crises—a few miles off Communist China's coast. Some months later, Dulles reaffirmed this line when he firmly rejected Chiang's calls to take back the mainland. American policy in the straits was committed to the preservation of the status quo. Each side should keep what it had and refrain from attacking the other. The Eisenhower administration thereby recognized what neither it nor its predecessor had been willing to admit openly before: that the Nationalist expectation of recapturing the mainland was a myth. At the same time, it tacitly acknowledged the Chinese Communist government as continental China's de facto government. It reconciled itself to the Communist conquest of the mainland. Containment had once more replaced liberation. The administration, moreover, resolved to back up its "disengagement" policy with force. In the straits, it could support its political position with sea and air power and the threat of using nuclear weapons to foil an invasion; ground forces were not needed. But in actuality, for all of his talk of U.S. readiness to use nuclear weapons in defense, Eisenhower had no more intention to use them on China than on Indochina. The president, as a military man, knew that not only were there no appropriate military targets, but also that the use of atomic weapons was not politically feasible. To drop a bomb once again on Asians would lead to outrage and condemnation from the whole world, including the NATO allies. The United States, despite its declaratory policy of massive retaliation, was in fact self-deterred.

In any case, for the moment, the situation in the Far East had been stabilized. The frontier between the American and Soviet/Chinese spheres had been drawn at the thirty-eighth parallel in Korea, in the Taiwan Straits, at the seventeenth parallel in Indochina, and at the line drawn by SEATO. Although it would not be clear until years later, by standing fast, the United States also helped stress Sino-Soviet differences to near the breaking point. For China, unification with Taiwan was a priority; the Soviet Union's indifference disappointed China. For the Soviet Union, however, Taiwan was not worth the risk of a war with the United States. Consequently, the tiny islands of Quemoy and Matsu had profound long-term effects. In the meantime, Soviet attention turned back to the Middle East.

The Middle East and the Suez War

In 1955 the United States completed its line around the Sino-Soviet periphery. Britain, with U.S. support, established the Middle East Treaty Organization (METO), which included Turkey, Iraq, Iran, and Pakistan. Also known as the Baghdad Pact, METO extended the NATO line from Turkey to India. With the exception of Iraq, this "northern tier" was drawn along 3,000 miles of the Soviet Union's southern frontier and therefore drew a sharp reaction from the Soviet Union. Although they had been rebuffed in Iran and Turkey, the Soviets had not surrendered their historic ambitions in the region. The Middle East linked Europe, Africa, and Asia. For Britain, the area—and especially the Suez Canal—had long been the lifeline to India, the crown of the old empire, and to its present Commonwealth. Of greater importance, Europe's economy was becoming increasingly dependent on the Middle East for oil (America was still self-sufficient). The power that could deny Europe oil would be able to dictate its future. In short, for the Soviet Union, the Middle East was the place to outflank and neutralize NATO. Its opportunity to attempt this came as a result of several situations: the bitter Arab-Israeli conflict, the Anglo-Egyptian quarrel, Egypt's expansionist ambitions, and the U.S. attempt to draw the line of containment just south of the Soviet Union's border.

The Beginnings of the Arab-Israeli Conflict

Arab antagonism toward Israel stemmed from the Balfour Declaration of 1917, in which Britain had pledged the establishment of a "national home" for the Jewish people in Palestine while promising the Arabs that the civil and religious rights of non-Jews would not be prejudiced. Zionists took this pledge as a promise to convert Palestine into a Jewish state; they considered Palestine, which had become a British mandate after the disintegration of the Ottoman Empire during World War I, as their ancient and traditional homeland.

If Britain's troubles were serious after Hitler's assumption of power in Germany, they became impossible after World War II. Hitler had slaughtered 6 million Jews in his concentration camps. Few of the survivors wished to remain in Europe, and many emigrated to Palestine. The Jews were determined to establish a Jewish state, while the Arabs feared that the Jewish immigration would crowd them out of what they also regarded as their rightful homeland. British troops were unable to keep the peace between the Arabs and Jews. Under these circumstances, Britain—already gravely weakened by the war and forced to curtail its commitments throughout the world—decided to end its burdensome mandate over Palestine.

In November 1947 the United Nations partitioned Palestine into two independent states, one Jewish and the other Arab. The Arabs refused to accept this solution. On May 10, 1948, as Britain ended its mandate, the Jews proclaimed the state of Israel, and the armies of the Arab League (Egypt, Jordan, Syria, Lebanon, and Saudi Arabia) invaded the new state. In the ensuing war, the Israeli army defeated the larger Arab armies, and the state of Israel became a fact of political life.

The Arabs, however, refused to recognize it as such. Although they signed an armistice in February 1949, they refused to conclude a peace treaty. They continued to regard the Jews as infidels who had no right to be in Israel. Moreover, they felt deeply humiliated by their defeat. The Arabs awaited their day of revenge; meanwhile, they continued to proclaim their intention to destroy Israel. They conducted constant guerrilla warfare against Israel. The Egyptians refused to allow Israeli shipping through the Suez Canal and blockaded the Gulf of Aqaba.

But Egypt, the leading Arab power, needed arms. In September 1955 Egypt stunned the West by concluding an arms deal with Czechoslovakia, acting for the Soviet Union. Under this arrangement, Egypt received a large quantity of arms, including planes and tanks. Egypt now thought that it had the means to achieve a decisive military victory over Israel. In April 1956 Egypt tightened the ring around Israel by forming a joint command with

Syria, Saudi Arabia, and Yemen. In October Egypt, Jordan, and Syria announced another joint command, "the principal concern of which is the war of destruction against Israel." This, in turn, raised a critical question for Israel: Should it strike now or wait until Egypt and its allies were ready for the "second round"? As Egypt solidified the encirclement of Israel, grew increasingly aggressive, and began to absorb the Soviet arms, the Israelis decided to strike before it was too late. All that was needed was the right condition for launching their preemptive attack.

Israel's opportunity came in October and grew out of Anglo-Egyptian antagonism. Britain had controlled Egypt since 1881, when it had established a protectorate there to safeguard its passage through Suez to India. A 1936 treaty between the two countries had converted this status into an alliance. Under the treaty's terms, British troops were confined to the Suez Canal zone, and their presence was declared to be neither an occupation nor an infringement of Egyptian sovereignty. To the Egyptians, however, British soldiers on their soil represented a violation of Egyptian independence, pride, and dignity.

The Anglo-Egyptian Quarrel and Nasser's Ambitions

World War II had intensified Egyptian nationalism and heightened the demand for a withdrawal of British forces. But negotiations on this question broke down, and other postwar events increased Egypt's anti-British sentiment. The Egyptians resented the Palestine partition plan, for which they blamed Britain as well as the United States. In late 1951 the Egyptian parliament abrogated the 1936 Anglo-Egyptian treaty, and in July 1952 the new military regime that took over the Egyptian government from King Farouk pressed with renewed vigor for the removal of British troops. The Eisenhower administration supported the Egyptian demand in the belief that Colonel Gamal Abdel Nasser, the real power behind the military coup, and the United States were natural allies. The military was believed to be anticolonial, progressive, and committed to improving people's lives and providing Egypt with a degree of political stability. If the United States helped Nasser to evacuate British troops from their Suez Canal base, the Egyptians might become allies in fact. Faced with U.S. opposition, and aware of its own unpopularity in Egypt, Britain signed a new Anglo-Egyptian treaty in 1954, by which it agreed to withdraw all its troops from Suez over a twenty-month period. British influence over Egyptian politics had come to an end. More important, having ended what it considered British colonial control, the new regime, which had overthrown the corrupt monarchy that it blamed for Egypt's defeat in the 1948 war, now wished to turn to its number-one goal: to avenge itself by destroying Israel.

The removal of British forces from Egypt did not eliminate British power from the region. Britain shifted from Egypt to Iraq, its longtime friend, whose royalist regime needed Western protection from Egypt's new military regime. Nasser did not see the Baghdad Pact as a means of containing the Soviet Union; he saw it as an instrument to preserve Western domination throughout the area and, because Iraq had always been Egypt's traditional rival for Arab leadership, he considered the pact a personal challenge as well. The pact completed Nasser's alienation from the West, for his ambitions reached beyond eliminating Israel and expelling the British. He saw himself as a modern Saladin, the champion of the Arab cause. He promoted Pan-Arabism as a way of expanding his influence and that of his country. As the former dominant influence throughout the region, the West became Nasser's target. Setting himself up as an adversary of the West, Nasser became a hero to the Arabs.

Eisenhower's and Dulles's expectations of establishing a close relationship with Egypt were headed for disappointment. Bent on containing international communism, they felt that U.S. policy was quite compatible with Arab nationalism and the formation of a close relationship with Egypt. There were only two obstacles to that goal: the British presence and the Arab-Israeli conflict. Once Britain had been persuaded to leave Egypt, the United States turned its attention to its policy on Israel. If the United States could show that it was not always biased toward Israel, it might enlist Arab nationalism for the containment policy. The U.S. political leadership clearly failed to understand the dynamics of Egyptian and Arab politics and rivalries, as events shortly after the formation of the Baghdad Pact demonstrated.

The pact was the instrument of its own destruction because it helped bind Egypt to the Soviet Union. Its failure testifies to the difficulties of containing Soviet expansion by drawing lines outside of Europe. In Western Europe, the states all shared a common perception of the Soviet threat and stood united against it. Outside of Europe, U.S.-Soviet competition intersected with regional rivalries, undermining the U.S. goal of containment and providing the Soviet Union with an opportunity to expand its influence. The Baghdad Pact became a target. It was in Moscow's interest to destroy the Western alliance along the Soviet Union's southern frontier; it was in Cairo's interest to gain a source of arms to destroy Israel and to put political pressure on the pro-Western regimes in the area. These overlapping interests produced the Moscow-Cairo axis. Moscow, as a result, leapfrogged over the territory of the Baghdad Pact members. For all practical purposes, the alliance was null and void. Worst of all, however, Moscow had established its influence in the eastern Mediterranean.

Cairo received its arms, and Nasser became a hero for the Arab people. He had defied the West by turning to the East; by championing the Arab cause and winning the allegiance of the Arab masses, Nasser could make it more difficult for pro-Western Arab regimes to oppose him. If they did, he could call for their overthrow and back those elements that supported him. In the meantime, he could seek to subvert these governments. By strengthening

Nasser, the Soviet Union became the Arabs' greatest friend. It had taken only one year from the signing of the Anglo-Egyptian treaty to the arms deal. But the price of the Moscow-Cairo axis was Israeli and British insecurity.

The United States further upset the West's position in the Middle East in July 1956 when it informed the Egyptian government that it would not help finance Nasser's pet project, the Aswan High Dam. The dam on the upper Nile was intended to raise Egypt's low standard of living by irrigating new land and providing electricity for industrial development. The American offer had been made shortly after the formation of the Baghdad Pact as a gesture of friendship toward Nasser. The retraction was a heavy blow to Egypt because the American loan was a prerequisite for further aid from the World Bank and Britain, and these offers, too, were withdrawn. The Eisenhower administration acted mainly because Egypt had moved close to the Soviet Union with the arms deal and had recognized Communist China as well.

Nasser regarded the American decision as a personal slap and national humiliation. A few days later, on July 26, he announced he would nationalize the Suez Canal and use the revenues collected from it to finance the dam. Arab nationalists were ecstatic, and Nasser's stature, already great, reached new heights. The British government reacted sharply to Nasser's seizure of the canal. Prime Minister Anthony Eden did not trust the Egyptian leader; although Nasser guaranteed that all ships, except Israel's, could pass through the canal, Eden feared that Nasser would use the canal as an instrument of political blackmail. Moreover, if Nasser could face the West with such a major act of defiance and go unpunished, Western influence would be destroyed throughout the Middle East. Other Arab governments would expropriate Western oil interests, and all opponents of Nasser would be forced to come to terms with him. Western prestige—especially British prestige because south of America's "northern tier" Britain was the leading Western power in the Middle East—had to be upheld. If it were not, the Cairo-Moscow axis would dominate the entire area and be in a position to strangle Europe. The British were determined to stand up to Nasser, and they insisted on some form of international control for the canal. The Egyptians rejected all proposals to wrest their newly won control out of their hands and denounced them as "collective colonialism." All attempts to bridge this gap failed.

The United States Displaces Britain During the Suez War

On October 29, only four days after Jordan's chief of staff announced that the time had come to launch the Arab assault on Israel, the Israeli army marched into Egypt. The Israelis quickly defeated the Egyptian forces on the Sinai Peninsula. The British and the French (who sought Nasser's downfall because of his aid to rebels trying to free Algeria from French control) intervened twenty-four hours later. But instead of facing the United States with a *fait accompli*, the result of a quick and effective intervention, they delayed and intervened ineffectively, dragging out hostilities. At this point, the United States saved Nasser. Although by withdrawing the Aswan Dam offer, the administration had precipitated Nasser's seizure of the canal and the British attack, it now opposed the use of force to settle this issue.

The reason was that, despite its disapproval of Nasser's action and the pro-Soviet direction in which he was leading Egypt, the administration saw Nasser's foreign policy as purely a reaction against Israel and Western colonialism. It remained convinced that if Israel had not existed, and if the Arab states had not long been dominated by the Western powers, especially Britain, the Arabs would not be anti-Western and pro-Soviet. The administration saw the invasion of Egypt as a golden opportunity to win Arab friendship. When Israel had proclaimed itself a state, the United States had recognized the new nation within eleven minutes. Here was a chance to show the Arabs that the United States was not as pro-Jewish as they thought, and that the United States could even be pro-Arab. Because Egypt's actions were also anti-British, the United States thought it wise to oppose the British attempt to reassert control over the canal. By saving Nasser, the United States could align itself with Arab nationalism; supporting Britain, France, and Israel would leave the Soviet Union as the sole champion of Arab aspirations.

American opposition to the invasion, in short, would identify the United States with the anticolonialism of the entire underdeveloped world, and particularly with the anti-Israel and nationalistic sentiments of the Arab world. Because continued evidence of British power in the Middle East only antagonized the Arabs, the removal of this power and its replacement by American influence would be in the interest not only of the United States but also of all the Western powers. In this way, the West's strategic and economic interests could be more adequately safeguarded. At least, that was the rationale for the United States humiliating its two main allies, thereby turning Nasser's military defeat into a political victory. It also would contrast favorably globally for Washington to oppose great-power intervention against a smaller state at a time when the Soviets were intervening in Hungary to suppress its aspiration for national self-determination.

America's opposition to the Suez invasion was the decisive factor in stopping the fighting. Egypt had already blocked the canal, and the Syrians had cut the pipelines running across their country from Iraq, making Britain dependent on the United States to replace its losses from the Middle East. The administration threatened to use this economic sanction if Britain did not cease the attack. Faced with this dire prospect—plus opposition to the invasion within Britain, the Commonwealth (Canada, India, and Pakistan), and the United Nations—the British government accepted a cease-fire and later withdrew its forces; France and Israel had little choice but to follow suit.

It is ironic in view of America's leading role in halting the attack on Egypt that the Soviet Union was to reap the benefits. After it had become clear that the United States would not support the British and French invasion, the Soviet Union threatened "to crush the aggressor." It sent notes to the British and French governments warning of possible rocket attacks on their countries and bluntly told Israel that its very existence was at stake. It even asked the United States to join forces with it to stop the war. And after the cease-fire, the Soviet Union and the People's Republic of China threatened to send "volunteer soldiers." In short, the Soviet Union risked nothing to deliver these threats, but it was the country that received most of the credit from the Arabs for saving Nasser by its threats to exterminate Israel and attack Britain and France. Losing Suez resulted in the collapse of British power in the Middle East, the strengthening of Arab nationalism, and the consolidation of Egyptian-Soviet links.

Nasser's great political victory increased his self-confidence. Supported by the Soviet Union, whose aim it was to weaken if not eliminate all Western power in the Middle East, Nasser continued his expansionist drive. Jordan abrogated the Anglo-Jordan Treaty by which Jordan had received an annual subsidy to maintain its economy; Egypt, Saudi Arabia, and Syria promised to replace the British funds, and Jordan announced that it would seek to establish a federal union with Egypt and Syria. The last two states did, in fact, join together into a union, called the United Arab Republic, in early 1958. Attempts to undermine the Iraqi government continued throughout 1956, and in the spring of 1957, the Egyptians organized riots against the government in Lebanon.

The Eisenhower Doctrine

After the Suez crisis Eisenhower urged Congress to support a new commitment to resist communism in the Middle East. A joint resolution of Congress, known as the Eisenhower Doctrine, passed in the spring of 1957 and declared that the United States considered the preservation of the independence and integrity of the Middle Eastern nations vital to American security, and that it was prepared to use armed force to assist any nation or nations "*requesting* assistance against *armed* aggression from any country controlled by international Communism [italics added]." It was difficult to understand what this doctrine meant. The Soviet Union did not border on any Arab state. Iraq, to the south, was already protected by the Baghdad Pact and, through its association with Britain and Turkey, by NATO; so the doctrine could not be directed against the Soviet Union. In any event, the Soviet Union had already leapfrogged the northern tier.

The Eisenhower administration was forced to reconsider its views of Nasser in light of his continued attempts to undermine Western power in the Middle East, his vicious attacks on all the Western nations, including the

United States, and his continued flirtation with the Soviet Union. At Suez, the United States had thought it could win his trust by demonstrating its friendship. But Nasser's actions proved this expectation was ill-founded. A complete reversal of policy was in order, and this required a "reinterpretation" of the Eisenhower Doctrine. First, the term *armed aggression* was no longer to refer only to the direct attack of one nation upon another but also to attempts to overthrow pro-Western governments through subversion; and second, *any country controlled by international communism* now included nations with close ties to the Soviet Union. In short, the target became Nasser's radical Arab nationalism. The revised Eisenhower Doctrine was still based on the same anti-Communist assumptions that had been the basis of the ill-fated Baghdad Pact; the principal difference was that it was intended to deal with a Middle East in which the Soviets had already destroyed the northern tier. Having helped to eliminate British power in the hope of winning Egypt's friendship against Moscow, the administration now found itself filling the vacuum left by British power to contain what it saw as the Moscow-Cairo axis.

The doctrine was applied first in Jordan, where King Hussein's dismissal of the pro-Nasser government led to a general strike, massive street demonstrations, and riots. Jordan's days as an independent state appeared to be numbered. Hussein charged in April 1957 that international communism was responsible for the efforts to overthrow him. The same day, the United States announced that it regarded "the independence and integrity of Jordan as vital." And to prove that it meant what it said, the administration dispatched the Sixth Fleet to the eastern Mediterranean and extended Jordan economic support for its army and economy. The Hussein government survived.

In the summer of 1958 an even more serious crisis arose when a group of nationalist officers led by General Abdul Karim Kassem overthrew the pro-Western government of Iraq. Although the new regime did not withdraw from the Baghdad Pact until some months later, this revolt, in effect, removed the pivotal state of the alliance. The United Arab Republic immediately recognized the new government, and the two countries quickly signed an alliance. There was little the United States could do but recognize the Kassem government. Arab nationalism seemed to be sweeping everything in front of it. Only Lebanon, Jordan, and Saudi Arabia were still outside the Nasser camp, and the first two were teetering on the verge of revolution. The whole Western position in the Middle East seemed to be on the brink of disintegration.

U.S. Action in the Middle East

The Eisenhower administration now resorted to force. Lebanon had been plagued for some time with civil war between Muslims and Christians.

The Muslims wanted close relations, if not union, with the United Arab Republic, and the Christians favored a pro-Western policy and the continued independence of Lebanon. With the Iraqi revolution, men and arms for the pro-Nasser elements began to be smuggled in from Syria. In Jordan, too, the situation took a turn for the worse. The Iraqi coup d'état was alarming to King Hussein, who also had his pro-Nasser masses and army officers. Jordan and Lebanon invoked the Eisenhower Doctrine and asked for military support. Now, ironically, the United States acted together with Britain. The United States sent 14,000 men into Lebanon, and the British sent 3,000 paratroopers into Jordan. The large size of the American contingent seems to have been a deliberate warning to the new Iraqi government against nationalizing Western oil resources. Kassem quickly gave the assurance that he had no such intention, and possible American intervention in Iraq was thereby forestalled. Loud Soviet hints of intervention also turned out to be hollow when countered by resolute American action. Both Britain and the United States withdrew their troops in late October.

The Anglo-American action saved Lebanon and Jordan. But it was also intended to have another important effect: to show Nasser and the Arabs that there were limits to Soviet willingness to come to their aid. Nasser's personal ambitions were, by themselves, important but secondary; the factors that had spelled success for Egypt's Pan-Arab policy were Soviet support and power. The Western powers, in thinking of counteraction against Egypt, could never eliminate the possibility of Soviet intervention. This, of course, only encouraged Nasser's expansionist drive. The Anglo-American action in Lebanon and Jordan disabused the Arabs of this notion. Prior to the intervention, the Soviets again had threatened to send "volunteers" to oppose the Western "imperialists" and had carried out conspicuous military maneuvers in Soviet central Asia and Transcaucasia. The firmness of the American position and the failure of the Soviet Union to do more than denounce the intervention and call for a diplomatic settlement made it very clear that there were limits to Soviet willingness to bail out the Arabs. This had a dampening effect on Nasser's anti-Western drive.

Another unexpected turn of events influenced this situation. The new regime in Iraq, instead of turning out to be pro-Nasser—as almost everyone, including Nasser, had expected—took the opposite position. It was not long before Kassem began to challenge the Egyptian ruler's leadership of Arab nationalism. Nasser recognized this threat of Egypt's traditional rival and attempted to overthrow the Kassem government. But the revolt by a group of pro-Nasser officers was quickly squashed. At the same time, the Soviet Union gave economic and military support to the Kassem government. Nasser's drive for Arab leadership was stalled: Jordan, Lebanon, and Saudi Arabia had remained independent; Libya and the Sudan had resisted his attempts to subvert them; Syria was restless in the United Arab Republic; and Iraq had become a rival for Arab leadership.

Nor was this situation materially changed by the events of the early 1960s: Kassem was overthrown, and Syria revolted to quit the United Arab Republic. Despite the Pan-Arab aspirations of Egypt, Syria, and Iraq, a true Arab union remained as elusive as ever. Syria and Iraq were unwilling to permit Nasser to dominate them, and Nasser was unwilling to form a union he could not control. The Egyptian leader's new emphasis on domestic reform—or what he called "Arab socialism"—therefore became crucial to his fight for Arab leadership, even though he continued his attempts to overthrow traditional pro-Western regimes and remained generally anti-Western in his policy positions.

Meanwhile, the United States had become almost a full-fledged member of the Baghdad Pact (now renamed the Central Treaty Organization [CENTO]) by joining its economic, military, and countersubversion committees. But south of CENTO's fragile line remained all the basic problems that had given rise to the turmoil after 1955: the conflicts among the Arab states, the Arab-Israeli quarrel, the overshadowing competition between the United States and the Soviet Union, and, above all, Arab nationalism and its xenophobia. Despite the region's vast oil wealth, the Arab masses remained very poor and suffered from illiteracy, malnutrition, and disease. Social discontent and political instability were the result. Above all, the American attempt to fill the vacuum left by the decline of British power and draw another "frontier" was unsuccessful. Ironically, it was the attempt to do this that drew the Soviet Union and Egypt together to destroy the northern tier, permitting the Soviet Union to jump over the line that was supposed to contain it.

The Soviet Shift Back to Europe

In Europe NATO had already drawn the defense line. The strength of this line on the ground depended on supplementing NATO forces with West German troops, and the NATO allies had chosen the European Defense Community to achieve this goal. But in August 1954, the French National Assembly rejected the EDC by a decisive majority; fear of Germany remained too great, and French nationalists wished to maintain France's identity and honor. This decision was a real blow to the efforts toward creating a situation of strength in Europe. The whole basis of NATO strategy and European integration was suddenly imperiled.

Dulles's response was to threaten an "agonizing reappraisal" of the United States' NATO commitments if the deadlock were not broken. Britain's Prime Minister Eden averted such a reappraisal by seeking a way of rearming West Germany with French approval. He found it in the forgotten Brussels Treaty. This organization was revised by the inclusion of Germany and Italy. The new alliance, which pledged all its members to come to one another's aid if attacked, was named the Western European Union (WEU). But the WEU had no forces assigned to it, and it had no responsibility for formulating a strategy to defend its members. These remained within the functions of NATO. The WEU's role was to channel West German troops into NATO, while maintaining a set of controls over West Germany similar to those included in the EDC. Furthermore, Britain agreed to keep a minimum number of troops on the Continent. Britain's pledge was a formalization of its responsibilities under the Dunkirk, Brussels, and NATO treaties. But to the French it seemed an important new commitment; they were now reassured that they would not someday be left to face German troops alone.

These commitments, embodied in the Paris Pact, came into force in May 1955. Ten years after Germany's defeat, the occupation came to an end, and the Federal Republic regained its sovereignty and entered NATO via the WEU. West Germany's military power could now be added to Western strength. Two important declarations were appended to these Paris agreements. In the first, the West German government subscribed to the principles of the United Nations, undertook "never to have recourse to force to achieve the reunification of Germany or the modification of the present boundaries of the German Federal Republic," and to resolve all disputes between itself and other states by peaceful means. In the second, the United States, Britain, and France declared that they recognized the Federal Republic as the only freely and legitimately constituted government entitled to speak for all of Germany, thereby indicating a policy of nonrecognition of the East German government. In addition, the allies would pursue German reunification by peaceful means, which in effect meant the preservation of a divided Germany. Finally, the Western powers stated that until "the conclusion of a peace settlement" they would continue to exercise their responsibilities with regard to the security of West Germany and West Berlin. NATO, like the European Coal and Steel Community (ECSC), it is worth emphasizing, was thus an instrument for defending Western Europe and harnessing German power for that collective purpose, as well as controlling and restraining that power.

The Birth of the Common Market

With Germany safely enrolled as a member of NATO, the WEU members now took a momentous step toward further economic and political integration. The six states that composed Little Europe had gained increasing benefits from this movement. On June 1, 1958, they established the European Economic Community (EEC), usually referred to as the Common Market, whose objective was to join them together into an economic union. Their plan was to achieve this in a twelve- to fifteen-year period. During this time, all six states would completely eliminate the tariffs and quota systems that hampered trade among them. They would also abolish restrictions on the movement of labor, capital, and services among them, with the exception of agriculture.

What were believed to be the chances for the development of this Common Market as it was being launched? The economic benefits were thought to guarantee it. As trade barriers were lowered and then eliminated, the increasing competition would result in the growth of efficient companies and the demise of the less efficient ones, unless they modernized or converted to new lines of production. All members were expected to gain. At its heart, the Common Market was a bargain between French agriculture and West German industry. Both stood to benefit enormously from a continental-size market. A final factor was that the community would collectively receive advantages against third parties. It was strong enough to demand reciprocal lowering of tariffs. All these advantages outweighed the burdens each nation would suffer as a result of economic dislocation and hardships, which in fact would be minimized by being extended over a period of years and by being shared among all members.

The principal advantage of the Common Market, however, was seen to be political, not economic. A common market needs common policies; only one set of rules—not six—can govern its competitive behavior. One nation cannot be allowed to pay its workers considerably lower wages than its neighbor to achieve a competitive advantage. There had to be some standardization of wages and of related items such as overtime, hours worked per week, and various welfare benefits. In the long run, the Common Market's success would lead to the adoption of common fiscal policies to control the ups and downs of the business cycle, a common currency, and a central bank. The economic "spillover"—from the original common market in coal and steel into a common market for all sectors of the economy—was expected to stimulate political unification. It was precisely the formation of a political union that had inspired the ECSC.

Initiated by France and strongly supported by West German chancellor Konrad Adenauer, the European Economic Community was the culminating act of the movement to tie Germany so closely to a European community that it would never again be able to use its power for purely national ends. The formation of what came to be called the Inner Six was nothing less than the last link subjecting Germany to European restraints and responsibilities. Its success would make it impossible for Germany ever again to pursue a unilateral course.

Not surprisingly, the Soviet Union reacted quickly against the Common Market and attempted to break it up. A strong Europe, economically prosperous and politically stable, would not only prove a powerful barrier to Soviet expansionist ambitions, but also might threaten the Soviet status quo in Eastern Europe. The West European societies exercised a magnetic attraction for the satellite countries. West Berlin, alongside Communist East Berlin, hampered Soviet control of East Germany. Hundreds of thousands of young, skilled and professional men and women left East Germany through West Berlin; it was an escape hatch that was depopulating the German Democratic Republic (GDR), as it called itself, of the very people it needed to run its society. But the real stake was the legitimacy of the GDR. As an artificial creation, not recognized by most states that recognized West Germany as the true representative of German interests, the loss of the younger generation for whose welfare the GDR supposedly existed deprived it of a rationale for existence. And if East Germany were to collapse, would Poland and other East European states not follow? If the existence of West Berlin and West Germany made the Soviet Union feel insecure about the status quo, Soviet apprehensions about a united Europe were even greater.

The Second Berlin Crisis

The stability of the Soviet position in central and Eastern Europe, as seen by Moscow, depended on two factors: one, gaining Western recognition of the East German "Democratic" Republic; and two, destroying the freedom of West Berlin. To achieve these objectives, the Soviet Union announced in November 1958 that at the end of six months it intended to end the four-power occupation and hand control of East Berlin and the routes leading into West Berlin over to the East Germans. The clear implication was that in the future, free access to Berlin would require that the Western powers deal directly and officially with the East German government.

The Soviet goal of eliciting Western recognition of East Germany was clearly subsidiary to the aim of strangling West Berlin. For what the Soviets were actually calling for when they declared the end of the four-power occupation was an Allied withdrawal from West Berlin, turning it into a "free city." This was, in effect, a demand for the incorporation of West Berlin into East Germany. Once Western troops had left the city, the West Berliners would feel isolated and unprotected, abandoned and completely helpless. The Soviet army and the East German army and police would surround them. In these circumstances, the defenseless West Berliners would have to come to terms with the East German regime. Conversely, if the West refused to sign a treaty turning Berlin into a "free city," the Soviet Union would then sign a separate peace treaty with East Germany, automatically abrogating the West's right to be in Berlin and making any further Western stay dependent on the terms that could be negotiated with the now "sovereign" German Democratic Republic. This would mean that the West would remain in Berlin by the consent of East Germany, which would then gradually intensify its pressure and undermine the West's position until it became untenable.

One way or the other, the Soviets planned to remove a troublesome thorn from their side. They would then be in a far better position to stabilize the status quo. The destruction of West Berlin would have accomplished not only the Soviet Union's defensive aims but also its long-standing offensive purpose of weakening its opponents, perhaps fatally. If the Soviets could drive the Western powers, especially the United States, out of Berlin, they would also be able to cut off the development of the Common Market before it gathered too much momentum and to shatter the NATO alliance. It was, above all, American power that guaranteed the freedom of the 2 million Germans living in West Berlin. If the United States were forced to abandon them, the Europeans would lose faith in America's ability to protect them. The Germans would be the first to read the lesson: because America could not guarantee their security, they would have to approach the Soviets independently.

The Soviets would certainly demand the abandonment of all Germany's political, economic, or military ties to the West. But without Germany, there could be no Common Market because Germany provided much of the capital its partners needed for their economic development. If Germany pulled out of the Atlantic alliance, the United States would have to send its troops home because it would be politically and strategically impossible to station them in France. Yet, these troops were a symbol of the American commitment to defend Europe; they were psychologically and politically indispensable. No written guarantees could be substituted for this living embodiment of America's stake in Europe.

Was America willing to defend Europe now that the United States was becoming increasingly vulnerable to a Soviet nuclear attack? This was, in the final analysis, the fundamental question posed by the Berlin crisis. The Soviet proposals had included the ultimatum that if West Berlin's status had not been "renegotiated" within six months, the East Germans would take control of the railroads and highways leading into West Berlin. If the East Germans then interfered with Western traffic and the West used force to break a blockade, Khrushchev stated that the Soviets would resist such force. The defense of West Berlin therefore raised the possibility of war. The Soviet challenge was clever: it presented the United States with a limited challenge and offered it the choice of surrendering West Berlin or risk war for its preservation. It was America's will that was really at stake in Berlin.

Soviet Technological Prowess and the U.S. Response

Berlin was a major test of postwar American policy, but it was not a repeat of the 1948 situation. At that time, Stalin had acted on two assumptions: first, that the far larger Red Army contingents would deter an Allied attempt to break through on the ground; and second, that the United States and Britain could not keep West Berlin alive. The first assumption proved to be correct, but the second was wrong. When Stalin realized this, he had to call off the blockade or shoot down Allied planes and risk a war. America's atomic monopoly favored the first solution. But in 1957, a year before the Berlin ultimatum, the Soviet Union had tested the world's first intercontinental ballistic missile (ICBM), and American determination to defend Berlin therefore became riskier and costlier. Moreover, the ICBM test had followed a series of spectacular Soviet accomplishments in space. Soviet Sputniks, or satellites, which flew around the world every 90 minutes, and the ICBM test were at the time considered impressive symbols of Soviet technological progress. In turn, they raised serious questions in the United States about its historic technological leadership and the future of the balance of power. Khrushchev, in fact, immediately talked of mass-producing ICBMs and asserted that the balance of nuclear or strategic power was shifting toward the Soviet Union. There was widespread public concern and anxiety in the United States about a future "missile gap," which, because ICBMs were faster than bombers, meant that U.S. strategic forces would become more vulnerable to a surprise attack and might no longer be as effective. Given the limited nature of the Soviet challenge and the all-or-nothing nature of massive retaliations, what strategy could the United States devise to prevent the Soviet Union from slowly choking West Berlin to death?

The crisis in Berlin was a test of the massive retaliation policy. How could massive retaliation, a policy intended to deter an attack on the United States or invasion of Western Europe, be used to prevent the strangulation of West Berlin? Could strategic air power, upon which the Eisenhower administration depended almost exclusively to preserve the line around the Sino-Soviet periphery, successfully accomplish this task against limited challenges? To be sure, the Soviets had to be very careful. The stakes for both powers were high. Since they confronted one another directly, a Soviet miscalculation could result in nuclear war. The problem was that American strategic power was *so* great that it could not be used; as a reaction to a limited challenge, it was not very credible. Would Moscow therefore be restrained by U.S. threats of massive retaliation in Berlin's defense when the United States had been self-deterred in Asia against far lesser threats to its interests?

The Berlin crisis, in brief, was the most serious confrontation Washington had faced since 1948-1949. The Truman Doctrine, Marshall Plan, Berlin airlift, and NATO had made it very plain to Moscow that Western Europe was an area of vital American interest. Soviet domination over the Western edge of the Eurasian continent was no more tolerable to the United States than German control. Presumably this knowledge had deterred the Soviets in the late 1940s, and it was the fear of war that had led them to direct their challenges to Third World areas.

Now, however, ten years after the first Berlin crisis, the Soviets had once more challenged the West in Europe. Indeed, in reopening the Berlin issue the Soviets were seeking to convey a new sense of confidence in their ability to deal with the West. That confidence seemed to reflect the Soviet claim that the strategic balance was changing in their favor. Clearly, Khrushchev was attempting to cash in on this claim, to undermine European confidence in the United States, and to drive a wedge between the European members of

NATO, especially West Germany, and their trans-Atlantic protector. This had been a constant Soviet goal since the early cold war.

Not surprisingly, the last years of the Eisenhower administration were gloomy—a mood expressed mainly by liberal Democrats, the authors of the containment policy. Although Eisenhower claimed there was no "deterrent gap," the succession of headlines about Soviet ICBM tests and Sputnik launchings all seemed to belie his words. American prestige and power were largely identified with technology; now the Soviets had gained a dramatic breakthrough in that area. After placing quite large weights, including a dog, in space, the Soviets derided the first American space shot. Khrushchev joked about the U.S. effort to launch "a grapefruit." More worrisome was the ability of the Soviets to bring the Sputnik back to earth at a designated spot; presumably they could do the same with their ICBMs. The bombers that had provided the United States with its deterrent shield were about to become vulnerable. Suddenly, the United States appeared to have lost the sense of security it had long possessed as a result of its isolation from world politics, its atomic monopoly, and its enormous strategic superiority. Sputnik, the "missile gap," and the 1958 Berlin crisis caused a deep pessimism about the future. This pessimism was not limited to America. United States Information Agency polls in Western Europe and elsewhere showed that others shared a general sense that the United States was falling behind the Soviets, that the balance was shifting, and that perhaps the United States had lost its dynamism.

c h a p t e r   s i x

Berlin, Cuba, and the Limits of Massive Retaliation

AMERICAN foreign policy has traditionally been based on a worldview of mutually exclusive conditions: war or peace, force or diplomacy, aggressors or peace-loving states. Peace was normal, war abnormal. Force was unnecessary in the absence of conflict and hostilities; it was to be used only in wartime to destroy the source of war itself. The concept of massive retaliation fit this American approach completely. It was an all-or-nothing strategy that could not be used short of a Soviet attack on the United States or Western Europe. At the same time, American presidents consistently rejected preventive war, both at the time of the nation's atomic monopoly and later, during the 1950s and 1960s, the period of gradually declining strategic superiority. Deterrence was the American goal; nuclear strategy was to retaliate after the opponent had struck first. If the United States were attacked, however, it would use massive retaliation, as in the two world wars, to punish and destroy the enemy in ways not conceivable until 1945.

Massive retaliation, by reducing the enemy's population centers and industries to rubble and radioactive dust, carried the American approach to war to its logical conclusion. Although some bombs were targeted on the small Soviet air force, the rapidly growing U.S. stockpile was to be used against all targets, military and economic, in one huge war-winning blow. The hydrogen bomb's megaton (equal to a million tons of TNT) explosive power, as opposed to that of the atomic bomb's kiloton (equal to a thousand tons of TNT), made that possible. In the words of a navy captain attending an air force briefing on the Strategic Air Command (SAC) plans at the time, the Soviet Union was to be left "a smoking, radiating ruin at the end of two hours."

In one sense, atomic weapons and the more destructive nuclear weapons enabled the United States to pursue an old American dream in a new and gruesome way. By making nuclear war too destructive to fight, by making the distinction between victor and loser in such a conflict increasingly meaningless, the deterrent strategy aimed at eliminating war itself. This old goal had been sought through the "war to end all wars" crusade, or through international organization and cooperation, or through free trade and economic interdependence among nations. The goal could now be realized because war had become, in the popular phrase, "unthinkable."

Precisely because they were so destructive, nuclear weapons could best be used to deter the possibility of an all-out attack and contain limited challenges, but they could not prevent them. Thus they were not an effective tool of foreign policy to deal with everyday problems. Even in the immediate postwar period, when the United States possessed an atomic monopoly, these weapons could not stop the Soviet Union from consolidating its grip on Eastern Europe, from attempting to seize a northern province of Iran, from pressuring Turkey, from permitting Yugoslavia and Bulgaria to intervene in the Greek civil war, or from urging the French Communist party to exploit France's postwar economic misery after 1947. Nor could atomic weapons deter the North Korean attack upon South Korea. The likelihood of massive retaliation had not prevented the Chinese Communists from helping the Vietminh or the Vietminh victory over the French in Indochina in 1954 or threatening Quemoy and Matsu. The Soviets had only to avoid attacking the United States or an area the United States had designated as vital to its security. Short of that ultimate provocation, the Soviet Union, the strategically weaker party during the first decade of the cold war, could—like the Chinese—raise tensions and challenge the United States.

The problem for the United States was how to maintain the circle of containment around the Sino-Soviet periphery against such limited challenges. As the situations in Berlin and Cuba were to show in the late 1950s and early 1960s, strategic weapons were necessary to prevent escalation of such challenges to war, but they also showed the need for conventional forces to defend U.S. interests. The chief lesson of the Korean War—that a capability for limited response was necessary to deal with less-than-total challenges, a lesson that the Eisenhower administration had rejected—could not be ignored. Indeed, as Soviet strategic strength grew during the 1950s, the Soviet and American nuclear forces increasingly deterred one another. Even though the Soviets had not yet acquired strategic parity, they could inflict enormous destruction on the United States with only a few hydrogen bombs. Thus the requirement for a conventional capability increased.

Deterrence and Challenge in the Nuclear Era

Mutual deterrence, or the "balance of terror," as Winston Churchill called it, would ensure the peace; indeed, in President Eisenhower's words, "there is no alternative to peace." His participation at the 1955 summit conference in Geneva with Soviet premier Nikolai Bulganin and Khrushchev, at the time first secretary of the Soviet Communist party, was generally recognized as testimony to this fact. War was no longer a rational instrument of national power; by simply meeting, the leaders of the two most powerful countries of the world were said to have "signed" a tacit nonaggression pact. Even though the United States had the capability to utterly destroy the Soviet Union, while the latter could "only" impose heavy casualties, this asymmetry in the ability to inflict destruction did not mean mutual deterrence did not exist. For neither country was willing to risk war and the loss of even two or three large cities.

Strategists and foreign policy experts, however, feared that U.S. policy was handing the Soviet Union an opportunity to break this stalemate. The age of nuclear plenty increased America's strategic dilemma. The Eisenhower all-or-nothing strategy, the critics said, meant that each less-than-total Soviet challenge—outside of Europe another Korea, or in Europe, a seizure of West Berlin (especially by Soviet-supported East German troops), or even an invasion of Western Europe that would not, however, launch a simultaneous attack on the United States—confronted Washington with the question whether the defense of American interests was worth the destruction of most of America's cities and a cost of lives ranging, depending on the size and scope of the attack, from an estimated 10 to 100 million and more. Faced with this prospect if it responded to such a "limited" Soviet challenge, the American government had a strong incentive to do nothing. In terms frequently used at the time, the U.S. dilemma was described as one of suicide or surrender, holocaust or humiliation. According to Henry Kissinger in 1957:

> It can be argued that the fear of all-out war is bound to be mutual, that the Soviet leaders will, therefore, share our reluctance to engage in any adventures which may involve this risk. But because each side may be equally deterred from engaging in all-out war, it makes all the difference which side can extricate itself from its dilemma *only* by initiating such a struggle. If the Soviet bloc can present its challenges in less than all-out form it may gain a crucial advantage. Every move on its part will then pose the appalling dilemma of whether we are willing to commit suicide to prevent encroachments, which do not, each in itself, seem to threaten our existence directly but which may be steps on the road to our ultimate destruction.
>
> To be sure, we shall continue to insist that we reject the notion of "peace at any price." The price of peace, however, cannot be determined in the abstract. The growth of the Soviet nuclear stockpile is certain to widen the line between what is considered "vital" and what is "peripheral" if we must weigh each objective against the destruction of New York or Detroit, of Los Angeles or Chicago.[1]

Was Berlin still a "vital" interest? or was it now only a "peripheral" one? These difficult questions confronted the United States in the late 1950s.

---

1. Henry A. Kissinger, *Nuclear Weapons and Foreign Policy* (New York: Harper & Brothers, 1957), 15-16.

The Soviet challenge was underscored by the small number of conventional forces on the Continent. These NATO troops had had two tasks. The first was to strengthen deterrence by making the U.S. commitment to defend Europe credible; Moscow could understand that once American soldiers were killed, SAC would be unleashed. The second, in case deterrence failed, was to implement the "forward strategy" by holding the Red Army at the border between East Germany and West Germany while SAC was destroying the Soviet Union. The policy of deterrence now, however, dictated yet a third operational assignment for NATO forces: to cope with challenges as in Berlin. It was simply unbelievable that the United States would risk suicide no matter what the level of Soviet provocation. Would suicide be preferable to reacting locally?

But this capacity to respond was missing in Europe. In large measure, this situation was a result of the Eisenhower administration's determination to "maximize air power and minimize the foot soldier." By January 1960 NATO had only seventeen or eighteen ready divisions. Moreover, the divisions had been equipped with tactical nuclear weapons to cope with the large number of Warsaw Pact forces. This, however, raised the same question as SAC: Would the weapons be used? Would NATO not grow increasingly reluctant to rely on these forces to respond to Soviet moves? When the original decision to equip Allied forces with nuclear battlefield weapons was made, it was believed that the Soviet Union would have few, if any, tactical nuclear weapons in the near future. The damage caused by such U.S. weapons would therefore be inflicted mainly on East Germany and Poland. The picture changed, however, when the Soviets acquired these weapons, ensuring that their use would be reciprocal. In these circumstances, the advantages that tactical nuclear arms were supposed to confer on the West began to diminish. Instead of protecting Europe, these weapons would devastate it. Europe is densely populated. Its cities are close to one another, and civil, military, tactical, and strategic targets are all intertwined. A nuclear ground war would be a catastrophe for Europe, probably spelling the end of its civilization. NATO's capacity to fight a limited tactical nuclear war, therefore, would not allow the West to escape the dilemma of suicide or appeasement. As someone supposedly said, the towns of Germany were just "two kilotons apart."

The concentration on massive retaliation—on NATO's sword—however, had reduced the need for conventionally armed ground forces. The very appeal of nuclear weapons to the United States and just as much, if not more so, to its European allies was that the nuclear deterrent would not require large expensive conventional forces; nuclear arms provided defense on the cheap. But in a situation of increasing nuclear stalemate, it was precisely such conventional forces that were needed to counter Soviet pressure. The lack of such NATO forces reinforced the need to stake the alliance's survival on each issue. Walter Lippmann had written rather critically right after the war that the bomb was the "perfect fulfillment of all wishful thinking on military matters; here is war that requires no national effort, no draft, no discipline, but only money and engineering, of which we have plenty. Here is the panacea which enables us to be the greatest military power on earth—without investing in time, energy, sweat, blood and tears." [2] Lippmann was in fact describing not just the United States, but all the Western democracies. But as the Soviet capacity to drop nuclear weapons on the United States grew in the late 1950s and early 1960s, "containment on the cheap" was over.

The Berlin Retreat

The reliance on SAC made it difficult for the Western powers, especially the United States, to impress the Soviet Union with NATO's unity and resolve. The United States was determined to stay in Berlin, but after stating that it would defend Berlin by massive retaliation, it sought to escape the consequences of its own military strategy. This it could do only by granting concessions. Shortly after the presentation of the Soviet ultimatum that West Berlin must be "demilitarized" in six months, Secretary of State John Foster Dulles spoke of accepting the East Germans as "Russian agents" at the checkpoints on the route leading into Berlin. Dulles also declared that Germany could be reunified by means other than free elections. Both statements threatened a complete abandonment of the long-held American positions of nonrecognition of the East German regime and of Germany's right of self-determination. The administration, already pressured by the British, also accepted the standing Soviet call for a summit conference. But the United States insisted on the prior fulfillment of two conditions: withdrawal of the Soviet six-month ultimatum and a foreign ministers' conference to hammer out a settlement of the Berlin issue and others relating to Germany. The purpose of a "meeting at the top" was, in the administration's opinion, essentially to ratify decisions already reached at a lower level. Eisenhower rejected a meeting that would settle nothing and end in a fruitless propaganda debate.

The Soviets reluctantly accepted the precondition of a foreign ministers' conference, but denied that the six-month deadline on Berlin was an ultimatum. However, they refused to budge from their position at the foreign ministers' marathon held in Geneva in the spring and summer of 1959. Rather, the West offered concessions. First, the United States allowed an East German delegation to attend the deliberations, thereby taking a step toward de facto recognition of the Soviet-installed regime. The Soviet Union had made East German presence a precondition for the meeting. Second, at the first sign of Soviet opposition, the West abandoned its plan for the

---

2. Quoted in Lawrence Freedman, *The Evolution of Nuclear Strategy* (New York: St. Martin's Press, 1981), 48.

reunification of Germany as a means of resolving the Berlin crisis. Third, the Western foreign ministers then offered to transform the allies' permanent status in Berlin for an interim settlement. In short, after years of stating that it was the Soviet division of Germany that was the cause of European instability, the United States and Britain accepted the Soviet claim that the principal source of the tension over Berlin was its "abnormal" situation and continued occupation by the allied powers so many years after the war.

The Soviets, however, refused to renew their endorsement of Allied rights in Berlin and reasserted that they would end the occupation regime. The Allies failed to obtain the Soviet guarantee they sought, but the fact that they had attempted to arrive at an interim arrangement for Berlin at all, and had been willing to grant concessions to obtain it, is eloquent testimony to the dilemma in which American strategy had placed them. In effect, the United States and Britain were willing to transform the Western position in Berlin in return for the withdrawal of the Soviet threat to the city. In an attempt to extricate themselves from the dilemma of suicide or surrender, the two countries placed themselves in the humiliating position of calling into question their well-established rights in Berlin. No wonder Khrushchev felt that all he had to do was maintain a high level of tension.

Khrushchev's bellicosity and rigidity paid handsome dividends. The more menacing he sounded and the more inflexibly he stood, the greater the number of voices in the West that called for more Western "flexibility" and "new approaches." Policies that had become almost untouchable over the years were questioned or condemned as dangerous. The controversy divided the West. The British denounced Chancellor Konrad Adenauer's "rigidity"; the Germans, in turn, accused the British of "appeasement." Franco-British relations cooled considerably. And both Adenauer and Charles de Gaulle demonstrated increasing suspicions of U.S. intentions and resolution. America's apparent willingness to discuss Berlin with the Soviets seemed to the German and French leaders to show little American conviction or courage to uphold an earlier position; to them, Eisenhower was showing far too much flexibility.

As if to prove Khrushchev's theory that his threats would have rewarding consequences, and to confirm de Gaulle's and Adenauer's apprehensions, Eisenhower invited Khrushchev to come to the United States in September 1959. His visit represented a tactical victory for the Soviets because Khrushchev knew that this summit conference could intensify the allies' apprehension of a separate United States-Soviet agreement at their expense; conversely, it might persuade Eisenhower that the crisis was caused by the rigidity of French and West German leaders whom Khrushchev would accuse of opposing the "normalization" of American-Soviet relations.

Khrushchev's visit to the United States did, however, have one positive result: the Soviet Union withdrew its threat to take unilateral action in Berlin in return for American willingness to negotiate on the problems of Berlin and

Germany at a four-power summit meeting, which was scheduled for May 1960 in Paris. For American policy makers, this meant another postponement of the painful decision on whether Berlin was worth the cost of war. But if the administration believed that the crisis had ended, that from then on it could negotiate leisurely on these issues and, if the Soviets did not accept its terms, preserve the status quo, it was quickly disabused of this notion. Khrushchev was soon reiterating his threat to sign a separate peace with East Germany.

The U-2 Spy Plane Incident

Shortly before the Paris summit, an event took place that shattered the conference after only one session and further postponed negotiations on Berlin. On May Day, 1,300 miles within Soviet territory, the Soviets downed an American U-2 "spy plane" loaded with photographic equipment for the gathering of intelligence data. The Eisenhower administration reacted to this unexpected and unhappy turn of events with considerable diplomatic ineptitude. In response to Khrushchev's announcement that the plane had been shot down, the U.S. government claimed that it had been engaged in meteorological observation and speculated that the pilot had flown off course. When the Soviet premier revealed the flight's true mission and produced an alleged confession by the pilot, the administration reversed itself. In a move unprecedented in diplomatic history, it admitted that the U-2 pilot had been taking aerial photographs of the Soviet Union and that it had lied in its previous announcement.

Nor did the administration stop there. It claimed that similar flights had been sent into Soviet skies for several years and strongly intimated that the flights would continue. The administration justified its actions, saying that Soviet secrecy made it necessary to gather information by this means to prevent a surprise attack. It is bad enough to be caught red-handed in spying and worse for the president to admit it; it is worst of all for him to assert that the United States would continue this behavior. In effect, the United States claimed the *right* to fly over Soviet territory. One need only imagine the uproar in the United States in this presatellite age if the Soviets had announced that they had the right to fly over American soil and take photographs of military installations.

The Soviets felt obliged to meet this challenge. For the Soviet premier to let it pass would be like acknowledging to the world, to his people, to his domestic enemies, and to his allies that he had surrendered to the United States the right to violate Soviet territory. Khrushchev could not survive such an admission. The course he took was to strike a belligerent pose in Paris. He launched a blistering personal attack upon Eisenhower, demanding his apology for past U-2 flights, a promise that the flights would cease, and punishment of those responsible for the spying operation. Eisenhower's assurance that no more reconnaissance missions would take place during his term of office did not satisfy Khrushchev, who apparently thought this meant but a temporary suspension. Khrushchev's other demands were rejected outright. Khrushchev thereupon suggested that the summit conference be postponed for six to eight months, and he bluntly told Eisenhower that he would not be welcome to visit the Soviet Union in June, as previously planned. In short, Khrushchev said that he wanted nothing more to do with Eisenhower and that he would wait to negotiate the Berlin problem with the next administration. A new crisis had been put off for a little while longer.

Kennedy's Berlin Crisis

It was inevitable, therefore, that the Soviets would raise the Berlin problem again once the new administration took over. Khrushchev was still convinced that the global balance was shifting in his favor, and he remained confident that he was strong enough to acquire West Berlin. President John Kennedy, fearing that Khrushchev might miscalculate, emphasized at a Vienna summit meeting America's determination to defend West Berlin; the United States would stand firm and protect the free half of the city. Khrushchev discounted these warnings. His response was characteristic: to test the president's resolution by reviving the original threat that the Berlin situation would have to be resolved within six months—that is, before the end of 1961. The Vienna summit turned out exactly opposite of what was intended: it resulted in the very type of Soviet brinkmanship against which Kennedy had sought to caution the Soviet leader.

Kennedy was thus quickly confronted with his Berlin crisis. Declaring his willingness to negotiate, he also stated that he did not expect the Soviets to confront him with a ready-made treaty with East Germany. The United States was not willing to discuss merely how the West would withdraw from the beleaguered city, thereby leaving it for the Communists to swallow. The West's right to be in the city stemmed from its victory over Nazi Germany. Western presence and access to the city and the freedom of West Berlin were not negotiable. Kennedy said, "We cannot negotiate with those who say: 'What's mine is mine, and what's yours is negotiable.' " More specifically, he asked, if the West refused to meet its clear-cut commitments in Berlin, where would it meet them?

But it was also clear on August 13, 1961, when the Communists built a wall dividing the city, that they had eliminated the escape hatch for East Germans. More than 200,000 East Germans escaped to the West in 1961 alone; 2.5 million had already migrated westward from 1948 to 1960—20 percent of East Germany's entire population! The wall ended West Berlin's usefulness as a "showplace for Western capitalism," and violated the quadripartite status of Berlin. The West did not knock the wall down with bulldozers for fear of military conflict with Communist—especially Soviet—

forces. This passivity intensified Khrushchev's conviction that the United States would not fight and that he could, slowly but surely, increase the pressure on NATO and drive the West out of Berlin.

This possibility, and the American fear that the Soviet leader might miscalculate Western resolve and accidentally trigger a war, accounted for the difference between Kennedy's and his predecessor's reactions to the Berlin crisis. Unlike Eisenhower, Kennedy used the tensions over Berlin to build up American military power; the new president was determined to show Khrushchev that the United States was not bluffing when it declared its intentions to defend West Berlin. Kennedy moved in two directions; indeed, he had begun to do so almost immediately after assuming office. One aim was "flexible response"; the United States needed more options than suicide or surrender. This increased flexibility was to be achieved by building larger conventional forces. In Europe, a conventional buildup would give NATO a credible defense, which did not immediately depend on tactical nuclear weapons or, if these failed to stem the Soviet advance, strategic weapons. Outside of Europe, the United States would also have a capability to respond to limited challenges.

The other critical aim was to reduce SAC's vulnerability during the changeover from bombers to missiles. Bombers located at known sites were highly vulnerable to surprise attack. Even in a situation of mutual deterrence, the possibility that many of the enemy's bombers might be destroyed on the ground remained an incentive to attack. If they could be destroyed, the retaliatory attack by a crippled remnant force might not be fatal to the attacking nation. In a crisis situation, this possibility could tempt either side to launch a preemptive strike—even if the other side had no intention of striking. But solid-fuel missiles, like the air force's Minuteman, could be widely dispersed and protected, or "hardened," in underground silos instead of being concentrated on a few above-ground bases; missiles were not yet accurate enough to hit such silos. And the navy's Polaris missiles would be mobile underwater so that the enemy would at no time know where to strike them.

The importance of these concealment tactics was that they deprived a surprise attack of its rationale. Obliterating the enemy's cities would benefit the aggressor very little if the enemy still retained its retaliatory capacity. Surprise, therefore, no longer conferred any significant advantage to the side that struck first. Indeed, there was no longer any need to hit preemptively because enough of the missiles would survive the first strike and be able to retaliate fully against the aggressor in a second strike. A first strike in these circumstances—which American policy makers generally conceded to the Soviets—would be completely irrational.

Invulnerable second-strike forces were believed to be the basis of *stable* mutual deterrence. Mutual deterrence, according to the arms control philosophy the Kennedy administration brought in, would not guarantee that war could be avoided. If the means of delivering nuclear bombs or warheads were vulnerable to attack, they might, particularly in crisis moments, tempt one side or the other to launch a first strike. Mutual deterrence in these conditions was unstable. Stabilizing the deterrent balance was therefore a priority for the new administration. The resulting deemphasis of bombers and their replacement by hardened land-based and mobile sea-based missiles occurred over a number of years.

In the meantime, Kennedy, as cautious as Eisenhower, vacillated between his determination to stay in West Berlin and his equally strong determination to avoid conflict. Like Eisenhower, he was willing to offer concessions and negotiate with the Soviets alone if West Germany and France remained diplomatically inflexible. The meager results of these bilateral American-Soviet negotiations were due primarily to Soviet unwillingness to concede the right to any Western presence in Berlin, which, in turn, was due to Khrushchev's conviction that he need only maintain Soviet pressure to evict the Western powers from the Communist-surrounded and divided city. If, during this early period of the Kennedy administration, as during the late years of the Eisenhower era, the Soviets were unwilling to risk the final test, they had shown they were not hesitant to push the issue to a point of high tension by seeking to create the belief that they were willing to risk war and thereby exploit the West's fear of nuclear hostilities. And although the United States had upheld the status quo, the manner in which it questioned its own position in Berlin and the concessions it offered in the name of flexibility demonstrated a lack of will and sense of purpose. This augured ill for the future if: (1) the Soviet leaders could keep their challenges below the level of provocation that might arouse an American nuclear response; and (2) the Soviets confined their challenges to the periphery of Western power, especially an isolated outpost such as West Berlin. As long as they followed these two fundamental precepts, they could continue to try to exploit the dilemmas of American strategy.

It was the second rule that the Soviets failed to follow when they shifted the challenge to ninety miles from the American mainland—to Cuba—where the United States had little choice but to respond in defense of what it conceived to be its vital interests.

Castro and the Missile Crisis

Cuba's revolutionary government dated from January 1, 1959, when its leaders overthrew the tyrannical dictatorship of Fulgencio Batista. During his struggle against Batista, Fidel Castro had identified himself with democratic government and social and economic justice and had gained widespread popularity among the Cuban people. This public support ensured the victory of his guerrilla army against the larger government forces. The Castro revolution was essentially a social revolution. In the opening months of its rule, the new government moved to remedy the conditions of the people by instituting land reform and by building low-cost housing, schools, and clinics. But some features of this social revolution were bound to clash with the interests of the United States.

Although the United States had been instrumental in freeing Cuba from Spain in the Spanish-American War at the turn of the century, it had subsequently passed the Platt Amendment, which granted the Americans the right to intervene at any time in Cuba for the preservation of Cuban independence, for the protection of life, property, and individual liberty, and for the discharge of Cuba's treaty obligations. By 1934, when the amendment was repealed, the United States had intervened militarily once (1906-1909); it also had established a naval base at Guantánamo Bay. American capital controlled 80 percent of Cuba's utilities, 90 percent of its mines and cattle ranches, nearly all of its oil, and 40 percent of its sugar; approximately 25 percent of the American market was reserved for Cuban sugar. Despite this special commercial link, it was not surprising that the Cuban revolution directed its long-pent-up nationalism and social resentment against a "Yankee imperialism" that dominated Cuba's economy. America's support of the Batista dictatorship until the moment of its collapse intensified anti-American sentiment. "Cuba, si! Yanqui, no!" became the Castro regime's rallying cry, the ceremonial burning of the American flag its ritual, and the confiscation of American property its reward. Yet Cuba in 1959 ranked fourth among Latin American nations in social and economic development (compared to high teens today).

This anti-American nationalistic feeling, deliberately fostered by Castro to increase the popularity of his regime, led to an increasing identification of his government with communism. If he was going to break with the United States, which Castro assumed would oppose his reforms, then he had to look to Moscow, its rival. Before long, Castro betrayed the revolution's original democratic promises and became a dictatorship with centralized control over all of the country's activities. All parties were abolished except for one—the Communist party, upon whose organizational strength Castro had become increasingly dependent. Castro also linked Cuba closely to the Communist bloc. The Soviet Union supplied Cuba with vast amounts of arms and accompanying military advisers. Cuban airmen were sent to Czechoslovakia to learn how to fly Soviet fighters, and a large number of Cuban technicians were trained in Communist countries. Cuba's armed services soon ranked second only to America's as the largest in the hemisphere. Diplomatic relations were established with all Communist countries except East Germany, and economic agreements were signed with many of the same countries, including East Germany. Cuba's economy became integrated into that of the Communist bloc; 75 percent of the island's trade was with countries behind the iron curtain. In January 1961, the United States cut off diplomatic relations with Cuba after a sequence of perceived provocations. If

Castro at that point had attempted to seize the Guantánamo base, there would have been an excuse for open American intervention.

Castro was too shrewd to risk a seizure, but he also ruled out an accommodation with the United States. Castro wanted to play a major role on the world stage. He could not achieve that role as the leader of either a pro-American or neutral country of 10 million people on a small Caribbean island. He could do so only as a revolutionary leader who took on his giant neighbor as an enemy. To stand up against the United States, he would need the support of the other giant. Castro turned down all friendly overtures from the United States after he took power: a new, sympathetic American ambassador was kept waiting for weeks before being allowed to present his credentials, and offers of foreign aid were rejected.

The Bay of Pigs

As Cuban-Soviet relations consolidated, the Eisenhower administration began to plan for Castro's overthrow. The new Kennedy administration in April 1961 launched an attempt by a small force of Cuban exiles—many of them former Castro associates who had become disillusioned by the premier's increasingly tyrannical rule, Communist sympathies, and alignment with the Soviet Union—to land in Cuba and attempt to overthrow Castro. The Central Intelligence Agency (CIA) had developed the plans for this operation and supervised their execution. The CIA assumed that, once the exiles had gained a beachhead in the Bay of Pigs, some units of Castro's army and Cuba's population would welcome the invaders as liberators. But the operation was a dramatic and appalling failure. The United States bungled because it launched a major foreign policy move, involving American prestige, on the glib assumption that a feeble beachhead operation would result in a mass uprising of Cubans against their government. The rumors and press reports, which conveyed the impression of a major invasion, made the failure appear even greater.

If nothing succeeds like success, it can also be said that nothing fails like failure. American prestige, already lowered by the Soviet Union's man-in-space achievement, sank to a new low. In Cyrus Sulzberger's pointed comment in the *New York Times,* "We looked like fools to our friends, rascals to our enemies, and incompetents to the rest." The administration had fallen victim to its own half-heartedness. The results of an unsuccessful invasion could have been predicted: an increase in Castro's domestic support, a revival of Latin American fears of "Yankee imperialism," a blunting of Kennedy's initially successful attempts to identify the United States with anticolonialism, and a loss of confidence in America's leadership by its allies.

But Kennedy was to set an unfortunate precedent for what was to become a pattern: to proclaim a Communist regime in the Caribbean-Central America area as a security threat to the United States, then use proxies in an effort to eliminate it, and finally to abandon these proxies when the "going got tough" because of a fear of escalation and war, and/or congressional and public opposition. If vital interests were really at stake, this course was unworthy of a great power. In short, the United States attempted to counter the Soviet exploitation of the new nationalist and social revolution to its south by "partial measures and through proxies. It has sought solutions on the cheap." [3]

Soviet Inroads in the Western Hemisphere

Thus, Cuba survived as a Communist base from which the Soviet Union could threaten the United States and subvert the security of the other nations in the Western Hemisphere. The importance of this cannot be underestimated. The American position in the Western Hemisphere had been preeminent. The Monroe Doctrine had announced to the world that Latin America fell within the American sphere of influence and that Europe's colonial powers were to keep their hands off. In subsequent decades the United States had intervened repeatedly, especially in the Caribbean-Central American area. Although the motives for intervention varied, principal among them was the fear that a European power might establish its influence in an area that could be called America's "strategic rear," or, to use a Churchillian phrase, its "soft underbelly." During the early 1940s the concern was with German power; after that, with Soviet power. A Marxist government had come to power in Guatemala in 1954. When it received arms from Czechoslovakia, the Eisenhower administration had intervened covertly to overthrow it, thereby setting a precedent for the Bay of Pigs. In short, the United States has never tolerated Latin American governments that leaned toward Germany or the Soviet Union, at least not in the smaller countries so close to the Rio Grande and Florida.

Castro's survival after the Bay of Pigs was a significant exception and meant that the United States no longer held a monopoly of power in the Caribbean-Central American area. This change resulted from the failure of covert intervention and the unwillingness to resort to overt intervention in the belief that it might alienate the rising Latin American middle class whose support the United States thought it needed. The United States wanted to remain what it had claimed to be since Franklin Roosevelt's time—a "good neighbor." Unfortunately, the Bay of Pigs disaster incited Soviet intervention. In Moscow, where unfriendly regimes were not tolerated but crushed, Kennedy's prestige plummeted. If it had been in the interest of the United States to eliminate Castro, then U.S. military intervention should have followed the bungled CIA attempt. A "serious" power does not tolerate its

3. Zbigniew Brzezinski, "America's New Geostrategy," *Foreign Affairs* 66 (Spring 1988): 691.

enemies so near and does not act squeamishly. It does what it has to do, regardless of international opinion. If Castro's elimination was not important enough for the United States to risk criticism, then the intervention should not have been launched in the first place. But to do so and fail suggested weak nerves and a lack of foresight. Worse, it suggested fear of the Soviet Union. Why else would the United States not intervene with its own military forces in an area so close to it, as it had many times before? Why should the Soviet Union not push a little further and see if Kennedy would tolerate a further extension of Soviet power?

The Importance of 'Not Losing' in Cuba

Once the Soviets saw that the Communist regime in Cuba was tolerated, they began to establish a missile base there. Washington had believed that the Soviet Union would not dare to do this in America's sphere of influence. In the fall of 1962, however, a U-2 spy plane suddenly discovered, to the great surprise and consternation of American policy makers, that the Soviets were building launching sites for approximately seventy medium- and intermediate-range ballistic missiles. That Khrushchev had dared to move his missiles so near the United States and apparently expected no counteraction beyond ineffective diplomatic protests, was a dangerous sign. War by miscalculation is the great danger; to prevent miscalculation is therefore an absolute necessity. But American actions had convinced the Soviet premier that the United States would not fight to protect its vital interests. If the overthrow of Castro were a vital interest, why did the United States not send its own forces once the exile forces had failed? If it were not a vital interest, why attempt such an operation at all? Khrushchev thought Kennedy too young and inexperienced; Kennedy, Khrushchev told an American visitor, was "too liberal to fight."

Khrushchev had a great deal to gain. A failure to respond to his move would prove to America's NATO allies what they feared already—namely, that the United States had become vulnerable to attack and could no longer be relied on to protect Europe. Inaction in the face of Soviet missiles so close to the American coast would have validated Khrushchev's claim of a shift in the nuclear balance. The promised renewal of Soviet pressure on Berlin after the midterm U.S. congressional elections, together with the likelihood of an even more cautious American reaction than before, would only have reinforced this impression. Only this time, the Soviets could deliver an ultimatum to get out or else. The threat was that the Soviets could for the first time cover a large part of the North American continent with their missiles, which would come flying in over areas where there was no adequate protection against them. The early warning systems against bombers and missiles were in the north because a Soviet attack had always been expected to come in over the Arctic. Not only was the United States vulnerable to attack, but also its prestige was on the line. The sudden and unchallenged appearance of the opposing superpower in the area where the United States had long been paramount would have eroded America's authority and status and encouraged the spread of Castroism throughout Latin America. All anti-Castro forces, including the indispensable and all too few genuinely democratic reformers, would have been demoralized and perhaps paralyzed by Washington's inaction.

The political and psychological implications of Khrushchev's limited challenge, therefore, were enormous. But for once Khrushchev had overplayed his hand. He had pressured the United States in the wrong place, and Washington could not avoid the test. If the stakes were high for the Soviet Union, they were even higher for the United States. Khrushchev might have wanted to "win" this one, but Kennedy felt that under no circumstances could he afford to lose it. Indeed, he had warned the Soviet leader against placing offensive missiles in Cuba; therefore, Kennedy had to compel their withdrawal to preserve his credibility and America's. From the outset, Kennedy realized that the central issue was Soviet and allied perceptions of the balance of power.

If earlier American actions and inactions had convinced Khrushchev that he could "get away with it," it was imperative to set him straight about this issue. Such confidence on Khrushchev's part, Kennedy realized, stemmed from a conviction that the United States no longer possessed the will to defend its interests. Such a notion was dangerous because, if it remained uncorrected, it would lead to an even greater challenge in Berlin—as Khrushchev had already announced. If the United States then declared it would stand firm there, but the Soviet leader did not believe it, a violent clash, possibly a nuclear war, might result. Characteristically, the Soviets had not committed themselves irrevocably in Cuba. They were willing to gamble for a big payoff, but they were also willing to suffer a serious setback to avoid a catastrophic clash. The Soviets were still seeking the limits of American tolerance in its hemisphere.

Kennedy therefore placed a blockade around Cuba to prevent any further missile shipments, and he demanded the removal of the missiles already in place. American firmness and determination left Moscow little choice. For once, the Soviets had to decide whether to fire the first shot—to break the American blockade of their missile-carrying ships—and risk a possible escalation of the conflict. The Kremlin backed down. The United States had enormous conventional, especially naval, superiority in the Caribbean. The United States also could have mounted an invasion if it had been necessary. In the absence of sufficient conventional forces to support his ally so far away, Khrushchev's only way of defending Castro was by risking nuclear war, which he was unwilling to do. America still had a huge bomber force, and Kennedy had already built up 200 ICBMs (of what a few years later was to be a 1,000-ICBM force). Khrushchev knew that he had fewer than 50 first-generation missiles, exposed above the ground. Berlin had been a vast strategic hoax. The Soviet Union had possessed no missile force to speak of despite its claims to the contrary. Starting in 1961, U.S. satellites had learned the truth: that there was indeed a missile gap, and it favored the United States. The shipment of Soviet missiles to Cuba was in all likelihood part of an attempt to reduce the nuclear imbalance that had resulted from Kennedy's rapid buildup, which had been stimulated by the years of Khrushchev's missile threats over Berlin and claims that he was mass-producing the new Soviet ICBMs. In any case, the resulting U.S. strategic strength set a clear upper limit to the pressure the Soviets could exercise on the United States. The level of tension therefore rapidly declined as America's determination and willingness to use its power became clear. In Secretary of State Dean Rusk's picturesque phrase, "We were eyeball to eyeball, and the other fellow just blinked."

Kennedy's critics had predicted that a Soviet humiliation in Cuba would compel Khrushchev to recoup his lost prestige by forcing the West out of Berlin (with the clear implication that the United States should let him do so or desist in Cuba). However, Khrushchev called off *both* challenges, apparently believing that America's superior nuclear strength, as demonstrated in the Caribbean, could also be marshaled in Berlin. Local conventional superiority, which the Soviet Union possessed around Berlin, was not the decisive factor. The missile crisis was therefore followed by years of détente. But the other results ought to be noted as well. One, the United States had publicly declared that it would not invade Cuba. This meant that although America had won a brilliant tactical victory, the Soviet Union had not suffered a strategic reversal. Its base in the Caribbean remained intact. Two, Moscow decided it would never be humiliated again. It needed to build up its strategic nuclear power to U.S. levels, if not surpass them. The missile crisis had therefore been instructive to the Soviets—nuclear strength was politically usable.

American Strategy and Frontier Defenses

The recurrent crisis over West Berlin from 1958 to 1962, plus the Cuban Missile Crisis, held several lessons for the United States if it wished to preserve the frontier line around what was then still considered a cohesive Communist world. First, despite U.S. retaliatory power, the Soviet leadership exploited opportunities to raise international tensions when it felt it could succeed and not provoke the United States. Moscow was fully aware of the dangers of nuclear war and of the need to avoid acts that would expose the Soviet Union to nuclear conflagration, but it did not allow this recognition to deter it from exploiting the West's fear of nuclear war and trying to alter the status quo in its favor, first by strategic deception, then with a weak strategic hand.

To ensure that tensions would not escalate beyond control, however, the Soviets either left themselves a diplomatic escape hatch or were willing to make timely withdrawals. When met by a determined countermove, the Soviets did not escalate the tension. The Soviet tactic was to put a ceiling on the tension, lest it provoke an American response that might escalate to a nuclear conflict, and therefore to seek an end to the specific crisis. The Berlin crises in 1958 and 1961 and the Cuban Missile Crisis in 1962 testified to the Soviets' confidence that, short of a major provocation, which they were not willing to offer, they could challenge the United States without fearing a nuclear response. Their rapid retreat was even stronger testimony to the Soviet desire to avoid a further upward spiral of tension that might reach dangerous levels.

The second lesson was that mutual deterrence is not automatic. Advancing technology may upset the stability of the deterrent balance. It bears repetition that simply possessing the bomb is insufficient; the key to a *stable* deterrent balance is an invulnerable retaliatory force. If country A's force is vulnerable to attack by country B, A may be tempted to strike B preemptively rather than have its forces caught on the ground. Or A may lead B to strike first because B also fears a preemptive strike. In the late 1950s and early 1960s, the Soviets claimed that they were mass-producing missiles that made American bombers vulnerable. If true, this meant that the U.S. deterrent capacity would decline as Soviet first-strike capability grew. It affected, in any case, the psychology of the policy makers in Moscow and Washington, emboldening Khrushchev and making Eisenhower and Kennedy more cautious—until the latter was forced to the wall.

The Soviet Union's willingness to challenge the United States in Europe, ten years after the first Berlin crisis, and the manner in which America reacted, were symptomatic of the effects of this perceived change in the balance. A Soviet claim of a shift in the nuclear balance led the Soviet Union to use "nuclear blackmail" or coercion to undermine the status quo. If Moscow could compel the United States to withdraw from West Berlin, NATO would collapse and the Soviet Union would become the hegemonic power in Europe. Only in Cuba in 1962, after it had become clear that Khrushchev had been bluffing and that he was not mass-producing ICBMs, did Washington once more regain its confidence and react vigorously. Preserving deterrence is a continuing, never-ending task, not because some change in the balance might precipitate war, but because it might affect the risks each side is willing to take as one side challenges the other.

The third lesson is that unregulated arms competition is potentially dangerous. In the rivalry between a democratic state and a totalitarian one, the totalitarian state had a distinct advantage in the presatellite era (1961). The Soviet Union could easily gather information on U.S. arms, but because the Soviet Union is a closed society, the United States could not accumulate information on the number and types of Soviet nuclear arms. After 1956, high-altitude U-2 aircraft were the principal American means of collecting information. Because these aircraft could not perform a complete daily surveillance of Soviet territory, Khrushchev could use his strategy of deception and claim that the Soviets had weapons that they did not, in fact, possess, and assert a capability to destroy the U.S. deterrent bomber force—a capability they also did not have. The United States could not be sure what was true. Earlier in the 1950s, the Soviets had flown the same few bombers around Moscow repeatedly to deceive Western military observers.

But without the type of arms control arrangements that were to become familiar after the 1950s, U.S. "worst case" assumptions about Soviet strength were understandable. When hard information on Soviet nuclear strength was lacking, the American reaction to the Soviet claims was the fear that bomber and missile "gaps" existed and that they favored the Soviet Union. The United States overreacted, for instance, by increasing the number of missiles beyond those originally planned. Meanwhile, once Moscow knew that Washington knew that it had lied, the Soviets felt compelled to compensate for its ICBM inferiority by placing in Cuba intermediate- and medium-range missiles, of which it had plenty. The subsequent missile crisis made leaders on both sides more aware of the need for arms control as a necessary complement to the unilateral acquisition of arms and the resulting action-reaction arms competition.

Fourth, even before the stabilization of the "balance of terror" in the late 1960s, the United States found it could not use its superior strategic forces to respond to limited challenges—hence the need for conventional forces. An all-or-nothing option was no option at all. Theoretically, a series of small defeats could turn the balance of power against America, and the United States would therefore be compelled at some point to take a stand to prevent the further deterioration of its position. But the Soviets might not believe in the firmness of such a commitment because massive retaliation and the threat of mutual suicide made it incredible. If America stood firm, however, the Soviet challenge would result in war by miscalculation. By its reliance on massive retaliation, the United States could in fact bring about the very war that massive retaliation was supposed to deter.

Fifth, reliance on massive retaliation foreshadowed the gradual weakening of the bonds of America's foremost alliance, NATO. The European allies had joined NATO to gain the protection of the U.S. nuclear deterrent. But in an era in which the United States would become increasingly vulnerable to a Soviet strike, what country could truly expect the United States to risk its survival to protect an ally? Would even a Soviet invasion lead the United States to use its strategic weapons? If the United States intended to carry out its retaliatory threat, Europe might be "saved from communism" by being reduced to rubble. Conversely, if America were unwilling to risk its existence for issues the Europeans deemed vital, then the alliance would gradually lose its reason for existence. There had to be an alternative to suicide or surrender.

Finally, as Berlin and Cuba demonstrated, the chief function of a military power was to draw and protect "frontiers." These frontiers were clear: along the inter-German border and through the middle of Berlin; at the thirty-eighth parallel in Korea and the seventeenth parallel in Vietnam; along the coast of China at Quemoy and Matsu; and at the "northern tier" of states from Turkey to Pakistan. Any attempt to cross these frontiers, either openly by direct attack or covertly by guerrilla warfare, risked hostilities. Admittedly, the lines drawn outside of Europe were extremely tenuous. The Central Treaty Organization (CENTO) and the Southeast Asia Treaty Organization (SEATO) were alliances in areas where nationalist forces opposed the Western-organized and Western-led alliances. They had little popular support in those regions, even in those states that were members. One result was that the Soviets might leapfrog the line, as they had in Egypt. Another result could be that the governments seeking to maintain this line would be unable, despite American help, to mobilize enough indigenous morale and support, as was to become evident in Vietnam during the 1960s.

Indeed, it might well be that the United States would have been better off had it not created what turned out to be poor replicas of NATO. That organization exists in an area in which nationalism supported containment against a clearly perceived potential external aggression; the less successful alliances were organized in non-Western areas where containment was widely perceived as an attempt to preserve Western influence and reactionary regimes. Nevertheless, because the lines drawn in Europe were clear, and neither superpower was willing to risk a clash, this delineation between their respective spheres of influence in the 1950s shifted the attention of the superpowers increasingly toward the Third World as an arena of competition.

The Third World During the Cold War Years

POLITICAL scientist Guy Pauker wrote at the height of the cold war,

> Four areas in the world are at present or potentially major power centers: the United States, the Soviet Union, Western Europe, and Communist China. In all four, productivity is on the increase, and the political system performs relatively well its integrating and decision-making functions. Despite major differences among them . . . these four areas are likely to be in a position to play major roles in political, economic, and cultural international affairs in the coming decade. In contrast, the Middle East, Southeast Asia, tropical Africa, and Latin America are apt to remain power vacuums during this period, owing to their lack of unity, political instability, economic stagnation, and cultural heterogeneity. It seems highly improbable that ten years from now any of the areas mentioned above will cease to be, respectively, a power center or a power vacuum.[1]

During the 1950s and 1960s the United States saw the power vacuums in the economically-developing countries as potentially dangerous. The cold war had started in Europe after World War II; the fall of Nationalist China and the Korean War had extended it to Asia after late 1949. But the birth of so many new states, as Western colonialism collapsed after 1945, underlined the importance of this new Third World. The international system was no longer divided into the First World, or Western world of industrial states, and the Second World, led by the Soviet Union. In 1946 the United Nations had 55 members; in 1950 the number was 60. But by 1955 there were 76 members; by 1960, 99; by 1970, 127; and by 1990, the figure was approaching 170. In a bipolar world, the "in-between" Third World was not

---

1. Guy J. Pauker, "Southeast Asia as a Problem Area in the Next Decade," *World Politics* (April 1959): 325.

a center of power but an attraction for the two superpowers. The United States and the Soviet Union extended the cold war in their rivalry for the support, if not the allegiance, of the former colonial states, which had refused during their early years of independence to align politically and militarily with either one. Moscow perceived the anticolonial revolt against the West as proof that the international capitalist order was disintegrating. The Soviet Union saw an opportunity for taking the new states into a partnership to build a Soviet-led Communist international order.

Conversely, Washington saw the challenge of Soviet communism and Chinese communism in the Third World as stemming not from conspiracy or military takeover but from the totalitarian model for modernization that communism offered the developing countries. The Soviet Union, discounting its rapid industrialization under Czar Nicholas II at the turn of the century, held itself up as a model of an underdeveloped country that had transformed itself into a modern industrial society in one generation. Said a leading U.S. scholar: "Whether most of these countries take a democratic or Communist or other totalitarian path in their development is likely to determine the course of civilization on our planet." [2] The developing countries' choice of which path to follow was seen as critical to American security and, more broadly, to an international environment safe for open societies and democratic values. The United States thought it vital to help the new countries develop, and it was a matter of basic self-interest rather than humanitarian concern for the poor.

The Revolution of Rising Expectations

The paradox was that the disintegration of Western colonialism after World War II provided the most eloquent testimony to its success. The Western powers, including the United States in the Philippines, had justified their imperial domination in terms of bringing the backward peoples of the earth the benefits of Western democracy, medical science, and technology. It was the "white man's burden," or duty, to educate the people so that one day they could govern themselves. The colonial powers apparently had taught their lesson well; they had ruled their colonies autocratically, while propagating the virtues of democracy. It was in the name of these ideals that the Western powers had come as colonizers; it was in their name, too, that the nationalist movements challenged their rulers and asked them to practice what they preached. The leaders of these nationalist movements had been educated in Europe or America, or in a Western school in their own country. They fought the European powers by using the principles of democracy and

---

2. Eugene Stanley, *The Future of Underdeveloped Countries,* rev. ed. (New York: Praeger Publishers, 1961), 3.

national freedom they had learned. They saw that these principles were incompatible with imperialism.

Once these countries became independent, however, they were left with a legacy of poverty, illiteracy, and disease. Annual per capita income in these nations rarely reached $100. To remedy the economic underdevelopment, to narrow the enormous gap between poor and rich nations, the developing countries turned to industrialization, which was to transform their traditional agrarian societies into modern, industrial, urban welfare states. Over the years, this transformation would have great political significance. Most people in the developing countries knew only their local communities, which held their loyalty. The concept of national loyalty was new to them. Consequently, the fledgling nation had to prove it could offer its people something they could not otherwise attain. By achieving an improved standard of living, the nation would demonstrate that it deserved the popular support and allegiance it needed to survive and grow.

The Consequences of Population Growth

The question that confronted the new countries in the 1950s—and today—is whether they could develop themselves economically. To a large extent the answer depended upon whether their economic progress was faster than their population growth, or whether their "population explosion" ate up any increase in national income. The world population passed 5 billion in 1986. In 1830 it was 1 billion; by 1930, it had doubled; by 1960, the figure was 3 billion; the fourth billion took only 15 years. The current population of over 5 billion will grow to almost 6.5 billion people by the year 2000, with 80 percent living in the developing countries. In 1900 there was one European for every two Asians; in 2000 the ratio will probably be one to four. In the Western Hemisphere, there will be two Latin Americans for each North American.

The concern was that, despite a later slowing of the population growth rate, the developing countries might still face the problem described by the Reverend Thomas Malthus—the constant hunger and poverty that result when the population grows faster than the means of subsistence. More than 150 years ago, Malthus, who was also an economist, predicted this fate for the Western world unless the population growth were limited by either "positive checks" such as wars or epidemics, which result in a high death rate, or by "preventive checks," which result in a low birth rate.

By contrast, the West made impressive economic progress following the Industrial Revolution, despite a huge population increase. Agriculture provided plentiful food, and industry raised the standard of living to heights never before attained. The West's recent history, therefore, would appear to refute Malthus's gloomy prediction. The fact was that the conditions that faced the developing countries were quite dissimilar from the West's. One of the chief differences was that the Western countries had far smaller populations when they began industrializing, and their population increase did not outdistance the economic improvement. But India, for example, began its modernization with a population of 350 million; India's population may reach 1 billion people by 2000. China, with a population of 547 million in 1950, reached 1 billion in the early 1980s. If the United States after the War of Independence had possessed a population density equivalent to that of Egypt, it would today have more than 2 billion people instead of just over 250 million. Under these circumstances, the United States would not have become a "developed" nation.

The European nations enjoyed an enormous benefit in the New World and in their colonial empires, which provided them with outlets to relieve their population pressures. About 60 million Europeans emigrated during the nineteenth and early twentieth centuries. The United States and Canada, rich in resources and fertile land, easily absorbed millions of immigrants and still increased their living standards. Australia, New Zealand, and South Africa experienced similar population and economic expansions, although on a smaller scale. From 1650 to 1950, the European population (excluding Russia) increased by approximately 300 million. By the 1950s there were about 400 million people of European descent living outside Europe. The colonies served Europe as a frontier similar to the American West, absorbing a population that might otherwise have led to overcrowding. This expansion to the colonies added materially to these nations' wealth. But the developing countries can find no such empty and rich spaces to absorb their surplus populations.

In Europe, moreover, the use of machinery in agriculture increased the food supply, but reduced the number of laborers needed to produce it. Unneeded farm workers went to the cities and into the factories. The ample supply of labor accelerated industrialization. Quite apart from modern technology, however, Europe was blessed with sufficient sunshine and rain. Temperate lands are more favorable to food production than tropical and monsoon areas, where many of the developing countries are found. Europe could grow sufficient food for its multiplying population; what it could not produce, it imported from the colonies and the New World in exchange for industrial products. Overseas trade enabled some European countries to support larger populations than their domestic food resources would otherwise have permitted. But the basic and critical point is that an industrial revolution must be preceded or accompanied by an agricultural revolution.

In the nonindustrialized nations, the majority of the population is still engaged in a primitive agriculture. Many of the new countries' governments, because they equate development with industrialization, have neglected to modernize agriculture. To their leaders, agriculture is the symbol of their former colonial status as producers of raw materials. Some countries experimented with intensive farming. Called the "Green Revolution," it used high-yield seeds, more chemical fertilizer, and insecticides, and increased food production enough to keep up with the population growth. By the 1980s, some even exported food. But many developing countries could not feed themselves: "If our population continues to increase as rapidly as it is doing," a former president of Pakistan said, "we will soon have nothing to eat and will all become cannibals."

This statement may seem exaggerated but it dramatizes the developing countries' overpopulation problem. There are simply too many poor people. This might have been all right if the sleeping masses had not awakened—if they had continued to accept their miserable lot as natural and not become conscious that it was a fate not ordained by God but made by man—if they had not made this discovery and demanded to eat more and live better. It is this "revolution of rising expectations" that creates the problem, for it will be impossible to fulfill these expectations unless there is a reduction in birth rates. The population pressure keeps the masses living close to the subsistence level, and such widespread poverty makes it very difficult to accumulate enough capital to stoke industrial growth.

In the West, the birth rate declined after 1850; with industrialization and the growth of cities came the spread of literacy and knowledge of artificial birth-control techniques. Malthus was right even for the West, because preventive checks were adopted. But the Third World has not yet reached a similar level of economic development, and knowledge of birth-control methods and the willingness to use them have spread very slowly.

The Developing Countries' Slow Pace of Modernization

To make any progress at all, the pace of economic development had to surpass the fast-rising rate of population growth. But many of these countries simply did not have enough capital. Internal savings in sufficient amounts could not be squeezed out of people living at subsistence level—at least, not without authoritarian controls. Another way to obtain capital was to earn it by trade. The developing countries were exporters of primary products or raw materials such as coffee, tea, rubber, and tin. But it was precisely this fact that in the past had limited their earning capacity. Because their economies upon independence remained tied to those of their former colonial masters, their exports rose or declined with every fluctuation in Western prosperity. If a major Western recession reduced the demand and price levels of natural resources (even oil until 1973), the resulting losses of income often exceeded the Western aid extended during the same period. Furthermore, markets may become glutted with certain items because of overproduction or substitution. A nation trying to raise its income by increasing production finds its competitors doing the same, which lowers world prices further. Another problem is that the Western industrial nations, whose ever-increasing demand for raw materials was supposed to furnish the capital for economic development, no longer needed them to the degree anticipated because of the development of synthetics. The lack of stabilized international commodity prices, similar to the parity prices paid to American farmers, plus the inventiveness of modern technology (for extracting resources from the ocean's seabeds, for example) limited the prospects of financing industrialization via earnings from raw materials.

Foreign investment was the third source of capital for economic development. Private capital was, however, in the initial period after independence, in short supply for the kind of long-range development that the developing nations needed. Most private American investments outside the United States have been made by a small group of oil companies to build refineries and to discover and pump out oil fields in Latin America and the Middle East. The reasons for the lack of private Western—and especially American—capital for foreign investment are obvious. The American economy experienced a boom for most of the cold war period, and investment capital stayed mainly at home. This was true for Europe as well. European capital concentrated on rebuilding, modernization, and expansion of its industrial base. American capital that did go abroad often went to the Common Market. Private capital is drawn to investments that will return sizable and relatively speedy profits.

Modernization, then, was the new nations' principal task, but they soon realized that it was *not* essentially an economic undertaking. More and more, modernization (of which economic development is a major ingredient) was seen as a political, social, and intellectual task. It was a revolutionary process frequently marked by political instability and violence rather than evolutionary, peaceful change. One reason for instability was that most of the new nations lacked administrative and political cohesiveness. Generally, the population had no single common culture or language; tribes opposed one another; different areas fought one another. The people had no natural loyalty to the state, no tradition of cooperation except on the one overriding issue of eliminating the colonial ruler. But once the struggle for independence ended, power tended to fragment. For example, India split violently into Hindu India and Muslim Pakistan following independence, and the latter dissolved further into Pakistan and Bangladesh—with the help of India, which also may split further as Sikhs seek greater autonomy, if not independence. The Congo (now Zaire) fell apart when the Belgians withdrew. Cyprus divided into Turkish and Greek factions. Biafra broke away from Nigeria, only to lose the subsequent civil war. Even where actual disintegration has not occurred, religious, linguistic, and racial differences and antagonists tend to tear apart the fabric of these states that lack any history of nationhood. In Burundi in 1972, for example, the Tutsi tribes reportedly slaughtered 120,000 Hutus; in 1988 this tribal violence recurred. In the late 1980s Sri Lanka, formerly Ceylon, a large island lying just off the southeastern coast of India, was tearing itself apart between Hindu Tamils and Buddhist Sinhalese. Nation building must therefore be the first task.

The absence of a strong sense of national consciousness was soon reflected in the way many of the leaders of the new countries built themselves up as symbols of nationhood. It was not difficult for them to do this because, as leaders of the movements for independence, their prestige was usually high. But the task was an essential one. Just as Louis XIV had proclaimed, they also said, *"L'état, c'est moi."* They *were* the state; without their presence as its symbol, the nation would not hold together as a unit. One-party rule or military governments exist almost everywhere in the Third World. In Africa, for example, the world's last continent to be freed from colonialism, three-fourths of its 345 million people lived under single-party or military rule by the late 1960s, ten years after independence.

Such policies might seem undemocratic, but they were widely justified by native rules and believed to be necessary by most Western observers and analysts. Most people in the new nations felt less loyalty to the state than to ancestors, family, village, or tribe. Wherever the opposition represented these centrifugal forces, an American-style democracy would lead not just to a change of government but to the disintegration of the state. The alternatives facing the leaders of these countries were said to be not democracy or dictatorship but statehood or disintegration.

Another reason that modernization was seen in a political and revolutionary context is that nationalist revolutions direct their opposition not only against the colonial ruler but also against the traditional governing elites if they remained in power after independence. Many of the developing countries were split into three main groups when they gained independence. The first was the ruling minority, usually composed of the landowners or merchants, whose vested interest lay in the preservation of the status quo. Their wealth and power derived from continuing, as in the old colonial days, to send their nations' crops and natural resources to the West rather than industrializing themselves and becoming economically independent. The second group, about 80 percent of the population in most developing countries, were peasants, villagers, small artisans, and shopkeepers—those whose energies have been spent largely on the struggle for day-to-day survival. This group, which had for centuries borne its hardships silently, awakened and demanded a better life. The third group, the urban intelligentsia, educated in Western ideas and committed to nationalism and modernization, voiced these resentments against the old way of life and articulated the new aspirations while it sought power to affect the political, social, and economic transformation of their societies. Change and more change was the demand of the day.

Without such social change—that is, the overthrow of the old ruling elites, modernization is inhibited. This is not a matter of "reform" but of revolution because the crucial issue relates to power. Who controls the nation—the old ruling elite committed to the preservation of the traditional, preindustrial society or those who seek to secularize, modernize, and industrialize the nation? Only one thing is certain: few who rule yield their dominant political, social, and economic position without a struggle.

New Seeds of Discontent

Instability can take root even where economic development occurs, where national bonds do not disintegrate, and where the modernizing elite is in control. The cause of this instability is that a slowly rising standard of living may not create an increasingly satisfied—and therefore happy and peaceful—population. Capital for investment can be accumulated only if it is not paid to the workers; low wages militate against mass consumption and allow the reinvestment of capital into further economic expansion. Although living conditions may improve, they will not satisfy the "revolution of rising expectations." Once the population realizes that it no longer has to live in the poverty and filth of the past, that change in this world is possible, that people can create a better life here on earth through their own efforts, they become dissatisfied. The gap between their expectations and achievements is particularly aggravating when the rulers live well, even ostentatiously. Those living less well become frustrated. In turn, this spawns social discontent and an increasingly sullen, hostile, and more radical mood.

Social instability and turmoil are further promoted by the intellectual and cultural changes that accompany the transformation of a traditional, static, rural society into a modern, dynamic, urban-industrial state. Many of the old customary and religious values that helped people to accept their place in society and conduct themselves throughout life simply collapse; people become disoriented, torn from their age-old moorings for which they have not yet found a substitute. Their ancestors had provided status and meaning in their lives; robbed of this, they become isolated and insecure atoms in a rapidly changing environment they neither made nor comprehend. Secular values, emphasizing materialism and progress, replace religious values that deny the importance of earthly existence and material possessions. A society in which individual effort is rewarded and people can rise socially according to merit replaces a society with a rigid social structure in which birth determined their place and religion often governed their mode of conduct.

Nationalism replaces local loyalty, and modern transportation and communication bring individuals to an awareness of the larger society in which they live and work. Impersonal ties to people far away in "their" country replace former face-to-face relations with neighbors, and they must learn new skills and ways of thought. In short, they must forget many of their old ways and cut long-time ties and adjust, readjust, and adjust once more. In the best of circumstances, these changes are difficult and agonizing, even if they do not arouse effective opposition from the traditional elite. The Iranians were undergoing this kind of upheaval in late 1978 and early 1979, when the religious leaders opposed the shah and his modernization, leading to his overthrow and the establishment of an Islamic republic, a theocracy, a throw-back to earlier centuries. Precisely because modernization was associated with secular values, no one in the U.S. government had taken seriously the possibility of the Ayatollah Ruhollah Khomeini's succession. The idea of an old man, a religious fanatic, coming to power was so at odds with contemporary ideas of modernization that the likelihood of its occurrence was dismissed as preposterous. Yet, for the poor and the lowly in a rapidly changing society in which tradition and customs were being eroded, religion retained a strong attraction and comfort.

Domestic Instability and Superpower Involvement

It is not surprising in these circumstances that the domestic transforma-tion of the developing countries had repercussions beyond their borders. The upheavals tended to disturb an international system largely defined by the frontiers drawn between the two superpowers' spheres of influence and by the nuclear stalemate. When the internal difficulties of the countries of the Third World spilled over into the external arena of international politics, or resulted in civil war or regional rivalries, they attracted the Soviet Union and the United States, thus leading to possible confrontation with the attendant danger of military conflict. These difficulties have attracted the two super-powers because they could either bring to power a group one superpower likes and the other dislikes or result in regional expansion and influence that could be perceived as benefiting one and hurting the other. If one superpower is unwilling to tolerate what it may consider, in terms of the overall balance of power, a local or regional setback, then it will intervene; or, if it fears that if it does not intervene then its opponent might, the result may be a preventive intervention. In both cases, it risks a similar move by its opponent. To quote Pauker once again: "Power vacuums are likely to disturb international relations increasingly. They are the natural targets for power centers wishing to extend their hegemony. They should be the object of anxious attention for those powers which want to strengthen the international balance." [3]

National Disintegration and Civil War: The Birth of Zaire

If a new nation disintegrates into two or more parts, those who seek to reunify their land or establish their new splinter states may appeal for help to sympathetic states that, for reasons of their own, may wish to see either a nation preserve its unity or a splinter state its independence. Such appeals were addressed especially to the Soviet Union or the United States. One of the more dramatic examples of the way the survival of a new state involved the

---

3. Pauker, "Southeast Asia as a Problem Area," 325.

superpowers occurred in 1960 when the Belgian Congo became independent. Patrice Lumumba, leader of the Nationalist party, became the country's new premier, and Joseph Kasavubu its first president. Almost immediately, the Congo fell into disorder. First, the rich mining province of Katanga, upon whose copper and cobalt exports the Congo was largely dependent as a major source of revenue, split off into a separate state. Katanga's president, Moise Tshombe, had the support of the powerful Belgian mining interests, eager to protect their investments. Then the army began to revolt because it resented the continued presence of its Belgian officers and wanted them replaced with native leadership. In a wild spree, the soldiers began to attack white women (including nuns) and children. The Belgian settlers' reaction was to flee. Among them were the experts the Belgians had expected to leave behind to help the Congolese in their early period of self-government. All public services now collapsed because the Congo lacked an educated native elite. The Belgians had never trained one.

In the midst of this situation, the Belgians flew in paratroopers to protect their nationals. Lumumba saw this move as a Belgian attempt to restore colonial rule, and he appealed to the United Nations to send forces to help him. It was at this point that the cold war was injected into the Congo. The UN troops, with no forces from the great powers, did not compel the Belgians to evacuate their paratroopers or agree to Lumumba's demand that they help him reestablish control over Katanga Province. Secretary-General Dag Hammarskjöld ordered that the international organization's forces were not to be involved in the internal squabbles of the Congo or employed by the contending political factions to gain power over their rivals. This, however, had the effect of underwriting the divisions of the Congo, and the country could not survive without Katanga. Lumumba turned against the United Nations, bitterly attacked the secretary-general, and accused Belgium and the Western powers, especially the United States, of conspiring against him. Lumumba's attacks grew increasingly racist. Finally, he asked the Soviet Union for help and received Soviet diplomatic backing, military supplies, and offers of troops, or "volunteers." Several neutrals, especially the United Arab Republic, Guinea, and Ghana, also extended their sympathy and support.

The United States now supported President Kasavubu (who dismissed Lumumba) and his army commander, Colonel Sese Seko Mobutu, who established a caretaker government composed of the Congo's fifteen university graduates. Mobutu also infuriated the Soviet Union by driving out all Communist-bloc personnel, who had been aiding Lumumba. The Soviets insisted that Lumumba was still the Congo's legitimate ruler and demanded his restoration; so did the neutrals, who supported this demand by threatening to remove their contingents from the UN forces. This would have left the Congo in utter chaos. The United States refused to budge, however, and continued to give its support to Mobutu, in whom it saw the best means of eliminating Soviet influence in the Congo and possible Communist penetration into the heart of Africa.

Soviet-American differences now became bitter. The Soviets, thwarted in the Congo for the time being, made two demands: Hammarskjöld's resignation and a veto over the secretary-general's activities. These demands were rejected. But by early 1962, after all efforts to unify the Congo had failed, the United Nations reversed its original stand. It finally adopted the policy of forcefully squashing the opposition. Although it took many months and cost lives, the country was "unified" through the deposition of Tshombe and his Belgian advisers and foreign mercenaries. Ironically, this restoration of national order, accomplished with UN support, was a victory for Lumumba, although he did not live to see it. (The CIA reportedly had planned Lumumba's assassination, but was beaten to it.) If the central government had not received American and UN support and had been unable to reunite the Congo, it, like Lumumba, would probably have turned toward the Soviet Union for help.

Nationalism and Regional Rivalries: The 1967 Arab-Israeli War

Even if a new nation does not disintegrate, the political leaders may invoke the only emotion the people ever shared to hold it together. This emotion is the nationalism fostered by the hatred of the former colonial power and is directed against both that country and, more broadly, "Western imperialism." Independence does not mean that colonialism is no longer an issue; rather, the fight against colonialism and imperialism becomes a useful tool to preserve national unity. The same technique may be used by a country with the even more common condition of a stagnant economy. The political leaders may then be tempted to preserve their power by finding foreign scapegoats to relieve internal stresses and strains.

It is simply easier and therefore more attractive for leaders to play a prominent and highly visible role on the international stage than to undertake the difficult task of modernization. The people can take pride in their leader's—and hence, their nation's—new status and identity in an international society that, under colonialism, had been denied importance and dignity. Kwame Nkrumah of Ghana, Sukarno of Indonesia, Muhammad Ben Bella of Algeria, and Nasser of Egypt were among the most prominent and skillful practitioners of the art of channeling domestic grievances into international attempts to expand their power during the 1950s and 1960s.

Nasser provided a dramatic example of how provocative this posture can be. Just as he had done in 1956, Nasser incited a war with Israel in 1967 when he faced increasing economic hardship at home and a militant anti-Israeli Arab nationalism in Syria, which was notoriously unstable. Increasingly preoccupied with "Arab socialism" and his fight for Arab leadership,

Nasser had not managed to launch Egypt on a path of self-sustaining economic growth after more than a decade of rule. Egypt was desperately short of funds to finance its development, buy food, support its sizable army, and provide enough jobs for its population. The birth-control program had failed to have any significant impact, adding 800,000 people annually to a population of more than 30 million. The pace of inflation was approximately 15 percent a year. Nasser's program of nationalization and expropriation had brought domestic investment to a near halt and discouraged foreign investment. His virulent anti-American attitude resulted in a cut-off of the American surplus food shipments. He had to buy food elsewhere and use up funds that might have been invested in development. The heavy expenditures on military equipment, probably amounting to one-third of Egypt's annual budget, also diverted funds from development.

Arab socialism, having lost its glamour, weakened Nasser's claim to Arab leadership and left him only the arena of foreign policy in which to recoup his prestige and hold on the Arab masses. But here, too, his stature had declined. He had reached the height of his self-proclaimed leadership of Arab nationalism a decade earlier when he seized the Suez Canal. Nationalism had also affected Nasser's neighbors. Iraq refused to subordinate itself to his direction, and Syria quit its short-lived union with Egypt in 1961. Nasser then resumed his verbal attacks on the traditional monarchies of Jordan and Saudi Arabia; Egyptian forces also helped the revolutionary forces who had overthrown the Yemenite monarchy supported by Saudi Arabia. Nasser was clearly seeking to extend his influence southward into the sheikdoms and sultanates of South Arabia, a British protectorate scheduled to become independent in early 1968. This would give him control over the Red Sea entrance to the Suez Canal. But the Egyptian army was unsuccessful in destroying the royalist supporters. In 1967 these intra-Arab rivalries, combined with economic failure, pressured Nasser to reassert his leadership of Arab nationalism.

The result was war. First, the Jordanians, in response to Nasser's hostility, taunted him with hiding behind the UN forces stationed between the Israeli and Egyptian forces at the close of the Suez War. Second, the Syrians, trying to displace Nasser as the leader of Pan-Arabism, openly and repeatedly called for Israel's destruction and stepped up their terrorist raids into Israel. After the Israelis retaliated, the Syrians claimed in May 1967 that the Israelis were assembling their forces for a full-scale invasion of Syria. This rumor, reportedly brought to Nasser's attention by the Soviet Union, which was seeking to exploit the Arab-Israeli-Western quarrel for its own purposes, was found to be untrue by UN observers. But Nasser, claiming to be the great hero of the Arab peoples, either felt compelled to act or saw in the invasion rumor his opportunity to regain his leadership of Arab nationalism. Whichever it was, there was bound to be trouble, particularly because, after eleven years of receiving Soviet training and arms, Nasser seemed confident that his forces could beat Israel, which this time would be fighting by itself, without the aid of France and Britain.

The Egyptian leader took several actions. He moved reinforcements into the Sinai desert. Next, he demanded and obtained the withdrawal of the UN peace-keeping forces; Egyptian and Israeli forces now confronted each other for the first time since 1956. In addition, he blockaded the Gulf of Aqaba, through which Israel received its oil and other goods. For Israel the gulf was a lifeline because Nasser barred Israeli shipping from the Suez Canal. Nasser knew Israel would consider a blockade intolerable and an act of war. In short, he was deliberately provoking a military conflict. Finally, Nasser signed an alliance with Jordan. This meant that Arab armies surrounded Israel: Syria in the north, Egypt in the south, and Jordan, with its highly regarded army directed to cut Israel in two at its narrow waist. All these actions were accompanied by increasingly shrill calls for a holy "war of liberation" and the extermination of all of Israel's inhabitants.

In these circumstances, war was inevitable, unless Israel were willing to accept a major political defeat, an unlikely prospect. Whether peace could be preserved, primarily by Nasser's lifting the blockade, depended on the United States and the Soviet Union. Washington was caught in a dilemma. On the one hand, the United States had recognized Israel's right to send ships through the gulf after compelling Israel to withdraw following its 1956 victory. The United States also recognized that if Nasser did not relent, a forceful test might be necessary. Seeking support from other maritime powers, the United States found them unwilling to use force. On the other hand, it was deeply involved in Vietnam and therefore reluctant to take on a second conflict. Furthermore, a key question for American policy makers was whether such a test would precipitate a clash with the Soviet Union, which had with great fanfare sent warships into the eastern Mediterranean, fully supported the Arabs in their aims, continuously denounced Israel as an aggressive tool of American imperialism, and perhaps even spurred Nasser on with the false story of an imminent Israeli invasion of Syria.

For Moscow, the Arab-Israeli conflict, as earlier, had global implications. If Western influence could be expelled from the Middle East and if the Soviet Union could establish itself as the dominant power over this oil-rich region, Europe would be weakened and perhaps even neutralized. Soviet political support and the naval show of force undoubtedly contributed to Nasser's intransigence. Certainly it helped to restore his reputation in the Arab world. Had the blockade been successful, the Soviet Union would have earned the Arabs' everlasting gratitude as the primary force behind Egypt's political victory. An effective blockade would have demonstrated the Soviet Union's ability to inhibit the American navy and would have eroded American commitments to Israel. The Soviet Union had an opportunity to replace the West as the region's leading power. For Moscow, the stakes in seeing Nasser achieve a political victory were enormous. Moscow, therefore, was unwilling to restrain Cairo's dangerous military moves and threats of war.

Because Washington was unable to arrange a diplomatic solution, the Israelis, who had not really expected one, attacked to seize the initiative in what had become an unavoidable clash. Routing the air forces of their Arab opponents in a brilliantly coordinated set of air strikes in the first hours of hostilities, they defeated the Egyptian army and reached the Suez Canal in three days—two days ahead of their 1956 record! They routed the Jordanian army and captured half of Jerusalem and the western bank of the river Jordan. Finally, they turned on the Syrian army and eliminated the bases from which Syria launched the terrorist raids and shelled Israeli settlements. Nasser's dreams of an Arab empire were shattered, despite his efforts to salvage his reputation by blaming his defeat on alleged American and British air intervention on behalf of Israel. Arab nationalism and intra-Arab quarrels had once again intensified the Arab-Israeli conflict and precipitated war. The bipolar competition for influence in the Middle East had once again exploited its problems, turning it into a "Balkans of the twentieth century," an inflammable area of political instability, regional rivalry, and great power conflict likely to explode at any moment and to cause war far beyond its borders. Domestic Arab problems only aggravated the tendency of leaders to engage in adventurism, to export internal dissatisfaction and grievances, to strike tough and inflexible poses, and to expose the world to the dangers of a superpower clash.

A World Divided into Rich and Poor Nations

The Soviet Model of Development

Washington, however, saw the new states' functional, not ideological, attraction to communism as the greatest danger to American security. Confronting an amalgam of political, social, and cultural changes (not just an economic transition), experiencing revolutionary transformations (not just evolutionary progress), the non-Western nations have no guarantee that they will successfully climb what Robert Heilbroner has termed the "Great Ascent"; even the attempt may well call for some sort of left-wing authoritarian rule.[4] In this context, the Soviet Union presented itself as a model of development. The Soviets' message was: "In 1917 Russia was also underdeveloped but now, within the space of one generation, it has become militarily one of the two superpowers, the second-largest industrial country in the world. You, too, can be industrialized quickly and live a better life." To people suffering from chronic hunger and poverty, it was thought that it probably did not matter that the Soviet Union had achieved industrialization by setting up totalitarian governments that brutally squeezed the necessary

---

4. Robert L. Heilbroner, *The Great Ascent* (New York: Harper Torchbook, 1963).

sacrifices out of the people; the loss of liberty did not mean much to people who had never known it anyway, who had lived for centuries under authoritarian governments, whether domestic or foreign. Soviet totalitarianism would at least provide the organization and efficiency to extract the sacrifices from the masses and the discipline to hold the nation together, to speed up the pace of the cultural revolution while controlling the social tensions produced by the early stages of development, and, where necessary, to depose ruthlessly the traditional ruling class blocking the path to modernization. In short, just as capitalism had been the instrument for modernization in the nineteenth century, Washington feared that Soviet communism might become a successful model for modernization in the twentieth. (After the Sino-Soviet schism, China too promoted itself as a model for Third World modernization, one superior to its European rival.)

Communism, therefore, was not seen primarily as a military threat in the Third World. In the newly politically aware and poorer areas of the developing world, communism was attractive because it promised a fairly rapid and disciplined way of bringing about political, social, economic, and cultural changes. The United States saw that the best way of competing with communism was to alleviate the conditions that were said to cause it. Poverty, ignorance, hunger, and social injustice were thought to provide the breeding ground for communism; curing these conditions and giving people hope for a better life were the means to defeat it. This would be achieved once the new nations' development had gained a self-sustaining momentum. Communism's appeal to attract adherents was strong during the initial phase of modernization. During this period, in the words of W. W. Rostow, later President Lyndon Johnson's national security adviser during the Vietnam War, Communists would act as "the scavengers of the modernization process. Communism is best understood as a disease of the transition to modernization." [5] If the West offered assistance, it was optimistically believed, the developing countries would evolve into Western-type, modern, urbanized, and industrial societies that would naturally look westward.

It was because of the competition of models that the United States and other Western states first offered the developing countries economic aid and technical assistance. In the final analysis, the fundamental problem was perceived to be the growing division of the world between rich nations and poor nations. Western aid was intended to close this gap, modernize the new nations without compelling them to use totalitarian methods, satisfy the revolution of rising expectations and thereby create politically and socially stable societies, and eventually promote the spread of democracy. This process, in turn, was expected to create a more peaceful world by giving

---

5. W. W. Rostow, "Guerrilla Warfare in Underdeveloped Areas," in *The Guerrilla—And How To Fight Him,* ed. T. N. Greene (New York: Praeger Publishers, 1962), 56.

developing societies a vested interest in the international order and Western values. It was clear that assistance to the Third World was justified mainly in terms of security considerations, not humanitarian reasons. A world divided into rich and poor nations was potentially explosive, for it set the majority of the poor against the privileged minority. Such a division was no more acceptable internationally than it had been within each of the Western nations one-hundred years earlier.

The Nineteenth-Century Precedent

The two situations were believed to be so similar that the "lessons" of the earlier experience were applied to the international division of wealth. As the Industrial Revolution gathered momentum in each of the European countries and America, it created a privileged minority that owned most of the wealth and a vastly unequal distribution of income. Laborers, including women and children, worked fourteen to sixteen hours per day, six or seven days a week, earned little beyond subsistence wages (and sometimes less), and lived in overcrowded slums. The rich got richer and the poor got poorer, a fact so obvious that one of Britain's great prime ministers, Benjamin Disraeli, spoke of England not as one nation but as two.

The prevailing laissez-faire philosophy argued that nothing could be done to alleviate this situation. Government intervention, whether to end the worst forms of exploitation, such as child labor, or to redistribute the income to help the poor lead a decent and dignified life, was rejected as contrary to the "iron laws of economics." Any outside interference with the workings of the market would stifle the private incentive and initiative that stoked the competitive capitalistic system. These laws, which condemned a large section of the population to a hopeless and miserable existence, received even further support from Charles Darwin's theory of evolution, with its emphasis on the "struggle for survival" and the "survival of the fittest." This philosophy, called social Darwinism, argued very simply that the rich were wealthy because their success in the competitive struggle had demonstrated that they were the most fit; conversely, the poor were destitute because they were unfit. It never occurred to social Darwinists to ask themselves whether everybody had had an equal start or opportunity in this struggle.

These philosophical justifications for poverty were ultimately rejected in all Western societies. The long working hours, the unsanitary, unsafe working conditions, and the teeming slums were a blot on the West's conscience. They were also politically shortsighted and economically foolish. Politically, the division of people into "haves" and "have-nots" could lead to revolution, with the bourgeoisie being overthrown by the working class, or proletariat; or, if it surrendered its domestic beliefs and values, the bourgeoisie could perhaps retain its power by establishing an authoritarian government and crushing any proletarian protests and uprisings. Neither of these alternatives was acceptable to the ruling middle classes. Nor did this policy of squeezing the workers for maximum profit make sense economically, since the less money people have, the fewer things they can buy. Thus, social justice made sense—morally, politically, and economically.

In every Western society, government in the late nineteenth century began to intervene increasingly in the economy. Growing public awareness eventually led to the regulation of business; the passage of wage and hour legislation; the abolition of child labor and "sweatshop" working conditions; the organization of trade unions; measures to counteract the swings of the business cycle; the implementation of the progressive income tax; and the initiation, during depressions, of unemployment insurance, public-works programs, and other "pump-priming" projects to increase the purchasing power of the people, thereby stimulating renewed demand and production. These measures, especially in the United States, widened and raised the base of wealth, giving rise to the twentieth-century mass market. They also led to a discovery so simple and yet so hard to understand that Europe, particularly continental Europe, learned it only after 1945: namely, that workers are also consumers. If they are paid good wages, they will also buy the goods they produce. This is profitable all around: workers are economically satisfied and therefore gain vested interest, politically, in the social and economic order; capitalists earn handsome profits by selling volume at reasonable prices, and they retain their social status and political influence.

U.S. Opposition to Social Revolution

The same problem of inequitable distribution of wealth was now regarded in a different way. This time the problem was the widening gap *between* nations, with the rich countries becoming richer, and the poor countries growing poorer. The iron laws of economics seemed to hold for poor countries the same fate they once did for the Western working classes. Had the Marxist prophecy that the exploited proletariat would overthrow the bourgeoisie been defeated domestically only to reappear internationally to defeat the West? Modernization was expected to give the new states a stake in the international system and to help create a world in which Western values would be more secure.

Although the nature of the problem seemed clear to many policy makers, the rationale for economic aid to assist the new nations' development never attracted the degree of public support that the more easily understandable military preparations against the Soviets did. What was probably required, as many suggested, was a progressive international income tax by which all the advanced Western nations would contribute 1 percent to 2 percent of their annual national income for development. The World Bank's Pearson Commission in 1969 endorsed the 1 percent figure. But by then no Western country was giving that much. Despite the rapid economic growth of the industrial states during the 1960s, their foreign aid spending had declined. This was particularly true for American aid to Europe, which, at the time of the Marshall Plan, had been 2.75 percent of the gross national product (GNP). Aid to the developing countries was always less than 1 percent of GNP. In short, at a time when the American GNP had risen by hundreds of millions of dollars, the national effort was out of proportion with its increasing capacity to pay and with the growing gap between the rich and poor nations.

Indeed, the term *economic aid* was something of a misnomer. After 1950 and the eruption of the Korean War, most economic aid was, in fact, military aid. Moreover, since Western Europe's recovery, most of this aid was channeled to allied countries: Turkey, Pakistan, South Vietnam, South Korea, Jordan, and Nationalist China. Even part of the money designated for economic assistance was "defense support," which was money to sustain the economies of allies such as South Korea or South Vietnam; without this support, these countries could not maintain their standing armies. The final sum actually allocated to economic development was also concentrated in relatively few countries. Most developing countries got next to nothing.

Apart from the lack of public support for foreign aid, U.S. policy toward the developing countries suffered from three other liabilities. The first was that American dollars were all too often offered with the explicit or implicit assumption that the recipients should associate themselves with U.S. cold war policies; that even if they did not formally ally themselves with the United States, they should often thank it for its generosity, praise it for the morality of its anti-Communist stand, and certainly refrain from criticizing it. The United States was reluctant to give dollars to nations that would not join its side. After all, could any nation really be neutral in a struggle between right and wrong? Was not democracy good and communism evil? If countries wanted U.S. money, surely the least they could do was "to stand up and be counted." But in these countries, the basic aspiration was to concentrate on internal matters, to raise the standard of living and strengthen their independence, and to minimize their involvement in the cold war. Most, therefore, preferred to remain nonaligned in the struggle between the West and the Communists, avoiding all "entangling alliances." Attempts to use economic aid as a means of forcing them into an American alliance system were counterproductive, as U.S. overtures to Nasser in the early 1950s had dramatically proven.

In preferring a generally nonaligned position, the developing countries believed they were following America's own example. After the United States gained its independence, it, too, avoided alliances and preoccupied itself with internal developments. As a developing country, the United States was aware that its newly realized independence meant very little without economic and political strength. Moreover, the United States had just thrown off the shackles of colonialism; its citizens had no desire to be once more tied to the

European powers. American policy makers, especially during the 1950s, forgot that it was the United States that had set this example.

The second liability that hampered U.S. policy toward the developing countries during the early cold war was the racial discrimination within the United States. The persistent segregationist practices and exploitation of blacks in both the South and the North were flagrant violations of the democratic principles of freedom and human dignity so often proclaimed by the United States. The peoples of the developing countries not only claimed equal status for their nations but also sought equality as human beings. Segregation in America reminded them of their colonial days when the white man had treated them as inferiors because of the color of their skin. Conditions in the United States began to change during the Kennedy and Johnson administrations. As blacks heard Martin Luther King articulate their aspirations for a life of more dignity and full participation in American life, as the ghettos exploded after King's assassination, the government began to outlaw certain discriminatory practices against blacks and to provide greater opportunities in jobs and housing.

However, racial problems continued to haunt the United States on the foreign front. In Rhodesia (now Zimbabwe) and South Africa, minority white-controlled governments, determined to stay in power, used abhorrent methods such as apartheid and strict police surveillance. The United States, despite its often-expressed disapproval of these policies, did not follow through with action. It imported Rhodesian chrome for years despite a UN embargo. American companies, although they provided their black workers with better working conditions and pay than local companies, lent support to South Africa through investment. America, the world's first state to articulate that all men were created equal, seemed all too often to say to the world that there was a qualifying phrase: "except blacks."

Third and more fundamental, U.S. relations with the developing states were hampered by the American lack of understanding of class struggle and social politics. America, "born free" as a bourgeois democratic society, had managed to avoid the kind of domestic conflicts over basic values that the countries of Europe experienced and that plagued many of the developing countries.[6] The United States had not experienced a genuine social revolution at its birth, for a revolution is characterized by violence; it seeks to destroy the institutions and social fabric of the old society and create a new society with new institutional and social class arrangements. Despite its self-proclaimed revolutionary character, the United States is, according to former senator William Fulbright, an unrevolutionary, conservative country.[7] Not surprisingly, therefore, America was not particularly sympathetic to revolutions and

---

6. See Chapter 1, 8.

7. J. William Fulbright, *The Arrogance of Power* (New York: Vintage Books, 1967), 72-73.

tended to associate revolutionaries with communism. Deviations from middle-class American values were likely to be condemned as "un-American" and sinful, to be rooted out so that the "American way of life" would remain pure and unadulterated.

The principal challenges to these values have indeed come not from within the system but from outside the U.S. borders, and the United States has reacted to foreign threats—German, Japanese, Soviet—in two ways. Internally, the government has hunted "subversives," a procedure that inevitably has infringed on civil liberties and endangered the security of traditional freedoms. Externally, government policy, before the atomic bomb, was the total destruction of the hostile regime so that American principles could survive untainted.

Thus, as already noted, the real or imagined Communist threat in the early 1950s led to McCarthyism, a search for heresy in which the goal of eliminating alleged un-American attitudes and behavior justified any means, including disregard for due process of law, the basic guarantee of all civil liberties. At times, this hunt went to frightening lengths, as when the United States Information Agency actually burned "suspect" books—and, even worse, when the careers and lives of people were jeopardized and sometimes ruined. In foreign policy, the reaction to the Communist threat was to support almost any regime, no matter how reactionary, if it claimed to be "anti-Communist." As a result, the United States often associated itself with governments whose days were numbered, that had alienated the masses: Chiang Kai-shek in China and Bao Dai in Indochina are but two examples that turned out badly.

This attitude was typical of American absolutism and inability to understand the deeper social struggles of Asia and the Middle East. In its attempt to contain communism—that is, to preserve the global status quo—the United States became committed to the domestic, social, and political status quo in these countries. In seeking stability, the United States was paradoxically trying to preserve freedom by supporting ramshackle autocracies that were unrepresentative of their peoples' aspirations. But this internal contradiction within the U.S. alliance system eventually had to resolve itself. American support for traditional regimes only bottled up the social and political resentment and ferment even more, thereby adding to the explosive forces that someday would burst forth and upset regional balances of power.

The Example of Latin America

Events in Latin America illustrate the way U.S. foreign policy, even when it took into account the need for development aid, became a prisoner of U.S. domestic experience. As a base for the subversion of other Latin nations, Cuba was much on the minds of U.S. policy makers during the 1960s.

Latin America

Successful subversion constituted a threat to the United States. Conditions in Latin America made Castro's success a real possibility: for example, the resentment against a history of U.S. interventions in the Caribbean and Central America; the large-scale, private U.S. capital investments and economic control of many Latin American economies; the persistent U.S. support for the privileged few who, usually closely linked to American capital, sought to preserve their position by ignoring social grievances and establishing right-wing military dictatorships; and finally, the misery, poverty, and illiteracy of the vast majority of the people, who, although they lived in the countryside, were landless.

Latin America shared two aspirations that were sweeping through all the developing areas: the urge for a better life for the masses and the desire of countries to determine their own national destiny. The United States has exercised its hemispheric domination indirectly, usually by alliance with the wealthy landowning governing class. Americans may believe that they are free of Europe's taint of colonialism, but that is not what Latin Americans think. The Monroe Doctrine had turned the southern part of the hemisphere into a U.S. sphere of influence; the United States did not have to resort to direct colonial rule. Invested American capital spoke louder than guns, and the U.S. government did not have to give political orders when a nation was a "banana republic." The economies of many Latin American nations remained backward, undiversified, and agrarian. They depended for a livelihood on the export of one or two raw materials or crops to the United States, their largest market. In good years, they earned money; in bad years, the ever-present unemployment, poverty, and hunger increased. Their livelihood was affected directly by the fluctuations of the business cycle, and by their sensitivity to American interests.

In these conditions, the success of Castroism was thought to depend on two elements. First, it would depend on how the Latin American governments reacted, whether they would undertake large-scale social and economic reforms or cling to their privileges. Public pressure for change was rising, but would this change be revolutionary or evolutionary? If the ruling classes remained as hostile to reform and as irresponsible toward public welfare as in the past, Fidel Castro might be able to export his revolution. Wherever there is social injustice, destruction of the *ancien régime* will appear as the only way of having a piece of land, enough food, or a job. Revolution and a "radical solution" become the only hope for a better life.

Second, the success of Castroism would depend on the effectiveness of U.S. policy directed toward alleviating the conditions that fostered popular resentment in Latin America. Whether the United States had the will to guide this revolution, however, was another matter. This was a task that required American acceptance of non-Communist left-wing movements and the expropriation of American property, neither of which would be easy because of the identification of reform with revolution and revolution with communism. Moreover, the United States was expected to invest billions of dollars in the Latin American economies to foster a self-sustaining rate of economic growth, to develop conditions in which private capital would be attracted to projects other than the extraction of raw materials or growth of single exportable crops, and to aid in the transformation of backward societies into modern, industrialized nations. In addition, Latin America's projected rapid increase of population lent urgency to development. The prospects of more radical revolutions might be avoidable only by an "alliance for progress."

To meet the challenge of the Latin American "revolution of rising expectations" President John Kennedy, soon after assuming office, established precisely such an alliance. He pledged $20 billion of primarily public money over the next decade to Latin America and, even more significantly, he emphasized the need for social change. Kennedy realized that, in the absence of the necessary reforms, the possibilities of economic and political development were slight. The alliance, in short, was a post-Castro attempt to abort future Castros.

Would the ruling oligarchies surrender their power, status, and prestige, and commit themselves to fundamental reforms? In the words of Herbert L. Matthews, then a veteran observer of the Latin American scene:

> In the whole of Latin America, the rich are getting richer and the poor poorer. This is the worst, the most difficult and the most dangerous feature of the area. The Alliance for Progress was created primarily to tackle this essentially social problem. . . .
>
> The most serious feature of this problem centers around agriculture and land reform. The frantic urge to industrialize that seized Latin America after the Second World War was, in part, satisfied at the expense of the agrarian sector. Yet virtually all the countries are from half to three-quarters agricultural. Latin exports are overwhelmingly agricultural and mineral.
>
> The abnormal and dangerous urbanization, caused by the flight of impoverished peasants from the rural areas to the urban centers, has led to some of the largest cities in the world and some of the worst slums. Countries with plenty of land were, and are, importing food at high cost.
>
> Most landowners are resisting the reforms that their governments and the Alliance for Progress desire. . . . Much will depend on whether the ruling classes see the need to make drastic structural reforms. Much, also, will depend on the state of the world and the world markets for raw materials, not to mention the ability of the United States to invest and to aid. . . .
>
> There are revolutions and revolutions. The fascist-military type in Latin America comes from the right; the socialistic-communistic from the left; and in between is the sort of peaceful, voluntary, gradual but genuine type of revolution which the Alliance for Progress is trying to promote.
>
> Latin America is such a dynamic area of the world that it is bound to have revolutions. The only unknown factor is: what kind?[8]

Castro's effect on the alliance was illustrated by the U.S. intervention in the Dominican Republic. The impetus for this event was the overthrow in 1961 of Rafael Trujillo, who had ruled as a dictator for thirty-one years. Following a brief period of political turmoil, Juan Bosch, a man of genuinely democratic convictions, was elected president. Seven months later, Bosch was overthrown by a military coup d'état whose leaders announced that they would reestablish a "rightist state." In April 1965 the pro-Bosch forces revolted against this right-wing military government. But, according to Washington, the leadership of this revolution swung increasingly toward communism. Communists were thought to be active in the movement against

---

8. *New York Times*, March 15, 1965.

the junta, and Washington feared they would gain control of the pro-Bosch forces and create a second Cuba in the hemisphere. The rebels claimed that, although some Communists might support their movement, their revolution was led by non-Communists who only sought a return to constitutional government. Before the evidence was clear that the revolution was in fact Communist-controlled, President Johnson ordered American armed intervention, even though this action once more raised the old specter of American intervention, so common in the days before Franklin Roosevelt's "Good Neighbor" policy.

The Dominican intervention demonstrated how obsessed the Alliance for Progress was with Castro. He was responsible for the alliance and for its failures. Without him, there would have been no large-scale efforts to seek the democratic development of Latin America. But the American fear that any Latin American revolution might become a Communist revolution, requiring preventive action, would not have sprung up without Castro. The overt U.S. intervention—the first in fifty years in Latin America—therefore undermined the Alliance for Progress, which had tried to persuade the region's ruling elites to undertake reforms if they wished to avoid revolutionary violence. Latin America's ruling classes could now relax because there was an alternative: American intervention would save them from the consequences of their own folly in holding onto an unjust way of life. American policy south of the U.S. border, as in other areas of the world, thus continued to be made in the context of the bipolar global struggle.

Was America's Third World Policy Imperialistic?

During and after the Vietnam War, it became fashionable among radical writers, often referred to as the New Left, to claim that American interventions such as those in Cuba, the Dominican Republic, and Vietnam were not accidental, nor was the failure to provide sufficient economic aid for the modernization of the new nations a mere oversight. Indeed, this argument maintains that, although these nations may have been newly formed in the sense of formal political independence, they were in reality economically controlled by the United States, the dominant economy in the "global capitalist system"; the so-called new and independent nations in fact remained in a subordinate status. *Neocolonial* was one of the terms popularly used to refer to this status. In European eighteenth- and nineteenth-century colonialism the European state had invaded a foreign land and established direct rule of the newly acquired colony. In an age of growing nationalism, American imperialism controlled its "colonial" appendages through less visible but equally binding economic chains: corporate investments, economic aid, and the needs of the Third World countries for advanced technology and for markets in which to sell their raw materials. In addition, the United States supported reactionary political and social elites who survived only with American political support that, when necessary, was supplemented with American training and arming of local police and military forces, bribes, coups d'état and—ultimately—U.S. military intervention.[9]

Why all this bother about the poor countries of the world? The answer is that they are, according to the radical critique, enormously profitable. Western industry needs cheap raw materials; the developing countries constitute potentially sizable markets for Western goods; and they provide places for the investment of private capital at large returns. Capitalist economies like that of the United States, the leading Western capitalist state, constantly need profits; without them, unemployment would increase, standards of living decline, and the struggle between capitalists and the proletariat or working class resume. This struggle is muted in the capitalist countries precisely because some of the enormous profits reaped by the capitalists from exploiting the developing countries trickle down to the workers in the form of higher wages and living standards. As long as this continues, the workers' revolutionary consciousness remains weakened and they will support the capitalist system. Without this trickle, the class struggle would resume. Therefore, even with the best of intentions, America, as a capitalist society and guardian of Western capitalism, could not surrender its "neocolonial control" over the developing countries. It was structurally necessary; if capitalism was to be preserved and domestic social revolution avoided, then the Third World countries had to be maintained as profitable dependencies and suppliers of raw materials. The American pursuit of counterrevolutionary and interventionist policies follows from this fundamental economic motivation driving the United States in the international arena.

Dependent, even more than *neocolonial,* has become the common term to describe these nations' standing in the global capitalist system (minus the Soviet bloc). To emphasize the character of the relationship of the United States and other capitalist states to the developing countries, the capitalist states were said to constitute the core, or center, of the international economy, the developing countries the peripheries. The developing countries' economies do not serve their people, nor is their purpose to improve the lives of their citizens. The cheap natural resources are sent to Western factories, where they benefit Western manufacturers and workers, and this has been an important reason for the dramatic increase in the Western standard of living

9. This section, while brief, was included because U.S. policy toward the Third World in the 1960s and 1970s is often described in imperialistic terms. This important alternative explanation deserves brief mention, therefore, as does the critique of it. I relied especially on Jerome Slater, "Is United States Foreign Policy 'Imperialistic' or 'Imperial'?" *Political Science Quarterly* (Spring 1976): 63-87; Robert W. Tucker, *The Radical Left and American Foreign Policy* (Baltimore: Johns Hopkins University Press, 1971); and Stephen D. Krasner, *Defending the National Interest* (Princeton: Princeton University Press, 1978).

over the last century. Thus, the developing countries are poor because they have been exploited, and the Western states are rich because they have been the exploiters. The international capitalist economy is unlikely to allow this relationship to change because the Western developed states benefit from it, and most developing countries remain too dependent on the capitalist states for capital, technology, and markets. The few that wish to resist and break the exploitative economic chains must use force. A successful war of "national liberation" against the pro-Western domestic ruling elite is needed to free them. Once in control of their own economy, which will be used for their people's welfare, these nations will have achieved genuine national independence.

This economically imperialist interpretation of American foreign policy from 1945 to the Vietnam years is testimony to the significance of faith and attitudes over facts. There is little evidence to support a purely economic interpretation. The survival of American capitalism and the achievement of the nation's high standard of living have not depended on exploiting the developing countries. The vast bulk of American private investments had been made in the American economy; and of the approximately 5 percent to 6 percent of American investment that was made abroad, most, even at the height of the Vietnam War in 1968, went to Western Europe, Canada, and Japan. In short, investment in non-Western economies was insignificant for the welfare of the American economy. In trade, the pattern was identical. The United States traded primarily with the other industrial countries. They had something to sell to one another. Here, too, the Third World states were not essential to the well-being of the American economy. Indeed, until the 1970s, the prosperity of the American economy did not depend on exports. It is primarily in the area of natural resources that the dependency argument carries a degree of plausibility, for clearly America, like other industrial countries, needed raw materials. But even here, with the possible exception of oil, the case is far from persuasive. Substitutes, alternative raw materials, and the domestic availability of a vast array of raw materials made the country less dependent on the Third World than the imperialist interpretation would suggest. (Admittedly, the cost of materials from domestic sources may be higher than from the developing countries, although not necessarily higher than the prices these countries hope to get or, in the case of oil, are already receiving. Moreover, as the price of oil rose in the 1970s, alternative sources of energy or oil from deeper wells became economically more feasible.) The United States, in fact, possesses many of the raw materials it needs, including energy resources, especially coal. The United States at the time of Vietnam had the world's highest standard of living and was at the same time a net exporter of raw materials.

What is equally clear is that the imperialist interpretation suggesting that capitalist countries either exercise control of Third World economies to make a profit, or, if they relinquish control, the capitalist economies collapse, could not be more wrong. Since 1945 the Western states that have achieved the highest rates of economic growth are Japan, West Germany, and the Scandinavian states, countries that had no colonies and that exercised no "control" over non-Western countries. They bought what they needed. Imperialist control was completely unnecessary for these states with "capitalist" economies; indeed, such control was inversely related to their prosperity. The former colonial states such as Great Britain and the last colonial state of all, Portugal, fared the worst of all Western economies. Domination of the developing countries is not required to have access to their raw materials. Indeed, and no doubt disillusioning to radical critics who would like the Third World countries to withhold their resources to bring down American capitalism, these nations, radical or not, sell their resources to all Western countries—if the price is right.

But to return to the main point: if economic control means equal political control, one would have expected the United States to resist the increasing country-by-country expropriation of American investments and property or the shifting of majority control from American multinational corporations— the alleged instruments of U.S. imperial control—to host governments; and one would also have expected the United States to intervene militarily to reverse the Organization of Petroleum Exporting Countries' (OPEC) four-fold increase of oil prices in 1973, which led to unemployment and inflation in the Western economies. Yet, nationalization was the trend in the post-World War II anticolonial age, and there was little that could be done about it except to acquiesce and officially protest—with anger sometimes, but not too much— and seek some compensation for the expropriated industry.

But the United States does not send in marines or overthrow governments to save a corporation's sugar fields or banana crops or even to lower oil prices. Economic and other pressures, as well as covert operations and overt interventions, have been used only where Washington perceived the stakes to be far broader than simple expropriation—that is, not where the stakes were corporate property, but where they were perceived to be far more important than money. In Guatemala in 1954, in Cuba in 1961, in the Dominican Republic in 1965 (and later, as we shall see, in Chile in the early 1970s, and Nicaragua after 1979), the American government intervened because it saw the governments in these countries and their international orientation in the context of cold war bipolarity. All these countries seemed to be aligning themselves with the Soviet bloc. And in Panama in 1989, the issue was its leader's involvement with drugs. The United States, as a great power, obviously has influence in the Third World, but the degree of influence depends on the issue and country. In general, it is a declining influence as the developing countries have asserted their nationalism.

American policy in the Middle East is probably the strongest refutation of the imperialist interpretation. If corporations did indeed control Washington, it is impossible to understand why the United States since 1948 has supported Israel so strongly, alienated most Arab states, jeopardized access to the oil needed so badly by Europe and increasingly by America, and risked the nationalization of Western oil companies (almost everywhere now controlled, even if not yet totally owned, by OPEC). In fact, what this policy shows is that economic considerations, if present and important, have not been dominant in the making of the nation's foreign policy.

American motivations in foreign policy must be sought elsewhere than in the economic realm. They derive primarily from security considerations and the fear of Soviet power and, after 1950, from the equation of the expansion of Soviet power and influence with the expansion of communism. It is hardly surprising that in a bipolar world the containment policy was extended to the Third World, even if at times the results were more counterproductive than beneficial to U.S. goals. The worst case of American intervention was to come in Southeast Asia, where the war in Vietnam was to undermine the rationale for U.S. postwar foreign policy.

Vietnam and the
Collapse of Containment

THE WORLD that emerged from World War II and dominated most of the twenty years from 1945 to 1965 was bipolar. The two superpowers, the United States and the Soviet Union, plus their allies, confronted one another directly in almost every area of the globe. In a series of actions and reactions, they drew "frontiers" between their worlds and extended their competition to the Third World. This bipolar world was dangerous because the distribution of power in the state system between two poles was so sensitive. Both were constantly alert to the slightest shifts in power lest they upset the equilibrium to give the adversary superiority. Each side perceived a gain of power and security for one as a loss of power and security for the other. Each viewed the opponent's moves, even if alleged to be defensive, as deliberate and offensive; moves in regions of secondary importance were ranked as significant and countered because they were seen as symbolically vital. Defining the "frontiers" around their respective spheres of influence and then guarding this territorial status quo against encroachment, subversion, or defection became the focus of the bipolar superpower competition.

Through this competitive process the United States became what some of its critics in the late 1960s and 1970s called the "world's policeman." Others, of a more Marxist disposition, referred to America's "empire"; in fact, it makes little sense to attribute the vast postwar expansion of power to economic motives. But the term *empire* is acceptable if attributed to security motives: a great power striving to preserve the balance of power in the state system. If, as we have argued, the superpower rivalry centers on the control of the Eurasian rimlands, then the U.S. role might be defined as *imperial,* as distinguished from the economically driven *imperialistic* search for colonies to exploit their markets and raw materials. Whatever it is called, the role was arduous, constant, and, to a large degree, successful in maintaining the frontiers of containment around the Sino-Soviet bloc—until Vietnam. In going to war there to defend one specific frontier, the United States became involved in an unconventional war it did not understand or know how to manage. The result was that it lost public support not only for the continuation of the war but also for the basic containment, or imperial, policy of which Vietnam was merely an application. In destroying the cold war consensus, the Vietnam War was a political defeat of the first rank for the United States.

The American and Soviet Empires

By the mid-1960s the United States had signed eighty treaties with forty-two separate states. The North Atlantic Treaty Organization (NATO), the Southeast Asia Treaty Organization (SEATO), the Central Treaty Organization (CENTO), and the bilateral security treaties with Japan, South Korea, the Philippines, and Taiwan organized the rimlands around the Sino-Soviet bloc. Western Europe was protected by 300,000 U.S. soldiers, and South Korea was similarly protected. American garrisons on their soil were their best guarantee against attack. The Sixth Fleet guarded the Mediterranean, protecting southern Europe and Israel and Western oil supplies and lines; the Seventh Fleet guarded the broad ranges of the Pacific to the Gulf of Tonkin. By a process of challenge and response, U.S. commitments had extended to virtually all continents, although its interventions in Latin America and Africa were only sporadic. America's projection of its power to all corners of Eurasia, with the accompanying alliances and basing of U.S. forces, resembling that of Britain in the nineteenth century, might therefore well be called "imperial." The USSR's territorial expansion and acquisitions since 1945 could also be so described.

Moscow and Washington were clearly the dominant voices at the time in their respective spheres, composed of allies and client states, which are allies in all but name, although there may be no commitment of defense involved. The magnitude of their power and the scope of their commitments defined the Soviet and American empires. A critical difference between them, however, was the nature of the relationships between the imperial center and the states within its empire. On this matter—the willingness of its members to be part of that empire, the independence they enjoyed as members of a larger collective association, and the manner in which alliance decisions were made—the contrast was striking.

Their Contrasting Characteristics

The Soviet empire (before its unexpected collapse in 1989) comprised the neighboring states of Lithuania, Estonia, and Latvia (which were annexed on the eve of the war with Germany) and other neighboring states in Eastern Europe and Outer Mongolia that were kept obedient by Soviet-imposed Communist regimes and/or Soviet forces on their soil. These troops have been used repeatedly to prevent defection or disloyalty to Moscow. Communist regimes that came to power on their own and controlled their own armies and police forces, such as in Yugoslavia and China, or where Soviet forces were withdrawn, such as Romania, have demonstrated different degrees of independence from Moscow. If Moscow considered leaders such as Tito, Mao Zedong, Imre Nagy, or Alexander Dubcek unreliable, it was even more suspicious of non-Communist rulers with whom it had signed friendship treaties, like Egypt's Anwar Sadat in the 1970s. This is why during that decade Moscow favored not only older Marxist regimes such as North Korea, Cuba, and Vietnam, but also newly self-proclaimed Marxist-Leninist regimes such as Angola, Ethiopia, Mozambique, and South Yemen.

The Soviet empire was more or less contiguous because until the 1970s the Soviets, following the czars, expanded basically around their own frontiers. Their success testified to the close relationship between territorial expansion and the strength of Soviet arms. In the Warsaw Pact area, certainly, there could be no question that Soviet rule had been imposed upon helpless and unwilling nations, except perhaps Bulgaria. Although several of the East European states gained a greater degree of autonomy after Stalin's death in 1953, they were careful not to become too independent, especially on foreign policy issues, to avoid Moscow's wrath and its fist. Indeed, it was probably not accidental that the Soviet Union's principal friends and admirers were found far away from Moscow; states such as Ethiopia and Nicaragua became loyal supporters after the Vietnam War.

The Soviet leadership kept a tight reign on power and dissent at home. It also showed little tolerance in Communist states where, if Soviet interests required, it could enforce its edict with the Soviet army. From the Soviet perspective, different views were wrong views and disagreement was heresy. The Soviet Union was the most powerful, the oldest, and the most experienced Communist state; that gave it the right to determine policy for other Communist states. Interventions in East Germany (1953), Hungary (1956), and Czechoslovakia (1968) demonstrated Moscow's determination to preserve its empire in Eastern Europe. The Soviet claim to intervene unilaterally to preserve socialism in its sphere became known after 1968 as the Brezhnev Doctrine.

By contrast, the American empire emerged over time as the United States reacted to Soviet moves. For the most part, American expansion in Eurasia was by invitation of the Soviet Union's potential victims. They wanted the United States to extend its imperial protection to them in preference to becoming Moscow's satellites. American power guaranteed their national independence; Soviet power meant the end of genuine independence.

In addition to its defensive nature, the American empire has three other notable characteristics. One, if it was not created in a "fit of absent-mindedness," as someone once said about the British Empire, it was created reluctantly, often despite U.S. preferences. After World War II, as the United States sought to retreat once more to the Western Hemisphere, the countries of Western Europe were worried that the United States would *not* help them, not that it would. The United States only gradually extended its commitments, usually because bipolarity seemed to leave it little choice. Two, it is fair to say that the United States did not think of itself as an imperial power. Americans generally do not feel France or South Korea is "theirs." To defend or to intervene in "its" empire, the United States must advance plausible reasons. Otherwise, both abroad and at home, there will be opposition to the use of American power, even if it is justified in the name of the containment policy. Finally, the U.S. relationship with its allies was different from that of the Soviet Union and its allies.

By sheer power the United States was in command; it was American power, especially nuclear power, that deterred a Soviet invasion of Europe. Japan and the members of NATO were under U.S. protection. Their alliances with the United States were in fact unilateral American guarantees for their continued independence. As a result the United States on occasion determined what alliance policy should be, but America's allies have rarely hesitated to express their views openly, including their differences with the United States. They considered themselves allies, not dependencies. If it wished to do so, France threw out U.S. bases and withdrew its forces from the integrated NATO army; Spain refused to renew the lease of U.S. bases unless Washington paid it more—the weaker party usually did well in these negotiations—without expecting retribution, let alone U.S. military intervention. The point was that U.S. alliances reflected the democratic character of the United States and its partners. The expression of different viewpoints was regarded as normal, and issues were usually decided by compromise. If there was no agreement, the alliance either could not act or individual members went their own way. The United States generally did not dictate to its allies. It might lead, but, however insistent it was, it could not compel them to follow unless they wanted to, which has been very obvious since the 1970s.

The United States had not always drawn its overseas frontiers wisely, however. Its attempt to replicate NATO outside of Europe was bound to run into trouble. The global strategy of containing communism tended to ignore the regional differences in the Third World. In Europe, NATO's members perceived a common Soviet threat; their nationalism sustained their determination to defend themselves. Outside of Europe, the new states' nationalism was directed at their former colonial masters. The new states were suspicious of the Western defense organizations, which, they felt, represented their former colonial masters. During the 1950s anticommunism made little sense to a country like Egypt, which sought Soviet help in its fight against Israel, which was supported by Western nations. Anticommunism meant little to most Asian nations; they admired the new Communist China, not the discredited Nationalist regime still backed by the United States. Unwilling to rely on the fierce sense of nationalism of the newly independent states to resist efforts to reestablish foreign domination, even by Communist states, CENTO and SEATO proved to be weak reeds upon which to rely for anti-Communist resistance.

In addition, alliances such as CENTO and SEATO stimulated regional rivalries. Pakistan, a member of both, was not interested in containing communism but in obtaining arms for its rivalry with India. The United States thereby alienated India, potentially the far stronger state and one of the Third World's few democracies, and drove it into Moscow's arms for political support and weapons. As a U.S. friend, India would have been a more effective barrier than Pakistan in the 1950s and later to Soviet probes toward the Indian subcontinent. Similarly, Iraq's membership in CENTO reinforced Egypt's anti-Western disposition because of their traditional rivalry for Arab leadership. Finally, the U.S. crusading style failed to understand that nationalism infected Communist states as much as it did non-Communist states, and, instead of exploiting conflicting national interests among members of the Sino-Soviet bloc, Washington incorrectly assumed its unity and that either Moscow or Beijing was in control of other Communist states' foreign policy.

The 'Center' and the 'Provinces'

Once this overseas empire was created, its preservation became a critical task for the United States. Pericles, Athens' ruler during its war with Sparta, told his fellow citizens that the empire "you hold is, to speak frankly, a despotism; perhaps it was wrong to take it, but to let it go is unsafe." Maintenance, however, demanded continuous vigilance and effort to protect these "frontiers," across several thousand miles of ocean. Strategic deterrence had been the principal means of preventing a major incursion of Western Europe, as well as a strike against the continental United States. Limited challenges were met by a variety of means: attempted coercion in crises was countered by a mixture of military and diplomatic tactics, and actual frontier crossings by "frontier wars." Characteristically, these challenges took place far away from the center of power, the United States. These places were, of course, where frontiers met and where the opponent found it easiest to cause trouble and the defender hardest to show resolution.

Because it was distant, the frontier might not seem clearly related to security interests at the center; it was also nearer to the opponent and its defense therefore involved great risks and expenditures. Indeed, such peripheral involvement seemed like an overextension of the center's power, which, it could be claimed, was not only dangerous but also expensive and unnecessary.

Yet these frontiers were guarded by America's armed forces, the Roman legions of our times. Occasionally in the former colonial areas of the world, the United States and the Soviet Union agreed to allow UN forces, staffed primarily by nonaligned members, to keep the peace and avoid a superpower clash.

A key feature of the American role was the U.S. belief that the empire's maintenance depended on its will to maintain it; the opponent had to believe that the United States would honor its commitments. It followed that if commitments to maintain a particular frontier were no longer credible—no matter how distant or unimportant this frontier may have seemed to some—the adversary might decide that other frontiers too could be crossed with impunity. It might be true that one frontier was more vital than another, but how was the opponent to know which one? An adversary might see the failure to honor a commitment in one area as an indication that another commitment elsewhere might also not be honored and be tempted to test the defender's will. A commitment, whether eagerly sought or reluctantly accepted, therefore, became a matter from which it was very difficult to withdraw without dangerous consequences. Commitments were interdependent.

Conversely, America's allies and friends knew that their defense depended on the United States, and they were constantly alert to signs of a weakening will. Because they knew that their defense might at times seem either hazardous or unimportant to their protector, they lived in a continuous state of apprehension that they would be left undefended. Although all the "provinces" looked to the center for protection, they did not see all imperial frontiers as equally important. Naturally, those in their particular area took priority. Fearful that the center's power might become overcommitted and weakened, they opposed the defense of other regional frontiers, as Europe has done repeatedly when the United States had become involved in Asia.

The third and final characteristic of the imperial power was that it commanded and trained foreign legions. NATO was always commanded by an American and had a highly centralized command structure and integrated forces. Only one of the provinces, France, removed its forces, although it remained dependent on the United States for its basic defense. When several of the provinces showed concern for their self-protection by building nuclear forces, purportedly for use in situations they deemed vital, but the center did not, the imperial power either tried to control these forces (Britain's) or opposed their development (France's). The provinces were not to decide when the empire would defend its interests and risk military conflict; these were for the center to decide. The United States also trained soldiers from non-Western states, some in America, some by sending military missions to these countries. Such a mission was present in South Vietnam. When the South Vietnamese army failed to deal effectively with the Communist Viet Cong guerrillas, the United States sent in its forces.

Vietnam as a 'Frontier War'

Foreign Policy Reasons for U.S. Involvement

The United States became involved in Vietnam because to American leaders the seventeenth parallel dividing North Vietnam from South Vietnam represented a frontier between the free world and the Communist world. Just as they had decided to defend South Korea when North Korea crossed the thirty-eighth parallel, so they now decided to come to the assistance of the South Vietnamese. Like the war in Korea, the Vietnam War was fought at a great distance from the center, in a place where the frontier was very accessible to the enemy.

But that was only the beginning of the problems for the United States. South Vietnam was a divided society; refugees from North Vietnam (approximately 1 million, about half of them Catholic) against indigenous South Vietnamese; Buddhists against Catholics; lowlanders against montagnards; and peasants against urban inhabitants. As in most new nations, loyalties were primarily local. Hostility to a central government was deeply ingrained because, as in most developing countries, the government historically has been that of the colonial power, as represented by the tax collector and recruiting sergeant. Transportation and communication were primitive and industrial development nonexistent. In addition, this was a new state that had emerged from the 1954 Geneva conference that ended the first Indochina war between France and the Vietminh forces; it had no established political institutions and a precarious economy. Not surprisingly, the Vietminh expected South Vietnam to collapse. The Geneva agreement called for a general election in 1956, and Hanoi assumed that a majority of the 12 million South Vietnamese would vote for Ho Chi Minh, who had led the nationalist struggle against the French. Obviously he would have most of the North's 15 million votes, and the country would be reunited under Communist control.

Ho's popularity was the reason that neither the United States nor the new government in the South favored the election. The United States wanted the seventeenth parallel to be accepted as the new frontier, and the president of South Vietnam, Ngo Dinh Diem, a fervent Catholic and anti-Communist, wanted to stay in power. Their opposition was decisive, irrespective of whether the unsigned Geneva declaration mandating the election was politically binding. Hanoi's chances for a peaceful takeover of the South ended, and so did its stance of reasonableness and restraint. At the time of the Geneva settlement, approximately 5,000 to 6,000 local guerrillas, presumably the Vietminh's political and military elite, went underground and began to live like peasants. About 90,000 went north; many later infiltrated South Vietnam. In 1959 the North Vietnamese began the armed struggle in the South. The second Indochina war had started. The guerrillas' immediate objective was to isolate the central government from the majority of its population and substitute Viet Cong control over the peasantry by killing the government's local representatives.

This war, in short, started in a way quite different from the Korean War. Korea had begun with a clear-cut, aggressive attack, which aroused the American public and united the principal Western allies against the common threat. It had also been a conventional war in which regular Communist forces had been checked by regular South Korean, American, and UN troops. By contrast, the French defeat at Dienbienphu had been a decisive moment in contemporary history, for, it demonstrated that *guerrilla warfare* could win against a larger, stronger, conventionally equipped army of even a major power. An internal uprising of guerrillas, directed and organized by the North, was therefore a shrewder manner of "crossing" the seventeenth parallel. It would lend the resulting struggle the aura of a civil war, which would make it less likely that the United States would come to the assistance of South Vietnam because of American doubts about the morality and wisdom of military involvement in such a conflict. Diem's increasingly autocratic rule and his failure to enlist the support of his population, especially the peasantry, through political, social, and economic reforms helped to prepare the ground for a successful guerrilla campaign and lent support to the view of the conflict as a civil war. It certainly provided the Viet Cong with fertile ground to mobilize support.

Another reason for involvement was that the war was seen in Washington as a test of its will, and meeting the test was believed to be necessary to maintain all frontiers. Until the non-Communist states of the area became more economically developed and possessed sufficient capabilities of their own, the Asian balance depended upon the United States. Commitments—and the administrations of Dwight Eisenhower, John Kennedy, and Lyndon Johnson all considered the United States to be committed to the defense of South Vietnam—were interdependent. The United States could not choose to defend West Berlin and Quemoy but not Matsu and South Korea. Washington believed that it could no more forgo the defense of the frontier in South Vietnam than in Greece and Turkey, in Western Europe and Berlin, or in Korea and Cuba. If one country fell it would, in its turn, knock down the next one and so on down the line like a row of dominoes; the political and psychological impact of an American pullout would be felt throughout the area, if not in other regions as well, and the series of losses would upset the balance of power. As all commitments were viewed as interdependent, being unfaithful to one risked the collapse of all. The memory of Munich and the appeasement of Nazi Germany, which had failed to avert World War II, was a stark reminder that to fight on the periphery now would prevent a bigger war later.

The assumptions underlying this perception were, of course, that the world was still bipolar and that the enemy was the Sino-Soviet bloc, which the United States continued to perceive as united, despite increasing evidence to the contrary. Signs of differences between the Soviet Union and China were generally explained as tactical differences on how the "Communist world" ought to wage its "war" against the United States, not as fundamental conflicts of national interests between the two powers. Even if these had been recognized, it probably would not have made much difference because "Red China," with its population approaching 1 billion and its revolutionary rhetoric denouncing "American imperialism," was viewed by Washington as far more militant and dangerous than Moscow. Ho Chi Minh and the Viet Cong were seen as puppets of China, applying Mao Zedong's guerrilla warfare tactics to destroy a non-Communist government in a country within the American sphere of influence. If they succeeded, Vietnam would be added to China's power and thus to the Sino-Soviet bloc's power; it would also be an example to other revolutionary forces in Asia and elsewhere that the United States, despite its nuclear weapons, could be defeated. Washington saw the North's war against the South as aggression similar to North Korea's against South Korea, even if North Vietnamese forces had not crossed the seventeenth parallel. Guerrilla warfare was just another variant of Communist aggression and therefore had to be defeated.

There was a double irony to this pattern of thinking. First, had the United States had diplomats in Beijing, they would have known that North Vietnam was not a puppet, that, historically, China and Vietnam had often been enemies, and that in the early 1960s China was in the midst of a domestic upheaval and that the last thing Mao, who was purging all whom he considered insufficiently revolutionary, would want to do was to risk a confrontation with the United States. As with China's earlier intervention in Korea, the United States again paid a high price for its refusal to recognize the mainland regime. Second, if the containment of China was a key goal of the U.S. intervention, the U.S. should have let South Vietnam fall. It should have done so because Ho was a nationalist, not just a Communist, and a united Communist and nationalistic Vietnam would have proven a stronger barrier to any possible Chinese ambitions of hegemony in Southeast Asia than a non-Communist South Vietnam governed by an unpopular regime.

Instead, the Vietnam War, undertaken in the name of containment, undermined containment. It involved the United States against an enemy in an area of only secondary interest in a war that lasted eight years, cost over 50,000 in dead and $150 billion in money. The beneficiary of this effort was the Soviet Union, the United States' primary enemy, which focused *its* resources on first catching up with and then surpassing the United States in missiles. Because of the popular backlash to the war and to military spending, the United States fell behind in the strategic buildup during the 1970s. Indeed, the key domino that fell was not South Vietnam but American public opinion.

Domestic Reasons for the Incremental Intervention

Yet, in a way, the U.S. intervention in Vietnam was by 1965 inevitable for, from the administration of Harry Truman to that of Richard Nixon, every president deepened the involvement in Vietnam. Although Truman at first opposed France's postwar efforts to restore its colonial rule, he changed his position to overcome French resistance to the American plan for the revival of Germany, especially its rearmament. After the Korean War erupted, the French war in Indochina became part of the global struggle against communism. At the time of France's defeat at Dienbienphu in 1954, Eisenhower, although deciding not to intervene militarily, backed the new government in South Vietnam, organized after France's defeat and withdrawal, with economic assistance and military training for its armed forces. This training was in orthodox warfare, not in the unorthodox or guerrilla warfare that had already been observed in Vietnam. SEATO was supposed to be the new state's security guarantee. Kennedy escalated this commitment by sending in 16,500 military advisers to help the South Vietnamese army; starting in the spring of 1965, Johnson raised this number and changed the nature of the commitment by sending in 500,000 American troops.

. Particularly significant during the years of piecemeal commitments was that at no point did policy makers in Washington ever ask themselves some fundamental questions about Vietnam: Was it vital to American security interests and, if so, how vital? If it had been vital earlier, was it still so in the early 1960s? Could the situation in South Vietnam be saved militarily, given the nature of the Saigon government and its seeming lack of popular support? If American forces should be sent, then in what numbers? And how could they be effectively used in an unorthodox type of war? What cost, if any, was South Vietnam "worth"? As incremental commitments were made whenever conditions in South Vietnam appeared ominous, these questions were never really debated at the highest levels of the government. American commitments and credibility virtually foreclosed any debate except how, when, and how much force was needed to save South Vietnam.

During the Kennedy period, military advisers managed to prevent total collapse, but by 1965 Johnson—who since Kennedy's assassination had concentrated on passing a major domestic reform program and getting reelected—could no longer operate on this basis and avoid the central question of what the United States ought to do. South Vietnam was about to be cut in two, and the Viet Cong would then be in a position to mop up first one part and then the other. In the face of this reality, Johnson sent in 200,000 troops that year, extending U.S. involvement and turning an incremental policy into a long-term commitment. After years and years of neglect and procrastination and with the situation growing worse daily, Washington had neither the time nor the inclination to make a carefully calculated basic decision; when the crucial decision was made, it was made by

Johnson, a new president—whose primary interests, experience, and skill were domestic—on the advice of the Kennedy staff and cabinet he had inherited. Long-range policy had become the prisoner of a number of earlier short-range decisions that had been made to tackle crises. Johnson's misfortune was that he could not procrastinate or make more piecemeal moves. He was stuck with the decision whether to escalate to prevent the defeat of the South Vietnamese army or be, as he phrased it, the first president in U.S. history "to lose a war." Each president had done just enough to prevent this defeat. Johnson's escalation was the logical culmination of his predecessors' decisions. But perhaps even more important than foreign policy considerations was American domestic politics. Originally, in 1947, anti-Communism may have been intended primarily as a means of arousing the public and mobilizing popular support for cold war policies while the nation in fact pursued more limited aims. However, once an administration had justified its policy in terms of an anti-Communist crusade and aroused the public by promising to stop communism, it opened itself to attacks by the opposition party in case of setbacks, even if they occurred for reasons beyond America's ability to prevent them. The out-party could then exploit such foreign policy issues by accusing the in-party of "appeasement," of having "lost" this or that country, and of being "soft on communism." This sort of accusation made it difficult to recognize the People's Republic of China, to build bridges to Eastern Europe, to negotiate with the Soviet Union, and especially to discriminate between areas of vital and secondary interest to U.S. security.

Democratic administrations were more deeply affected by this political rhetoric than Republican administrations. The Democrats were in power when Nationalist China collapsed; the Democrats were accused of "treason," of "selling out" China, and they lost the 1952 presidential election as a result. The desire to avoid accusations of being "soft on communism" had pushed Truman to advance northward across the thirty-eighth parallel before the 1950 midterm elections and made it impossible for him to negotiate any settlement of the war that would leave Korea divided. The wish to avoid similar accusations made it impossible for John Kennedy, who had campaigned on a tough anti-Castro platform, to reject the Eisenhower-initiated plan to invade Cuba, even though the new president had serious qualms about it. It led the Kennedy and Johnson administrations to make their piecemeal commitments in Vietnam, lest the Democrats be charged with the "loss of Indochina" as well as China, and it influenced Lyndon Johnson to bomb North Vietnam and to escalate the war by sending in the army. But even Eisenhower, a conservative Republican president and victorious general who had led the Allies to victory over Germany—a man who could hardly be accused of disloyalty—had felt sufficiently threatened by the Republican right that in 1954 he did not pull the United States out of Vietnam. He kept America in Vietnam by supporting the new South Vietnamese government. Each president thought each step in the growing involvement in Indochina to be less costly than doing nothing and disengaging from Vietnam. In the context of U.S. politics, defeat was believed to be unacceptable. The costs of nonintervention in terms of the loss of public and congressional support were calculated to be much higher than the costs of intervention.

These examples illustrate the high price the United States consistently paid for its penchant to crusade and to moralize power politics: overreaction, diplomatic rigidity, and overt or covert interventions that it might otherwise never have launched. National style was a principal cause for the long delay in recognizing China and the failure to exploit Sino-Soviet differences. Worse, it was the main reason for misunderstanding Asian communism, including the war in Vietnam. It was certainly a key reason, if not *the* reason, for the subsequent intervention. Because the domestic costs of losing a country to communism were so high, those in power felt compelled to intervene with the Central Intelligence Agency (CIA), marines, or army to avoid such losses. The desire to avoid accusations of appeasement, of betraying the nation's honor, of weakening its security was keenly felt. This was especially true just before elections, and there was always an election coming up.

The Misconduct of Counterguerrilla Warfare

The United States virtually ignored the political structure of South Vietnam, which was the key to the successful use of American arms. For years the United States had supported Diem, a devout Catholic, whose authoritarian rule and aloofness from the mainly Buddhist population had alienated most of it. By the time the military overthrew and murdered Diem, with Kennedy's knowledge and tacit blessing, the Viet Cong already controlled much of South Vietnam; the social, political, and economic reforms needed to win the war had been neglected too long. That the United States had acquiesced in the coup against Diem should have alerted future administrations; that Kennedy had said Diem had "gotten out of touch with the people" testified to the political bankruptcy in Saigon, as well as to the questionable wisdom of having begun the military intervention in the first place. Even with Diem gone, South Vietnam's governments were unable to rally popular support for a vigorous prosecution of the war against the Viet Cong. But Saigon's succession of corrupt, reactionary, and repressive regimes apparently never reawakened thoughts in the minds of U.S. policy makers of Chiang Kai-shek and his Nationalist government in postwar China.

At the time of China's fall the Truman administration had decided China could not be saved, except perhaps—and it was only *perhaps*—with enormous military and economic costs, which it felt the American public would not be willing to pay. In addition, these costs would have diverted the nation's resources and efforts from its area of primary interest in Europe where American security was at stake. In Dean Acheson's words, as noted before: "Nothing that this country did or could have done within the *reasonable* limits of its capabilities" could have changed the result in the conflict between Mao Zedong and Chiang Kai-shek.[1] In short, containment could not be achieved through a sieve. By attempting containment in South Vietnam, Truman's successors in Democratic administrations risked major domestic discontent. They also risked a public questioning of the fundamental assumptions of American postwar foreign policy that had led to the war.

Guerrillas and Social Strategy

Certainly, the possibility of achieving a quick victory over the Viet Cong was remote, for a guerrilla war is totally different from traditional Western warfare. The militarily weaker side resorts to guerrilla tactics because it has no other options. The aim of a guerrilla war is to capture the government from within and to do so by eroding the morale of the army and by undermining popular confidence in the government, thus isolating it. To achieve this objective, it is not necessary to inflict a complete defeat on the government's forces or to compel them to surrender unconditionally. Indeed, until the final stage of the war, guerrillas do not even meet these forces openly, and then they do so only to apply the *coup de grâce*. Guerrilla war is therefore a protracted conflict in which the guerrillas use hit-and-run tactics—here, there, everywhere—and engage only those smaller and weaker government forces they can defeat. To cope with this strategy, year in and year out, the government troops must be dispersed to guard every town, every hamlet, and every bridge against possible attack. Unable to come to real grips with the enemy and defeat it in battle, and suffering one small loss after another, the army becomes demoralized and its mood defensive.

Although such tactics gradually weaken the military strength of the army, the guerrillas' main effort is directed at the civilian population. As the weaker side, the guerrillas aim to wrest the allegiance of the population from the government, and, without popular support, the government simply collapses. The guerrillas do this in two ways. First, by increasing their control of the countryside, where most of the people live, and by winning battles with government forces, they demonstrate to the peasants that the government cannot protect them. The execution of the village headmen, who are generally government representatives, or of other people who may have helped the government forces, proves this most vividly. Second, and even more important, the guerrillas exploit any existing popular grievances. Communist guerrillas do not pose as Communists, and they do not usually receive support because they are Communists. The populace supports them because it believes the

---

1. Department of State, *United States Relations with China* (Washington, D.C.: Government Printing Office, 1949), xvi. Italics added.

guerrillas will oust the government with which it is dissatisfied and that a new government will meet its aspirations.

Mao said that guerrillas need the people as fish need water; without popular support, the guerrillas would not receive recruits, food, shelter, and information on the government forces' disposition. Unlike conventional warfare, in which each army seeks the destruction of the other's military forces, guerrillas seek the support of the people. A government that has the allegiance of its population does not provide fertile soil for guerrillas; where social dissatisfaction exists, however, guerrillas find an opening. The guerrillas gain the support of the peasantry because they successfully represent themselves as the liberators from colonialism or foreign rule, native despotic governments, economic deprivation, or social injustice. In this way, they isolate the government in its own country.

Counterguerrilla war is therefore not purely military; it is also political. Although the government under attack must try to defeat the guerrillas in the field, its principal task is to tackle the political, social, and economic conditions that bred the support for the guerrillas. Fundamentally, counterguerrilla warfare is an extremely difficult and sophisticated form of war to wage—far more so than the traditional clash of armies—because the war cannot be won without thoroughgoing reforms. Yet these reforms have to be carried out in the midst of battle. Such a war is also likely to take years; five to ten years is not at all unusual. And finally, it takes approximately fifteen counterguerrilla fighters to one guerrilla—in short, a sizable army, and one trained in counterguerrilla tactics.

What all this means is that the United States finds such a war extremely difficult to fight. America likes its wars "strictly military." A war that is concerned primarily with social and political reforms runs completely counter to the American approach. The war's length would also cause great frustration, because the United States likes to get its "boys home by Christmas." If this new kind of warfare did not yield swift and successful results, the American temptation would be either to pull out or to seek a shortcut to victory by purely military action.

The Military Battlefield: Vietnam

American policy makers misplaced their confidence in the nation's military prowess and its ability to change the guerrillas' "rules of the game." In 1965 the illusion of American omnipotence had not yet died. Had not the United States successfully confronted the Soviet Union in Cuba and compelled it to back down? Could there really be much doubt that its well-trained generals in command of armies equipped with the newest and latest weapons from America's industry and under the leadership of that most efficient Pentagon manager, Secretary of Defense Robert McNamara, could beat a few thousand "peasants in black pajamas"? With its sizable forces and its superior mobility and firepower, could not America find the enemy's troops and destroy them, compelling that enemy to desist from taking over South Vietnam? Characteristically, then, the emphasis was strictly military.

In Vietnam, the war required forces to secure villages and to stay in them to root out the Viet Cong cells and show the villagers that Saigon did care about them. Instead, the military carried out massive search-and-destroy operations. The guerrillas, even if driven away from the villages, returned after the helicopters had left and continued to control the countryside. Because such large-scale operations could not be launched without preparation at the base camp and were usually preceded by airstrikes and artillery bombardments of the area in which the troops would land, the Viet Cong often disappeared and the whole operation ended in frustration.

American military men clearly did not understand the political nature of counterguerrilla war. They had been trained for conventional battle, and their strategy was to use maximum firepower to wear the enemy down in a war of attrition. The military was confident it could do this because its helicopters provided superior mobility and modern technology gave it the necessary firepower. The measure of success became the daily body count of Communist dead. The war was also extended by air to the North. The purpose of bombing the North was clearly not military, although the United States claimed its purpose was to stem the flow of men and supplies coming south. Guerrillas can live off the land and capture many of their weapons from their enemies; in any case, the sustained American attacks on Chinese supply lines in North Korea during the Korean War had shown that air power alone was unable to stop the flow of supplies to the fighting zone. The aim of the attacks was political—to persuade North Vietnam to stop the war. The gradual extension of these attacks was intended to stress that the United States meant to protect South Vietnam and would not withdraw, that the price Hanoi might have to pay for victory would be disproportionately costly, and therefore that it had better desist.

But the bombing did not weaken Hanoi's will to prosecute the war, nor did it cut the supplies sufficiently to hamper the fighting in the South or greatly reduce troop infiltration. Hanoi's persistence, in turn, led to increased military and political calls for more air strikes and new targets. Those who advocated increasing the air war did not acknowledge that air power could not by itself win the war; rather, they insisted that it could, if it were used with maximum efficiency. Air power, in short, came to be seen by some as an immaculate way of fighting the guerrillas, of efficiently inflicting great destruction on them, throttling their supply lines, breaking their morale, and finally compelling them to end the conflict at little cost in lives.

This objective, however, remained unattainable. Even the more stable military regime of Nguyen Van Thieu and Nguyen Cao Ky, which sought to legitimate itself in the election of 1967, failed to implement a program of social and economic reform until 1970 when it adopted a major land reform program. It was particularly remiss in not earlier carrying out a necessary redistribution of land from the usually absentee landlord to the peasant. Without such reforms, the Viet Cong grew stronger. Militarily, every increase of American forces was met by increased infiltrations of both guerrillas and conventional troops from the North to the South. Nevertheless, the U.S. government issued optimistic battle reports and forecasts of victory on a regular basis.

The 1968 Tet (or Vietnamese New Year) offensive, launched on the last day in January, was the Johnson administration's Dienbienphu. Tet showed once and for all—and Americans could see it nightly on their television sets— that despite the repeated optimistic predictions the enemy had again been badly underestimated. It had launched a major countrywide offensive and attacked Saigon, Hué, and every other provincial capital; a Viet Cong squad had even penetrated the American embassy compound, thereby scoring a significant symbolic victory. The subsequent fighting (which in fact destroyed the Viet Cong so that afterward the North Vietnamese army actually assumed the main burden of fighting the Americans) was bloody and destructive. Above all, the Viet Cong had clearly demonstrated that neither an American army of a half-million men nor the far larger South Vietnamese army could give the people living in the urban areas security—and the Communists presumably already controlled much of the countryside.

The Political Battlefield: The United States

American power and its effectiveness in unorthodox warfare were shown to be greatly exaggerated. Tactically, American forces had seized and retained the offensive, claiming the destruction of large numbers of enemy soldiers. But strategically the Viet Cong had maintained the upper hand, and the Americans were on the defensive. And by using about 80 percent of their forces to find and destroy North Vietnamese troops in the relatively unpopulated central highlands and frontier regions, they were unable to secure *and* protect the 90 percent of the population living in the Mekong Delta and coastal plains. The pursuit of victory through physical attrition could not be transformed into military or political advantages. Indeed, in question was not just America's protective capacity but also its wisdom. Having left the cities unprotected, except for elements of the South Vietnamese army, allied forces then had to fight their way back into the hearts of the various cities and towns the Viet Cong had infiltrated. If, after almost three years of American help, South Vietnam was still that insecure and the enemy that strong, the wisdom of continuing the war, let alone sending further American reinforcements, was bound to be intensely debated.

This was particularly so because so many Americans perceived the war to be morally ambiguous, if not downright immoral. There had never been a clear-cut crossing of the seventeenth parallel dividing North Vietnam and

South Vietnam, which made less believable the accusation that Hanoi was an aggressor. The undemocratic Saigon government and its apparent lack of popularity gave credence to the view of the war as a rebellion or civil war against Saigon's repression. (Interestingly, in 1950, the South Korean government had a similar autocratic reputation, but the attack across the thirty-eighth parallel focused attention on North Korean ambitions and justified the American intervention. No one in the United States raised questions about defending a "corrupt dictatorship.") The massive, sometimes indiscriminate, use of American firepower, which led to widespread destruction of civilian life (although less than in Korea); the creation of thousands of refugees; and, reportedly, the hostility of the peasants, whose support was vital for military success, had already pricked the conscience of many Americans concerned with their nation's historic image as a compassionate and humane country. The tanks rumbling into cities after Tet, the divebombing of apartment houses, the civilian suffering, personal tragedies, and just general carnage, left television viewers—who saw only one side of the war and not, for example, the deliberate slaughter of 3,000-5,000 professional people and bureaucrats in the city of Hué—asking themselves if there was any point in "destroying a country in order to defend it."

Within the United States, the Tet offensive caused antiwar feelings, which had been growing throughout 1967 as the war continued, seemingly without end, to coalesce. Johnson's initial support eroded on both the right and the left, with the right demanding an end to the war through escalation and the left through deescalation, if not withdrawal. (Sometimes, in fact, the same people held both views.) The articulate opposition to the conflict by a number of liberal and moderate Republican and Democratic senators, especially the chairman of the Senate Foreign Relations Committee, J. William Fulbright, made the opposition of many politicians, professors, students, journalists, editorial writers, and television commentators respectable instead of "un-American." Indeed, after Tet, Fulbright and his committee became an alternative source of interpretation and policy recommendations to the president. Although the Viet Cong was virtually destroyed during the Tet fighting, the United States suffered a political defeat. The guerrilla strategy of *psychologically exhausting* the opponent had succeeded. The American strategy of *physical attrition* was the wrong one. The military won all the battles, including Tet, but lost the war as the public grew tired of it.

The Vietnam War involved two battlefields. The first, in Vietnam, was bloody but inconclusive militarily. The second, in the United States, was not bloody, but it was decisive politically. As the war dragged on, the nation's will to continue it declined. In a total war like the two world wars, when the United States sensed its security, if not its survival, was at stake, all issues were subordinated to the prosecution of the war. In a limited war, important issues may be at stake, but the security threat to the United States may not be apparent. How could the loss of South Korea or South Vietnam diminish

U.S. security? Neither North Korea nor North Vietnam could invade the United States. During hostilities, politics go on as usual, with most domestic interest groups pursuing their interests and preferences; butter is not automatically subordinated to guns. But, as the costs of the conflict rise in terms of lives, inflation, and taxes, public disaffection also grows. So do antiwar demonstrations and parades, some of which spilled over into clashes with the police and supporters of the war.

The guerrillas were well aware of the two battlefields and of which one was more important. General Vo Nguyen Giap, the North Vietnamese strategist who had overseen his country's victories against France and the United States, spoke of the impatience of democracies at war. He saw that a strategy in which the war seemed never to end, in which the minimum purpose was simply not to lose, would eventually erode the opponents' will to continue. As the war dragged on, as the casualties and costs mounted, the democracies would throw in the towel. It was their "home fronts" that were decisive, where the "real battle" would be won. The Tet offensive was deliberately launched as the 1968 political primaries were about to begin in the United States, where opposition to the war had become widespread.

Disagreement over the war led two senators from the president's party, Eugene McCarthy and Robert Kennedy, to contest Johnson's renomination as the Democratic standard-bearer. Running as "peace candidates," they provided a rallying point for the growing numbers of Americans disenchanted with the war. Then, in March 1968, at the end of the speech that laid the basis for the Paris peace talks, the president announced that he would not run for a second term. Lyndon Johnson's tragedy was that he had come into office seeking a "great society" in America; instead the war destroyed him. The changing American mood was evident in the 1968 campaign. Vice President Hubert Humphrey, nominated in Chicago after bloody clashes between police and antiwar students (many of them McCarthy supporters) and bitter disagreement among the delegates over the Vietnam platform, was mercilessly heckled during most of the campaign. As a member of the administration, he found it difficult to disavow the war; when he took his own "risk for peace," it was very late in the campaign.

In these circumstances of Democratic disunity, former vice president Nixon, a longtime hawk, found it inexpedient to charge the Democrats with a "no-win" policy; instead he softened his views on the war. Indeed, in his speeches the menace abroad suddenly ran a poor second to the "moral decay" at home. Generally, both candidates fell over themselves in their eagerness to abandon both anti-Communist slogans and the war, offering instead hopes for an "honorable" peace in Vietnam and for "law and order" at home. Halting Communist aggression was abandoned as an issue; stopping further costly foreign adventure—"no more Vietnams"—became the issue. In Vietnam, the only question was when to get out and on what terms. By not losing, the North Vietnamese had won; by not winning, the United States had indeed lost.

A New Mood of Withdrawal

The United States was weary, disillusioned, and ready to retreat from its imperial role. This mood manifested itself in the attempt to curb presidential power in foreign policy, especially the power as commander-in-chief to commit American forces to battle. Under the Constitution, the president is chiefly responsible for the conduct of foreign policy, which made the office the target of those opposed to these policies. During the 1950s the conservatives had wished to limit presidential authority because the president was, in their minds, not anti-Communist enough and might, acting on the advice of the "pro-Communists" in the State Department, sell the country down the river. Starting in the late 1960s the liberals sought to restrain the president's authority because, in their opinion, the president, the military-industrial complex, and the Central Intelligence Agency (CIA) supporting him were too anti-Communist and were intent on involving the country in too many costly adventures abroad.

Conservative or liberal, the remedy for the "imperial presidency's" alleged abuse of its authority and its virtually solo determination of foreign policy was identical: to reassert the control of Congress in the formulation of external policy and to restore the constitutional balance that purportedly had been upset. The president presumably would be restrained so that, for conservatives, he would no longer be able to "appease" America's enemies or, for liberals, be able to act in an interventionist, warlike manner. The abuse of power by Nixon, a conservative president who resigned his office rather than be impeached, reinforced the liberal sentiment to curb presidential powers and compel a more restrained and moderate policy.

A second symptom of the new mood was that priority should be paid to the nation's domestic problems. These problems became apparent when in the 1960s the affluent society, as it was called in the 1950s, began to reveal its seamier and more violent sides, such as urban slums, air and water pollution, and the dissatisfaction of the poor and disenfranchised, who were primarily blacks, Puerto Ricans, native Americans, Chicanos, and Asians. Critics of the war wanted to spend money to improve the quality of life for all American citizens. Instead of crusading for democracy abroad, they argued, the United States should start crusading to make *America* safe for democracy. Liberal critics of the war in Vietnam quoted Edmund Burke to the effect that "example is the school of mankind, and they will learn at no other." The example should be one of a free society enjoying its freedom fully.

These blessings could not be fully realized in a nation whose excessive preoccupation with foreign affairs drained its powers and resources, both human and material. A "strong" foreign policy was unlikely to bring with it any lasting greatness, prestige, and security; rather, the constant expenditure of energy in adventures abroad would ruin the domestic base. The cold war preoccupation was corrupting of American society. Institutional imbalance was eroding constitutional processes, particularly when powerful and energetic presidents, in the name of national security, not only committed the nation to war but also appeared to sanction plots to assassinate foreign leaders such as Fidel Castro (with Mafia help), lied to the American people and Congress about what they were doing or why they were doing it (intervention in Vietnam), acted covertly (bombing Cambodia for years), and in various ways violated the constitutional rights of some American citizens. And the large-scale devotion of the country's financial and intellectual resources to its external commitments meant a corresponding neglect of domestic issues. Extensive involvement in the world, in short, was tainting the American promise and vision; the priority of foreign over domestic policy had to be ended. This idea had always been at the heart of the old isolationism: America could take care only of its own needs, serve as an example for humankind, and remain pure in a morally wicked world if it stayed out of or minimized its political involvement in it. The consequence of assuming an active role internationally was to endanger, not protect, American democracy.

Perhaps the most revealing symptom of America's reaction to Vietnam was the reassertion of the deep-seated attitude toward the exercise of power internationally as immoral and corrupting. Once power politics could no longer be justified in moral terms of democracy versus dictatorship, as in the two world wars, the sense of guilt over using power returned. Vietnam seemed to prove that in the exercise of power the nation had forsaken its moral traditions and violated its own democratic and liberal ideals. Not surprisingly, sensitive people deeply committed to human values—and daily watching the exercise of power in the form of violence in history's first televised war—repented their former support of containment-through-power as if in giving that support they had been unwitting sinners. Fulbright, who had been a leading advocate of postwar foreign policy as moral conflict, now attacked America's global role as evidence of an "arrogance of power." [2] He did not merely assert that the United States had overextended itself and that its commitments needed to be cut down to its capacities. Nor did he say that Vietnam had been an unwise commitment, although the basic policy of containment had been correct. He stated something far more fundamental: that all great powers seem to have a need to demonstrate that they are bigger, better, and stronger than other nations and that it was this arrogance of power, from which the United States now suffered, which was the real cause of international conflict and war.

In brief, it was the exercise of power per se that, regardless of a nation's intentions, made it arrogant. Power itself is corrupting; even if justified in moral terms, its use is immoral except in clear, unambiguous cases of self-defense. No idea could have been more characteristically American. Power is evil, and its exercise tantamount to the abuse of power; abstention from power

---

2. J. William Fulbright, *The Arrogance of Power* (New York: Vintage Books, 1967).

politics, providing an example to the world of a truly just and democratic society, is a more moral policy. America should be loved for its principles and for practicing what it professes, rather than be feared for its might. Democracy and power politics were simply incompatible.

Toward Détente

After 1962 the United States and the Soviet Union sought a relaxation of tensions, and both had clear motives for doing so. For the United States, the two chief reasons were the assassination of President Kennedy and the country's increasing involvement and preoccupation with Vietnam. Johnson focused his attention on domestic problems. He did this in part because of the shock of the assassination and the need to calm the nation and provide continuity in the government. Domestic affairs also were a natural choice for him. A Texan and devoted disciple of President Franklin Roosevelt, Johnson was determined to create what he called a Great Society for white and black Americans alike and, in the process, outdo Roosevelt in the achievement of social reforms. He had little experience or interest in foreign policy. His main interest in being elected to a full term was to have the opportunity to carry out his social program. Starting in 1964, however, the rapidly deteriorating situation in Vietnam began to compete for his attention and energy. As the U.S. intervention deepened and antiwar protests mounted, the conduct of the war became Washington's focus. Domestic politics were subordinated to foreign policy, which was more and more affected by public opinion as the war dragged on with no end in sight.

The Soviet Union also needed the cooling of American-Soviet relations. The humiliating withdrawal from Cuba in 1962 had been a major factor in the overthrow of Khrushchev by his disciple Leonid Brezhnev two years later. Brezhnev needed time to consolidate power and decide on the direction of Soviet domestic and foreign policies. More important, the Soviet leadership blamed its defeat in Cuba on the strategic superiority of the United States. The Soviets could not have risked escalating the conflict in Cuba by defying the ban on further missile shipments or even by making their missiles operational. With only 150 bombers of doubtful quality and 50 missiles against 1,300 U.S. bombers fully supported by air-refueling aircraft plus 200 missiles, Moscow would have invited the Soviet Union's total destruction. Therefore, the principal task of the Brezhnev regime was a massive military buildup, which would last into the 1980s and include both strategic and conventional forces. When Brezhnev took over the reins of government, the Soviets possessed about 200 ICBMs. By the time Nixon assumed office in 1969, the Soviets had overtaken the United States in numbers of land- and sea-based missiles by 1,900 to 1,710; and, by the time of the first Strategic

Arms Limitation Talks agreement (SALT I) in 1972, the figures stood at 2,350 and 1,710, respectively.

One of the first signs of the changing relationship between the superpowers, in fact, was the beginning of arms control talks. After the missile crisis, both sides were determined not to repeat such an incident. Among their first agreements were the limited test-ban treaty and the establishment of the hot line, which made it easier for the two powers to communicate at times of great tension and thereby reduce the possibilities of miscalculations. Johnson had also proposed that the superpowers talk to one another about their strategic forces. These SALT talks were scheduled to begin in 1968 but were postponed by the United States to protest the Soviet Union's invasion of Czechoslovakia.

But it is fair to add that the 1960s, which for the United States had started with a major victory in Cuba, ended in disaster with Vietnam. The Eisenhower administration, so stodgy in appearance and apparently not overly concerned by Soviet missile and space achievements (or with achieving racial equality in the United States), had seemed to many—especially Americans of liberal persuasion—to be a reason for pessimism. Kennedy's youthfulness and his attractive family had signaled a national change of mood. In his famous inaugural address, the new president, characterizing his ascendancy to the office as a shift to a younger and more energetic generation, had called upon his fellow citizens to place the nation ahead of themselves—to ask what they could do for their country, not what the government could do for them. And he had promised that his generation, committed to freedom as strongly as previous generations, would "pay any price, bear any burden, meet any hardship, support any friend, oppose any foe to assure the survival and success of liberty."

The first years of the Kennedy administration were years of optimism and activism. America stood triumphant after the missile crisis. But the triumph changed quickly as a result of defeat in Vietnam; the Soviet strategic buildup; the murder of a beloved president who had style, grace, and a sense of humor; and the ugliness of racial violence that attended the integration of American society. U.S. foreign policy in the 1970s was to find itself essentially on the defensive as Moscow claimed that what it called the "correlation of forces" had shifted toward the Soviet Union. By correlation of forces, the Soviets included not only the military balance but also other components of power such as willpower, national unity, and economic vitality. Marxism emphasizes the social and economic basis of political and military power. America's lack of will and unity was obvious after Vietnam; the decline of the U.S. economy, the basis of American power, became evident during the oil shocks of 1973 and 1979. The low point was reached in 1979 when Iranian youths took over the American embassy in Tehran following the collapse of the shah's pro-American government, and for 444 days 52 Americans were held hostage.

From Cold War I
to Détente

THE VIETNAM War left the United States disillusioned with anticommunism as a rationale for global involvement. The price was too high. Before Vietnam, the nation could be mobilized to stop Communist aggression; after Vietnam, the concern became avoiding engagement in further adventures overseas. Even more basically, anticommunism had been weakened by the increasing pluralism of the formerly cohesive Sino-Soviet bloc.

In the bipolar world, it had been relatively easy to moralize about power politics precisely because the bipolarity had been one of power *and* ideologies. Globalism, which had made sense as long as any Communist expansion meant an addition to Soviet strength, could be explained in terms very understandable to Americans; that is, democracy versus dictatorship. But it was one thing to "fight communism" as long as there was only one communism to fight; when communism became fragmented, which sort were they to fight? Were all Communist states, because they were Communist, enemies of the United States? Or did the United States now have to distinguish among them, determining which was hostile, which friendly, which neutral—in short, which posed a true threat. More specifically, in these new circumstances, what changes in the distribution of power could America safely allow, and where, if anywhere, and against whom did it still have to draw "frontiers"? These questions were more difficult to answer than during the simple days of bipolarity because each situation would now confront policy makers with alternative policies, thereby arousing great debate and intense controversy. In addition, anticommunism would no longer be as useful a means of eliciting popular support because the United States might well be supporting one Communist state against another.

From Idealpolitik to Realpolitik

One crucial question the decline of anticommunism posed for the future conduct of American foreign policy, therefore, was whether, in the absence of anticommunism, the United States would "dirty" its hands by playing straight and unadorned power politics. When realpolitik was synonymous with idealpolitik, it had been easy to be a leader and organize various coalitions whose basic task was to push back when pushed. The state system's requirement to maintain the balance of power could be performed by the United States government so long as it could disguise from its own people what it was doing and pretend it was engaged in a noble task. But could a nation that has historically condemned power politics adapt its outlook and style to a world in which justifying foreign policy in terms of ideological crusades was outmoded; could it "play the game by no other name" in an increasingly multipolar world? More specifically, how could the United States, disabused of anticommunism and disenchanted with a world in which the forces of good could no longer crusade against the forces of evil, mobilize congressional and popular support for its foreign policy? Or would America, no longer believing it had an ideological mission, sway from occasional fits of moral passion and crusadism to moralistic isolationism or—if the latter were no longer possible in the late twentieth century—to a major withdrawal from the world? Would the country, having enjoyed its drug of anticommunism and the resulting "high" of global responsibility and exercise of world power, now swing to the "low" state of reaction and withdrawal?

The incoming administration of Richard Nixon in January 1969—which, after Nixon's resignation in 1974 because of the Watergate scandal, would become the Nixon-Ford administration—confronted a novel postwar situation: how to conduct foreign policy without a consensus. The administration thought it could substitute a policy based on the traditional logic of the state system. This dramatic shift away from a style that stemmed from the nation's domestic values and experiences to a balance-of-power rationale was somewhat surprising because Nixon, as U.S. representative, senator, and vice president, had been an exponent of virulent anticommunism, of the "illusion of American omnipotence," and of an inflexible moralism that rejected having anything to do with Communists lest one be tainted with an "un-American" virus. But as president, he and his national security adviser Henry Kissinger, a German-born Jewish immigrant and Harvard professor who became secretary of state in Nixon's second administration, rejected the traditional American justification for participating in foreign affairs. Indeed, the Nixon-Ford years might well be called the Kissinger era. Kissinger articulated and justified the Republican approach to foreign policy; personally carried out much of its private as well as public diplomacy; and provided an element of continuity amid the transfer of power from a disgraced president to his unelected, or appointed, successor. Kissinger so dominated these eight years that one wag noted that he was the only national security adviser and secretary of state ever served by two presidents. His diplomatic exploits earned him widespread admiration and popularity; he was frequently pictured in cartoons as "Super-Kraut," a pudgy figure decked out with a cape as he flew through the sky from one set of negotiations to another. His successors in Jimmy Carter's administration continued to feel his presence, not least because national security adviser Zbigniew Brzezinski, a Columbia University professor and one-time Harvard colleague of Kissinger, and Secretary of State Cyrus Vance, were constantly being compared with Kissinger—usually unfavorably.

The Kissinger Philosophy

The philosophy underlying American foreign policy during the Kissinger years from 1969 to 1977 began with the assumption that international politics was not a fight between the good side and the bad side. All states, Communist or non-Communist, had the right to exist and possessed legitimate interests. A nation, therefore, did not launch crusades against an adversary on the assumption that differences of interests represented a conflict of virtue and evil. The better part of wisdom was to learn to live with other states, to defend one's interests if encroached upon, but also to attempt to resolve differences and build on shared interests. International politics was not just conflict, but cooperation as well. Differences, admittedly, would not be easily or quickly reconciled; states' views of their interests were usually deeply held and not easily relinquished. Summit meetings were important as part of a negotiating process, but one summit could not solve all problems, and to raise false hopes that it would was to produce the cynicism and disillusionment that would endanger diplomacy itself. Good personal relations among leaders might smooth this process, but they were not a substitute for hard bargaining, and accords basically reflect the ratio of power between the nations that the leaders represent.

How should the United States deal with a Communist dictatorship whose values and practices it abhorred? The most the United States could expect was to influence its international behavior in a responsible direction; American power was too limited to transform another nation's domestic behavior, and to make agreements dependent on such a transformation would be counterproductive and raise tensions. American demands would be resisted, and this, in turn, would jeopardize accords on international issues that might otherwise have been resolvable. The United States was not omnipotent and had to abandon its habit of crusading to democratize adversaries. Negotiating with a Communist regime, such as that of the Soviet Union, was necessary if peace and security were to be preserved. The key, of course, was the balance of power, but it was necessary to try to accommodate the legitimate needs of the principal disturber of that peace. Power neutralizes countervailing power, and satisfying the interests of other great powers would be more likely to produce acceptance of the present international system than continued frustration and hostility to an international system in which they had little vested interest. No state could be completely satisfied, but it could be relatively satisfied.

Kissinger's view, then, concentrated on the powerful actors. Although he brought the rhetoric and style of American foreign policy more in line with the operational norms of the international system, there was also an essential continuity in policy. The Soviet-American balance remained the preoccupation; it was still the Soviet Union, as a great power, whose influence needed to be contained and behavior moderated. This unity of rhetoric and action—the explanation of U.S. policy in terms of power, balances, spheres of influence, prestige, national interests, and the limits of American power, as well as the specific rejection of ideological justifications and crusades—represented the "socialization" of American foreign policy by the state system. The United States now explained its actions on the international scene much as all great powers before it did in terms of the logic of the balance of power.

During its first two years, the Carter administration did not always share Kissinger's preoccupation with the balance of power and American-Soviet rivalry. Its concern was to lower America's profile in the world, to ensure that there would be "no more Vietnams," which it attributed to the global containment policy. Carter questioned whether this policy had not resulted from an exaggerated fear of the Soviet Union and had therefore been an overreaction. He asserted that his administration would not be driven by "an inordinate fear of communism." Indeed, even more fundamentally, the Carter approach to foreign policy questioned the entire postwar policy of his predecessors, both Democratic and Republican. He saw the war in Vietnam as the end product of not only containment but also of the whole "realist" approach. Was the critical problem not the immoral—or at best, amoral— "power politics" philosophy on which operational, as distinct from declaratory, American foreign policy since World War II had been based?

Indeed, Carter for a brief time embraced a new vision of a more "interdependent" world, which focused not on security issues but on economic or welfare issues; not on superpower competition but on closing the gulf between the rich and poor nations. He emphasized cooperation among nations seeking to advance collective human interests, not an international hierarchy based on power and the use of force, not conflict in which each nation acts primarily in terms of its national interest. By eliminating the Soviet Union as America's principal problem, he could reject "power politics"; by emphasizing lifting the world's poor and human rights, he embraced what he saw as America's historical moral mission. He needed only to continue the détente to keep international tensions low and achieve a series of arms control agreements as a prerequisite for changing American foreign policy.

The Decline of American Power and Need for Détente

The Nixon, Ford, and Carter administrations all pursued détente because changes in the United States and the state system made a relaxation of tensions necessary. Within the United States the change was that the nation had become weary of its foreign policy burdens. This mood, often portrayed in this post-Vietnam era as neoisolationist and anti-national security, was illustrated by the attacks on the "imperial presidency," by the 1973 War Powers Resolution, cuts in the defense budgets, and by restrictions on CIA covert operations. The president was to be restrained by a more assertive and watchful Congress; the freedom to use the instruments of overt and covert intervention abroad were to be limited. In the pre-Vietnam era of containment, Congress had rarely questioned the president's authority to use the armed forces or CIA to carry out U.S. policy. But after Vietnam, the criticisms of America's "global policeman" role were widespread and emphasis was placed on the nation's "limited power," suggesting a more restricted role in what was popularly regarded as the post-cold war era. Indeed, the Carter administration—coming to power shortly after the collapse of South Vietnam in 1975—thought the cold war was finished. Nixon and Gerald Ford were constrained by the public mood of neoisolationism, but Carter represented that mood until 1979. For Nixon and Ford, détente was therefore necessary until the nation could "recover its nerve" and once more play the leading role they felt was required to protect U.S. interests against Soviet expansion; for Carter, it was necessary because the United States was living in a more complex post-cold war era in which an activist anti-Soviet policy would needlessly rekindle the superpower conflict.

Another change, around 1970, was in the balance of power—a longer-term reason for détente. The Soviet Union had attained strategic parity. The balance between the two superpowers had long been between the U.S. Strategic Air Command (SAC), later supplemented by the navy's nuclear submarines, and the Red Army. The American bombers and missiles deterred the Soviet Union by threatening to destroy its cities. The Soviet Union gained its intercontinental capability and capacity to destroy the United States from its massive buildup that began after 1964. From the 1950s to the late 1960s, however, America's strategic power was balanced not by Moscow's bomber and missile force, which was relatively small, but by the Red Army. The powerful Soviet army, it was believed, could overrun Western Europe and quickly defeat North Atlantic Treaty Organization (NATO) forces.

The American-Soviet balance had been asymmetric: the United States had held strategic superiority and an intercontinental reach; the Soviet Union, conventional superiority and a regional reach. But by 1969 the balance had become symmetrical; the Soviet Union's strategic power had caught up with that of the United States, and the Soviets could now hold America's population, as well as Western Europe's, hostage. Moreover, this Soviet buildup showed no sign of slowing down, not even after the number of Soviet ICBMs had caught up with the number of American missiles. It was to keep on building.

Even during the period of U.S. strategic superiority, Moscow had been willing to risk limited challenges, such as in Berlin and Cuba, but it had remained cautious during confrontations; if there was resistance, it could retreat and call the challenge off. U.S. power had set limits to how far the Soviets felt they could push. But the strategic balance was now shifting, and the Soviet leaders had at the very least achieved parity; so a continuation of the containment policy by means of threats of force would become more risky and costly. The Soviet leaders had gained a new sense of confidence in their power. Their country was at last truly an equal of the United States. In 1945 the Soviet Union did not have the atomic bomb; much of the country lay in ruins. Even after the American atomic monopoly had been broken, the United States retained a decisive strategic superiority. As late as 1962 the Soviet Union was not strong enough to resist when the United States compelled it to pull its missiles out of Cuba. But only a quarter of a century after World War II, it had caught up. The Soviet Union now belonged to the most exclusive club in the world. The potential danger of this development was clarified when the Soviet foreign minister informed the world that no important issue anywhere could be resolved without the Soviet Union. In brief, the Soviet leaders were in a confident and assertive mood.

Closely related to this shift in strategic power was the Soviet Union's emergence as a global power. Although its leaders' ambitions might be worldwide—the Soviet Union saw itself as the nucleus of a new and more humane postcapitalist world, as well as a great power—its reach had been limited to Eurasia, and attempts to extend its power beyond Eurasia had been largely unsuccessful. The Congo and Cuba were painful reminders that the Soviet Union was not, like the United States, a country with a worldwide capacity to project its power. The Soviet Union had concluded from its experience in Cuba that strategic power paid off politically because it could be used not only to deter but also to intimidate and compel the adversary to retreat. The achievement of strategic parity with the United States was thus symbolically significant.

But, in addition to this growing strategic power, the Soviet Union had also engaged in a parallel massive conventional buildup, particularly of a modern surface navy and airlift capability. This meant that as its ability to neutralize America's nuclear force grew, its capacity to project its conventional power beyond Eurasia also grew. The Soviet naval buildup, which by the late 1970s had produced a navy that exceeded that of the United States in numbers of combat ships (although it did not yet have large U.S.-type aircraft carriers), was not needed for defense. Soviet allies were territorially contiguous, not spread out overseas as were those of the United States; nor was the Soviet Union dependent on imports of oil and other natural resources, as were all the Western allies. Would the Soviet Union, in these new circumstances, be content to expand its influence only on land and in nearby areas? Or would it, as a result of its new might, feel a confidence that had been absent before, act more boldly, take greater risks, and reopen old issues and challenge the United States in new areas farther away from the Soviet Union? Now that it had lost its strategic superiority, would the United States, by contrast, be more reluctant to react?

Kissinger compared the Soviet Union's emergence as a world power to Germany's appearance on the world scene in the early twentieth century. In both cases, the challengers were land powers. The symbols of their aspiration and determination to expand were the navies they built; nothing could have carried greater symbolic weight for Great Britain and the United States, the two greatest naval powers in their respective times. Germany's emergence and desire to be a world power with its overseas colonies resulted in World War I. How could the Soviet Union's newly gained power and its determination to pursue a *Weltpolitik,* or global policy, to achieve its "place in the sun" (as the Germans had called it) be managed peacefully so as not to threaten American security interests? Clearly, as a badge of its newly achieved equal status, Moscow also sought its overseas "colonies," basically Marxist-Leninist states that would become members of the Soviet "empire." As they had been for Germany, these colonies, usually of limited strategic value and needing to be subsidized economically, were geopolitically important as a symbol. Thus, the question of the Soviet Union's massive military buildup raised questions not just about the military balance and its stability but, more fundamentally, about its ultimate intentions and whether the emergence of a true "structure of peace," to use Nixon's phrase, were possible.

Managing the New Relationship

Nations whose power has declined normally adjust by reducing their commitments or by seeking new allies or greater contributions from current allies; they generally also seek to reduce threats to their interests by diplomacy. The United States did not curtail its obligations but sought to preserve them by its détente strategy. As a political means for managing the superpowers' adversarial relationship, this strategy sought to secure these interests at a lower level of tension and cost than those required by the policy of cold war confrontation and frequent crises. The American-Soviet balance would still be bipolar, but it would be somewhat more complex and fluid than in the earlier cold war era. But U.S. foreign policy was now explained differently: Nixon's predecessors, while also pursuing a balance-of-power policy, felt compelled to justify their policy as a crusade. From Truman on, U.S. presidents had frequently been trapped by their anti-Communist rhetoric and felt forced to be more inflexible and interventionist than perhaps they would have been. For twenty years they had been unable to abandon the fiction that Taiwan was China and to establish a formal diplomatic relationship with the real China on the mainland, the People's Republic. The Nixon-Kissinger balance was to include the PRC. Beijing could be used to get the Soviets to act with restraint and to show greater willingness to compromise if they wished to avoid closer Sino-American relations and cooperation against the Soviet Union. The Nixon tripolarity was a tactic devised to make the superpower bipolarity work more smoothly and securely.

Furthermore, the still fundamentally bipolar balance was to be supplemented by a network of agreements and a set of rules of mutual restraint beneficial to both powers. Bipolar competition was to be supplemented by agreements and rules profiting both, thereby presumably enhancing each country's stake in cooperation with the other. The key Kissinger word was *linkage.* If a series of agreements and understandings on matters such as arms control and trade could be arrived at, the more expansionist-minded Soviet Union, because of the benefits of these agreements and understandings, would gain a vested interest in good relations with the United States. While the Soviet Union was to be faced, as before, with continued parity and a strong American military, this "stick" was to be supplemented with enough "carrots" to make a restrained foreign policy more appealing. Indeed, military sanctions against the Soviet Union at a time of strategic parity was becoming riskier for the United States. So the offer of economic rewards for restraint or self-containment was particularly appealing to the Soviets.

There was another meaning to linkage. It meant that the various U.S.-Soviet issues would be linked together diplomatically. Progress on one front would be tied to progress on another; the Kremlin could not expect to make gains on one issue that interested it but refuse to meet American interests on others. If it did so, there would presumably be a penalty exacted by way of lack of progress on issues of interest to the Soviet Union or by withholding benefits Moscow was seeking. During the Nixon-Ford years linkage was often explicitly declared to exist; it was officially denied by the Carter administration (although it was on occasion pointed out that certain Soviet actions could not but affect American public opinion or congressional support for administration policies). Cooperation and mutual concessions were obviously preferable. The adversarial part of the relationship was to be balanced by the partnership element in a new adversary-partnership. The overall purposes were to lower tensions between the superpowers, to confront fewer crises, and to encourage diplomatic negotiations; the new policy did not mean an end of American-Soviet conflict and competition. A détente was not an entente cordiale.

For Kissinger (as for Brzezinski later, if not always for Carter and Vance), then, détente was not only a strategy selected to secure American interests at a lower level of tensions and costs but was also a continuation of containment at a time when the United States had lost its strategic superiority and its extensive role in world affairs was widely questioned by its citizens.

Détente was to achieve its purpose by exploiting the Sino-Soviet split and by using American technology and food as nonmilitary "weapons." It should be noted that this political-diplomatic strategy was not utopian; it did not assume that the Soviet Union had become a benign power or that the cold war was over. Détente was intended to be a realistic strategy for a time when, because of neoisolationism at home and the shift in power internationally, the United States was no longer in a position to compete as vigorously with the Soviet Union as in the days before the Vietnam War. Détente was the continuation of containment by other means.

Disengagement from Vietnam

Before the relationships among the United States, the Soviet Union, and China could be reshaped, the United States had to unburden itself of the Vietnam War. Vietnam was a drain on U.S. resources and a political albatross around the Nixon administration's neck. But Nixon's and Kissinger's perceptions of great-power relationships heavily influenced their thinking about acceptable terms for withdrawal. One course open to Nixon, which would have brought him popular acclaim, was to pull out all American forces immediately on the grounds that the United States had fulfilled long enough its obligations to defend Saigon. But in the president's view the central issue was not getting out of Vietnam, but *how* to get out.

The Nixon administration was determined neither to just withdraw or to accept any settlement that was tantamount to a defeat, namely, a coalition government in Saigon controlled by the Communists. Nixon believed that establishing détentes with the Soviet Union and China would not be feasible if America's prestige—reputation for power—were tattered. The president wanted to modify U.S. relations with the two largest Communist states, especially the Soviet Union, the more powerful of the two. Why should the Soviet Union, rapidly building up its strategic power, settle for parity and mutually acceptable peaceful coexistence if it sensed that America was weak and could be pushed around? Why should China tone down its revolutionary rhetoric and conduct a more traditional state-to-state diplomacy, and indeed move closer to the United States, if it could not count on American strength and determination to resist what it saw as Soviet attempts at hegemony in Asia? In short, the country had to "hang tough" in Vietnam to normalize relations with the Soviet Union and China.

Nixon and Kissinger therefore devised a twofold strategy. First, American ground troops were to be gradually withdrawn to cut the costs of the war and make further hostilities tolerable for the "silent majority," which Nixon felt was loyal, although fatigued, and would support him in an "honorable" ending of the war. But in addition to silencing his domestic critics, Nixon hoped the continued involvement of U.S. forces, especially in the air, would provide an incentive for Hanoi to negotiate an end to the war. This incentive would presumably be all the stronger if the president's strategy worked at home, that is, if it removed Vietnam as a principal issue in the next election and facilitated Nixon's reelection. Hanoi, then confronted with the prospect that the war could last longer than four more years, would have a reason to settle the war diplomatically. The second part of the president's policy was the "Vietnamization" of the war. South Vietnam's forces were to be trained better and supplied with modern arms so that they could bit by bit take over the ground fighting. This would counter the criticisms and pressures that had multiplied in Congress, on campuses, and elsewhere for faster troop withdrawals and for the abandonment of Saigon.

The danger inherent in the president's strategy was that the North Vietnamese would attack after American troops were withdrawn but before the South Vietnamese were ready to meet the enemy in battle. In March 1970 Cambodia's Prince Norodom Sihanouk, who had long tolerated the Communist troops and supply lines in his country, was overthrown by an anti-Vietnamese military regime that wanted Communist troops out of Cambodia. The Communists moved toward the Cambodian capital to unseat the new government. Nixon decided to intervene, which reignited domestic dissension. After four demonstrating students at Kent State University were shot to death by Ohio National Guardsmen, many campuses erupted, and a number of colleges and universities were completely shut down. Protesters once again turned out for peaceful mass demonstrations in Washington and in other cities. The reaction to U.S. policy in Cambodia made it clear that it would be foolhardy for the president to repeat such an action.

Saigon's army unfortunately remained the key to the success of the president's strategy. In the spring of 1972, with the U.S. army withdrawn from the battlefield, North Vietnam launched an unexpected large-scale attack across the demilitarized zone between North Vietnam and South Vietnam. The South Vietnamese army performed poorly and only American air support staved off even worse losses.

Nixon was therefore in a quandary on the eve of a summit conference in Moscow to advance détente. The Soviet Union had supplied Hanoi with modern arms, and, whether it knew the date of the North Vietnamese offensive, Nixon thought the USSR should have restrained its ally. As a great power, the Soviet Union must have known that a major South Vietnamese defeat would be humiliating to its adversary on the eve of vital negotiations from which Moscow had as much to gain as Washington. The president was unwilling to negotiate under the shadow of defeat.

With Vietnamization in danger, Nixon "re-Americanized" the war by ordering extensive bombing of the North and blockading North Vietnam's ports with mines. The aim was to stop the flow of Soviet and Chinese supplies. Because the war was now a conventional one, dependent on oil and heavy weapons and large amounts of ammunition, air power might be more effective than it was during guerrilla operations. Simultaneously, Nixon also offered Hanoi just about all it could reasonably expect: the complete withdrawal of all American forces from Vietnam within four months if all prisoners of war were returned and an internationally supervised cease-fire. The Communists could keep their forces in the South—a significant concession previously offered only in secret talks. Equally important, the president did not insist on the survival of Nguyen Van Thieu's government. He specifically said that the United States' withdrawal "would allow negotiations and a political settlement between the Vietnamese themselves." This new set of proposals provided a concrete and serious basis for negotiations. But Hanoi rejected the offer. It appeared to want the president to do the one thing he refused to do—guarantee Communist control in Saigon. His proposal, in fact, had seemed to suggest that the North Vietnamese should do this job for themselves, if they could.

The North Vietnamese also faced a dilemma. Despite the heavy bombing and blockade, the Soviet Union had gone ahead with the summit meeting. China no longer opposed a negotiated settlement of the war. Moscow and Beijing both gave priority to their relationships with Washington. Hanoi was politically isolated. Yet the North Vietnamese leaders had sought their goal of a unified Vietnam for so long, paid such a high price for it, and been so often cheated out of the fulfillment of their dream by their adversaries that they were suspicious of Nixon's offer and resentful of the declining Soviet and Chinese support.

But a month before the U.S. presidential election, Hanoi, probably fearing that Nixon's reelection might make him less accommodating, signaled its willingness to accept something less than a total victory. By late October Hanoi had negotiated a tentative Indochina settlement. The terms included an internationally supervised cease-fire that would halt all American bombing and mining and bring about withdrawal of all U.S. forces within two months; separate future cease-fires were expected in Laos and Cambodia. Prisoners of war would be exchanged. A series of mixed political commissions, composed of elements from the Viet Cong, the Saigon government, and neutralists, would then be established to work out a new South Vietnamese political order leading to a new constitution and the election of a new government. Provisions and personnel were to be supplied on a one-to-one basis for both sides.

The Nixon administration felt it had achieved an "honorable peace." The North Vietnamese, after having declared for years that the Thieu government would have to go as a precondition for a cease-fire, now accepted Thieu as the leader of the government faction. Thieu remained in control of a sizable army and large police forces with which he administered most of the country and all the urban centers, leaving only minor areas and a small percentage of the population under the control of the Viet Cong and the approximately 145,000 North Vietnamese troops. The Thieu faction therefore seemed to have a good chance to compete politically and militarily with the Communists after the fighting ended. Thieu stalled against this tentative October 1972 settlement because the United States had accepted the presence of North Vietnam's troops in areas of the South from which U.S. and South Vietnamese troops had been unable to dislodge them. Although Thieu could object, he held no veto. The end of fighting in the Vietnam War came in January 1973 for the United States. The administration could now focus its primary attention on improving relations with China and the Soviet Union, and the United States would no longer pour its resources into a war that deeply divided the country.

Détente with China

When the Nixon administration came into office in January 1969, the United States had no official relationship with the People's Republic of China. The Chinese were opposed to resuming relations with the United States as long as Washington recognized the Nationalist regime on Taiwan, which they regarded as PRC territory. But Nixon recognized the changing circumstances and considered it vital to bring mainland China into the diplomatic constellation. Calling the regime by its chosen name, the People's Republic of China, ending regular patrolling of the Taiwan Straits by the Seventh Fleet, and lifting trade and visitation restrictions against China, Nixon opened the way for a personal visit to China. This visit served in part to symbolize to the American public and Congress, long hostile to dealing with Beijing, the dramatic shift of American policy and in part to begin clearing away mutual misperceptions and defining some of the more outstanding issues and problems impeding improved Sino-American relations.

Therefore, it would be a mistake to speak of détente only in terms of the relationship between the United States and the Soviet Union. There were two détentes—one with the Soviet Union and one with China. Indeed, it may be argued that détente with China was the greater U.S. achievement because of the tremendous hostility that had existed between the two countries since 1950. At least with the Soviet Union, the earlier period of high tension, confrontation, and recurring crises, particularly since the Cuban Missile Crisis, had been balanced by increasing cooperation in arms control. In any event, there can be little doubt that détente with China was a prerequisite to détente with the Soviet Union because by bringing China into the superpower balance the Soviet Union's incentive to improve relations with the United States would increase.

The Nixon administration could exploit the rivalry between the Soviet Union and the People's Republic of China because relations between these two allies had become deeply embittered. The Soviets had too long dominated the Communist world. As the capital of the first Communist-controlled nation, Moscow had since the early 1920s controlled the international Communist movement and formulated its policies. After World War II it had established control over the states of Eastern Europe. Of these states, only Yugoslavia was controlled not by Moscow but by its indigenous Communist party. When Yugoslavia resisted Stalin's efforts to impose control, it was ejected from Stalin's empire. The birth of Communist China—another state controlled by the indigenous party—therefore represented a real problem for the Soviets. The Chinese leadership, while Communist, was like that of Yugoslavia, highly nationalistic and therefore not likely to subordinate itself to the Kremlin. The potential for a schism was therefore built into the relationship. That the leaders of these two huge Communist states shared an ideological framework did not dampen their growing policy differences toward the United States and the Third World—with Moscow generally taking a more accommodationist attitude and Beijing a more hard-line one—but accented their rift. Precisely because ideology defined the general purposes of the movement and provided the framework through which events in the world are analyzed, it became a divisive factor. Moscow had long been the Communist "Rome," and the ruler in Moscow therefore became the Communist "pope" when he assumed power. If an ideology claimed to represent the truth, there could only be one correct interpretation and application of the doctrine. No ideological-theological movement can tolerate two popes. A schism—and a fight for the leadership of the movement—was therefore inevitable. Hence Moscow denounced Mao for having deserted Marxism-Leninism and, by fragmenting what had been a united Communist front against the United States, for having aided the devil's cause, imperialism. Denouncing the actions of the Soviet Communist party as "Khrushchevism without Khrushchev," the Chinese charged that the party had been seized from within by "revisionists" who were in fact capitalists, cooperating with Washington to contain China! Beijing called for the overthrow of the Soviet leaders.

The Sino-Soviet schism was thus, by the late 1960s, dramatically visible. The epithets hurled between Beijing and Moscow reached a ferocity unknown since the early days of the cold war. The Soviets called Mao "Hitler" and compared the Chinese with the Mongol hordes who overran Russia a millennium earlier; and the Chinese talked about the "Soviet revisionist clique" as a "dictatorship of the German fascist type," and quoted Karl Marx as saying that Russia's aim had been, and always would be, world hegemony. As the struggle against the Soviet Union intensified, Mao and his followers were more careful to avoid conflict with the United States. During Vietnam, for example, China continuously counseled Hanoi that revolutions had to be self-sufficient; it repeatedly stated that only an American attack on China would precipitate Beijing's intervention. In brief, North Vietnam should not and could not count on active Chinese help to help defeat American forces in South Vietnam. Rhetorically, Mao's policy was militantly anti-American, but in action it was restrained. (U.S. policy makers never realized this, however, and thinking of the Korean War analogy, did not dare send U.S. forces into North Vietnam, the organizer of the war in the South.) Thus, the incoming Nixon administration had a grand opportunity to exploit the Sino-Soviet conflict, to bring about closer Sino-U.S. relations, and to end a hostile twenty-year relationship that had been strategically very harmful, if not disastrous, for the United States.

U.S. Chance to Outflank the Soviets

The Sino-Soviet split gave the United States an opportunity to bring pressure to bear on the Soviet Union; the clearly implied message to the Soviet leadership was that their obstinacy would compel Washington to align itself more closely with Beijing. To the Soviets, already fearful of China, such an alignment had to be a nightmare. It might encourage China to be more hostile, as well as renew tension on the Soviet Union's other front in Europe. Similarly, Beijing had for years complained loudly about alleged American-Soviet collusion to isolate and contain China. But as the Soviet Union began to move huge numbers of troops eastward to defend its frontier with China, and on occasion let a rumor slip about the possibility of an attack on China, Beijing—apparently convinced that Nixon was pulling out of Vietnam—was interested in detaching Washington from any possible cooperation with Moscow against China. Even more important, better relations with the United States would presumably restrain the Soviet Union from attacking China, for the Kremlin could not be sure that Washington would not support Beijing in such a contingency.

In the Shanghai communiqué released at the end of Nixon's historic visit, the United States and China declared their opposition to the hegemony of any power in Asia; they were clearly referring to the Soviet Union. Thus Sino-American relations began despite Taiwan. The Communist position had long been that Beijing would not establish any relationship with Washington before official U.S. ties with Taiwan were cut. Such ties with the rival claimant to power was, Beijing claimed, interference in a domestic matter. That, in these circumstances, the People's Republic would reverse itself and sign the Shanghai communiqué constituted evidence of its fear of the Soviet Union; the eagerness to attract China into an anti-Soviet coalition was reflected in America's declaration that it would gradually remove all its forces and installations from Taiwan and not interfere in a "peaceful settlement" between the Communists and Nationalists of their differences, including the future of Taiwan, which was acknowledged to be a "part of China."

President Nixon's trip to Beijing in 1972 symbolized a dramatic change in Sino-American relations, ending once and for all the irrationality of a situation in which the United States for almost a quarter-century had ignored the existence of the world's most populous country, a nation with great potential power, a significant stake in Asia's future, and an ideological rival of the Soviet Union. And just as Washington, during the 1950s, had feared the Sino-Soviet coalition, and Beijing, during the 1960s, had frequently pointed to an alleged Soviet-American collusion to isolate China, so Moscow now became apprehensive of closer Sino-American relations because it gave the United States a persuasive lever—if skillfully used—in its negotiations with the Kremlin. The American shift of policy from Taiwan to Beijing was long overdue. Domestic politics had too long blocked a rational adjustment and exploitation of the Sino-Soviet conflict, a conflict in which tensions may rise or fall from time to time, but one that is likely to continue despite leadership changes in both countries. Their quarrels reflect differences of interest more profound than mere differences of personalities.

Indeed, the succession struggle in China and the change in the presidency in the United States did not stop progress toward full normalization. On January 1, 1979, the People's Republic of China and the United States exchanged diplomatic recognition and ambassadors. This was followed in March by an official visit to Washington by China's apparent strong man, Deputy Premier Deng Xiaoping. The timing of this last step toward normalization had come from Beijing, which confronted large modern Soviet forces along its 4,500-mile northern frontier with increasingly obsolete weapons. At the same time, it looked to the West to help it modernize everything from building hotel chains and steel mills to exploring China's enormous estimated oil reserves. For the United States, the final shift from Taiwan to Beijing meant ending diplomatic recognition of Nationalist China and abrogating the Taiwan defense treaty, requiring the withdrawal of the last American military personnel stationed in Taiwan. In return, Beijing appeared to accept the American position that this problem be resolved peacefully, although it expressed anger at the United States for continuing to supply the Nationalists with weapons to defend themselves against a possible Communist invasion.

The likelihood of invasion was not great anyway. For one thing, Beijing lacked the air and naval capacity to cross 100 miles of water to launch such an attack. More important, however, Beijing, having turned primarily to the United States and Japan to help it modernize, would not risk taking an action that would alienate both of these countries, especially the United States, which it also needed to balance Soviet power. That an invasion of Taiwan would be politically counterproductive was further underlined by the fact that Tokyo (which had recognized Beijing earlier than Washington) maintained very close and profitable commercial relations with Taiwan, and the United States expected to do the same. Having long insisted on a peaceful resolution of Communist-Nationalist differences, the United States could easily resort to force and defend Taiwan should Beijing some day violate the understanding about the peaceful resolution of this problem.

With recognition of the mainland came new directions in trade. Although the United States at first did not sell arms to Beijing in order not to provoke Moscow, it was willing to let its European allies sell China arms, such as jet fighters and antiaircraft and antitank missiles. The United States limited its own sales to dual-purpose equipment such as radar, trucks, and transport planes, which could be put either to civilian or military use. Ronald Reagan's administration, in an effort to forge stronger links with China against the Soviet Union, offered to sell Beijing arms. As China had limited funds to buy arms on a large scale, the significance of this move was more political than military. It signaled to the Soviets the growing Chinese-American links. The United States and China also cooperated in jointly operating an electronic intelligence-gathering station in China to monitor Soviet missile tests.

The Implications of Sino-American Relations

For the United States, hostility between the two largest Communist states was preferable to a united Sino-Soviet bloc. A strong China, dividing the Soviet Union's attention between East and West, benefited NATO. Washington, therefore, had a vested interest in supporting the new post-Mao Chinese leadership, which opposed Moscow and looked toward the West and Japan. Fundamentally, the United States was taking advantage of its adversaries' dilemma and resorting to the time-honored tactic of "divide and rule." In the past, America always had to choose between China and Japan: when the United States was friendly to China before World War II, Japan became the adversary; and when Nationalist China collapsed, the United States became an ally of Japan and enemy of the new China. Now the possibility of closer Washington-Beijing-Tokyo cooperation appeared increasingly possible. The new China connection, however, was not without risk. The danger was that the United States would align itself too closely with China and that such an alignment would be regarded as unfriendly and provocative by Moscow. The same would be true for Beijing if, in seeking to improve its relationship of détente with the Soviet Union, Washington pulled too close to the Kremlin.

One dramatic example of this dilemma occurred shortly after the United States had officially recognized the PRC and its deputy prime minister toured America vehemently denouncing Moscow. Beijing, concerned with what it saw as increasing Soviet-Vietnamese collaboration to the south—which it interpreted to be part of a growing Soviet influence and attempt to encircle China—struck at Vietnam. Angered by Vietnam's expulsion of almost 200,000 ethnic Chinese, by border conflicts, and especially by Hanoi's signing of a friendship treaty with the Soviets in late 1977 (followed by Vietnam's invasion of China's friend, Cambodia), China decided to "teach Vietnam a lesson" by crossing the border and inflicting heavy casualties. The resulting border war demonstrated once again that a common ideology was not enough to prevent conflict and that nationalism was as divisive a force within the Communist sphere as in the rest of the world. The danger for the United States was the possibility of a Soviet military reaction. An attempt "to teach China a lesson," if it was more than a limited incursion into China, could affect American interests and draw the United States more deeply into the Sino-Soviet quarrel. Moscow already saw Washington's normalization of its relationship with Beijing as collusion and tacit support of China's military action, although Carter explicitly opposed this invasion of Vietnam, as he had opposed Hanoi's earlier invasion of Cambodia. Thus, the possible advantages for the United States of "playing the China card" against Moscow were matched by the dangers of China's "playing its American card"; and the possibility of Moscow's someday "playing its China card" against America could not be completely excluded. Yet on the whole, the United States and the People's Republic of China were driven together by their respective security interests and shared fear of rapidly growing Soviet power. Geopolitics prevailed over ideology. From the American perspective, the world was obviously less threatening with China as a friend.

Arms Control as the Centerpiece of Détente

Arms control over the years gained increasing importance in relations between the United States and the Soviet Union, and for very good reasons. The two powers have been rivals since the closing days of World War II, and their rivalry has reached into almost every region of the world. As a result, profound distrust and mutual fear, if not hatred, have characterized their relationship. The arms race was an expression of their deep political differences. The danger was, of course, that the arms race, fueled by continuing conflict, would at some point spill over into a nuclear war. One way each side has tried to avoid such a cataclysmic end is to build up its nuclear forces as a defense; the other is to meet and negotiate agreements that reduce the chances of war breaking out. But, as the basic conflict continued and nuclear weapons were unlikely to be abolished, the next best tactic was to "manage" the nuclear arms balance by instituting arms control agreements.

During the 1960s arms control had dealt largely with issues such as the establishment of a "hot line" between the Kremlin and the White House for quick communication in a crisis, a limited ban on testing nuclear devices, and, through the United Nations, an agreement on the nonproliferation of nuclear weapons. In the 1970s these negotiations shifted to each side's strategic forces. Indeed, the Strategic Arms Limitation Talks (SALT) stood at the center of détente. More specifically, SALT had four objectives. The first was to make the arms race more predictable by establishing the numbers of strategic weapons for each side. It was hoped that such knowledge would reduce the anxiety of the arms race; uncertainty and the fear that the opponent might be gaining superiority in military strength fueled competition. The Soviets had begun a steady, large-scale military buildup in strategic and conventional weapons after the Cuban Missile Crisis. By the time Nixon became president, the Soviets had overtaken the United States in numbers of deployed missiles, and the missile production continued. Normally, a new arms race would have been likely. But given the antimilitary mood in the United States following the Vietnam War and congressional hostility to increased defense spending, the pressure on the Nixon administration to negotiate mutually accepted ceilings on missiles was intense. The alternative would be a huge missile gap in favor of the Soviet Union.

SALT's second aim was to ensure parity. The assumption was that if the two sides had approximately the same number of warheads and bombs, neither side could launch a crippling strike against the other. More specifically, parity was a condition in which no matter who struck first, the attacked side would still have the capability to retaliate and destroy the aggressor. When each power possessed missiles with single warheads, even with reasonably accurate warheads, a two-to-one superiority was needed to launch a devastating first strike. Short of such a superiority, the United States and the Soviet Union would each retain a sufficient retaliatory capability to assure the continuation of deterrence.

The third purpose of arms control was to reduce threats to each side's deterrent forces. By the early 1970s, the deterrent balance was threatened not only by the continuing Soviet strategic growth but also by technological innovations that were widely believed in the United States to be undermining the stability of American-Soviet deterrence. One matter of concern was the development of a new defensive weapon. The Soviets had deployed antiballistic missiles (ABMs) around Moscow and were thought to be working on a second-generation ABM for possible nationwide deployment. If ABMs could shoot down enough incoming American ICBMs and reduce the destruction inflicted on the Soviet Union to an "acceptable" level of a few million casualties, the ABMs would undermine U.S. deterrence, which depended upon its capacity to impose "assured destruction."

In turn, this defensive weapon stimulated the United States to improve its offensive technology, specifically, the development of the multiple independently targeted reentry vehicle (MIRV). MIRV is an ICBM with multiple warheads that can separate in flight, change trajectory, and fly independently to assigned and dispersed targets. The advantage of MIRV was that the large numbers of warheads would be able to overcome any ABM defense, meaning that the United States would still be able to destroy Soviet society in a retaliatory blow.

But MIRVs also threatened to destabilize the deterrent balance. It was one thing for the United States and Soviet Union to possess missiles with single warheads, even if those warheads were reasonably accurate. If side A had 1,000 missiles and side B 1,400, B still did not have the two-to-one superiority it was assumed necessary to destroy A's missiles. But it was another if both possessed the same number of missiles—let us say, 1,000—but A's missiles could carry ten warheads and B's could carry only three, the ratio of warheads would be greater than three to one. This would permit A with only 200 missiles to launch a first strike to disarm the latter. Multiplying the warheads and providing them with greater accuracy thus undermined the stability of the nuclear balance because it placed a premium on attack. Whichever side got in the first blow was likely to win because it might be able to prevent any major retaliation.

This was a potentially dangerous situation. When both sides possessed such counterforce weapons (weapons aimed at the other side's weapons), their mutual fear of a preventive war, and especially of a preemptive strike during a crisis, would make both jittery. Each would fear that if the other struck first, it would be unable to retaliate with sufficient force to destroy the other; the very vulnerability of the opponent's forces, therefore, provided an incentive to attack first. Each would feel it had to "use them or lose them." This was particularly so if the preempting side possessed ABMs. An ABM defense might not be able to cope with a full-fledged attack; but it might be able to limit the damage from a crippled second strike attack.

The fourth reason for SALT was that it was necessary for détente. On the one hand, a failure to arrive at an agreement or at least to continue the SALT dialogue was bound to have a deteriorating effect on their overall political relationship. On the other, only a relaxation of tensions could provide the diplomatic atmosphere that would enable the two nuclear giants to arrive at an arms agreement that would leave them feeling more secure, sanctify the strategic parity between them, and avoid new costly offensive and defensive arms races. SALT, in brief, became a symbol of détente. With it, détente seemed to blossom; without it, it seemed to fade. Success or failure to achieve a SALT agreement became the barometer of U.S.-Soviet relations.

The first set of agreements, known as SALT I, was signed by President Nixon and Soviet Communist party leader Leonid Brezhnev in May 1972. SALT I had taken two and a half years to negotiate and incorporated two agreements. The first, a treaty, limited each nation's ABMs to 200 launchers, later to be reduced to 100 each (the United States built none because such a small number of ABMs could not prevent a catastrophic strike). For all practical purposes, by eliminating the ABM, the two powers ensured that their deterrent retaliatory forces would be able to retaliate while also avoiding a renewed offensive arms race in response to large-scale defensive deployments.

The second agreement, a five-year interim agreement, essentially froze offensive missiles at the number each side possessed at the time. This meant 2,358 ICBMs and SLBMs (submarine-launched ballistic missiles) for the Soviet Union (of which 300 were very large missiles, the SS-9s) and 1,710 ICBMs and SLBMs for the United States. Bombers, in which the United

States had in 1972 a numerical superiority over the Soviet Union of three to one, were not included in the accords. Given the American lead in MIRVs, the accord on offensive weapons meant that the larger number of Soviet missile launchers was matched by the large number of U.S. bombers plus the technological superiority of American missiles and their greater number of warheads. Each side retained the right to improve its weapons within the overall quantitative agreement, thus preserving parity (or, officially, *sufficiency*). Although no on-site inspection to check for violations was agreed on, both sides pledged not to interfere with each other's reconnaissance or spy satellites, which would be the principal means to check compliance with both accords. What the freeze meant was that neither side could launch a crippling first strike against the other.

Basically, SALT I was a trade-off: a freeze on Soviet missiles against low numbers of ABMs. The United States wanted to stop the ever-growing number of Soviet ICBMs; the Soviets, fearful that the American ABM would be technologically superior and more effective than their own, wanted to halt a U.S. deployment before it started. Moscow at first offered only an ABM agreement, but Nixon resisted; he would not sign a defensive arms agreement without an offensive arms agreement. How could he limit the numbers of ABMs deployed by the United States without knowing how many ICBMs the Soviet Union intended to produce? The defensive and offensive arms races were inextricably intertwined. There could be no missile ceilings without an accompanying ceiling on defensive weapons (an argument that Moscow was to pick up and use against the United States after President Reagan in 1983 proposed a space-based U.S. defense against missiles).

SALT I was to be the beginning of a process, a continuing dialogue and effort to control the arms competition; the offensive freeze was to be a prelude to a more lasting agreement. The two nuclear giants also appeared to recognize their special obligation for the preservation of peace by complementing SALT I with certain standards of behavior. They pledged to avoid confrontations, to exercise mutual restraint, and to reject efforts to gain unilateral advantages.

SALT II was therefore regarded as critical to a long-term effort to stabilize mutual deterrence. President Ford, after Nixon's resignation, arrived at the guidelines for SALT II with Brezhnev at a 1974 meeting in Vladivostok. This time each side would have an equal number of strategic weapons: 2,400 missiles and bombers, 1,320 of these delivery systems could have MIRVs. Despite this broad agreement, it was seven years after SALT I that Brezhnev and Carter signed SALT II. It was a complex series of agreements, carefully balancing off the varying interests and different force structures of the two powers. But SALT II became controversial in the United States.

Proponents said it provided for some reduction of strategic launchers from the Vladivostok ceiling of 2,400 to 2,250. This change meant that the

Soviets would have to reduce their force levels by about 150 older missiles. This set a precedent for SALT III, whose main purpose was to bring about a major reduction of strategic forces. Critics noted, however, that the SALT II ceilings were so high that it was the very opposite of any reasonable interpretation of the words *arms control;* other critics asserted that, despite the equal numbers provided for both sides, the treaty would give the Soviet Union strategic superiority because Soviet missiles were considerably larger, could carry more and bigger warheads, and were more accurate. The Soviets, therefore, would acquire a sizable first-strike force that by the mid-1980s would be capable of destroying up to 90 percent of America's ICBMs. A "window of vulnerability" was opening over the American deterrent.

Defenders of SALT II argued that it could not be expected to undo what technology and earlier political decisions had done. For example, having developed MIRV to overcome possible extensive Soviet ABM deployment, the United States continued with MIRV, even after Moscow had agreed to the virtual elimination of ABM. That decision came back to haunt the United States. The Soviet Union's 1,400 land-based missiles would not be a threat to the 1,000-Minuteman force if each Soviet missile possessed only one warhead. U.S. vulnerability stemmed from the combination of big Soviet missile launchers with the large number of warheads they could carry. At best, SALT could reduce the consequence of this development, and it attempted to do so by limiting the number of Soviet land-based MIRVs and the number of warheads they could carry, especially the SS-18 (the successor to the SS-9), which could carry upwards of thirty warheads. Still, both liberal and conservative critics scored points—liberals, because SALT II was not a step toward major reductions, conservatives because the 300 SS-18 missiles with ten warheads per missile and the more than 300 SS-19 missiles with six warheads per missile *each* carried potentially more warheads and total megatonnage than the *total* American ICBM force. Each therefore posed a potentially formidable threat to Minuteman's survivability and America's deterrent capability.

SALT II's supporters asserted that the treaty in fact would permit the United States to undertake programs that would reduce the vulnerability of American deterrence. The treaty allowed the United States to deploy 200 new land-based MX missiles which, because of their planned mobility, decreased the likelihood of their being destroyed in a Soviet first strike. Also, because it was larger than the Minuteman and could carry ten large, accurate warheads, the MX gave the United States a counterforce capability. Additionally, it could deploy twenty extremely accurate, long-range, subsonic, air-launched cruise missiles (ALCMs) on some B-52s at a time when the Soviets did not have a comparable ALCM. Finally, the United States also could proceed with the replacement of its older Polaris submarines with the new Trident submarines, each with twenty-four missile tubes (as opposed to sixteen on the older submarines); the Trident I missile, with a range of more than 4,000 miles, would be placed in some Poseidon submarines as well, thus giving U.S. nuclear missile submarines a far vaster range of ocean in which to hide. In the meantime, testing of the more accurate Trident II, with a range of more than 6,000 miles, could proceed.

The primary debate about SALT II was between the administration and its conservative critics and revolved around two main issues. The first was whether the real vulnerability of U.S. ICBMs was as great as the 90 percent theoretical vulnerability the critics claimed. An attack on the U.S. deterrent force would have to hit simultaneously the ICBMs, SLBMs, and bombers that compose the American triad. Even if all ICBMs were destroyed, they represented only about 25 percent of U.S. strategic power. The two other elements had an enormous retaliatory capability of their own, which was growing. Would any Kremlin leader take the chance of launching a first strike, gambling that Soviet forces could destroy a sufficient number of U.S. deterrent forces so that they would no longer be able to inflict overwhelming losses on the Soviet population? Would the Soviets, as Carter's defense secretary, Harold Brown, said, gamble on this "cosmic roll of the dice"?

The administration said no, but the critics feared the worst. The Soviets, they claimed, were driving for strategic superiority and rejecting parity. Their force development testified to their commitment to a first-strike capability, not a second-strike or retaliatory capability. The Soviets, they asserted, not only rejected the belief that nuclear war was unthinkable but also articulated a strategy of fighting a nuclear war and winning it. In the final analysis, the defenders and critics of SALT II differed most about how aggressive and ruthless the Soviets were. Proponents pointed to the unwillingness of the Soviet leadership to take great risks, precisely to avoid a possible clash with the United States. Conservative critics minimized the record, insisting that the Soviets were ruthless, determined to achieve global domination, and that for the first time they had the power with which to pressure the Western powers and even risk an attack upon the United States, whose deterrent forces the critics maintained were vulnerable.

The second issue was the Soviet Union itself. If the Soviets had not invaded Afghanistan, Carter might have gained the Senate's consent for SALT II, the prerequisite for deep reductions in SALT III. A majority of the American people and senators favored the treaty, but not the two-thirds of the Senate required for ratification. The invasion led the president temporarily to withdraw the treaty from Senate consideration. For several years, Carter had argued that SALT was so important that the negotiations ought to continue and that, when concluded, SALT II should be ratified despite repeated Soviet efforts to expand their influence. But the brazenness of the Soviet use of force in Afghanistan led the president to resort to the Kissinger-like linkage he had consistently rejected and that his conservative critics had long demanded. In the final analysis, it was Soviet behavior—the continued military buildup and the meddling in the Third World—that killed the treaty. Concern about this behavior had reinforced the more specific fears about a Soviet first strike. The growing American disillusionment with détente also led to the collapse of Kissinger's other weapon, the economic one. From the Soviet perspective, the failure of détente to yield arms control and trade benefits reinforced their determination to seek unilateral advantages. This was a recipe for cold war II.

Trade and Technology as Incentives for Soviet Self-Containment

In the early days of détente American policy makers were willing to fortify the incentives for Soviet political and military restraint with economic help. The Soviet economy as it entered the 1970s was in serious trouble. After rapid advancement in the 1950s and early 1960s, its 5 percent growth rate headed down to 2 percent by the early 1970s. The economic decline was particularly notable in those branches of industry associated with the second industrial revolution: computers, microelectronics, and petrochemicals. In short, the Soviet Union was behind and falling further behind the West in those industries that were most important for economic growth. The implications of this decline could not be ignored; it damaged the Soviet Union's appeal as a Socialist state, hampered its ability to compete with the United States, and potentially threatened its future superpower status.

Even in agriculture the growth in production had fallen sharply below expectations and official plans. Workers on the land, like workers in the factory, were far behind their American counterparts in per capita production. The Soviet Union's continued inability to provide a balanced diet—indeed, in some years just to avoid widespread hunger—was not just the result of poor weather, but of the ideologically determined organization of an agrarian economy administered by a rigid bureaucracy. By contrast, the small private plots that peasants were allowed to own produced much of the Soviet Union's poultry, pork, vegetables, and other staples. Just as the regime was failing to live up to its promise of more consumer goods, it was falling short of its goal of a more nutritious and varied diet, including more meat. During the 1970s, the Soviet workplace was characterized by high absenteeism, drunkenness, corruption, and shoddy production. The Soviet Union was also the only industrial society in which the peacetime life expectancy of males was declining and infant mortality rising.

Brezhnev could not forget that Nikita Khrushchev's promises of a higher standard of living had played a large part in his fall from power. He had raised popular expectations and then failed to meet them; the same thing could happen to Brezhnev. In a system where the leadership is determined to maintain a monopoly on political power and control, it seeks popular approval—legitimacy—by providing multiple social benefits at low costs: jobs, housing, health care, retirement benefits, and similar social services. The Soviet standard of living may not be high by Western standards, but as long as it improves gradually, the regime can claim to be fulfilling its aim of ameliorating the lives of its citizens. Conversely, a decline has serious implications. The Kremlin had to look no further than Poland. In 1970 the poor state of the Polish economy and worker dissatisfaction with food shortages and a lack of consumer goods had led to riots in several cities and the collapse of the government, which, even in a Communist-controlled state, had to be replaced. (Similar unrest occurred in 1980-1981.)

Soviet concerns about their ailing economy and falling behind in the scientific-technological revolution presented the Kremlin with two choices: to look toward the West for a "technological fix" to help stimulate the economy or attempt a basic structural reform of its highly centralized and rigidly bureaucratized system. The Soviet leadership chose Western technology, machinery, food, and the proffered Western credit to buy them as the only recourse. Structural reform was rejected because it was not only antithetical to the regime's basic ideological beliefs about private property, the profit motive, and free market, but it ran contrary to the deeply vested interests of the governmental bureaucracies committed to central planning, a command economy, and self-preservation. Decentralization of authority—devolving authority to factory and farm managers and their work forces—was judged as too risky because it might threaten the party's control of political power. Importation of Western goods and food was less risky than such a fundamental reform. Trade with the United States, with its scale of production, high technology that the Soviets envied, and agricultural abundance, was especially desirable to Moscow since it preferred dealing with its principal adversary. Because it had little to sell the United States, it offered to let Americans develop and exploit the huge Soviet deposits of raw materials, especially in Siberia; the American capital to help finance this extraction would presumably be repaid in oil, natural gas, and other mineral resources in the future. The Soviets also looked to the United States for food in years of shortages, which occurred more and more frequently.

The Nixon-Ford administration believed these economic problems would give the United States leverage. Trade obviously was profitable for American industry and agriculture, but the main reason for permitting it was political. American productivity, it was hoped, would provide a powerful material reinforcement for a Soviet foreign policy of restraint and accommodation made necessary by the desire to prevent closer Sino-American "collusion," to achieve strategic arms agreements to stabilize mutual deterrence, and to gain American recognition of Soviet parity and equal status with the United States. Kissinger put it negatively: "Economic relations cannot be separated from the political context. Clearly, we cannot be asked to reward hostile conduct with economic benefits even if in the process we deny ourselves commercially profitable opportunities." But Kissinger's idea of using economic means to achieve political purposes was undermined by the Senate, which approved offering the Soviets trade and credits on the condition (specified in an amendment offered by Senator Henry Jackson and Representative Charles Vanik) that Moscow would allow more Soviet Jews to emigrate. Considering the amendment an intervention in its domestic affairs, the Soviet Union rejected the trade agreement. No great power—let alone the Soviet Union, which claimed to be a nation in which class distinctions and religious and other forms of prejudice no longer existed—would publicly admit that it mistreated part of its population and allow itself to be placed on probation by a foreign nation in return for trade. As a result, the Soviet Union conducted its business with Western Europe instead of the United States, and a potentially powerful American weapon remained largely useless. And to the extent that the Soviets' primary motive for détente was economic, as many observers thought, the lack of payoff reduced their incentives for maintaining détente.

Détente: Real Change or Political Tactic?

The Jackson-Vanik amendment was an early indication of a growing American skepticism about détente. High expectations had been generated by the 1972 summit conference where Nixon and Brezhnev had signed SALT I and the 1973 summit at which they had set down the principles to govern the superpower relationship. But then a number of events took place that raised questions about Soviet sincerity. Was their more moderate behavior in foreign policy genuine or was détente a tactical adaptation to a new international environment but still part of an expansionist policy? Did it reflect a Soviet willingness to live and let live with the West on the basis of strategic parity, acceptance of the status quo, and mutual restraint? Or, having learned from experience that a hard line and an iron fist tended to arouse and unite the West, were the Soviets using détente with its summits and smiles as a way of relaxing the West's guard and shifting the balance? Were they using détente to gain a superiority of power by lowering Western defense budgets, weakening NATO, and acquiring Western technology and economic assistance? Was détente anything but a "selective détente" in which the Soviet Union reaped general benefits from the lowering of tensions while unilaterally exploiting opportunities that increased its influence?

The Arab-Israeli War of 1973

The situation that first and most dramatically raised these questions was the 1973 Arab-Israeli war. Only a few months after the second summit, which had reaffirmed the general rules of conduct between the two superpowers, Egypt and Syria attacked Israel on Yom Kippur, the highest of all Jewish holy days, the Day of Atonement. What shocked Washington and other Western capitals was the Soviet role. Egypt was ruled by Anwar Sadat, an Egyptian nationalist who had succeeded Gamal Abdel Nasser. Egypt had become increasingly frustrated by Israel's continued occupation of Egyptian territory up to the east bank of the Suez Canal. This territory, captured by Israel in the Six-day War in 1967, looked as if it might remain in Israeli hands for a long time because Israel had no incentives to surrender it. The Arab states continued to be hostile to its existence. Even after losing the war of 1967, they refused to sit down with Israel to negotiate a settlement; Israel's victory therefore did not bring peace, only another cease-fire.

But Israel thought it was a peace of sorts. Israel was militarily superior and not likely to be attacked. The American-Soviet détente also benefited Israel because the Soviet Union, having improved its relations with Washington, was not about to permit Cairo to jeopardize them. Indeed, having once risked U.S.-Soviet relations by supplying arms to North Vietnam, Moscow made sure that the offensive arms Cairo wanted for an attack on Israel were not delivered. Only Egypt's defenses were bolstered, and the territorial status quo became frozen.

But Sadat, succeeding the much-loved and charismatic Nasser, was unwilling to live with this status quo. He was subject to strong pressures from other Arab states and domestic pressures to seek revenge against Israel. Sadat also realized that Moscow would be no help in persuading Israel to relinquish the Arab territory captured in 1967. Only the United States, Israel's friend, could help him achieve this goal; implicit in this emphasis on the return of the 1967 territory was a reciprocal willingness to recognize Israel's existence. But the United States, preoccupied with Vietnam, China, and the Soviet Union, was unresponsive, even after Sadat in 1972 threw out some Soviet military advisers in an effort to entice Washington to take the initiative in seeking a peace agreement.

Frustrated, Sadat therefore launched the Yom Kippur War, taking Israel by surprise. The Egyptian army achieved initial success in crossing the Suez Canal and driving into the Sinai desert, which it could not have done without large amounts of Soviet arms and equipment. Reluctant to risk détente by helping to precipitate another Arab-Israeli war, as it had in 1967, Moscow (once informed of the Egyptian-Syrian determination to go to war) was also unwilling to risk losing influence in the Arab world by opposing them. Thus, Moscow changed its mind and delivered offensive arms, including ground-to-air missiles and highly accurate antitank missiles.

When indeed the Egyptian and Syrian armies proved successful in the opening round of fighting, the Soviet Union began a huge airlift of war materiel and opposed any cease-fire calls that were not linked to a pullback by Israel to the 1967 frontiers. Moscow also called on other Arab governments to join the war and approved the Organization of Petroleum Exporting Countries' (OPEC) oil embargo against the United States. And when the

United States responded with its massive airlift of military supplies in the face of enormous Israeli fighter plane and tank losses, Soviet denunciations of the United States were stepped up. In the United States, this Soviet behavior was seen as incompatible with détente.

Once Israel had recovered from its shock and had driven the Syrians back from the Golan Heights, its forces concentrated on Egypt, crossed the Suez Canal to the west bank, and moved to cut off supplies to the Egyptian forces on the east bank and to encircle them. At this point, the United States and the Soviet Union agreed on a cease-fire resolution in the UN Security Council. The United States took this step because it felt that no peace could be arranged if Egypt were again humiliated in war—indeed, the psychological boost derived from its initial successes had to be preserved if Egypt were to make any concessions in a peace settlement. Moreover, the Soviet Union might feel compelled to enter the war to rescue its client state. But the shooting continued, and the Israelis drove to encircle and destroy the Egyptian army on the eastern side of the Suez Canal. Sadat now asked the United States and the Soviet Union to use their own forces to impose their cease-fire resolution. The United States declined to intervene with its forces, but the Soviet Union threatened to do so unilaterally. The two superpowers now confronted one another, as American military forces were placed on a worldwide alert. Moscow backed off, however, and the United States, also eager to avoid an escalation, pressured Israel to end its military advance. These moves assured the cease-fire.

Civil War in Angola

The second example of selective détente came in 1975 in Angola, a country rich in oil and mineral resources and geographically dividing "white supremacist" Africa—Rhodesia and South Africa, which controlled South-West Africa, or Namibia—from black Africa. As a Portuguese colony, it had helped to protect the two racist states from black liberation movements. But as Portuguese colonialism came to an end, Angola's interim government, which was composed of three factions based on tribal allegiances, underwent a power struggle. This rivalry continued after Angola became independent, and the different factions attracted outside support. Some claimed that the large-scale, decisive Cuban military intervention occurred after repeated South African military strikes into Angola, as well as intervention from Zaire (formerly the Congo, now governed by a pro-Western leader) on behalf of two of the rival factions. But the Ford administration saw it differently. The Soviets first shipped in military supplies and Cuban military advisers, which were followed later by Soviet jet fighters, mortars, rockets, armored cars, ground-to-air missiles, and a Cuban military force of more than 12,000 men to help the pro-Soviet faction. The administration viewed the Cubans as Soviet proxies and the attempt to influence the outcome of the conflict in Angola as an expression of "Soviet colonialism."

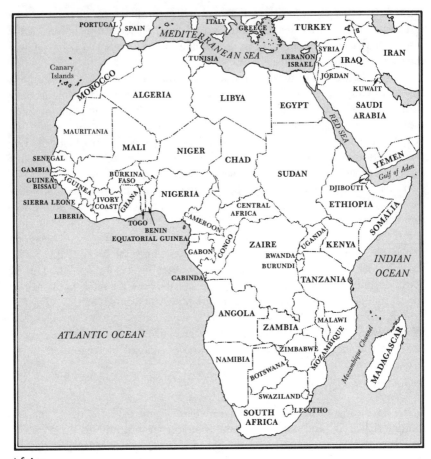

Africa

The result was to reintroduce great-power rivalry and confrontation into southern Africa. Rejecting U.S. military intervention, Washington provided covert arms aid to the faction opposing the Soviet-supported ones. But this effort not only did not match that of the Soviet Union but was cut off by the Senate, fearful of another Vietnam in an area that did not constitute a vital American interest. Rejecting the contention that Angola might become another Vietnam, Ford and Kissinger conceded that Angola was not a significant American interest. They emphasized, however, that Soviet behavior could not for that reason be ignored. Angola might be far away, but, in their view, it was a test case of the superpower relationship. Soviet actions were simply incompatible with détente; it was another case of their selective détente, of the Kremlin's seeking unilateral advantage from the general relaxation of tensions.

Angola was probably a turning point in détente. The Soviets had been allies of the Egyptians since 1955; it was understandable that they would not wish to risk a two-decade investment of political prestige, economic aid, and military assistance by not shipping Egypt offensive weapons or by informing Washington of the impending attack in 1973. But to Kissinger, Angola was far beyond any Soviet sphere of influence, and the Soviet action constituted a military intervention to impose a regime of Soviet choice. The Soviet Union's response was to defend its behavior by asserting that support of national liberation movements, including armed intervention, was not incompatible with détente. Détente did not mean the end of the struggle against imperialism. "What's mine is mine, what's yours is negotiable," President Kennedy had once said in summing up the essence of Soviet foreign policy. Had things really changed, détente notwithstanding?

The Carter administration's answer was more schizophrenic than that of its predecessor. For the administration was divided between the "globalists" and the "regionalists." For globalists like National Security Adviser Brzezinski, the prime concern was Soviet-American rivalry; a gain of influence for the Soviets was a loss of influence for the United States. For regionalists like Secretary of State Vance, these types of quarrels had to be resolved locally by addressing the causes that had given rise to them. The globalists maintained that Soviet-Cuban intervention added the element of superpower competition that could be ignored only at great cost to American prestige and to the credibility of American power, as well as strategic position. The regionalists countered that if these conflicts, which had ethnic, racial, regional, or nationalist origins, were resolved on their merits, the Soviets would be deprived of opportunities to meddle. But for the United States to intervene with military assistance and advisers on the anti-Communist side, which often did not have sufficient popular backing, would be to escalate the conflict, needlessly engulf a local problem in a global contest, and, in this way, risk another Vietnam. Political problems, they asserted, could not be solved by the use of force. Haunted by Vietnam because many of them had participated in the decisions leading to the U.S. intervention, they now believed that the United States had given too much priority to the East-West conflict, and that the containment policy was responsible for the nation's past overcommitments and follies in foreign policy.

Soviet Involvement in Ethiopia

Moscow's next move in Africa came in 1977 as Somalia, the Soviet Union's closest African ally, a country in which it had a naval base at Berbera and which it had supplied with arms, supported the Western Somali Liberation Front in the Ogaden region of Ethiopia (Somali troops had invaded Ethiopia to fight alongside the Front). Somalia had long claimed that this area, populated by ethnic Somalis, was part of Somalia. Ethiopia, already facing disintegration as it confronted other rebellions and secessionist attempts, especially the attempt by Eritrea to establish itself as an independent state, rejected the claim. Like other African and Third World nations, it recognized the borders existing at the time of independence—that is, borders drawn by the colonial powers—as its legal national boundaries. Because Ethiopia is about ten times as large as Somalia with its population of just over 3 million, the Soviet Union supported Ethiopia with an estimated $1 billion of military supplies, military advisers, and 20,000 Cuban advisers and troops to squash the Ogaden rebellion. It was willing to risk alienating Somalia and the loss of its naval base and some air facilities facing the Indian Ocean because the stakes were even greater in Ethiopia than in Angola.

There was irony in a Soviet-supported Marxist regime attacking another Soviet-supported Marxist regime, which the Ethiopian government had become after the overthrow of Emperor Haile Selassie in September 1974. But, as Soviet relations with Washington worsened, Moscow saw its opportunity to enhance its influence in the strategic Horn of Africa. Across the Gulf of Aden lay Saudi Arabia. Washington's fear, therefore, was that the Soviet Union might gain control of the southern entrance to the Red Sea, which led to the Suez Canal and Israel, and that it would pose a threat to the important oil routes from the Persian Gulf to the West.

The Carter administration's reaction was divided. Brzezinski, like Kissinger, tended to see the Soviet-Cuban activities in Africa in the context of the American-Soviet rivalry. So did the Defense Department, which wanted to send military aid to Somalia to displace Soviet influence. Among the states urging American help for Somalia, a Muslim country, were Saudi Arabia, the Sudan, and Egypt, all worried by the expansion of Soviet influence and the need to protect the oil routes through the Suez Canal or around the Cape of Good Hope.

Secretary of State Vance and the State Department's African desk, however, tended to see the problem as essentially an indigenous one in which American intervention would be counterproductive and lead to deeper involvement, which would be costly and tarnish America's reputation. Moreover, in a continent where national boundaries lacked geographic and ethnic logic and where virtually every state had its tribes with separatist hopes, the United States—which in the early 1960s had supported the UN effort to prevent Katanga (now Shaba Province) from splitting away from the Congo (now Zaire)—could not now intervene to help Somalia without alienating most African states. Short of preventing Cuban and Ethiopian troops from crossing over into Somalia after recapturing the Ogaden, the United States could do little. The situation, as it existed, simply favored Moscow.

Carter's Reaction to Afghanistan

The Carter administration's division between the globalists and regionalists continued in the following years and the president alternated between them. The split did not end until the Soviet invasion of Afghanistan. The

1978 coup in Afghanistan by pro-Soviet elements had been overlooked, but 85,000 Soviet troops, which were sent in during the last week in December 1979, were hard to ignore. Fierce resistance by Muslim tribesmen to radical and antireligious reforms appeared to threaten the Soviet-supported regime. Perhaps the Soviets also feared that the Islamic fundamentalism then sweeping Iran and Pakistan might engulf Afghanistan, which lay between these two countries, creating an insecure situation on the Soviets' southern border where approximately 50 million Soviet Muslims lived. In any event, Moscow invoked the Brezhnev Doctrine, that once a nation had become Socialist, it was not again to be surrendered to counterrevolution (as the Soviets defined these terms). The march of history toward socialism was inevitable and irreversible. But this doctrine previously had been asserted only in Eastern Europe—in Hungary in 1956 and Czechoslovakia in 1968. Now the Red Army was to ensure history's progress outside of the Soviet sphere in a Third World country.

The Soviets probably expected no more of an American response than words condemning Soviet action as deplorable, but no action. Clearly, they believed vital security interests to be at stake and did not give much thought to American reactions. In truth, there was little to lose. Détente hardly survived. SALT II was dying in the Senate; Carter, to rescue the treaty, had promised to increase defense spending and to build the new MX missile, and he was intent on matching Soviet intermediate-range nuclear forces (INFs) aimed at Western Europe with U.S. INFs in Western Europe (where, to Soviet consternation, they could reach the Soviet Union). The Soviet Union had received little of the trade, technology, and credits it had expected, and it was denied the most-favored nation commercial status, which China had received. Nevertheless, such a disregard for American reaction, implying contempt for American power, was rather new.

For Carter and Vance, who had pinned so much of their hope in détente on SALT II and restrained themselves from countering Soviet behavior in the Third World in order not to jeopardize American-Soviet relations, the Soviet invasion was a shock. Carter publicly confessed his earlier optimistic views when he said that the Soviet action had "made a more dramatic change in my opinion of what the Soviets' ultimate goals are than anything they've done in the previous time I've been in office." No president in the postwar era has more dramatically testified to his naiveté. Brzezinski, for whom this type of Soviet behavior held no surprise, but who until then had limited influence on Carter's policy toward the Soviet Union, began to gain influence; Vance's star, once bright, faded quickly.

The president, swinging with events, now became a "hard-liner." He halted high-technology sales, embargoed feed grain shipments, and imposed a U.S. boycott on the Olympic Games scheduled for Moscow in the summer of 1980. Most important of all, in the context of growing Soviet influence in the Horn of Africa and the collapse of the pro-Western shah in Iran and his replacement by a militant anti-American regime (see chapter 10), Carter announced his own doctrine. Even if Soviet motivations for the invasion of Afghanistan had been basically defensive, the consequence was nevertheless a major advance of Soviet military power toward the vital Persian Gulf-Indian Ocean oil line to the West. After three years of nonresistance to Soviet moves, the president suddenly became fearful of a Soviet pincer movement on Saudi Arabia and the other oil kingdoms in the Gulf region. Having previously denounced those still primarily concerned with the East-West conflict as globalists and cold warriors, Carter shifted gears toward the end of his term and embraced the approach he had previously rejected.

Détente thus came to an end. Carter undoubtedly had been correct that not all regional conflicts were tests of superpower strength and credibility; but events had demonstrated that some became so because of Soviet intervention. In fact, few purely regional quarrels existed. Ironically, then, détente collapsed because of a series of regional conflicts that the administration had tried to isolate from the American-Soviet rivalry—only to find that it could not do so. Soviet activities in the Third World were evidence that the Soviet Union did not consider this rivalry over. Quite the opposite: it sought to exploit both the United States' post-Vietnam reluctance to act and its illusion that Third World problems could be separated from the superpower competition.

The Erosion of U.S. Alliances

The whole concept of détente was bound to pose several problems for the United States. Alliances are normally drawn together by common perceptions of an overriding external threat. But what cements the bonds of such relationships when that threat is no longer seen as great—indeed, as vastly reduced—by the principal members of the coalition? Is it not inevitable that the strands of such entangling alliances become untangled? In Europe, among America's most important allies, that appeared to be the situation.

In the days when all members of the alliance had seen the Soviet threat as serious, NATO had been a reasonably cohesive organization. To be sure, the alliance had become strained because its European members, although still dependent on the United States for their security, had recovered from the war and wanted a greater voice in the alliance. The common perception of external danger had sufficed to keep the bonds of the alliance close.

In the era of détente, however, the various nations were no longer so willing to give priority to alliance interests. Washington, for example, now negotiated directly with the Kremlin on key issues, as relations with Moscow became in some respects more important than those with NATO members. Not surprisingly, the European states also went their own way, and economic issues proved especially divisive within the Atlantic community. During the immediate postwar era economic policies such as the Marshall Plan had been consistent with and supported American political-military policy. But now economic relations were at odds with the other strands of NATO policy.

NATO Develops Cracks

As the 1970s began Europe was no longer the weak, divided, and demoralized continent it had been after 1945. Indeed, the emerging Common Market was an increasingly powerful economic competitor. During the cold war, the United States had been a leading proponent of European union; a strong United States of Europe would be a significant contribution to the U.S. balance with the Soviet Union. The competitiveness of an economically unified Europe was thought to be worth the risk. In a period of détente, however, as the European unification movement stalled, and differences between the United States and Europe grew (especially as Europe's heavily subsidized agriculture became productive and exportable, which reduced U.S. agricultural exports to Europe and competed with it elsewhere), past policy often appeared counterproductive because of the economic losses it entailed.

The European-American relationship was also strained by the continued sense of vulnerability of the Europeans because of their dependence on the United States for defense. Their concern revolved, on the one hand, around their fear of abandonment. As the United States became more vulnerable to Soviet attack, the Europeans wondered if they could continue to rely on American protection. Without sufficiently large and credible nuclear forces of their own, their security was entirely in American hands. But, as Soviet intercontinental missile forces grew, what would happen if the Soviets made demands considered vital by the Europeans but not by Washington? Could the small British or French strategic force deter the Soviet Union? The U.S. management of the Berlin crises from 1958 to 1962 had not reassured them—especially France and West Germany—of Washington's steadfastness as its risks and costs of defending the alliance rose. At the same time, they also feared entrapment. The Europeans had been deeply concerned over the diversion of U.S. resources and attention away from them during the Korean and Vietnamese wars. They also worried that the United States, in its new global role, might involve them in an all-out war resulting from a confrontation, such as the Cuban Missile Crisis, or from an escalation of a limited conflict, such as the Vietnam War. While the Europeans worried about U.S. recklessness, the United States resented their lack of political sympathy and support for its ventures outside of Europe. This feeling deepened U.S. disappointment over the failure of the Europeans to play a far greater role in their own defense.

The alliance was further divided by the psychological fact that while the United States had become a global power, the European states, having shed most of their empires, had largely relinquished their former extra-European role and had concentrated on their economic growth and their European role. As former great powers, the European states naturally resented their rapid postwar decline in prestige and status and their dependence on a vigorous, self-confident, and, in their eyes, youthful and often impetuous newcomer who might disregard their counsel—advice that, the Europeans felt, was based on greater experience and wisdom.

Thus, by the late 1970s, as the United States was increasingly disillusioned with détente, the allies were intent on preserving it. The Americans had become increasingly concerned with the growth of Soviet military power and the expansion of its political influence in the Third World. The Europeans virtually ignored Soviet activities outside their continent, as if relieved that Soviet energies were directed away from Europe. Compared with the confrontations and frequent Berlin crises of the cold war, the decade of the 1970s had been a period of peace and calm in Europe. For West Germany especially, the period had seen the stabilization, if not legitimation, of the European territorial status quo: the 1971 four-power settlement of the Berlin issue, the 1973 mutual recognition of West Germany and East Germany and their entry into the United Nations, with the subsequent increasing trade and person-to-person contact across their boundary. The West Germans saw this situation as the closest thing to reunification. Thus, while the United States wanted less détente, Europe sought to maintain a détente separate from U.S. policy while still preserving American military protection. It did so by distancing itself from the new harder-line, anti-Soviet rhetoric and actions emerging from Washington.

Carter's economic boycott of the Soviet Union after the Soviet invasion of Afghanistan, therefore, received little enthusiasm or support, as did the United States' rather painless boycott of the summer Olympic Games in Moscow. After Afghanistan the French and German leaders journeyed eastward to salvage their separate European-Soviet détente. As the Soviets achieved strategic parity, Western Europe appeared to become more accommodating. Increasingly, America's allies denounced American behavior as reckless and dangerous because it might provoke Moscow.

Indeed, the fundamental question raised in the post-Vietnam period was whether, thirty years after the war, Western Europe, with a population of well over 300 million, highly developed industry, and a long military tradition, had the will to defend itself. Or had it become too used to being defended by the United States? The mood of accommodation was strong, and pacifism and neutralism were gaining respectability. The British Labour party, out of power and under the strong influence of its left wing, favored unilateral nuclear disarmament and declared its opposition to American nuclear bases in Britain; it almost came out for Britain's withdrawal from NATO. On the Continent, governments—with the major exception of France—were also sensitive to public opinion. In West Germany the Social

Democrats, formerly strong supporters of NATO, swung, like the Labour party, to the left.

Events outside of Europe, like the Yom Kippur War, were also divisive. The Europeans, almost totally reliant on Arab oil for their well-being, were reluctant to antagonize the Arabs and risk an oil embargo. Therefore, although the Syrians and Egyptians had started the war, there was little backing for the United States in its support of Israel. While Europe supported American efforts to seek a comprehensive peace between Israel and its neighbors after the 1973 war, the deadlock on the Palestinian issue, as well as others, led the Common Market countries to take an independent stand.

The Europeans' sensitivity and vulnerability on the question of oil supplies was also in evidence during the period following the seizure of the American hostages in Iran (chapter 10). In several key areas of the world, therefore, Western Europe did not follow the lead of the United States except reluctantly and only when unavoidable. Some sanctions, such as against Iran, were invoked largely for symbolic purposes, not because of any painful effect they might have. They were intended primarily to assuage the United States, which felt that Soviet actions in Afghanistan and the humiliation of America in Iran demanded more than verbal protests. The key, however, was that the Europeans sought above all to restrain the United States from doing anything that they perceived as rash and dangerous. As these events unfolded, détente led Greece and Turkey to a military clash over the island of Cyprus. This disintegration of NATO's flank in the eastern Mediterranean was made even worse when Congress, pushed by the Greek-American lobby, cut off all military assistance to Turkey even though Greece had precipitated the conflict.

SEATO and CENTO Dissolve

While the Western alliance was straining, the Southeast Asia Treaty Organization (SEATO) collapsed completely. It formally dissolved in 1975 after the fall of South Vietnam and its takeover by the North. All expectations had been that Hanoi would make its big push for victory in 1976 during the American presidential campaign. But a rather routine fight turned into a rout as President Thieu of South Vietnam, allegedly short of military equipment as a result of congressional cutbacks of funds for South Vietnam, sought to withdraw troops from northern South Vietnam and to concentrate them in the more populated areas. Hanoi, undoubtedly as surprised as Washington at the sudden collapse of Saigon's army, quickly sent its troops southward to keep up with the retreating South Vietnamese. Thieu had made his decision to pull back in mid March; Saigon fell on April 30. South Vietnam's leaders now reaped their reward: having inherited France's colonial legacy, they had been overly concerned with their own power and had relied too much on American assistance and forces instead of developing a social strategy to boost the morale and mobilize the support of their people.

The war was finally over. Despite a U.S. show of force when the Cambodians seized the American merchantman *Mayaguez* and the recovery of the ship and its crew, there was no way to halt the erosion of American influence in Southeast Asia. Communist troops also won in Cambodia, and the Communists gained political power shortly thereafter in Laos. Everywhere in Southeast Asia was anxiety and nervousness—the result of what was seen as an American defeat in Vietnam. In these circumstances SEATO did the only thing it could do—bury itself. No one wept at the funeral.

The Central Treaty Organization (CENTO) died more slowly. First, with the splitting off of Bangladesh from Pakistan, which had also been a SEATO member, India emerged as the dominant power on the Subcontinent. Pakistan, which had joined both alliances primarily to receive U.S. arms for its adversarial relationship with India, no longer had much interest in either. In the meantime, it had moved close to China, a regional rival of India. Turkey, at the other end of the alliance's geographical area, was still nursing its wounds after the U.S. arms embargo and suffering from increasing domestic instability. In between, Iran was now the only reliable friend of the West in Southwest Asia.

After Britain had withdrawn from "east of Suez," Iran had become America's local policeman in the Persian Gulf because the United States, given its own isolationist mood, was incapable of filling the vacuum left by the disappearance of British power (as it had done shortly after World War II in Turkey and Greece). The shah, whose throne had been restored to him in 1954 by the CIA, was a strong supporter of U.S. policy. He had, among other things, sent oil to Israel during the 1973 war, backed Egypt's efforts to make peace with Israel, and not embargoed oil shipments to the United States in 1973-1974. In return, the Nixon-Ford administration had supplied him with all the weapons he requested for building up large and modern Iranian armed forces. But the shah, who, as an absolute ruler, seemed so safe as the guardian of Western interests in the region, lost his power at the end of 1978. Fundamentalist Shi'ite Muslim leaders inspired their followers to protest against the shah's rapid modernization and the accompanying Westernization that was destroying the traditional religious society as well as eroding their own status and influence. They, together with secular left-wing and constitutional forces, protested the shah's despotic rule and pro-Western policies. The shah was widely perceived by Iranians as a tool of the United States, doing its bidding. And so he fell, and his "foreign" regime was replaced by a more orthodox Islamic republic. Iran quit SEATO, to be followed shortly by Muslim Pakistan.

The collapse of the shah's government was a tremendous strategic loss for the United States, but whether it could have done anything to prevent his fall remains controversial. The shah's concentration of all political power in his own hands forced the opposition, especially the Western-educated middle class seeking a more democratic Iran in which it would play a large political role, to join together with the more traditional opposition led by the clergy. At the same time, the Carter administration was paralyzed by internal disagreement. On one side Brzezinski kept Iran's strategic position and role foremost in his mind, urging that the shah be told that the United States would support him fully, even if he used the army to suppress the crowds in the streets. On the other side, the State Department was largely hostile to the shah, repelled by his human rights record; it also believed that a successor regime would be made up of those seeking democracy in Iran and that if the Ayatollah Ruhollah Khomeini came to power, he would be a figurehead only. Khomeini was a religious figure, thought to be too old and without the necessary experience in government to play an active, let alone dominant, role. The State Department, almost looking forward to the shah's collapse, advised against supporting him; if he fell, the United States would be rid of an embarrassing supporter and could replace him with pro-Western, prodemocratic forces. It was a risk-free policy that would presumably strengthen the U.S. position in the Gulf.

The president, who had stressed human rights in his election campaign and pointed to the shah, among others, as an example of his predecessor's amoral, if not immoral, policy, was as usual caught between conflicting views. The disagreements in Washington were such that the subsequent fall of the shah and Khomeini's triumph were greeted with relief. As happened so often before—for instance, in the Eisenhower administration's analysis of Nasser— the Carter administration's understanding of Khomeini was superficial, consistent with its own hopes of what would happen. Perhaps Carter's misapprehension is forgivable, for, after all, who in Washington or any other Western capital would in this secular age have given serious consideration to the strength of a religious movement and the possibility that it would transform Iran into a medieval theocracy? Modernization after all, if it meant anything, meant secularization, an emphasis on life here on earth. Western scholarship's explanations of the "stages of economic growth" through which the developing countries would have to pass, emphasized only that traditional society was an obstacle to progress. The possible emergence of an Iran dominated by the clergy was so alien to all Western thinking that it was not taken seriously; there was no precedent for such a reaction to efforts at modernization.

The result, in any case, was that the whole area was suddenly in crisis. The overthrow of the shah and his replacement by a fundamentalist Islamic, militantly anti-American regime; the increasing insecurity felt by the Saudis, who had watched the United States stand by helplessly as another monarchy fell; the spread of Soviet influence in Ethiopia and South Yemen on the Arabian peninsula; plus the Soviet invasion of Afghanistan amounted to a collapsing American position throughout the area and a greatly increased danger to the vital oil supplies that the United States and its allies needed. Thus, in the irony of ironies, Carter found himself forced to declare that the United States would fight to guard these oil resources. The United States under the Carter Doctrine was now committed to the defense of the Persian Gulf countries.

The United States learned two lessons about its role in the world: first, no local power, especially if it is suffering from internal weaknesses, can substitute for American power, and second, no matter how strong its preference to play a less prominent role in the world, the United States as a superpower has extensive interests that it cannot evade. The world will not sit still while the United States decides whether it wants to play international politics or not. These lessons had to be learned again in the post-Vietnam era in which the United States was left with only one major alliance in Eurasia—NATO—and NATO's power and resolve to act collectively in the common interest were growing more questionable.

Disillusionment with Détente

Any evaluation of détente reflects one's expectations. In the context of America's national style, it is not surprising that views of détente swung from euphoria in 1972 to increasing disillusionment as early as 1973 or 1974. The national mood wavered between opposite and mutually exclusive categories: isolationism or intervention, peace or war, diplomacy or force, harmony or strife, optimism that the United States can reform the world or cynicism about an evil world that resists reform and, in the process, corrupts the reformer—all of which suggested withdrawal from the world as a solution. Thus, détente was widely believed to be the opposite of cold war.

The Nixon administration's overselling of détente and slogans like "negotiation, not confrontation" reinforced the expectation that the cold war was over and that the two superpowers had put their conflicts and crises and the danger of war behind them. Raising people's hopes too high is bound to lead to disillusionment when subsequent events do not live up to expectations. The problem is that each administration tends to package its foreign policy in slogans that emphasize how its policy differs from that of its predecessors; and, anticipating the next election, it wants to make that policy look appealing and successful. Despite the high degree of continuity of American foreign policy, the United States has indulged itself by turns in the rhetoric of containment, liberation, frontiersmanship, and détente.

In addition, détente as a state of existence that combined both conflict and cooperation was more difficult than the cold war for people to understand. It is easier to explain a relationship that is essentially one of confrontation or cooperation. The cold war aroused people; détente relaxed them, as if it were the same thing as entente, meaning friendship. In fact, détente means a reduction of tensions, not an absence of tensions or superpower rivalry. To regard it as if it were such an absence was bound to produce disillusionment.

Indeed, in its conception, détente was intended as another form of containment for a period of domestic neoisolationism, superpower parity, and Sino-Soviet schism. The cold war stick was to be supplemented by the carrot of détente, and issues were to be linked, explicitly or otherwise. The Soviet Union was to be constrained from foreign adventures with force, or the threat of force, plus the withholding of agreements it desired. The United States hoped that Moscow, enticed by Western goods, technology, and credits, would restrain itself to avoid the loss of such benefits and of agreements such as SALT. In other words, Moscow would be given the incentives to practice self-containment!

But this U.S.-Soviet adversary-partnership was not static; the mix of these two elements varied according to circumstance. In 1972 the Soviets wanted Western, especially American, trade, technology, and credits, a slowdown of the Sino-U.S. rapprochement, a strategic arms agreement, plus millions of tons of American wheat. But in 1973 the Soviet harvest was good; SALT I had been signed, but there had been little progress toward SALT II; the Senate had not yet decided what terms of trade and credit to offer the Soviet Union; and, perhaps most important, Nixon's authority was rapidly eroding as the Watergate scandal unfolded. Whereas in 1972 Moscow withheld the offensive arms Sadat wanted and, as a result, suffered the humiliation of having its advisers thrown out of Egypt, in 1973 the Soviet Union did not need the United States for food and was still waiting for détente's economic payoff. The Soviet Union may also have been unsure about signing any arms agreements with Nixon and felt he might be unable to react to any challenges; therefore, Egypt received not only the arms with which to launch its war against Israel but also the Kremlin's hearty political endorsement. In short, détente is not one thing that stays the same year after year. It changes with conditions.

As emphasized earlier, two of the basic reasons why the United States first adopted détente as a diplomatic strategy was the country's pervasive mood of withdrawal and relative decline after the Vietnam War. This attitude made containment of the Soviet Union very difficult at the exact time it had become a global power. Détente was not a set of self-denying rules. If the Soviet Union faced favorable situations to exploit, should it shun these opportunities just because the United States was in no mood to resist? Self-restraint as a policy is asking a great deal of any major power, especially one that had just achieved strategic parity. Nixon and Ford felt very constrained by public and congressional forces, although Nixon opposed the potential Soviet intervention in the Yom Kippur War, and Ford attempted to resist Soviet-Cuban moves in Angola. The Jackson-Vanik amendment for all practical purposes robbed them of the "economic weapon." The Watergate scandal and Nixon's resignation were critical in weakening the presidency as an institution. The passage, over Nixon's veto so soon after his landslide reelection, of the War Powers Act, which restricts the president's ability to use force, was symbolic of the shifting of power from the executive to the legislative branch, whose purpose was to restrain the United States's role in international affairs. The nation had had a "bellyful" of an interventionist foreign policy. It wanted a rest, a détente. Symptomatic of this post-Vietnam mood were restraints imposed on the presidency and the CIA, the chief arms of overt and covert intervention, and the cutbacks of the defense budgets as a percentage of the GNP to pre-Korean War levels at a time of unprecedented Soviet military spending. Carter shared the mood and attitudes of the middle 1970s: that the United States had overextended itself in the world; that it had incorrectly estimated the Communist danger and overreacted; that American power had, especially in Vietnam, been misused; that the cold war had ended, and it was time to play a less prominent role in the world.

As the 1970s were passing, Americans were increasingly reluctant to use American power because of their sense of guilt about its uses in the past. It was as if the exercise of *American* power, not the expansionist efforts of the Soviet Union, were the main problem. Restraint of the United States, not the containment of communism, appeared to be the chief task if the world were to become a more peaceful place. The Carter administration's constant refrain was "the limits of American power." The phrase made good sense on one level: the United States was not omnipotent and could not indiscriminately commit itself everywhere. It made less sense if it meant—as it often appeared to—that the United States was virtually impotent and could not, therefore, influence events or resist adverse trends. Deeply embedded in the administration's attitude was the old American feeling of shame about the use of power in a morally ambiguous world, as if using it had made Americans wicked. Vietnam seemed to be obvious evidence of evil.

The best course for the United States, therefore, was to withdraw from the international scene, renew and purify itself by concentrating on its domestic affairs, and build a fully free and socially just society whose example would radiate throughout the world. Power politics would be replaced by social politics; America's foreign policy would be its domestic policy. In the words of a former chairman of the Senate Foreign Relations Committee, America should "serve as an example of democracy to the world" and play its role in the world "not in its capacity as a *power* but in its capacity as a *society.*"[1] Virtue, not power, would be the hallmark of American foreign policy; other nations would be attracted to the United States by the merit of its principles, not by its superior strength.

Apart from the collapse of the cold war consensus, another issue was whether the American political system was suitable for the conduct of a policy of cooperation and confrontation that relies upon an ever-changing mixture of sanctions and incentives. How could a Senate that favored détente attach a

---

1. J. William Fulbright, *The Arrogance of Power* (New York: Vintage Books, 1967), 256.

provision about Jewish emigration to a commercial agreement with the Soviet Union or cut off funds for arms being sent to the anti-Communist factions in Angola or not adequately fund military budgets? How can a president expect détente to continue without Soviet unilateral exploitation if he refuses to use wheat as leverage because he is unwilling to alienate the vote of farmers who prefer cool cash to cold war (or if he does use it, as Carter did after Afghanistan, only to find strong farmer resistance)? What if the president does not want to link arms control to other issues and Congress favors it (or vice versa)?

The built-in executive-legislative conflict resulting from separate institutions sharing power has always made it difficult to formulate foreign policy. The United States' first major experience after a century of isolationism, World War I, ended in a peace treaty that the Senate defeated. It was Congress's strong opposition that led President Franklin Roosevelt to resort increasingly to executive agreements in his conduct of foreign policy from 1939 to 1941. During the cold war, the shared presidential and congressional perception of great external threat plus agreement on America's foreign policy aims had generally toned down the conflict between the two branches and increased the president's influence with Congress. But in the absence of a clear-cut and overwhelming perception of danger during the détente years and the presence of intense disagreements about the roles and purposes of America in the world after the war in Vietnam, the president and Congress often pulled in different directions. Given the lack of access to U.S. industrial technology and the failure to achieve a significant arms control agreement, even after years of difficult negotiations and America's signature on SALT II, a Soviet leader might well ask why the Soviet Union should restrain itself. This was especially so at a time when in the United States the executive was weakened and Congress's main concern was avoiding further Vietnams. Almost every policy became caught in a bitter dispute between Congress and the president, making it easier for the Soviet Union to expand its influence with impunity.

Probably any great power rival would have behaved as the Soviet Union did. The United States, after all, during the heyday of détente, had bombed Moscow's ally, North Vietnam. After the Yom Kippur War, the United States had promoted a Middle East peace settlement by making itself the arbiter between Israel and the Arabs and excluding the Soviet Union from playing a key role in the area. But Moscow was especially likely to exploit America's paralysis of will and any opportunities to enhance Soviet influence. The Soviet Union believed itself to be engaged in an irreconcilable struggle with international capitalism led by the United States. For the Soviet Union, détente did not mean an end of the competition; it only meant competing at a lower level of tension so that the rivalry would not erupt in nuclear war. It was not its fault if Americans did not want to hear the message that the "class struggle" or "ideological struggle" would go on, that Moscow would give its blessings and assistance to "national liberation" movements in the Third World. The Soviet leaders had no intention of betraying their historical obligation to assist the inevitable struggle of peoples for freedom from Western neocolonial controls.

Indeed, détente was a particularly favorable situation in which to promote this struggle. Détente, to the Soviets, was the product of a shift in the balance of power as a result of the new strategic parity in nuclear weapons. Before parity, U.S. strategic superiority had allowed Washington to intervene all over the world and to intimidate Moscow and compel it to be cautious. But now that U.S. nuclear forces had been neutralized and deterrence had become truly mutual, the United States had to act more cautiously. In fact, that is why Washington pursued détente. Note the cause and effect carefully: it was the growth of Soviet nuclear forces that induced the United States to behave with greater self-restraint. And the obvious corollary: the greater the military power the Soviet Union acquires, the better; American compromises and concessions in negotiations were offered *only* because of Soviet strength. This perception of American behavior was nothing less than a rationale for a continuing arms buildup. The implications of this became so clear that by the late 1970s the Carter administration began the U.S. rearmament effort; the continued Soviet military buildup after SALT I was a major factor disillusioning American opinion with détente.

Now that the Soviet Union was less likely to be opposed by the United States and Moscow had in its own eyes achieved equality with Washington, the world was a safer place for Soviet expansion, which was another reason why the United States was disillusioned with détente. The achievement of strategic parity and the acquisition of new Soviet "colonies" in the Third World were directly linked. They were the product of the Kremlin's new *Weltpolitik*. Like the Soviet navy, they represented for Moscow—as colonies and a navy had once for Germany—the geopolitical status symbols of the Soviet Union's new standing in international politics.

The Search for Consensus and Human Rights

A major problem to emerge from détente was how the United States could conduct its foreign policy without a domestic consensus. In the absence of external threat, the United States has historically wanted only to be left to its own devices; when provoked, however, the country has been easily mobilized and united for its foreign policy crusade. As the cold war anti-Communist consensus disintegrated in Vietnam and the country tired of being the world's policeman, Kissinger's abandonment of the missionary style and the moralistic justification for foreign policy seemed very much in order. His emphasis on states and their legitimate interests, instead of moral causes and the division of the world into saints and devils, assumed a clear-cut distinction between a nation's foreign and domestic policies. The United States had an obligation to itself to defend its interests and, in doing so against another great power, it could use a range of diplomatic, military, and economic tools. It could seek to restrain an adversary with carrots or sticks or a mixture of both.

But the United States should abandon ideological goals because they spill over into crusades and hinder the diplomatic process by making the recognition of, or compromise with, allegedly immoral states virtually impossible. To make changes in the adversary's domestic structure and ideals a part of the negotiating process and perhaps a prerequisite for other agreements is bound to be unproductive—indeed, counterproductive, because it may well harden the opponent's positions and raise tensions. A Soviet leader, Kissinger contended, may make concessions in private diplomacy (as Brezhnev did when he arranged with Kissinger to allow a large number of Soviet Jews to emigrate), but to try to compel a Kremlin leader to change the way he governs the Soviet Union, a sovereign nation, will expose him to accusations of "coddling capitalism" and selling out "Socialist interests" and may even endanger his tenure.

Yet, in asking for the abandonment of America's traditional national style, which had allowed the country to play its foreign policy roles in the past, what was Kissinger substituting? The answer was basically the balance of power, which was not a new or exciting idea that would arouse Congress and the public. It was difficult to sustain support for a policy that involved elements of conflict and cooperation with the Soviet Union and that tried to use rewards and sanctions in an ever-changing mix as conditions changed. Personal charisma and diplomatic successes gained public attention and support (for SALT, the opening to China, and the attempts to move the Middle East toward peace). But the increasing public cynicism about détente, the Watergate scandal, Kissinger's own reported involvements with wiretaps, and the succession of an unelected president (and vice president) eroded support for détente and led to increasing attacks on its architect. "Superkraut" had been shot down, and American foreign policy continued to operate without a consensus.

Perhaps no consensus was possible in the 1970s. Therefore, the Nixon-Ford administration adopted the only course it could: operate without one and rely on dramatic policy initiatives, achievements, summitry, and Kissinger high-wire acts. The difficulty of creating consensus was shown by Carter, who thought he could find it in America's self-proclaimed historical role as the defender of democracy and individual liberty. "Human rights" became the platform on which he expected to mobilize popular support; the liberal tradition, which Kissinger was accused of having abandoned in favor of his amoral geopolitics, had been reunited with American foreign policy. The nation, it was now proclaimed, once more stood for something, having reclaimed its democratic heritage and a moral basis for its foreign policy. Jimmy Carter, the born-again Christian, had become the redeemer of the American tradition.

Carter's policy ran into trouble abroad almost immediately. The Soviets, as Kissinger had predicted, did not care for Carter's emphasis on human rights, which they felt was specifically directed against them. Moreover, they interpreted political opposition, freedom of assembly, and free speech—all tenets of human rights—as dangerous to their system and "counter-revolutionary." The president's policy and his support for Soviet dissidents was viewed in Moscow as a fundamental attempt to undermine the Soviet system. Predictably, it led to a stiffening of Soviet diplomacy on SALT, postponement of a final agreement from the time when its approval by the Senate might have been relatively easy, a sizable reduction of Jewish emigration from the days when Kissinger had handled this problem privately, and a greater crackdown on dissidents.

Indeed, some critics suggested that precisely because the United States could apply sanctions for the violation of human rights more easily to its friends and allies than its adversaries, the policy was applied mainly to friendly countries that were generally aligned with the United States on foreign policy, thereby jeopardizing American security as well as the human rights of individuals in the affected country. In Iran, as we have seen, human rights abuses led the U.S. government to give the shah what at best was only half-hearted support while in effect expecting that his overthrow would result in a regime led by westward-looking democrats. Instead, the result was an Islamic theocracy that was not only militantly anti-American but also proved as brutal as the shah's secret police. The ousted ruler was replaced by an even crueler and more repressive despot. It had happened earlier in Vietnam, after South Vietnam collapsed and Hanoi took over, and in Cambodia, where the Communists slaughtered an estimated 2 million people out of a population of 8 million.

A further result of the emphasis on human rights was to expose America's double standard of judgment, if not its hypocrisy. How could President Carter square his human rights stand with his strategic interest in normalizing American relations with China? Or that when he needed to complete the SALT II negotiations, the president toned down his denunciations of Soviet infringements of human rights? The same doubt about Carter's sincerity was also raised by his pre-1979 support and praise for the shah of Iran; the United States needed the shah to help stabilize the Persian Gulf area, although it was known that he ruled his country with an iron fist. Clearly, in all these instances the problem for the administration was one of deciding priorities; failure to decide whether to give priority to human rights or security where these values clashed meant that the pursuit of both enhanced neither. This is not to downgrade human rights in U.S. policy. That, indeed, could not be done because such rights express the profound commitment of the nation to the values upon which it was founded. Such values must be as much a part of U.S. policy as power. But they cannot be pursued regardless of consequences.

Thus, neither Kissinger nor Carter could find a new basis for a consensus on U.S. foreign policy. The balance of power as a justification remained alien to the American tradition, and Carter's human rights policy was unworkable. Yet Carter was not that far off the mark, at least traditionally. The United States historically has explained its international involvements in terms of the defense of democracy or human rights against the onslaught of undemocratic and antidemocratic regimes. Indeed, during the first stage of the cold war, the anticommunism inherent in the containment policy was legitimated by the liberal Democratic administrations of Truman, Kennedy, and Johnson by their human rights concerns. Liberals were concerned about civil rights and social justice at home; these also had to be advanced and protected abroad from the Soviet Union and its allies.

Ironically, it was after Carter that a conservative president reunited anticommunism and human rights, at first in support of right-wing regimes that ignored human rights, but then to help transform a number of them into democracies. In the meantime, Carter tried to divorce human rights from the American-Soviet conflict and marry them to his concern for the lot of people living in the developing countries. Here is where the majority of humanity lived, and, in the emerging interdependent world, Carter's focus was to be on the relationship between the Western industrial democracies and the poorer Third World in the creation of a more peaceful and more decent "world order."

Conflict with—and in—
the Third World

THE DEVELOPING countries benefited from the cold war, although many of them criticized the superpowers for their cold war preoccupations and their consequent neglect of the poorer nations of the world. Far from neglecting them, in fact, the United States and the Soviet Union gave them attention and resources that were wholly disproportionate to the Third World's power. The reason, as we know, was the bipolar distribution of power, which conferred on these new nations, most of whom were not only poor but also weak, a greater leverage than their own strength and influence warranted. Confronted by two nations competing for their allegiance and loyalty, the Third World countries could lean first toward the East, thus attracting Western economic and military aid and political support, and then toward the West, thereby attracting similar assistance from the East. The replacement of bipolar competition by the newer adversarial partnership in the early 1970s meant that their bargaining capacity declined. Nonalignment also became more acceptable to the United States in these circumstances.

If the change in the superpower relationship was the fundamental reason for the decreased American attention and aid to the Third World, then the results of previous assistance efforts reinforced "donor fatigue." It had become clear after two decades that the optimistic expectations of "instant development" had underestimated the difficulties and complexities of modernization. Aid seemed never-ending. Moreover, aid had not even been particularly successful in winning friends and gaining influence. In the absence of traditional means of control, the friendship of countries receiving aid was unreliable and inconstant. American aid, as a consequence of all these changes, had not only been reduced to its lowest point—less than half of 1 percent of the gross national product (GNP)—but the emphasis had shifted from capital development to technical assistance and an increasing role for private enterprise, meaning basically the multinational corporations. In 1979 U.S. aid was only 0.2 percent of the GNP, behind the aid given by Sweden, Norway, the Netherlands, France, Britain, and West Germany.

As the 1970s began, the lot of the developing countries appeared grim. With a few exceptions, they were still far from modernized. The optimism had faded that foreign aid would stoke their modernization or, later, that "trade, not aid" would permit them largely to earn their own way and to finance their own development. Food shortages in Africa and Asia were stark reminders of what could happen. After years of trying to lift themselves up by their own sandal-straps, they still faced formidable problems in their attempts to modernize. The hopes of the 1950s and early 1960s had turned into disappointment, even despair, as many of these countries remained mired in backwardness. The expectation of the former colonial states that they could realize their dream of a better and more rewarding life for their peoples was unfulfilled. Poverty, illiteracy, ill-health, and overpopulation, among other problems, continued to coexist with dreams of national dignity and material welfare.

The New International Economic Order and Nonalignment

The Western states might point out that the causes of the persistent poverty of so many of these newly emerging countries were of their own making: the fragility of nationhood; the low priority given to agriculture, resulting in hunger; the high birth rate, which defeated the most valiant efforts of economic growth; the large amounts of money spent on arms; and, all too frequently, widespread inefficiency and corruption. The developing nations rejected the argument, however, that the responsibility for their failure to modernize was internal. They pointed to the external system—the international economy—in which they were the sources of raw material for Western industry. When demand declined, or several non-Western suppliers competed with one another for the same markets, or Western industries found substitutes or synthetics, the prices of their resources went down. As prices declined, so did the capacity of the developing countries to earn foreign exchange with which to buy Western industrial products, which have tended to rise in price. In short, their earnings declined while the cost of Western-made goods rose. In addition, when these countries developed some industry and exported to the West, they often ran into protective tariff barriers. In short, even if they worked harder, it was of little use. The structure of the international economy was against them and kept them in a subordinate position, as suppliers of cheap raw material for the rich Western states. Third World countries therefore seemed condemned to poverty.

As they saw it, they were dependencies. They may have gained political independence, but in reality they remained economically chained to the

Western industrialized economies. Their status remained neocolonial because their economies were geared, not to the needs of their own markets, but to those of the developed countries' markets. As exporters of raw materials, they depended on Western demand and access to Western markets; therefore, they were the victims of Western economic policies, obviously made in the interests of the Western countries who were favored by the law of supply and demand. The international market was stacked against the weak and poor and favored the strong and rich. That is why, they claimed, that after decades of working hard and despite foreign aid they remained less developed. For Western nations, the Third World's status as a supplier of relatively cheap raw materials was a matter of self-interest. Why should the industrialized world favor their development? Their dependency status in an international economic and political order dominated by the West, as the Third World nations perceived it, limited their ability to grow economically; their integration into the global economy has benefited the dominant Western nations with a high standard of living and left the developing countries poor.

The developing countries, it ought to be emphasized, were arguing not just that the Western-controlled international economic order gave an advantage to the strong over the weak. Their main point was that they were poor because they had been exploited by the West. They had been plundered during the colonial days, and this plunder continued as they sold their resources cheaply on the international market. In this context, their demand for a new international economic order was a claim for a redress of past wrongs. Having used their power unfairly to take from the poor countries what rightfully belonged to them, the argument went, the rich nations were obligated to make restitutions in the name of social justice and decency. The transfer of wealth from the West to the Third World was therefore seen as repayment of a moral debt, or conscience money. Whatever the real mix of internal and external reasons, then, for the slow development of the Third World, the "revolution of rising expectations" had become the "revolution of rising frustration." This was the reason for the increasingly strident demand for a new order, which was essentially a demand for a redistribution of wealth from the rich nations to the poor nations.

It was in this context that during the 1973 Arab-Israeli war the Organization of Petroleum Exporting Countries (OPEC) raised oil prices fourfold from $3 to $12 a barrel and that its Arab members for a while embargoed shipments of oil to the United States and the Netherlands, both supporters of Israel. The oil companies, which according to the imperialist interpretation were supposed to be such powerful multinational corporations that they dominated the economies and countries in which they operated, were shown to be without much power. They were at the mercy of the governments of the countries in which they operated. The so-called imperialist states, whose governments were presumably controlled and directed by the capitalists, did not mobilize to squash the governments that were said to be their puppet regimes. Confronting a vital threat to their well-being and security from countries that had no military power to speak of, the industrial democracies did not even debate the issue of military intervention. Had this event occurred a few decades earlier, they would not have hesitated to resort to force rather than face the possibility of being destroyed economically. In 1973 they talked of accommodation and acquiesced.

OPEC's action was widely viewed in the Third World as symbolic of a general protest against their lot by developing countries. OPEC was regarded as a kind of "vanguard of the (world's) proletariat," or poorer nations. This mood of anger, resentment, and revolt was clearly directed against the West. Ironically, the effects of the quadrupling of oil prices were felt most keenly by other non-Western nations. The sharp increase in oil prices threatened their plans to industrialize and handicapped their efforts to grow more food with technologically intensive, oil-based agricultural techniques. But whatever fears they had about the future, these countries stood united with OPEC. Materially and rationally, though, they should have aligned themselves with the First World—the Western industrialized nations—to compel OPEC to lower its prices to a more acceptable level.

Despite the increased suffering brought on by the steep rise in oil prices, the Third World countries did not form a coalition with the United States, Western Europe, and Japan to force lower oil prices. This can be partly explained by their fear of irritating OPEC, partly by their hope for promised but largely undelivered OPEC economic help (most went to fellow Muslim nations, where it was spent on arms), and partly by their desire to imitate OPEC. But the basic reason was that the Third World identified emotionally with OPEC. The organization's action was widely perceived by these countries as "getting even" for past exploitation. It gave them a good feeling that for once the weak had turned the tables and made the strong suffer. The German word *Schadenfreude* says it best: pleasure received from seeing someone who deserves it really suffer, or "get his." The sight of the rich and privileged nations who had so long ruled them as the "lesser breeds" being humiliated and quaking before their old colonial slaves was just too delicious. While OPEC quickly gained immense wealth, the rest of the Third World received an enormously satisfying "psychic income." That was why OPEC's action inspired so much hope. The suppliers, instead of competing against one another and keeping prices low, organized themselves into a cartel to control access to the oil and its price. Perhaps OPEC had provided the example to the developing countries of how they could raise their commodity prices and earn the funds they needed.

For among these countries, the demands for a new international economic order consisted of more stable commodity prices, indexing those prices to Western inflation rates, more foreign aid, and preferential tariffs so that they could sell their products on Western markets. They felt they had the resources Western industry needed, and, without them, Western industry and society would be in serious trouble. The rich nations appeared vulnerable, and the poor nations seemed to have gained real leverage. Increasingly, observers noted the new First World-Third World confrontation and asserted that it was becoming at least as important as the conflict between the Soviet bloc and the Western allies.

The OPEC-developing country coalition held into the 1980s, even after oil prices had hit $32 a barrel after the shah of Iran fled the country in 1979, followed by the subsequent decline of Iranian oil production (some of which was made up by other Persian Gulf countries), and the resulting tighter supplies in a world with an ever-expanding demand. Bitterness toward the West intensified, and, as their frustration and anger grew, the nonalignment of the developing countries increasingly appeared to be changing into alignment with the Soviet Union and its ideological friends. The Soviets had charged all along that the poverty and misery of the non-Western world were the results of Western capitalism and imperialism. Still, it seemed odd to find Vietnam, Afghanistan, North Korea, and Cuba accepted as nonaligned nations and odder still that their 1979 conference was held in Havana. It seems oddest of all that when Vietnam was cruelly driving its Chinese population out of the country, usually in boats that would not survive long ocean journeys, its behavior was not condemned as racist, and that neither Vietnam's invasion of Cambodia nor the earlier genocide of the Cambodian people was condemned as aggression or a crime against humanity. The Soviets and the developing countries would not have hesitated to use such phrases had the United States acted in similar ways. Nevertheless, this coalition between the Soviet Union and the nonaligned nations was by and large tactical. The nonaligned countries were nationalistic, and they had not fought for national independence only to lose it to Soviet imperialism. Yet it was a sign of the times that this coalition existed and that only a small number of Third World governments criticized the direction of the non-aligned movement and defended American policies.

Oil as a 'Weapon'

The sharp rise of prices in the wake of the shah's collapse left no country untouched. In the United States and among its principal industrial allies, high oil prices stoked inflation, brought on unemployment, created a stagflation (a simultaneous inflation and recession), slowed down economic growth, lowered standards of living, brought about the largest redistribution of wealth in history from the West to the OPEC nations, created large Western imbalances of trade, and sharply lowered the value of the dollar. The "energy crisis" of the 1970s did not merely cause occasional inconveniences such as long lines of cars waiting to buy gas or higher prices to be paid at the gasoline pump. It profoundly upset entire economies and changed ways of life, as evidenced by smaller cars and lower speed limits in the United States. Moreover, the energy crisis raised the questions of how the Western states, which had paid for welfare programs by means of rapidly growing economies, could still afford such programs, and if they would have to reduce defense expenditures in order to continue such programs. Or would they be able to maintain strong defenses only by cutting social expenditures? Plenty of "guns" and "butter" no longer appeared affordable.

OPEC's Success and Third World Expectations

Mao Zedong once said that "power grows out of the barrel of a gun." OPEC thought he would have been equally correct had he referred to a barrel of oil. By organizing themselves into a cartel, the petroleum-exporting countries were rejecting the open market that the developing countries had been claiming favored the consumers and not the producers. In the past, each producer, seeking to enhance sales, maximized production, which caused an excess of supply and kept prices low. The cartel sought to maximize its profits and influence by seeking to control both the levels of supply and prices. If it could control enough of the world supply of oil, so that outside suppliers could not make up for a cutback in the cartel's total production nor meet the expanding needs of consumer countries, it would hold the bargaining chips. A second condition was also important, namely, that the resource the cartel controlled was of such importance to the consuming nations that they could not do without it. The demand, in brief, was intense, and it was less painful to accept higher prices than to tell OPEC "to drink its oil." These conditions would presumably confer leverage to the producers of oil.

Oil is a vital commodity and is irreplaceable. It cannot be recycled. It takes large-scale capital investments and many years to explore, find, and drill for new oil. Similarly, new technologies to exploit solar energy or shale oil also require enormous investments of time and money. Finally, other energy sources such as nuclear power are controversial or, as with coal as well, are deemed environmentally undesirable. No short-run substitute is readily available for economies that have long depended on relatively cheap oil and have neglected research and development.

No wonder that the developing countries were delighted and held high hopes in the wake of the 1973 price hikes. OPEC's actions gave rise to two expectations: one, that OPEC would use its leverage to raise the prices of natural resources from the other Third World countries; and two, that the other producers of resources could follow OPEC's example by organizing their own cartels, limiting supplies and raising prices. Maybe, finally, the developing countries could acquire the large-scale funds for investment in modernization that foreign aid and free trade had not raised.

The expectation of a resource coalition against the West was not fulfilled, and First World-Third World negotiations on changes in the economic rules of the game were not very fruitful. The fact is that if we use the rather over-simplified distinction of rich and poor nations, in the 1970s the rich were becoming the "declining rich," while OPEC and a few other Third World countries were becoming the nouveaux riches. The latter's fundamental interest lay basically with the richer nations, not the poorer. Even more radical states such as Libya, Algeria, Iraq, and Iran—all of them "price hawks"—have not withheld oil at their nation's cost to advance the collective welfare of all Third World states, although all were generally hostile to U.S. policies.

Conversely, OPEC has not refrained from raising its prices because of any social conscience and concern about the devastating impact these raises have on less prosperous states. OPEC's foreign aid for some of them remained puny in comparison with what the rising prices have extracted from these nations; this is money that could no longer be invested in their own development. Third World unity, in fact, was fragile, if it existed at all. It was a handy term to describe countries that shared certain social and economic conditions, emotions and attitudes about colonialism and modernization, and voting patterns at the United Nations. But on material issues that affect each of them differently, there was division. The OPEC countries followed their national interests, even if the cost involved great injury to the developing countries.

Nor was OPEC's example of much relevance for most of the developing countries with other resources. Nonoil mineral resources exerted less leverage: there were more readily available substitutes; industrial scraps could be recycled; conservation, stockpiling, and new sources of minerals, including seabeds, were available options. Furthermore, there are barriers to setting up cartels. First, in many areas producing raw materials producers are far more numerous than in OPEC, which could complicate the task of organizing a united front. Second, the developing countries that would benefit from a cartel were those already better off because they had a product in demand; the poorer nations, less blessed by nature, would not benefit and, given the higher commodity prices that they had to pay, would be worse off. Third, the most difficult barrier was that the role of these countries as the suppliers of raw materials for the industrial world is in part a myth.

Western countries produce most of the world's resources. The ironic fact is that most developing countries are net importers of raw materials! Of the nonfood, nonfuel commodities, the Western industrial nations in the mid-1970s supplied 60 percent, the Communist states 20 percent, and the developing countries 30 percent. And most of the world's food exports—as shown by repeated Soviet imports of wheat and the threats of starvation in certain areas of Africa and Asia during the 1970s—are from the rich countries, especially the United States. Therefore, there would not be a straight transfer of wealth from the rich to poor. It was not only unlikely that the West would soon confront a series of commodity cartels, but also unlikely that such cartels could do much to lessen Third World poverty.

Economics and Political Pressure

These conclusions, however, were not of much comfort in the West while OPEC retained its key position as an oil producer. The economic effects of rising prices were not the only matter of concern; the possibility that a political price might be exacted by the oil producers was also worrisome. Would Saudi Arabia maintain high oil production and restrain prices to some extent if the United States could not fashion a solution of the Palestinian problem satisfactory to the Arab states and obtain Israeli withdrawal from Arab lands captured in 1967? If the United States supported South African domestic and foreign policies toward its neighbors, would Nigeria—second only to Saudi Arabia as an exporter of oil to the United States in the 1970s— then refrain from exploiting its oil weapon? Indeed, had not America's more evenhanded policy in the Middle East since 1973 been partly the result of the fear of the Arab OPEC's use of another oil embargo? Were the West European countries not influenced by the possibility of an oil cut-off when many of them received Yasir Arafat, head of the Palestinian Liberation Organization (PLO), as if he were already a head of state, thereby conferring upon the PLO a degree of legitimacy?

Economics is not a new instrument of state policy. Indeed, during the cold war, economics had become a well-known means of advancing American interests, especially the Marshall Plan and the various foreign aid programs for the developing countries. The United States had on other occasions resorted to embargoes, such as cutting off Cuba's U.S. sugar quota to punish Fidel Castro in his early days in power for moving closer to the Soviet bloc. In Chile, the United States cut off loans from international agencies and prevailed upon American banks not to support Marxist president Salvador Allende, and, after the Iranian seizure of U.S. hostages and the Soviet invasion of Afghanistan, it attempted to use economic coercion either to change the targeted nation's behavior or to exact a price for that behavior.

But economic means are usually of limited effect in gaining short-range or medium-range goals. Foreign aid has won few reliable friends; cutting off access to American markets or embargoing food is not helpful as a coercive tool if other markets or other sources of supplies are available. Castro, finding his American market cut off, found a market for Cuban sugar in the Soviet bloc; after Afghanistan, the Soviets bought much of the grain they needed from other countries once the U.S. embargo took effect. In addition, publicly announced sanctions such as these usually have the opposite effect: they usually unite the targeted nation, mobilize popular support for its regime, and provide a scapegoat for the regime's failures.

What is striking about OPEC's efforts to use oil as an instrument in international politics is its intellectual impact in the United States. Instead of reinforcing the traditional interstate perspective because of oil's potentially coercive effect, the embargo produced an image, widely shared in academia, government, and the mass media, of a more interdependent world, dedicated to enhancing the material welfare of its peoples. The shock of the energy crisis, despite the pain it had caused in the West, was seen as beneficial in the long-run. Interdependence among nations would transform the very nature of international politics.

Interdependence: Global Transformation or Escape from 'Power Politics'?

In one sense, the interdependence of nations—if it meant mutual impact or vulnerability—was obvious. The multiple and profound effects on the West of OPEC's actions have already been mentioned. This interdependence involved the non-OPEC nations of the Third World as well. Recession in the West reduced the demand for raw materials, which lowered their prices, which in turn produced less foreign aid and raised the prices of Western machinery and other goods. With smaller earnings of foreign exchange, the ability of these countries to import high-priced oil declined too, unless they borrowed heavily from Western banks. Another consequence of this interdependence was that national planning by itself could not lead to full economic recovery, that the actions of other countries had a profound impact. For example, U.S. attempts to cope with stagflation depended on the stability of OPEC's oil prices rises and production. The price shocks of 1973 and 1979 taught that lesson in the most painful way.

The OPEC countries were also deeply enmeshed in this interdependent world. Without the industrial countries, they could not sell their oil, so that ruining the Western states was presumably not in their self-interest. If they wished to modernize, they needed Western assistance, for the West had the industry and technology. The West could also supply a country such as Saudi Arabia, which believed it had a major security problem, with the most modern weapons and the men to train its forces. In addition, American political support for the Saudi government was desirable because the regime was conservative and concerned with political stability. The government was staunchly anti-Communist and always worried about radical Arab regimes that leaned toward Moscow.

In a rather obvious sense, then, the nations of the world had become more interdependent. Price rises, production cuts, inflationary forces, and recession all reached across national frontiers. No nation was any longer "an island unto itself." In an interdependent world, nations obviously could hurt one another. But why were broader conclusions drawn, suggesting that the very nature of international politics and the historical pattern of state behavior would be replaced by a new world politics whose characteristics would be quite the opposite of the old "power politics"? Why were so many observers, mainly American, so optimistic about this growing international interdependence? Why did interdependence become the new wisdom during the 1970s and have such wide appeal among President Jimmy Carter's policy makers and among American news commentators and academics?

The Appeal of Interdependence

The attractiveness of interdependence was its promise of a more peaceful and harmonious world consistent with American values and an escape from the more troublesome world of power politics. Moreover, transnational economic and technological forces made this more humanitarian planet "inevitable." The assumptions underlying interdependence as a model of the future were both multiple and interesting. First, it is asserted that in an ironic paradox, nuclear weapons have ensured the peace. The superpowers' strategic nuclear arms are weapons of denial and deterrence, and their existence makes the use of conventional arms less likely because of the danger of escalation of hostilities. The likelihood of major war between them, even among their allies and friends, is therefore not great. When wars occur, however, as in the case of Vietnam, the conflict may last a long time and be expensive to wage in terms of lives lost, money, and increased social divisions—in short, the costs may be excessive in relation to the goals. Hence future Vietnams were unlikely.

Second, as a result, attention has turned from security to economic or welfare issues. These issues have become increasingly salient not only because security seems more assured but also because the democratic societies of the West have become more and more preoccupied with economic growth rates, consumerism, and ever-higher standards of living, and the developing countries are bent on modernizing and on satisfying their own people's expectations for a better life. The key issues are economic and social rather than military and involve values such as social justice and human dignity rather than violence and destruction.

Third, nations cannot fulfill their socioeconomic goals by themselves. Western societies, for example, run largely on imported oil. The non-Western countries, in their turn, seek Western technology and food. Nations no longer completely govern their own destiny, and no government by itself can meet the aspirations and needs of its people for a better life. Worldwide cooperation is not just desirable but a necessity if goals such as peace, political stability, human welfare, and individual dignity are to be achieved on earth.

Fourth, on the traditional issues of security, the state system assumes the separation of states and conflict among them, but on these bread-and-butter or welfare issues only cooperation will enhance each nation's prosperity. Whereas in international politics one nation's increase in power and security is seen by its adversary as a loss of power and security for itself, on economic issues each country's welfare was perceived to depend on the existence of prosperity in other countries. Economically, they gained or lost together; one did not gain at the other's expense. Precisely because in an interdependent system nations are vulnerable to one another, they need to work out problems together. Such cooperation requires a greater willingness to resolve disputes peacefully and a higher degree of mutual understanding and international harmony. Unlike cold war security issues, which were bilateral, the issues of oil or other resources or population or environment require multilateral negotiations. Many nations are affected—indeed, usually different nations on different issues. By "the logic of interdependence," they have to find collective solutions to their common problems.

Fifth, and very important, force and the threat of force are said to play a minimal role in these welfare issues, again in strong contrast to the primary role they play in security issues. The downgrading of force is largely attributable to the fact that countries with which the United States would negotiate these issues are allies and friends. Even if the threat or application of force were effective once or twice, frequent threats or use of it could only alienate countries that are needed on these social and economic issues. Although many of the nations with which the United States must deal on these prosperity issues are comparatively weak militarily, they are not helpless or without leverage of their own. They have commodities that, if production were shut off, would hurt the consuming nations. Militarily weak states such as the major oil-exporting nations therefore have formidable bargaining power. But the traditional way of calculating power, by adding manpower, industrial capacity, military strength, and other factors, does not reveal this. The old hierarchy of states determined by military strength was therefore more and more irrelevant, and the emerging world order would be more genuinely egalitarian.

At least, power politics would be less relevant. The emphasis would be on cooperation among nations and their common interests, and the prime values to be sought would be human welfare and dignity. Nations clearly continue to exist, but their military fangs are to be drawn and their aggressiveness subordinated to the task of building a better future for all peoples. The national interest could be satisfied by serving the human interest. Interdependence, in brief, supposedly restrains national egotism and enmeshes nations in a web of interlocking relationships that compels them to cooperate for the "good of mankind."

Interdependence is unquestionably in part a description of current reality, but it is *also*—usually implicitly—a cry to move "beyond the nation-state" to a "world without borders" by dissolving, so to speak, power politics in welfare politics and "planetary humanism." Without denying the reality of existing economic problems posed by Third World poverty and hunger, the emphasis on interdependence was in part an attempt to escape from the structure of the present state system with its inherent conflicts and dangers. It is a plea for humankind to cooperate despite national differences to make "spaceship earth" a truly decent and fit place for all people to live and enjoy life free from oppression and want.

Indeed, what could be more characteristic of America's national style than interdependence, with (1) its distinction between economics, which is thought of as good because it is identified with social harmony and material benefit, and politics, which is equated with conflict, destruction, and death; and (2) the normative commitment to a better future for humanity, to be achieved by a rational response to the allegedly inexorable forces of economics and technology? At one time, free trade was thought to be the answer to war and a unifier of nations because commerce would benefit all of them and presumably give them a vested interest in peace. Then economic development was advocated as the key. Is interdependence not just another idea in search of a more peaceful and harmonious world because the earlier proposals have *not* done away with power politics?

Interdependence and American Guilt

Moreover, is the timing of the idea of interdependence not coincidental with, as well as a reaction to, Vietnam and "realism" as a way of understanding and conducting American foreign policy? There is a certain irony to the advocacy of interdependence. Vietnam created a strong reaction to globalism, which was dismissed as an overreaction of the cold war. Yet, under the guise of interdependence, globalism has been resurrected as the best way for nations to coexist and resolve not security issues but welfare or prosperity issues—population, resource depletion, energy, food, and the maldistribution of wealth.

It is not surprising that this new philosophy of global change strongly influenced the Carter administration's policy. Carter came to power just after South Vietnam's final collapse, when the United States was sick and tired of the war and the power politics that allegedly had been responsible for the country's involvement. Many of the administration's top officials, who as leaders or members of the bureaucracy under Lyndon Johnson or Richard Nixon had participated in the decision making about the war, shared the widely felt sense of shame about the war. They felt guilt about this abuse of American power, as well as other misuses (such as covert political interventions). Henry Kissinger's balance-of-power approach, therefore, was dismissed as dated; the world had moved beyond the days when this allegedly older, or "European," approach seemed relevant. The incoming administration claimed that it would be more sensitive to the "new" realities of a more complex world and no longer a prisoner of the old cold war myth of superpower competition and confrontation, which in the past had received strategic priority and had led the United States to support right-wing dictatorships in the name of freedom. The administration, therefore, would move beyond the balance-of-power politics of East-West relations to "world-order" politics and a focus on North-South relations (between developed and developing countries).

East-West matters, then, were no longer regarded as of central concern except in the sense of working together for arms control to reduce the superpowers' nuclear arsenals, to prevent the outbreak of a catastrophic war, as well as to reduce the spread of nuclear weapons to nations that did not yet possess them. Détente remained a prerequisite for doing "good works" in the developing areas of the world.

This image of the post-Vietnam War world with its distaste for national egotism and use of power and the reassertion of an older and allegedly more moral American approach to foreign policy—nicely disguised as interdependence and a transformation of world politics—testified to the strength of that approach and its set of attitudes and ways of perceiving the world. Yet the emergence of interdependence as the new intellectual fashion together with the disutility of force as the new wisdom came at the very moment when the Soviet Union became a global power, American strategic superiority vanished, and the "imperial presidency" was weakened. Thus, while the new administration was deemphasizing the East-West balance-of-power conflict and focusing on North-South world-order cooperation, the Soviet Union, perceiving the balance to be shifting in its favor, saw opportunities to exploit and expand its influence militarily in the Third World.

But the East-West struggle was not just an old and bad memory. It was still very much alive, even if the United States preferred not to compete actively and told itself that containment no longer seemed wise or relevant because history, the nationalism of the new nations, and the shift in emphasis from national security to global welfare, would limit and defeat such old-fashioned expansionism. The Soviets showed that they shared neither the belief that international politics had changed nor the view that force had become an increasingly inept, if not irrelevant, instrument of policy. At the time, the Soviet Union was estimated to be outspending the United States on its military forces by at least 25 percent, perhaps by as much as 50 percent. Given an economic base believed to be about half that of the United States, this very heavy emphasis on "guns" at the cost of "butter" for the Soviet people suggested that these forces were intended for more than just defense. With its simultaneously increasing political-military involvement in the Third World, the Soviets taught the United States once more that there was no escape from the world of great power conflict.

Undoubtedly, the United States, on occasion, has made mistakes by overemphasizing East-West relations; some of them, particularly with regard to China, were costly. But experience has also shown that ignoring or downplaying these relations also leads to grave errors. It is one thing to learn from the past and correct errors; it is quite another to dismiss the very nature of international politics, whose chief characteristic, one might argue, was its strong sense of continuity. Soviet behavior—the continuing growth of Soviet military power, interventions in the Third World by proxies (Cubans especially), and the outright use of the Red Army in Afghanistan—made one question inevitable: Had Kissinger and preceding administrations been so wrong in granting priority to American-Soviet competition, in emphasizing military power or in thinking that the East-West struggle sometimes intersected with North-South issues?

From Globalism to Regionalism and Back Again

The Carter administration's emphasis on the creation of a "new world order," with its central focus on the relationship between the Western industrial world and the developing countries, left no doubt of its answer to that question—namely, that it was precisely this preoccupation with American-Soviet competition that had led to U.S. involvement in Vietnam. By applying the superpower struggle to regional and even domestic rivalries, the United States in the past had become needlessly embroiled in situations it should have avoided and had become identified as a reactionary power supporting the status quo rather than needed changes. The Carter administration cited the Nixon administration's intervention in Chile and its own policy toward Panama in support of its contention that regional issues should be seen as such and solved accordingly. The United States would be better off, said the new administration, not upgrading quarrels from regional to global if it wished to avoid aligning itself with forces opposed to democratic values and nationalism in the Third World.

Chile

The United States' Latin American policy had historically regarded South America to be within America's sphere of influence. Although Washington had gradually become more accommodating to the nationalism of its Latin neighbors, it remained sensitive to what it perceived to be radical left-wing revolutions and regimes that might bring Soviet influence close to America's shores. When in 1970 Chile elected the Marxist Allende to the presidency, the Nixon administration, while behaving with diplomatic correctness, sought first to prevent Allende from becoming president and, after that failed, to make life difficult for him and encourage a military coup d'état. In a less overt way than John Kennedy with the Bay of Pigs invasion or Lyndon Johnson in the Dominican Republic, the new Republican administration used the CIA for the same anti-Communist reason as preceding administrations. Yet, ironically, the reasons for the Chilean coup, when it came, stemmed essentially from Allende's own actions and the domestic reactions these precipitated. The CIA may have helped to hasten the coup, but the causes of the crisis were internal; by 1973 Allende's end was merely a matter of time. Indeed, Chile provided a most persuasive example of why the United States should *not* intervene.

It is important to stress this point because Allende has become something of a martyr, frequently portrayed as a revolutionary who was fairly elected to seek reforms and better the lot of the poor and underprivileged, only to be blocked and finally overthrown by a fascist conspiracy on behalf of a reactionary ruling class in league with capitalist America. Had he lived, Allende's reputation would have been stained by the failure of his political leadership; his suicide at the time of the coup elevated his reputation to a level he could never have achieved as leader of Chile's "road to socialism."

Allende came to power with 36 percent of the vote, only two points ahead of his next competitor in a three-way race. In the runoff vote in the Chilean congress, he received the support of the centrist Christian Democratic party. At the start of his rule the opposition supported much of his program, including the nationalization of the American-owned copper mines, banks, and major industries and land reform. Although it should thus have been possible for him to work within Chile's constitutional norms with a democratic consensus, Allende believed in class struggle. He deliberately pursued a policy of polarizing Chileans, which did more to consolidate the professional middle and lower-middle classes in opposition to him than to broaden his worker-peasant base of support.

As he pursued his program, his vow to maintain constitutional rule fell by the wayside. Representing a sizable minority, but hardly "the people," he could have governed only had he gained the majority support in the Congress, which he did not have. He survived by increasingly bypassing the Congress and the courts. The Christian Democrats joined the rightist opposition, and class polarity was then matched by executive-legislative polarity. Allende had eliminated the middle ground of Chilean politics and emasculated the spirit of the constitution.

The nucleus of Allende's opposition came from the lower-middle class, which was hurt by an inflation rate of more than 300 percent by 1973, shortages of all kinds in the shops, and worries that their small businesses might be wiped out by inflation or government takeovers. In 1972 and 1973, small truckers, those who owned only one or two trucks, went on strike and were joined by shopkeepers, doctors, lawyers, engineers, bus and taxi drivers, and airline pilots. Between the strikes even the workers in the largest copper mine struck.

The military during this period became increasingly politicized. Asked by Allende at several points to participate in his cabinet to reassure those worried about law and order in the midst of strikes, street marches, and illegal seizures of land by the president's followers, the military at first served Allende as it had his predecessors. What precipitated the military's intervention was the rapid growth of paramilitary forces among Allende's extreme left-wing followers, who had always believed in armed confrontation with "reaction," and the call for an insurrection in the navy by a close Allende friend and party leader; both events apparently occurred with Allende's complicity. The country was on the verge of civil war when the military struck. It did not need American urging.

Not that the United States had been friendly to Allende. After the expropriation of American property without compensation, Washington cut off American credit and pressured international financial institutions to follow suit. But Allende more than made up his American losses with credits from Communist states, other Latin American countries, and West European countries. Chile also had rich copper mines. Had Allende imitated Nasser, he would have survived U.S. pressure and hostility by arousing his people's nationalist ardor. But that was why Allende did not survive; he declared himself to be president of only some Chileans—against other Chileans. Such polarization of society, a galloping inflation, and increasingly unconstitutional rule were hardly recipes for political success. Had the CIA abstained from meddling, responsibility for the Chilean coup would properly have fallen on Allende; he destroyed himself politically. The CIA's intervention drew attention from this, reaping the blame on behalf of the United States. Whatever it says for or against American intervention in its sphere of influence—if such a sphere can still be considered important and relevant in this intercontinental age—Chile, like the earlier Bay of Pigs, makes a persuasive case for nonintervention, as the Carter administration contended.

Americans, perhaps because of the democratic nature of their society, on the whole seem rather clumsy at covert intervention and feel morally uneasy about it. Perhaps most reprehensible and in some ways symbolic were the several attempts to assassinate Castro, involving the Kennedy administration, the CIA, and Mafia figures—certainly an immoral alliance for murder in the name of national security. And, unlike in a television play, this unholy alliance failed in all of its attempts. In Chile, a country as far away from the United States as the Middle East, the question is surely whether the United States had the right to try to upset the constitutional election of any political figure, either in the name of American national security or for the broader consideration of the preservation of democratic values—values Washington did not later insist on in Chile or in other parts of a largely nondemocratic globe. One major result has been that the United States reaped widespread condemnation for its intervention and that Chile became for many liberal people a *cause célèbre,* just as the Spanish civil war had become a symbol of the conflict between fascist and progressive forces in the world.

The Panama Canal

The Carter administration's contention that local problems could be handled more appropriately on a local basis meant above all support for those domestic or regional forces that were identified with nationalist aspiration. Symbolic of the new attitude was the acceptance of a change in the status of the Panama Canal Zone. Negotiations had begun in the 1960s, were carried on throughout the Nixon-Ford administration, and finally concluded under Carter. For Latin America, the disposition of this issue was critical. This was not a strictly American-Panamanian issue; all of the Latin American states— left, centrist, and right—supported Panama in its determination to assert its control over a piece of territory that America treated as if it were its own. Would the United States try to keep its control of the zone, which would lead to violence between the American forces there and the Panamanians, or would it accommodate itself to the nationalism of Panama and all the states to its south?

Theodore Roosevelt had carved Panama out of Colombian territory in order to build the canal for the growing American navy at the turn of the century; the 1903 treaty between the two countries had granted the United States "in perpetuity the use, occupation, and control" of a ten-mile-wide zone to build, run, and protect the canal, although the sovereignty of this territory was to remain vested in Panama. The result was a virtual colonial situation. The American role in that small country became dominant. The Canal Zone cut Panama in two and was run by the U.S. Army. Panamanians in the zone were subject to American law administered by American courts. All business enterprises were operated by the United States; Panamanians were denied the opportunity to compete. And the American government held large tracts of land and water needed by Panama's rapidly growing population. What all this amounted to is that the United States acted as if it were sovereign in the zone when in fact it possessed only certain treaty rights over a piece of Panamanian territory.

The Panamanians also felt that they had received rather scanty economic benefits from the canal; fair or not, the contrast between the standards of living of those living in the zone and those living outside was grating and humiliating. Political discontent had become so high in 1964 that nationalist frustrations burst into riots when Panamanian students tried to fly their country's flag next to the American one at the zone high school. American students resisted, and twenty-one Panamanian and three American students were killed in the subsequent brawl. The confrontation was a symbol of what faced the United States should it seek to preserve its control "in perpetuity."

By the middle 1970s the canal's economic benefits to the United States were declining with shifting world trade patterns and the increasing use of supertankers and container ships too large to pass through the canal. Even its military value was being reduced by a two-ocean navy with huge aircraft carriers, which could not go through the canal, and nuclear submarines, which would have to surface to pass from one ocean to the other (providing intelligence to the Soviets of their whereabouts). The Canal Zone issue, like the flag issue, had become primarily symbolic. American liberals recognized the need for change to meet Panama's aspirations for territorial integrity and real instead of nominal sovereign control; if denied, Panama might become "another Vietnam." But American conservatives, very strong in Congress, bitterly resisted a new treaty, which would restore the zone to Panama by the end of the twentieth century while ensuring America's right to continued use of and protection for the waterway. According to conservatives, the "American Canal in Panama" would become "another Suez," symbolic of American decline, another instance of a once-powerful America groveling before a tiny country. Common sense prevailed in the end, but not without a struggle in Washington.

The canal obviously could be better protected with the Panamanians' consent than without it. Should the Panamanians actively work against protection with sabotage and violence, the United States would be compelled to send large military forces to protect the zone from "the natives." Stories of American troops shooting Panamanians would make ugly headlines, as would the public confrontation in the United Nations. In the world organization, the United States would stand virtually alone against a solid bloc of developing nations. The symbolism of the issue was domestic and international. For many Americans, and not just some in Congress, the Canal Zone was "American," but anything less than eventual Panamanian control over its own territory was unthinkable. A new treaty would demonstrate a change in American attitudes toward the nationalist aspirations of its southern neighbors and show that the United States had reassessed its formerly dominant position in its hemisphere. Already Peru, Venezuela, Bolivia, and Argentina had asserted themselves strongly against the United States, and American influence throughout Latin America was clearly on the wane. The real stake in Panama, in brief, was America's new global image and role. In April 1978, by only one vote more than the two-thirds required for a treaty, the Senate ended thirteen years of negotiations and a lengthy national and Senate debate by voting to turn the canal over to Panama by the year 2000.

This became part of a new pattern in Latin America. President Johnson had intervened in the Dominican Republic to stop left-wing forces from taking over the government, but Carter pressured the Dominican generals to stop their opposition to the election of a left-wing president. In Nicaragua, Carter opposed the dictatorship of Anastasio Somoza, which collapsed in a popular revolution in 1979; his predecessors had frequently supported despotic regimes like Somoza's. Carter thus ended up favoring the Sandinistas, who during Somoza's days were domestically supported by such elements as the Catholic church and the business community, even though they were externally supported by Cuba.

These policies were characteristic of the administration's attempt to be sensitive to the nationalism of Third World countries in its pursuit of world-order politics, with the primary emphasis on the North-South relationship. The administration accepted the risk that the new regimes might turn toward Cuba and the Soviet Union for friendship and eventually repress all domestic opposition forces, including those working for genuine democracy. But supporting right-wing dictatorships, it felt, would certainly doom U.S.

interests. Popular resentment and anger would eventually lead to their overthrow; American identification with the status quo would alienate the new rulers. Unlike Vietnam, the argument went, the United States had to place itself on the "right side" of historical development. Thus, the new administration favored social and political change and tried to identify U.S. policy with such change rather than oppose it.

Southern Africa

In Africa, this attitude meant that U.S. policy moved away from identification with the white-supremacy regimes of Rhodesia and South Africa and toward a closer alignment with the black states of the continent. Fear of the Soviet Union was admittedly present, for the United States worried that if the guerrilla wars in South-West Africa (Namibia) and Rhodesia (Zimbabwe) could not be ended by political settlements, the Soviets and Cubans might not only provide arms and training for the guerrillas but also send Soviet advisers and Cuban troops to help. The West would then be at a definite disadvantage because it would be identified with white racist regimes. But the fundamental purpose was to align U.S. policy with the prevailing African sentiments that were strongly opposed to the white-dominated governments.

The United States therefore sought to promote South-West Africa's independence from South Africa, which had governed the former German colony since World War I, and to bring about a cease-fire in its guerrilla war and majority rule under U.S.-supervised elections. Rhodesia, however, was the more critical area. Its leader was Ian Smith, who had separated Rhodesia from the British Commonwealth in order to maintain the rule of 300,000 whites over almost 7 million blacks. After years of resisting any change, Smith was compelled by the increasing cost and drain on manpower imposed on Rhodesia by the black nationalist guerrilla war, as well as by economic sanctions, to shift his position. Proclaiming his willingness to accept "majority rule," Smith said free elections would be held. As a token of his intent, he formed a transitional government, which included several moderate black leaders who were believed to have popular appeal. Smith hoped that the "internal settlement" would end the war by attracting black support at home and isolating the guerrillas in their bases in neighboring Mozambique. Presumably, such a settlement would also gain American and British approval and lead to a lifting of economic sanctions.

The externally based Patriotic Front rejected the internal settlement as a fraud, asserting that it was a clever device to preserve white privilege and power. Virtually all black African states backed the Patriotic Front, led by Joshua Nkomo and the more militant, Marxist-oriented Robert Mugabe. In these circumstances, the Carter administration argued that Anglo-American support for the internal settlement and lifting of economic sanctions would be disastrous and would end the attempts to arrange for talks among all Rhodesian leaders, including the guerrillas. But sentiment for the internal settlement was growing in Britain and in the United States. It appeared to be a solution to the civil war without risking the possibility that the guerrilla leaders would capture power.

The newly elected Conservative government in Britain, however, decided to make one final effort to reach an overall settlement. Despite the widespread belief that a conference including black domestic and guerrilla leaders, as well as the white representatives, would fail, the British succeeded in bringing the various factions to agree to forgo a military solution and abide by the results of a free election. More surprises were in store. The election was won by the more radical Mugabe and not, as expected in London and Washington, by Nkomo. Mugabe at first showed himself to be a pragmatist and did not dispossess the white farmers and businessmen, whom the newly named Zimbabwe needed to remain prosperous. These results meant that the Carter administration had been saved by the British from choosing to alienate either the black states of Africa or the U.S. Senate, which had voted to lift economic sanctions. (In 1984, however, Mugabe declared that Zimbabwe would become a one-party, Marxist-Leninist state.)

One problem remained, as noted earlier: the Soviet Union was determined to exploit Third World situations to expand its influence. In a way, this was an old pattern. During the cold war the problems of the Third World had affected the superpowers and led to several conflicts. Soviet political strategy after Joseph Stalin's death had been to support the first generation of nationalist but non-Communist leaders of the newly independent countries. They might be bourgeois but their nationalism was directed against the West. In this way, a coalition could be forged to weaken the West. But by the early 1970s many of these leaders had either died, or they or their successors had turned against the Soviets, who had made enormous political, economic, and military investments in the Third World. Moscow lost positions of influence in the Sudan and Egypt, which turned toward the West; earlier, it watched in dismay as President Sukarno of Indonesia turned from the Soviet Union to China before he was overthrown and Indonesia turned to the West.

Although the Soviets did not abandon the policy of support for anti-Western nationalist regimes, they limited it to where it could still be pursued, as in Iraq and Syria, for example. The Soviets increasingly turned to helping Marxist or pro-Communist factions gain power and then defending them. They helped the North Vietnamese with arms supplies during the last phase of the Vietnam War; helped their friends capture power in Angola; assisted Marxist officers to seize power in Ethiopia; supported the pro-Moscow Marxist regimes in Afghanistan and South Yemen; and, by extending a treaty of friendship and cooperation to Hanoi, allowed North Vietnam to invade Communist Cambodia and replace the pro-Beijing regime there with a pro-

Soviet government. In the mid-1960s only Cuba, North Korea, and North Vietnam identified themselves as Marxist-Leninist states in the Third World. By the late 1970s there were six more: Afghanistan, Angola, Ethiopia, Mozambique, Nicaragua, and the People's Democratic Republic of Yemen. Moreover, North Vietnam had expanded and controlled all of Vietnam, as well as Cambodia.

These pro-Soviet regimes appear not to have enhanced long-term Soviet influence. Communist states, like non-Communist states, have increasingly been divided by nationalism, a force even stronger than communism— witness, in Asia, the conflicts between the Soviet Union and China, China and Vietnam, and, until it invaded Cambodia, Vietnam and Cambodia. But Soviet intervention did have two disturbing effects. The first was a rise of regional tensions. In Southeast Asia, the Vietnamese conquest of Cambodia and imposition of a Hanoi-controlled government led to China's punitive invasion of Vietnam, which, had it advanced toward Hanoi or lasted longer, might have led the Soviet Union to punish China by a similar limited border crossing. There was fear among Vietnam's neighbors of its expansion and dominance throughout Indochina and other Southeast Asian countries.

In Southwest Asia, in the area from the Horn of Africa to India, the combination of domestic instability, regional conflicts, and growing Soviet influence had created a more immediate, dangerous, and unstable situation. Zbigniew Brzezinski called the area an "arc of instability." Soviet-Cuban influence in Ethiopia and South Yemen on the Arabian peninsula especially worried the Saudis. Their anxiety about Soviet influence, moreover, was paralleled by anxiety about their internal stability. They saw that the shah of Iran, who, like them, had been using his enormous oil funds to modernize rapidly, was overthrown by a clergy upholding traditional Islamic society and opposed to Westernization. The Soviet invasion of Afghanistan enhanced this anxiety.

Fear in the area was widespread. Pro-Soviet Iraq, seeking to take advantage of Iran's weakness and domestic preoccupation, attacked Iran in an attempt to replace it as the primary Persian Gulf power. Iraq also sought to become the preeminent Arab state and to strengthen its role as spokesman for the Arab cause now that Egypt, traditionally the leading Arab power, had been isolated as a traitor to that cause. But the war divided the Arabs, with Syria and Libya supporting Iran and Jordan supporting Iraq; this division increased the rivalries in the area. Saudi Arabia and the other oil kingdoms became fearful of possible air strikes against their oil fields because they too supported Iraq. And Pakistan, which sent troops to Saudi Arabia to help defend the royal regime, worried over what the Soviets might do as 2 million Afghan refugees fled into Pakistan, many of whom returned to their homeland to fight with weapons bought and supplied by the CIA.

Always fearful of India, the Pakistanis were rumored to be developing a nuclear bomb to match India's. Iraq also appeared to be seeking the bomb, a matter of great worry to the Israelis, who presumably already possessed a number of them or could produce them quickly. The Israelis, having watched the Iraqis organize the Baghdad front and reject Arab peace negotiations with Israel, therefore attacked the Iraqi nuclear reactor. The Middle East-Persian Gulf area was as much a tinderbox as ever. And because of its close relationship with Israel and even more because of its dependence on Middle Eastern oil, the United States could not avoid involvement as the superpowers' rivalry was superimposed on these regional problems. The Carter Doctrine was simply open recognition of the vital interests at stake for the United States in this critical region.

The second effect of Soviet intervention was the impact on détente itself. The Soviet Union continued to fish in the troubled Third World waters because the potential gains were high and the costs virtually zero. The problems in Africa or Asia might well be regional, but Soviet-Cuban military interventions in Angola and Ethiopia and pro-Soviet coups in Afghanistan and South Yemen had transformed these local disturbances into aspects of the wider Soviet-American competition for influence. Yet before the invasion of Afghanistan in 1979, no penalties were imposed, and so long as the Soviet Union believed that the United States was paralyzed by memories of Vietnam and the change in the balance of power, Moscow had no reason to desist. The Carter administration abandoned the virtually automatic response to Soviet involvement in the developing regions that had characterized American foreign policy during the earlier, bipolar, cold war days and first few years of détente. But the administration's incomprehension both of the consequences of Soviet-Cuban interventions for American interests and of the world's perception of American power and will as weak were very harmful. Increasing sensitivity to the nationalism of the Third World and sympathy for the social struggles and causes involved, while clearly desirable, therefore appeared to be an insufficient response. The East-West context continued to intrude. Nowhere was this more vividly demonstrated than in the Middle East, which had within a few years become critically important to U.S. security and prosperity.

The Middle Eastern Linchpin

By the 1970s the Middle East, with its unstable governments, militancy, high emotions, and its ability to suck the superpowers into its regional quarrels, more and more resembled the Balkans in the early twentieth century. Even before Carter, the Nixon, and later the Ford, administration resolved to avoid the past pattern in which the Israelis won a military victory but were unable to translate it into a political settlement. The Israeli victories had left the Arabs humiliated and resentful, more determined than ever not to accept the right of Israel to exist and willing only to prepare for another

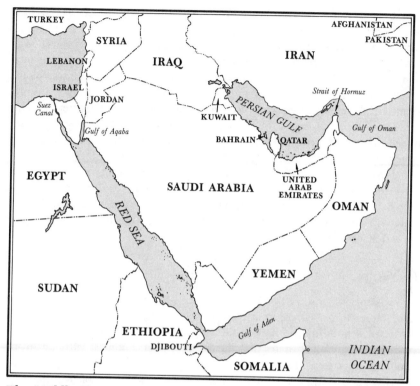

The Middle East

round in the struggle. In the American evaluation, the 1973 war had shown a number of things: Israel could be caught by surprise, Arab armies could learn how to use modern weapons effectively, the intolerable cost in manpower losses to Israel of a war lasting longer than a few days, the grave difficulties for the Israeli economy when much of its manpower is mobilized, and the political isolation of Israel in a world in which most industrialized nations, whatever their fear of the Arab oil weapon, were generally unsympathetic to Israel's policy, especially with regard to the Palestinians. All this spelled further trouble for Israel, whose only friend in the world now was the United States. But in the face of oil embargoes and higher energy costs, would the United States continue to support Israel, which was still holding the territories it had captured in 1967?

For Kissinger, the urgency of attempting to reach a Middle East settlement was obvious, and the time seemed favorable. Anwar Sadat had declared his willingness to accept the existence of Israel and make peace with it on the basis of the 1967 frontiers. The Arab armies for the first time had shown bravery and skill and recovered some self-esteem; diplomatic concessions in these circumstances might be easier. Their earlier defeats had led only to inflexibility. An Arab-Israeli peace would have other desirable consequences as well. The chief one was avoiding an American-Soviet confrontation that could escalate into a superpower war. Each of the Arab-Israeli wars had held the possibility of such a confrontation, and in 1973 that possibility had come frighteningly close. Would another Arab-Israeli war prove to be the incendiary device setting off World War III? Another consequence was the reduction of Soviet influence in the area and its replacement by American influence. American support for Israel had been a principal reason for this Soviet influence. Playing a more evenhanded role and arranging for peace, which would achieve security for Israel as well as satisfy Arab territorial and political purposes, would enhance America's position in the area. Peace would also secure a reliable source of oil, which was particularly critical at a time when the United States was becoming an oil importer; but this appears to have been a less important consideration.

Two Approaches to Middle East Peace

Kissinger's strategy for peace was a step-by-step approach. There were many issues to be settled; to attempt to solve them at one time with all the parties present would be impossible. In a public conference at Geneva, co-chaired by the United States and the Soviet Union, the most extreme Arabs would set the pace; to take a moderate position in this atmosphere would seem a betrayal of the Arab cause. The presence of the Soviet Union was likely to lend support to the militants, because it profited from continued turmoil in the area. And such a conference would openly bring out Israeli-American differences. A step-by-step approach would start with the easier issues and proceed to the more difficult.

The first task was the disengagement of the Israeli forces and the Egyptian and Syrian forces after the war. Next would be a further Israeli withdrawal from the Sinai and then the Golan Heights. The two issues that would be the hardest and most emotional were the establishment of a Palestinian state, a cause espoused by the terrorist Palestine Liberation Organization, with whom the Israelis would not talk directly, and control of eastern Jerusalem, called the Old City. By successfully resolving the initial issues, a momentum would be established to help resolve the other matters; and success would divide the moderates from the more militant regimes, strengthening the former and weakening the latter.

Kissinger was successful in achieving two unprecedented interim agreements—first the disengagement of the hostile forces on the Egyptian Sinai and Syrian Golan fronts, and later a further withdrawal by the Israelis from two strategic passes and an oil well in the Sinai. Throughout the process the Soviets denounced Kissinger. Becoming cooler toward the Egyptians, who expected the Americans to pressure the Israelis to leave, the Soviets threw their support behind the more militant Syrians. By its agreement, Egypt, as the Syrians saw it, had left them to face Israel all by themselves. To the Syrians, as well as to many other Arab states and the PLO, these acts were tantamount to a sell-out of the Arab cause. Egypt was isolated in the Arab world.

The Carter administration, on coming into power and somewhat more concerned with the energy situation than its predecessor, viewed this situation with alarm. Carter and Brzezinski believed that the step-by-step approach had reached its end. It had, in their view, some fundamental liabilities. One, Israel was required in each step to give up territory for promises that, when all steps had been taken, it and its neighbors would sign a peace treaty and Israel would be accorded legitimacy. But by then it would no longer have any bargaining chips. Two, the incremental approach avoided the central problem of the Palestinians, whose grievances would have to be met if a genuine peace were ever to be established. The Kissinger way—dealing with the easy problems first in the hope of gaining sufficient momentum and trust among the negotiating parties to resolve the difficult issues later—frittered away precious time and thereby perhaps jeopardized the possibility of peace. The greatest danger was that if the key differences between Israel and the Arabs were not resolved, Sadat would either be outflanked by more militant Arabs; be overthrown within his own country; or, to survive politically, if not physically, be forced to play the role of the new Nasser. Time, in brief, was not on the side of the United States.

An Egyptian-Israeli Breakthrough

The Carter administration proposed that all parties resume negotiations at Geneva. Kissinger had fashioned his strategy to exclude the Soviets; only at the final conference would the Soviet Union attend as the cochairman. Carter decided to approach the Soviets and enlist their cooperation. Moscow had influence with the more militant Syrians and the PLO, and it therefore had the capacity to cause a lot of trouble and block negotiations. If Moscow participated in the peace negotiations, however, it would retain a degree of influence in the Arab world if and when a peace treaty was signed, reduce the possibility of a superpower clash, and help strengthen détente with the United States.

Neither Jerusalem nor Cairo was happy with the Soviet-American accord in late 1977. Israel did not want to face all its enemies simultaneously, and Egypt had already broken with Moscow, which now favored Syria, Egypt's rival. Israel and Egypt decided to bypass Moscow and Washington and negotiate directly. In a dramatic and internationally televised visit to Jerusalem in November 1977, during which he addressed the Israeli Knesset (parliament), Sadat, the leader of the Arab world's strongest nation, in effect extended recognition to the Arabs' archenemy. He expressed his hope that there would be no more war. The impact was euphoric as a comprehensive peace—a peace with all of Israel's Arab enemies—seemed near.

Begin and the Settlements Policy

The mood did not last long. Sadat apparently believed peace was easily and quickly achievable because he had taken the significant psychological step to reassure the Israelis that his peace offer was genuine, not a trick. Israel would withdraw to its 1967 frontiers from the Sinai, the West Bank, Syria's Golan Heights, and Jordan's East Jerusalem and would recognize the Palestinians' legitimate rights; and, in return for their land, the Arabs would sign a peace treaty and Israel would gain the legitimacy and peace with security it had sought since birth. The Israelis had always asserted that if only the Arabs would negotiate with them directly, implying recognition, they would be willing to return the territories taken in 1967. Israel had specifically disclaimed annexationist ambitions. The Labor government after the 1967 war had accepted UN Resolution 242 committing Israel to the withdrawal from the captured land (or, given some adjustments for security reasons, from almost all).

But Israel's new coalition government was led by Prime Minister Menachem Begin, leader of the principal opposition party, Likud, who had spent his parliamentary life in opposition, and he had other ideas. He proposed to withdraw from the Sinai desert, but offered the Palestinians on the West Bank and in the Gaza Strip only autonomy, or self-rule, not self-determination. Begin referred to the West Bank by its ancient Hebrew names, Judea and Samaria; he claimed that they were not occupied territory to be returned but liberated territory to be kept as a part of the Greater Israel of which Begin had long dreamed. He left no doubt that he expected to establish Israeli sovereignty over both the West Bank and Gaza, each of which contained several hundred thousand Arabs. In the meantime, the Israeli government announced that Jewish settlements in the Sinai and West Bank would remain and encouraged more settlements.

To Sadat, Begin's plan for the West Bank and Gaza meant the perpetuation of Israeli military occupation under the guise of autonomy. And without a settlement of the Palestinian issue satisfactory to the Palestinians and the withdrawal of Israel from the conquered Arab territories, he could not sign a separate peace with Israel. After Sadat's trip to Jerusalem, Syria, Libya, Iraq, Algeria, South Yemen, and the PLO had already condemned Sadat and formed a "rejectionist front." Sadat, in turn, had broken diplomatic relations with the five states. But there were limits to his freedom of maneuver.

Bilateral negotiations therefore broke down and the United States reentered the negotiating process. The effect of U.S. mediation in the stalled

Israeli-Egyptian negotiations, however, was to bring into the open what Kissinger had expected to avoid with his step-by-step approach—namely, American-Israeli differences on how to achieve peace. Carter, like Kissinger, felt that Sadat was offering Israel the security and peace it had so long sought, and if this opportunity were not seized the result would be politically disastrous for Israel and economically disastrous for the West.

The president thought three conditions were necessary for a solution in the Middle East. First, UN Resolution 242 meant the return of most of the Arab territory Israel had captured in 1967. Only minor adjustments for security reasons could be allowed. Second (and in this respect the administration went far beyond any of its predecessors), it boldly asserted that the key to peace was the Palestinian issue. More specifically, it said that the Palestinians had the right to participate in the peace-making process, and Carter himself soon publicly declared that the Palestinians had a right to a "homeland," a deliberately vague term but one that nevertheless carried great symbolic weight. Third, in return for such Israeli concessions, the Arab states had to commit themselves not only to ending their state of hostilities with Israel but also to signing a peace treaty followed by diplomatic exchanges and trade and tourism agreements. The Israelis had been insistent on this point, but the Arabs were balking at such normalization, declaring that it would take a whole generation for this to occur after so much bitterness and anger.

Begin was at odds with the first two positions. He had reinterpreted UN Resolution 242, accepted by his predecessors, to mean that Israel was not required to withdraw from the West Bank and Gaza. He was also opposed to a Palestinian state which he, and indeed most Israelis, felt would constitute a danger to the existence of Israel. The issue that most clearly symbolized U.S.-Israeli differences was the policy on Israeli settlements in the occupied lands. Ever since 1967, the United States had consistently opposed these settlements as illegal. The Carter administration repeated this while it watched with disbelief as the Israeli government actively encouraged new settlements on the land the Arabs were reclaiming. It appeared as if Israel were deliberately setting out to destroy the one chance it had ever had to gain legitimacy and peace; it certainly impressed Washington and Cairo as an act of bad faith to begin new settlements in the midst of peace negotiations.

Repeated American efforts to halt this policy and encourage the Israelis to hold out more hope to the Arabs for the eventual recovery of the West Bank and Gaza were all in vain. By contrast, Sadat appeared reasonable and conciliatory. He had with great courage provided the psychological breakthrough with his trip to Jerusalem. He had shown characteristic sensitivity to Israel's security needs by being willing to listen to various ideas for demilitarizing or thinning out forces in certain areas, and he had been willing to accept Israel's demands for a peace treaty and the subsequent normalization of relations not after twenty-five years, or even five years, but immediately.

The Camp David Accords

Yet, the stalemate continued. As the three-year, second interim Sinai agreement was about to run out in October 1978, Carter gambled and invited Begin and Sadat to meet with him at Camp David. The invitation was a gamble because had this summit meeting produced no results, the president's prestige, already low, would have been even more seriously impaired, American mediating attempts would have run their course, and Israeli-American relations would have been set back even further. But the president, perhaps for the first time in his administration, showed persistence and skill and after twelve days of patient negotiations emerged with a series of agreements, including a commitment by the two men to sign a peace treaty within three months.

Sadat made most of the concessions. He did not gain a commitment to an eventual Israeli withdrawal from the West Bank and Gaza Strip, or full Palestinian self-determination. The Israelis, however, promised to recognize "the legitimate rights of the Palestinians," to permit West Bank and Gaza Palestinians to participate in future negotiations on these areas and ratify or reject a final agreement, and to halt temporarily new Israeli settlements on the West Bank. But Israel vetoed the participation of the PLO leaders in such negotiations or the establishment of a Palestinian state; on these issues Israel's position remained intact. Yet Israel gained a separate peace treaty with the strongest of its Arab neighbors; without Egypt the others could not by themselves take on Israel. Thus, for a seemingly small investment Israel had gained the enormous dividend of a real sense of security because Jordan or Syria alone or together were too weak to wage war against it. That was why, as noted, Syria had opposed Sadat's journey to Jerusalem and the subsequent bilateral negotiations. Once the threat of war with Egypt had ended, Israel would have no reason to return the Golan Heights to Syria.

Sadat, however, had taken a chance. Rather than selling out, he appears to have felt that a peace agreement would start a momentum for further agreements with Israel. The first Arab reaction to Camp David, however, was negative. Jordan and even Saudi Arabia joined the rejectionist group of Syria, Iraq, Libya, Algeria, and South Yemen in condemning Sadat, who became more isolated than ever. Under these circumstances, Carter's courageous personal intervention—his trip to Egypt and Israel—produced the necessary diplomatic breakthroughs and brought peace between these two long-term enemies. Yet the subsequent treaty did not bring a stable peace to the area. On the eve of the Israeli-Egyptian peace treaty in March 1979, Begin in a defiant mood told his parliament and the world that Israel would never withdraw to its 1967 borders, Jerusalem would remain Israel's "eternal capital," and that there would never be a Palestinian state on the West Bank and Gaza. If Israel, with Egypt now neutralized, were unwilling to accommodate the grievances and aspirations of the Palestinians, Jordanians, and Syrians, the peace process would grind to a halt.

The ink on the Israeli-Egyptian peace treaty was hardly dry when Israel announced the formation of new settlements on the West Bank. Israel was ensuring that the West Bank would belong to Israel. Not long afterward, the Israelis began to dispossess the Arabs of their land. Because this policy enhanced pro-PLO sentiment, the military occupation became increasingly repressive and censorship tightened. And American policy appeared to be the prisoner of Israeli policy, although Israel was the dependent state. The United States supported Israel almost without reservation, even though in America's judgment Israeli policy often seemed self-defeating, short-sighted, and annexationist. No pressure was exerted by the United States on Israel to be more accommodating; instead, Washington continued to finance and militarily support an increasingly untenable political situation.

The Arabs, of course, held the United States responsible both for a peace treaty that had omitted resolving the key Palestinian problem and for an Israeli policy that was calculated to make a comprehensive peace impossible. Symbolic was the unilateral Israeli decision to incorporate East Jerusalem into Jerusalem and declare that the city would never again be divided. The action aroused great anger throughout the Arab countries. The Arabs blamed Israeli policy on American acquiescence. American efforts to be more evenhanded after 1973 appeared in the eyes of the Arabs to have ended in a return to the pre-1973, one-sided support of Israel, regardless of how provocative Israeli actions were. Did the United States not know its own interests? This question was particularly asked in traditional and conservative, as well as pro-Western and anti-Communist, Saudi Arabia, upon whose oil the United States now greatly depended and whose position in the Arab world had been endangered by Washington's stance.

The Saudis did not like the position in which they were placed by American Middle East policy: a separation from Egypt, which, under Sadat, was also a moderate, pro-Western, and anti-Communist state; a "distancing" from the United States in order to avoid too close an identification with it; and a fear that if the peace negotiations stalled, Soviet and radical Arab influences would again rise while the influence of the United States would decline once more. Thus, while the Saudis were being asked to raise oil production to meet American needs and restrain the "price hawks" among the oil producers, their confidence in the wisdom of U.S. policy and American leadership declined. This lack of confidence was reinforced by the perception of an increasing lack of credibility of American power as the shah of Iran was overthrown; the Soviets, whose influence was already established in Ethiopia and neighboring South Yemen, invaded Afghanistan; and the Saudis, along with the rest of the world, watched the new Islamic Republic of Iran humiliate the United States by seizing American diplomats in their embassy in Tehran. For fourteen months following the seizure, the United States appeared impotent and incompetent to deal with the situation.

Iran and the End of the Vietnam Syndrome

The year 1979 witnessed, as noted earlier, the crumbling of U.S. positions in Southwest Asia. Deterioration began in Iran, second only to Saudi Arabia in non-Communist world oil production, with the overthrow of the shah. Iran's oil production fell off sharply, and the resulting tightening of world oil supplies led to a huge escalation of oil prices to approximately $32 a barrel (more than $40 in some markets), with devastating effects on inflation and unemployment in the industrial world, especially in the United States. Most important of all, however, was the spectacle of a disintegrating American position in an area of absolutely vital importance for the United States.

The low level to which American resolution and power had fallen was symbolized by the invasion of the American embassy in Tehran in November 1979 by a mob of militant students, who seized fifty-two American personnel. This outrage occurred after the deposed shah, suffering from cancer, had been admitted to the United States for medical treatment. (He died a few months later in Egypt.) The revolutionary authorities gave the unprecedented action—not even Hitler or Stalin had tried to seize enemy diplomats—their blessing and support. The subsequent efforts by the Carter administration to gain the safe release of the Americans became high public drama. Under the watchful eyes of the cameras of the three major U.S. television networks, the American public was repeatedly exposed to pictures of crowds, like well-rehearsed choruses, chanting their hatred of America, the "Great Satan," as it was called by the Ayatollah Ruhollah Khomeini, Iran's chief religious leader and *imam,* or leader, of all Shi'ite Muslims. "Death to America," the crowds screamed constantly. In frequent interviews Khomeini and other Iranian leaders lectured the American public for America's support of the shah and spoke mockingly of the U.S. naval power gathering in the Indian Ocean. They virtually dared the president to use it.

In the 444 days following the taking of the hostages, the world watched as the Carter administration tried one means after another to gain their release: appeals to the United Nations and the International Court of Justice, both of which were ignored by Iran, and a series of economic sanctions, which were largely ineffective because Japan and Western Europe needed Iran's oil more than the United States did. All was in vain: the holding of the hostages was a symbolic act of defiance and revenge for the shah who was portrayed by the new regime as an American puppet who had cruelly exploited Iranians on behalf of U.S. interests. As the administration's patience wore thin, it attempted a rescue mission in the spring of 1980. The mission was called off when three of the eight helicopters malfunctioned in a brutal sandstorm, leaving the operation short of the six considered necessary to proceed. One helicopter collided on the ground with the refueling aircraft for the flight out of Iran, killing eight servicemen and injuring five others. The mission's failure dramatically symbolized the humiliation and apparent helplessness, clumsiness, and impotence of the United States, as well as the low level of readiness, competence, and reliability of its armed forces.

Two events helped to gain the hostages' release on January 20, 1981. The first was the Iraqi attack on Iran in the fall of 1980. The war suddenly made the U.S. economic sanctions, especially the freeze on Iranian money in U.S. banks, painful for Iran because its military forces were largely American equipped; the need for spare parts and the cash to buy them and other goods grew as oil production in Iran fell to almost nothing. The second event was the November victory of Ronald Reagan, the former governor of California, in the U.S. presidential elections. Because he had run on a tough foreign policy platform and denounced the Iranians as "barbarians" and "kidnappers," the Iranians expected harsher measures from Reagan, including military action. In these circumstances, diplomacy finally proved successful. The fifty-two diplomats and marines were released just after Reagan's inauguration in a gesture fraught with symbolism. A humiliating chapter in American history had ended. In the exuberance of the welcome that the ex-hostages received upon their return to America, one could almost hear the refrain "never again," for in a real sense, America itself and the U.S. government had been taken captive and held hostage.

Until the war in Vietnam, the United States had been extensively involved in the world, and it had justified its role as anti-Communist. As in the two wars against Germany, the cold war was a moral cause: democracy versus dictatorship. After Vietnam, the reaction had set in, illustrating the usual American pattern of swings from isolationism to crusading and back again. The mood of disillusionment and disengagement from the burdens of more than two decades of American-Soviet conflict—plus the accompanying sense of shame and guilt about the uses to which American power had been put—found their outlet in the Carter administration's rejection of the "inordinate fear of communism"; the emphasis on America's "limited power" and restraint in its exercise; the avoidance of force or covert intervention in the domestic affairs of other states; a preference for North-South cooperation to erase poverty and broaden human rights—or, at least, reduce the worst abuses of them; a distaste for East-West relations, except for arms control; and a repudiation of old-fashioned power politics in favor of reorienting U.S. policy toward the forces said to be transforming world politics.

Interdependence as a theory fit the temper of the 1970s like a glove. If balance-of-power considerations were indeed becoming less critical and economic forces and global welfare more important, there was little reason to worry about the Soviet Union despite its steadily growing military power. The reasons advanced for not worrying were many: the Soviets were just catching up with the United States; they had to worry over China as well as the North Atlantic Treaty Organization; and, given the frequency of past invasions, they were insecure. But, it was forecast, once they had achieved parity with the United States, they would stop. When they did not stop, new explanations said it did not really matter: nuclear weapons were suicidal and conventional ones too costly to use; the Soviets were just wasting their money; the Soviet leaders were clearly in need of education for thinking that past patterns of behavior would be just as useful in the future.

In any event, whatever the level of Soviet military capability, there was little need to worry about Soviet intentions. By the middle 1970s, it was commonplace to regard the cold war as over. The Soviet Union was said to be a status quo power; it might still mouth ideological slogans and revolutionary global aims, but these had about the same practical effect on Soviet policy, the argument went, as most Western churchgoers' Christian beliefs had on their everyday behavior. At worst, Soviet Russia—like czarist Russia—might still harbor imperial ambitions like those of other great powers throughout history, but these were limited, not at all comparable to the universal goals of revolutionary powers. The Soviet Union in the 1970s was no longer considered a revolutionary power. Nationalism in the Third World, the determination of former colonies to assert their identity and interests, would ensure that they would not become Soviet colonies.

The upshot was predictable of this unwillingness to face fully the "real world," to explain away continued superpower competition, to minimize concern for the results of this competition while it remained largely one-sided, and the reluctance to assert American power. The Soviets calculated that they could defy the United States with impunity. Perhaps indicative of this state of affairs was Carter's handling of the issue of the Soviet combat brigade that U.S. intelligence had discovered in Cuba in the summer of 1979. Although the brigade had probably been there for years and Brzezinski recommended against demanding its withdrawal, the president, pushed on the issue by domestic politics, took a hard-line position. He first declared that this "status quo was not acceptable." When Moscow said that the troops were there merely to train Cubans, Carter accepted this reassurance and accepted the very status quo he had a few days earlier found unacceptable. Moscow refused to budge on this issue, even though it might—and did—hurt the chances of SALT II's passage through the Senate. Rather than risk a confrontation or a delay of SALT II, Carter changed his mind. The issue was undoubtedly publicly overblown and not comparable in its importance to Soviet moves in Africa and elsewhere, but Carter's ineptness and impotence seemed to symbolize post-Vietnam America. Is it any wonder that shortly thereafter, having seen the United States frequently change its mind, hesitate, or remain passive since Angola in 1975, the Soviet Union felt it could invade

Afghanistan without fear of U.S. retaliation? Or that Iran thought it could seize American diplomatic personnel with impunity and that the sizable U.S. naval forces gathered in the Indian Ocean after the seizure were only a bluff?

Yet, the capture of the hostages and invasion of Afghanistan dispelled much of the post-Vietnam atmosphere and led to a demand for a more vigorous policy. Khomeini and Leonid Brezhnev may have done the United States a favor, just as it had taken a German submarine attack on U.S. ships (World War I), a Japanese attack on Pearl Harbor (World War II), and a Soviet coup in Czechoslovakia (cold war) to mobilize the nation when the public mood was one of disengagement and relaxation. After years of neoisolationism, the two successive slaps in the face in November and December of 1979, may have been necessary to demonstrate that impotence can result only in national shame. Carter sensed this shift of mood as he took a harder line toward the Soviets. But it was Reagan who received the full measure of the benefit of this shift of mood. He had long taken a hard line toward the Soviet Union, and, although inflation and the weak state of the U.S. economy may have been the primary factors for Reagan's election, the fact remains that because of OPEC and the collapse of the shah, the domestic economic issue was inseparable from American foreign policy and the U.S. position in the world. As on earlier occasions when America had felt provoked, its reaction was predictable. The pendulum of public opinion swung back part of the way to a recognition of the continuation of American-Soviet rivalry and a more vigorous reassertion of American interests and power.

Reagan and Cold War II: Reviving U.S. Military and Economic Capabilities

IN JANUARY 1981 Ronald Reagan took the oath of office as president of the United States. A mediocre actor, conservative spokesman for General Electric, and former governor of California, Reagan as president was to be known neither for his intellect nor for long hours spent in the White House devoted to the nation's business. He was to become famous for what was politely called his "hands-off" style of management of foreign policy, that is, paying little attention to the details of policy formation and execution. But he brought to the office he occupied for two terms (the first president to do so since Eisenhower) two skills that were to help transform American-Soviet relations. Reagan had strong anti-Communist instincts and a powerful ability to mobilize public opinion.

He proved to be the right man at the right place at the right time. America was pessimistic about the future and uncertain about the use of its power as the 1980s began; Carter had damned his own presidency with his whining epitaph of a national "malaise." Reagan restored the nation's pride in itself and made it feel good again about the nation's mission in the world: the defense and promotion of democratic values. The nation was also concerned about the military balance. Reagan believed the Soviets were winning the arms race and therefore spent his first term overseeing a rapid and extensive rearmament program, crowning it with the Strategic Defense Initiative (SDI), a vision of a space-based defense of the country against Soviet missiles. NATO was concerned that the Soviet deployment of SS-20 missiles was upsetting the nuclear balance in Europe; Reagan was determined to go ahead with the counterdeployment of U.S. intermediate-range nuclear forces (INF). Although this decision had originally been made by Carter, considerable public outcry against it had placed the decision in some doubt. Plenty of voices counseled postponing deployment or cutting the numbers of missiles to be deployed or accepting the Soviet proposal to include the British and French nuclear forces in a trade-off.

The new president, like the nation, felt that Moscow had used détente to advance its global strategic interests. He was determined to reverse these gains. The Soviet leaders had claimed the right to expand their country's influence under the doctrine of "national liberation," while simultaneously claiming the right to keep what they had gained under the Brezhnev Doctrine. In short, Moscow claimed that communism was irreversible. Reagan, with his instinctive anticommunism and angered by Soviet behavior in the 1970s, made that behavior the centerpiece of his foreign policy. His predecessors had made arms control the centerpiece of their policies. The president rejected the thesis that arms control negotiations were so important because the arms race made superpower conflict so fraught with nuclear hazards that negotiations must not be jeopardized by anything more than futile protests against Soviet expansionist efforts. Reagan gave priority to the various regional conflicts and decided to put off all arms control negotiations. He had disapproved of SALT II. If arms agreements were to be negotiated in his administration at all, they would aim for deep reductions, especially of the larger Soviet forces. But such negotiations would not be held until the United States, with its rearmament effort, was able to "negotiate from strength."

Just as Leonid Brezhnev's exploitation of détente helped to bring Reagan into the presidency, so Reagan assisted in Mikhail S. Gorbachev's emergence. The reduction of tensions between the superpowers by 1987, so unexpected at the beginning of the decade, has often been attributed to Gorbachev himself. The new Soviet leader was said to be the first enlightened ruler since the 1917 Revolution. He represented a new generation, more critical of the failings of the Soviet system, sharing the Soviet people's great desire for material improvements; most of this new generation came from an urban rather than rural background and had some exposure to foreign travel. Had Brezhnev or his immediate successors, Yuri Andropov and Konstantin Chernenko, survived, Gorbachev's domestic and foreign policy changes might not have occurred.

An alternative interpretation suggested that the improvement in superpower relations was due to the Soviet system that, threatened by a stagnant economy and a declining standard of living, faced the possibility that by the beginning of the twenty-first century the Soviet Union would lose its superpower status. Thus, Gorbachev—or any leader of the country—had to undertake drastic domestic reforms. For Gorbachev to focus the necessary attention on the domestic economy, he needed a relaxation of political tensions with the United States. New arms control agreements would permit him to reduce the heavy military expenditures and to invest more funds in the civilian economy. Reagan was thus, in a sense, lucky. He happened to be in office at a moment when the Soviets needed to retrench in foreign policy. The president was thus the beneficiary, but he could claim little of the credit for the resulting improvement of American-Soviet relations.

These interpretations do not, however, recognize the role that Reagan played in increasing the pressure on the Soviet Union to reform its system. The Reagan military buildup meant further Soviet investments in arms and rendered Soviet deterrent forces vulnerable to attack, as the Soviet buildup in the 1970s had done to American strategic forces. The American INF deployment in Europe meant that instead of the SS-20s strengthening the Soviet position, they rendered the Soviet Union less secure because INF missiles could reach the Soviet Union. In addition, the president's program for a strategic defense of the United States, the Strategic Defense Initiative (SDI), which was criticized by almost all American scientists as impractical, worried the Soviets because whether or not it succeeded in realizing Reagan's vision of a missile-proof shield over the United States, the research might lead America to another quantum leap in technology at a time when the Soviet Union was already concerned about the gap between itself and its rival. And the Reagan Doctrine of supporting guerrillas against the Marxist governments the Soviets had either helped into power, as in Angola, or helped keep in power, as in Nicaragua, made Moscow's support of its empire an economic drain and military burden, especially in Afghanistan.

In brief, the Brezhnev foreign policy, which at first had appeared so successful—with its achievement of nuclear parity, conventional forces with a global reach, and acquisition of imperial outposts—had become counterproductive: It had stimulated a strong American reaction, held NATO together and, with Japan and China, left the Soviet Union surrounded by enemies. Reagan, in short, increased the strains on the Soviet Union enough so that it could no longer "muddle along" as in the 1970s, hoping that Western technology and trade would rescue it from having to risk more fundamental structural reforms of the political-economic system. Moscow no longer had any choice.

It was in this sense that Reagan helped Gorbachev achieve power. By increasing the strains on the Soviet system, he left it no alternative but to retrench abroad, to cut military spending, and to subordinate foreign policy to domestic affairs. Initially thought to be reckless and widely condemned as a cowboy (especially in Europe) because he appeared trigger-happy to many, the president left office with the superpower relationship on the best terms it had been since 1945. Thus, despite some setbacks (Nicaragua), scandal (the Iran-*contra* affair) and, worst of all, a huge federal budget deficit that helped to make the United States, once the world's largest creditor nation, its greatest debtor, Reagan left office in January of 1989 with the highest public approval of any postwar president.

Reagan's Anti-Soviet Rhetoric

When Ronald Reagan came into office, the national disillusionment with détente was widespread and the term *cold war II* was a frequently used term. The president's long-term hostility toward communism in general and more specifically toward the Soviet Union fit the new postdétente mood. No more was heard about "world-order politics," the priority of North-South issues over East-West issues, or the limits of American power. Quite the opposite: the president often sounded like an old-fashioned evangelist rather than a born-again Christian. Reagan never suggested that he thought the United States had abused its power or that it should feel ashamed or guilty about the past exercise of power. Vietnam had been an "honorable" war. He denounced Soviet communism as "the focus of evil in the modern world." He said, "There is sin and evil in the world, and we're enjoined by Scripture and the Lord Jesus to oppose it with all our might" [1] and Soviet leaders would lie, steal, cheat, and do anything else to advance their goals.[2] Opposition to the Soviet Union, therefore, was a religious as well as a political imperative.

Reagan spoke of the march of freedom and democracy leaving "Marxism-Leninism on the ashheap of history," of the "great revolutionary crisis" of the Soviet political-economic system, and the "decay of the Soviet experiment." Of Eastern Europe he said, "Regimes planted by bayonets do not take root"—that is, the Communist regimes had no legitimacy. He stated that the United States could not accept the "permanent subjugation of the people of Eastern Europe"; that the Yalta conference had not divided Europe into Soviet and American spheres of influence (which was true because the Soviets had promised free elections in the countries of Eastern Europe and then placed Communist regimes in power at bayonet point).[3] In making the point that democracy and freedom were the waves of the future, the president was giving the Soviets a dose of their own medicine, for the Soviets constantly denounced the United States and forecast the "inevitable end" of Western capitalism. More important, he was questioning the legitimacy and longevity of communism as a social and political system not only in Eastern Europe but also in the Soviet Union.

The Soviet leaders, surprisingly thin-skinned, were greatly irritated. Many American critics, too, thought of Reagan's predictions about communism being swept aside by the tide of democracy as only so much rhetoric. By the end of his second term, however, as non-Communist tyrannies were being swept away and Communist regimes were being exposed to greater demands for liberties from within, Reagan's prediction looked less like

---

1. Remarks to the National Association of Evangelicals, March 8, 1983, in Strobe Talbott, *The Russians and Reagan* (New York: Vintage Books, 1984), 113.
2. *New York Times,* January 30, 1981.
3. Address to members of Parliament, June 8, 1982, in Talbott, *The Russians and Reagan,* 89-104.

right-wing rantings than accurate and intuitive insights into historical development.

Reagan's rhetoric undoubtedly contributed to the worsening of relations with the Soviet Union in the early 1980s. In September 1983 the Soviets shot down a South Korean Boeing 747 jetliner with 269 people aboard, which had flown off course over Soviet territory. They then lied for a week that they had not done it, after which they finally admitted the act. The Soviets then had the temerity to charge that the United States had been using the Korean jetliner as a spy plane. In response, the president denounced the downing as an "act against humanity." It confirmed his view of the Soviet regime as uncivilized and brutal. (When the United States shot down an Iranian jetliner over the Persian Gulf in 1988, having mistaken it for a fighter jet, Reagan accepted responsibility in more sober language and offered compensation to the bereaved families). The Soviets responded in kind, denouncing the president for piling slander on the Soviet Union and socialism. They also boycotted the Olympics held in Los Angeles in 1984 (as the United States had done in 1980 following the Soviet invasion of Afghanistan, when it withdrew from the Olympic games held in Moscow, which the Kremlin had intended to exploit as a glorification of Soviet socialism and superpower status). The Soviet boycott in a presidential election year was deliberate; the Soviet Union intended to underline the message that Reagan's anticommunism and militarism were the sole source of the new superpower chill.

Reasons Behind the Rhetoric

The harsh denunciations of the Soviet Union, undiplomatic perhaps but not totally inaccurate, were not mere statements of the president's personal ideology. They served at least two specific purposes. First, they were intended to remobilize American public opinion after the years of détente. To be sure, Reagan's election was itself a sign of the public's growing cynicism about détente and anger at America's recent humiliations in foreign policy. The stronger anti-Soviet rhetoric and more assertive post-Vietnam role, in fact, had started with President Jimmy Carter. But Carter was more strongly identified with the American hostages in Iran and his confession that he had misunderstood Soviet intentions until the Soviet invasion of Afghanistan. Reagan, to whom détente had all along been an illusion based on the unwarranted belief that the Soviets had changed their character, sought to arouse American opinion for the longer term. The angry mood would pass; the public during the 1970s, after all, had shared the hopes that the cold war was dead. The nation's attention needed to be refocused on the Kremlin's leaders.

The second function of the president's war of words was to send the Soviet leaders a message, especially at a time the Soviet Union was having a severe geriatric problem. First, Brezhnev died in late 1982; his successor,

Andropov, died just over a year later in early 1984; and his successor, Chernenko, in ill health when he took over, died just over a year later in 1985. Gorbachev, who had risen rapidly to the top of the Soviet party hierarchy, partly as a result of being close to key leaders, especially Andropov, who had served as head of the KGB, now became the Soviet Union's fourth leader since Reagan had assumed office. Gorbachev's early career spanned the years of growing Soviet military strength, expansion of influence beyond Eurasia, and America's declining appetite for an activist global role. Reagan's blunt declarations sent the new Soviet leadership the signal that the Vietnam syndrome was a thing of the past, that America's will to resist Soviet expansion was back. The president's purpose was to avoid confrontations and possible military clashes. The signals were perhaps intentionally sharp so that the Soviet Union would not act, as it had during the 1970s, in the belief that America would not react. Minor military actions against small Soviet proxies like Libya and Grenada—actions that the United States could not lose and were not costly—were intended to drive this message home. In that sense, the tough words were essentially a substitute for riskier deeds.

In fact, the early Reagan years were characterized by *rhetorical* confrontations, but no real encounters. In policy terms these were quiet years; there were no crises. Despite his cowboy reputation, operationally, the president was cautious and careful. Indeed, to the extent the Soviets saw him as a leader spoiling for a fight, they were no doubt strengthened in their conviction that they needed to act with restraint. Reagan's foreign policy was basically a return to the classical containment policy of the immediate postwar years. The primary emphasis was on East-West relations, on the Soviet Union as a Communist expansionist state, and on the need to contain that expansion, including in the Third World, by force, if necessary. Like his predecessors, Reagan had a "doctrine," but with his own twist. From the Truman Doctrine until the war in Vietnam, the basic purpose of U.S. foreign policy had been to prevent or limit the further expansion of Soviet power. The Reagan Doctrine was a response to Soviet gains in the post-Vietnam period. The doctrine's aim was to undo these gains by supporting insurgencies in some of the countries to which Soviet power had been extended in the 1970s. It expected thereby to legitimate the insurgents' challenge to these nations' pro-Soviet regimes. In a sense, the Reagan Doctrine was an American version of Nikita Khrushchev's "national liberation" strategy. Supporting "freedom fighters" became a centerpiece of the Reagan version of containment. It was U.S. actions like these, together with Reagan's hard-line rhetoric, that concerned Moscow, which has always been more impressed by action than by words.

An Old Policy Revived

Despite his strong anti-Communist ideology and rhetoric, then, Reagan's foreign policy continued his predecessors' anti-Soviet stance. Relations with

China clearly illustrate both the president's personal anticommunism and his administration's strategic sense. The reconciliation of the United States with China in the 1970s had been motivated in part by the Soviet Union's growing power; that is, the United States and China had strategic reasons for moving closer together from positions of mutual dislike and hostility. The president's ideological sympathies, however, were with the Nationalist Chinese on Taiwan. His administration at first appeared to downgrade the PRC's military strength and political influence, even though China held down about fifty Soviet divisions along its long frontier with the Soviet Union. Moreover, by pursuing a tough anti-Soviet policy, the president offered Beijing few reasons to be more accommodating toward Washington. Why should China offer concessions to the United States when its president was so hostile to the Soviet Union? Chinese concessions would be far more likely if Washington were also negotiating meaningfully with Moscow and Beijing wished to prevent the establishment of closer relations between the two superpowers.

But China could not go too far in breaking with the United States lest the Soviet preeminence that had originally driven China toward America be reestablished. Nor could the United States afford to break with Beijing either and to face once more, as during cold war I, an alliance of the two Communist states. The president was faced with a problem. Clearly, Reagan's heart lay with the defunct Nationalist regime on Taiwan. At one time he even talked of upgrading the United States mission there to a full-fledged embassy, even though the United States had officially recognized the People's Republic in 1979 and transferred its embassy to Beijing from Taiwan. Reagan's policy bordered on the old "two Chinas" solution, despite the 1972 Shanghai communiqué issued at the end of Nixon's visit that stated there was only "one China." After the Chinese several times expressed irritation over American arms sales to the Nationalists, the Reagan administration signed an agreement in 1982 in which the United States for the first time agreed to cap the quality and quantity of arms sales to Taiwan and eventually to phase them out. Beijing, in turn, restated that its basic policy was to seek peaceful reunification with Taiwan, not to take it by force.

Ideology and pragmatism thus struggled with each other in the Reagan administration, strongly reflecting the president's own inner conflicts. Taiwan almost became an obstacle to maintaining the more important strategic relationship between the United States and the People's Republic of China, but the president's visit to China in the spring of 1984 was a concession to strategic reality, as well as a bid for reelection. Given his lack of any dramatic foreign policy successes during his first term and great public concern that he might get the United States into a war somewhere—in Central America, if not with the Soviet Union—the president needed a successful trip to China to show he was a peacemaker and superpower leader. In this instance, Reagan's domestic needs dovetailed with the country's strategic needs. Indeed, the forthcoming election had already brought about a moderation of Reagan's language concerning the Soviet Union; it had even led him to endorse arms control negotiations, something he had denounced while he was concentrating on a U.S. arms buildup.

Unilateral Rearmament

By 1981 any president would have been concerned about Soviet intentions as well as capabilities. Carter's defense secretary, Harold Brown, noted that: "As our defense budgets have risen, the Soviets have increased their defense budgets. As our defense budgets have gone down, their defense budgets have increased again." Reagan had once asked, "What arms race? We stopped, they raced." During the 1970s American defense expenditures had fallen to the 1950 (pre-Korean War) low of 5 percent of the nation's gross national product (GNP) at a time when the Soviet Union, despite an economy only half the size of the United States', was spending substantially more than the United States on defense. From 1950 to 1969 congressional cuts in defense budget requests had averaged only $1.7 billion annually, compared with $9.2 billion in cuts for nondefense programs. The six Nixon-Ford defense requests were cut by an average of $6 billion annually, while the nondefense budget was increased by an average of $4.7 billion. The 1970s were rife with antimilitary sentiment, neoisolationist hopes, and cries for "domestic priorities" and for reductions of the defense budget; they witnessed "the most substantial reduction in American military capabilities relative to those of the Soviet Union in the entire postwar period." [4] Any administration coming to power after a decade and a half of Soviet efforts to exploit America's Vietnam-induced isolation and a weakened American presidency would have been concerned. The Soviet Union possessed a growing first-strike capability against an increasingly vulnerable U.S. deterrent force, the military balance was shifting in favor of the USSR as the buildup of Soviet strategic and conventional forces continued and the Soviets were increasing their capability to project power beyond Eurasia. It was in the context of Soviet perceptions of a changing "correlation of forces" that the Soviets had exploited Third World situations to increase their influence by means of military advisers and arms, proxies such as the Vietnamese in Cambodia and the Cubans in Africa, and, of course, their own troops in Afghanistan.

The administration was especially worried about the state of America's deterrent forces. A key task was to do something about the vulnerable Minuteman land-based ICBMs and the aging B-52 bombers and Polaris submarines (all weapons systems built in the 1950s and mid-1960s). American strategic forces needed to be modernized to ensure their continued

---

4. John Lewis Gaddis, *Strategy of Containment* (New York: Oxford University Press, 1982), 320-322.

deterrent capability. At the center of the administration's rearmament program was the MX (missile experimental) ICBM. As large as the Soviet SS-19, the MX could carry ten warheads like the even larger Soviet SS-18. The MX aroused enormous controversy for two reasons. First, the administration rejected Carter's method for deploying the MX missiles in a mobile fashion so that they would not be vulnerable to a Soviet first strike, as were the stationary Minuteman missiles, the backbone of the U.S. land-based deterrent. The reasons for this rejection were (1) the high cost of mobile deployment and (2) Utah and Nevada, the two states Carter had selected for MX basing, did not want the MX and had voted Republican in 1980.

But in deciding to deploy the MX in Minuteman silos, the administration negated a major reason for wanting it: to make the ICBM component of the deterrent less vulnerable. In addition, according to the critics, the MX's accurate warheads were capable of hitting Soviet silos. This meant that if the MX were deployed in vulnerable Minuteman silos, it would be particularly likely to attract a preemptive Soviet strike, especially during a crisis in which the Soviets might expect an American first strike. The United States would either have to "use them or lose them." The danger was that the MX would create a mutual hair-trigger situation that, in turn, could lead to a nuclear war that neither side wanted. Each would feel it had to take that risk because if it failed to strike first, its ICBMs would be destroyed.

The second and even more critical reason why the MX aroused enormous controversy was the administration's talk of *limited nuclear options, protracted nuclear war, nuclear war fighting, and "prevailing" in a nuclear war*. These phrases did not mean that the United States was no longer committed to deterrence. It was. But what if deterrence failed? The United States had to think of this possibility, according to administration spokesmen (and, it must be added in fairness, according to the secretaries of defense in the Nixon-Ford and Carter administrations); it followed from the Soviet deployment of large numbers of accurate warheads on its big missiles. What if, in a crisis, the Soviets attacked only or primarily American ICBMs? Was not the retaliatory capability of American submarines and bombers still so enormous that the Soviets would not dare a first strike? Would not the second-strike threat still prevent a first strike? The administration feared it would not.

Why not? A Soviet first strike aimed at ICBMs, generally deployed far away from large cities, would leave the vast majority of Americans alive and most cities still standing. An American retaliatory blow with the remnants of the U.S. deterrent forces—bombers and SLBMs—however, would destroy much of the Soviet Union's population and many of its cities because these were largely imprecise weapons, usable mainly against urban-industrial areas. Only ICBMs were sufficiently accurate to be used to strike back at Soviet military targets, especially its remaining ICBMs. So? Why did it matter if the United States struck back at cities or at missiles? The key question was what would happen if the Soviets, after their initial blow, announced that they had carried out their attack with 30 to 40 percent of their strategic forces, and that if the United States retaliated against Soviet cities they had enough missiles left to strike again against American cities they had deliberately avoided attacking before? In short, would a Soviet threat of a *third* strike not deter the American *second* strike? Would a president order a second strike, knowing that if he did so he would be signing the death warrant for most of America's population? Or would he, faced with that possibility, do nothing? No one could say. He might retaliate regardless of the consequences. But the real issue is whether any president should be confronted with this awful choice. The MX was proposed as a means of avoiding having to cope with such a situation. Should deterrence of a "limited nuclear attack" fail, then the United States could respond in kind to punish the Soviet Union in equal measure, prevent further escalation, and compel it to desist. Most of all, it was expected that the existence of the MX would deter the possibility of such a limited strike, thereby avoiding future crisis confrontations in which Moscow could intimidate Washington. The MX—first thought of during the Nixon-Ford administration and first proposed for deployment by the Carter administration—was intended to strengthen deterrence.

Critics, however, thought the whole scenario either bizarre or improbable. Given the historical Soviet unwillingness to risk the survival of their homeland, it was thought the Soviets were unlikely to engage in a limited nuclear strike. And critics further pointed out that nuclear weapons were far too destructive to be used discriminately against military targets only. In any event, the momentum of an initial nuclear exchange would inevitably escalate to a full-scale war. What was truly frightening about Reagan's (and before him, Nixon-Ford's and Carter's) limited nuclear war scenario, they said, was the possibility that the policy makers might really believe that a limited nuclear war could be waged and that society, suffering "only" a few million casualties, would survive; if they thought this, they might be tempted to resort to a nuclear war. The likelihood that this might occur was increased by MX, which was basically a first-strike weapon and also part of a larger buildup of strategic weapons that could hit Soviet military targets with great accuracy. Among these weapons were the new B-1 bomber, capable of penetrating Soviet defenses, the Trident II submarine missile with its accurate warheads (scheduled for deployment in the 1990s), and a variety of cruise missiles. The critics saw these weapons acquisitions as part of a larger U.S. effort to regain strategic superiority and to shift to a war-fighting, or counterforce, strategy, which would intensify the arms race and risk nuclear war.

Instead, they argued that mutual assured destruction (MAD) was unavoidable and that the MX was therefore unnecessary. In the final analysis, they contended, plans for a limited nuclear war and the MX were based on the claim that Minuteman had become 95 percent vulnerable to destruction. But this figure was based on simulated computerized war games;

in a real-life operation, the Soviets could not achieve such a high kill rate and could therefore not count on an absence of American retaliation, including retaliation by U.S. ICBMs. Neither the Soviets nor the Americans had any experience in nuclear war, which would involve coordinating hundreds of missiles and thousands of warheads and targeting them with split-second timing and accuracy on the opponent's multiple and widely dispersed nuclear forces. If either side launched a first strike, it was unlikely to be carried out with the efficiency and effectiveness of a war plan; such a plan would be degraded by what professional soldiers knew as the "friction" of war (or, what many Americans refer to as Murphy's Law: if something can go wrong, it will). Therefore, according to the critics, much of the Reagan strategic buildup was not only unnecessary but also downright dangerous.

Against Bilateral Arms Control

After the disillusionment with détente, whose centerpiece had been arms control, it is doubtful that there would have been any strategic arms control agreement in the early 1980s, even if Carter had been reelected. Given the extensive Soviet arms buildup during the decade of détente, it was not surprising that unilateral rearmament received priority over bilateral arms control; indeed, this rearmament program had begun under Carter. Reagan, however, expanded it.

Nevertheless, despite considerable public support, the administration's initial $1 trillion, five-year rearmament program stimulated enormous controversy (for the two terms the total was almost $2 trillion). This was so even though much of defense spending went for personnel and for weapons that were needed. It was the administration's harsh anti-Soviet rhetoric, its seemingly reckless talk of limited nuclear war—which appeared to suggest that U.S. policy was shifting from deterring nuclear war to getting ready to fight one—and its absolute determination to increase defense spending over that already scheduled that conveyed an impression that the administration relied too much on military strength and, if not, then it was spoiling for a fight. It seemed that the United States was largely responsible for the arms race. The momentum of the Soviet Union's program of arms acquisition across the board since the mid-1960s and its impact on the balance of nuclear and conventional balances often appeared to be forgotten in the uproar over the administration's rearmament program.

The Peace Movement Gathers Strength

Reagan therefore inspired a widespread "peace movement" in the early 1980s. Its adherents ranged from academia to religious institutions, especially the Catholic and Methodist bishops, who questioned the morality of nuclear deterrence, a policy based on the threat to use nuclear weapons in order to prevent their use. Both sets of bishops opposed the *use* of nuclear weapons. But if such weapons could not be used even in retaliation, how could deterrence be made credible? Was the goal of peace moral but the means of preserving it immoral? Would a nonnuclear deterrence be moral even if it failed to prevent war? And would one side's renunciation of nuclear weapons mean that the other side would not use them? The bishops certainly did not advocate large-scale conventional rearmament as an alternative to a nuclear defense. In the meantime, antinuclear books and films became popular, climaxing in an ABC-TV spectacular, "The Day After."

Besides the immorality of nuclear deterrence, the second major theme of the peace movement was that nuclear war would mean the end of civilization, the "last epidemic," as a doctor's organization phrased it. This theme was given strong support by new scientific arguments that the smoke produced by the many fires resulting from nuclear attacks would shut out sunlight, plunging the world into darkness for several months, and causing a prolonged freeze, or "nuclear winter," leading to the extinction of most plant and animal life. Even if the attacker had successfully eliminated most of the opponent's retaliatory capability, climactic catastrophe would follow and spread over the globe. The aggressor might be a winner—but for two weeks only. In brief, most of these antinuclear writings and films concluded that if humans were to survive, nuclear weapons not only had to be eliminated but also, if possible, a world government had to be established that would end national rivalries. The public mood, which had initially favored the Reagan rearmament program, had shifted.

Yet there was really little that was novel about these antinuclear books and films. By 1980 the horror of nuclear war had been common knowledge for thirty-five years. That was, after all, why the United States had adopted a deterrent strategy. And it was the suicidal nature of these nuclear arms that had encouraged the belief that nuclear deterrence would prevent an all-out Soviet attack on the United States and preserve peace among the superpowers. Moreover, although deterrence could fail, it *had* a historical record. The superpowers had not exchanged as much as a rifle shot in Europe where they confronted one another. Their nuclear power and their mutual fear of suicide had given them forty years without hostilities on the Continent, Europe's longest period of peace in the twentieth century. Indeed, nuclear weapons had eliminated war among *all* the great powers, not just the superpowers.

While the antinuclear movement appeared to confuse the issue of threatening nuclear force to bolster deterrence with its use, it had gathered enormous momentum by 1982. The danger of nuclear war appeared to be the nation's first concern. In New York City, three-quarters of a million people turned out for the largest political gathering in American history. For these demonstrators and the others marching, meeting, and debating the nuclear issue across the country, the ultimate goal was to eliminate nuclear weapons, but the immediate focus was to achieve a nuclear freeze. Proposals for a freeze on the testing, production, and deployment of nuclear weapons to stop the arms race were passed (or almost passed) by many town-hall meetings and by voters in ten of the eleven states on whose ballots it appeared in the midterm 1982 election. Congress, especially the Democratic House, reflected this antinuclear mood, and, after coming within two votes of endorsing a nuclear freeze in 1982, it endorsed a modified version of the freeze in 1983. All 1984 Democratic presidential candidates but one came out in favor of a freeze.

Reasons for Opposition to Arms Control

This mix of concern, unease, and occasional pacifism was not appeased by the administration's professions of peaceful intent. What particularly hurt the administration as it rebuilt American military strength was its evident hostility to arms control. In part, this hostility reflected a strong distrust of the Soviets, which implied that agreements with them were not desirable. Alleged Soviet violations of SALT II were constantly cited. In part, it was the belief of the president and many in his administration that past arms control efforts were the chief reason for America's purportedly declining strength vis-à-vis the Soviet Union. Indeed, Reagan was the first postwar president who specifically said when he came into office that U.S. military power was inferior to the Soviet Union's, an assessment with which few outside of the administration (and probably not too many in it, including the Joint Chiefs) agreed. Spokesmen for the administration asserted that arms control restrained the United States, but had not inhibited the Soviet buildup. Given this perspective, administration skepticism, if not opposition, to arms control was not surprising.

In part, this negative view of arms control was also a reaction to an increasing domestic clamor for arms control as a substitute for an arms buildup. Arms control was originally conceived as supplementing the defense effort. Military strength was the basis of a peaceful superpower relationship; arms control was to ensure the stability of the deterrent balance. But during the 1970s, popular opinion and Congress resisted large increases in defense expenditures. The military, it was charged, "had plenty"; the armed services' emphasis on the growing Soviet threat was self-serving, intended only to increase their budgets. Arms control in this context appeared not so much as a supplement but as an *alternative* to an expensive and unilateral defense buildup in order to achieve security. Indeed, such an effort was often said to undermine arms control! It was charged that new arms were not only unnecessary but also would endanger future agreements. This disassociation of arms control from defense policy and the pursuit of arms control in its own right, regardless of any linkages to the Soviet exploitation of foreign policy opportunities to expand its influence, ignored the fact that arms control agreements could not by themselves make peace more secure. It was often forgotten that arms competition was a symptom of the underlying superpower rivalry; arms control could neither end that conflict nor be a substitute for maintaining strength. That is why the Reagan administration gave priority to Soviet behavior, focusing on regional conflicts rather than arms control, as its predecessors had done.

The administration therefore continued to concentrate on building up U.S. arms, announcing it would postpone any arms negotiations until the United States could "negotiate from strength," and its goal would then be, not to cap the arms race, but to radically reduce the number of nuclear weapons. But postponing new arms control talks proved difficult; public opinion equated arms control with disarmament and even more so with a sincere search for peace. The pressure on the administration grew. When negotiations finally started in 1982, the administration claimed it was shifting the emphasis from arms limitation—setting ceilings on launchers—to drastic reductions. It changed the name from SALT (Strategic Arms Limitation Talks) to START (Strategic Arms Reduction Talks). The real motive for this change was to make its approach politically appealing at home, to deflect domestic criticism, and to weaken the freeze movement while the buildup continued. The initial proposals were clearly propagandistic and meant to be rejected by Moscow, thus winning time for the administration. That is how many Americans saw it too.

The lesson was clear: a president can arm the United States if necessary, but only if the public also sees a genuine effort to control the arms competition and to improve the superpower relationship. The Reagan administration had not learned that lesson. Thus, when Reagan suggested various options for the MX's deployment, he created enormous opposition; for the first time since 1945 Congress initially refused to fully fund a major new weapon requested by the president. It gave him only 50 of the 100 requested (which, in late 1986, the air force suggested might be placed on special railroad cars so that during crises they would be less vulnerable). To Congress, Reagan's arms control proposals all appeared to be a way of gaining legislative support for the MX. So Congress turned the tables on the administration: if Reagan wanted the MX, he would have to negotiate seriously on arms control.

The president got the message. Public pressure and the 1984 election moved him toward expressing a desire for arms control and to talk to the Soviets. He also finally had a Soviet leader with whom he could talk; Gorbachev had begun to consolidate his power. But the chances of success were never good. American proposals continued to call for a massive Soviet reduction of the SS-18s and SS-19s, while the modernization or buildup of the U.S. deterrent continued. This included the MX, which the administration did not want to trade. (The president later confessed his ignorance of the fact that the Soviet Union, unlike the United States, relied mainly on ICBMs and that the U.S. offer had been one-sided.) The Soviets were not likely to give up the heart of their strategic force cheaply, even had the United States been willing to give up the MX, and even if it had 100 operational MXs. This would not have sufficed for a trade against half of the more than 300 SS-18s and 300 SS-19s. As it was, MX was only a potential weapon, while the Soviets had already deployed their missiles.

SALT II Provisions Renounced

The best that could be achieved in these circumstances was that the two superpowers observe SALT II. Despite his frequent criticism of it as "fatally flawed," the president committed the United States to live within its terms. He even accused the Soviets of violating this agreement, which the United States had refused to ratify! But in 1986, the day after Thanksgiving, the Reagan administration, which had repeatedly denounced SALT II because of expressed concerns about Soviet compliance, asserted that its limits were no longer "operational." Theoretically, there were now no longer any limits on either American or Soviet acquisitions of offensive arms. The Soviets made the most of the propaganda opportunity created by the U.S. renunciation of SALT by announcing that for the time being they would not follow the American example. But the Soviet Union was in a better position than the United States to increase the numbers of missiles and in 1986 it deployed a new SS-24 mobile ICBM with ten warheads. American production lines, except for the MX, were shut down, and the huge federal budget deficit constrained Washington's capability to respond to any large Soviet buildup. These had been the chief reasons the Joint Chiefs of Staff had opposed the president's renunciation of SALT II, that earlier the United States had stated it would not "undercut."

There was, on the one hand, an illogic to the U.S. action. It would legalize an increase of the same Soviet ICBMs that the Reagan administration had from the beginning labeled as destabilizing. Most illogical was that the renunciation of SALT II would magnify the problems of the president's favorite program, SDI. To destroy incoming missiles is difficult enough even with the thousands of warheads allowed under SALT II; that task would be infinitely more difficult if the Soviets could multiply missiles and warheads by several thousand beyond those permitted by mutual agreement. But, on the other hand, if the administration was seeking to increase pressure on Moscow, there was a rough logic to its action. As already noted, the United States was slated to deploy counterforce weapons to enhance Soviet strategic vulnerability. The threat to exceed the SALT II limits may thus have been intended to worry the Soviet leadership, raising its incentives for deep cuts in its forces. Ironically, however, it was Reagan's proposal for SDI—whose hardware was far in the future, unlike the MX or Trident II—that concerned the men in the Kremlin more.

The Strategic Defense Initiative

Reagan first introduced SDI in the midst of the controversy about arms spending, the MX, and arms control. The proposal was quickly dubbed "Star Wars" by its critics because of its reliance on sophisticated space-based technologies glimpsed only in movies, such as lasers and particle beams. The purpose of SDI was to render nuclear missiles "impotent and obsolete." This, in turn, would protect America's population. Mutual assured survival would replace mutual assured destruction. Was it not better to save lives on both sides, the president asked, than to kill the population of the aggressor in revenge for a first strike?

The best time to destroy an incoming missile is in its initial five-minute boost phase. In the second, or mid-phase, period of flight, defense becomes more difficult because the warheads separate, vastly multiplying the number of targets to be destroyed. Those warheads that survive could be destroyed by a ground-based defense like the old ABM system in the third, or terminal, phase as they seek their targets on earth. According to official descriptions, SDI would be a "layered defense" using different technologies to destroy attacking missiles during each phase of the ballistic trajectory. This amounted to placing a protective shield over the United States.

SDI's Domestic and Security Purposes

For the president this plan served several purposes, the first of which was domestic and political. Under attack for increasing the defense budget while cutting social services, criticized for being a warmonger, Reagan was able to seize the initiative with SDI. Instead of always defending himself, he could pose as a man of vision who would end the threat of missile attacks and ensure that the population of the United States, of the Soviet Union, and, indeed, of the world would survive. He had gone arms control advocates one better, not by stabilizing the balance of offensive missiles, but by banishing their life-threatening potential.

If the churches condemned nuclear deterrence as immoral, was his scheme for a strategic defense not the incarnation of morality? And if this movement condemning nuclear deterrence spread in other Western societies as well, strategic defense might be the most politically acceptable option. With SDI, in fact, Reagan undermined the antinuclear movement by stealing its thunder. It did not like nuclear weapons. Neither did he, so he would get rid of them. Reagan was not faking. He may have been the nation's most conservative postwar president, but on nuclear issues he was a radical abolitionist. He could have headed any of the left-wing organizations calling for the elimination of nuclear arms. Reagan dismissed the distinction between stabilizing and destabilizing nuclear weapons, as he did the role that they had played in deterring war. He clearly was uncomfortable with the deterrent strategy to which all of his predecessors had been committed, and, therefore, at the Reykjavík summit in 1986, he agreed with Gorbachev to the total elimination of all nuclear weapons within a ten-year period. He did so without consulting his top advisers, including the Joint Chiefs of Staff and his national security adviser, or the NATO allies, which were dependent on the United States for their security. Once he returned home, Reagan was quickly persuaded by, among others, Britain's tough prime minister Margaret Thatcher, to change his mind (or, as some might phrase it, recover it from his insane binge on getting rid of the nation's deterrent in one afternoon). Nevertheless, in Reagan's mind, nuclear weapons remained "bad" weapons and were therefore to be rendered harmless by U.S. technological prowess and ingenuity.

Second, SDI's utopian side was matched by a more pragmatic consideration: if it worked, it would outflank the Soviets. For years the Soviets had invested heavily in first-strike weapons. SDI not only reduced the value of the Soviet investment in ICBMs but also ensured there would be no nuclear war. What would be the point of attacking if these missiles could not penetrate the defensive shield above the United States? Third, although population defense was the fundamental and long-term SDI goal, defense of the U.S. ICBM force could start more quickly. To protect population, a defense has to be virtually perfect. If only 80 percent effective—and that would be very high—then 20 percent of, for example, 2,000 warheads could get through, destroying urban America. But a defense against missiles can be "leaky." If it takes two warheads to destroy one missile, and an 80 percent effective SDI destroys 1,600 incoming warheads, the remaining 400 will destroy 200 U.S. missile silos. This would leave 800 of the U.S. ICBM force for retaliation. Even a less-than-perfect SDI, therefore, would relieve the American fear that its ICBMs were vulnerable and increase Soviet uncertainty that they could launch a successful first strike. If the Soviets were unsure that they could destroy a sufficient number of ICBMs, there would be no point in striking at all. SDI would restore the credibility of the U.S. deterrent and the stability of mutual deterrence.

The contradiction at the heart of SDI was that it would be ten, twenty, or more years before anyone would know if population protection was really feasible; ICBM protection was possible in the near future. But SDI, Reagan emphasized, aimed to do away with missiles (if they could not penetrate a defense, they might as well be mutually abolished as both superpowers acquired such defenses); ICBM protection assumed these missiles would survive. SDI's aim was to make mutual deterrence—the reciprocal hostage relationship—safer.

The critics questioned the long-range goal of SDI from the start. The technology would be extremely complex; the first time it was needed, it would have to work perfectly, an unlikely prospect for a system of so many interacting parts, each of which was technologically highly sophisticated. The Soviets could overcome SDI much less expensively by multiplying both missiles and warheads (as the United States had done when it added MIRVs to its missiles to overcome the ABMs being placed around Moscow, fearing that the Soviets were beginning a nationwide deployment). The Soviet Union would also seek its own SDI. The Soviets would figure out that, although SDI would be unable to protect the United States from a massive Soviet first strike because of all its technological shortcomings, it would be able to defend the United States against a crippled Soviet retaliatory strike *after* an American first strike against Soviet strategic forces. This Soviet fear that SDI might be a prelude to an offensive American strike rather than a defensive system was a counterpart of the same American fears in the early 1970s that the Soviet ABMs, together with their large numbers of ICBMs and their warheads, were part of a Soviet first-strike scenario; the ABMs would protect the Soviet Union against a U.S. retaliatory force greatly weakened by a Soviet first strike.

In short, according to the critics, SDI would lead to intensive defensive and offensive arms races in which the defensive technologies, even if they gained the upper hand, would do so only temporarily. Moreover, the system would be extremely expensive, threatening the budgets for other strategic and conventional forces; these expenses would rise even more because SDI, unable to defend against bombers and cruise missiles, would need to be supplemented by an additional defensive network. Therefore, it was dubious that the United States or the Soviet Union would be any more secure. Arms reductions through bilateral negotiation was the better course.

Soviet Concerns and Arms Proposals

If the critics were correct, why did the Soviets denounce Reagan's "arms race in space" and "militarization of space"? Why, after walking out of all arms control negotiations when the United States refused to suspend its deployment of medium-range missiles in Western Europe to counter the Soviet SS-20 deployment, were the Soviets so eager to resume talks? Clearly, SDI worried them. Why? Their scientists must surely have questioned SDI's ability to prevent major missile penetration. One reason might have been that the Soviets really were as fearful of an American first strike as the Americans had been of a Soviet first strike since the early 1970s. Another had to be that SDI research and development might result in American technology taking a quantum jump; this fear of falling behind spurred even America's allies to cooperate with SDI, although they doubted its military value. And, of course, Soviet technology was already behind. In addition, the Soviets could not afford economically to engage in an arms race, especially a high-tech arms race.

The Soviets, therefore, were eager to delay, if not stop, the deployment of SDI. The United States continued to worry about the Soviet first-strike capability. A "grand compromise" seemed the obvious solution: a radical cut in Soviet ICBMs, including the SS-18s that the United States feared the most as a first-strike weapon, in exchange for SDI, or at least a delay of SDI. At the Reykjavík summit, Gorbachev repeated an earlier offer of a U.S.-Soviet 50 percent reduction of strategic forces in return for confining SDI to laboratory research. (This offer was a prelude to the total elimination of all nuclear weapons.) He insisted, however, on reaffirming the 1972 ABM Treaty, which, while permitting ABM research, did not allow the development or testing of space-based defensive systems. The president, insisting that this interpretation of the treaty was too "restrictive" and offering a more "permissive" interpretation that would allow the United States to do everything short of deployment, rejected Gorbachev's offer on grounds that if SDI were limited to the laboratory, that would be the end of it. The result was an impasse. It was clear that the Soviets would not cut their strategic forces until they knew whether these forces had to cope with SDI; the restriction on strategic defense research must precede radical force reductions. This was exactly the same argument Nixon had used when the Soviets proposed an ABM agreement. He could not accept that, he had said, until he knew whether the Soviets would end their continuing offensive buildup; if it continued, the United States would need more ABMs because the two were related. Reagan, however, convinced of the correctness of his long-range vision, refused to trade SDI for Soviet ICBMs. No strategic arms control agreement was possible in these circumstances.

When the Reagan administration came to power, its primary concern was the perceived "window of vulnerability"; it intended to make U.S. land-based missiles less vulnerable to a Soviet first strike. When Gorbachev offered Reagan a 50 percent reduction of Soviet missiles, a potentially enormous reduction of U.S. ICBM vulnerability, the president turned him down. What had become the most potent "bargaining chip" since SALT had begun had apparently become unnegotiable. This was ironic because SDI was only a vision with a research program. Only the future will tell if SDI is technically feasible and cost-effective. A future president will make the key decisions on deployment. Nevertheless, Reagan rejected Gorbachev's terms that SDI be confined to the laboratory and not deployed for a ten-year period in return for a drastic cut of those very Soviet missiles against which SDI was supposed to guard the country. SDI therefore remained, on the one hand, the chief block to a conclusion of START. But, on the other, it did not prevent continued negotiations on radical strategic arms reductions.

By the time Reagan left office, the two powers had resolved some of their principal differences and, according to the Soviets, had completed 70 percent of an agreement. But the critical deal on SDI remained undone.

NATO, Détentism, and Disengagement

The Reagan administration's attacks on détente, its preoccupation with rearmament, the shift in U.S. military doctrine to nuclear war fighting, the reluctance to engage in arms control negotiations, and willingness to use force as in Grenada upset the NATO allies in Europe. Even SDI caused considerable unease because, if the United States ever could defend itself against Soviet missiles and achieve the almost complete military security that Reagan stated was its basic goal, then America's need for allies might decline and it might once more be able to withdraw in safety into isolationism.

Having complained during the Nixon-Ford administration of American-Soviet collusion and during the Carter administration of American vacillation, Western Europe now charged that American policy was too hard-line. Western Europe was determined, therefore, to preserve its own separate détente with the Soviet Union. Two events demonstrated the great differences of attitude and policy between Europe and Reagan's United States.

Poland and the Rise of Solidarity

The first event took place in Poland, where domestic changes threatened the Polish Communist party's monopoly of power and control. Ironically, it was in Poland, a so-called people's democracy and a Communist state that purported to represent and protect the interests of the working class, a truly spontaneous Marxist workers' revolution against their exploiters (the Communist party!) occurred in 1980. Stimulated by a failing economy as a result of poor political leadership, bureaucratic planning, and mismanagement, the workers demanded the right to form their own independent trade union, which would have the right to strike. Such a demand was unheard of in a Communist country where the party claimed to embody the workers' aspirations. In wanting their own union, the Polish workers were rejecting this claim and challenging the basis of the party's legitimacy.

Strikes brought the government down, just as strikes in 1970 had replaced another set of leaders who had mismanaged the economy. This time, however, economic conditions were far more severe. The new political leadership recognized the right of the workers to form their own union, called Solidarity. In effect, this meant a loss of the party's monopoly of power. Solidarity's demands were not only economic but also political. The union wanted Catholic mass to be televised on Sundays, Solidarity meetings to be broadcast, censorship to be restricted, corrupt officials to be removed from office, and a farmers' union to be recognized. As the party-controlled government retreated before each demand, the demands increased and the party withdrew further in the face of strikes and threats of strikes. It was a heady experience for a still very Catholic and nationalistic people who hated the Soviets and who had been denied freedom so long.

With its successes, Solidarity grew more militant. At its first national conference, it publicly asserted that it was "the authentic voice of the working class" and announced support for other East European workers who might wish to form independent unions. Domestically, it favored free parliamentary elections, free speech, and a voice in government policy, including the running of the economy. Although the Soviets accused Solidarity of provocative behavior—seeking "political power"—they refrained from invading Poland.

This restraint contrasted sharply with Soviet behavior in Hungary (1956) and Czechoslovakia (1968), where the Soviet army had intervened when the Communist party's monopoly of power was threatened. And Poland, the nation through which every Western invader of Russia had marched and through which the Soviet Union had projected its power into the center of Europe since 1945, was geographically far more critical than those two countries had been. As the situation grew more intolerable in Moscow's eyes, the danger of the Polish "disease" spreading to other East European states, perhaps even to the Soviet Union, led the Soviets to hold very visible Warsaw Pact military maneuvers in hopes of frightening the Poles. The Soviet Union could afford neither a weakening nor a collapse of its hold on Eastern and central Europe, nor a dilution of controls at home.

But the risks and costs of intervention were also great. The Soviets recognized that Solidarity was not just a trade union seeking better working conditions, but that it represented a well-organized mass movement. The Soviets faced the possibility of a clash with units of the Polish army, the costs of occupation, and the difficulties of pacifying the population and getting it to work. In addition, the cost of paying off Poland's $27 billion debt to the West would be a drain at a time when the Soviet economy was in trouble; maintaining the separate détente with America's European allies would become more difficult; and the possible establishment of a better relationship with the new U.S. administration would be jeopardized. Reagan could exploit a Soviet invasion of Poland to rally the NATO allies. Therefore, for more than a year Moscow demonstrated remarkable restraint. When the move against Solidarity finally came, it was the Polish military and police who arrested the union leaders and imposed martial law on Poland.

Whether Moscow ordered the intervention or the Polish government acted on its own to forestall Soviet action, there can be little doubt of increasing Soviet pressure on the Polish authorities to crack down on what the Soviets called "anti-Socialist" and "counterrevolutionary" elements. Solidarity, by winning the sympathies of almost 10 million members, about one-third of the population, was a living refutation of the party's claim of representation; it symbolized the bankruptcy of communism. Unable either to produce a decent standard of living or to tolerate a minimal degree of freedom, communism in Poland had lost legitimacy. Force was therefore necessary to maintain the party in power; in reality, it was the army that was in power and had replaced the party. Poland was occupied by its own army! In response, the United States imposed some economic sanctions on both Poland and the Soviet Union, more symbolic of American displeasure than punitive. But in Western Europe, one almost heard a collective sigh of relief that the Red Army had not invaded Poland. The Polish army's crackdown was considered a domestic affair, not a matter over which détente was to be sacrificed.

American Economic Warfare and Alliance Discord

Europe's attempt to preserve its separate détente with Moscow, including its profitable trade relationship, also ran headlong into Washington's determination to squeeze the Soviet Union economically. In contrast to the détente policy of the 1970s, which had attempted to balance the military stick with the economic carrot, to provide the Soviet Union with incentives for greater self-restraint in foreign policy, the Reagan policy concluded that offers of trade, technology, and credits had not worked. The Soviet civilian industrial and agricultural economies continued to be weak, except in the military sector. Why should the West help strengthen the economy of a hostile state? Lenin said the capitalists would sell the Communists the rope with which they would hang the capitalists. Was the West, in its eagerness to trade and sell its latest technology, not selling the Soviets that rope and even providing the money for its purchase at low-interest credit? And would the chief beneficiary of this Western "subsidization" of the Soviet economy not be the Soviet armed forces? By putting up trade barriers instead, the West could increase Soviet economic difficulties and compel the Soviet leaders to move resources to the civilian sector from the military to prevent the standard of living from declining even further, thus creating a Soviet version of the Polish disease. Only an increase in the Soviet quota of "pain" might compel the Soviet Union to relax international tensions and moderate its behavior.

Given the different European and American perspectives on relations with the Soviet Union and the role of trade, it was not surprising that soon after the Reagan administration took office, conflict erupted over the construction of a Soviet pipeline that would carry Soviet natural gas to Western Europe. Overwhelmingly dependent on imported energy, Europe was eager to diversify its energy sources and become less dependent on the Arab members of OPEC. The Reagan administration fiercely opposed the pipeline, which was to be built by the Soviets but financed by the Europeans. The principal reason was the fear that Western Europe over the years would become more and more dependent on the Soviet Union for its energy, giving the Soviets the political leverage that might gradually undermine NATO. Another reason was that the pipeline would allow the Soviets to earn hard currencies with which they could buy Western technology. The Europeans denied that their energy purchases would make them dependent on the Soviet Union or politically amenable to Soviet pressure. Indeed, they argued that greater Soviet moderation was more likely to be produced by an extensive network of economic relationships.

To force the Europeans to comply with American policy, Reagan ordered American companies, their branches in Europe, and European firms licensed by American corporations to produce American technology not to sell to Moscow the items needed for the building of the pipeline. These items were for the most part large turbines. The emotional and political fallout that resulted led the European governments to order their firms to comply with national policies and go ahead with the Soviet deal. Washington responded by imposing sanctions against these firms! Reagan became the first president to impose sanctions against U.S. allies (the companies, rather than nations, were penalized to minimize European resentment, but there was no doubt at whom American anger was aimed).

Secretary of State Alexander Haig opposed the president's course on this issue. He predicted that the Europeans were determined to go ahead; to oppose them was to risk dividing members of the alliance even further at a time when they should be closing ranks. It was also hypocritical since this most anti-Communist of anti-Communist administrations had as one of its first acts in office lifted the Carter grain embargo to benefit U.S. farmers. The pipeline was one of the issues over which Haig resigned, and his successor, George Shultz, spent many of his early days in office trying to defuse it. The pipeline controversy was a symptom of the increasing divisiveness among NATO members which, in this instance, hurt the alliance more than the Soviet Union, the intended target.

The Missile Debate in Europe

By the early 1980s, indeed, it had become commonplace to say that the West Europeans wanted to pursue an independent political policy while still counting on the United States for their defense; they wanted, it was said, to "uncouple" themselves politically from Washington but to remain "coupled" to it militarily. Even the military relationship was called into question when West European opinion appeared to go back on a decision, collectively agreed to by the United States and Western Europe, on how to meet the threat of the new, mobile, and powerful Soviet SS-20 intermediate range nuclear missiles that had three warheads each. The West German government had first raised the issue of the SS-20 deployment and requested the United States to counter these missiles aimed at Western Europe. The proposed American force of 572 missiles to deter the 270 SS-20s deployed in the western Soviet Union (plus 171 in its Asian territory, but movable to the west) was to consist of 108 Pershing IIs (with one warhead each), whose range was sufficient to hit western Russia, plus 464 subsonic ground-launched cruise missiles (GLCMs).

Since the beginning of NATO, the Europeans had wanted the alliance strategy to emphasize deterrence. Europe had had its bellyful of wars in the twentieth century. The NATO army, therefore, was to serve as a "plate glass," which, once the Soviet invasion occurred, would sound the alarm and call in the United States' strategic forces. The army's purpose was not to fight a long war like World War II, even when it was reinforced by 300,000 American soldiers. The presence of the troops emphasized America's stake in Europe and clarified to Moscow that any attack would result in war with the United States. The army's role was to "couple" Europe's defense to American strategic forces. The fear of nuclear retaliation by the United States, it was reasoned, would deter the Soviet Union from invading Western Europe.

The Soviet SS-20s threatened to uncouple Europe's defense from the American deterrent. NATO ground forces, it was claimed, were no match for the Warsaw Pact forces. Nor could NATO's tactical nuclear forces any longer compensate for the lack of manpower, including reserves. The SS-20s would deter a NATO escalation from conventional to tactical nuclear weapons. But were the American strategic forces not still the instrument of last resort? Perhaps they were, but perhaps not. Ever since the first Soviet missile test in 1957, the key question had been: Would the United States risk its own survival for the defense of Europe? Some had answered this question with a no; most had been uncertain, although United States strategic forces at the time were superior to those of the Soviet Union. Since the 1970s and the emergence of strategic parity, the answer to this question had grown even more doubtful. It was one thing for the United States to attack the Soviet Union when the Soviets could not attack the United States, or when America had a vast strategic superiority; it was quite another to do so when the Soviet Union could retaliate fully. Was America's strategic deterrence still credible? Washington's standard reply was yes, but in Western Europe there was more doubt than ever that this was so.

The Pershing IIs and GLCMs were supposed to reassure the allies. Because the Pershings could strike targets in the Soviet Union itself, the Soviets presumably would consider such a strike an act of American aggression and would retaliate against American missiles in Europe *as well as* the United States to forestall an all-out attack by U.S. ICBMs. The Pershings were to let the Soviets know that any attack on Western Europe could not be limited to that area and to reassure the allies that their defense was still "coupled" to the American deterrent.

Instead of being strengthened, however, the NATO "marriage," in the words of the French foreign minister, came close to a divorce. Huge crowds throughout Western Europe (except in France) demonstrated for months against the proposed deployment of the American missiles, with the greatest opposition in West Germany. The Protestant churches, the universities, the Social Democratic opposition party, and a new political movement, which called itself the Green party and was a mixture of environmentalists (against all things nuclear), pacifists, neutralists, and antiestablishment figures, were all opposed to the deployment, the Greens militantly so. The street demonstrators' accusations were many: America was stoking the arms race; America intended to fight a war limited to Europe; America was the aggressive party in the cold war. Moscow was not considered the chief threat. It was Washington, which had defended Western Europe since 1949 and had not yet deployed a single Pershing II, that was charged with being the bigger menace to peace.

Certainly, the demonstrators did not represent majority opinion in their respective countries. In all NATO countries, support for the alliance remained high; so did faith in deterrence. Nevertheless, the peace movement reflected widespread concern about Reagan's antidétente foreign policy and an increased fear of war. (The U.S. invasion of Grenada was widely viewed in Europe as equivalent to the Soviet invasion of Afghanistan.) These concerns came together in the decision to deploy more U.S. nuclear weapons in Europe. In the words of a West German journalist:

> The impending arrival of a new generation of land-based missiles thrust to the forefront of the collective psyche the irreducible dilemma of contemporary defense. Nuclear weapons not only buttress deterrence; they also drive home the fatal consequences of its failure. "Old nuclear weapons," half-forgotten, suggest a sturdy shelter; "new" nuclear weapons remind their beneficiaries that they are also the potential victims. . . .
>
> Nations that depend for their security on others want the best of all possible worlds. The Europeans want full protection but minimal risks; they will the end, which is the credibility of American power, but not necessarily the means, which entails the reassertion of American power— be it in the form of Euromissiles or confrontationist policies towards the Soviet Union.[5]

Ironically, the antinuclear demonstrations that took place in Western Europe stymied American-Soviet negotiations on INF. The Soviets shrewdly exploited the protests. If they might prevent the American deployment, why should Moscow make any concessions to stop the Pershings and GLCMs emplacement? Further, by repeatedly saying that they were eager to negotiate the issue, the Soviets appeared reasonable and put the United States on the defensive. The president felt compelled to respond to the demonstrations in Europe and to the Soviet initiative. He proposed a "zero option" whereby the United States would not deploy any of its Pershings and cruise missiles if the Soviets dismantled all of their INFs, including the SS-20s. It sounded good; all intermediate-range missiles were to be eliminated. What could be more beneficial for peace and more moral than doing away with a whole class of dangerous weapons? The United States, however, did not expect Moscow to accept this offer. The zero-zero option was a public relations move; by turning it down, the Soviets would enable the U.S. deployment to go ahead as a clearly necessary and defensive move, the street demonstrations would decline, and the blame for the American missile buildup in Europe would be placed at the Kremlin's door.

---

5. Josef Joffe, "Peace and Populism: Why the European Anti-Nuclear Movement Failed," *International Security* (Spring 1987): 16, 17-18.

The intra-NATO "missile crisis," however, had by then done considerable damage to the alliance. If, for many Europeans, the protests against deployment expressed their concern about Reagan's foreign policy, their desire to reduce the risk of war, and (more subconsciously perhaps) their knowledge that they depended on the United States for protection and that this protection was not free of cost or risk, then, for many Americans, the protests were a reminder that the Europeans did not appear ready to take the measures necessary for their own defense. Although their combined population and industrial output exceeded that of the Soviet Union, America's European allies were still unwilling to raise the size of their conventional forces. They wanted to continue relying on the American strategic deterrent at a time when the superpowers strategically neutralized one another.

One result was to stimulate demands in the United States for the withdrawal of some or all American forces from Europe over a period of years. Most of the American defense budget allocated for hardware and maintenance was not spent on strategic forces; half went for the upkeep of the more expensive conventional forces whose primary mission was the defense of Europe. When the alliance had been formed, the European nations vividly remembered the failure of appeasing a totalitarian regime, the defeats and suffering of World War II, their postwar collapse, and the need for American protection against the new threat from the East. By the 1970s and 1980s the memory of having appeased Nazi Germany was fading; the story of this appeasement was not even a part of the history or consciousness of the new generation that had grown up in a peaceful Europe. Protected by the United States, that generation, as many older Europeans, had seemingly forgotten the realities of international politics and took peace for granted.

In France, which had fielded forces that had been withdrawn from the integrated NATO structure and was deploying a growing independent French deterrent force, the popular historical association of national independence and pride in the nation's armed forces was still alive. Moreover, there were no massive antinuclear and anti-American demonstrations. Indeed, Socialist president François Mitterrand told the West German parliament in 1983, "I'm against the Euromissiles. But I notice two terrible simple things about the current debate: Pacifism is in the West and the Euromissiles are in the East. I consider this an unequal relationship." [6] Such an imbalance, he predicted, would ensure war, not avoid it.

But elsewhere in Western Europe, defense had apparently become an American responsibility. Parties that were formerly stalwart defenders of NATO, such as the British Labour party and the West German Social

---

6. Quoted in Flora Lewis, "Missiles and Pacifists," *New York Times,* November 18, 1983.

Democrats, now literally deserted the alliance. Given that circumstances vastly differed from when NATO was founded, one had to wonder whether, if NATO had been proposed in the 1980s, there would be an alliance at all, and if so, which countries would join it?

NATO Threatened from Within

By the mid-1980s one thing was thus very clear: the intermediate-range nuclear weapons issue was not primarily a military issue but a critical political one. The decision to deploy the Pershing IIs and the GLCMs had been an alliance decision. Attempts to negotiate with the Soviets a reduction of their constantly growing SS-20 force against a smaller U.S. deployment had been fruitless. Moscow refused to accept *any* American deployment and rejected the principle of superpower equality. The Soviet purpose was clearly to manipulate Europe's fear of war to drive a wedge between the NATO allies, especially between Europe and the United States. Would the alliance survive? The Soviets had no reason to compromise in separate arms control negotiations on this issue; they had every reason to test the strength of the European peace movement in the hope of aborting the American deployment. The Soviets could deploy their missiles and target every European capital, but the United States could not deploy missiles in Europe that could hit the Soviet Union. What Moscow has is not negotiable, what NATO has is, was the message.

Could NATO, having made a key decision, stay with that decision? Or would NATO be unable to stick with its defense and diplomatic strategy or to resist pressures from within that were abetted by shrewd Soviet political propaganda? The alliance itself was at stake. The gravity of the situation was magnified by recent elections in Britain and West Germany in which governments in favor of the American deployment had been elected. The democratic process was therefore also at stake. Would governments elected by clear majorities give in to the peace marches? Was the alliance and the viability of democratic elections to be negated by the politics of the street?

For Moscow the missile debate was a means of undermining the alliance. NATO had not confronted such a serious issue since German rearmament in the early 1950s and the Berlin crisis after 1957. These two issues had involved the future of the alliance, its ability to face down intimidation and remain united. Above all, they had involved a struggle for West Germany, NATO's strongest European member, without whose territory the alliance could not defend itself. Moscow obviously wanted to detach it from NATO, and Washington wanted to keep West Germany within the alliance. Given the political stakes for each superpower, should it have been a surprise that American-Soviet relations reached a low point in the early 1980s, regardless of who the leaders were? Neither side was willing to compromise in what it regarded as a fundamental test of wills. Despite considerable pressure on Reagan to be more accommodating, he insisted on going ahead with the deployment. When that began during the winter months of 1983-1984, was it really a surprise that Moscow walked out of all arms. control negotiations in order to raise the fear of war in Western Europe and to push it into a greater neutralism and pacifism?

For a time the missile crisis faded as the deployment occurred. Then, in a complete turnabout Gorbachev, in a surprise move, accepted an earlier Reagan proposal for zero intermediate-range missiles for both powers. The Soviet leader needed a relaxation of international tensions in order to give priority to domestic affairs and the rebuilding of the Soviet economy. The administration's determination had paid off. It had not abandoned the deployment, nor, when the Soviets responded by walking out of all arms control negotiations, had it delayed deployment, despite widespread calls to do so. Unable to achieve Soviet goals with threats, Moscow capitulated. The zero-zero solution was a significant achievement, trading about 1,400 Soviet warheads for just over 300 U.S. warheads. This move eliminated an entire class of weapons rather than—as in SALT I and II—placing limits on their deployment; and Moscow also accepted intrusive verification procedures to monitor the agreement. More fundamentally, in retrospect, the Soviet turnabout was the first sign that the Soviet Union needed a cease-fire in the cold war. U.S. resolution had paid off, collapsing not the NATO position but that of the Warsaw Pact.

But two things became apparent during this episode. First, the Europeans' confidence in the United States had diminished since Vietnam. During the Nixon-Ford détente years they had complained about possible U.S.-Soviet deals at Europe's expense; during the Carter years, of vacillation and weakness; and during the Reagan years, of too much machismo or "Ramboism." Europe's fear of war had also risen. Not Soviet behavior but the "arms race" was seen as the critical danger, as was "provocative" American behavior. These attitudes translated into growing public doubts about the value of NATO despite general support for the alliance. While the first cold war was characterized by U.S.-Soviet conflict and U.S.-European cohesion, the second cold war was characterized by U.S.-Soviet conflict *and* U.S.-European disagreement.

Second, the European members of the alliance remained unwilling to reexamine the assumption they had accepted for more than forty years— namely, that the Soviet Union was the naturally dominant Eurasian power against which Western Europe cannot mobilize sufficient counterbalancing power without outside help. Such an assumption was demeaning for states that have for centuries been the leading international actors and that, by the 1980s, had become the prosperous dependents of a protector whose foreign and defense policies they increasingly distrusted and which, in turn, had become increasingly restive in that role.

The Declining American Economy
and Global Commitments

In a fundamental sense, the critical problem facing the Reagan administration from the day it took office was not the Soviet Union or NATO, but the state of the American economy, which had been in the doldrums since 1973. No president in the 1980s could afford to neglect this problem because without a growing economy the United States could not support a global foreign policy. America had long been the world's leading industrial power, and its huge productive capacity was the basis of victory in the two world wars. Most especially, the enormous wealth created by American industry and agriculture had made it possible for the United States to accept commitments in many areas of the world and simultaneously to afford sizable deterrent forces and a conventional military capability.

The key question that American policy makers after World War II repeatedly asked themselves was whether a particular area or country was of vital interest to the security and/or prosperity of the United States. If they decided it was, the appropriate policy followed. The question of affordability was only rarely asked; rather, it was assumed. Only conservatives on occasion asked whether the United States could afford a Marshall Plan or large deterrent and conventional forces. The Eisenhower administration was particularly concerned with the question of costs, federal deficits, and balanced budgets. But in the words of presidential candidate John Kennedy, the country could afford anything it needed for its security. Although funds obviously were not unlimited, the assumption was that the nation was wealthy enough to support a high standard of living at home and a global policy abroad.

The 1950s and 1960s were decades of very rapid economic growth. It became commonplace to refer to the United States as an "affluent society," to Americans as the "people of plenty." Wages for workers rose rapidly during this period as trade unions grew powerful and negotiated sizable annual pay raises. American industry apparently could afford such raises in an increasingly consumer-oriented society while still earning handsome profits. The Kennedy and Johnson administrations vastly expanded the welfare state. The payments made by older programs such as Social Security were frequently raised, and new programs were initiated. Some, like Medicare, started small but grew rapidly in cost as more people became eligible for them and the benefits were adjusted to meet inflation. These entitlement programs were made possible because the economy was growing rapidly and producing sufficient wealth to support both a high standard of living and welfare payments, as well as an extensive foreign policy. President Johnson went to war in Vietnam thinking he could finance both the Great Society programs and the war (which originally was expected to last two years and involve only 200,000 troops) without increasing taxes.

The enormous expense of the Vietnam War, plus the dramatic rise of oil prices, which simultaneously produced high inflation and large-scale unemployment, put a brake on the economy. Instead of growing rapidly, it stagnated. The United States could no longer afford both guns and butter. It had to make choices: an economy that was growing only slowly could not afford constantly rising wages, rapidly rising annual welfare costs, and expensive foreign policy commitments. When the economy slows down, growth in one program comes at the cost of others. In a democracy these choices are painful: workers do not gladly accept pay cuts; voters are unhappy with a slowdown in the increase in welfare programs, let alone cuts; and, although defense cuts are often advocated and followed in these circumstances, the nation also needs to guard itself against foreign threats.

Reaganomics and U.S. Competitiveness in the International Economy

Reagan, asserting that defense spending had been held back during the 1970s, stepped up military spending and cut back the growth of social programs. Politically, of course, this can be done only for so long. The longer-term solution, according to the Reagan administration, was to stimulate the economy so that it would once more grow as rapidly as it had during the 1950s and 1960s. But the American economy had changed greatly since the 1960s. Although American agriculture was the most bountiful in the world, and the export of food was a major source of earnings in foreign trade, by the middle 1980s overseas markets were declining. Other developed countries like Britain and France had become food exporters, as had developing countries such as India, China, Thailand, and Indonesia. The future of American agricultural exports looked dim as conflict over markets became an increasingly tense and divisive issue among the United States, its allies, and other friendly nations. The traditional smokestack industries like steel were especially hard hit because they had become increasingly uncompetitive internationally and had declined. There were many reasons for this decline: underinvestment in the American economy because of high U.S. wages, a desire to be nearer overseas markets, and the Common Market's tariff barriers against imports. American industry was going overseas where it could save transportation costs and where wages were lower, especially in Third World countries. American manufacturers could avoid the Common Market's tariff wall by building factories in Western Europe. Industry considered its actions rational: goods could be produced more cheaply outside of the United States, and large-scale markets and opportunities were also opening up abroad. Goods, for consumers both abroad and at home, it argued, would be less expensive and more competitive with foreign goods while also increasing corporate earnings.

Another reason was that America's allies and friends, whose economies it had helped to rebuild following World War II, became by the 1970s major industrial competitors. Older industries such as textiles, steel, shipbuilding, and automobiles (in Europe) were rebuilt, and new industries such as automobiles (Japan) and electronics (Japan, Taiwan, and South Korea) were started. Smugly believing they would always be number one, and because they were accustomed to having the enormous domestic market virtually all to themselves, U.S. industries had not made the necessary investments in (nonmilitary) research and development. American textiles, steel, shipbuilding, automobiles, and even electronics became successively unable to compete with goods mass-produced by new technologies. The American techniques of mass production had now become global, and, together with the lower wages in other countries, especially in the developing nations, than those paid to well-remunerated, unionized American workers, the resulting products undersold U.S.-manufactured products. This is the principal reason why U.S. industries, to stay competitive and profitable, go overseas. This process is referred to as the "deindustrialization" of America. Abandoning some industries like electronics, the surviving U.S. industries all too frequently produced shoddy and unreliable products. It was the Asian and European, especially West German, competition that made the country aware of its economic decline and need to change its way of doing business. American industries had to learn the hard way that not only did they have to compete for foreign markets but they also had to fight for the U.S. domestic market.

Industries like steel foundered. In 1986 U.S. Steel, once the symbol of American industrial might, changed its name to USX as it cut back further on steel production. Japanese steel, produced by more modern methods, could be shipped to the United States and sold more cheaply than steel made in Ohio. Although the automobile industry invested money, it kept mass-producing the same large, gas-guzzling, showy cars year in and year out, expecting customers to trade them in every few years for another large car. When the oil crisis hit, the industry was caught without small, fuel-efficient, well-made automobiles. Japan had them and captured a sizable sector of the market, which has since increased. Even the high-technology sector of the economy (supercomputers, semiconductor chips, machine tools, robotics, biotechnology, telecommunications, and aerospace technology among others), often acclaimed as the basis for future economic growth and prosperity, experienced difficulties. The Japanese especially appeared increasingly to be emerging as the world's most advanced country in nonmilitary technologies. By 1987, near the end of Reagan's term, the U.S. trade deficit—the gap between imports and exports—in high technology with Japan was almost as large as that in cars. The total deficit of $25 billion in 1980 had risen to $161 billion. But Japan was hardly alone in this respect, even if it was the largest of the 110 countries with which the United States had a trade deficit; the others included not only the other country the United States had defeated in World War II, (West) Germany, but also such states as Bangladesh and Sri Lanka.

Among the reasons for this deficit were American capital investments and funds for nonmilitary research and development, among the lowest in the Western industrial world (Canada, Western Europe, and Japan); U.S. corporate preoccupation with quarterly profits and dividends to the detriment of long-term investments and research; and the decline of the American labor force, a reflection of lower U.S. educational standards. Japanese and West German school children attended school longer each day and up to two months longer per year. These children learned more science and mathematics, knowledge of which fuels all contemporary innovations. Lastly, there was a lack of corporate enterprise. Even when the United States had achieved technological breakthroughs, as in video recorders, microwave ovens, and robots, American manufacturers chose not to produce them. Almost all of these products are now produced by the Pacific Rim countries. In the United States during the 1980s, capital investment and modernization took second place to a merger mania and leveraged buyouts of companies. Even though this was financially profitable for a small group of investment bankers and lawyers, this shuffling of paper money did not add one whit to the nation's economic growth.

The economic rise and competitiveness of Japan and the "little Japans" (South Korea, Taiwan, Singapore, and Hong Kong), and Europe—scheduled in 1992 to complete its economic integration and to become a more productive and efficient economy, which will also be more competitive in international trade—threatened to disrupt the alliance relationships further with "trade wars." The decline of the American economy was in part natural. Its postwar dominance was the result of the collapse of the European economies, and it lasted only until, with American assistance, they recovered. But in large part, it was clearly self-inflicted. And protectionism of uncompetitive U.S. industries—the political reaction to failing industries and loss of jobs—was no more the answer to reviving the economy than "Japan-bashing" because of Japan's access to the U.S. market while not allowing reciprocal access to its own. For while the removal of Japanese barriers would reduce the huge American trade deficit with Japan, the fundamental problem was the increasingly uncompetitive U.S. economy.

The Imbalance Between Economic Power and Political Commitments

The economic base of the U.S. international role was eroding. America's superior productive capability had been the basis for its victory in World War II; after the war, the economy had underwritten America's role abroad. The decline raised the critical question whether the economy could still support a foreign policy that kept 300,000 men in Western Europe, defended Japan, was committed to the Persian Gulf and was increasing its commitments in Central America. Could it do all these *as well as* support higher wages and extensive welfare programs and still find the investment capital necessary to restimulate the growth of the private sector? Given the expenditures needed to make the American economy internationally competitive, including investment in education, transportation, and basic urban services, all of which contribute to U.S. competitiveness, how much could the nation afford to spend on commitments abroad and on defense? Would these commitments divert funds from social programs, thereby risking domestic dissatisfaction, hardship, and conflict? Should ailing industries be protected with tariffs and subsidies or should they be compelled to become more efficient (assuming they can survive), even if that means forcing wages downward? How much should the government become involved through tax policies in the reindustrialization of America?

The Reagan administration had placed its greatest emphasis, once in power, on economic growth and controlling inflation. It sought to do so by "supply-side" economics, that is, by stimulating the economy with lower taxes to stimulate investments. But it did this while increasing the defense budget. The result was a loss of revenues and a huge budget deficit of more than $200 billion. As the government competed with industry for capital to cover the deficit, interest rates rose. This in turn attracted huge foreign investments, boosting the value of the dollar. The result was that American export prices shot upward, devastating exporting industries. At the same time, import prices dropped, undercutting American firms at home. While American consumers and tourists benefited from this state of affairs, American farmers, overproducing and heavily dependent on exports, were badly hurt; many smaller family-owned farms went bankrupt. Industry also suffered as lower earnings meant less investment capital. In 1986 the United States became the world's largest debtor nation, with a bigger debt than all the developing countries put together. More than 2 million jobs were lost in industries that export, which resulted in widespread demands for protectionism. But protectionism could not arrest the decline of the economy or boost its ability to compete against the world economy. It would only disrupt the flow of trade, hurt friendly nations and allies, perhaps endangering important political and military ties.

When the United States reversed course and, with the collaboration of its trade partners and competitors, forced the value of the dollar down, making American products cheaper and more competitive and foreign products more expensive, the trade deficit narrowed sharply. But by 1989 it was clear that this strategy could not make it disappear; the sizable gap that remained, despite the slump in oil prices during the decade, could be overcome only by a revived and more competitive economy. In the meantime, foreigners, possessing enormous sums of dollars, used them to buy up huge tracts of American farmland, shopping centers, hotels, and urban real estate that had become cheap to buy because of the lowered value of the dollar. America was "for sale." Such familiar names as Alka-Seltzer, Baskin-Robbins, Bloomingdale, Burger King, Firestone, Geritol, Pillsbury, CBS, RCA, MCA Studios, Columbia Pictures, Rockefeller Center, Smith Wesson, Timex, and *TV Guide* are but a few of the American corporations now foreign-owned.

In the final analysis, the United States must give priority to rebuilding its economy by following its own earlier history. The United States, like Germany, at the turn of the century did not just compete with Britain, then the world's leading industrial power, in areas in which it had attained industrial primacy, such as steel and shipbuilding; both countries developed new products such as chemicals, electrical devices, and automobiles. The United States has had a history of successful transformations from older to newer industries. The question is whether it can do so again. One thing is certain: if the United States cannot revitalize its industry and recapture its technological edge, the decline of the American industrial base will continue. A productive and competitive economy has been the basis of America's prosperity and power sustaining its postwar global role and its high standard of living. The foundations of that power and living standards were eroding. No great power, not even the United States, which has been a military and economic superpower (unlike the Soviet Union, which has been only a military one), can afford to become increasingly dependent on foreigners for essential technologies, including some for its most advanced weapons systems, and not do the research and development needed to maintain its scientific and technological leadership (ranging from supercomputers, the next generation of memory chips, to high- definition television) and not lose control of its own economic destiny, and, thus, its political future. As many developing nations have long argued, the greater the share of a nation's production controlled by foreigners, the more dependent that nation becomes on decisions made elsewhere, either by foreign governments or financiers or corporate managers. And all great powers have been creditor, not debtor, nations. By 1990 the interest payment on the U.S. debt was greater than the federal government's total budget at the height of the Vietnam War, and greater than the Bush administration's spending on agriculture, education, environment, public housing, science, and transportation. Indeed, debt payment on the deficit came in as the government's third most expensive program, right after social security and defense, and it threatened to climb into first place if serious deficit reduction measures were not undertaken.

Closing the Ends-Means Gap

Past administrations had already made efforts to deal with the growing gap between the nation's ends, or objectives, and means, or power. The defeat in Vietnam, the resulting domestic constraints on the use of American power, the growth of Soviet military power, and especially the rise of Japan and, to a lesser extent, Western Europe as major economic powers, had all been indicators of the passing of the bipolar era and the relative decline of American power. Any nation confronting commitments exceeding its power can cope with this gap in several ways. Among these it can reduce its commitments, reduce the threat to its interests, or increase its power; that it can do either by greater alliance burden-sharing—shifting more of the cost of defending the allies to them—or by mobilizing greater resources of its own.

The Nixon administration, which made the first effort to deal with this growing gap between ends and means, did not reduce U.S. commitments; nor have any of its successors. Indeed, despite Vietnam and the cries for shedding the nation's "global policeman" role, American commitments expanded after Vietnam, first to Southwest Asia (the Persian Gulf area) and then to Central America. Nixon and Kissinger set the precedent by focusing on reducing the threats to these interests. The rapprochement with China, ending with official U.S. recognition of Communist China in 1979 by the Carter administration, was the most dramatic effort to deal with the non-Soviet threat. Another was the Nixon-Kissinger attempt to exploit Egyptian president Sadat's determination to change sides in order to gain back the Sinai; this too was climaxed by President Carter's achievement of peace between Egypt and Israel at Camp David. Carter also concluded negotiations, initiated by President Johnson, on the Panama Canal, turning it over to the Panamanians by the twenty-first century. Collectively, these were considerable diplomatic achievements. One need but "consider how different the world would look and what the demands would be on U.S. resources if China were threatening aggression against American interests in Asia, if Egypt were a Soviet ally and military base, and if the Panama Canal were under intermittent attack by guerrilla-terrorists." [7]

Other efforts to deal with the commitments-power gap were less successful. The effort to find substitutes for American power in some areas of the world, e.g., Iran as America's policeman in the Persian Gulf, foundered on their internal weaknesses and American human rights concerns. Burden sharing was not much more successful, as most of the NATO allies, facing their own internal economic problems and pressures for maintaining their generous welfare systems, did not undertake the defense expenditure increases they had pledged to meet. The Europeans remained as unenthusiastic about larger conventional forces as they were when NATO was founded. In part, they had always feared that Moscow might be tempted to launch an attack if it really thought that the Western allies would fight a conventional war. What deterred the Soviet leadership was the fear of a nuclear war; they were concerned that the American effort to rely initially on a conventional defense was part of an effort to confine the fighting to Europe and spare the United

---

7. Samuel P. Huntington, "Coping with the Lippmann Gap," *Foreign Affairs* (America and the World 1988), 454-458.

States from nuclear devastation. But the Europeans had also gotten used to "defense on the cheap." By confronting the Soviet Union from the beginning with the threat that any invasion of Western Europe would immediately become an all-out nuclear war that would destroy the Soviet Union, the Europeans felt they could rely mainly on U.S. nuclear deterrence and avoid raising large, expensive armies. America's allies still preferred "massive retaliation," even though conditions had changed since the 1950s and the United States was no longer immune from a Soviet attack.

The failure to induce its allies to assume more of the defense burden not only made the reduction of the non-Soviet threat more important but also lent special urgency to dealing with the Soviet threat. The resulting effort focused basically on arms control: SALT I, which dealt with the offensive-defensive linkage, and SALT II, which set equal ceilings on the strategic forces. These treaties were to be followed by SALT III reducing these forces. The expectation was that these efforts would lessen the cost of the arms race, as well as the Soviet capabilities and incentives to threaten U.S. interests.

Brezhnev's belief that the Soviet arms buildup is what made the Americans interested in détente, and that he could unilaterally exploit that détente to enhance Soviet influence, led the Reagan administration to close the end-means gap by rebuilding American military power. Like its predecessors, the administration was unwilling to reassess America's commitments throughout the world. Its emphasis was on rebuilding the means. Since the allies were not going to make much of a contribution to this effort, it would do so unilaterally. Its rationale was that only by rebuilding American military strength could the United States at some future point "negotiate from strength." In the meantime, the administration also extended American commitments in the Third World.

Cold War II
in Central America
and the Middle East

D ESPITE Americans' growing concerns about "imperial overstretch," President Ronald Reagan's administration expanded U.S. commitments in the Central American-Caribbean area, just as the Carter administration had in the Persian Gulf.[1] Neither felt it had much choice; both were concerned about stopping the growth of Soviet influence. But the Third World was no longer "a homogeneous area of underdeveloped nationalists, full of 'vacuums' waiting to be filled by one superpower or the other."[2] The containment policy, therefore, had to take into account the Third World's more complex realities: the instability of many governments; the proliferation of regional conflicts, including ethnic and religious differences; the increasing use of terrorism; the bursts of intense nationalism, often directed against the United States; and the economic stagnation of many countries, some of which were deeply mired in debt.

Despite his conviction that Third World problems had to be viewed through the prism of the East-West struggle, Reagan found containment in the developing regions a frustrating experience. Memories of Vietnam and congressional restraints on the use of the armed forces made it impossible to deal with the Marxist regimes in Nicaragua as other presidents had dealt with them: by covert or overt intervention. And the Middle East-Persian Gulf area remained as volatile as ever, if not more so because of the Iran-Iraq war and Iran's determination to spread Islamic fundamentalism. The president found himself completely stymied in advancing the Arab-Israeli peace process.

1. Paul Kennedy, "The (Relative) Decline of America," *Atlantic Monthly*, August 1987, 29-38.
2. Robert Osgood, "Reagan's Foreign Policy," in *Reagan's Leadership and the Atlantic Alliance*, ed. Walter Goldstein (New York: Pergamon-Brassey's, 1987), 27.

Moreover, his administration was weakened and his reputation damaged when it was revealed that the United States had sold arms to Iran to gain the release of U.S. hostages in Lebanon and then used the excess profits from the deal to finance a covert war against the Nicaraguan government over the opposition of Congress.

Intervention in Central America

Virtually from the day Reagan took office, his administration placed El Salvador, a country the size of New Jersey with a population of 5 million, within the context of superpower conflict. The roots of El Salvador's problems were—as in Nicaragua, Guatemala, Honduras, and even in democratic Costa Rica—largely domestic. All except Honduras had been rapidly modernizing since 1960, but their economic growth had benefited mainly a small elite of landowners, businessmen, and generals while leaving the mass of the urban population and peasantry poor. In addition, a high birth rate weakened the semifeudal structure in the countryside and forced many peasants, many of whom did not own land, to move to cities. Here they were exposed to new ideas and saw a better way of life to which they aspired. With governments unable to meet their peoples' new expectations, these countries suffered rising social discontent and tensions. Their attempts to modernize failed to undermine the traditional, conservative political systems; and the high price of imported oil caused high inflation. Military regimes or militarily supported regimes prevented social reform and political change. Peaceful change being impossible, the authoritarian governments in Nicaragua, El Salvador, and Guatemala increasingly faced the opposition of leftist guerrillas.

The first result of guerrilla action, the collapse of the regime of Anastasio Somoza in Nicaragua in 1979 and the victory by the Sandinistas, led to increased disturbance throughout the region, as the extreme left and right sought to achieve or preserve power through violence. America's major setback to its primacy in the area had begun in the 1960s when Washington tolerated the Soviet presence in Cuba. Now U.S. influence eroded further. Somoza's fall, coming after forty years of rule by his family, regarded as friends of the United States, encouraged armed, left-wing forces to make a military bid for power. The traditional right-wing authoritarian governments (except in Costa Rica) responded fearfully with force. Each side attacked elements of the other side, the right even assassinating nuns and priests, including an archbishop in El Salvador. Moderate political leaders who advocated peaceful reform and change, such as some of the Christian Democrats who came to power in El Salvador, were targets for assassination. The moderates had difficulty controlling right-wing death squads and factions of the military who, while fighting against leftist guerrillas, were allied with these death squads. Such killings further polarized society in these countries.

Nevertheless, the Reagan administration made El Salvador an international issue because, after years of Soviet-Vietnamese-Cuban successes in the Third World, the administration was determined to send Moscow a message to stop expanding Soviet influence by means of proxies. Asserting that the Salvadoran government of Napoleón Duarte was moderate, the administration decided that Duarte had the best chance of carrying out domestic social reforms while preventing a radical left-wing assumption of power. Therefore, the Reagan administration backed him with shipments of military equipment and fifty U.S. advisers to the Salvadoran government forces. This assistance, it was claimed, was necessary to counter the arms sent to the Salvadoran guerrillas by Cuba, Ethiopia, Libya, and Vietnam at Soviet direction. Further, it was alleged that most of these arms had been shipped via Nicaragua, which was punished for its complicity by a cut-off of American economic aid.

In addition to arms, the Communist states were said to be giving the Salvadoran guerrillas money, training, and advice. The war in El Salvador, the State Department claimed, was a "textbook case of indirect armed aggression by Communist powers." Because of Washington's determination to publicize and stop Soviet-Cuban expansion in the Third World, especially so close to the United States, the war received widespread international attention. Washington was concerned that if, after Nicaragua, El Salvador also fell to left-wing guerrillas and established a second Marxist mainland regime, the rest of Central America would follow. But the threat was defined as applying to not only Panama or Mexico but also to the wider U.S. position throughout the world. "If Central America were to fall," the president asked, "what would the consequences be for our position in Asia, Europe, and for alliances such as NATO? If the United States cannot respond to a threat near our own border, why should Europeans or Asians believe that we are seriously concerned about threats to them?"[3] In brief, U.S. stakes were judged very high in Central America, and the nation could not ignore or be indifferent to the danger of governments with close ideological and military ties to the Soviet Union.

Whether El Salvador was the right place to take a stand against Soviet communism and its proxies or whether the revolution should have been allowed to follow its natural course was energetically debated in the United States. Critics of the administration's plans, especially the Democrats in opposition, argued that the arms were not the principal cause for the civil war but, rather, the appalling domestic social and economic conditions and political repression. The United States should not support the privileged few

---

3. Ronald Reagan, "Central America: Defending Our Vital Interests," U.S. Department of State, *Current Policy*, No. 482, April 27, 1983.

who had long exploited the poor. Social justice demanded nonintervention; so perhaps did expediency if the United States wished to avoid being identified with the losers, as it had been so many times before. The Vietnam War was frequently cited as a reminder of the dangers of supporting the wrong side— an unpopular political elite whose vested interest lay in the preservation of the status quo. In any event, no purely military solution was possible. Much was made of human rights violations in El Salvador. The United States, which stands for human rights, it was said, should not be backing a regime whose security forces were so brutal. Moscow would be the only winner. Indeed, in Western Europe as well as in many Latin American countries, especially Mexico, El Salvador's northern neighbor, the Salvadoran guerrillas were thought to deserve more support than the government because they would create a more equitable society.

Rejecting these arguments, Reagan officials pointed to Nicaragua, where the Carter administration, not wishing to block a "progressive Third World revolution" and preferring to be on the "right side" of history, withdrew support from Somoza, initially believing that the successor government would bring Nicaragua a more democratic regime and social justice. But, once in power, the Sandinistas began to consolidate their hold on government, gradually suppressing the voices of criticism as counterrevolutionary. They postponed general elections while building an army larger than Somoza's and establishing relations with Cuba and the Soviet Union. The question was not how Marxist the regime would become, as it turned against the Catholic church, the business community, professional organizations, trade unions, and student groups that had helped it to depose Somoza, but how dictatorial it would become and how closely it would align with Havana and Moscow. The Sandinistas imposed censorship on opposition newspapers, restrained activities by other political parties, extended control over worker and peasant organizations, and strengthened its police and security apparatus. They also turned toward Cuba and the Soviet Union. The United States therefore reassessed its policy even *before* the arrival of the Reagan administration and its organization of the *contras*, the fighters trying to overthrow the Sandinista government.

But if the Reagan administration did not intend to repeat in El Salvador what it regarded as Carter's error in Nicaragua, American public opinion was not enthusiastic about becoming involved in that tiny country. Economic and military aid, but not military intervention, it was willing to tolerate. Congress made that aid contingent on an improvement of the Salvadoran regime's human rights record. This left the administration little choice but to support the Salvadoran government while encouraging it to continue its social reforms and to discipline any soldiers and security forces accused of killing civilians. A key aspect of American policy was to legitimate the regime by holding general elections.

The left, however, opposed participation, and the guerrillas threatened those who tried to vote. Nevertheless, to the surprise of American observers and others watching the election for fraud and intimidation, more than 80 percent of the electorate turned out. The results of the 1982 election were ironic. The Christian Democrats, who were in power, received the largest vote of any single party, but the several right-wing parties together polled a larger vote and organized a coalition government. Those who had opposed the Christian Democrats and the reform-minded military officers, both supported by the United States, were therefore the beneficiaries of the American-sponsored free election. Duarte was out. The election, however, demonstrated that the formerly strong support for the guerrillas among peasants, students, and workers had eroded.

Nevertheless, the war went on. The army was poorly led and trained. As death-squad killings of civilians continued and no government official or soldier was convicted of any of the thousands of murders, Salvadoran politics became further polarized between right and left. Reagan wanted to send in more military advisers and greater military assistance. But Congress, continuing to be haunted by memories of Vietnam and questioning whether the Salvadoran army could win the war, no matter how much aid it received, opposed the president on sending in more advisers and only reluctantly supported him with funds for military and economic assistance.

The Shift to Centrist Politics

Locating a moderate center was the key to mobilizing support domestically and, it was hoped, to achieving success in El Salvador. The United States in the Third World had often appeared trapped between reactionary forces on the one hand, whose rigid commitment to the status quo only intensified revolutionary sentiment and endangered American interests, and radical forces on the other, which tended to be Marxist and to look to Havana and Moscow. But it was rescued from this trap by the 1984 Salvadoran presidential elections and legislative and municipal elections in 1985, which brought Duarte back to power. Duarte's election strengthened the Reagan case for assistance to El Salvador because Reagan could rightfully claim that the United States was not supporting the right wing as an alternative to the radical left. Washington sent Duarte military aid and encouraged domestic reforms, without which military assistance could not win the war. It hoped in these ways to avoid both another Cuba in Central America and another Vietnam.

As a result of U.S. training, aid, and advice, the Salvadoran army's mistreatment of civilians was reduced. It also became a better fighting force, driving the guerrillas to resort to urban assassinations as they suffered defeats in the field. The guerrillas therefore stepped up their campaign of economic ruin, knocking out bridges, electrical pylons and destroying crops. This destruction, in turn, required continuing large-scale U.S. economic assistance to ensure Duarte's political survival. Although the rebels were unlikely to win the civil war, they continued this war of attrition. In the meantime, the fundamental problems of Salvadoran society—its vast social inequality, class divisions, and authoritarianism—persisted. American policy had denied the guerrillas victory; it now found itself committed to the more difficult and elusive task of building a nation from a deeply fragmented society. Rising unemployment, inflation, and the failure to implement any fundamental social and economic reforms resulted in the narrowing of Duarte's base among the workers and peasants. He grew increasingly unpopular. He was also dying from cancer. All efforts to arrange a cease-fire and a political settlement of the war ended in failure. In 1989 Duarte lost the presidential election to the right-wing party; he had not been strong enough to make peace or impose reform to end the economic distress in his country. In the meantime, the roots of the insurgency—poverty and the economic grip of a small privileged elite—remained.

The Reagan Doctrine
and the Latin American Focus

In the broader context the Reagan administration's policy in Central America was not merely to hold the line in El Salvador, but to reverse what it saw as Soviet gains in Third World contests in Angola, Ethiopia, Yemen, Afghanistan, and Cambodia after the Vietnam War. The Soviets and their allies had been using force, directly in Afghanistan, indirectly through proxies elsewhere. By contrast, in the United States there was a widespread feeling that the use of force had become counterproductive, that it was so clearly immoral that short of an attack on the United States or its allies in Western Europe, force was not a legitimate means for protecting or advancing American interests. "Force will not solve political problems" had become a commonplace. In this atmosphere of American nonintervention, neither Moscow nor Havana was penalized for intervening; the absence of sanctions, indeed, provided them with an incentive to exploit favorable political opportunities. The Reagan administration had been skeptical from the beginning about the notion of the disutility of force. The U.S. invasion of Grenada in 1983 was intended to raise the risks and the costs for the Soviets and Cubans should they continue to try and extend their political and military control in this hemisphere, as well as elsewhere. Asserting that it had intervened just in the nick of time to prevent Grenada from becoming a "Soviet-Cuban colony," the administration called Grenada a "warning shot."

Cuban-Soviet presence on Grenada had been of concern to the administration earlier. Grenadians, it ought to be added, overwhelmingly welcomed the intervention, which rescued them from Cuban control and domestic repression. As it turned out, many of the 700 Cuban "construction workers" resisted the American landing, which the president called a "rescue mission," not an invasion. Soviet military personnel, North Koreans, and East Germans were also present on the island. Caches of arms were found, as well as documents showing that larger shipments of arms were to be transported in the future, presumably to be sent to leftist rebels in Latin America or used for training guerrillas. For Cuba, the invasion of Grenada was certainly a blow. Fidel Castro lost a bridgehead and influence in the Caribbean and in Central America where he announced he would not be able to help Nicaragua if it were invaded. The U.S. action was obviously aimed at Nicaragua. American pressure against the Sandinistas had been increasing for some time with the support of the *contras* and the stationing of sizable American naval forces off both the Atlantic and Pacific coasts of Nicaragua. Grenada was intended to escalate this pressure and demonstrate to the Sandinistas, Cubans, and Soviets that the United States would once more use force if the administration thought it necessary. The Soviet Union and its proxies might mock the United States for attacking a minuscule state, but presumably they would exercise more restraint in the future—at least in Central America and the Caribbean.

But Grenada, as El Salvador and Nicaragua, was a reminder that the United States could no longer assume, as it had historically, the security of its borders. The nation's ability to project power to Europe, Asia, or the Middle East, all far away from the United States, was predicated on peace in the Western Hemisphere. By contrast, this strategic luxury had been denied the Soviet Union, which has historically had to be concerned with the security of its long frontiers. It was to enhance his country's sense of security that Joseph Stalin transformed Eastern Europe into a Soviet buffer zone and that Leonid Brezhnev later formalized the Soviet right to intervene in that area to prevent "counterrevolutions," which might jeopardize socialism. The Brezhnev Doctrine, announced at the time of the Soviet intervention in Czechoslovakia in 1968, had already been practiced in East Germany in 1953 and Hungary in 1956. The Monroe Doctrine historically had reserved the Western Hemisphere as America's sphere of influence. But, if it was anything, the Monroe Doctrine was really a "Caribbean Doctrine," making that area America's buffer zone. (Tierra del Fuego, the southern tip of South America, was, after all, farther away than Western Europe.) Castro's survival in Cuba had altered this situation.

The Reagan administration viewed the Central American region as America's "soft underbelly," a potential "Eastern Europe." The reason was the combination of unstable political conditions throughout the area and the rise of Soviet-Cuban-Nicaraguan influence. Washington therefore thought it was confronted with three undesirable options: much larger defense spending to guard against future efforts to expand Communist influence and the stationing of larger military forces, including carrier battle groups, in the area; a reduced role and capability to defend more distant areas, including Western Europe; or eliminating the regime in Nicaragua that had transformed the nation into the first "Cuba" on the mainland. It was the third option that the administration actively pursued.

The administration was convinced that the Sandinistas harbored ideologically motivated ambitions beyond their own frontiers. Because they also accepted support from Havana and Moscow, Washington saw them as a continuing source of instability and tension in an area of vulnerable states. The Sandinistas' pledge to confine themselves to Nicaragua was regarded with skepticism by those who recalled their pledge before they assumed power in 1979 to political pluralism, a mixed economy, and a nonaligned foreign policy. By the dynamics of their own revolution, the Sandinistas were expected to support "fraternal" revolutionary movements among their neighbors; theirs was a "revolution without frontiers."

What the Reagan administration sought in Nicaragua was to undo the Sandinistas' increasing monopolization of power and to turn Nicaragua back to the immediate post-1979 period when the popular anti-Somoza revolution had produced a new government composed of the major groups that had helped to overthrow the dictator. Past administrations had been committed to containment and had not hesitated to intervene to save a friendly regime from being attacked externally or from within by the Soviet Union and/or its friends. However, except for episodic efforts such as Truman's effort to "liberate" North Korea, or Kennedy's Bay of Pigs operation in Cuba, it had never been the official policy of the U.S. government to unseat Soviet-supported regimes. Eisenhower's administration had spoken of the "liberation" of Eastern Europe but had never acted on that wish. Containment was a defensive doctrine. The new Reagan policy went "beyond containment" and was inclined to take the offensive.

Dubbed the "Reagan Doctrine," it aimed to undo the results of Soviet expansion not only in Nicaragua but also in Angola and Afghanistan, the Soviet Union's neighbor. Afghanistan was included, although the Afghan resistance had been receiving assistance from President Carter even before Reagan took office. (President Ford had also tried to help the opposition in Angola until Congress cut off the funds.) All three countries had become Marxist states, but the new governments had not yet consolidated their power, and all faced resistance movements. The Soviets had justified their Third World expansion with the doctrine of "national liberation" and then asserted that communism was irreversible once a society had become Marxist. Reagan now adopted his own national liberation strategy against governments that had not come to power by means of democratic processes; in his eyes, such regimes lacked legitimacy. Moscow had placed them in power and, unlike his predecessors (with the partial exception of Carter in Afghanistan), he refused to accept Moscow's claim that civil wars were over once governments were in place. The domestic conflicts were not over until popular governments, acceptable to the people (and presumably to Washington), were in power. In short, the Reagan Doctrine set out to disprove the

Brezhnev Doctrine's claim that once a nation had become part of the Soviet bloc, it could never leave.

The president's version of national liberation was, of course, not applied to all Third World states, but only to some of the Soviet Union's recent acquisitions. The doctrine was based on certain assumptions: that the Soviet Union had become overextended in the 1970s; that the "correlation of forces," as Moscow called it, after favoring Moscow in the 1970s, was shifting back to the United States as a result of its military buildup; that the Soviet Union's most critical problems were domestic; that, except for Afghanistan, only peripheral Soviet interests were involved; that the Soviet Union would not want to risk a confrontation with the United States; and that a democratic tide was sweeping through the Third World. In practice, the Reagan Doctrine amounted to little more than bleeding the targeted governments and especially Moscow; if they wanted to stop the hemorrhaging, they would have to negotiate a political solution with the insurgents. The insurgencies were not strong enough to overthrow the Marxist regimes, but with American help they could keep the wars going.

Theoretically, the Reagan Doctrine was flawed by a contradiction. Its aims were ambitious, but its means were modest—less than a billion dollars a year. Either the means would have to be greatly increased or the ends reduced. An increase of the means was precisely what many in Congress feared. Sooner or later, if the insurgents failed, the end could be achieved only by American forces, at least in Nicaragua, which the administration considered a vital interest. Given the involvement of American prestige, could the United States allow the insurgents to lose? Would it not be claimed that American resolve was at stake? In short, was not escalation (and the possible loss of public support) built into the Reagan Doctrine and its ambitious goals? That the United States might at some time have to escalate its efforts or cut its losses was demonstrated by the Soviets in 1985-1986.

They showed that they were both able and willing to support their friends by stepping up the war in Afghanistan and raising their military assistance to the Nicaraguan and Angolan governments. The new Soviet leader, Mikhail Gorbachev, appeared determined to maintain his country's imperial outposts. In Nicaragua the result was that the *contras* suffered severe losses. Basically defenseless against Soviet-supplied helicopter gunships, they were driven out of Nicaragua into neighboring countries. In Angola Jonas Savimbi, the leader of the insurgents, came to the United States to appeal for more military aid after his troops suffered severe setbacks at the hands of government and Cuban forces. And in Afghanistan, where the fierce resistance had already involved the Soviet Union in a war longer than that against Nazi Germany, the Soviet helicopter gunships appeared to be turning the war in its favor.

In the circumstances of the mid-1980s, the dilemma of raising the means or cutting the ends—accepting the "loss" of the countries to the Soviet

Union—could be avoided only if historical trends were judged favorable. That is precisely what the Reagan administration claimed. A democratic revolution was sweeping the Third World; modest means could achieve immodest ends. For evidence, the administration pointed to Latin America. During the Reagan years—besides El Salvador, Grenada, and Haiti (in whose transformation it had been involved)—the administration cited Argentina, Bolivia, Brazil, Guatemala, Honduras, Peru, and Uruguay as having become democratic. Whatever the reason for this phenomenon—administration policy, the sudden political blossoming of Iberian culture in Latin America after Spain and Portugal became democratic in the 1970s, or sheer coincidence—the administration expressed its optimism that this was part of a global trend. The Soviet bloc, by denying human freedom and dignity to its citizens, was running against the tide of history. This was why, at the periphery of the bloc, there were revolts against governments that had come into power and were kept there with Soviet bloc help. The United States, as a free society, Washington asserted, was duty bound to support such struggles for national independence and self-government. Thus, the administration married anticommunism and human rights.

The Salvadoran Precedent

Admittedly, early administration pronouncements on the superpower struggle in the Third World did not sound as if the United States would be a contributor to this democratic tide. The clear-cut preference for pro-American authoritarian regimes over pro-Soviet ones had not seemed particularly compatible with American values, even if it could be justified strategically or by events in Iran and Nicaragua. The rise of Duarte in El Salvador, however, provided the Reagan administration, despite its rhetoric, with a democratic politician and party to back. (Congress, too, deserves credit for this development for compelling the administration to switch from total anticommunism to support for democracy by insisting that, in return for military aid, El Salvador would have to demonstrate greater respect for human rights. This helped to win the military's support for Duarte because of its desire to continue receiving U.S. weapons.) In brief, even in the midst of a civil war, there were elements upon which to build democracy; social justice and strategic concerns did not always have to be incompatible. The Salvadoran center was admittedly fragile, beset by guerrillas on the left and resistance to reforms on the right, but it curbed the death squads and created a more hospitable climate for democratic politics.

But when the voters elected the right-wing Arena party in 1989, the fragile Salvadoran democracy was threatened. Although the Bush administration let it be known that it would not accept a right-wing reversion to its pre-Duarte behavior, the murder of a half-dozen Jesuit priests by government soldiers jeopardized American support for the elected Salvadoran government.

The army also suffered several setbacks when the rebels launched a Tet-like offensive in San Salvador in December 1989.

Nevertheless, the Salvadoran precedent of support for a democratic center was widely recognized after the events in the Philippines in 1986. The United States had long supported President Ferdinand Marcos. In August 1983 opposition leader Benigno Aquino returned home from exile in the United States and was assassinated at the airport by Marcos supporters. As public opposition to the Marcos regime grew, the United States urged him to restore democracy, economic growth, and military reforms. His despotism, economic mismanagement, widespread corruption, and the military's abuses were also fueling a rebirth of the Communist guerrilla army called the Nationalist People's Army (NPA). In the absence of basic reforms, the guerrillas might defeat the poorly trained and badly led Philippine army. Marcos, however, refused to heed these suggestions and, to prove his legitimacy to the Americans, called for a snap election, confident he could control the outcome, as he had done before. But this proved to be his undoing. The opposition ran Aquino's widow, Corazon Cojuangco Aquino, for the presidency; she had become both a symbol of democracy and a rallying point. Marcos tried to alter the election results with widespread fraud, but, as the election was closely monitored by U.S. watchdog organizations and covered by the U.S. media, the fraud was not difficult to discover. Marcos lost his legitimacy even while "winning" another term. When top army commanders defected, Marcos fled to Hawaii and Corazon Aquino became president.

Almost simultaneously the Reagan administration helped Haiti get rid of Jean-Claude "Baby Doc" Duvalier, who had succeeded his father as dictator. The United States first advised Duvalier not to use force against protesting crowds and then furnished him with an airplane to flee to France. The Reagan administration now declared its new policy: "The American people believe in human rights and oppose tyranny in whatever form, whether of the left or the right." [4] The United States would support those struggling for democracy and oppose not just radical left-wing regimes but also pro-American right-wing authoritarian regimes. And it did so. In 1987, after considerable turmoil in South Korea, which had flared on and off for years, the military-supported regime promised free elections for the presidency. Administration pressure on South Korea's rulers had helped smooth the long-awaited transition.

Had the Reagan administration gone Carteresque? Was it now doing what it had accused Carter of doing in Iran and Nicaragua, that is, "destabilizing" conservative pro-American regimes? The administration rejected this comparison. The impetus for change in the Philippines and Haiti

---

4. President Reagan's March 14 Message to Congress, *New York Times,* March 15, 1986.

had been indigenous. American help had come only as the despots' power was already crumbling because of popular revolts. Most important, in the Philippines, the opposition appeared genuinely democratic, reform-minded, and pro-American. By implication, however, this also meant that in countries where there was no democratic center as a political alternative, American pressure might make things worse, not better. In Chile American pressure resulted in an election that opened the way for the restoration of democracy; in other countries, it was less likely to work, as American pressure on the shah of Iran for political and social liberalization had demonstrated. In Iran, like Nicaragua, the center had been a mirage. Presumably, therefore, in the absence of a democratic center that had a genuine chance of blossoming, right-wing authoritarianism would still be preferable to left-wing totalitarianism. But where democracy had a chance to grow, it was the best antidote to communism.

The Criteria for Success or Failure

For the most part, however, the Reagan administration invoked its claim of a global prodemocratic tide to support the resistance movements in Afghanistan, Angola, and Nicaragua, although the insurgencies it supported in the name of spreading freedom were of questionable virtue in that respect. In Afghanistan, the opponents to Soviet rule were Islamic fundamentalists who, if they won, were more likely to establish an Iranian-style theocracy than a democracy. Still, that they were a genuine resistance movement could not be doubted. In Angola, Savimbi, the rebel leader representing Angola's largest tribal group, was trained in the PRC and was quite willing to rely on South Africa for help. And in Nicaragua, some of the principal *contra* commanders were former members of Somoza's detested National Guard. In fact, suspicion of the Somocistas was a major cause for the *contras'* inability to exploit the growing alienation of Nicaraguans from the Sandinistas.

Admittedly, the 20,000 *contras* could not be effective, let alone win, when Congress, fearful of another Vietnam, cut military aid and/or substituted "nonlethal" or "humanitarian" aid of food, medicine, and such items—although the administration funded the *contras* secretly so that they could survive until Congress changed its mind again—while the Soviets supplied $500 million in arms over a period of five years. Nevertheless, an effective guerrilla movement should have been better able to exploit the worsening social and economic conditions in Nicaragua and been able to spark the kind of devotion and following the Sandinistas did in an earlier era.

Partly because of this, the *contra* war never gained much popular support in the United States. Quite the opposite: Congress, especially the Democratic-controlled House during the first six years of the Reagan presidency, generally opposed the war. Moreover, the president was never able to convince the public that U.S. security interests were endangered by the Sandinistas. Indeed, it was widely believed that the administration, determined to overthrow the Nicaraguan regime, had not seriously pursued a diplomatic solution. The lack of domestic support drove the administration to fund the war illegally both during the years that Congress had cut off military assistance to the *contras,* as well as after, when Congress resumed funding (see below).

The contrast to Afghanistan was instructive. The Soviet invasion meant that the resistance to the Soviet-imposed government had genuine popular support. The resistance fighters fought courageously and successfully against the Soviet army despite their general lack of modern weapons. Many states throughout the world were sympathetic to the rebels; the Moslem states were largely united in their condemnation of Moscow. Unlike the U.S.-supported *contra* war, which most states in the region and elsewhere opposed, America's covert assistance to the Afghan resistance was not condemned by neighboring states; and it had congressional and popular support in the United States.

Lack of congressional and public support for the *contras* left Reagan only one option as the presidents of Costa Rica, Nicaragua, El Salvador, Honduras, and Guatemala agreed to a regional peace plan in 1987. Reagan supported it because if the plan failed and if the failure could be clearly attributed to the Sandinistas' unwillingness to open up Nicaragua to genuine democratization, as stipulated by the peace plan, the president might regain support for further financial assistance of the *contras.* But this was not to be. The Democrat-controlled Congress remained disenchanted with the *contras* and used the peace plan as a reason not to fund any more military aid; such assistance, it was claimed, would only thwart efforts to bring peace to Nicaragua and the area. The administration's plan to overthrow the Sandinistas, thus, seemingly ended in failure. This appeared even more certain when in early 1989 the five Central American presidents, over the protests of the United States, called for the disbandment of the *contras,* most of them in Honduras, by December. But there was no enforcement provision, so the *contras* remained alive—but barely. Congress had deprived them of money for weapons. More important, Daniel Ortega and his *commandantes* had consolidated power during their ten years in office, and they expected to be able to use their control of the government, including the police and army, to ensure an electoral victory that would give them international legitimacy and eliminate any possible rationale for further U.S. assistance to the *contras.* They certainly did not expect to lose and to relinquish their power; as good Marxists, they believed they represented the masses. But despite Sandinista control of the government and efforts to intimidate opposition candidates and rallies, as well as hold up congressionally approved funds for the opposition, Daniel Ortega lost to Violeta Chamorro—widow of the anti-Somoza newspaper editor whose assassination had rallied the Sandinista-led revolution that brought the dictator down.

A Final Evaluation

Whoever should receive the credit for the defeat of the Sandinistas—the *contras* and Ronald Reagan, or the five Central American presidents led by Costa Rica's Oscar Arias, or the Nicaraguan people who, with international observers present at polling stations, had the courage to vote against an oppressive regime, or the Sandinistas themselves for believing they could survive an unpopular draft and a mismanaged economy in a relatively free election—there was no doubt of the consequences. For the Salvadoran guerrillas, the loss of Nicaraguan political support and military assistance constituted a serious setback to their campaign to overthrow the government or negotiate a favorable settlement that would give them a share of the power. For Castro, who had been the idol for the Sandinistas and to whom they had always looked for help and support, it meant further isolation as he increasingly appeared to be the only remaining revolutionary, and an outdated one at that. And for Nicaragua, the solid defeat of the Sandinistas gave that country a second opportunity for building a democracy, for reintegrating the *contras* into the fabric of Nicaraguan society, for reconciling political opponents, and for reestablishing cordial relations with the United States.

Whether the results of the Nicaraguan elections are attributed to the Reagan Doctrine or not, the doctrine has to be judged at least a partial success. It was a cost-effective means of putting pressure on Moscow, which had to spend an estimated $10-20 billion a year (compared to less than $1 billion annually for the United States) to preserve the gains it had achieved in the 1970s. In 1988, therefore, a number of the regional conflicts in which the United States and the Soviet Union had been engaged came to a conclusion. In Afghanistan, Gorbachev, realizing the war was an unending drain and a political embarrassment, decided to withdraw Soviet forces. After years of fruitless negotiations, the Cubans agreed to pull their forces out of Angola, and the South Africans agreed to pull back their forces and grant independence to Namibia, which they had governed since World War I. These arrangements were followed by a settlement of the Angolan civil war, in which the guerrillas had been supported by the United States and South Africa. In Cambodia, the Vietnamese agreed to withdraw their army, which had invaded that country earlier and overthrown the pro-Chinese Pol Pot regime, responsible for the genocide of 1-2 million of its own 8 million people. Gorbachev had to resolve these regional quarrels because by 1987 it had become clear that he needed to conserve his resources for investment in the stagnating Soviet economy. The prerequisite was an armistice in the cold war so that the Soviet leader could greatly lower spending on the huge Soviet military establishment and unpromising foreign policy involvements. But the Soviet Union did not suffer a set of total defeats or the United States a series of unqualified triumphs. In Afghanistan, Angola, Ethiopia (where America's Arab friends, notably Saudi Arabia, had supported the opposition), and Cambodia, the Marxist regimes retained power. The United States had compelled the Soviet and Vietnamese withdrawals, but it had not achieved its declaratory goal of replacing Marxist regimes with democratic governments.

The Reagan Doctrine had also demonstrated how limited U.S. influence had become in Latin America. If Nicaragua provided one example of constraints on the use of American power, especially force, the other example was Panama. After its strongman, General Manuel Noriega, had been indicted for drug-running by two grand juries in Florida, the United States tried for several years to squeeze him out economically; while effectively undermining the economy and hurting the pro-American middle class, these measures failed to remove Noriega. He had his drug money and secured the loyalty of the armed forces by paying them well and regularly; the collapse of the Panamanian economy and the lot of the citizenry did not budge him. During a coup attempt in early 1989 in an admittedly confusing situation and with poor intelligence, the U.S. government and American forces stationed in Panama stood by passively. This was despite the United States' avowed goal of removing Noriega from office and its broader commitment to ending the inflow of cocaine from Colombia, where the government was at war with the powerful Medellin drug cartel in an effort to keep them from taking over the government.

Noriega too, feeling cockier than ever, now tempted fate. Calling himself the "maximum leader," he declared war on the United States and his forces started harassing American personnel. Stung by previous charges of ineptitude, if not lack of courage, President Bush, who since the failed coup attempt had ordered the military to draw up plans for an invasion, gave the signal to go ahead in December 1989. Almost universally condemned in the United Nations and the Organization of American States (OAS), which had proved impotent to alter the situation in Panama after Noriega had disallowed the election he had lost to the opposition parties, the U.S. government's action was viewed with widespread approval by the American people; and U.S. troops were welcomed as liberators by the Panamanian people. But the capture of Noriega may yet embarrass Washington, including the president. Noriega's defense lawyers will undoubtedly use the general's trial to focus on the U.S. government's use of Noriega to support the *contra* war against the Sandinistas.

Ironically, until Panama, a principal block to the use of American power, especially the use of force, had been the military itself. The memory of Vietnam and the loss of popular support during that conflict was one reason; another was what the military considered civilian interference in the conduct of the war. The post-Vietnam military wanted to be assured before any future interventions that it would have congressional and public support and that the nation would be committed to victory. To the military that meant that once the government had decided to intervene, it would be allowed to win a victory by using force fully without any political constraints. Since these conditions were impossible to assure beforehand, the armed forces opposed all interventions, including Lebanon, Grenada, Nicaragua, and Panama. The chief spokesmen for the use of force to support U.S. foreign policy were civilians, especially Secretary of State Shultz during the Reagan years. Thus, the military reinforced the national post-Vietnam reluctance to use force. But the fact that force could not be used in Nicaragua, and was used finally in Panama only after all other measures had failed and Noriega had provoked Bush, testifies to the general failure of U.S. political policy in Latin America and how little the Monroe Doctrine still mattered in this era of nationalism.

The Middle East and the Effort
to Organize an Anti-Soviet Strategic Consensus

The oil in the Arabian peninsula and in some of the nearby countries had made security in this area critical for the United States and the West since the early 1970s. But the region was both threatened and unstable. With a sizable army in Afghanistan on the border of Pakistan (a nation caught between the Soviet sphere and unfriendly India), and with the use of air and port facilities in Ethiopia and South Yemen, the Soviet presence in the area and its threat to the oil and shipping lines were real in the early 1980s. The increasing nearness of Soviet power and influence frightened Saudi Arabia and the other oil kingdoms, which were already confronting the possibility of domestic instability as a result of the presence of foreign workers, such as Palestinians and fundamentalist Islamic groups opposed to Western-style modernization.

The Carter Doctrine was a symbol of America's vital interest in the area. The superpower rivalry was thus imposed on the instability of key countries, as well as on regional rivalries, such as those between India and Pakistan and Iran and Iraq. Arab unity was shattered by the Iran-Iraq war. Libya and Syria supported non-Arab Iran, while former adversaries of Iraq such as Jordan helped it; even Egypt, the target of Iraq's Rejectionist front, sent arms. And, of course, the politics of the area could not be separated from the Arab- (minus Egypt) Israeli quarrel. The area was a veritable tinderbox.

The Reagan administration pursued a twofold foreign policy strategy toward the Middle East-Persian Gulf area to reduce this insecurity. First, based on the assumption that Saudi Arabia, the key oil country, kept its distance from the United States because it lacked confidence in American leadership and power, the new administration decided to upgrade the U.S.-Saudi relationship by agreeing to sell the Saudis the fuel tanks and air-to-air missiles they requested for their F-15 fighters, as well as five Airborne Warning and Control System (AWACS) aircraft. Reagan vowed the United States would not permit Saudi Arabia "to be an Iran," thereby upgrading Carter's commitment to protect Persian Gulf states against external forces. This statement implied that the United States would protect the Saudi government even against internal insurrection.

If reassuring Saudi Arabia of its special relationship with the United States and of America's ability and willingness to protect the kingdom's security was fundamental U.S. political strategy, what about the Arab-Israeli conflict? Reagan administration officials were fond of stating that the region's various rivalries and domestic instabilities were only marginally related to the Arab-Israeli struggle, thereby suggesting that, if the United States could establish its power in the area and the pro-Western Arab regimes then felt more secure, then oil supplies for the West would also be more secure. The key issue was American leadership and the credibility of American power, not the self-determination of the Palestinians, the critical issue blocking a more comprehensive Arab-Israeli peace.

The second part of the Reagan strategy, therefore, was to stress the anti-Soviet nature of its policy. Fundamentally, this attempt to forge an anti-Soviet "strategic consensus" was intended to overcome the Arabs' resistance to joining forces with the United States because of the U.S. policy on Israel. Specifically, Reagan's purpose was to gain the cooperation of countries such as Egypt, Jordan, Saudi Arabia, and Pakistan, as well as Israel. They should all give priority to containing Soviet influence and subordinate their local quarrels to this more important task. This approach amounted to downplaying the central Arab-Israeli conflict and postponing a settlement of the most critical problem preventing a settlement, that of the Palestinians.

It was not a successful strategy. The Israelis were very anxious about any weapons sold to any Arab state, and Saudi Arabia, as an Arab state, could not ignore the Palestinians and other issues of concern. In fact, the Saudis argued strongly that the increasing frustration and anger about the lack of progress on the Palestinian issue was the *main* danger to the U.S. interest in keeping the oil flowing, and that *all* Arabs, not just Israel's neighbors, felt the same way. In short, the countries in the area gave priority to their quarrels while the United States searched for ways of resolving both the oil and the Arab-Israeli problems, problems that refused to be divorced from each other.

Events Undermining Reagan's Policy

Four events took place to frustrate the administration's policy for the region. The first was in Lebanon, Israel's small northern neighbor, which several years earlier had disintegrated into civil war between Christians and

Muslims. The Christians, long the wealthier and more politically influential, sought to retain their position by suppressing the Palestinians, whose presence had become sizable after Jordan's King Hussein had driven them out of his country during the early 1970s. Sympathetic to their fellow Arabs and their aspirations for a greater say in Lebanese affairs, which would reflect their rapidly growing numbers, the Palestinians, heavily armed, constituted a threat to the integrity of Lebanon. They upset the agreement of the Christians and Lebanese Muslims for a domestic redistribution of power because the more militant left-wing forces felt that they could militarily defeat the Christians with the help of the Palestine Liberation Organization (PLO) and win most of the political power. Syria opposed a solution that would probably have led to a Christian secession from Lebanon and the establishment of two states, one Christian and one Muslim. It sought Lebanon's survival and political integrity, first through political mediation and, when that proved unsuccessful, through military intervention. Syria did so for several reasons but mainly to establish its dominance in Lebanon, hoping to incorporate it into Syria's sphere of influence.

An uneasy peace, frequently violated, was the result. A Christian-Israeli alliance formed because the two groups shared an interest in containing, indeed in weakening, PLO influence. The Syrians, in their turn, were more sympathetic to the Muslim majority fighting the Christians. The character of Lebanon's civil war thus changed as each side was supported by an external power. As a result, Israel and Syria almost came to blows in 1981.

The second, and even more dramatic, reminder for the Reagan administration that the Arab-Israeli conflict could not be subordinated to an anti-Soviet strategic consensus was the Israeli attack in June 1981 on Iraq's nuclear reactor just before it became operational. Although Iraq had signed the nuclear nonproliferation treaty, Israel defended the attack by pointing to Iraq's possession of a reactor, Iraq's leadership of the Arab states opposed to the Camp David peace process, and Iraq's very leader, Saddam Hussein, who Israeli prime minister Menachem Begin described as a "tyrant" and "crazy." Indeed, Hussein did use poison gas against Iranian troops during his eight-year war with Iran, as well as against his country's own Kurdish minority. In any event, Israel's notion of self-defense as encompassing the right to attack a potentially hostile neighbor that had the ability to develop its own nuclear weapons (presumably to attack Israel) was clearly a broad one. Nevertheless, while Washington during its confrontation with Iraq in 1990 was to take a different view, in 1981 it viewed Israel's airstrike as politically damaging because it revived Arab perceptions of Israel as the prime foe in the region, defusing U.S. efforts to portray the Soviets as the chief threat.

The third jolt to the Reagan strategy of subordinating the Arab-Israeli conflict to an anti-Soviet strategy was the reelection of Begin as prime minister of Israel. Begin, having made peace with the only Arab state that had potential power to be a threat to Israel, saw no reason to be accommodating on other issues. Washington had hoped that the Labor party would win the election and take a more flexible approach when the peace process was resumed. Instead, the most right-wing government in Israel's existence came to power. Begin appointed a foreign minister who had opposed the peace with Egypt and a defense minister who as agriculture minister had implemented an aggressive policy of settling the West Bank. Symbolic of Begin's conviction that the West Bank was part of Israel, he put his *interior* minister in charge of the Palestinian autonomy talks. Begin had always pursued Israeli interests, as he defined them, regardless of American preferences, offering occasional demonstrations of the natural order of things turned upside down—of a small country manipulating its far stronger protector. He was able to do so because most U.S. presidents were genuinely concerned about Israeli security and also feared domestic repercussions if they pressured Israel.

The fourth blow was the biggest of all to the administration: the assassination of President Anwar Sadat of Egypt in October 1981. Both Israel and Egypt immediately announced that they remained committed to carrying out the remaining provision of their peace treaty. Still, uncertainty over the future increased. Israel remained bent on annexing the West Bank. Sadat's whole policy had been based from the beginning on the expectation that the United States would pressure Israel; in that respect, the United States had clearly failed him. No American administration had been willing to take that domestically risky political course. None had been willing even to speak out publicly about the U.S. interpretation of Camp David and how the peace process was supposed to evolve, or to say that Begin's policy was a reason for Egypt's isolation in the Arab world, for the criticism of—and opposition to—Sadat at home, and for the increasing perception in the region that the United States was either a one-sided or ineffective mediator.

The Palestinian issue was not the only question on which Washington and Israel differed, as Begin quickly demonstrated when, unexpectedly and without consulting the United States, he formally annexed Syria's Golan Heights, an area important to Israeli security. When the United States, feeling that cooperation between the two countries was a two-way street, voiced its displeasure, Begin lashed out, accusing the administration of practicing anti-Semitism, breaking its word, and treating Israel like a "banana republic." The Israeli actions raised a key question: could Israel and the United States work together for peace? The American assumption had always been that a Middle East peace could be built on an exchange of the Arab territories that Israel had conquered in the 1967 Arab-Israeli war for Arab acceptance of Israel; the Israeli withdrawal from the Sinai suggested that Israel shared that belief. But increasingly since the peace treaty with Egypt, it had become clearer that Begin's Israel preferred the expansion of territory to peace with its neighbors based fundamentally on the pre-1967 borders. Negotiations were replaced by annexation—of East Jerusalem, the

Golan Heights, and, for all practical purposes, the West Bank and Gaza. Could the United States in these circumstances still assume that Israel would withdraw from these areas in return for Arab acceptance of Israel, and more fundamentally, that American and Israeli interests coincided?

The Israeli Invasion of Lebanon

The 1982 Israeli invasion of Lebanon to crush the PLO and solve the political problem of the Palestinians by purely military means dramatically underlined the question of U.S.-Israeli common interests. The Israeli pretext for the invasion was the danger to its citizens in its northern settlements from PLO artillery and rocket fire. Once the invasion began, it became clear that the Israeli goal was Beirut because West Beirut, the Moslem half of the city, was where the PLO had its headquarters. If the Israeli forces could militarily defeat the PLO and politically humiliate it, they would be doing more than ensuring the safety of Israeli citizens; crushing the PLO would also, it was hoped, destroy Palestinian nationalism on the West Bank and either force the Palestinians to move to Jordan or submit to permanent Israeli domination. A third aim was to place Lebanon more firmly in control of the Christians, who were friendly to Israel, and thus enhance Israeli security on its northern border.

But the siege of Beirut backfired, demonstrating once more that a military victory cannot always be transformed into a desirable political settlement. Every night for several weeks, television showed Israeli warplanes, tanks, and artillery pounding West Beirut, bringing destruction and human misery, and world criticism of Israel grew. Even though it was the PLO that decided to fight in the city among the civilian population, the heavy Israeli fire greatly damaged Israel's reputation in the West. In its previous three wars, Israel had attacked only after it had been struck or was certain an attack would occur. No such danger to Israeli security had existed before the invasion of Lebanon. The invasion was widely viewed as an unprovoked offensive action. The massive use of force, however, achieved the central Israeli aim: the expulsion of the PLO from Beirut. Abandoned by their fellow Arabs as well as their Soviet friends, the PLO finally gave in and accepted an American-negotiated truce that kept Israeli forces out of West Beirut and provided for a multinational peace-keeping force composed of Italian, British, French, and American troops to supervise their exit to the twenty-odd Arab countries.

Yet, ironically, in victory the Israelis defeated themselves. Seeking to crush the PLO and thereby Palestinian nationalism, they made the Palestinians the central political issue. The artillery fire and pounding from the air of West Beirut deeply affected American public opinion, including President Reagan. The president now accepted that the Palestinian problem could not be subordinated to regional anti-Soviet policy; that the Arab-Israeli problem was a separate issue; and that the key to resolving that conflict, as well as establishing closer and more cordial relationships with the Arab countries, including the oil producers, was resolving the future of the Palestinians. The Israeli government now found itself alienated from the United States and faced by an American initiative it had neither expected nor welcomed. Clearly separating himself from Begin's policy, Reagan proposed a new peace plan whose basic features were genuine autonomy for the Palestinians living on the West Bank and Gaza and the association of the West Bank with Jordan. In short, there would be no Palestinian state, which Israel constantly declared was unacceptable because it would pose a security risk. But there would also be no Israeli annexation of the West Bank; instead, Israel was expected to withdraw from most of it. The initial Arab and PLO reaction was to show interest, but Begin's immediate reaction was a swift and total rejection.

The Sabra-Shatila Massacres

Israel appeared to be isolating itself in the world, even among Jews. The always loyal Jewish community in the United States largely supported the president in his peace efforts. The World Zionist Congress, meeting in Israel at the time, denounced Begin's effort to annex the West Bank. And then came the real shock, a human tragedy that placed the Israeli invasion, Begin, and his defense minister, Ariel Sharon—the man largely responsible for Israel's policy on the West Bank and the invasion of Lebanon—in the global limelight. In Lebanon Bashir Gemayel, the newly elected pro-Israel leader of the Christian, or Phalangist, militia was assassinated on the eve of becoming president. Begin and Sharon immediately sent Israeli forces into West Beirut in violation of the truce (the multinational peace-keeping forces had been pulled out), ostensibly to protect the Muslim population from Christian revenge. But the real aims were to gain control over West Beirut and to make the United States (which had arranged the truce that was supposed to keep the Israelis out of West Beirut) look helpless. This, in turn, would undermine the support the president needed from the moderate Arab states for his peace plan. Once in West Beirut, the Israelis called on the Christian militia, the Phalangists, to go into the Palestinian refugee camps to rout out any remaining PLO terrorists. The stated purpose was to save the lives of Israeli soldiers. But the Christian forces proceeded to slaughter several hundred Palestinians, mainly women, children, and old men, in what became known at the Sabra-Shatila massacres.

The Israelis, along with the rest of the world, were shocked. To what extent were Israel's leaders and army implicated? At best, knowing of the hatred and past killings between Christians and Moslems, the Israeli authorities should have known better than to send the Phalangists into the Palestinian camps in the wake of their leader's death, presumably at the hands of Muslims. Begin denied any Israeli responsibility and harshly denounced the critics. When he refused to establish an impartial judicial commission of inquiry, the president of Israel, normally a symbolic figure, intervened and publicly called for such an inquiry as a moral necessity. Street demonstrations occurred, and Jewish leaders in Europe and America joined to protest Begin's decision. The prime minister was compelled to change his mind. For many Jews in Israel and outside, Begin and Sharon had squandered Israel's most precious asset, its self-respect and the respect of the world. The findings of the judicial commission did, indeed, hold Israel "indirectly responsible" for the massacres.

If Begin and Sharon appeared morally callous and Israeli policy too eager to use force to resolve problems, the events in Lebanon also showed the Arabs' lack of foresight and courage. Although neither the Arab states nor the PLO completely rejected Reagan's peace plan, they soon reaffirmed their commitments to an Israeli withdrawal to the 1967 borders, to a Palestinian state, and to the PLO as the representative of the Palestinian people. Nothing had changed. Little attention was paid to King Hussein's reported warning that if the Reagan initiative were allowed to die, Israel would determine the West Bank issue once and for all with its settlements. There was little time left for the Arabs to negotiate, reverse the Israeli policy of annexation, and gain American backing. The time may have passed for a Palestinian state, and the Reagan plan might be the most that could still be achieved to advance Palestinian goals.

The Arab leaders were unwilling to take the initiative. This included Hussein, who would not proceed without PLO consent. Despite its military defeat, the politically weakened PLO was allowed to exercise a veto to prevent the moderate Arab states from exploring the Reagan plan. There simply was no leader of Sadat's stature who was willing to seize the opportunity and announce a willingness to accept Israel and negotiate with it on the basis of the American formula. The postponement of negotiations and a settlement also risked transforming the character of Israel, a state composed of 3.5 million Jews ruling over 2 million Arabs (750,000 Israeli Arabs, more than 800,000 Palestinians on the West Bank and 500,000 in Gaza), whose high birth rate threatened Israel's Jewish character, its democratic character if it denied them the vote, and its humane character if it kept them as second-class citizens, treated them as noncitizens without basic rights as on the West Bank, or uprooted most of them and drove them out.

The failure of Arab and PLO leaders to take risks meant that the situation on the West Bank was bound to deteriorate: Jewish settlers would increase in numbers and determination to make it part of Israel; and the 60 percent of the West Bank population that was under the age of twenty—a youth that had never known anything but Israeli occupation—would become politically radicalized and intensely nationalistic. The young people were drawn to Arafat as a symbol of their desire for a Palestinian state, even as efforts were made to relegate him to the political sidelines and his leadership of the PLO was contested by the Syrians.

Who Gained? Who Lost?

Nor did the United States escape unscathed from Lebanon. It too blundered there as a result of Lebanese politics and regional rivalries. The Israeli defeat of the PLO in 1982 had shifted power back to the Christians and had led to the formation of an Israeli-supported, Christian-dominated government. As the price for withdrawing their troops, the Israelis demanded a normalization of Lebanese-Israeli relations. This, it was widely assumed, would then lead to a simultaneous Syrian troop withdrawal, allowing Lebanon once more to govern itself. Israel demanded more than security arrangements for its northern border with Lebanon—the original pretext for the invasion—because the Israelis had suffered high casualties and the war had for the first time led to domestic protests. The government needed to justify these losses and pacify the opposition. Peace with another Arab state appeared to be a prize worth Israeli sacrifices. Lebanon's fragile Christian-dominated government was reluctant to accede to Israeli terms, however, because most of its Arab population would refuse to go along. But Lebanon finally accepted an American-mediated agreement because that appeared to be the only way to get the Israelis and Syrians out.

Not only were Lebanon's Arabs opposed to the Christian-dominated government and its acceptance of Israeli terms for peace but most important, Syria, which had opposed the Israeli-Egyptian accords, now rejected the terms of this peace and refused to withdraw its 50,000 troops. As Israeli forces, tired of the casualties, pulled back to southern Lebanon, Syrian influence grew. During the months that the Israelis had refused to pull back and had pressured the Lebanese government to accept the normalization agreement, the Soviets had reequipped the Syrian armed forces, badly defeated by the Israelis in 1982, and had sent 7,000 military advisers to Syria. This strengthened Syria's resolve and its hand in settling Lebanon's future. The Syrians now supplied the military hardware the various Arab militias needed to attack the Lebanese government and its small and poorly trained army.

In the midst of this escalating and fiercely fought civil war, the multinational peace-keeping force, which had returned to Beirut after the slaughter in the Palestinian camps, no longer had a peace to keep. The approximately 1,500 U.S. marines, even with the fleet offshore, were in no position to impose domestic peace. Nevertheless, without ever announcing it, Reagan changed the marines' mission. He judged it important to preserve the Lebanese government from its domestic opponents and their Syrian supporters. Their victory over the government, whose jurisdiction at the time did not extend beyond Beirut's city limits (if that far), was likely to result in a basically anti-American, anti-Israeli government controlled by Syria, which had close relations with the Soviet Union, Libya, and Iran. The role of the marines and the fleet was therefore shifted from keeping the peace to enforcing it on behalf of a pro-American and pro-Israeli Christian-led government. This meant that the United States was now supporting one side in a civil war, and the Arab factions saw the marines and the navy offshore as enemies. They began to fire on the Beirut airport, where the marines had dug in to protect themselves. The marine position proved indefensible. Pro-Iranian Shi'ites filled a truck with gas-enhanced explosives equal in tonnage to an atomic bomb and, in a suicide mission, destroyed a barracks where the marines were sleeping. The marines lost 241 men as a result of this terrorist attack, which could not possibly have been organized without Syrian knowledge, if not help. An earlier suicide mission on the U.S. Embassy in Beirut had also caused a large number of deaths.

With an election in 1984 and Lebanon a political liability for him, the president pulled the marines out. For the United States, the withdrawal of the marines and the collapse of the Christian-dominated government and the Lebanese-Israeli treaty was a bitter defeat. The Reagan administration had tried to demonstrate to Arab moderates that, unlike its predecessor, it would be a staunch friend they could rely on in a crisis. The result in Lebanon suggested the contrary. The United States apparently was an unreliable and weak friend with little stomach for a fight with Syria, a small and tough adversary, which after the Israeli and American withdrawal sought to establish control over a Lebanon rapidly disintegrating in civil war. The friends of America—as in Vietnam and Iran—had lost again. This was in fact the lesson that America's enemies wanted the states in the region to learn (and which, to counteract, led the United States in 1987 to send its navy into the Persian Gulf to show its support for the Arab Gulf states in the Iran-Iraq war). In the meantime, the Reagan administration, dispirited after its bumbling in Lebanon and the loss of the marines and weakened by the Iran-*contra* scandal, had neither the imagination nor the will to risk taking the initiative in the peace process before the situation grew even more unstable and violent. So it continued to stand passively by.

The Intifada

In December 1987 Palestinian youngsters, throwing rocks at Israeli troops, began what became known as the "intifada," a protracted uprising that was to change Palestinian society. After years of Israeli occupation, Arafat's unwillingness to recognize Israel and resort to diplomacy—although the Israeli government insisted it would never negotiate with his terrorist organization—Hussein's reluctance to act unilaterally, and the Arab states' preoccupation with the Iran-Iraq war and disregard of the Palestinian problem, the Palestinians took matters into their own hands. The resulting uprising, widely supported by the West Bank and Gaza Strip Palestinians, gave the Palestinians a new sense of pride and identity. Despite the Israeli soldiers' policy of breaking the hands and arms of the stonethrowers they

Israel and the Occupied Territories

caught, despite hundreds of Palestinians shot, thousands wounded, widespread detention, usually without trial, on the mere suspicion of having taken part in the resistance, the blowing up of the homes of any families whose members were suspected participants, deportations of some believed to be leaders of the intifada, long closings of Palestinian schools and universities, and curfews imposed on Palestinian villages and towns, the sacrifices unified the Palestinians. It also gave the Israelis an impossible task of pacification. The use of force to resolve what was essentially a political problem cost Israel not only a few lives and a lot of money, but also, above all, its moral standing in the world.

In July 1988 King Hussein, after years of frustrating attempts to organize a common front with PLO leader Yasir Arafat for a joint diplomatic approach to Israel, abandoned any claim to the West Bank, which Jordan had ruled from 1948 to 1967. Hussein declared that he respected the desire of the PLO to be recognized as the sole legitimate representative of the Palestinian people to establish a Palestinian state. This unexpected move stunned everyone. The United States had counted on Hussein as a principal negotiator. Arafat, besieged by radical Palestinians supported by Syria, which opposed any diplomatic solution that recognized Israel, was now saddled with responsibility for the West Bank. Before his withdrawal, Hussein had financially supported the Palestinians living there. As head of a many-splintered umbrella organization, many of which opposed negotiations with Israel, Arafat was now confronted with Hussein's challenge to put up or shut up. If he failed to economically assist the Palestinians in the West Bank, speak on their behalf, and make some progress toward a peaceful solution, the Palestinians might well abandon him and ask Hussein to negotiate some kind of confederation with Jordan. As the widely recognized symbol of Palestinian nationalism, Arafat, in short, now had to assert his leadership lest West Bank Palestinian leaders of the intifada displace him, taking over the Palestinian movement that they, not Arafat, had mobilized.

Hussein's move was also a blow to the Israeli Labor party. The party was engaged in an election campaign in which its position was to seek a negotiated solution exclusively with Hussein, considered a reasonable and moderate leader, rather than with Arafat. The Likud party, the party of Begin and now Yitzhak Shamir—the party of the status quo—reaffirmed that it would never negotiate with the PLO or surrender an inch of Israeli territory, which included what it defined as the liberated 1967 territories. The election results, in which neither won a majority while the conservative orthodox parties gained votes, led to another coalition government. In short, after years of a Likud-Labor Coalition government, the domestic stalemate continued as Israeli society proved unable to decide whether to negotiate or not, to give up the West Bank and Gaza or not in a territory-for-peace exchange. In the meantime, Israel was faced internally with a growing Palestinian boycott of Israeli goods and externally with nations afraid to buy Israeli goods, fearing Arab retaliation. Moreover, its inefficient state-run industries and businesses, combined with boycott pressures, created an economic stagnation and rapidly rising inflation, both of which were intensified by the cost of dealing with the intifada.

Under great pressure, Arafat in December 1988 recognized Israel, accepting U.N. resolutions 242 and 338, which called for a return of Israel to secure borders (the 1967 borders with minor changes to provide for Israeli security); he also denounced terrorism. But Arafat's recognition was within the context of U.N. resolution 181, which affirmed Israel's 1947 frontiers, one-third the size of contemporary Israel, and called for the return of the Palestinian refugees into what would be left of Israel, thus destroying its Jewishness. His renunciation of terrorism, in addition, was also qualified, for he approved of Palestinian resistance within Israel. Nevertheless, the Israeli government expressed its consternation that Arafat had seemingly met the conditions Henry Kissinger had established in 1975 as a prerequisite for American diplomatic contacts with the PLO. This consternation was aimed at Washington, where, in its closing days in office, the Reagan administration, taking the domestic heat off its Republican successor, opened talks with PLO spokesmen. Whether the PLO or Israel were ready for negotiations or were merely resorting to tactical maneuvers was unclear.

Arafat's recognition of Israel was indirect and ambiguous, and the promise to end terrorism qualified. Did the PLO, which remains deeply divided on whether to accept Israel and pursue diplomatic options, really want a genuine settlement? Such a course might produce something short of an independent Palestinian state, which Israel and the United States oppose. And even if it gained a Palestinian state, would that satisfy the PLO, or would the new state be merely the base from which further territorial demands would follow? Was Arafat's move just a clever tactic to gain American support, isolate Israel, and increase the pressure—especially U.S. pressure—on Israel? Given its record (the PLO has never lost an opportunity to miss a peaceful solution), was it finally ready for peace with Israel or merely for dismantling Israel piece by piece? PLO spokesmen's statements to Arab audiences suggested the latter; statements for Western audiences were more positive.

On the other side, was Israel ready to negotiate and make concessions for peace? The West Bank settlers, for the most part religious zealots who would like to drive the Palestinians out and into Jordan, were unlikely to give up their settlements peacefully. Likud was committed to a vision of a Greater Israel. It was unlikely that even Labor would surrender most of the West Bank. The Israeli government reacted sharply to Bush administration Secretary of State James Baker's speech calling on Israel to give up once and for all "its unrealistic vision of a Greater Israel" and reach out to the Palestinians "as neighbors who deserve political rights." While Baker also counseled the Palestinians to "reach out to Israelis and convince them of your peaceful intentions" and telling them that "no one is going to deliver Israel to you," Prime Minister Shamir dismissed the administration's advice for direct talks between Israeli officials and "Palestinians living in the territories"—not the PLO—as "useless." Nevertheless, under great pressure from the Bush administration, Shamir devised a plan to hold elections in the West Bank and

Gaza and let the Palestinians run their own affairs and elect leaders who would eventually negotiate with Israel. Was it sincere? Or was it a tactical move to avoid alienating the United States at a time when the PLO finally seemed ready to negotiate? After all, Shamir's formula for Palestinian autonomy was basically a resurrected version of the Camp David formula, which Israel had always defined so as to continue its occupation and control. Even then, Shamir was forced by his party to place such restrictive conditions on such an election that, for all practical purposes, the party denounced elections as a way of solving the Palestinian problem. Territory was not—as in all U.S. peace plans since Kissinger—to be exchanged for peace.

In fact, Shamir's party has for years taken the lead in discouraging the emergence of a moderate Palestinian leadership by jailing or deporting Palestinian spokesmen. Likud has not been willing to acknowledge the existence of a legitimate Palestinian Arab nationalism. Once Begin had made peace with Egypt, he set out to eliminate Palestinian nationalism and the PLO; this quest ended in the disaster of the Lebanon invasion and Begin's resignation from office. The logic of denying Palestinian nationalism has been the logic of endless conflict, escalating violence, and Israel's self-destruction of its once high reputation. Thus, appearances of moderation and a willingness to negotiate coexist with civil insurrection, military repression, and growing religious fanaticism as 3.5 million Jews try to rule 2 million Arabs who, representing more than thirty-five percent of the population already, feel no links to Israel by flag, language, historical experience, or nationalist feelings and common loyalty. Israel, facing a security problem that is in this respect more internal than external, therefore faced a situation in which it might have to decide whether giving up the West Bank is worse than retaining it. It cannot subdue the intifada, even with an army larger than the one that conquered the West Bank in five days in 1967. Can it really, then, protect Israeli Jews, who now seem engaged in a permanent civil war? In this domestic war, Israeli Arabs are increasingly identifying with the Palestinian Arabs, and more and more Israeli Jews are seeing the West Bank and Gaza as part of a single state controlled by the Jewish population.

Two things, however, were clear: one, if rejectionism continues to rule, only greater frustration and violence can result; and, two, despite American insistence on direct negotiations, the few successes in resolving Israeli-Arab differences occurred when the United States became actively involved as a mediator. American passivity in the years since the disastrous Lebanon invasion may be understandable, but it also meant that in reality the United States acquiesced in a status quo that had become unbearably volatile. This became even more apparent as Israel's government fell in 1990 because it refused to implement its own peace plan. Prime Minister Shamir formed a new government that was even more conservative than any of its predecessors. Composed of Likud hard-liners and several tiny extreme right-wing parties, the Shamir government was collectively referred to in the Israeli press as "right-wing crazies." Some of its members favored the use of massive force to squash the intifada; others favored mass deportations of Palestinians from the West Bank. The government's main declared goal was to deal with the massive immigration of Soviet Jews—expected to be 650,000 to 1 million by mid-1991—and the expansion of Jewish settlements in the West Bank and Gaza Strip. This influx of Soviet Jews (who were seeking to escape resurgent anti-Semitism in the USSR) will likely forestall the day when Israel's Jewish majority will be overtaken by the higher birth rate among the Arabs. Shamir's party therefore welcomed their arrival, which probably made peace talks even more of a charade than before. In addition, Israel thwarted an attack attempted by a Libyan-supported, hard-line faction of the PLO on bathers on Tel Aviv's beaches. Arafat's refusal to condemn the attack and discipline its leader, a member of the PLO's executive committee, jeopardized U.S.-PLO talks, which were based on Arafat's commitment *not* to engage in terrorism; Arafat's disinclination to do more than disassociate himself from the attack also placed in question once more his commitment to Israel's right to exist, which the PLO Charter specifically rejected.

The constraints on the American sponsorship of the peace process were thus being narrowed as the hard-liners in Israel, the PLO, and Arab states appeared to be in the ascendancy. Since the Israeli-Egyptian peace, Israel's problem had been mainly the Palestinians. That issue was now being fused once more with the hostility of the Arab states, at least the more extreme ones such as Iraq. With the cold war fading and other regional quarrels being settled in 1989 and 1990, the Middle East stood out as the stark exception. "I have to tell you," said Secretary of State Baker, "that everybody over there should know that the [White House] telephone number is 1-202-456-1414. When you are serious about peace, call us." This U.S. assessment of the peace process and the future of U.S.-Israeli relations was deeply pessimistic. But Iraq's invasion of Kuwait in August 1990 and its attempt to establish its dominance over the Persian Gulf forestalled a serious rupture between the United States and Israel, at least for a time.

Terrorism and the Iran-*Contra* Affair

While the Reagan administration after Lebanon practiced diplomatic abstinence in the Middle East, it became more and more concerned with terrorism. The kidnappings continued in Lebanon. The Americans and French were particularly targeted by pro-Iranian Shi'ite groups like the Islamic Jihad and the Party of God, which had bombed the U.S. Embassy and the marine barracks. These groups were also involved in the seizure of a TWA airliner, during which they murdered an American sailor in civilian clothing. Other Palestinian groups were also active, including the PLO and groups opposed to Arafat and to any moderate Arab leaders who might favor peace negotiations with Israel. Especially ruthless was a faction led by archterrorist Abu Nidal. Members of this group seized an Italian cruise ship, the *Achille Lauro,* in the Mediterranean, killing an elderly American in a wheelchair. In other terrorist incidents, a bomb exploded on a TWA airliner during landing, and several people were killed; an Egyptian airliner was hijacked; a simultaneous attack was carried out on the Rome and Vienna airports, injuring and killing many, including an eleven-year-old American girl. Several other plans, like the bombing of the U.S. Embassy in Rome, were aborted.

The common link in all these attacks was that the terrorists were state-sponsored: Iran and Syria backed the groups in Lebanon, and Libya and Syria the extremist Palestinian groups. Such state-supported terrorism (providing camps and training, furnishing weapons and money) was a "poor-man's war"; the Soviet Union's Eastern European allies also supported these efforts actively. Terrorism was a way of striking at an enemy whose military strength was too great to face in a state-to-state confrontation. The enemy was the United States, and all Americans were targets—soldiers, officials, and tourists. There were no "innocent" Americans; even those who worked and taught for years in Arab countries were not exempt.

The motives for terrorism varied. To the ayatollah, America was the representative of a secular (and, therefore, atheistic), dynamic, successful Western civilization that was undermining Iranian traditions and customs, including the influence of the clergy. Opposed to modernization, seeking to revive the glories of Islam, and to expand its influence, Khomeini wanted to completely eliminate American influence from Southwest Asia and the Middle East. For Syria, the goal was Greater Syria that included Lebanon, Syria's preeminence in the Arab world, and the proof that "all roads lead to Damascus" in any Middle East negotiations. Syria was not much concerned with the fate of the Palestinians, except to use them for its own purposes. And Libya's Muammar Qaddafi believed himself to be a revolutionary leader and global figure. But how could he play a prominent role on the world stage as leader of a country with fewer than 4 million people? He sought to do so by making himself a champion of the Arab world and by seeking the elimination of the state of Israel as well as by supporting other terrorist groups whose stated goals were radical. Obviously, Palestinian grievances were a genuine cause for some, but, even if the Palestinian problem were solved, the settlement would be unacceptable to many. Terrorism would continue against those who had accepted the settlement, as well as against Israel. Whatever the motives, the terrorists considered themselves at war with the United States, if not the West.

Personal ambition, dedication to a higher cause, and hatred of the United States by certain leaders of specific countries are, then, key ingredients. But because Americans think of their fellow citizens who are kidnapped or killed as innocent bystanders, the other side of the coin—the role the United States plays in the world—needs to be examined. As a global power whose decisions and policies affect other governments, often unfavorably, the United States is deeply involved in the affairs of many nations. Given its enormous power and that its isolationism is not a genuine alternative, the United States has no other choice but to play this role. As Israel's close supporter, the United States is not seen as an innocent bystander when Israel invades Lebanon and destroys Beirut, or when the United States intervenes militarily in Lebanon's civil war. There are states and factions within states that strongly oppose U.S. policies and blame the United States—and, therefore, all Americans—for what happens to them. There are no "innocent" Americans in their eyes. As the weaker parties, they fight by any means they can, not by the "rules" of warfare. The terrorists do not see themselves as madmen, but as fighting back against an omnipresent and interventionist United States. This does not mean that the United States, or any other nation beset by terrorists, should not react, as it would with any other adversary state.

Reagan, who had been inaugurated as the Iranian hostage crisis was ending, had long promised retaliation against terrorism waged on Americans. But as one attack after another occurred on American installations in Lebanon, no retaliation occurred. The United States managed to intercept the *Achille Lauro* hijackers in a flight over the Mediterranean. But the United States did not react militarily until the attacks on the airports in Vienna and Rome and a bomb blast in a West Berlin discotheque full of U.S. servicemen. According to U.S. intelligence, the Libyans were deeply involved in these terrorist incidents. It turned out later that the Syrians may have been responsible for the attacks, but the United States struck Libya, not Syria, with its thousands of Soviet military advisers and ground-to-air missiles. Qaddafi, a troublemaker for all his neighbors, was generally disliked by other Arab governments, and they probably would have quietly cheered his demise. After the United States sent aircraft carriers into international waters claimed by Libya, to which the Libyans responded by firing a few missiles, the United States launched a quick strike at Libya, which was followed by a larger attack, partly from carrier aircraft and partly from bombers based in England. The main target for some of these bombers was reportedly Qaddafi himself.

Apart from the British, no European government supported the attack. Even British public opinion was strongly against it, and there were demonstrations in many European cities against the United States. The main U.S. attack had occurred only after Washington had repeatedly sought to get its allies to act with it to impose economic sanctions on Libya, a country highly dependent on foreigners, mainly Europeans and Americans, for the operation of its oil fields and other industries. But the Europeans, fearful of negative economic consequences, had refused to go along. After the United States had acted unilaterally, and probably only to prevent another U.S. military act, the Europeans reduced the number of personnel in Libyan "people's bureaus" (embassies) and restricted their freedom to travel. Some months later, after an attempt to place a bomb aboard an Israeli airliner in

London, the British government, convinced of Syrian involvement, broke relations with Syria. At that point the European governments agreed to an arms embargo and restrictions on Syrian diplomats. Ironically, at the very moment that a European consensus on terrorism was emerging, the Reagan administration was undermining its own position on terrorism and eroding its credibility in the conduct of foreign policy.

Iran Scores Again

Iran came to haunt the Reagan presidency, as it had Carter's. Carter had come to grief over fifty-two U.S. hostages held for more than a year in the embassy at Tehran; Reagan now came to grief over six U.S. hostages seized by Iranian-supported terrorists in Beirut. Claiming that the United States had wanted to deal with Iran because it was strategically important and that it would be beneficial to make contacts with "moderate" elements in the leadership before the question of Khomeini's successor was settled, the president—after a leak in a Middle East newspaper—admitted that he had sent arms shipments to Iran. He also stated that he wanted to try to end the six-year Iran-Iraq war, which, if won by Iran, the larger state, threatened to spread Islamic fundamentalism to the oil sheikdoms in the Persian Gulf and the Middle East.

It was a bizarre explanation that raised more questions than it answered. However persuasive the geopolitical rationale for approaching Iran might be, did it have to be accompanied by arms? How could giving arms to Tehran possibly help end the war? Why were negotiations not quietly conducted in some neutral country? Among the Khomeini loyalists, were there in fact moderates? Would not their contact with Robert McFarlane, Reagan's national security adviser, expose these moderates, if they existed, and end their influence? Above all, how could the president square the shipment of arms with the U.S. arms embargo against Iran, his own consistently strong stand against terrorism, his efforts to mobilize allied support, Iran's earlier humiliation of the United States, and Iran's involvement in the attacks on the U.S. Embassy and annex in Beirut and the marine barracks?

It soon became clear that geopolitics was not the real reason for approaching Iran, but merely a convenient justification to cover the administration's embarrassment once it had been caught doing what it publicly and repeatedly had condemned other countries for doing. The U.S.-Iran opening was a straight arms-for-hostages deal. Ransom money had even been raised from a private source. Apparently, the deal was that all six hostages were to be released with the arrival of the first arms shipment. When none were freed, instead of calling the trade off, the administration made three further shipments. Each time, one hostage was released, making it obvious that, for all the president's denials, his motive had been to gain the release of the hostages. Moreover, by trading on a one-to-one basis, the administration was giving the terrorists an incentive to replace the freed captives, which is exactly what they did by kidnapping three others. All of this went on despite the opposition of the secretaries of state and defense, who were cut out of the decision-making process as a result. John Poindexter, the president's national security adviser, and his staff, usually a coordinating and advisory body, now played the key operational role, for which it was not well equipped.

Worse, however, was that little consideration was given to how the arms-for-hostages deal would look if it became public or to the damage it would inflict on the administration and on U.S. relations with its allies and moderate Arab governments. First, the United States would be exposed as hypocritical—asking its allies to honor the U.S. arms embargo against Iran while it shipped arms to a country President Reagan himself had condemned as an "outlaw state" run by "misfits, Looney Tunes, and squalid criminals." Second, having slowly mobilized allied support for some actions and sanctions against state-sponsored terrorism, the United States undermined its credibility, and probably weakened the new allied resolve. Third, it also shocked and dismayed its Arab friends, all deadly fearful of an Iranian victory over Iraq. An Iranian victory would endanger the oil sheikdoms, including Saudi Arabia, where in 1987, after provoking a bloody riot in Mecca, Iran had called for the overthrow of the Saudi regime. If Iran won the war, it would control the Persian Gulf with two-thirds of the world's known oil reserves, enhancing its ability to eliminate U.S. influence from the Middle East.

It was for these reasons that in 1987 the United States tried to recoup its influence in the region by making a potentially dangerous move vis-à-vis the conflict. Iraq had failed to achieve a quick victory after its 1979 attack on Iran, and the war had become a grim war of attrition. Given Iran's three-to-one superiority in men, it would ultimately wear down Iraq, which had superiority in arms. Iraq in 1984 therefore attempted to bring the war to an end by attacking oil tankers doing business with Iran, as well as Iranian loading facilities, in an effort to shut off its oil exports and strangle Iran financially. In late 1986 Iran retaliated by attacking Kuwaiti tankers. Kuwait, one of Iraq's informal allies along with Saudi Arabia and other oil sheikdoms, contributed to Iraq's war effort. Moreover, Kuwait allowed its harbor to be used for transshipment of Soviet arms for Iraq. In the wake of Reagan's dealings with Iran, Kuwait appealed to the Soviet Union for protection of its tankers. Moscow agreed, whereupon the United States, which had also been asked but had not responded, said it would reflag eleven Kuwaiti tankers as U.S. ships and protect them. That an Arab state would ask Moscow to play a role in the Gulf, *the* geopolitical prize of the late twentieth century, may have been the most damaging result of the Reagan approach to Iran.

In fact, the United States, by trying to rebuild its influence with the oil kingdoms and moderate Arabs and to limit Soviet encroachment in the area, had involved itself in the war and had tilted toward Iraq. The danger to U.S. ships in the Gulf was real; an Iraqi pilot mistakenly launched two missiles at the U.S. frigate *Stark*, killing thirty-seven men. Congress reacted strongly, recommending that the reflagging be postponed, if not canceled. What would the United States do if the Iranians attacked the tankers or U.S. naval escorts? And if the Iranians used their land-based short-range missiles to cut off the oil flow from the Gulf, would the United States retaliate by attacking the air bases or missile launchers? Would it strike preemptively rather than retaliate? The possibilities of escalation were endless. Luckily, the war did not escalate. The Iranians, by now subject to frequent Iraqi missile attacks on their cities and poison gas attacks on their frontline troops, were not reckless enough to take on the United States as well. There were, to be sure, some minor clashes, followed by measured American retaliation; the U.S. Navy even shot down an Iranian airliner, having mistaken it for a jet fighter, with a large loss of life. But Iran was essentially politically isolated and tired of its eight-year war and its huge loss of life, estimated at about 1 million. Iran therefore finally assented to a cease-fire. The United States' intervention, its steadfastness in the face of Iranian threats, and its restraint in action helped to recoup much of the prestige the Reagan administration had lost among the oil kingdoms because of its policy in Lebanon and the Iran-*contra* affair. Iran's efforts to neutralize Kuwait and to undermine the other Persian Gulf states' support of Iraq had failed. The Reagan policy, ill-planned and open-ended, succeeded at a low cost in life. It helped to stiffen the Gulf states' resolve to resist Iran, drew in the navies of the NATO allies in a cooperative effort, contained Iranian expansionism, and helped to bring the Iran-Iraq war to an end. Little did the United States know that in helping Iraq in its war against Iran it was preparing Iraq for a second attempt to establish its dominance over the Persian Gulf.

The *Contra* Connection

In the United States, however, the administration's competence, sense of judgment, and policy-making procedures remained the central issues in the arms-for-hostages deal when it was revealed that profits from the arms sales to Iran had been placed in a secret Swiss bank account. These profits were used to fund the Nicaraguan *contras* during the period from late 1984 to 1986, when the Congress had expressly forbidden the use of U.S. funds for this purpose. In fact, in an end run around Congress, the administration had shifted the conduct of the *contra* war from the Central Intelligence Agency (CIA) to the National Security Council (NSC) staff. But on the hostages and *contras*, the national security advisers, first McFarlane, a former marine colonel, and then vice admiral Poindexter, both staff officers with little foreign policy experience or competence, were not in charge. Both operations were reputedly run by the CIA director William Casey and his point man in the NSC, Oliver North, a marine lieutenant colonel.

Referred to in the later congressional investigation as the only "five-star" lieutenant colonel in the U.S. military, North supervised the arms-for-hostages deal. He also directed the raising of private funds for the *contras* through individuals, mainly people formerly involved with military intelligence, from tax-exempt organizations, and from wealthy U.S. citizens and foreign governments. Moreover, North commanded a vast network of arms dealers, ships, and airplanes to supply the *contras,* for whom he also provided tactical intelligence and advice on how to conduct the war. Although CIA agents, an ambassador, and other public officials were also enlisted to help in various tasks (from fund raising to pressuring Central American governments to allow this network of what were in fact U.S. agents to operate in their countries), the total effort amounted to an attempt to "privatize" foreign policy.

The NSC thus became a "shadow government," which, in turn, organized a "private CIA" and a "private Treasury" to direct and fund the *contra* war effort. The U.S. Constitution, however, requires that foreign policy be made by the president and Congress in a publicly visible manner; nowhere does it sanction private groups to conduct the nation's policy. The State Department would not be needed anymore or, for that matter, Congress, which in the American political system has the right to decide whether to support policy by appropriating the necessary funds to carry it out.

Although Reagan remained personally popular and the nation was not ready for another Watergate—the scandal that forced Richard Nixon from office—the violation of the presidential oath to "take care that the laws be faithfully executed" was raised again. The abuses of power this time were the selling of arms in violation of a law banning such sales to states that sponsor terrorism; the failure to notify Congress's intelligence committees of this covert operation; the diversion of funds from the sale to buy arms for the *contras;* and the private solicitation of money for the *contras* in the United States and abroad. Even the president had solicited funds from Saudi Arabia, and he had also met with individual Americans who had contributed generously. When discovered, the NSC attempted a cover-up to minimize the president's role in these events. Relevant documents were shredded. Throughout the operation, the administration kept any knowledge of what it was doing from Congress. Furthermore, as the story broke, the president first denied knowledge of many of the details of these events, making it appear as if McFarlane, Poindexter, and North, who had spent most of their adult lives acting as links in chains of command, would suddenly and blatantly flout the law and take the foreign policy of the United States into their own hands.

Public opinion polls showed that most Americans thought Reagan was lying, and the congressional hearings made it plain that he was actively involved and informed, especially on the *contras.* He suddenly reversed gears and claimed that he knew everything except for the diversion of funds and that the congressional restrictions did not apply to him or his staff. When Congress had first forbidden military assistance, the administration had claimed repeatedly that it was obeying the law. Obviously, the secrecy with which the Iran and *contra* operations were carried out suggested that the administration knew very well that it was breaking the law. All the participants, once they were caught, claimed only to be acting for patriotic motives, but in several cases, the patriotism seemed well greased by private gain.

Poindexter testified that he had never informed Reagan of the diversion of funds, but he added that he had made that decision so that the president would—as often occurs in secret operations—be able to deny knowledge of what would be an explosive political event and embarrassment if revealed. North stated that he had offered himself as the fall guy if news of the operations ever leaked to the press and the public, but he was told by the CIA director that he might not be big enough and that Poindexter might have to play that role. Poindexter's apparent willingness to take the blame made the case that the president was lying all the more convincing. (When facing indictments brought by a special prosecutor appointed by Congress, both men later sought to reverse themselves and to place the blame on Reagan.)

Reagan had damaged himself badly by this affair. He was, after all, the presidential candidate who had accused his predecessor of weakness in dealing with the Iranian hostage situation. He had consistently projected an image of toughness and confidence, and he had claimed that the nation could "stand tall" again. Many Americans shared this new sense of patriotism and regarded the president as the man who made them proud again and who could—and did— stand up to the Soviets. But Reagan had almost done the impossible by making Carter's hostage policy look good; Carter had not sent arms to Khomeini. Even the president's admirers and supporters were puzzled. What saved Reagan's reputation as president was that after Poindexter resigned, his replacement, Frank Carlucci, was both experienced and pragmatic; and when Carlucci succeeded Defense Secretary Weinberger over at Defense, and Lieutenant General Colin Powell became Reagan's sixth national security adviser, the president for the first time had not only three moderate advisers on foreign policy—number three being Secretary of State Shultz—but three men who worked well together. It is not surprising that it was in 1987-1988 that the Reagan administration made its major breakthrough in the cold war; Gorbachev, too, by 1987 had realized how much the Soviet economy was ailing and that he needed relief from the arms competition with America and the cost of maintaining the Soviet Union's imperial outposts. The result: the cold war began to thaw. But North-South relations continued to be troublesome.

The Third World: Democratic Capitalism, the 'Debt Bomb,' and OPEC's Decline

While the administration got into domestic trouble in pursuing the Reagan Doctrine in Nicaragua and by trading arms for hostages with Iran, its general attitude toward the Third World was one of benign neglect. It was involved in the Third World mainly because it saw developing regions in light of Soviet activities and the continuing superpower competition for influence. Revolutionary changes, seen as either Soviet-inspired or exploited, were opposed. The "globalist" viewpoint prevailed once more. But the administration's attitude was unsympathetic toward Third World demands for a new international economic order and complaints about Western capitalist exploitation, or "imperialism." It held a rather similar point of view of the world's poor as it did of the domestic poor; namely, that they were poor because they did not work hard enough. That is, developing countries should not look for Western "charity" to do for them what they would not do for themselves. From the beginning, the administration emphasized that the developing countries were responsible for their own welfare, just as it held individuals responsible.

In 1979, the last Carter year, the United States gave only 0.20 percent of its gross national product to the developing nations, ranking it ahead of only Austria and Italy among all Western nations. The stress was now on "the magic of the marketplace," private enterprise, investments, and international trade. Selling goods in the huge American market was, Reagan emphasized, the best recourse for nations interested in economic progress. In 1980 non-OPEC countries earned $63 billion with their exports to the U.S. market, representing more than half of these nations' manufactured goods. An improvement of the American economy would presumably help them sell even more of their exports as the U.S. demand for their goods would rise. The administration could claim that the priority it had given to the U.S. economy was not only the best domestic course it could pursue but also the best foreign policy for the Third World.

As it did with regard to the Soviet Union, the administration was quick to react to Third World complaints that their problems were not their own fault and assertions that the West owed them aid and technical assistance because of past and present exploitation. The administration considered these charges unfair and rejected them. It also attacked the Third World's preference for socialism as a system allegedly superior to capitalism for encouraging development. The administration not only argued that developing nations most deeply involved in the present international economy were the best off, but also that the policies of these self-styled Socialist states were to blame for the lack of development. There was considerable evidence to support this contention, such as the conspicuous consumption and corruption among the governing elites, the long neglect of agriculture so that many of these nations could no longer feed themselves but had to import food, and the vast spending on military hardware. The administration therefore recommended a course of self-help by means of greater domestic austerity, high savings, and productive investments.

At Cancún, Mexico, in 1981 at a meeting of twenty-two developed and developing countries, including China and India, the latter group of nations tried to impress upon the U.S. president their situation and their needs. They urged that "global negotiations" between the rich and poor countries deal with problems such as the distribution of wealth, food, and energy. The president, however, continued to stress the virtues of democratic capitalism and the creation of new wealth rather than the redistribution of existing wealth. He also pointedly noted that the Soviet Union's absence from the conference was a tacit admission that it had nothing to contribute, despite its claim that the world's economic problems were the result of capitalism and all solutions lay with socialism. "Who's feeding whom?" Reagan asked. (The Soviets' response was that they had not cared to attend a meeting of the "civilized plunderers" and "the plundered.") The United States was taking a critical and adversarial position, reminding the developing countries that the American experience had combined economic development, political freedom, and respect for human dignity.[5] This emphasis on private investment and trade, rather than government assistance, was the focus of the president's Caribbean Basin plan. The plan would help the non-Communist Caribbean and Central American nations combat further domestic radicalization by dealing with their social and economic problems.

The American decision not to accept Third World charges that their poverty was caused by an exploitive Western-dominated international economy, or that the West was morally obligated to assist the developing countries by creating a new international economic order, spilled over into a general critique of their self-professed nonalignment. This nonalignment had already been losing credibility—the 1979 conference had been held in Havana—as the movement embraced Communist states like Cuba and Vietnam, which, like the Soviet Union, boycotted the Olympic Games in 1984, and accused the United States of gross injustices but refused to accuse the Soviet Union. How seriously could these denunciations be taken when most of the Third World's non-Communist leaders did not represent democratic opinion and when many preserved their power with brutality and repression and were guilty of aggression? How seriously should their accusations be taken of white South African treatment of blacks or Israeli treatment of Palestinians, when not a word was said about human rights abuses by Third World states of their own or other citizens? Or when in calling for the withdrawal of Soviet forces from Afghanistan, the reference was only to "foreign forces," when the United States was always denounced by name? In any event, as evidence of America's mood, the United States withdrew from the United Nations Educational, Scientific, and Cultural Organization (UNESCO) in 1983 on the grounds that it had become thoroughly politicized, and constantly attacked Western values, institutions, and interests.

The Reagan administration's vigorous defense of American policies and its unwillingness to acquiesce in what it regarded as unjustified and one-sided

---

5. The Reagan administration's attitudes toward the Third World are well expressed in Peter Berger's "Speaking to the Third World," *Commentary*, October 1981, 29-36.

attacks were symptomatic of a new mood in America not to put up with such hypocrisy. Yet at the same time there could also be no doubt that the Third World was of increasing importance and concern to the United States. The developing countries rivaled Western Europe and Japan as a large export market. The United States also depended on the developing nations for tin, natural rubber, bauxite, and other strategic materials besides oil. And, of course, prosperous developing nations were less likely to suffer domestic instability, which might threaten American security interests. Negatively, the enormous $970 billion debt which, by 1985, thirty developing nations owed Western banks, also demonstrated the growing economic closeness of the First and Third Worlds. Of this amount, almost $400 billion was owed by Latin American states, most prominently by Brazil ($104 billion), Mexico ($98 billion), Argentina ($45 billion), and Venezuela ($38 billion). The fear was that one or more of these countries might refuse to pay its growing debt and bring down major Western, including American, banks.

The needs of the Third World could not be ignored. In the early 1980s, these countries suffered from the lowest nonoil commodity prices in thirty years. Their earnings were down because of the West's recession; so was Western aid. Their alternative was either to tighten their belts or continue their economic development. Western banks, holding huge amounts of "petrodollars" the oil producers had deposited, were only too eager to lend that money and earn handsome profits. They did not worry too much about collateral, especially from oil-producing states like Mexico. The developing countries did not worry either; the high American inflation rate meant that they expected to repay the dollars borrowed with cheaper dollars in the future.

But the dollar rose sharply in value as not only commodity prices but also oil prices fell. This combination of existing debt and falling prices created a huge "debt bomb" whose explosion could hurt borrowers and lenders alike. Even to repay their annual interest on loans, the developing countries had to borrow more money at a time interest rates were going up, and Western banks extended further loans to avoid defaults. To receive new loans, however, the developing countries were required to balance their budgets and cut government spending, including the subsidies for all sorts of social programs. In countries with many poor, the resulting malnutrition and social dislocations led to rioting, strikes, and general social upheaval because many of the hard-earned benefits gained over the last four decades were wiped out: increasingly, the middle classes were also pauperized by the runaway inflation. The unconscionable cost in human suffering led to the idea of debt repudiation; the attractiveness of this solution for the debtors grew as billions more kept on flowing out of their countries to repay the banks than they received in loans from those banks, and their standard of living continued to plummet. Only the fear of losing credit ratings prevented this radical solution. Clearly it was in America's interest to do something, if only to save some banks from collapse and to stabilize the growing number of new and fragile

Latin democracies, such as Venezuela, Argentina, and Brazil, which were among the leading debtors. Moreover, assistance to the debtors ultimately would benefit the United States because it would enable these countries, once good customers, to resume buying U.S. goods and help to reinvigorate the economy. The United States, therefore, shifted toward the position that economic growth was more likely to enable the Latin American countries to pay off their debts. More money was to be made available to them from not only commercial banks but also from the World Bank, and private enterprise and market-oriented policies were to be encouraged.

This policy did not succeed, however, because the banks were understandably reluctant to lend more money. The Bush administration therefore proposed forgiving part of the debt to ease the lot of the Latin American nations (much of the debt would probably be uncollectable anyway). Mexico made a major effort to restructure its economy by eliminating government-run industries and encouraging foreign investment in order to encourage a more efficiently run private sector. It was the first country to negotiate debt reduction with the banks. It received a 20 percent reduction; whether that would be enough to revitalize Mexico's economy remained to be seen, although most observers expressed skepticism.

What remains clear, however, is that the debt crisis was part of the greater issue of the division of wealth between the rich and poor states and was not just a financial problem. It was also clear that the developing countries would have to rethink their ways of development. By the 1980s many of them were increasingly attracted to private enterprise as state-owned enterprises foundered. More basically, they increasingly questioned their earlier attitudes that profits and private markets, identified with capitalism, were selfish and exploitive while the public sector was selfless and oriented to improving everyone's lot. Socialism, as they had usually called their economic system, had proved disappointing, especially in comparison to the economic successes of Asian societies. Not just Japan, but also other newly industrialized countries, such as Hong Kong, Singapore, South Korea, and Malaysia, had adopted free-market policies and were very export-oriented; that is, they were integrated into the international economy that so many developing countries had pilloried for their continued lack of economic progress. By the latter part of the 1980s, therefore, the developing countries were less confrontational on aid, trade, and Third World development issues.

One other reason for their newly chastened mood was the collapse of OPEC. OPEC's huge price escalation after the fall of the shah in 1979 proved its own undoing, for it led to genuine Western conservation of energy (in 1983, U.S. oil imports from the Gulf were down to less than 5 percent of total U.S. oil imports, Europe's to 25 percent, and Japan's to 50 percent). High oil prices also created a deep recession that idled many factories and workers, which lowered the market for OPEC oil even further. OPEC's policies encouraged an increase in the supply of non-OPEC oil (for example, from Mexico, Alaska, and the North Sea) and the use of alternate energy sources like coal. The result was an oil glut, and the real price paid for oil fell below the official price of $34 per barrel.

The only way OPEC could ensure its future as a cartel and regain control over oil prices was to cut production. But in general, the countries with larger populations, such as Nigeria, Iran, and Algeria, expected the less-populated Arab Persian Gulf countries to absorb most of the cuts. Presumably, these countries needed less money; Saudi Arabia was expected to accept the biggest cuts. But the cartel members had many conflicts with one another; worse, Iraq was at war with Iran; and, needing to finance the war, Iran refused to accept its OPEC-set production levels. Given the members' conflicting interests, OPEC found it impossible to control production. Even when OPEC finally agreed on new production levels and lowered the official price to $28 per barrel, it was unable to keep that price up. Saudi Arabia, tired of losing revenues while its market share declined, decided to increase its production and regain its share of the world oil market. Oil prices plunged briefly to $9 to $10 a barrel.

Although this decline in oil prices was undoubtedly beneficial to economic growth, resulting in lower inflation and interest rates in the oil-importing countries, it worsened the lot of oil producers and debtors like Mexico and Nigeria. Many Westerners now enjoyed watching the OPEC members' misery as their revenues plunged. The danger was that by the mid-1990s the increased consumption as a result of the cheaper oil prices would lead to another oil crisis as demand rose, a demand that only OPEC, still possessing the world's largest oil deposits, could satisfy—at higher prices, of course. OPEC, seemingly on the ropes, was thus hardly dead. By early 1987 oil prices had already recovered to $18, twice the mid-1986 level, and were rising slowly. U.S. imports by the end of the decade were back up to the level of the late 1970s, only slightly less than the 47.7 percent in 1977; with U.S. production falling, the nation was not only again becoming dependent on imports, but was also adding to its huge trade deficit (about 44 percent of it constituted oil imports) and exposing itself once more to political events in the unstable Middle East.

Thus, as the Reagan administration was coming to its close, the health of the American economy remained one of the two critical issues facing the American people as the debt problem and greater oil imports and potentially higher prices threatened to aggravate the nation's already grave economic problems: overconsumption, underinvestment, aging machinery, neglected infrastructure, insufficient nonmilitary research, poor workmanship, an insufficiently skilled labor force, and bad management by bloated corporate bureaucracies that have not been receptive either to risk taking or to innovation. The other problem, which had hampered post-Vietnam policies toward the Soviet Union and the Third World from Nixon to Reagan, was the absence of a foreign policy consensus.

The Absence of a Foreign Policy Consensus

The key symptom of the public's increasing skepticism about foreign commitments was the fact that the two parties no longer shared the same perception of the world and the U.S. role in it. Indeed, the two have essentially changed positions. During cold war I, the Democratic party was the most interventionist and most strongly anti-Soviet (and anti-Chinese during the days of the Sino-Soviet alliance) in its behavior. This reflected not only the views of its southern conservative anti-Communist wing and the party's efforts to ward off Republican accusations that it was the party of appeasement, but also the party's essentially dominant liberal orientation. The liberal wing, essentially northern and committed to democratic values and social justice at home, was equally concerned with the protection of democratic values from Soviet totalitarianism abroad. Because the Democratic party was essentially liberal, it was also a cold war party. The term *cold war liberalism* was the phrase usually used to describe this pattern of thought. By contrast, with the exception of its eastern moderate wing, which supported postwar Democratic foreign policy, the Republican party, primarily conservative, remained to a large extent isolationist, especially toward Europe. Its rhetoric was fiercely anti-Communist, but it was directed toward the Democrats, accusing them of "coddling communism." In 1952 Eisenhower ran for the Republican presidential nomination because he feared that if the conservative senator, Robert Taft of Ohio, were nominated and won the election, the party would abandon the nation's foreign policy commitments. Eisenhower's main task for eight years was in fact to gain his party's support for the nation's international role.

Since the Vietnam War, the two parties have flip-flopped. The Republicans now became interventionist in foreign policy, while the Democrats were much less so, unwilling to use force or the threat of force to support foreign policy objectives. Indeed, they were much more likely to define these objectives very selectively. The old cold war liberals, who belonged to the Hubert Humphrey-Henry Jackson wing of the party, have essentially disappeared. Liberalism—that is, the commitment to democratic fulfillment, social justice, and egalitarianism domestically—had to a large extent been divorced from a hard-line foreign policy stance. Ironically, this stance was alive and well in the Republican party.

The Republicans, whether during Nixon's détente or Reagan's cold war II, still saw the world as the Democrats used to. For them, the world remained basically bipolar politically and militarily; international politics revolved mainly around issues of security; the prime focus for American foreign policy was the East-West conflict, including its manifestations in the Third World; and the principal threat was the Soviet Union, a totalitarian expansionist power whose military ability exceeded any conceivable defensive needs and endangered the military balance. In short, for the Republicans (except the small and dwindling number of moderates who were close to the old Democratic liberal viewpoint), the key issue remained freedom versus tyranny, democracy versus totalitarianism. Containment of Soviet power could not be abandoned.

The post-Vietnam or post-cold-war liberal Democrats' focus through the late 1980s was not on East-West issues, but on North-South ones. The problems the party wanted addressed were poverty, overpopulation, hunger, ill health, and lack of education. Once the party of cold war crusaders, it now regarded the use of force with a distaste reminiscent of the Founding Fathers' attitude toward "entangling alliances." In turn, as noted earlier, this Democratic stance reflected the party's concern with interdependence and other global issues such as the inequitable distribution of wealth in the world, the Third World debt problem, the scarcity of natural resources, and environmental pollution, which cut across national boundaries. These problems confronting all humanity were said to be the critical issues for the future, more important than national and ideological differences between the superpowers and their allies. Building a new world order should therefore be the focus of attention and effort rather than the continuation of old-fashioned balance-of-power politics with its undue concentration on national interest, national security, and military power, all of which endanger the survival of the world. In an increasingly interdependent world, therefore, the Democrats, because of their commitment to social change in the Third Word, were more sympathetic to left-wing forces who propose such changes and hostile to right-wing forces, even if they were pro-American.

The Soviet Union had almost been eliminated by definition. Democrats favored détente and especially arms control as ways of reducing superpower tensions, stabilizing the deterrent balance, and allowing resources that otherwise would have been invested in the arms race to be used to erase Third World poverty. In 1984 the Democratic platform stated that the "gravest political and security changes" stem from "poverty, repression, and despair." Economic aid, political and economic reform, and support for democratic values must be the "primary instruments" of U.S. influence in the Third World. Force would be of limited usefulness against such problems. Bayonets cannot create democracy. (Actually, a Democratic administration used precisely such instruments to create democracy in Germany and Japan.)

The Reagan administration, not surprisingly, therefore, saw a Soviet-Cuban-Nicaraguan security threat to the United States in Central America, while the Democrats, critical of a status quo they condemned as unjust, saw the problem in that area as essentially domestic. They viewed El Salvador and Nicaragua as the products of years of American-supported repressive rule. Their proposed solution was to bring democracy and the elimination of poverty to El Salvador and to attract Nicaragua away from Moscow and Havana by offering it help rather than opposing it and driving the Sandinistas into the arms of the Communists. In both cases, the Democrats were resolutely opposed to the Reagan administration's military intervention. While the Republicans were concerned about "another Cuba," Democrats warned against "another Vietnam." Initially, they were also very critical of the Grenada invasion, changing their minds only as it became clear that public opinion overwhelmingly supported the president. The evidence clearly indicates that since Vietnam the two parties have seriously disagreed on foreign and defense issues. How much became evident on the issue of supporting the *contras*.

The Democrats' anti-interventionist mood was very visible on one issue above all: multilateralism. During the Truman-Kennedy-Johnson presidencies, the Democrats' activist and interventionist policies had been conducted through various multilateral organizations: the United Nations, the OAS, and SEATO. The United States had used these organizations to legitimate its actions: the intervention in Korea was carried out under the UN, the one in Vietnam under SEATO, and the one in the Dominican Republic under the OAS. In no case did these organizations act as a major restraint on the United States.

Since Vietnam, the Democrats have remained committed to multilateralism, but their purpose has changed. Their advice to act through the UN or OAS is advanced as a substitute for action because the majorities in these bodies usually disagreed with U.S. policies. The Soviet bloc and Third World countries constituted the majority in the UN General Assembly; even the OAS, which in 1965 formally supported the American intervention in the Dominican Republic, in 1983 would not have approved the U.S. invasion of Grenada. That is why the United States had to find the rather obscure Association of Eastern Caribbean States, an organization almost no one had heard of, to legitimate its action. The Republicans, now the party of interventionism, preferred to act unilaterally and viewed alliances and multilateral organizations mainly as constraints on America's freedom to do whatever was necessary in its own interests.

By the late 1980s, as the threat of Soviet expansion faded and the country's perception of the "Communist threat" declined—refocusing on crime and drugs, the decaying infrastructure, environmental degradation, and the enormous debt burden—a new consensus appeared to be emerging around three issues: one, to pursue negotiations with the Soviet Union to resolve differences and create a more cooperative, stable, and peaceful bilateral relationship while simultaneously keeping up America's guard; two, to reserve American power, especially the use of military force, only for the most vital interests that the country—the president and Congress—can agree on; and three, to focus on the increasingly critical issue, not the Soviet threat to the military security of the United States, but the economic threat from America's allies, especially Japan, to the nation's economic well-being.

Ending the Cold War:
Negotiating the Terms of Peace

WOULD a new administration analyze American-Soviet affairs in terms of its continuities or discontinuities? This question faced George Bush when he became president in January 1989. In the few years since Mikhail Gorbachev came to power, the changes in Soviet domestic politics and foreign policy had been extensive and unprecedented. A wholesale domestic transformation was accompanied by a substantial reduction of tensions with the United States and increasing cooperation on arms control and regional issues.

Indeed, many observers (including George Kennan, a former Foreign Service officer and the founding father of the containment policy) proclaimed that the cold war was over; others, more cautious, suggested it was coming to a close. President Bush said he would not use the term *cold war* and referred instead to a period "beyond containment," in which the principal task would be "integrating the Soviet Union into the community of nations." But after what he himself called the "revolution of '89" in his 1990 State of the Union address, Bush said the changes of 1989 had been so striking and momentous that they marked "the beginning of a new era in the world's affairs."

As Reagan left office American-Soviet relations were better than they had been since the two had been allies against Nazi Germany during World War II. How could that be? How, in a few years, could such a profound transformation of superpower relations have occurred? Was Gorbachev's emphasis on the priority of domestic affairs and on a conciliatory foreign policy an admission of defeat in the cold war? Would future American-Soviet relations be more "normal"? Was the cold war really over? And what were the policy implications of the change in American-Soviet relations?

The Rapid Turnabout in U.S.-Soviet Relations

The rapidity of the change in the two superpowers' relationship was certainly astounding. The cold war spanned more than four decades, exceeding the time that elapsed from the beginning of World War I (1914) to the end of World War II (1945). The transformation of American-Soviet relations is the more surprising because the 1970s had been a period of great uncertainty, confusion, and stumbling for the United States; by contrast, the Soviet Union had appeared confident and optimistic about the future course of international politics. Having withdrawn from Vietnam without victory—some would say defeated—the United States was domestically divided. Its economy, and that of the other Western nations, had suffered oil shocks and stagflation in 1973 and 1979, the year the Somoza government fell to the Sandinistas in Nicaragua; the Iranians seized the U.S. embassy and fifty-two American hostages; the Soviets invaded Afghanistan; the Vietnamese, after invading Cambodia in December 1978, established a pro-Soviet government there; and a pro-Soviet Communist faction seized power in Grenada. It was a decade to deflate any country's self-confidence. Many Americans, feeling guilty about what was claimed to be an abuse of power in Vietnam, counseled a return to isolationism. By the late 1980s Americans, while still cautious about protracted military interventions and involvements, had recaptured much of their patriotism and pride in America's mission of defending and, where possible, advancing democratic values. Although Reagan's talk of a recession of the Communist tide and the inevitable global sweep of democracy was at first widely dismissed as self-serving, right-wing propaganda, the fact remains that the president, whether through faith or intuition, proved by the end of his second term to have been correct.

Soviet policy was at a high point in the 1970s. It attained strategic parity, a conventional capability to project Soviet power beyond Eurasia, and it sought to attain geopolitical advantage to exploit America's mood of withdrawal. The Soviet leadership saw the USSR's growth of military power as part of a shift in the "correlation of forces" from West to East. That strength would allow Moscow to exploit opportunities it saw in the Third World to weaken the West while simultaneously deterring American military countermoves. Brezhnev and his colleagues believed that the more military power they acquired, the greater would be the American need to be accommodating. In addition, by encouraging Third World governments to adopt Leninist one-party governments, Moscow believed that Soviet gains would be irreversible and cumulative. Convinced that the United States was a declining power, Moscow calculated that Washington had no choice but to adjust to these new circumstances and accept the consequences.

The apparent successes of the Soviet Union were, however, deceptive. Two reasons account for what was, in fact, a flawed policy. One was the failure of the Soviet economy. The economic growth rate, 5 percent in the

1960s, and only 2 percent by the early 1970s, was standing still at virtually 0 percent a decade later. Capable only of producing a plentiful supply of weapons, the Soviet economy was characterized by an absence of consumer goods and food. By the late 1980s the Soviets were importing basic items such as razor blades, soap, and pantyhose, among other things, and some basic staples like meat and sugar were rationed. Harvests failed repeatedly since the early 1970s, and food had to be imported from the United States and other countries (czarist Russia had been a food exporter). Basically, the centralized Soviet economy was nearing a breakdown. Gorbachev, who when first appointed general secretary in 1985 had believed that economic growth could be stimulated by more discipline in the workplace, less worker absenteeism and drunkenness, and higher productivity, by 1987 realized the severity of the crisis he faced.

A second reason for the Soviet turnabout was the cost of Brezhnev's foreign policy. With a GNP half that of the United States and a military budget that the CIA estimated at 16 percent of GNP (compared to 6 percent for the United States and 3 percent for the Europeans), the civilian economy was starved. In fact, later Soviet figures showed that military spending was between 25 percent and 30 percent and the Soviet GNP closer to one-third the U.S. GNP. The continuous arms buildup across the board and Moscow's expansionist activities in the Third World produced fear and suspicion of Soviet intentions. The result was the very encirclement the Soviet Union long had feared. In Europe, the SS-20s led to an American counterdeployment. In Asia, the growing Soviet threat allowed the United States to play divide-and-rule, attracting China to the West in a major shift of power. The Soviet Union, like Germany at the turn of the century, thus created its own worst nightmare and increased its sense of vulnerability.

The Reagan administration's hard-line policies made Soviet foreign policy even more costly, thereby contributing to Gorbachev's awareness that the Soviet Union faced a systemic crisis. Simply put, it built up American power to create incentives for the Soviets to negotiate. The strategic modernization program was intended to devalue the ICBMs on which the Soviets had spent so much for so long: the MX, Trident II, and the B-1 bomber, to be followed by the Stealth B-2, were all counterforce weapons. SDI, too, to be developed and deployed for defensive purposes only (according to President Reagan), was seen in Moscow as fitting within a broader offensive, counterforce strategy whose purpose was declared to be "prevailing" in a nuclear war. Unable to defend the United States from a full-scale Soviet nuclear attack, SDI would be able to protect the country against a retaliatory Soviet strike crippled by an initial American disarming attack. In addition, the American Intermediate Nuclear Force (INF) threatened Soviet territory from Western Europe. The Soviet Union was therefore confronted with not only a costly arms race when it needed huge capital investments at home, but also a high-tech arms race when it could not even keep up with contemporary Western technology. The Reagan administration also bargained very hard by appearing uninterested, indeed unenthusiastic, about arms control negotiations, "hanging tough" when negotiations did start, insisting on deeper cuts involving asymmetric Soviet reductions than any of its predecessors had demanded, and insisting on verification procedures for arms agreements far more intrusive than those the Soviets had in the past consistently rejected.

In addition, American-supplied weapons made the fighting in Afghanistan costly and placed victory out of reach, kept the civil war going in Angola, while China and the United States made Vietnam's pacification of Cambodia impossible. Although the administration did not succeed in overthrowing the Sandinistas in Nicaragua, the Soviet effort to sustain the latter was the only cheap part of an otherwise unending financial drain, as was the continuing civil war in Ethiopia. The imperial outposts that had looked so promising only ten years earlier now lost their luster; and sustaining proxies like the Cubans and Vietnamese was too expensive. Gorbachev had no choice but to see what Marxists have always prided themselves on recognizing: objective reality. The Soviet Union, with a structurally unsound economy, surrounded by a Western coalition of NATO, Japan, and China, and led by the United States with a resurgent economy (despite its rapidly increasing federal and trade deficits, suggesting deeper long-term threats to its viability), Gorbachev was forced to recognize the need for rapprochement with the United States.

The Soviet weakness and consequent desire for an end to the cold war first became apparent in 1987 when the USSR delegates walked back into the INF talks they had earlier walked out of and accepted virtually the entire package of U.S. demands. Even more significant, Gorbachev and his supporters made a series of pronouncements that contradicted long-held Soviet doctrine and positions: (1) the "all-human value of peace" took precedence over the class struggle, meaning that the unilateral pursuit of advantage to extend socialism could jeopardize the peace; (2) Soviet (and American) security could not be achieved unless there was "common security," suggesting that if one side armed and then the other responded in kind, as in the past, it would leave the initiating side less, not more, secure; (3) force and the threat of force should no longer be instruments of foreign policy; (4) security should be achieved by political means, that is, resolving disputes by compromise; (5) "reasonable sufficiency" would be the new standard by which the Soviet Union would in the future judge the military strength it needed; (6) its forces in Western Europe, organized for surprise attack and a lightning, or *Blitzkrieg*, strike toward the English Channel, would be reorganized in a "nonoffensive defense," or "defensive defense," so that NATO, whose war plans called for no advance eastward, could feel reassured; and (7) negotiations between NATO and the Warsaw Treaty Organization (WTO) should reduce the levels of manpower and arms and, wherever asymmetries favored one side, the stronger power—like the Soviet

Union in, for instance, tanks and personnel carriers—should reduce to the level of the weaker side rather than the reverse. As a symbol of his goodwill, Gorbachev in late 1988 committed the Soviet Union to a two-year unilateral 10 percent cut of its armed forces, promising the withdrawal of six tank divisions, bridging equipment and units, and other offensive means from the front facing NATO.

In the Third World, Moscow deemphasized the revolutionary struggle for national liberation and raised questions about the future of socialism in the developing countries. In addition, by withdrawing from Afghanistan and helping to resolve several other regional conflicts, Gorbachev was reducing Soviet foreign policy costs and diminishing the likelihood of new conflicts with the United States and the chances that the current ones would undermine the emerging improvement in U.S.-Soviet relations, as they had done in the previous decade. Gorbachev realized that while Soviet influence had been extended beyond Eurasia, its new client states were economic basketcases requiring unending assistance. More broadly, Gorbachev sought to deprive the American-led coalition encircling the Soviet bloc of an enemy. His "charm offensive" (as some called his diplomatic-propaganda campaign), including visits abroad, was very effective in Europe, especially in West Germany, where "Gorby" rated far higher as a statesman and peacemaker than either presidents Reagan or Bush. The Soviet leader also normalized relations with China in 1989. Among two of the many dramatic moves to improve the Soviet image, Moscow confessed that its intervention in Afghanistan had violated Soviet law and international norms of behavior, and, after years of denying accusations that it had violated the 1972 ABM treaty, admitted the violation.

Gorbachev therefore changed priorities and launched his program of *glasnost* (openness) and *perestroika* (restructuring) to revitalize Soviet society and the economy. He realized that the two were intimately related: without more openness in Soviet society, without harnessing the energies of the Soviet people, long used to suppression and obedience, the Soviet economy would not recover from its stagnation. Thus Gorbachev advocated strengthening civil liberties, more freedom in the press, arts, literature, scholarship, and even in the reexamination of the darker side of Soviet history, hitherto kept secret. He urged decentralizing the economy, cutting back on the pervasive role of the Moscow-based central planning bureaucracy, and permitting the profit motive and market forces a greater role in stimulating production, including a degree of private ownership and entrepreneurship.

But it quickly became clear that *glasnost* and *perestroika* would not succeed unless the political system were restructured. Gorbachev therefore called for the removal of the party from the daily management of the economy and other sectors of Soviet life; permitted real but limited competition in party and legislative elections; allowed the Soviet parliament, or Supreme Soviet, to assert itself; ensured secret ballots; fixed terms of no more than two five-year terms for party, government, and legislative officials; created a powerful new post of president of the Soviet Union (which he himself filled, giving him the two most powerful positions in the Soviet Union); and tolerated nonparty popular political groupings. But despite Gorbachev's exhortations and reform efforts, there was strong resistance from the 19 million party and government bureaucrats, who had a vested interest in the status quo. Change threatened their jobs, status, and privileges. The political system that Gorbachev wanted to change might well be described as a system of the bureaucrats, by the bureaucrats, and for the bureaucrats.

Opposition to Gorbachev was further fueled by the fear that the loosening of central controls could be harmful, if not fatal, politically. It was the Russians who in the Soviet Union, as in czarist Russia, controlled most of the levers of power and were particularly concerned that such a devolution of power away from Moscow might result in more political self-determination by the more than one hundred non-Russian nationalities. Economic decentralization would then spill over into political decentralization. In other words, the fundamental structural reforms required by the Soviet Union might threaten not only the party's sole control of power but also Moscow's imperial control over its own vast country. The repeated unrest in the Baltic republics (Estonia, Latvia, and Lithuania), especially the demands for independence, and similar agitation in Georgia and the central Asian republics, were in this respect very worrisome. This uneasiness was compounded by the successful efforts by the countries of Eastern Europe to throw off *their* Communist yokes. The Soviet Union faced the real possibility of becoming the Soviet *Dis*union. Quite contrary to Marxist analysis, then, the political substructure determines the fate of the economy rather than the other way around; the Soviet political system had become the greatest obstacle to economic modernization. That is why, preoccupied at home, Gorbachev needed to end the cold war.

The Peace Process

What were some of the indicators by which the U.S. government could judge whether, in fact, the cold war was drawing to a close or was indeed over? The Bush administration was initially unsure, although the president acknowledged that the United States had an interest in the success of *perestroika*. In the context of forty years of cold war, of previous hopes that the cold war was over (hopes that had been repeatedly dashed), the administration—and especially the president—tended to think the better part of wisdom was to be cautious. If Gorbachev were to fall and be replaced by a hard-line conservative, the United States did not want to be caught out on the proverbial limb. Nevertheless, the secretary of state acknowledged that Soviet "new thinking" in foreign and defense policies promised possibilities that ten years earlier would have been unimaginable. Therefore, uncertainty about

Soviet reforms was all the *more* reason to seize the opportunities represented by Gorbachev. After a period of hesitation, the administration endorsed Gorbachev; maintaining him in power was good for the United States. The assumption behind this policy was that any replacement would be a Communist hard-liner. Only in 1990 did this assumption become more questionable as Gorbachev's rival on the left, Boris Yeltsin, began to lead a growing democratic political opposition.

In any case, events were moving rapidly, both within the Soviet Union and outside. Predicting the future in these circumstances was a risky enterprise: the changes had come so quickly and to Western observers (and Soviet ones, no doubt) had been so unexpected, that it was virtually impossible to forecast what the Soviet Union would be like in five years or even one. The year 1989—the Year of the Collapsing Dominoes in Eastern Europe—had been truly revolutionary; 1990—the Year of the Disintegration of the Communist System in the Soviet Union—saw at least as much upheaval as the Bolshevik Revolution which, seventy years after its inception, was collapsing. What was clear, however, was that the Soviet Union was operating from a position of weakness, and Gorbachev's foreign policy amounted to a "diplomacy of the decline"—or, perhaps more aptly, of retreat.

The result was that regardless of who held power in Moscow, the United States had a grand opportunity to advance its interests. Any ruler of the Soviet Union, if it survived essentially intact, would face the same domestic constraints on the conduct of foreign policy. As the victor in the cold war, the question for the United States was what were its terms of peace? What kind of post-cold-war world did the United States wish to see? It had, therefore, to define its own purposes. Even if Gorbachev did not survive, the United States needed to take advantage of the time he was in office to restructure American-Soviet relations and make future Soviet foreign policy less reversible. American influence on Soviet internal affairs was limited, but, if the United States was responsive to Gorbachev's policies and proposals, it could assist the process of domestic change and help him. But in the final analysis, the success of *perestroika* depended on events within the Soviet Union. Washington's principal recourse, therefore, was to act in terms of American interests vis-à-vis the Soviet state given that both superpowers were phasing out the cold war and creating a new post-cold-war order.

Although the Soviet Union's position was weak in these negotiations—a weakness that was to worsen as Eastern Europe defected, ethnic nationalism grew, and communism as a political and economic system withered—the country had not surrendered unconditionally. Nor had the United States won a total victory, as it had in World War II against Germany; it could not impose its terms on Moscow. Moreover, a victory that humiliated the loser would result in a peace built on sand. World War I had ended with a victor's peace imposed on Germany; it lasted only as long as Germany remained weak. After World War II, both Germany and Japan were treated in a more conciliatory fashion; therefore, neither was bent on revenge. For a durable peace, the Soviet Union, too, had to find the post-cold-war international order acceptable. The two powers engaged in genuine negotiations about the terms on which the cold war was to be ended, as well as the construction of the new balance of power. The ending of the cold war depended basically on the fulfillment of four conditions: (1) dismantling Stalin's empire in Eastern and central Europe, (2) decolonizing Brezhnev's Third World outposts, (3) reducing arms and stabilizing the balance, and (4) ensuring human rights and continued liberalization in the Soviet Union.

Dismantling Stalin's Empire in Eastern and Central Europe

A prime indicator of Soviet willingness to end the cold war was its acceptance of Eastern Europe's wide-ranging moves away from Communist party control. The conquest and subsequent Stalinization of Eastern Europe, together with the division of Germany, split the continent after the war. This division was at the heart of the cold war confrontation, and only self-determination for Eastern Europe could end it. Events there were critical because each of the major wars of this century has broken out there. The disintegration of the Austro-Hungarian empire led to the eruption of World War I; Germany's attack on Poland began World War II; and the Soviet expansion into Eastern Europe and the Sovietization of the area—symbolized by the brutal coup in 1948 in Czechoslovakia—led to the cold war. Reversing Soviet policy in Eastern Europe was a critical step toward ending it.

American policy during World War II had been sensitive to Soviet security concerns in Eastern Europe, but the United States was also committed to national self-determination. President Franklin Roosevelt thought that Soviet security could be compatible with democratic elections. Where Communist parties did well, they could be included in coalition governments, reflecting the popular will. Critical in the president's thinking was that smaller countries living in the shadow of the Soviet Union naturally would take their huge neighbor's security concerns into account in formulating their foreign policies. Roosevelt's thinking reflected that of a traditional great power: small nations living within a superior power's sphere of influence do not have to have governments that reflect the latter's ideological and political values. They *do* need to be willing to make a virtue out of necessity: to make the best of their geographical situation, to be aware of their constrained freedom and maneuverability, and to be alert to the interests of the regionally dominant power.

The Soviet ideological outlook, however, defined security in Marxist terms. Security could be ensured only if class enemies were kept out of power. The governments bordering the Soviet Union therefore had to be Communist.

Even coalition governments in which the party controlled the major levers of power—military and police—were unacceptable. Eastern Europe therefore was to become a sphere of dominance, with each country having not only Communist governments controlled by Moscow but also ideological conformity. Soviet troops were stationed throughout the area to assure that dominance and control and adherence to Soviet-style socialism. Without this military presence and occasional interventions, these governments, unpopular with their people, would not have survived.

Could Moscow now separate its ideology from its definition of security? That was the main question in 1989. The initial reaction came when the Communist party in Poland was unable to form a government after its disastrous showing in the relatively free June elections in which the Solidarity movement clearly demonstrated overwhelming popular support. Because the party had been repudiated, Solidarity, which had received a *de facto* mandate to govern, was asked to organize the government. Poland thus formed its first postwar non-Communist, indeed anti-Communist, government. The military and police, including the security police, were left in Communist hands, however, to reassure Moscow about the future course of Poland, a country that the Germans had twice marched through in the twentieth century to invade the USSR. In addition, Lech Walesa, Solidarity's leader and spokesman, stated that Poland would remain a member of the WTO. This sort of political sensitivity was what Roosevelt had in mind.

Gorbachev appeared willing to accept such a non-Communist Poland and a more traditional sphere of influence in Eastern Europe for several reasons. One was his preoccupation with domestic matters. Another was that Eastern Europe had not proved to be a security belt but, instead, had added to Soviet insecurity. Its people were sullen and resentful of the Soviet-imposed regimes, and they had not forgotten that earlier efforts to rid themselves of these regimes had been suppressed militarily. Gorbachev did not want to be confronted with an explosive situation, which, among other things, would be a major, if not fatal, setback to the emerging détente with the West. More acceptable and legitimate governments would avoid this confrontation and thus enhance Soviet security. Furthermore, given the strains on the Soviet economy, he could not afford continued subsidies to Poland and the rest of Eastern Europe, all of whose economies were in trouble. It made eminent sense, therefore, to unburden his straining economy and "dump" Eastern Europe on the West, especially West Germany's bankers. Finally, by accepting a traditional sphere of influence, he could resolve a principal issue that had precipitated the cold war.

To make the best of the situation, Gorbachev announced that Socialist countries had no right to intervene in each other's affairs. The clear implication was that the Brezhnev Doctrine was dead. Gorbachev now claimed that each country was responsible for its own destiny. Indeed, Gorbachev paid a symbolic visit to Finland in late 1989. In a country that had always been sensitive to Soviet security interests, yet maintained a democracy, Gorbachev specifically declared that the Soviet Union had no moral or political right to interfere in the affairs of its neighbors in Eastern Europe; he held neutral Finland up as a model of a relationship between a big and little country that were neighbors and had different social systems. Shortly afterward, Moscow and its four WTO allies that had jointly invaded Czechoslovakia in 1968 condemned that invasion as "illegal" and pledged a strict policy of noninterference in each other's affairs; Moscow issued its own separate declaration of repentance as well. The leader of Hungary's renamed Socialist party announced that the collective declaration marked a formal repudiation of the Brezhnev Doctrine.

The result was that 1989 was the year of Eastern European dominoes. In Poland a Communist government had allowed its popularity to be tested in a national election and suffered an overwhelming and humiliating rejection; in Hungary, the parliament dropped the word "People" from the country's formal name, and the Communist party renamed itself the Democratic Socialist party to survive a Polish-style disaster in the multiparty elections of 1990. (Even so, the party was able to keep only 30,000 of its original 720,000 members.) Similarly, Czechoslovakia dropped "Socialist" from its formal name, and the Polish and East German Communist parties also sought to shed their Stalinist skins to better compete in the 1990 elections. In East Germany 200,000 people, mostly young skilled workers vital to its industry, fled the country (mainly via Hungary) for West Germany when the most hard-line regime in Eastern Europe initially refused to follow the Polish and Hungarian examples. All these events demonstrated vividly that communism had lost its appeal. Indeed, the events of 1989 and the momentum they gathered suggested that the legitimacy of all Communist regimes throughout the area was in doubt; even those who had grown up under communism rejected its philosophy. Zbigniew Brzezinski called it the "terminal crisis of Communism."

The changes were undoubtedly most dramatic in East Germany (population 16 million), where the hemorrhage of its youth threatened to depopulate the country and mass demonstrations finally led to the replacement of its inflexible Communist leader. In what was a genuine people's revolution, Soviet troops stood by instead of propping up the regime, and the new party leader promised radical changes, including free elections. As a token of his promises of reform, he lifted all restrictions on travel and emigration. In the hours after that announcement, hundreds of thousands of East Germans swarmed across the Berlin Wall; altogether, 1.5 million East Germans poured across the Wall that first weekend to celebrate. In one of history's ironies, the capital that fifty years earlier, in Adolf Hitler's time, represented the most evil of modern regimes, now represented hope. Since 1961, when the Wall was built, it had become the symbol of what the cold war was all about—tyranny versus freedom. Its opening on November 9,

1989, exactly fifty-one years after Hitler had unleashed his storm troopers against German Jews, therefore symbolized, more than any other event, the ending of the cold war. But the successor regime was doomed; evidence of privilege and corruption among the former Communist rulers infuriated the already aroused masses in the streets, leading to the collapse of the Communist party leadership that only a few weeks earlier had still ruled East Germany with an iron hand.

After the opening of the Berlin Wall, the winds of change swept over Czechoslovakia. What was happening there also had great symbolic importance, although not widely noted at the time because of the tumult in the Eastern bloc. The great powers had inflicted tremendous injustices on Czechoslovakia, the only central European democracy before World War II. It was betrayed by France and England in their efforts to appease Hitler in 1938. It was violently transformed into a Communist nation by the Soviets in a 1948 coup. And its efforts to humanize Czech communism (the Prague Spring) were crushed by Soviet tanks in 1968. The collapse of the Communist regime in Prague was, therefore, also a sign of the times.

Everywhere in Eastern Europe, in what Ronald Reagan had once called the "evil empire" (which many at the time thought was an excessively anticommunist and provocative term), people were saying just how evil that empire had been and were militantly expressing their anticommunism. They demanded not just the reform of Communist parties but their removal from office, ending what many of them viewed as a forty-year-long foreign occupation. The call was for free elections, an end to the Communist party's leading role in the affairs of their countries, and interim governments composed mainly of non-Communists.

In addition to the genuinely popular uprisings in 1989 in Poland, Hungary, East Germany, and Czechoslovakia, events in the Soviet Union and China, where a vibrant prodemocracy movement in Beijing thrived before it was brutally crushed in June, suggested that the erosion of communism's appeal and legitimacy had extended to the two largest and most powerful Communist states. Only in Bulgaria and Romania did the local Communist parties manage to run under new names, with claims that they had reformed, and easily win the first free elections after the collapse of the Soviet-supported governments.

The United States responded by expressing support for the governments seeking to liberalize. President Bush did this with his visits to Poland and Hungary in 1989. But the United States did not want to arouse Soviet security concerns further. Gorbachev, therefore, sought a tacit understanding with Bush: the Soviet leader would continue to support, if not encourage, the transformations in Eastern Europe, and he would not crack down militarily on the changes, even if they went faster and farther down the road to "desovietization" and "decommunization" than Gorbachev—like everyone else—had anticipated. The Soviet leader presumably had thought that the changes in Eastern Europe would end with reform-minded Communists like himself in power, not the sweeping aside of all Communists. In any event, in return for Soviet nonintervention, the United States agreed it would not seek to exploit the geopolitical transformations now underway in the Soviet empire. Nor would it jeopardize Soviet security or humiliate Moscow more than was already being done by the popular rejection of communism among its WTO allies. Washington also said it would make some concessions, on trade, for instance, to help Gorbachev rebuild the Soviet economy and show some tolerance for his internal problems. Because it was in the U.S. interest as well to manage the changes in the Soviet Union and Eastern Europe peacefully, the Gorbachev-Bush bargain held. This deal even applied for a time to the Baltic republics. Gorbachev considered them part of the Soviet Union, while the United States had never recognized their annexation.

Nonviolence was chosen not only by the rulers (although Gorbachev certainly urged this course on them) but also by the masses. For forty years the Soviet-imposed regimes had exploited and oppressed their peoples. Violence from below would have been natural as these regimes relented. Indeed, the transitions, starting in 1989, were almost unnaturally smooth and nonviolent. Revolutions—for that was what was going on in Eastern Europe—are rarely peaceful. After all, 1989 was the bicentennial celebration of the French Revolution; this act of popular liberation was paradoxically a violent affair. But such violence in the liberation of Eastern Europe could jeopardize the whole process of change and possibly endanger Gorbachev in the Soviet Union.

Only in Romania was there violence because the regime used force in its attempt to stay in power. Hundreds of people were killed as its dictator, Nicolae Ceausescu, sought futilely to buck the trend in the rest of Eastern Europe. But he failed as army units defected to the opposition and fought Ceausescu's security forces. Captured as they attempted to flee, Ceausescu and his wife, Elena, the second most powerful figure in the regime, were executed after a hasty trial on Christmas Day. Resistance to the popular revolution quickly faded after that. Interestingly enough, Moscow thought of sending military assistance to the opposition and Washington declared it would not oppose Warsaw Pact intervention to get rid of the regime. But, with that single exception, it was the nonviolence that stood out. Czechoslovakia's new president, the playwright Vaclav Havel, set the tone by calling for his fellow citizens to act with dignity, honesty, and honor. The slogan of the demonstrators massed in the streets was "we are not like them."

Equally important, Washington thought it best to allow Eastern Europe's evolution to occur within the broader European context. The reasons were multiple: the U.S. budget deficit; the desire to reduce America's military role in Europe; the need to focus more on domestic problems, particularly on reinvigorating the economy; and not least, the determination to encourage the emergence of the European Community (EC). The EC and

Comecon, the Eastern bloc's trading organization, already had exchanged recognition in 1988; and since then Hungary and Czechoslovakia have made their own trading arrangements with the EC. East Germany, because of its relationship with West Germany, was in all but name a member even before the possibility of a reunified Germany arose. After 1989 states like Poland and Hungary were expected to be offered some sort of associate EC membership when they became democratic. The United States, contributing almost $1 billion, mainly for Poland, wanted to encourage the EC members to send financial help to the liberalizing countries of Eastern Europe. As it was, the U.S. commitment was only a modest percentage of the aggregate Western amount planned.

West Germany, the most prosperous member of the EC, subsequently offered Poland $2.2 billion in aid and financial relief, France $642 million; the European Community also decided on an aid package to Poland and Hungary and reached an agreement with the Soviet Union on a ten-year trade pact. In addition, French president François Mitterrand called on the Europeans to establish an investment bank, to be called the European Bank for Reconstruction and Development, with about $12 billion in capital, most of which was to be invested in Eastern Europe's private sector to assist the region in its move from centrally planned to market economies. It was President Bush's conviction, to reemphasize the point, that Western Europe should play a more active role and bear more of the burden than in the past in deciding Europe's future, including the integration of nations into the broader European structure that, with the exception of Czechoslovakia, had little experience with democracy or free markets. During his 1989 trip to Europe Bush welcomed a stronger united Europe. After decades of talking about the devolution of power to America's allies, it finally appeared to be occurring. This trend coincided with Europe's growing self-confidence.

Indeed, the EC's role in these momentous events could not do anything but grow. Even before the 1989 revolutions, the EC had decided to revive its movement toward a single market. It was a wise move given the likelihood that the U.S. deficit plus a diminished Soviet threat would lead to a significant reduction of American forces in the 1990s. The EC was also mindful of stiff Japanese—and to a lesser extent, U.S.—economic competition in the last decade of the century. The EC declared that it would make a new and, it was hoped, final push in 1992 toward its long-proclaimed goal of a United States of Europe. A single market and eventually a single currency remain a prelude to a European political federation, which would ultimately be able to conduct common foreign and defense policies. If the task of helping Eastern Europe was now an additional motive for an enlarged EC role, another—and perhaps more important one in the long run—was the rebirth of the German problem. For more than forty years, East and West had lived with a divided Germany. They preferred it that way because each remembered the havoc a powerful Germany wrought in this century by launching two world wars. A split

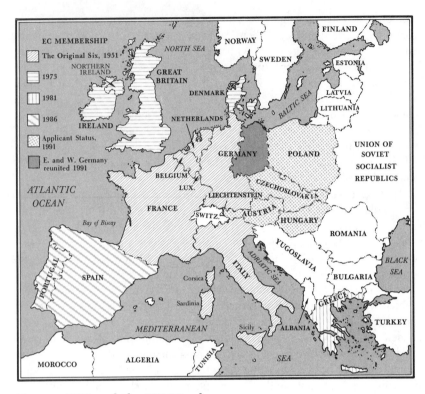

Europe 1990 and the EC Members

Germany at least was unlikely to initiate another war. NATO had been organized not only to contain the Soviet Union but also to restrain Germany; in addition, one purpose of the movement toward a united Europe had been to harness German power to broader European goals.

The terminal crisis of communism in Eastern Europe, however, undermined this status quo. Poland can reform itself, even decommunize, and still be Poland. Hungary, communist or not, still would have legitimacy as a nation. Moreover, Poles or Hungarians cannot flee to another part of their country sharing the same language and basic culture. But East Germans could. And the only way to stop the depopulation of East Germany short of police methods was to reform East Germany and to make living there more attractive to its citizens. But such liberalization, however, proved the adage that the cure is worse than the disease. Two thousand East Germans a day fled to West Germany, endangering the survival of the East German state, the viability of its economy, and the delivery of social services; moreover, as the government's authority waned, sentiment in East Germany for unification grew stronger every day. If East Germans in a free election were to vote out the Communist party and move toward political pluralism and free markets,

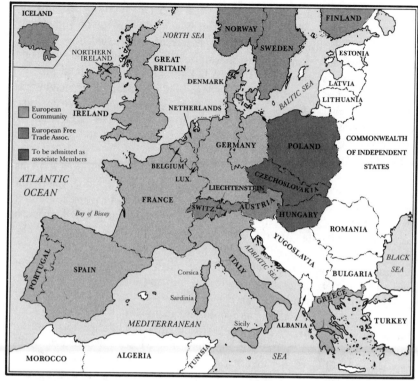

Europe 1992

why should East Germany continue to exist at all? Nationalism could not legitimate it. A democratic and free-market East Germany that truly lived up to its name, German *Democratic* Republic, would seek unification with the larger, richer, and democratic Federal Republic. And how could West Germany refuse to accept such an offer to reunify? It could not, and the March 1990 East German election, to everyone's surprise won by the followers of West German chancellor Helmut Kohl, ensured reunification. The large vote for the Christian Democrats and the Social Democrats, both tied to their West German counterparts, amounted to a death sentence for the German Democratic Republic and an endorsement for a "buy-out" by the richer and more powerful West Germans.

A reunited Germany, even a democratic one, however, posed all sorts of problems and potential instabilities. In fact, the collapse of the WTO and the inevitable, increasingly imminent, reunification of Germany meant constructing a new European balance of power. To make a united Germany acceptable to Moscow, the West proposed that a united Germany should be a member of NATO. This proposal contained two types of reassurances for Moscow. First, no Western armies, including German troops assigned to

NATO, would be stationed on former East German territory in view of Moscow's certain opposition to the presence of NATO troops on the Polish border. Second, during a three- to four-year transition period, the 380,000 Soviet troops would remain on East German soil (of a reunited and sovereign Germany that was a member of the NATO alliance and that would pay for the upkeep of these troops!). Germany also would guarantee its neighbors' borders, restate West Germany's pledge that it would not seek to acquire nuclear weapons, and accept a limit of 370,000 on the size of Germany's armed forces, below West Germany's 474,000 level in 1990 and well below the 667,000 level of the two Germanies.

Gorbachev's initial proposal was based on the memory that the Germans defeated czarist Russia in World War I and that the Soviet Union, although it repelled the German invasion in World War II, did so at a cost of 20 million lives. He therefore insisted that Germany be reunited only if it became a neutral, disarmed state. But this was unacceptable to virtually everyone else and it was probably not even thought to be the best solution by Moscow. For the question was whether a united but neutralized Germany would become once more a nationalistic, dangerously destabilizing force on the Continent. Pushed by his former allies to accept a NATO Germany, Gorbachev then proposed a reunited Germany that would be a member of both the WTO and NATO alliances. This too was rejected as merely another formula for neutrality. The United States felt confident that Moscow would eventually accept the NATO Germany favored by all members of the Western alliance, the West German government, the new East German one, as well as most WTO members. The Soviets, having lost the cold war, were thought to be in too weak a bargaining position to insist on anything else.

But Gorbachev, weak or not, continued to resist the Western solution to the German problem. The collapse of East Germany spelled the end of a major Soviet cold war goal: hegemony over Europe by neutralizing West Germany. Indeed, the Soviet Union's gains in World War II all had been lost. Together with the collapse of its empire in Eastern Europe plus the pullback of Soviet forces, the scheduled withdrawal of Soviet troops from East Germany spelled the end of the conflict over Europe that had been the central struggle in the cold war. Even more humiliating, a reunited Germany would likely emerge as the financial and economic center of Europe, the dominant power in Eastern Europe, and the principal source for capital and machinery for the Soviet Union. During the cold war, because of its far superior military strength, the Soviet Union had been the dominant power; in the post-cold-war period, when economic considerations and power were more significant and the Soviet Union needed German help, the Soviet-German relationship was likely to be reversed, resembling more the period before both world wars.

In July 1990, only four months after declaring that German membership in NATO was "absolutely out of the question," Gorbachev bowed to the inevitable, accepting a reunited Germany in NATO; his acceptance was made easier by the promise of eight billion dollars' worth of German credits to help the failing Soviet economy. Nevertheless, like his acceptance of a larger number of U.S. troops than Soviet troops in post-cold-war Europe, Gorbachev's acquiescence to German membership in NATO was a clear recognition of who had lost and who had won the cold war. Although it had none of the drama of a VE Day or V J Day, which marked the end of the war in Europe and the Pacific in 1945, history will note July 16 as the day the Soviet Union surrendered in the cold war. Indeed, the American insistence on Soviet acceptance of Germany's admission to NATO appeared in large part driven by the need to clarify this issue.

The reemergence of modern Europe's central problem—that of Germany—which, when the Berlin Wall fell, was thought to be years away from complete reunification, was imminent. The only issue had been what kind of security arrangements could be arranged to contain German power in the new post-cold-war Europe. On February 13, 1990, the two superpowers agreed on a framework for ending the forty-five-year division of Germany. First, the two governing Christian Democratic parties quickly agreed after the March election to a monetary and financial union by July 1990, the merger of the two governing Christian Democratic parties on October 1, and German reunification on October 3. Second, the four victors, having given their consent, the issue would be submitted in November for formal approval to the thirty-five-nation Conference on Security and Cooperation in Europe (CSCE, comprising sixteen NATO countries, seven WTO nations, and twelve neutral states), founded in Helsinki in 1975, at which time the participants had promised to commit themselves to respect existing frontiers (including the East German-Polish border) and to observe human rights.

Only one more date in 1990 was important, and that was December 2, the time scheduled for an all-German election of an all-German parliament. The new year would therefore start with the convening of this parliament and formation of a new government. This reunited Germany will be Europe's most powerful economic actor. Germany, like Japan vanquished in World War II, was once more becoming a principal actor in the newly emerging multipolar international system.

Decolonizing Brezhnev's Third World Outposts

A second symptom of the Soviet resolve to end the cold war was Soviet cooperation in resolving regional conflicts in the Third World. Gorbachev's reversal of Soviet expansionism was dramatic. The Soviets withdrew from Afghanistan and later admitted that the invasion had been a mistake, a symptom of their foreign policy's overreliance on force. In Angola, after prolonged failure to negotiate the exit of 50,000 Cuban troops from that country in return for South Africa's withdrawal from Namibia—from which territory the South Africans had frequently attacked Angola in pursuit of guerrilla forces operating in Namibia—a deal was negotiated under which the Cubans would withdraw in return for the independence of Namibia. Vietnam's withdrawal from Cambodia, which Vietnam had invaded to overthrow its murderous pro-Chinese government (which had killed more than 1 million of its own population of 8 million people), also was arranged. In both cases, the backing of the Cuban and Vietnamese operations in support of Marxist governments had been costly. Moscow wanted to cut its losses from these seemingly unending struggles, prolonged in part because of U.S. support for the rebels. The Soviet Union's overseas empire was proving too expensive.

Moreover, Soviet expansionism in the Third World had hindered U.S.-Soviet relations a decade earlier, thus constituting a reason to end these involvements. Presumably, the desire to avoid trouble with the United States was likely to prevent further expansionism. Even in the Middle East, Moscow moved, initially, toward rapprochement with Israel, with which it had broken diplomatic relations in 1967, and later to the re-establishment of relations; it also backed the U.S. idea of an Israeli-Palestinian dialogue. Instead of supporting the more radical parties and obstructing American peace efforts, the Soviet Union indicated that it preferred partnership with the United States. It has been reported, for example, that the Soviets cut back the arms they had for years been sending to Syria, Israel's strongest and most inflexible neighbor.

There was one important area where the Soviets continued to supply arms to anti-American forces despite soothing words about wishing to help seek peaceful settlements, and that area was Central America, where Congress, by cutting military assistance to the *contras,* made the Soviet effort pretty much cost-free. Soviet arms shipments to the Sandinistas continued; although the amounts were reduced, shipments from Cuba and Eastern Europe made up the difference. Soviet-made weapons also reached the guerrillas in El Salvador, where they launched a number of attacks in the capital city in 1989. The Bush administration strongly protested these policies of support as "cold war relics," diplomatically choosing to call these countries "Brezhnevite clients" during the informal summit meeting that Gorbachev and Bush held in December 1989 off the Mediterranean island of Malta.

Gorbachev denied sending weapons to Central America, but Bush would have none of it. Cuba and Nicaragua were Soviet clients. Washington clearly expected Moscow, which elsewhere had pressured its proxies to reach regional settlements, to do the same in America's backyard. Undoubtedly, Cuba's Fidel Castro, who had denounced the Soviet Union's retreat from socialism and considered himself one of the few true remaining Socialists, would resist counsels of restraint, although Cuba depended on Moscow for its economic survival. But even without Soviet arms shipments, Cuba and Nicaragua had, if not a surplus, then at least sufficient weapons to ship to the Salvadoran guerrillas. The more critical issue was the 1990 February election in Nicaragua, which, if fairly and freely conducted, held out the promise of resolving the disputes in Central America. Gorbachev reportedly prevailed on the Sandinistas to permit free elections such as those held in Eastern Europe. The Sandinistas, like Ferdinand Marcos in the Philippines, were supercon-fident of a victory in an election while they held the reins of power. Such a victory promised them greater legitimacy and the discrediting of any further U.S. support for the *contras*.

The Sandinistas completely underestimated the chances of the opposition winning the elections in a country wracked by civil war, drained of young men, and disabled by a huge inflation and a ruined economy. The Nicaraguans, tired of civil war and economic stagnation, in an election supervised by the United Nations, voted the Sandinistas out of office, thus making the *contra* issue moot. It was a stunning upset, totally unexpected by the Sandinista leadership. The consequences of the election could be equally dramatic if it isolated the leftist guerrillas in El Salvador and Cuba's Castro, weakening them both. In Nicaragua, national reconciliation, disbanding the *contras*, rebuilding the economy, ensuring a democratic and more just society, and reestablishing good relations with the United States were to be the new tasks. But such tasks depended on whether the new government could constrain the Sandinistas, who declared that they intended to "rule from below." They mobilized the civil service unions, calling for intermittent strikes, presumably for more pay (which the government could not provide because the Sandinistas had left the country almost bankrupt), but really to protest government efforts to reestablish a free market, thus undoing the Sandinistas' prior nationalization programs.

What happened to the Sandinistas and, more broadly, the collapse of the Soviet empire in Eastern Europe and in the Soviet Union itself, was not lost on the rebels in El Salvador. Long, previously unsuccessful negotiations to end that country's civil war became more productive, and in 1991, again with the help of the United Nations, the government and guerrillas agreed to end the conflict, although many details remained to be worked out on the guerrillas' place and role in Salvadoran politics after peace was reestablished.

While pro-Soviet governments remained in power in Afghanistan, Angola, and Cambodia, efforts continued either to replace them or broaden them to include other factions of the population. In Afghanistan, the United States and the Soviet Union agreed to stop supplying weapons to the opposing sides. In Angola, negotiations continued on the formation of a new govern-ment for the post-civil war period. And in Cambodia, the lengthy and often acrimonious negotiations held under UN auspices finally resulted in an agreement acceptable to all the contending parties, promising to end that bitter civil war as well. The only remaining source of real friction between

Washington and Moscow was Cuba. Although Castro felt Gorbachev had betrayed socialism and swore that socialism would continue to be practised on his island even if it were abandoned virtually everywhere else, Moscow discontinued its multibillion dollar subsidy in 1991, announcing that future economic relations with Cuba would be on a strict trade basis. The Soviet military training mission also would be withdrawn. The Soviet Union, itself seeking economic help from the West, was responding to American insistence that at least the United States would not consider such assistance while Moscow continued to provide Castro with $5 billion annually. Thus the Soviet retraction of power from the Third World continued.

Reducing Arms and Stabilizing the Balance

A consistent long-term U.S. goal in the superpower relationship has been to provide for a more stable arms environment through appropriate arms control agreements. More specifically, U.S. policy sought three objectives. The first, especially in view of Gorbachev's uncertain tenure, was to reach agreements to reduce strategic and conventional arms; once achieved, such arms reductions would be politically and economically difficult to reverse. The second was to reduce, if not eliminate, the likelihood of surprise attack. The third was to reduce the burden of defense spending and to realize a "peace dividend" to be spent on domestic needs. (For Gorbachev, this financial benefit was probably the driving force behind all his arms proposals. As the U.S. budget deficit grew, Bush also wanted to see a reduction in defense spending.)

From the beginning of the SALT process, SALT III was intended to greatly cut the strategic arsenals of both powers; SALT II had placed ceilings on these arsenals. Renamed START (Strategic Arms Reduction Talks) by the Reagan administration in order to emphasize radical reductions—a 50 percent cut—the objective was to cut the Soviet land-based missiles, which, with their multiple and accurate warheads, constituted the principal threat to the survival of American ICBMs. In short, reductions per se were not the objective; the aim was *stabilizing* reductions. By the time the Reagan administration left office, the START negotiations were substantially completed. Each side agreed to a ceiling of 1,600 delivery vehicles, an aggregate of 6,000 strategic weapons, and a ballistic missile warhead limit of 4,900. Although the overall cut in strategic forces was closer to a 30 percent reduction, it did cut the most destabilizing forces, ballistic missiles, by 50 percent; the Soviets would, for instance, cut their 308 SS-18 force (with ten warheads apiece), which had long worried U.S. policy makers, to 154. Nevertheless, the negotiations were stymied by a number of obstacles that slowed reaching an agreement until 1991.

The chief obstacle from the very beginning was SDI. The Soviets were persistent in stating that they would not reduce their ICBM force until they knew whether they would have to cope with American strategic defenses. But Reagan clung to his vision of SDI, and therefore the Soviets refused to sign a START treaty. To break the deadlock, Moscow in 1989 announced its willingness to sign a START treaty; the condition was that the United States would abide by the 1972 ABM agreement. While the two issues were finally "de-linked," at least formally, START's fate depends on Washington's future decisions about SDI development. The program admittedly had lost its main advocate and faced great technical difficulties and increasing congressional disenchantment at a time of a huge federal deficit, but support for SDI had become a token of party faithfulness to the right wing of the Republican party. Moreover, the war with Iraq *(see Chapter 14)* gave a scaled-down version of SDI a new lease on life because Iraq is only one of twenty or so smaller countries thought to be seeking missiles and weapons of mass destruction—nuclear, biological, and chemical—against which this kind of defensive system was considered the most effective.

Another major obstacle was the mobile ICBM. Often advocated as a solution to the problem of the increasing vulnerability of silo-based ICBMs, the Soviets had by the late 1980s deployed two mobile systems. The U.S. Air Force wanted to shift its fifty MX missiles with their ten warheads apiece from fixed silos to railroad flatcars during crises; many arms control advocates strongly preferred the U.S. deployment of a single warheaded mobile missile named the Midgetman. But the Reagan administration's position was to seek a ban on all mobile missiles because of the difficulties of verification. As the cold war waned, however, Congress became increasingly opposed to spending the large sums on either making the MX mobile or buying the Midgetman. Another possible solution was the reduction and eventual elimination of all missiles with multiple accurate warheads.

Bush, in fact, made a move toward this goal with an initial proposal to eliminate all mobile ICBMs late in the START negotiations. This came to naught because the Soviets already had deployed mobile land-based missiles (indeed, in 1990 they had reportedly doubled their 1989 arsenal of 190), and the United States had not. The president repeated his offer to negotiate the elimination of mobile MIRVed ICBMs later in 1991 when he ordered the removal of all U.S. tactical nuclear weapons from American forces on land, air, and sea, and a stand-down of the bombers and missiles that had previously been on twenty-four-hour alert. Both the rail-mobile MX and mobile Midgetman also were abandoned. Gorbachev, reciprocating, said that the Soviet Union would voluntarily reduce its warheads to 5,000 and he offered to negotiate radical reductions to about half of the remaining strategic forces once START had been ratified by both countries. Thus the arms race was being reversed.

In terms of conventional forces, after 1987 Gorbachev had talked repeatedly about a shift from an offensive military doctrine to a defensive one, as well as sizable military budget cuts as the Soviet Union scaled its forces back to "reasonable sufficiency." He promised and carried out unilateral reductions of Soviet forces, including the withdrawal of frontline troops and tanks, facing NATO. For WTO forces to shift to a strategy that could repel an attack but not launch a massive surprise attack on NATO, followed by a *Blitzkrieg* thrust into Western Europe, was obviously very much in the West's interest. Such a shift would constitute a significant change once brought into Soviet force structure and military exercises. It would greatly relieve Western fears caused by the sizable Soviet forces and Soviet military doctrine; and it would be a major sign that Soviet intentions had fundamentally changed. Until 1989, however, there remained a large gap between many of the Soviet statements about military cuts and restructuring and Soviet action because Soviet defense spending remained very high.

The conventional arms reduction negotiations, called the CFE (Central Front Europe) negotiations, sought to reduce Soviet forces in Eastern Europe (565,000 strong in 1988; 380,000 of them in East Germany) and American forces (326,000 troops, the bulk of them, 243,000, stationed in West Germany), to 275,000. CFE also sought equal numbers of tanks, armored personnel carriers, artillery pieces, and combat aircraft for NATO and WTO. But events in Eastern Europe were moving so fast that in January 1990 President Bush called for a further U.S.-Soviet reduction of troops to 195,000 in central Europe, with 30,000 more American troops outside of that area. Gorbachev, surprisingly, accepted the U.S. proposal in the 1990 CFE agreement, even though this cutback would leave the United States for the first time since the war with more troops in Europe than the Soviet Union. Militarily this was unimportant, but politically and psychologically it was further evidence of Soviet weakness. In any case, the 195,000 troop ceiling was unlikely to be the last word on reductions because of the strong domestic pressure in the United States to further cut U.S. forces to about 75,000. (By late 1991, they were down to 150,000.)

Such reductions seemed possible because by 1990 the Soviet-led alliance, organized to protect the Soviet-imposed Socialist systems, had fewer Socialist systems to defend as Eastern Europe began to "decommunize" in 1989; in these circumstances, Moscow could no longer count, if it ever could, on the armies of Czechoslovakia, Hungary, Poland, East Germany, Bulgaria, and Romania for any joint military action against the West. In addition, the first three of these countries have asked that Soviet forces be withdrawn from their soil. Moscow agreed to withdraw its forces from the first two countries by mid-1991; and Poland, by the end of 1992. In any case, WTO died shortly afterwards, to be formally buried in 1991.

Would NATO also disappear? That was unlikely, at least in the short run. The alliance continued to have several functions. One was to continue to guard the West against the possibility of a renewal of the Soviet threat. There was at the time still a widespread concern that Gorbachev might be overthrown by the old elite that opposed his domestic reforms and foreign policy shift away from the cold war. Even after the August 1991 attempted coup against Gorbachev, which led to the Soviet Union's demise *(see next section)*, the successor state retains significant military power. It may remain peaceful and friendly toward the West, but the West will not want to rely on goodwill alone. Another objective, although for diplomatic reasons it could not be spoken of openly, was to restrain the new Germany. Would its reunification give rise to yet another round of the "German problem"? The Europeans, after twice needing American power to defeat Germany, were unsure that they could manage a unified Germany by themselves. Retaining NATO would keep American power in Europe. In addition, the United States wanted the alliance as an institutional link and through it to influence the shape of the new emerging European order as the EC moved to greater economic and political integration.

NATO's long-term survival was more in doubt. Once Soviet troops were withdrawn from the former East Germany, at the latest by 1994, there would no longer be a rationale for keeping U.S. troops in Germany. German public opinion would increasingly regard them as occupation troops, indicating that Germany was not to be trusted despite a forty-year alliance. Moreover, American public opinion and Congress would not long support the continued presence of large numbers of American forces after the demise of WTO, the democratization of Poland, Hungary, and Czechoslovakia, and the pull-out of Soviet troops from Germany. Most important, however, was that the Soviet threat had vanished. France and Germany already have proposed the eventual formation of a European army and common foreign policies toward the Soviet Union, the United States, the Middle East, and certain policy areas like arms control and nuclear nonproliferation. While professing that such a plan—admittedly, years off—would be compatible with NATO, they see as inevitable the decrease of U.S. military presence in Europe and therefore a smaller security role for NATO as well in the post-cold-war era.

Despite these revolutionary changes, the "peace dividend" was relatively modest. The U.S. defense budget of almost $300 billion in 1990 was slated to decrease by only 25 percent by 1995, a figure that could go up to 30 percent due to the disappearance of the Soviet Union. The weakening of the party, secret police, and military-industrial complex removed a critical obstacle to the negotiation of deeper cuts in strategic nuclear and conventional arms and, therefore, greater savings. Both sides felt more secure; both could anticipate investing the savings realized from further arms reductions in the civilian sector of their economies. Nevertheless, such negotiations will be complex and require major concessions by each side; they will be difficult to conduct because Washington will no longer be negotiating with the Soviet Union but with the eleven-member Commonwealth of Independent States

Table 13-1   Commonwealth of Independent States

Area and Republics	Populations (to nearest hundred thousands)
Slavic Europe	
Belarus (formerly Byelorussia)	10,200,000
Moldova (formerly Moldavia)	4,300,000
Russia	147,400,000
Ukraine	52,000,000
The Caucasus	
Armenia	3,300,000
Azerbaijan	7,100,000
Georgia[1]	5,500,000
Soviet Central Asia	
Kazakhstan	16,500,000
Kyrgyzstan (formerly Kirghizstan)	4,400,000
Tajikistan (formerly Tadzhikistan)	3,600,000
Turkmenistan (formerly Turkmen)	3,600,000
Uzbekhistan	19,900,000

1. Currently seeking independent statehood, although may join CIS eventually.

(CIS) that replaced it in late 1991 *(see Table 13-1)*.

The major republics, on whose soil the strategic nuclear weapons are based, are Russia, Ukraine, Belarus, and Kazahkstan. Ukraine and Belarus have declared that they want to be nuclear-free states, leaving Russia as the prime inheritor of the former Soviet Union's nuclear arsenal; Kazakhstan has said it will keep some nuclear weapons as long as Russia does. To overcome the difficulty of negotiating with so many republics and encourage the three non-Russian republics to destroy their nuclear weapons, the United States acted unilaterally, announcing that it intended to reduce sharply its land- and sea-based MIRVed missiles, the backbone of the U.S. strategic nuclear forces. As Washington expected, this move elicited a response from Boris Yeltsin. Declaring that he did not consider the United States an enemy, and that his ultimate goal was the elimination of all nuclear weapons, Yeltsin said that Soviet missiles would no longer be targeted against American cities or military sites. Presumably, he too intended to make substantial cuts in the former Soviet strategic nuclear arsenal, also composed largely of missiles with multiple warheads, and use the money saved from the defense budget to help his transition to the free market economy he launched in January 1992. Thus, the possibilities of an accelerating arms race in reverse looked promising.

Human Rights, Reform, and the Disintegration of the Soviet Union

Perhaps the most important indication of the Soviet Union's willingness to end the cold war was its changing human rights policy. For years the United States had emphasized the need for improvement in this area. The reason for this is obvious: all other changes depended on the continued opening of Soviet society and politics. During the decades in which the Soviets invested in arms and heavy industry, the standard of living was sacrificed for the power of the state. The West, therefore, had to be reassured and know that it was no longer possible for the USSR to restrict consumption and invest disproportionately in the accumulation of arms.

Indeed, by 1990 there was no question that the Soviet system was undergoing a rapid and profound transformation. The disintegration of the economy led to a concomitant delegitimation of the political regime, which was further weakened by conflicts between Moscow and a number of Soviet republics. Demands for autonomy, if not independence, erupted in many republics, and ancient ethnic feuds reemerged. These events threatened the integrity of the Soviet state and compelled the regime to move Soviet tactical nuclear warheads out of the Baltics and the volatile southern republics to parts of the Russian republic it considered more politically stable. Most of all, the Communist party was showing increasing signs of disintegration and was losing its authority to impose decisions on the nation. In the Baltic, it was faced with the Lithuanian Communist party's defection from the Soviet party and its identification with Lithuania's demand for independence; in Azerbaijan, the Soviet army had to be sent in not only to restore order between the Azerbaijanis and Armenians, but to prevent the Communist government from falling into the hands of the Azerbaijani popular front—much as Communist regimes in Eastern Europe had fallen to the opposition groups there. In several cities and areas, party officials had to resign because of popular outrage over their corruption and privileges. Indeed, in Moscow, Leningrad, and other cities the emerging democratic political opposition inflicted embarrassing defeats on the Communists by winning majorities in elections.

Gorbachev, alert to popular disenchantment with the party, gradually shifted his base of power from the Communist party (whose conservative apparatus continued to resist his reforms) to the elected Supreme Soviet and the presidency, a post he held along with the general secretaryship of the party. He went even further by calling on the party to give up its seventy-year constitutional monopoly of power, although he clearly considered the party to be the most capable of guiding the nation through its turmoil. But for the party to remain the political vanguard, it would have to earn the Soviet people's trust, and this would require it to restructure itself. Gorbachev suggested that at some future point rival political parties might be established.

Equally revolutionary was Gorbachev's embrace of the free market for the failed Communist economy. Having already repudiated Lenin, Gorbachev now dumped Marx as well. Seventy-three years after the Bolshevik revolution, the Soviets reversed themselves; markets would replace bureaucracy, and capitalism would succeed socialism (and the freedom to worship would replace atheism). But Gorbachev, however revolutionary his rhetoric and declarations, hesitated to implement his reforms because one result would be a flow of power away from Moscow and the central government he headed. Another might be a social explosion. He feared that the end of subsidies to Soviet citizens for rent, food, health care, and education, and the end of subsidies for industry, would result in sharp rises in inflation and unemployment. And he could not discount the old guard's opposition.

In principle, then, the party had renounced both its political-economic dictatorship and intellectual heritage, but the real question was whether it had all happened too late. Could a political leadership that, after five years of growing economic shortages, which now included even bread and cigarettes, that no longer enjoyed sufficient political authority or popularity, take the tough measures required to implement wholesale economic changes? Had Gorbachev become the captain of the Soviet *Titanic* as the party increasingly lost control to the Supreme Soviet, the legislatures of the republics, municipal governments, popular fronts, and increasingly assertive workers' unions, all of which sought a greater devolution of power and policy? The strongest challenge to his power in a situation of the Communist system's declining legitimacy came from Yeltsin, who in May 1990 was elected to the presidency by the Supreme Soviet or legislature of the Russian Republic. Russia occupies two-thirds of the territory of the former Soviet Union and has almost half of its population and most of its oil, natural gas reserves, and coal. Yeltsin was quick to sense the popular disaffection with the power and privileges of the Communist party. Once Gorbachev's protégé, Yeltsin became his fiercest critic and archrival because the Soviet leader was, in Yeltsin's judgment, too timid to move quickly to change the system.

On the day after his election by the Russian parliament, Yeltsin challenged the system by proposing Russia's economic autonomy and a radical decentralization in which republic law took precedence over Soviet law and the president of the Soviet Union would have no greater authority than the presidents of the fifteen republics. Indeed, not only would Russia claim sovereignty and determine the prices of its natural resources, but also it would make its own agreements with the other members of the Soviet Union. And just to make his challenge clear, Yeltsin also announced that in 1991 he would seek to make the Russian presidency a popularly elected office, which he won overwhelmingly. His victory provided another contrast to Gorbachev, who had been elected by the Supreme Soviet. By being elected president of the Soviet Union's largest republic by the people for the first time in its thousand-year history, Yeltsin acquired a legitimacy Gorbachev did not have. At the

Communist Party Congress a few weeks later, Yeltsin warned the largely conservative party functionaries that the party must change its name and undemocratic methods or face inevitable "historical defeat"; he reminded them of the fate of the Communist parties in Eastern Europe. Criminal trials for party leaders, Yeltsin warned, were not beyond the realm of possibility if the party clung to its old ways and remained "in opposition to the people." Having delivered this warning, Yeltsin, together with the reformist mayors of Moscow and Leningrad, the nation's two largest cities, resigned from the party despite Gorbachev's efforts to maintain unity and an appeal to the radicals to help him fight the conservatives.

In a sense, Yeltsin's resignation was a symptom of a growing national disenchantment with the party and Gorbachev's declining popularity. The congress was barely over before the Ukraine, the Soviet Union's second-largest republic (the size of France), with a population of more than 50 million, declared its sovereignty and its laws above those of the Soviet Union. It also claimed an independent foreign policy role by stating it would be a neutral state, would not participate in military blocs, and would ban the production and deployment of nuclear weapons on its territory. The Ukraine's action was followed by a similar declaration from Byelorussia (now renamed Belarus); eventually all of the Soviet Union's fifteen republics issued sovereignty declarations, asserting either outright independence or more cautious assertions of their rights. Gorbachev's Soviet Union was indeed becoming the Soviet Disunion.

By late 1990 Gorbachev had become more and more irrelevant in domestic affairs. Yeltsin set the pace and scope of change by supporting the drive for independence by the Baltic republics and proposing a "500 days" plan for the radical transformation of the Soviet economy into a market economy. The revolution Gorbachev had unleashed threatened to devour him. During the annual May Day (May 1) parade in 1990, he had already observed protesters shouting slogans like "Down with the Red Fascist Empire," "Down with the KGB," "Seventy-two Years on the Road to Nowhere," "Gorbachev Resign," "A President Elected by the People," and "Socialism? No Thanks!"

Gorbachev found himself maneuvering between the increasingly radical forces on the left and the forces of reaction on the right, represented by the traditional instruments of Soviet power—the military, secret police, and Communist party bureaucracy—which had survived all his attempts at reform. They were the elite; they therefore had a strong vested interest in the status quo and had blocked most of Gorbachev's reforms. But to hold the union together, to stem the republics' nationalism, Gorbachev now aligned himself with the forces of "law and order." He dismissed many of his former liberal allies in the struggle for *glasnost* and *perestroika,* began cracking down on the Baltic republics, and reimposed a measure of censorship. The new course alienated his own foreign minister, who resigned in protest and warned the country of the possibility of a new dictatorship.

Gorbachev's new allies, however, tried to decrease his power and enhance their own because they felt that he was leading the country to chaos and anarchy, that he had retreated from Eastern Europe and given up the Soviet Union's World War II gains for increasing cooperation with the enemy, the United States and the West. In reaction, Gorbachev swung back to ally himself with the reformers. He made his peace with the republics. He promised the presidents of the nine republics who agreed to stay within the union, including Yeltsin, to turn the Soviet Union into a new voluntary federation in which all republics would have the right to join or be independent, choose their own forms of government, and exercise most of the power over their natural resources, industry, foreign trade, and taxes. He promised a new constitution and a newly elected central government.

Just as the new All-Union Treaty was to be signed, the hardliners struck. Fearing that their power was waning and that soon it would be too late, they launched a coup, arresting Gorbachev while he was on holiday. But the coup plotters failed to understand the effects of the six years of Gorbachev's policies. Led by the popularly elected Yeltsin, who showed enormous courage, the people of Moscow rallied behind Gorbachev, resisting those who would reimpose the old dictatorship. Even units of the military and secret police opposed the coup, which quickly collapsed. The result was to change the Soviet Union the world had known since 1917.

All the republics now wanted their independence from Moscow and central authority. The three Baltic republics were let go, and their independence as nations recognized by Moscow. At this point, seven of the twelve remaining republics, including Russia, planned to stay together in a loose confederation because they were still economically interdependent, although the agriculturally and industrially important Ukraine would not commit itself to creating a "common economic space" and a single currency, the foundation for a free market economy. What was absolutely clear was that the old regime had disgraced and discredited itself by the coup attempt. Statues of Communist leaders like Lenin were removed from public squares (Stalin had already come down earlier during the heyday of Gorbachev's reform program); the old imperial flag designed by Peter the Great flew over the Russian parliament, the center of the resistance to the coup; and Leningrad was renamed St. Petersburg, its pre-revolutionary name, in accordance with the wishes of its citizens. Many said that it was also time to remove Lenin's body from the mausoleum in Red Square.

The failed coup also resulted in the death of the Communist party. Yeltsin took sweeping measures against the Russian Communist party, closing all its offices and newspapers. Gorbachev, sensing the mood of the country and trying to salvage some of his authority—the crowds in Moscow during the coup had called Yeltsin's name, not Gorbachev's—ended the party's role as watchdog of the military, secret police, and government

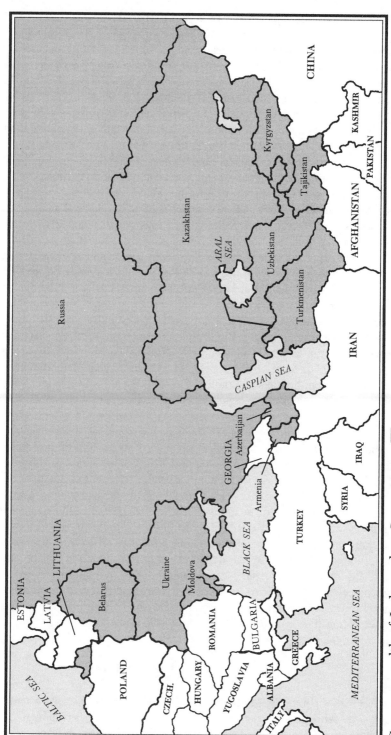

Commonwealth of Independent States 1992 ▨

bureaucracy and disbanded its leadership. For all practical purposes, the party as a governing body was dead. It could no longer block the path to democracy and radical economic reform. The revolution of 1917 had been undone in a stunningly rapid turn of events.

Yet, at the moment of decision, the seven republics that had endorsed the new union would not commit themselves, leaving its fate in the hands of their nationalistic parliaments. When the Ukraine voted on December 1, 1991, for independence and became Europe's fourth largest nation, it became clear that endless negotiations while the economic situation neared catastrophe could not stop the rapid rate of Soviet disintegration. With even a weak confederation now dead, Russia was left as the successor state to the Soviet Union. Indeed, this status had become overwhelmingly clear when the central government declared bankruptcy in November 1991 and Russia assumed its debts and promised to fund what remained of the central government's ministries. In capitalist language, this act constituted a buy out of the former Soviet Union. Russia also claimed the Soviet Union's permanent seat as one of the five great powers on the UN Security Council.

The Soviet Union was formally buried on December 8, 1991, when, in an act of desperation to stop the complete disintegration of the nation, the presidents of the three Slavic republics, Russia, Ukraine, and Byelorussia, representing 73 percent of the population and 80 percent of the territory of the Soviet Union, decided to establish a commonwealth of fully independent countries and invited other republics to join. The new Commonwealth of Independent States assumed all international obligations of the Soviet Union, including control over its nuclear arsenal. Coordinating bodies would be established to decide on cooperative policies in foreign affairs, defense, and economics. Subsequently, the commonwealth agreement was signed by eleven of the remaining twelve Soviet republics after the defections of the three Baltic states; the twelfth, Georgia was consumed by civil war. It remains to be seen whether the CIS will, in fact, survive or will eventually fall victim to the republics' nationalist and ethnic tensions and the pursuit of their individual interests. Indeed, will some of the republics themselves survive intact or will they subdivide further? What was clear is that Gorbachev had become a historical relic, the president of a country that no longer existed. On December 25, 1991, the red hammer and sickle flag that had flown over the Kremlin was lowered, seventy-four years after the Bolshevik Revolution. The Soviet Union had disappeared from the world's map.

A Marshall Plan for the CIS?

One of the major issues facing the West even before the coup attempt of 1991 was whether to assist the Soviet Union while it was undergoing its transformation. Gorbachev had withdrawn from Eastern Europe, allowed

German reunification, called off the cold war, signed two important arms control agreements—a conventional agreement between NATO and WTO and a strategic agreement sharply reducing the American and Soviet nuclear arsenals—and helped resolve several regional conflicts. The West had a vested interest in maintaining Gorbachev in power. The threat to him was not seen as coming from the democratic forces on the left but from the party officials and bureaucrats on the right. Should the West not try to keep him in power by sending economic aid to ease the lot of the Soviet people? Without such aid, the withdrawal of subsidies to the Soviet consumers and industry were expected to cause massive popular dissatisfaction as inflation and unemployment soared. Would that dissatisfaction not be the final blow to Gorbachev and be an incentive for the forces of reaction to seize power?

The Europeans already had provided some help. Germany, grateful to Gorbachev for permitting the reunification of the country after four decades of division, was providing more than $30 billion in credits and subsidies, some of which was to be used to support Soviet troops in what had been East Germany until their scheduled withdrawal in 1994. The United States had provided in excess of $1 billion to the Soviet Union to buy food from U.S. producers. But such piecemeal assistance, it was widely argued, needed to be replaced by a long-range strategy. The West would offer Gorbachev a "grand bargain": in return for implementing the necessary changes toward a market economy, the West proposed a multibillion dollar aid program over a number of years. At each stage of reform, more money would be released; in this way, the Western states would ensure that the money would not be wasted. If changes occurred and a free market economy emerged, the gains in security and the subsequent lower defense budgets would more than make up for the expense of this new Marshall Plan.

But critics called the proposal a "grand illusion." The aid given to Poland and other East European states was cited as the better road to follow. These states had thrown off the Communist party and government apparatus first. Aid in such circumstances could be useful in helping these countries begin their economic recovery. By contrast, the old Soviet elite was still clinging to power, constraining Gorbachev's reforms. Extending aid in these conditions would be pouring money down the proverbial rat hole. Nothing would change.

The West Europeans were generally in favor of the grand bargain; the United States and Japan thought the plan was a grand illusion. This debate was reinvigorated as the Soviet Union was declared officially dead and the new CIS took its place. In the words of the director of the Central Intelligence Agency, "All of the former Soviet republics face enormous economic, social, and political problems that will make the transition to democracy and a market economy difficult and potentially dangerous. The economy is in free fall with no prospects for reversal in sight. Severe economic conditions, including substantial food and fuel shortages in some areas, the disintegration of the armed forces and ongoing ethnic conflict will combine this winter to produce the most significant disorder in the former USSR since the Bolsheviks consolidated power." Secretary of State James Baker emphasized that the West's security interest would be deeply affected by the outcome of what was happening in the CIS. The West had a huge stake in the success of the new association. If it faltered in its efforts to build peaceful, democratic, and economically stable societies, possibly reverting to internal repression and external aggression, its future relations with the West could be jeopardized. The West could risk neither an economic collapse and a possible restoration of a dictatorship nor total disintegration and chaos in a country still equipped with thousands of nuclear weapons. Moreover, would not aid to assist a shift to free economy and away from militarization be offset by savings from defense budget cuts?

Baker therefore announced emergency airlifting of food to stricken CIS cities and a meeting in early 1992 of NATO, Japan, South Korea, Persian Gulf partners like Saudi Arabia, and international financial institutions, to collectively deal with "the wreckage of Communism" by addressing the longer-term problems of stabilizing the economy, establishing democratic institutions, and helping the republics destroy their nuclear weapons. While the conference focused on better coordinating aid rather than any increases of aid, such assistance was considered hardheaded and self-interested, reflecting U.S. and Western security concerns. The overriding question, however, remained whether the CIS would survive the same divisive nationalist, ethnic, and economic forces that had destroyed the Soviet Union. Above all, would Russia manage to avoid further subdivision, and would Yeltsin and other elected leaders survive the anger of their hungry constituents facing increasing unemployment, galloping inflation, and shortages in the stores? Would there yet be some right-wing reaction as people, who had little experience in democracy or free market economics, became more desperate and despairing?

Retrospect
and Prospects

NOW THAT the cold war is over, can we say that the United States has won and that the containment policy was successful? Or would it be more correct to say that the Soviet Union lost the cold war and that its defeat was basically self-inflicted? In the latter view, the containment policy did not play an essential role in bringing defeat about; indeed, even the failures of containment contributed to the Soviet Union's downfall. If the United States "won," then it was by default because the Soviet Union's demise was basically attributable to its system.[1] Its excessive centralization of power, of bureaucratic planning and supervision of every detail of Soviet life, economic and otherwise, its command economy and ideological rigidities all contributed to its undoing. Seventy years after the Revolution and at a staggering cost in human lives (estimated generally at more than 50 million dead), the Soviet standard of living was so low that even Eastern Europe, with its own severe economic problems, had by contrast appeared affluent for much of the period since World War II. According to the former Soviet Union's own statistics, about 40 percent of its population and almost 80 percent of the elderly live in poverty. Reportedly, one-third of its households had no running hot water, and another third had no running water at all. The Soviet Union was the only industrial society in which infant mortality had risen and male longevity declined. A large percentage of its hospitals had no hot water or adequate sewage facilities, and lacked basic sanitation.[2] Indeed, conditions were so bad that the Soviet Union had increasingly been described, not as an industrial society, but as an advanced developing society with nuclear weapons! Other

---

1. John Mueller, "Enough Rope," *New Republic,* July 3, 1989, 14.
2. Zbigniew Brzezinski, *Game Plan* (Boston: Atlantic Monthly Press, 1986), 37, 236-238.

societies have achieved the same level of social deprivation as the Soviet Union at far lesser cost. In Zbigniew Brzezinski's words, "Perhaps never before in history has such a gifted people, in control of such abundant resources, labored so hard for so long to produce so little." [3]

Ironically, it was the economy, which was supposed to have demonstrated the superiority of socialism, that failed. Deliberately isolating itself from what it saw as the global capitalist economy, the Soviet Union had intended to build an economy that was efficient and productive, assuring a bountiful life for the workers and peasants who had so long been deprived. Instead, the centralized command economy meant no domestic competition among firms, and its self-exclusion from the international economy ensured that it remained unchallenged by foreign competition. The Soviet economy thus became a textbook case of what free traders have long argued are the results of protectionism: inefficiency, lack of productivity, unresponsiveness to consumer wants, and a lack of technological innovation. The fact is that in 1987, after the failure of the initial economic reforms, Gorbachev declared that his country had economically stagnated so badly that he described it as being in "chapter eleven," in other words, bankrupt.

It is not surprising, then, that the Soviet Union became a new phenomenon among great powers: a one-dimensional power. Other great powers throughout history normally have been not only great military powers but also great economic and financial centers that have been distinguished by their art, culture, ideological beliefs, and political systems. Britain was a democracy and London was the world's financial center. The United States more recently has also served as the exemplar of democracy, and the dollar has replaced the British pound as the postwar international currency; American culture—from blue jeans to rock music to films and television programs—has worldwide global appeal, including behind the now-dismantled iron curtain. But the Soviet Union's postwar prestige was built entirely on its military power: its valiant resistance to and victory over Nazi Germany, its conquest of Eastern Europe, its notable achievements in space, its sizable and expanding peacetime forces and—before Afghanistan—its reputation for invincibility. In contrast to previous great-power struggles between nations with comparable levels of development, the cold war was a rivalry between a military *and* economic superpower, the United States, whose open society and free-market productivity held enormous appeal, and a military superpower, the USSR, whose totalitarian political system and command economy lost much of their appeal within the Soviet bloc and in most of the Third World as they provided neither freedom nor affluence.

To be sure, at one time the Soviet model had possessed political and ideological appeal. In the West it attracted intellectuals who, after the Great

---

3. Ibid., 123. Also see Brzezinski, *The Grand Failure* (New York: Charles Scribner's, 1989).

Depression, believed capitalism could not provide social justice, a decent standard of living, or steady employment to its workers. In countries like France and Italy it appealed to working classes that had benefited little from their own economic systems, and, with the post-1945 breakup of colonial empires, to leaders in many developing countries who saw the Soviet Union not only as an opponent of Western colonialism but also as a model of development for their own rapid industrialization. But as the benefits of the Western democratic welfare state and market economies became apparent (in contrast to the human and material deprivations engendered by the Soviet system and as evident in its own stagnant economy), Soviet communism lost most of its appeal—except to a few in the developing countries who saw in Marxism-Leninism a means of gaining and consolidating power in their countries, usually with the help of the Soviet Union and/or proxies like the Cubans.

Communism's focus and efficiency in producing military hardware also contributed to the defeat of the Soviet Union in the cold war. Its emphasis on producing weapons was understandable to a degree. As a state with few natural protective barriers, frequently invaded throughout its history, first Russia and then the Soviet Union kept sizable standing forces for its defense. Its twentieth-century experiences with Germany did nothing to relieve long-held concerns for its safety. The Soviet outlook on politics as a constant struggle and its perceptions of enemies everywhere—including the People's Republic of China (PRC), which was defined as a heretical state sliding back to capitalism!—greatly aggravated the longtime Russian sense of insecurity. Indeed, this fear is often referred to as paranoia. But whether Soviet expansionism stemmed from a defensive preoccupation with security or from an offensive ideological goal of aggrandizement, Moscow's drive for absolute security left other states feeling absolutely insecure. It is no wonder that it drove all of its great power neighbors (Western Europe on one side, China and Japan on the other) into an encircling alignment with the United States. The surprise would have been if in these circumstances the Soviet Union had not driven itself into virtual bankruptcy.

It has even been argued that Soviet successes, like the expansions in the 1970s, considered setbacks to the United States at the time, were actually counterproductive, adding to the Soviet Union's woes. Angola in 1976, Ethiopia in 1977, and Afghanistan, Grenada, and Nicaragua in 1979 are supposed to have given the Soviet bear a bad case of indigestion. Indeed, the logic of this thesis that the more the Soviet Union expanded, the greater the cost, is that the containment policy was not an essential ingredient in stopping Soviet expansionism; indeed, it was precisely when containment failed that the Soviet Union's burden became too great to bear.[4] Soviet expansion, this suggests, would thus have reached its limits even in the absence of American countervailing power.

---

4. Mueller, "Enough Rope," 15.

Did the United States Win or the Soviet Union Lose?

There can be little doubt that the Soviet economy and paranoia contributed to the Soviet Union's downfall. Communism certainly deserves more credit than it has perhaps received for its role in its own collapse. But to conclude from this that the containment policy was not necessary, or, if necessary, was not a key ingredient in the fading of the cold war, is to differ with the Soviet Union's potential victims. As the United States attempted to withdraw from Europe after World War II, as it had after World War I, countries like Iran and Turkey, followed by those in Western Europe, pleaded with the United States to help them. These countries could not have resisted Soviet pressures by themselves. All saw their independence and national integrity at stake. They saw America's expansion of power as their only protection. The collapse of all the former great powers of Western Europe left the Soviet Union as the hegemon in Eurasia. Had the United States retired to isolationism, the countries on the periphery of the Soviet Union on the eastern Mediterranean, as well as the countries of Western Europe, would have had little choice but to submit to Soviet terms.

The major reason for the U.S. reentry into the European balance was to prevent the Soviet Union from capturing and organizing the largest pool of skilled workers, scientists, engineers, and industrial potential next to the United States. Allowing the Soviet Union to dominate Western Europe—indeed, Eurasia—and to control its resources would have constituted a tremendous shift of the balance of power toward the East; such a shift was as unacceptable to the United States after 1945 as had been the shift toward Germany in the two world wars. Because the United States is protected by oceans on two sides, the western rimland of Eurasia was its first line of defense, frustrating its continental challenger from dominating the Eurasian landmass; the latter obviously considered America's postwar presence in Europe as an obstacle to the fulfillment of its ambitions.

Western Europe remained the pivotal strategic stake throughout the cold war. In Berlin in the late 1940s, as well as late 1950s, early 1960s, and again during the INF crisis in the late 1970s and early 1980s, the Soviets repeatedly tried to intimidate the Western nations, to divide them (especially West Germany from the United States) and to drive the United States back to its shores. It was the containment policy here, as elsewhere, that made Moscow cautious about expanding its power. Had there been no American opposition, who can say that the Soviets would have failed to organize Western Europe and made themselves into a far more productive state, affording both a reasonable standard of living and formidable military power—and presenting an overwhelming threat to the United States? All that can safely be said is that the ancient rule of states is a prudent one: power must be met by countervailing power. A balance among states is the only guarantee that they will retain their independence and enjoy their way of life. Power is the best antidote to power. Without containment, the inefficiencies of the Soviet system might not have mattered much; and as a hegemon, the Soviet Union would not have had to engage—let along overreact—in a costly, continuous arms competition.

The aim of containment, however, was not only to block Soviet domination of Western Europe and the rest of Eurasia, but to win time for the Soviet leadership to reexamine its aims and its outlook on world affairs. Fundamentally, the American definition of the cold war rested largely and correctly on an ideological explanation of Soviet behavior. In George Kennan's original explanation, the United States had

> it in its power to increase enormously the strains under which Soviet policy must operate, to force upon the Kremlin a far greater degree of moderation and circumspection than it has had to observe in recent years, and in this way *to promote tendencies which must eventually find their outlet in either the breakup or the gradual mellowing of Soviet power. For no mystical, messianic movement—and particularly that of the Kremlin—can face frustration indefinitely without eventually adjusting itself in one way or another to the logic of that state of affairs.*[5]

In retrospect, these words were prophetic. Containment achieved its aim and, by doing so, compelled the Soviet Union to moderate its behavior. But for U.S. policy over the past forty years, the Kremlin would not have "mellowed."

The importance of the containment policy becomes even more evident when contrasted to the period before it was put into effect. If the principal causes of the cold war were the structure of the postwar state system and the Soviet style in foreign policy, America's national style made its own contribution. By failing to take a firm stand against Soviet policy during World War II, after it had become evident from repeated episodes that accommodating Soviet interests in Eastern Europe and Asia was impossible, the United States has to accept some of the blame for the subsequent cold war. This is not to say that the United States passively accommodated Soviet security concerns, but only that it did not oppose Stalin early enough, that it continued to cling to its hope for postwar amity with the Soviet Union despite Soviet behavior in the late stages of the war, and that after hostilities had ceased, it dissipated its strength immediately in a helter-skelter demobilization. Stalin respected American power and was a cautious statesman; but when President Roosevelt informed him that American troops were to be withdrawn from Europe after two years, Stalin did not need to concern himself about American protests against Soviet actions in Eastern Europe. Protests were one thing, action another. Not until after the war did the United States act and draw the lines beyond which Soviet expansion would not be tolerated.

---

5. George Kennan, *American Diplomacy, 1900-1950* (Chicago: University of Chicago Press, 1951), 127-128 (italics supplied).

Containment was, of course, not a flawless policy. Once the cold war started, U.S. misperceptions, like Soviet ones, fed the superpower conflict. Washington frequently exaggerated Soviet military capabilities. Fears of Soviet superiority—the bomber gap in the 1950s, the missile gaps a few years later, the ABM gap in the mid-1960s, and "the window of vulnerability" in the 1970s—helped to fuel the arms competition already well under way owing to Soviet insecurity. In addition, the U.S. emphasis on anticommunism meant American policy was often insensitive to the nationalism of the new nations. The METO and SEATO alliances, as a result, proved weak reeds for containing communism, alienating important states such as Egypt and India, which shifted toward the Soviet Union, aggravating regional rivalries, and aligning the United States with discredited regimes like Nationalist China. Indeed, in the name of anticommunism, Washington often supported authoritarian, right-wing regimes in the Third World; it saw no democratic alternatives to the regimes it backed other than left-wing pro-Soviet and/or Chinese ones, which were unacceptable.

The U.S. government also consistently exaggerated the monolithic nature of international communism. The fall of Nationalist China, the Korean War, and the Communist Chinese intervention in that war transformed the containment policy, which originally was limited to responding to Soviet moves in the eastern Mediterranean and Western Europe, to a global anticommunism. The events of 1949 and 1950 led to virulent anticommunism in the United States, with the Republicans (notably Senator Joe McCarthy) accusing the Democrats of being "soft on Communism" and winning two presidential elections. Future Democratic administrations would therefore not be able to exploit the growing differences between the Soviet Union and China; instead, seeking to avoid being charged with the "loss of Indochina," as they had been with the "loss of China," Democratic administrations intervened militarily in Vietnam. The American penchant for crusading, already vividly demonstrated in two "hot" wars, was not to be denied in the cold war. But this failure to distinguish between vital and secondary interests—this inability to discriminate between different Communist regimes—resulted in a war that the United States could not win, divided the country deeply, and undermined the domestic consensus that had been the basis of the cold war. Ironically, however, Vietnam destroyed American anticommunism, and U.S. policy shifted back toward the containment of Soviet power, but this time in "alliance" with the PRC.

The Soviet Union was only one of the two challenges the United States faced at the end of World War II. The other was the atomic bomb, and the two were to be intimately related in the years that followed. What is most striking about the American-Soviet relationship, as both powers armed themselves heavily with nuclear weapons, is that the two superpowers have successfully avoided sparking a war from any of their political quarrels, confrontations, crises, limited wars, and interventions: Iran (1946), Greece

(1947), Berlin (1948-1949), Korea (1950-1953), East Germany (1953), Hungary (1956), Berlin (1958-1961), Cuba (1962), Czechoslovakia (1968), Vietnam (1964-1973), the Arab-Israeli wars (1956, 1967, 1973), Afghanistan (1979), Poland (1981), and the Korean jetliner incident (1983). The existence of "the bomb" disciplined the conduct of the superpowers' foreign policy. The age of the "absolute weapon" that could destroy the nations that dared use it was also the age of deterrence, crisis management, limited wars, and wars by proxy. The nuclear peace was kept for more than forty-five years. Indeed, the nuclear age not only avoided a superpower war but also *eliminated all great-power wars*, a feat due in no small measure to the caution exercised by American and Soviet leaders, who were fearful of committing mutual suicide.

Nevertheless, most of the credit for avoiding a nuclear catastrophe belongs to American leadership. Until 1949 the United States held an atomic monopoly; and until the 1970s it had strategic superiority. At the time of the Cuban Missile Crisis in 1962, the Soviet Union had fewer than fifty missiles, all of which were deployed above ground and whose liquid fueling would take several hours. Yet the United States, largely invulnerable for much of that period, certainly during the mid- to late 1940s and early 1950s, at no time used its nuclear weapons to respond to challenges, whether these were Soviet efforts to subvert Iran, pressure on Turkey, the seizure of power in Czechoslovakia, the blockade of Berlin, or the invasion of Korea. Even in the late 1950s, after the Soviets had tested the first thermonuclear device and thereby gained the capability to impose vast destruction and loss of life on the United States if only a few of their bombers got through, the Strategic Air Command still could have launched a preemptive strike to disarm the small force of intercontinental Soviet bombers. U.S. leaders did not resort to nuclear weapons because they and the American people were morally and politically opposed to using weapons of mass destruction, and a preemptive strike against an enemy contravened both the American tradition of fairness as well as the law that Congress declared war. Instead, they emphasized a second-strike deterrent policy and arms control. Had Stalin possessed a nuclear monopoly or superiority, would he have been similarly restrained in advancing the Soviet Union's expansionist goals? Or Khrushchev or Brezhnev? The answer would seem to be no.

But nuclear weapons, while they enabled the United States to pursue peace and security—avoiding both a world war and restraining Soviet expansion—also provided another, generally much overlooked, advantage: defense on the cheap. These weapons allowed the American people—and the West Europeans—to enjoy peace and security without any significant sacrifice of their prosperity and freedom. Quite the opposite: both blossomed while Soviet military capabilities grew. But for these new and awesome arms, the United States could not have demobilized its armed forces either as rapidly or to the same degree as it did after World War II. Instead, it and its NATO allies would have had to maintain large standing armies. The price of such forces, with their enormous requirements of everything from manpower to tanks, artillery, armored personnel carriers, and fighter aircraft, would have been extremely high. Furthermore, such funding of a permanent and sizable military would have set back the postwar economic "miracles" in the United States and Western Europe, in which standards of living reached all-time highs. It also would have constrained the expansion of the welfare state on both sides of the Atlantic. In addition, funding such large standing armies would have limited the allies' ability to provide economic aid to the developing countries (and earlier, the generous U.S. funding of the Marshall Plan to revive Europe in 1948). It might even have compelled the United States and its allies to transform themselves into garrison states with whatever sacrifices in democratic liberties this might have demanded as long as the Soviet bloc was highly armed. In short, maintaining the balance of power might have jeopardized the very liberties the United States and its democratic allies were seeking to defend. The alternative of accepting a militarily inferior position in order not to surrender either prosperity or freedom, however, was an even riskier course. Nuclear weapons saved the Western states from having to choose among unpalatable alternatives; they permitted peace, security, freedom, and prosperity without undue sacrifice.

If containment was critical to the defeat of the Soviet Union in the cold war, and nuclear weapons enabled the United States and its Western allies to preserve their security and freedom while simultaneously enjoying the highest standards of living in their histories, two conclusions seem clear. The first is that the nature of regimes is crucial. For all of the attention paid to nuclear weapons and the importance of arms control in stabilizing the nuclear balance, it was the Soviet regime that constituted the principal threat to U.S. and allied security. Yet during the Reagan administration's first term, which began in 1981, the public debate in the United States (as in Western Europe) appeared almost totally preoccupied with the inherent danger of nuclear arms. Groups ranging from the Physicians for Social Responsibility to the hierarchy of the U.S. Catholic church to all but one of the 1984 Democratic party presidential candidates to the major television networks feared that Reagan's rearmament program would ignite a nuclear arms race and nuclear war. Nuclear arms, in short, were defined as the overwhelming danger to the peace of the world.

Although most of these weapons still exist, no one today worries about an all-out nuclear war. The reasons are the changes in the Soviet Union: the economic collapse of the Soviet Union; Gorbachev's "new thinking" and suing for peace in the cold war; the elimination of the Soviet-imposed regimes in Eastern Europe and the disappearance of the WTO; the disintegration of the Soviet state, especially after the failed coup of 1991; and the subsequent elimination of the Communist party as the governing party, disintegration of the Soviet Union, and new leadership roles of political figures who profess commitments to democratic aspirations. Thus, while former Soviet nuclear capabilities, now under Russian control, remain huge, the change in regime produced a drastic reduction of the threat of war. Russia's president, indeed, has declared that he does not consider the United States an adversary anymore.

The second conclusion is that American leadership in organizing opposition to Soviet policies was pivotal. After World War II, it was the states threatened by Soviet expansion that most sought a countervailing U.S. expansion of power. In the 1980s it was U.S. leadership that stood firm and organized resistance to the Soviet manipulation of the INF issue to break the Western alliance; it was Moscow that finally broke and capitulated. It was U.S. leadership that conveyed to the Soviet Union that it could not win the arms race. Faced with the expense of a new arms competition that it could not win because it was falling farther behind the United States technologically, Moscow finally called off the cold war. And it was U.S. leadership that led Moscow to recognize the futility of its Third World expansion; trapped by costly, endless civil wars in which the United States backed those fighting the Soviet-supported governments, Gorbachev negotiated a series of regional settlements. Moreover, as if to reemphasize the above points in the immediate post-cold-war era, Saddam Hussein in Iraq left little doubt that it was the nature of his regime that was the main threat to peace and security, and that American leadership was indispensable in organizing the resistance and defeating his bid to become the dominant Persian Gulf power with control over the world's oil supplies.

The First Post-Cold-War Crisis

As the cold war was ending, certain expectations were widespread. The world would finally enjoy a period of peace, international tensions and defense budgets would decline, and the so-called peace dividends would translate into lower taxes or better-funded social programs, or both. Military power, it was thought, would play a considerably smaller role in the world, and economic power would be the most important means of exercising political influence. Both Japan, with its global corporations, its technological advances, and its investment in real assets overseas, and Germany would play leading roles in the world. The United States would play a lesser role.

This was the thinking until August 2, 1990, when Hussein, exceedingly self-confident following what he believed to be a victory over Iran, directed his large battle-tested army to invade neighboring Kuwait. The Iraqi army, equipped with the Soviet Union's best military weapons plus Chinese-made missiles and domestically produced poison gas, quickly overran the Kuwaiti capital but provoked nearly unanimous international outrage that resulted in direct U.S. military intervention. The ensuing crisis demonstrated that the widely believed demise of military power and the end of U.S. leadership in the world were premature.

During the Iran-Iraq war Kuwait had loaned Iraq $15 billion and pumped oil on its behalf. Now $80 billion in debt because of his eight-year-long war and dependent on oil exports for income, the Iraqi strongman saw Kuwaiti coffers as one way to ease his country's financial crisis. Earlier he had sought to increase Iraq's revenues by forcing up OPEC oil prices. He did so by threatening Kuwait and the other Persian Gulf oil kingdoms that overproduced their OPEC-set quotas and kept oil prices below $20 a barrel. Despite OPEC's agreement to raise prices, Hussein's army invaded oil-rich Kuwait, thereby wiping out his debt, seizing Kuwait's oil fields, and increasing his influence over OPEC production and pricing. Money, in short, precipitated this attack. The debtor wiped out his creditor in an international version of an old-fashioned stick-up.

With his army now poised on the border of Saudi Arabia, which also had lent him billions during the war, and the Arab world afraid of him, Saddam Hussein was in fact seeking broader aims than just reducing his debt and bolstering his income. By demonstrating that his was the most powerful state in the Persian Gulf and the Arab world, he sought to achieve at least two additional objectives. One was to intimidate the Persian Gulf oil kingdoms and to assert his dominance over the Gulf, which he thought was his due after his alleged victory over Iran, the previous claimant. The other was to establish his leadership over the Arab world, a goal he had tried to achieve by his attack on Iran. Hussein had thought he could impress the other Arab states by quickly defeating Iran, now no longer a close friend of the United States and in the midst of revolution and turmoil. Egypt, traditionally the leader of the Arab states, had lost that status when it made peace with Israel and was seen by other Arab states as having gone too far to accommodate the United States; and Syria, another frequent rival for Arab leadership, was left isolated as Moscow scaled back its cold war efforts. There was really no one, therefore, to oppose Hussein's bid for power.

Iraq's leader was no doubt also eager to settle a score with Syria, which had supported Iran during the war, and to champion the Palestinian cause, especially in the Israeli-occupied territories. Such moves were designed to help him become the Nasser of the 1990s but had the effect of highlighting, once again, the myth of Arab unity. At war almost constantly since assuming Iraq's presidency in 1979, Hussein also had threatened that he would "scorch half of Israel" with chemical weapons if it attacked the nuclear reactor Iraq was rebuilding in the wake of Israel's 1981 attack. U.S. estimates were that Iraq would acquire nuclear arms within three to five years. Later, he broadened that threat: if Israel attacked *any* Arab state, not just the Iraqi nuclear reactor, Iraq would use chemical weapons against it.

Ultimately, as leader of the Arab world, his real target was the United States. By establishing Iraq as the dominant power in the region, Hussein could then lead an anti-American alliance in a "holy war" against Israel, the pro-American Persian Gulf oil kingdoms (Saudi Arabia, Bahrain, Qatar, the United Arab Emirates, and Kuwait) and other moderate states such as Egypt. (Jordan's King Hussein, long pro-Western, but fearing that the hard-line Israeli government might try to drive the Palestinians out of the West Bank into Jordan, thus destabilizing his regime, had moved toward Iraq for support. He was now trapped between Washington and Baghdad.) But Saddam Hussein represented a danger even to a hard-line state like Syria, which had aligned itself with Iran against Iraq during their war. Twice already Hussein had shown that he was quite willing to invade his neighbors and that past friendship provided no protection.

As a result of Iraq's occupation of Kuwait (Iraq and Kuwait together held 20 percent of the world's oil reserves), oil prices shot up immediately, worsening the U.S. trade deficit, threatening a rising inflation rate, and further weakening an economy already perched on the verge of a recession. Indeed, as Iraqi forces massed near the Saudi Arabian border in August 1990, the possibility that Saddam Hussein might soon control 40 percent of world oil reserves and gain control over oil production levels and pricing led the industrial democracies to act. Aware of the threat posed by Hussein to their well-being and to that of the developing countries, the NATO countries and Japan froze Iraqi assets and those of the deposed government of Kuwait. This was accompanied by a UN-sanctioned embargo on Iraqi oil and Iraqi-controlled Kuwaiti oil. Iraq was vulnerable to such economic pressures over the long term. Turkey and Saudi Arabia turned off Iraqi pipelines that had been built in the 1980s to bypass Iranian interference with Iraqi oil shipments through the Gulf. A Western naval blockade of the Gulf would enforce an embargo. The big question was whether Iraq's principal customers would continue the embargo over the weeks or months necessary to bankrupt the Iraqi economy.

None of the options was cost-free: the embargo meant a decrease in production of 4 million barrels per day and higher oil prices, although that might be mitigated to some degree by increased production by other oil-producing states. But these options posed risks because Saddam Hussein was a man with formidable military forces and without any scruples (as he showed once again by holding thousands of Western citizens as human shields at sites the Iraqis feared would be bombed). An Iraqi invasion of Saudi Arabia presumably would lead to U.S. intervention if the Saudis requested it—by no means a certainty at the outset of the crisis, given Saudi Arabia's weakness and fear of Iraq. Indeed, the Arabs' first reaction was to warn against "outside" intervention, stating that they would settle their own problems. But the Saudi rulers, concerned about their survival after seeing Kuwait's king flee his country, decided to request U.S. military assistance as Iraqi forces in Kuwait were poised on the Saudi frontier and the Arab states were unable to devise a response. The United States sent in jet fighters and tens of thousands of troops, in addition to large naval forces already on the

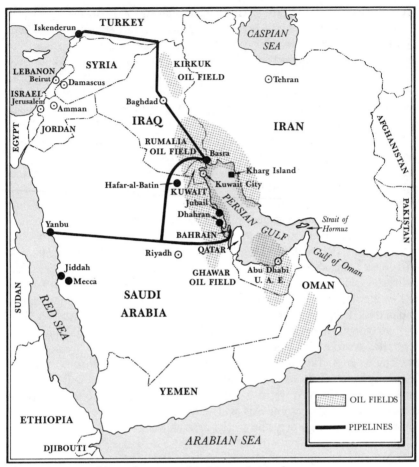

The Persian Gulf, with Key Oilfields and Pipelines

way to the Gulf and the Mediterranean. The president stated U.S. aims as the defense of Saudi Arabia and the restoration of Kuwait as an independent state.

It was another lesson in power politics: After the collapse of British power "East of Suez," Washington had first tried to use Iran as a surrogate for American power. When Iran sought hegemony over the Gulf following the Islamic revolution, Washington supported Iraq in its efforts to block Iran's ambition. Now that Iraq had decided to assume that same quest, the United States found there was no substitute for U.S. power to keeping a balance in that area of the world. This might be no short-term task, particularly after Saddam Hussein unexpectedly offered Iran peace terms in which Iraq conceded all the disputed territories that it had used as a pretext for attacking Iran in 1980. In short, it would have nothing to show for its "victory" in the eight-year-war, although it eliminated the threat on the Iran-Iraq frontier and freed up troops to be moved elsewhere; the concessions to Iran, Iraq probably hoped, might also help it break the economic blockade, but Iran respected the UN sanctions. Hussein's withdrawal from the territory he had won in the war with Iran, however, made an unconditional pull-out from Kuwait less likely because he would have nothing to show for his aggression this time either. And because President Bush had publicly stated an Iraqi withdrawal from Kuwait as one of his goals, and Bush could not back down without a loss of face and political support at home, a peaceful resolution of this crisis would be difficult to achieve.

The Bush administration proceeded with the largest U.S. troop buildup since the Vietnam War. In August it sent over a force of 100,000 troops, which was then increased to 250,000, to deter an attack on Saudi Arabia. The Bush administration decided to double that force in November to face the approximately equal number of Iraqi forces in Kuwait and southern Iraq and 3,500 Iraqi tanks. The administration declared that the possibility of a war with the United States and allied forces might compel Saddam Hussein to withdraw from Kuwait and restore its government. But, if it did not, the coalition forces would be large enough to force the Iraqi army to pull out of the country whose people it was treating with barbarous cruelty.

Faced with possible economic strangulation, confronted by the likelihood that retreat would mean relinquishing his dream of regional hegemony—perhaps even his hold on power in Baghdad—would Saddam Hussein surrender Kuwait? He had annexed his prize, declaring it to be a province of Iraq. Would he not wait out the embargo while he attempted to stir up the Arab masses against "American imperialism" and the oil-rich Arab rulers who, he charged, were subservient to the West? Hussein might even try, as he repeatedly threatened, to attack Israel, or provoke it by sending troops into Jordan in an attempt to lead the Arab masses in a crusade against what he would call a joint U.S.-Israeli assault on the Arab world. Perhaps he would use terrorist attacks; after all, some of the area's most vicious terrorist groups were sheltered in Baghdad. The Iraqi leader was a big risk taker, commanded powerful forces, and was cold-blooded enough to use poison gas. In a war, he vowed to destroy the Saudi oil fields on which the West was so dependent, as well as the Kuwaiti fields; faced with defeat, he might even try to destroy his own.

But could the West really accept Saddam Hussein's fait accompli in Kuwait and avoid the risks and costs inherent in a confrontation over Saudi Arabia when in a few years this ruthless dictator with his enormous ambitions would possess nuclear weapons and missiles? This was a contest over power and domination. The stakes were clear: Hussein's control over oil prices and the survival of Arab regimes opposed to his attempt to become master of the area. Having accepted the challenge, the United States could not afford to back off without endangering its security, its economic future, and its superpower status. If it failed its Arab friends in their moment of peril, they might never trust it again; rather, they would submit to Iraq. The question was not whether to answer the Iraqi challenge, but whether to confront it at once or later under worse circumstances. Would a diplomatic solution that did not eliminate the Iraqi war machine, in fact, be a solution at all?

Indeed, in what was supposed to be a postmilitary international system, the Iraqi strongman changed everything: using blackmail and force to attain his commercial and political ends, Hussein threatened untold damage to international commerce and the world economy. He also reminded the world that it remains a very dangerous place and that military power continues to play a pivotal and very visible role. Indeed, quite apart from the oil, Saddam Hussein, like Libya's Colonel Qaddafi, posed serious problems for the post-cold-war world: not only did they represent threats to neighboring countries, but increasingly, as they acquired long-range missiles, to states farther away. Toward the end of the Reagan administration, the United States had considered bombing suspected Libyan chemical weapons-producing facilities. If Iraq had pulled out of Kuwait and the crisis had been resolved diplomatically, it still would have left in power a man who not only had large military and poison gas capabilities but who was also actively seeking nuclear weapons. How would the crisis have evolved if Saddam Hussein already had put together a nuclear arsenal, which he would have done if Israel had not bombed his reactors in 1981. Would the man who resorted to poison gas in his war with Iran and who used chemical weapons against his own country's Kurdish minority have hesitated to use an atomic or hydrogen bomb? Was any outcome of the crisis acceptable short of the destruction of Iraqi chemical-, nuclear-, and missile-producing facilities? Would a postponed crisis not reappear in a few years when Iraq might possess missiles with a range to hit Europe and possibly the United States (Iraq had tested a three-stage rocket)? The estimated time for an Iraqi bomb ranged from three years to ten years, but after the conflict, it turned out that the Iraqi nuclear program was far more advanced than the United States had thought. Iraq was probably within twelve to eighteen months of having two or three bombs. In any case, postponing a showdown had little appeal.

The stage was set for a showdown. The United Nations gave Saddam Hussein a mid-January deadline to withdraw from Kuwait. If he refused, force would be used to eject him. This remarkable UN unanimity was not matched by the U.S. Congress. It insisted that President Bush come to it and gain its assent before he used force. Bush at first tried to avoid going to the Democratically controlled Congress, fearing that it would turn him down, embarrass and humiliate the United States, and undermine its goals. The Democrats, the party of intervention in Vietnam, were still haunted by that war. While declaring that they supported the president's goals of defending Saudi Arabia and restoring independence to Kuwait, they argued that economic sanctions would achieve these objectives. Within six months, perhaps a year, possibly two years, Iraq would have to comply because, with its oil exports cut off, it would run out of money. Clearly, the Democrats wanted to avoid a war that could cost heavy casualties; the commonly projected figures were 5,000 to 20,000. The Iraqi army, said to be the fourth largest in the world, had gained eight years of experience in the war against Iran, and specialized in defensive warfare. The Democrats' counsel for patience and economic sanctions, therefore, did not mean that if the strategy failed to achieve the aims the president had set, the Democrats would later vote for the use of force. They would not. It was simply incredible that in the fall of 1991 or in the spring or summer of 1992, with the presidential campaign in full swing, that going to war was a real option.

In these circumstances, Bush was initially tempted to rely on the UN vote for legitimizing the use of force. But in early January 1991, with the UN deadline nearing, he changed his mind and decided that he needed congressional approval before taking the nation into war. After intense debate, Congress approved. The Senate vote was in doubt until the last moment; only ten Democrats, only one of whom was from north of the Mason-Dixon line, voted with the Republicans to approve, 52-47, the resolution backing the use of force after January 15. While the margin in the House was more comfortable, the fact remains that 80 percent of Senate Democrats and 70 percent of House Democrats, including the entire Democratic leadership in both Houses, voted against supporting the president. The vote raised once more the question posed in every presidential election since Vietnam: if the Democrats opposed the use of force in this situation when the aggression was so unambiguous, the stakes so great, and the UN's support so powerful, when would they use force in defense of vital U.S. interests?

War was now likely. The president had decided that economic sanctions would be ineffective. The concerns about these sanctions were several. One was that the U.S.-European-Arab-Soviet coalition would not hold. Before August 1990 the suggestion of such a disparate alliance would have been dismissed as impossible. Any one of many events could blow the coalition apart and almost did: trouble between the Israelis and Palestinians, outraging Arabs whose cooperation with the friend of Israel against another Arab state was a risky and courageous course; the resignation of the Soviet foreign minister, jeopardizing Soviet cooperation and the effort to demonstrate to its former rivals that the Soviet Union had truly changed its behavior; and economic pain for some of the members of the coalition who were financially harmed by their participation in the sanctions imposed upon Iraq. Another concern was that most embargoes spring leaks after a while.

When the January 15 deadline passed and Saddam Hussein had not withdrawn, the United States and its allies decided to use force. The Iraqi dictator either did not expect the United States to go to war against him or he thought that if it did, attacks against his forces would result in heavy U.S. casualties. He apparently anticipated that once the United States suffered losses, criticism of the war and pressure from a Vietnam-like peace movement would compel Washington to desist. After watching the United States pull out of Lebanon without retaliating despite 241 casualties, Saddam Hussein seemed convinced that the United States, as powerful as it was, would lose its stomach for continuing the war. Iraq, therefore, if it did not lose, would—as Vietnam had done—win the war, even if it lost the individual battles.

As in his attack on Iran, in his invasion of Kuwait, Saddam Hussein had badly miscalculated. His forces were quickly routed in a display of force that was as stunning as it was probably unexpected. As General Colin Powell, the chairman of the Joint Chiefs of Staff, had put it when hostilities began: the strategy would be to isolate Iraqi forces in Kuwait and then "we would kill them." In an air war that lasted five weeks, allied air forces flew around the clock for over 100,000 sorties. In phase one, they took out all Iraqi command and control posts in order to prevent communications between the political and military leaders in Baghdad and the forces in the field; they also destroyed air fields and went after protected fighter planes. (Those that survived were flown to Iran!) In phase two, they destroyed bridges and roads to stop all supplies of food, water, and ammunition from reaching the Iraqi forces in Kuwait. In phase three, these forces, now cut off, were subject to constant pounding. Only in the final phase, did the ground forces launch their attack. Within 100 hours, they had surrounded the Iraqi forces and defeated them. Prisoners flocked in from the beginning of the ground assault; most were only too glad to surrender and get some food and water. The war had lasted forty-three days, and U.S. casualties were a miraculously low 130 dead in battle and 268 dead for the whole period. Only after suffering a defeat, did Saddam Hussein revoke his annexation of Kuwait.

The war, however, did not result in Saddam Hussein's removal from power. That had not been the UN's goal, and, had the United States marched on Baghdad, the coalition might have come apart. The Arabs wanted to end Saddam Hussein's threat to his neighbors, but they were against his overthrow, and Washington wanted no part of governing a nation in civil war. In the wake of Hussein's defeat, the Kurds and the Shi'ite Muslims, who constitute the majority of Iraq's population, rebelled against their ruler, a Sunni Muslim, but they were not strong enough against the remnants of Saddam Hussein's Republican Guard. True to his character, Hussein sought revenge as millions took refuge in Iran and Turkey and in the cold mountains on the Turkish border. Portrayed on television, the refugees' misery aroused international sympathy to such a degree that the United States and Britain felt compelled to send troops into northern Iraq and, disregarding the issue of Iraqi sovereignty, declared it a "safe haven" to protect the Kurds. Allied troops were later replaced by UN personnel, and Iraq was warned not to send its troops or aircraft into the area or they would be shot down. Despite Hussein's well-known brutality, however, Bush and the allies did not want to see Iraq disintegrate because they expected it to continue playing a role in the regional balance of power. They did not want all the surrounding countries, especially Iran, and to a lesser extent, Syria, to divide the country up in their own bids for regional hegemony.

A more serious problem, from the international perspective, is that Saddam Hussein did not obey the terms of the cease-fire agreement. He was supposed to cooperate with the UN in destroying his nuclear, chemical, and biological mass-destruction weapons and facilities as well as his missiles. But he tried to hide as many of the laboratories and weapons as possible from international inspectors. It took repeated U.S. threats to bomb to force compliance, but even these threats did not bring about full compliance. This was worrisome for it became clear that allied claims to have destroyed Iraqi nuclear and other facilities were exaggerated; defectors revealed the existence of nuclear facilities not previously known. It turned out that Iraq was much closer than previously believed to producing several atomic bombs and that it was also working on a hydrogen bomb. The war against Iraq had, in a sense, been a preventive war. It would be better to fight in 1991 than later when Iraq's ruthless dictator would have a nuclear arsenal.

But now it seemed that despite the victory in the war the potential threat would remain until Saddam Hussein and his regime were finished. The expectation that Saddam Hussein would soon be replaced by one of the military figures around him was false. The continuation of the economic sanctions, which the United States and Britain said they would maintain until Hussein was removed from power, was hurting the Iraqi people but not their ruler and his hand-picked associates, including the military. Only continued U.S. pressure was likely to help the UN inspectors gain full information on Iraq's weapons of mass destruction and make it possible to destroy them.

The Gulf war had some disappointing results, serving as a reminder that most wars have unintended consequences. The peace treaty at the end of World War I created the causes of World War II; that conflict produced the four decades of the cold war. But the Persian Gulf war also had some positive results. In the Middle East, it led to the opening of the first peace conference between Israel and the Arab states, with the Palestinians represented as part of the Jordanian delegation, in accordance with Israeli demands. While Israel had always refused to deal directly with the Palestine Liberation Organization (PLO), the West Bank Palestinians, tiring of the intifada and the PLO's past refusal to negotiate with Israel, asserted themselves in the wake of Iraq's defeat by agreeing to Israeli terms to limit negotiations to a three-year interim autonomy with no prior agreement on the ultimate status of the occupied territories. The PLO, which previously had wanted to talk only about the creation of a Palestinian state, had to accede. Its embrace of Saddam Hussein, and the Palestinians' cheering at the landing of SCUD missiles on Tel Aviv, had upset Israelis, even those who until then had argued that the Palestinians' legitimate grievances had to be taken into account. This had reinforced Israeli resolve not to deal with the PLO. But the PLO's stance had also alienated the

Arab Gulf regimes that had previously bankrolled it, as well as more moderate Arab states. The organization by its action, in short, largely isolated and weakened itself, even with the Palestinians who professed loyalty to it.

The fact that the conference could be organized at all was important. Undoubtedly, the Arab governments allied with the United States during the war pointed out that if the United States demonstrated that it was only interested in protecting Arab oil fields and remained unconcerned about solving Arab political grievances, their alignment would jeopardize them and make them vulnerable to the criticisms of anti-Western radicals and supporters of Saddam Hussein. These governments might ask: If the United States was opposed to Iraq's acquisition of territory by force, why was it not similarly opposed to Israel's? Thus, while the Palestinian problem was deferred by the war, the new military and strategic relationships the United States had forged with the Arab states was a major factor responsible for a new effort to resolve the Israeli-Palestinian differences, as well as Israeli-Arab ones.

Admittedly, the prospects for the conference, which was likely to be prolonged if it did not break down quickly, did not look promising. The U.S. position has long been one of trading land for peace, as in Israel's return of Sinai for peace with Egypt. Israel's governing Likud party had made peace with Egypt because without Egypt, the strongest Arab country, Syria and Jordan were too weak to make war. That, in turn, meant that the Arabs could do little but protest Likud's claim that the West Bank and Gaza were liberated rather than occupied territories and part of a historical Greater Israel. Israeli settlements would over time strengthen Israel's hold and claim. Even before the conference, the United States and Israel clashed over this issue. Israel asked the United States for a $10 billion loan guarantee to help it settle the incoming flood of Soviet immigrants. Washington, suspecting that the immigrants would not be discouraged from settling in the West Bank and other disputed territories, asked the Israelis to postpone the request until after the peace conference had started; it wanted to maximize its leverage and make sure first that the Israelis would attend and be in a conciliatory mood. The Israelis, realizing that if they were unwilling to be flexible and angered the United States, knew their bargaining capability would decline; they therefore wanted the money before the meeting.

Since the Nixon and Ford administrations, the U.S. position was that the Israeli settlements were illegal and obstacles to peace. The United States continued to send Israel billions of dollars of foreign aid anyway. The Israelis had come to take not only this aid for granted but also that Washington would assist Israel with additional funds in special situations. Bush was the first president who tried to use the money to change Israeli policy toward settlements in the occupied territories. He said that perhaps the United States would guarantee all or a part of the loan Israel wanted, but not right away. It was not the cost that was the issue, since Israel's record of paying back loans was unblemished. Bush was sending a message: U.S. assistance would no longer be unconditional. Each time Secretary Baker had visited Israel to arrange the peace conference, the Israelis had defiantly planted a new settlement.

Yet, when Bush decided that enough was enough, that the United States should not be expected year after year to help support Israel while it proceeded to pursue policies that Washington regarded as obstacles to peace, the Israeli government reacted furiously. It decided to challenge the president by going over his head to Congress, where in the past it had usually been successful. Unfortunately for the Israelis, the American public, in the midst of a recession, looked unfavorably at foreign aid, believing that U.S. money ought to be spent at home dealing with its domestic problems. Moreover, Americans were growing increasingly disenchanted with the Israeli government's policies. Given President Bush's political strength on foreign policy issues, Congress did not challenge the president. But this incident previewed trouble on a central issue. The Israeli government had declared that it would not trade land for peace, although a majority of Israeli public opinion favored such a trade; instead, its formula was "peace for peace."

Whether the United States could persuade all the parties to the peace conference to make the necessary compromises remains to be seen. While all the Arab states attended, Washington had no guarantees that they would offer reconciliation and security in return for Israeli concessions. No other state can, however, try to reconcile these long, bitter, and suspicious enemies. The American position was certainly unique. After the Soviet collapse, it was the only power left that had the political influence and military power to maintain some kind of international order. The test had been Iraq's aggression. The United States had to react not only because the immediate consequences of Saddam Hussein's acts were unacceptable, but because the post-cold-war's biggest security challenge was to create a safer and more peaceful world. But it was one thing to deal with aggression; an even more imposing challenge facing the great powers, and especially the United States, was whether they could create the basis of a more permanent peace in the Middle East, the world's most volatile and explosive area.

The Economy: Is the United States Following Britain Again?

It is ironic that at the very moment of victory in the cold war the American economy was deteriorating. The cost of the intervention in the Persian Gulf and higher oil prices could not have come at a worse time for the United States. Indeed, the war was the first major American military operation in which the United States sought a significant financial contribution from its allies, both for sustaining the military force in the Gulf and to assist Turkey, Egypt, and Jordan. These countries lost billions of dollars as a result of the oil and trade cut-offs and the ousted oil workers who would no longer be sending their paychecks home. Long before 1990, an economist looking at the size of the U.S. trade deficit had remarked that the United States would have to ask Japan's permission before it could fight another war. In fact, the contrast between the United States still playing its global role and seeking billions of dollars not only from Japan, but from other allies such as Germany and the oil kingdoms, was striking. Without their financial help, justified by the claim that Washington was protecting their interests as well, the country could not really afford this venture, given the weakened state of its economy.

The nation's twentieth-century role had been based on a once-vigorous economy that had helped win both world wars and created the highest standard of living in the world: a mass-production economy that built high-quality goods. Any product labeled "made in America" was sought all over the world. The United States did not depend on overseas markets for its economic health; it did not need to export much or to import many raw materials. Rich in resources, the nation's industry could provide the American consumer with abundant goods and create what in the 1950s was called the "affluent society." At the same time, it could sustain large-scale economic aid and rearmament plus two limited wars since 1945.

But even before the first shock of higher oil prices in 1973, the U.S. economy had been showing signs of weakness. By the late 1970s the rise in energy prices had demonstrated brutally and swiftly not only that the economy was vulnerable to external events but also that America's industries were unable to compete in the global economy. The flood of imports during the 1970s that so satisfied consumer demand had to be paid for; in the 1980s imports rose even more as the American consumer went on a binge of spending, largely on credit.

At the same time, unfair trading practices by other countries could not hide the weaknesses of industries ranging from the old smokestack factories to the latest high-tech products, including computers, microchips, robotics, and machine tools. America's farmers, who had been a mainstay in paying the nation's trade bills, suddenly found they were too productive in a world in which even the developing countries had learned the techniques of producing food. In addition, the lack of discipline in U.S. budget policy, as among consumers, added further grave damage to the economy. Ronald Reagan, America's most conservative president, who always called for balanced budgets, cut taxes while vastly increasing military spending, thereby creating the biggest deficits in U.S. history. High interest rates attracted foreign capital to cover the deficit but made it more expensive for Americans to invest in industry. The accompanying high dollar and the subsequent flood of cheaper imported goods produced a further decline of U.S. economic growth and investment. But the president refused to raise taxes, and Congress, led by the

Democrats, refused to accept deeper cuts in the social programs than the administration had already made. The country apparently was unconcerned, wanting both social spending and low taxes, while continuing to indulge in mass consumption and saving little for future investment. With tax increases seemingly unlikely, Social Security untouchable, and domestic spending cut about as much as was politically tolerable, the United States was strategically and financially overcommitted.

The story of the industrial economy was frighteningly reminiscent of Britain's economic history. In 1887 Britain assembled the world's most powerful fleet to celebrate Queen Victoria's Diamond Jubilee. It was an impressive demonstration of power: 21 battleships and 54 cruisers among the total of 154 warships. But underneath this show of raw military power, the economy, which had made all this possible, was already showing signs of rot. Britain, the first nation to industrialize, often could not hold its own against German and American goods, even in its home market. With a large imperial market to sustain it and unused to competition, British industry had grown complacent.

Germany and the United States, admittedly, were larger countries with bigger industries, and, in the course of time, Britain would have lost ground to them in world markets. But the decline of British industry was not inevitable and unavoidable. Having done so well for so long, British manufacturers saw no need to change traditional attitudes toward business management, production, labor relations, and salesmanship. These attitudes resulted in a lack of research and development and technological innovation; a low level of investment in new machinery, which was considered too expensive; an educational system that deemphasized science, technology, and business management; and cultural values that frowned on commerce and business, the very activities that had energized Britain earlier in the nineteenth century. British power declined as a consequence, and that was a major reason why the United States was drawn out of its long isolationist stance.

In the late 1980s some of the symptoms of Britain's economic decay were evident in the U.S. economy: underinvestment and overconsumption; outdated machinery; a neglected infrastructure, from roads and bridges to education; insufficient research and development, with too much of it going into military rather than economic needs; poor workmanship and a labor force not skilled enough in the post-mass-production information age; and poor management by bloated corporate bureaucracies that have not been receptive either to risk-taking or to innovation. Is American power therefore fated to decline as did Britain's? When Britain became aware of Germany's growing might and challenge, it formed alliances to supplement its military power and defend its global commitments. Specifically, it organized alliances with Japan and with two former rivals, czarist Russia and France. This devolution of military responsibility failed. Russia suffered a revolution in 1917, France was defeated in 1940, and Japan turned into an enemy.

German power was simply too great, but fortunately Britain could fall back on the United States. Starting in the 1970s, with the vast improvement in the West European and Japanese economies, the United States began urging its allies to take on a greater share of the defense burden as Soviet military power continued to grow and Soviet political influence spread in the Third World. At the same time, the United States sought regional allies, such as Iran in the 1960s and 1970s, and arrived at an accommodation with the People's Republic of China. But the U.S. effort to place some of its defense burden on NATO, Japan, and smaller allies failed. Upon whom could the United States shed some of its imperial burdens?

Until the Iraqi invasion of Kuwait, the Soviet collapse had made that question less relevant. Indeed, a "peace dividend" was expected to be realized by the savings in the defense budget as a result of scrapping or buying fewer certain strategic weapons systems, bringing back most of the troops from Europe, and cutting the size of U.S. forces. This, in turn, could help reduce the federal budget deficit and be used to invest in the many programs to prepare America for a world in which economic competition would presumably largely replace military competition; a world in which America's cold war allies and friends, especially Japan and the Pacific Rim countries, as well as a reinvigorated Europe with a thriving united Germany at its center, will be the nation's principal post-cold-war competitors. But defense budget reductions have not yet created substantial cuts.

No great power in history has been a debtor nation. The United States from World War I to the late 1980s was the world's leading creditor nation. But it started the 1990s as the world's largest debtor; its federal budget deficit is so huge that interest payments on it alone are larger—it is worth emphasizing—than all federal programs except defense and social security (ahead of education, welfare, roads, prisons, or environmental protection). Its trade surpluses for the first seventy years of this century have turned into trade deficits that simply will not go away (except with Europe, with whom the deficit has recently turned into a small surplus), even though the country remains the world's largest exporter. It has become the number-one host nation for foreign investments, giving foreigners controlling interests over U.S. industries. The American banking system is fragile, saddled with huge Third World debts that will never be repaid, and beset with a savings and loan crisis whose bailout will cost taxpayers several hundred billion dollars. And in this information age in which there is a premium on knowledge, especially of science and math, the nation has an educational system that, while spending more money per student than any country except Switzerland,[6] has a scandalous drop-out rate, producing functional illiterates and students who place among the lowest, if not the lowest, in the industrial world

---

6. Earl H. Fry, "Strategic Choices and Changes in the International Political Economy," *Naval War College Review* (Spring 1990): 31-52.

in subjects ranging from math and science to U.S. geography and history.[7] It will require political leadership of a high order to turn the economy around for the coming international economic rivalry and competition, and for the United States to remain in control of its own economic and political destiny.

The United States will be competing not only against Japan, but also against a rejuvenated Europe. While Japan opens an ever greater gap between itself and the United States in critical technologies of the future (after taking only twenty years to transfer the semiconductor industry across the Pacific), the twelve members of the European Community (EC) are beginning their final drive toward economic and political integration in 1992. In part, the reason for European unity is defense. As the cold war ends and Soviet troops withdraw from the center of Europe, the Europeans realize that U.S. troop strength will be further reduced and that they must assume a far greater role in its own defense. But, more important, if Europe is going to be competitive in the new post-cold-war world, it is imperative for it to unify its market of 350 million and to create mass production industries with greater investments in research and development. Indeed, because the EC has such potential, there is a long line of applicants. Poland, Hungary, and Czechoslovakia in the East have applied for associate membership and eventual full membership. The EC also has signed an agreement with additional West European states, members of the European Free Trade Association: Austria, Sweden, Finland, Liechtenstein, and Switzerland, all neutrals during the cold war, and Norway and Iceland, two NATO members. These countries will increase the population of the trading bloc to 380 million people (the first three have already applied for full EC membership). Thus the future may not lie along the Pacific Rim alone. But clearly, keen economic competition among Japan, the EC, and the United States will be the wave of the future.

The Fundamental Democratic Purpose of American Foreign Policy

It was the productivity and technological leadership of the U.S. economy that allowed the nation to wage the cold war and defend the cause of human freedom. In every war, hot or cold, the critical question is what are the contestants' political objectives? What would each like the world to look like at the end of the war? The principal American objective at the beginning of the cold war has usually been described as "security." To ensure it, the United States reestablished the balance of power in postwar Europe. But the balance is a means to an end. Washington's concern after the war, as before the two world wars, was not just the security of a piece of real estate called

---

7. Tamara Henry, "Report: Schools Waste Money," *Gainesville Sun,* May 14, 1990.

America; it was the security of a *democratic* America.

The United States could not survive as a lone democratic island surrounded by totalitarian seas, as President Roosevelt once put it. American democratic values could flourish only in an environment in which other democratic states survived as well. That is why Washington's concern during the cold war—a conflict of power *and* ideologies—was to support the democracies, old and new, in Western Europe and Japan through alliances— and to support one state, Israel, that has no formal alliance with the United States (although, for all practical purposes, it might as well have).

Indeed, as the cases of West Germany, Italy, Austria, and Japan suggest, the expansion of American power and influence in the world is by and large associated with the promotion of democracy. Our World War II enemies, once dictatorial, are today stable, free societies. If one looks at the societies liberated by the Soviet Union during World War II, the contrast is striking. No East European country could, until Gorbachev, be described as a "free society"; past attempts to move toward greater freedom were squashed by the Soviet army in East Germany, Hungary, and Czechoslovakia, and by the Polish army in Poland. East Germany had to build a wall across Berlin and a barbed-wire fence along its entire border with West Germany to prevent its citizens from escaping. As South Vietnam was collapsing in 1975 before the advancing North Vietnamese armies, much of the population, as in East Germany earlier, "voted with its feet," moving southward. After the unification of Vietnam, thousands more risked their lives fleeing from their country in small boats, and many were drowned. And when Cuba allows its people to leave, they do so by the hundreds of thousands.

All fled *from* Communist rule. These flights were as close as these societies ever came to holding plebiscites. It was symbolic, too, that in the summer of 1989 when the prodemocracy movement in China was demonstrating in Beijing, the student leaders erected a "goddess of democracy" modeled after the Statue of Liberty. After the movement was violently crushed by the authorities, this goddess became the symbol for its sympathizers all over the world.

Admittedly, over four decades the United States acquired many dictatorial allies and friends, usually of right-wing coloration, which weakened Washington's democratic rationale and laid open its foreign policy to the charge of hypocrisy. The reason for this kind of alliance in the case of South Korea, for example, was that the security of another ally (Japan) required it. The United States therefore supported its regime for many years. Similarly in Europe, the desire for air and naval bases to strengthen NATO, composed of the principal remaining democracies in the world, led to the inclusion of Portugal as an ally and Spain as an associated power, at a time when both were governed by right-wing authoritarian regimes. It is, of course, preferable to have democratic allies, but this is not always possible in a world in which most states are not democratic. Security and democracy occasionally are bound to appear as conflicting values. Which value is to be given priority is a difficult, often agonizing choice. If in the name of security a democracy indiscriminately picks up a large number of dictatorial allies to enhance its power, to acquire strategic position, or to play off one country against another, it may indeed corrupt its purposes. If in the name of democracy it refuses to align itself with any undemocratic regimes to keep its hands clean, it may remain pure but weaken itself against its principal adversary. In the real world, a democracy must at times sup with a dictatorship, be it of the right or left, although when it does so it needs to eat with a long spoon.

The question is not whether a democracy should ever ally itself with an undemocratic government or come to its rescue if it sees that its *own* security is involved—as, for instance, Britain did when it went to the rescue of an undemocratic Poland attacked by Nazi Germany in 1939, or Britain and the United States when they were allied with the Soviet Union against Hitler, or the United States when it sought to bolster undemocratic Turkey and Greece against perceived expansionist pressures from the Soviet Union in 1947—but how often, for what purposes, for how long, and at what level of commitment such an association should be forged. On these issues, honest men and women can and do differ vigorously. In the absence of war, it cannot be proved that America's relations with Portugal and Spain, for example, contributed to the prevention of hostilities and therefore to the protection of Western Europe. Perhaps the peace could have been kept without them and we need not have stained our cause. Perhaps the United States could have achieved its diplomatic objective of restraining the Soviet Union even without aligning itself with Tito's Yugoslav dictatorship after 1948 or, after 1972, with the regime in China.

In any event, given the democratic nature of American society, the pros and cons of aligning with right- or left-wing despotisms tend to be debated so that the tradeoffs between the values of democracy and security become clear, even if disagreements remain about the exact mix that policy should reflect. The pressure not to sacrifice democratic values on the altar of security, at least not in a permanent alliance, stems from the fact that America is a democratic society. This means first of all that the nation's leaders are products of American values and are committed to them. In addition, the watchfulness of Congress, the press, and private human rights groups constrains the ability of administration officials to align themselves with authoritarian regimes and then to look the other way when gross violations of basic human rights occur. This is not to say that such things do not happen; only that the pluralism of U.S. society and the institutional system of checks and balances constrain political leaders from abusing their power or disregarding their nation's fundamental beliefs and values more than in any other society. Pressure from Congress and the press on El Salvador and the Philippines, for example, compelled the executive branch to concern itself with democratic reforms in these two countries.

It is worth remembering that a fair number of America's authoritarian allies and friends, such as in Portugal and Spain (and many of their "children" in Latin America and the Philippines) as well as in Greece, have collapsed, been overthrown, or have begun to evolve in a more democratic direction. It is also worth a final reminder that the reformers who opposed U.S.-supported right-wing regimes often turned out to be left-wing revolutionaries who, once they did gain power, were at least as insensitive to democratic values and individual freedom as their American-supported predecessors had been. Indeed, usually they were more so. Fidel Castro and Ho Chi Minh may have portrayed themselves as more humanitarian and democratic than the leaders they overthrew. But once in power, their suppression of the values they claimed to represent was efficient and total.

In any event, the principal thrust of American policy since World War II, as before the war, has remained the preservation of a balance of power that would safeguard democratic values in the United States and other basically democratic countries. Indeed, this has been a consistent policy since World War I, whether the threat came from the expansionism of the right or of the left. American policy makers in the twentieth century have opposed both types of regimes, for they threatened not just U.S. security but also, more broadly, the international environment in which democratic values could prosper. And this was the crux of American opposition to the Soviet Union: that its great power constituted a threat to Western values and Western-style open societies. For communism, as reflected in the organization of pre-Gorbachev Communist societies, was the antithesis of societies that believe in individual freedoms, whether of speech or religion, in free party competition and genuine political choice, and in a distinction between state and society. It was America's counterbalancing power that protected democratic values. Without that power, Soviet power and the Soviet Union's social values and order would have prevailed. Freedom in the world since 1945 has been intimately tied to American power. As former secretary of state Henry Kissinger once succinctly expressed it, "If we do not lead, no other nation that stands for what we believe in can take our place."

That is the reason human rights remains a central issue, and why the greater respect for and observance of such rights in both Communist and non-Communist societies is important. The United States, as the leading democratic power in the world, sought a post-cold-war world in which its values would be the wave of the future. It was with the spread of freedom to Eastern Europe and the beginnings of a more open society in the Soviet Union that the cold war ended. More important, *the United States, in being true to its democratic tradition, has made the world safer for democracy as the twentieth century draws to a close.* The basic condition for freedom has been the defeat of the two major forces—fascism and communism—that threatened that freedom and had the power and the will to implement that threat. The end of the cold war is witness not only to the end of the Soviet challenge but also to the defeat of the second totalitarian challenge to Western-style democracy in this century.

The Nazis will forever be identified with the concentration camps of Auschwitz, Bergen-Belsen, and Treblinka, where they systematically murdered millions of people, including 6 million Jews, and the unleashing of World War II which, before it was over, cost the lives of 17 million soldiers and 34 million civilians. Just as the Nazi system was epitomized by Hitler, the Soviet system remains identified with Stalin and his cruel collectivization of the Soviet peasantry, the deliberate starvation of the Ukrainian peasants in the early 1930s, and the purges and other crimes that claimed the lives, conservatively estimated, of 20 million people and imprisoned and deported 20 million more. Stalin, not Hitler, was the great mass murderer in history; he also was in power twice as long.[8] Thus, while the "decommunization" of Eastern Europe and the retrenchment of Soviet power are to be celebrated, the defeat of the two regimes that have been the greatest suppressors of human rights has global significance.

The U.S. victory in the cold war coincides with its own economic woes, and the country needs its own *perestroika*, but the nation still has reason to be proud of its overall record. During the forty-five-year cold war in which it was the leader of the Western coalition, there was no nuclear war, Soviet expansionist ambitions were checked, and democracy flourished while the United States preserved and revitalized its own democratic traditions and guarded those of its allies in Western Europe. Surely, this record testifies to the fundamentally correct policy of firm opposition to the Soviet Union and the power of democratic ideas in the conduct of American foreign policy. The United States has also avoided treating its former enemies, Germany and Japan, in a vengeful manner; indeed, it helped them back on their feet economically and welcomed them into the Western alliance of democratic nations. Similarly, after winning the cold war, it refused to gloat, seeking instead to attract the Soviet Union, or its successor state, as a partner in the creation of a more secure Europe and a post-cold-war international order. All in all, not a bad record.

---

8. Robert Conquest, *The Great Terror* (New York: Oxford University Press, 1990).

Appendix A

U.S. Alliances in Europe and Asia

Alliance	Dates	Membership
NATO (15 members)	1949-	Belgium, Britain, Canada, Denmark, France, Greece, Iceland, Italy, Luxembourg, Netherlands, Norway, Portugal, Turkey, United States, West Germany
ANZUS [1] (3 members)	1951-	Australia, New Zealand, United States
Philippine Treaty (2 members)	1951-	Philippines, United States
Japanese Treaty (2 members)	1951-	Japan, United States
Republic of Korea (2 members)	1953-	South Korea, United States
Republic of China (2 members)	1954-1978	Taiwan, United States
SEATO (8 members)	1954-1975	Australia, Britain, France, New Zealand, Pakistan, Philippines, Thailand, United States
METO (later CENTO minus Iraq), 1955-1979. (Initially 6, later 5, members if the United States is counted, although not a full-fledged member)		Britain (chief sponsor of this alliance), Iran, Iraq (until it pulled out after 1958 overthrow of monarchy), Pakistan, Turkey, United States

Note: The United States also has alliances in all but name with Israel, Egypt, and Saudi Arabia. Although no treaties of defense exist, long commitments and/or continued strategic or economic interests have made these countries virtual allies, as the 1990 Iraqi crisis was to dramatically show for the two Arab states.

[1] The United States suspended the alliance in 1986 because of New Zealand's banning of visits by nuclear-powered and nuclear-armed ships. The United States stated that it therefore no longer felt obligated to come to New Zealand's defense.

Soviet Alliances in Europe and Asia

Alliance	Dates	Membership
Sino-Soviet (2 members)	1949-1979	PRC, Soviet Union (expired 1980)
Warsaw Pact[2] (7 members)	1955-1991	Bulgaria, Czechoslovakia, East Germany,[3] Hungary, Poland, Romania, Soviet Union

Note: The Soviet Union has signed a number of treaties of friendship and cooperation: India (1971), Iraq (1972), Egypt (1971, abrogated in 1976), Somalia (1974, abrogated in 1977), Angola (1976), Mozambique (1977), Ethiopia (1978), Afghanistan (1978), Vietnam (1978), South Yemen (1979), Syria (1980), and the Congo (1981). Although Moscow emphasized that the purpose of the treaties was consultation, the implication was that they involved defense commitments; the aim was to deter the United States from any actions against these nations.

[2] The Soviet Union had signed bilateral alliances with Czechoslovakia, Poland, Romania, Hungary, and Bulgaria in the 1940s.

[3] East Germany withdrew in 1990 to become part of a reunited Germany.

Appendix B

Selected Principal Events

1945   The Yalta Conference seeks to organize postwar world.
World War II with Germany ends.
World War II with Japan ends after two atomic bombs are dropped.
President Franklin Roosevelt dies.
Vice President Harry Truman succeeds.
United Nations is established.
Soviet military forces occupy Poland, Romania, Bulgaria, Hungary, and Czechoslovakia.

1946   United States confronts the Soviet Union over Iran, and Moscow withdraws its troops.
Winston Churchill, Britain's wartime prime minister, delivers "iron curtain" speech at Fulton, Missouri, warning of Soviet threat.

1947   Truman Doctrine commits the United States to assist Greece and Turkey.
Plan for the economic recovery of Western Europe is devised by Secretary of State George Marshall, formerly U.S. chief of staff and architect of victory during World War II.
George Kennan, a Foreign Service officer, provides the government with the analysis that becomes the basis of the containment policy of Soviet Russia.
India becomes independent.

1948   Soviet coup d'état takes place in Czechoslovakia.
Soviets blockade all ground traffic from West Germany to West Berlin and the Western airlift starts.
Vandenberg resolution of U.S. Senate commits American support for the Brussels Pact of self-defense.
Marshall Plan is passed by Congress.
North and South Korea are established.
The state of Israel is established and receives immediate U.S. recognition.
Truman wins upset election.
Stalin expels Yugoslavia's Tito from Communist bloc.

1949   North Atlantic Treaty Organization (NATO) is formed.
Soviet Union ends Berlin blockade.
East and West Germany are established.
Soviet Union explodes atomic bomb.
Nationalist China collapses and Communist China is established.
U.S. troops are withdrawn from South Korea.
Truman announces Point Four foreign aid program for developing countries.

1950   Soviet Union and Communist China sign thirty-year treaty of mutual assistance.

North Korea attacks South Korea by crossing the thirty-eighth parallel.
United States intervenes on behalf of South Korea.
Communist China intervenes after U.S. forces advance into North Korea toward China's frontier.
Senator Joseph McCarthy begins his attacks on government for treason and "coddling communism."

1951 General Dwight Eisenhower is appointed Supreme Allied Commander in Europe and Truman sends U.S. forces to Europe.
U.S.-Japanese mutual security pact is signed.
Truman fires General Douglas MacArthur in Korea for proposing that the United States attack Communist China.
European Coal and Steel Community (ECSC) is formed.

1952 Eisenhower is elected president.
Greece and Turkey join NATO.
Britain tests its first atomic weapon.

1953 Joseph Stalin dies.
Armistice negotiated along thirty-eighth parallel in Korea.
Soviet Union intervenes in East Germany to quell revolt.

1954 United States explodes first hydrogen bomb.
France is defeated at Dienbienphu in Indochina.
United States threatens to intervene in Indochina.
Vietnam is partitioned at the seventeenth parallel at the Geneva Conference.
Southeast Asia Treaty Organization (SEATO) is formed.
U.S.-Korean pact is signed to prevent a renewal of the war.
U.S.-Nationalist China defense treaty is signed.
Central Intelligence Agency overthrows Guatemala's left-wing government.

1955 Communist China shells the Nationalist Chinese (Taiwanese) islands of Quemoy and Matsu.
The Formosa resolution authorizes Eisenhower to use force, if necessary, to protect Taiwan against a possible Communist Chinese invasion.
Middle East Treaty Organization (Baghdad Pact) is formed.
West Germany joins NATO, and Soviets establish "their NATO," called the Warsaw Treaty Organization.

1956 United States withdraws offer to help finance Egypt's Aswan High Dam.
Egypt nationalizes the Suez Canal.
Suez War breaks out after Israel attacks Egypt, and France and Britain intervene.
UN forces are sent to Egypt to keep the peace between Israel and Egypt.
Soviets suppress Hungarian revolt and almost intervene in Poland.
Soviet leader Nikita Khrushchev attacks Stalin at twentieth Communist Party Congress.

1957 Soviet Union tests intercontinental ballistic missile (ICBM).
Soviets launch two Sputniks, or satellites, into space.
British test hydrogen bomb.

Eisenhower Doctrine commits the United States to assist Middle East countries that resist Communist aggression or states closely tied to the Soviet Union, such as Egypt.

1958   United States lands marines in Lebanon, and Britain lands paratroopers in Jordan after Iraqi revolution.

Soviet Union declares it would end the four-power occupation of Berlin and turn West Berlin into a "free city."

The European Economic Community (the Common Market) is established.

First of several Berlin crises erupts.

Communist China shells Quemoy and Matsu again.

1959   Khrushchev visits Eisenhower for Camp David meeting over Berlin issue.

Fidel Castro seizes power in Cuba.

Central Treaty Organization (CENTO) replaces the Baghdad Pact.

1960   Soviets shoot down U.S. U-2 spy plane over the Soviet Union.

Paris summit conference collapses over U-2 incident.

The Congo becomes independent from Belgium, causing the first superpower crisis in sub-Saharan Africa.

UN forces sent to the Congo to help resolve the crisis.

France becomes an atomic power.

John Kennedy wins presidential election.

1961   Kennedy launches abortive Bay of Pigs invasion of Cuba.

Kennedy proposes Alliance for Progress for Latin America.

Soviets send Yuri Gagarin into orbital spaceflight.

Kennedy holds summit conference with Khrushchev in Vienna.

Kennedy sends first military advisers to South Vietnam.

Soviets build Berlin Wall.

1962   U.S. sends John Glenn into orbital spaceflight.

In Cuban Missile Crisis, the United States blockades Cuba to compel the Soviets to withdraw their missiles.

Chinese-Indian frontier conflict erupts.

1963   French president Charles de Gaulle vetoes Britain's entry into the Common Market.

"Hot line" established between the White House and the Kremlin for direct emergency communications.

Atomic test-ban treaty is signed.

Kennedy is assassinated and Lyndon Johnson succeeds him.

1964   Congress passes Gulf of Tonkin resolution, raising the U.S. commitment to the defense of South Vietnam.

Khrushchev falls from power and is replaced by Prime Minister Aleksei Kosygin and Communist Party Secretary Leonid Brezhnev.

1965   United States starts bombing North Vietnam and sends American land forces into South Vietnam.

Protests against the war start.

United States intervenes in the Dominican Republic.
War erupts between Pakistan and India.

1966   People's Republic of China becomes a nuclear power.
France withdraws its forces from NATO's integrated command structure but remains a member of the alliance.

1967   Six-day War between Israel and its Arab neighbors takes place.
Greek colonels seize power in Greece.

1968   Tet offensive in South Vietnam escalates demand for U.S. withdrawal from Vietnam.
Johnson withdraws from presidential race.
Richard Nixon elected president.
Vietnamese peace talks begin in Paris.
Nuclear Non-Proliferation Treaty is made.
Soviet Union intervenes in Czechoslovakia to quell revolt.

1969   Brezhnev Doctrine is proclaimed asserting the right of Soviet Union to intervene in Soviet sphere to suppress "counterrevolution."
ABM deployment is narrowly voted by Senate.
United States tests MIRV.
SALT talks start.
"Vietnamization" program starts. South Vietnamese are to do more of the fighting while the United States begins troop withdrawal.
Ho Chi Minh dies.
United States lands men on moon.
Lt. William Calley, Jr., stands trial for My Lai massacre of civilians in South Vietnam by U.S. troops.
First of several Sino-Soviet border clashes occurs.

1970   West Germany, East Germany, the Soviet Union and Poland conclude treaties recognizing Poland's western border and acknowledging Germany's division into East and West Germany.
Senate repeals Gulf of Tonkin resolution.
U.S. invasion of Cambodia causes widespread student protests, which escalate after National Guard kills four students at Kent State University.
Chile elects a Marxist, Salvador Allende, president.

1971   India and Pakistan go to war over the Bangladesh (East Pakistan) secession effort.
PRC joins the United Nations.
Four-power Berlin settlement is reached ensuring Western access to Berlin.

1972   Nixon visits Communist China, beginning a process of normalizing relations after two decades of hostility.
North Vietnam invades South Vietnam.
Nixon retaliates by expanding air war against North Vietnam and blockading the harbor of Haiphong.
Nixon visits Moscow for summit conference with Soviet leaders, signs Strategic Arms Limitation Treaty (SALT I) and ABM treaty.

Watergate affair starts with police arrest of five men who had broken into
Democratic party headquarters.

Soviets buy enormous quantities of U.S. grains, raising U.S. domestic
prices.

Paris peace talks, close to success, break down, and the United States
bombs North Vietnam heavily during Christmas season.

Nixon reelected president in a landslide that carried every state but
Massachusetts.

1973   Henry Kissinger is appointed secretary of state while remaining the
president's national security adviser.

Vietnamese peace agreement is signed.

United States and China establish liaison offices, or informal embassies, in
Washington and Beijing.

Yom Kippur War breaks out in Middle East.

Arab members of the Organization of Petroleum Exporting Countries
embargo oil to the United States because of U.S. support for Israel.

Britain, Denmark, and Republic of Ireland join Common Market,
increasing membership to nine countries.

OPEC quadruples oil prices.

U.S.-Soviet Mutual and Balanced Force Reductions talks in Europe start.

West and East Germany exchange recognition and ambassadors, acknowledging Germany's division into two countries.

Congress passes the War Powers Resolution over Nixon's veto.

Vice President Spiro Agnew resigns and Gerald Ford succeeds him.

Allende is overthrown by military in Chile.

1974   India explodes "peaceful" nuclear device.

Congress asserts right to veto large arms sales to other nations.

Annual Nixon-Brezhnev summit conference further reduces small
numbers of ABMs the United States and Soviet Union are
allowed by SALT I.

Kissinger negotiates first agreements between Israel and Egypt and Syria
as part of his "step-by-step" diplomacy intended to achieve a comprehensive regional peace.

Nixon visits Egypt, Syria, and Israel.

Nixon resigns and Ford becomes unelected president; New York governor
Nelson Rockefeller becomes vice president.

Ford and Brezhnev set Vladivostok guidelines for SALT II negotiations.

1975   Soviet Union rejects American-Soviet trade agreement because of the
Jackson-Vanik amendment.

South Vietnam collapses and a unified Communist Vietnam is established.

Cambodia falls to Cambodian Communists.

Cambodians seize U.S. merchantship *Mayaguez,* and the United States
reacts forcefully to free crew and ship.

SEATO dissolves itself.

Helsinki agreements, including Western recognition of Europe's division
(and Soviet domination in Eastern Europe), arrived at by Western and
Eastern states.

Congress passes arms embargo against Turkey.

Lebanese civil war erupts.

Francisco Franco dies and King Juan Carlos starts to lead Spain to democracy.

In Angola three major factions struggle for control as Portugal grants independence.

1976   Soviet-Cuban forces in Angola win victory for Marxist-led faction over pro-Western factions.

Syrian forces intervene in Lebanon.

Mao Zedong dies.

Jimmy Carter elected president.

1977   Carter announces U.S. withdrawal from South Korea (to be reversed later).

Carter sends letter to leading Soviet dissident, and another dissident visits the White House.

Soviets denounce Carter's human rights campaign as violation of Soviet sovereignty.

Carter submits new SALT II plan to Soviet Union, which quickly rejects it because it is not based on Vladivostok guidelines.

Carter halts plans to produce B-1 bomber and instead chooses to deploy air-launched cruise missiles on B-52 bombers.

United States and Panama sign Panama Canal treaties.

Somalia expels Soviet advisers and denounces friendship treaty with Soviet Union.

Soviet-Cuban military help for Ethiopia grows.

Menachem Begin is elected prime minister in Israel.

Egyptian president Anwar Sadat pays historic visit to Israel, offering peace and friendship. Other Arab states denounce him.

1978   Soviet-Cuban military intervention in Ethiopia's war against Somalia forces latter out of Ogaden.

Soviet-inspired coup occurs in Afghanistan.

Camp David meeting of the United States, Israel, and Egypt arrives at "framework for peace" between two former enemies. Other Arab states denounce framework because it did not provide for a Palestine solution.

Senate approves sale of jet fighters to Israel, Egypt, and Saudi Arabia.

Panama Canal treaties approved by Senate.

Carter postpones neutron bomb (tactical warhead) production.

United States ends arms embargo on Turkey.

Shah leaves Iran.

Rhodesian prime minister Ian Smith announces "internal solution" to the race problem—the formation of a black-led government.

1979   United States officially recognizes the People's Republic of China (PRC). It also breaks ties with government on Taiwan as official government of China and ends mutual defense treaty.

China briefly invades Vietnam to punish it for the invasion of Cambodia in 1978, which overthrew a regime friendly to China and replaced it with a pro-Soviet and pro-Vietnamese one.

Shah's regime in Iran replaced by Islamic republic led by Ayatollah Ruhollah Khomeini.

U.S. Embassy in Tehran seized and employees held hostage by militant Islamic students after shah is hospitalized in United States for cancer treatment.

United States freezes Iran's financial assets in United States and boycotts Iranian oil.

Oil prices shoot upward as Iranian oil production drops and world supplies tighten.

SALT II Treaty signed by Brezhnev and Carter at Vienna summit conference.

Soviets send 80,000 troops into Afghanistan to ensure survival of pro-Soviet regime.

NATO decides to deploy 572 theater nuclear weapons to counter Soviet "Eurostrategic" missile buildup.

1980   U.S. mission to rescue hostages in Tehran ends in disaster before it reaches embassy.

SALT II "temporarily" withdrawn from Senate by Carter after Soviet invasion of Afghanistan.

Carter embargoes shipments of feed grain and high technology and declares United States will boycott summer Olympic games in Moscow.

Carter Doctrine commits United States to security of Persian Gulf oil-producing states if they are externally threatened.

United States organizes Rapid Deployment Force to back up the Carter Doctrine.

Iraq attacks Iran.

Ronald Reagan elected president.

1981   U.S. hostages released moments after Reagan assumes presidency.

AWACS deal with Saudi Arabia is approved by Senate.

Reagan declares United States will not allow Saudi Arabia to become "another Iran."

Begin reelected in Israel.

Sadat assassinated in Egypt.

Reagan decides on large program to rebuild U.S. military power, including 100 MX missiles and 100 B-1 bombers.

Polish government imposes martial law.

United States imposes economic sanctions on Poland and on Soviet Union, believed to be behind Polish crackdown.

1982   Reagan announces economic assistance plan for Caribbean Basin (the Caribbean and Central America) as he supports El Salvador's government against rebel forces and attempts to isolate the Sandinistas in Nicaragua despite congressional criticism.

Israel invades Lebanon, attempting to destroy the PLO.

U.S. marines are sent into Beirut as part of a multinational peace-keeping force to supervise the PLO's leaving.

China and the United States sign agreement on the reduction of U.S. arms sales to Taiwan.

Brezhnev dies and is succeeded by Yuri Andropov, former head of the Soviet secret police.

Argentina invades the British Falkland Islands, long claimed by Argentina. Britain reconquers the islands.

United States imposes—and later, lifts—sanctions on U.S. and European companies selling equipment to the Soviets for building of a natural gas pipeline to Western Europe.

Secretary of State Alexander Haig resigns.

1983   Reagan denounces the Soviet Union as an "evil empire."

Bipartisan Scowcroft Commission recommends deployment of 100 MX missiles and eventual replacement of missiles equipped with MIRVs with mobile, smaller missiles with single warheads. Congress accepts these recommendations.

Catholic bishops in pastoral letter deplore nuclear deterrence for its immorality. French bishops endorse deterrence as "service to peace."

Two hundred forty-one marines killed in suicide truck-bomb attack on their barracks in Beirut.

Soviet Union shoots down Korean 747 jetliner with 269 passengers aboard after it strayed into Soviet airspace.

U.S. forces, together with troops from six Caribbean states, invade the island of Grenada. They depose the Marxist government, return Cuban worker-soldiers to Cuba, and withdraw.

United States begins deployment of Pershing II and ground-launched cruise missiles in Europe. Soviet Union responds by breaking off all arms control talks.

1984   Bipartisan Kissinger Commission recommends extensive economic and military assistance to Central America to combat domestic poverty and Soviet-Cuban intervention. Congress critical of administration policy.

Andropov dies and Brezhnev's confidant, Konstantin Chernenko, succeeds him.

Reagan is reelected.

United States pulls marines out of Lebanon.

Napoleón Duarte wins Salvadoran presidency, defeating right-wing candidate.

Congress cuts off all military assistance to the *contras* in Nicaragua.

Latin American debtor countries meet at Cartagena to discuss the debt problem and repayment.

United States declares Iran a supporter of international terrorism.

1985   Chernenko dies and is succeeded by Mikhail Gorbachev.

Africa, especially Ethiopia, which is engaged in a civil war, suffers from widespread starvation.

Christian Democratic party, led by Duarte, wins majority in Salvadoran National Assembly.

Various terrorist groups hijack a TWA plane flying from Athens to Rome, seize an Italian cruise ship, and attack Israel's El Al passengers at the Vienna and Rome airports.

Reagan orders limited economic sanctions against South Africa; Congress imposes harsher sanctions in 1986.

Reagan and Gorbachev hold their first summit conference in Geneva, Switzerland.

1986   Ferdinand Marcos and Jean-Claude Duvalier are forced to flee their respective countries, and the Reagan administration proclaims its new human rights policy, opposing dictatorships of the left and right.

Congress approves $100 million for the Nicaraguan *contras.*

The United States attacks Libya for terrorist acts. Syria is shown to be involved in terrorism, and Britain breaks diplomatic relations with Syria after abortive attempt to blow up Israeli airliner.

World's worst nuclear accident takes place at Chernobyl in the Ukraine. Sweden breaks news of radioactivity coming from the Soviet Union.

Reagan and Gorbachev meet in Iceland, and Reagan refuses to trade limitations in SDI research for deep cuts of Soviet strategic missiles and a mutual elimination of all intermediate-range missiles in Europe.

United States exceeds SALT II limits and declares that the unratified 1979 treaty is no longer "operational."

Iran-*contra* scandal breaks.

OPEC's oil price falls to $9 to $10 a barrel, but then stabilizes at $18 a barrel.

Spain and Portugal join the European Economic Community.

U.S. dollar is allowed to drop substantially against Japanese yen and West German mark to improve U.S. exports and reduce huge trade deficit, but action proves ineffective.

1987   Congressional hearings into Iran-*contra* scandal raise doubts about Reagan's effectiveness for the remainder of his term.

The United States and the Soviet Union agree to a worldwide ban on short- and intermediate-range missiles, the so-called double zero option, ending years of tension over Soviet SS-20 missile deployment.

The United States reflags Kuwaiti oil tankers in the Persian Gulf and escorts them with U.S. warships to protect them from possible Iranian attacks.

Five Central American presidents devise a plan for peace in their area. The *contras* and Sandinistas are to negotiate an end to the civil war, and the Sandinista government commits itself to hold general election by spring 1990.

Palestinians in December begin the *intifada,* or uprising, protesting both the continued Israeli occupation of the West Bank and opposition to a Palestinian state, and, more indirectly, the PLO failure to seek a diplomatic solution.

Gorbachev at the seventieth anniversary celebration of Bolshevik Revolution denounces Stalin's historical legacy and defends his program of *perestroika.*

1988   George Bush elected president.

Gorbachev, at first national party conference since 1941, proposes to restructure Soviet government with strong presidency, selected by a more popularly responsive Supreme Soviet.

United States Navy shoots down Iranian commercial jetliner with 290 people aboard over Persian Gulf.

Iran and Iraq agree to a cease-fire in their eight-year-long war.

Panama's strongman, General Manuel Noriega, is indicted for drug running by two Florida grand juries.

The right-wing Arena party wins majority in Salvadoran Legislative Assembly.

PLO and Yasir Arafat declare the right of all states in the region to live in peace with secure boundaries: proclaim a Palestinian state in the West Bank and the Gaza strip; recognize Israel; and reject terrorism.

The Soviet Baltic republics assert their desire for autonomy, if not independence; ethnic clashes in the southern Soviet Union between Azerbaijanis and Armenians lead to increasing violence.

Gorbachev makes dramatic announcement at UN of unilateral military reductions, including sizable cuts in troop levels and tanks (50,000 and 1,000 respectively), and other offensive weapons of the forces facing NATO.

1989   Gorbachev elected president of the Soviet Union, an alternative base of power to the Communist party.

The Baltic republics push for independence; ethnic violence erupts in Georgia; hundreds of thousands of coalminers strike, setting the Soviet economy even further back.

Free elections in Poland result in the overwhelming repudiation of the Polish Communist party. Solidarity forms the first non-Communist-led government in Poland and Eastern Europe.

Hungary allows emigration to the West; tens of thousands of East Germans flee via Hungary to West Germany. Mass demonstrations in East Germany protest regime celebrating its fortieth year; cabinet resigns. Hard-line Communist party leaders are replaced, and, on November 9, the Berlin Wall is opened by the new government, which restores the people's right of emigration.

The Hungarian Communist party changes its name to Hungarian Socialist party, and the parliament drops the word "People's" from the Republic of Hungary.

Czechoslovakia and Bulgaria follow the reformist path of Poland, Hungary, and East Germany. Only in Romania does government resist and use force, but its leader Nicolae Ceausescu is nevertheless overthrown and executed.

CFE (Central Front Europe) negotiations begin in Vienna to reduce Warsaw Pact and NATO forces to equal ceilings, generally requiring larger Soviet cuts of manpower and weapons.

Soviets announce that differences over SDI should not stand in the way of an agreement in the Strategic Arms Reduction Talks (START), although Moscow expected the United States not to violate the 1972 Anti-Ballistic Missile (ABM) treaty.

Soviet Union withdraws its troops from Afghanistan, although the pro-Soviet government there survives. The foreign minister declares that the 1979 intervention in Afghanistan "violated the norms of proper behavior."

Gorbachev in neutral Finland states that the Soviet Union has no moral or political right to interfere in the affairs of its neighbors. It and the other Warsaw Pact states that intervened in Czechoslovakia in 1968 apologize to the Czechs. Together with the Soviet noninterference, which allowed the changes in Eastern Europe to occur, this declaration is tantamount to a repudiation of the Brezhnev Doctrine.

President Bush tours Poland and Hungary to show U.S. support of the democratization and de-Sovietization in Eastern Europe. But because of the huge U.S. budget deficit, he can offer only limited financial assistance. Western Europe, especially West Germany, offers larger sums.

Bush and Gorbachev meet off the island of Malta in the Mediterranean and state that they hope that by the June 1990 summit in Washington the two countries will achieve major arms control agreements in both conventional and strategic arms.

On the way to Malta, Gorbachev meets the pope in Rome, a first for a leader of an avowedly atheistic movement.

The Ayatollah Khomeini dies in Iran.

Huge prodemocracy demonstrations take place in Beijing. The Communist leadership violently suppresses the demonstrations.

In El Salvador the right-wing ARENA party candidate wins the presidency. Guerrillas launch attack in the capital.

Opposition candidate wins Panamanian presidential election; General Noriega voids the result. Coup led by Panamanian officers fails. Noriega declares Panama to be in "a state of war" with the United States. Bush orders military intervention. Noriega surrenders and is brought to the United States for trial.

Five Central American presidents agree to close *contra* camps. The Nicaraguan government agrees to hold an election by early 1990.

Cuban troops begin withdrawal from Angola under Angolan-Cuban-South African agreement under which Namibia is to achieve its independence.

1990   Lithuanian Communist party breaks from the Soviet party and becomes spokesman for independent Lithuania.

Armenians and Azerbaijanis continue their ancient feud while the local Communist party loses control to the Azerbaijani popular front. Gorbachev sends in the army to restore order and keep the party in power.

Gorbachev, in a revolutionary statement to a plenum of the Communist party, renounces the constitutionally guaranteed Communist monopoly of power and declares his support for an eventual multiparty system as well as the private ownership of the "means of production," repudiating Marx as well.

Eastern European free elections in the spring produce non-Communist governments, except in Romania and Bulgaria, where the Communists, under a new name, win by large majorities.

After the East German election in March, East and West Germany begin negotiating reunification. On July 1, they create a financial and economic union. Two weeks later, Gorbachev agrees that a reunited Germany can choose to join NATO. On October 3, the two Germanies unify. In November, the Conference on Security and Cooperation in Europe endorses Germany's unity. On December 2, elections in both Germanies produce the first postwar all-German parliament.

The Soviet Union's two largest republics, Russia and the Ukraine, declare their sovereignty and assert that their laws are superior to those of the Soviet Union. Other republics follow.

In Nicaragua the Sandinistas risk a free election and lose badly. The *contras* disband.

1991   January 1, 1991, an all-German parliament and government are sworn in.

Iraq, refusing to withdraw from Kuwait, is forced out in forty-three days by the U.S.-led UN coalition. Iraqi forces were defeated by five weeks of devastating air attacks followed by a mopping-up operation on land.

Saddam Hussein seeks to evade the cease-fire terms requiring him to disclose the whereabouts of Iraqi missiles, as well as all biological, chemical, and nuclear facilities, to UN inspectors so that they may be destroyed. President Bush threatens renewed air attacks, causing Iraq to provide UN inspectors more information.

The United States and the Soviet Union sign a START agreement, reducing strategic weapons by 30 percent, although cutting the most destabilizing Soviet missiles by 50 percent. Agreement followed conventional arms reductions between NATO and the Warsaw Treaty Organization (WTO).

The WTO formally dissolves itself. Soviet troops leave Hungary and Czechoslovakia. (They are scheduled to leave Poland by late 1992 and what used to be East Germany by 1994.)

Boris Yeltsin, Gorbachev's rival, becomes the first elected leader of the 1,000-year-old Russian republic.

A coup against Gorbachev is launched by conservative party elements. Yeltsin defies the coup attempt and it fails. Gorbachev survives but his authority declines further as Yeltsin establishes his primacy among Soviet leaders.

Estonia, Latvia, and Lithuania are granted independence and plans for a new federation collapse as the republics too seek independence from Moscow. As the old Soviet Union disappears, it remains unclear what will take its place.

The Western industrial nations consider a Marshall Plan for the Soviet Union.

After efforts to establish a confederation founder due to bickering over sovereignty and fear of a revival of the central government, Russia, Byelorussia, and Ukraine declare the Soviet Union officially dead and form a Commonwealth of Independent States. Other republics are invited to join.

The European Free Trade Association, consisting of Austria, Switzerland, Sweden, Finland, Liechtenstein (neutrals during the cold war), and Norway and Iceland (NATO members), establish a common free trade area with the EC.

Poland, Hungary, and Czeckoslavakia are granted associate status in the EC, giving them access to the free trade area by the end of the century.

Selected Bibliography

Most of the entries in this bibliography are books. Readers who wish to keep up with contemporary foreign and defense policies will find the articles in *Foreign Affairs, Foreign Policy,* and *International Security* useful and relevant. This is especially so for *Foreign Affairs'* annual *America and the World.*

American Society and Style in Foreign Policy

Almond, Gabriel A. *The American People and Foreign Policy.** New York: Praeger Publishers, 1960.

Boorstin, Daniel J. *The Genius of American Politics.** Chicago: Phoenix Books, 1953.

Crabb, Cecil V. *Policy Makers and Critics.** New York: Praeger Publishers, 1976.

Dallek, Robert. *The American Style of Foreign Policy.* New York: Alfred A. Knopf, 1983.

Hartz, Louis. *The Liberal Tradition in America.** New York: Harvest Books, 1955.

Herberg, Will. *Protestant, Catholic, and Jew.* Rev. ed.* New York: Anchor Books, 1960.

Hofstadter, Richard. *The Paranoid Style in American Politics.** New York: Vintage Books, 1967.

Kennan, George F. *American Diplomacy 1900-1950.** Chicago: University of Chicago Press, 1951.

Krasner, Stephen D. *Defending the National Interest.** Princeton: Princeton University Press, 1978.

Morgenthau, Hans J. *In Defense of the National Interest.* New York: Alfred A. Knopf, 1951.

Osgood, Robert. *Ideals and Self-Interest in America's Foreign Relations.* Chicago: University of Chicago Press, 1953.

Packenham, Robert A. *Liberal America and the Third World.** Princeton: Princeton University Press, 1973.

Potter, David M. *The People of Plenty.** Chicago: Phoenix Books, 1954.

---

* Asterisked titles are available in paperback editions.

American Foreign Policy

Allison, Graham T. *Essence of Decision.* Boston: Little, Brown, 1971.

Aron, Raymond. *The Imperial Republic.** Cambridge, Mass.: Winthrop, 1974.

Bell, Coral. *The Diplomacy of Détente.* New York: St. Martin's, 1977.

Bowker, Mike, and Phil Williams. *Superpower Détente.* Newbury Park, Calif.: Sage Publications, 1988.

Brzezinski, Zbigniew. *Game Plan.* Boston: Atlantic Monthly Press, 1986.

Clemens, Diane S. *Yalta.* New York: Oxford University Press, 1970.

Draper, Theodore, et al. *Defending America.* New York: Basic Books, 1978.

Dukes, Paul. *The Last Great Game.* New York: St. Martin's, 1989.

Fleming, D. F. *The Cold War and Its Origins, 1917-1960,* 2 vols. Garden City, N.Y.: Doubleday, 1961.

Fulbright, J. William. *Old Myths and New Realities.** New York: Vintage Books, 1964.

_____. *The Arrogance of Power.** New York: Vintage Books, 1967.

_____. *The Crippled Giant.** New York: Vintage Books, 1972.

Gaddis, John L. *The United States and the Origins of the Cold War, 1941-1947.** New York: Columbia University Press, 1972.

_____. *Russia, the Soviet Union and the United States.** New York: John Wiley & Sons, 1978.

_____. *Strategies of Containment.** New York: Oxford University Press, 1982.

_____. *The Long Peace.** New York: Oxford University Press, 1987.

Gati, Charles, ed. *Caging the Bear.* New York: Bobbs-Merrill, 1974.

George, Alexander, ed. *Managing U.S.-Soviet Rivalry.** Boulder: Westview Press, 1983.

Gilbert, Felix. *To the Farewell Address.* Princeton: Princeton University Press, 1961.

Halle, Louis J. *The Cold War as History.** New York: Harper & Row, 1967.

Harbutt, Fraser J. *The Iron Curtain.* New York: Oxford University Press, 1986.

Hilsman, Roger. *To Move a Nation.* Garden City, N.Y.: Doubleday, 1967.

Hoffmann, Stanley. *Primacy or World Order.* New York: McGraw-Hill, 1978.

Hyland, William G. *The Cold War is Over.* New York: Times Books, 1990.

Kennan, George F. *American Diplomacy, 1900-1950.** New York: Mentor Books, 1952.

_____. *Memoirs.* Boston: Little, Brown, 1967.

_____. *The Clouds of Danger.** Boston: Atlantic/Little, Brown, 1977.

Kuniholm, Bruce R. *The Origins of the Cold War in the Near East.* Princeton: Princeton University Press, 1980.

Larson, Deborah Welch. *Origins of Containment.* Princeton: Princeton University Press, 1985.

McNamara, Robert S. *Out of the Cold.* New York: Simon and Schuster, 1989.

Mandelbaum, Richard, and Strobe Talbott. *Reagan and Gorbachev.** New York: Vintage Books, 1987.

May, Ernest R. *Lessons of the Past.** New York: Oxford University Press, 1973.

Muravchik, Joshua. *The Uncertain Crusade.* New York: Hamilton Press, 1985.

Osgood, Robert, et al. *America & the World.** Baltimore: Johns Hopkins University Press, 1970.

_____. *Retreat from Empire?** Baltimore: Johns Hopkins University Press, 1973.

Rosenau, James N., and Ole R. Holsti. *American Leadership in World Affairs.** Boston: Allen & Unwin, 1984 (see also *International Studies Quarterly,* December 1986).

Sainsberry, Keith. *The Turning Point.* New York: Oxford University Press, 1985.

Schlesinger, Arthur, Jr. *The Imperial Presidency.** Boston: Houghton Mifflin, 1973.

Smith, Gaddis. *Morality, Reason, and Power.* New York: Hill & Wang, 1986.
Steel, Ronald. *Pax Americana.** New York: Viking Press, 1967.
Talbott, Strobe. *The Russians and Reagan.** New York: Vintage Books, 1984.
Tucker, Robert W. *The Purposes of American Power.** New York: Praeger
Publishers, 1981.
Wildavsky, Aaron, ed. *Beyond Containment.* San Francisco: Institute for Contempo-
rary Studies, 1983.
Wilmot, Chester. *The Struggle for Europe.* New York: Hayes & Brothers, 1952.
Yergin, Daniel. *Shattered Peace.** Boston: Houghton Mifflin, 1977.

Revisionist or New Left Histories

Alperovitz, Gar. *Atomic Diplomacy.** New York: Vintage Books, 1967.
Barnet, Richard. *Roots of War.** New York: Atheneum, 1972.
Kolko, Gabriel. *The Roots of American Foreign Policy.** Boston: Beacon Press, 1969.
Kolko, Gabriel, and Joyce Kolko. *The Limits of Power.** New York: Harper & Row,
1972.
La Feber, Walter. *America, Russia, and the Cold War 1945-1980.** New York: John
Wiley & Sons, 1981.
Oglesby, Carl, and Richard Schaull. *Containment and Change.** New York:
Macmillan, 1967.
Paterson, Thomas G. *Soviet-American Confrontation.* Baltimore: Johns Hopkins
University Press, 1973.
_____. *On Every Front.** New York: W. W. Norton, 1979.
_____, ed. *Kennedy's Quest for Victory.** New York: Oxford University Press, 1989.
Sherry, Michael. *Preparing for the Next War.* New Haven: Yale University Press,
1977.
Williams, William Appleman. *The Tragedy of American Diplomacy.* Rev. 2d ed.
New York: Delta, 1972.

Critical Evaluations of New Left Histories

Maddox, Robert J. *The New Left and the Origins of the Cold War.* Princeton, N.J.:
Princeton University Press, 1973.
Richardson, J. L. "Cold War Revisionism: A Critique," *World Politics,* July 1972,
579-612.
Schlesinger, Arthur, Jr. "The Origins of the Cold War," *Foreign Affairs,* October
1962, 22-52.
Tucker, Robert W. *The Radical Left and American Foreign Policy.** Baltimore:
Johns Hopkins University Press, 1971.

American Military Policy

Abel, Elie. *The Missile Crisis.** New York: Bantam Books, 1966.
Blechman, Barry M., and Stephen S. Kaplan. *Force Without War.** Washington,
D.C.: Brookings Institution, 1978.
Blight, James G., and David A. Welch. *On the Brink.* New York: Hill & Wang,
1989.
Brown, Harold. *The Strategic Defense Initiative.* Boulder: Westview Press, 1987.
Bundy, McGeorge. *Danger and Survival.** New York: Random House, 1988.
Carnesdale, Albert, and Richard N. Haass, eds. *Superpower Arms Control.**
Cambridge, Mass.: Ballinger, 1987.

422   *Selected Bibliography*

Dinerstein, Herbert. *The Making of a Missile Crisis.** Baltimore: Johns Hopkins University Press, 1976.
Epstein, William. *The Last Chance.* New York: Free Press, 1976.
Freedman, Lawrence. *The Evolution of Nuclear Strategy.** 2d ed. New York: St. Martin's, 1989.
George, Alexander L. *The Limits of Coercive Diplomacy.** Boston: Little, Brown, 1971.
George, Alexander L., and Richard Smoke. *Deterrence in American Foreign Policy.** New York: Columbia University Press, 1974.
George, Alexander L., Philip J. Farley, and Alexander Dallin. *U.S.-Soviet Security Cooperation.** New York: Oxford University Press, 1988.
Gompert, David, Michael Mandelbaum, Richard Garwin, and John Barton. *Nuclear Weapons and World Politics.** New York: McGraw-Hill (for the Council on Foreign Relations, 1980s Project), 1977.
Gray, Colin. *The Soviet-American Arms Race.* Lexington, Mass.: Lexington Books, 1976.
Harvard Nuclear Study Group. *Living with Nuclear Weapons.* Cambridge: Harvard University Press, 1983.
Herken, Gregg. *Counsels of War.** Expanded ed. New York: Oxford University Press, 1987.
Horelick, Arnold L., and Myron Rush. *Strategic Power and Soviet Foreign Policy.* Chicago: University of Chicago Press, 1966.
Jervis, Robert. *The Meaning of the Nuclear Revolution.** Ithaca: Cornell University Press, 1989.
Kahan, Jerome H. *Security in the Nuclear Age.** Washington, D.C.: Brookings Institution, 1975.
Kissinger, Henry A. *Nuclear Weapons and Foreign Policy.** New York: Harper & Brothers, 1957.
_____. *The Necessity for Choice.** New York: Anchor Books, 1961.
_____. *The Troubled Partnership.** New York: Anchor Books, 1966.
Krepon, Michael. *Strategic Stalemate.* New York: St. Martin's, 1984.
_____. *Arms Control in the Reagan Administration.* Lanham, Md.: University Press of America, 1989.
Levine, Robert A. *Still the Arms Debate.* Brookfield, Vt.: Dartmouth Publishing, 1990.
Lakoff, Sanford, and Herbert F. York. *A Shield in Space?* Berkeley and Los Angeles: University of California Press, 1989.
McNamara, Robert S. *Blundering into Disaster.** New York: Parthenon Books, 1987.
Mueller, John. *Retreat From Doomsday.** New York: Basic Books, 1989.
Newhouse, John. *Cold Dawn.* New York: Holt, Rinehart and Winston, 1973.
Payne, Keith P. *Strategic Defense.* Lanham, Md.: Hamilton Press, 1986.
Scoville, Herbert, Jr. *MX.** Cambridge: MIT Press, 1981.
Smoke, Richard. *National Security and the Nuclear Dilemma.* 2d ed. New York: Random House, 1987.
Stares, Paul B. *The Militarization of Space.* Ithaca: Cornell University Press, 1985.
Talbott, Strobe. *End Game.* New York: Harper & Row, 1980.
_____. *The Master of the Game.** New York: Knopf, 1988.
Thayer, Charles W. *Guerrilla.** New York: New American Library, 1963.
Tirman, John, ed. *The Fallacy of Star Wars.* New York: Vintage Books, 1984.
Tucker, Robert W. *The Nuclear Debate.* New York: Holmes & Meier, 1985.
Wolfe, Thomas W. *The SALT Experience.* Cambridge, Mass.: Ballinger, 1979.

American Policy in Postwar Europe

Barnet, Richard J. *The Alliance—America, Europe, Japan.* New York: Simon & Schuster, 1983.
Calleo, David P. *Europe's Future.** New York: W. W. Norton, 1967.
_____. *The Atlantic Fantasy.* Baltimore: Johns Hopkins University Press, 1970.
_____. *Beyond American Hegemony.** New York: Basic Books, 1987.
Cook, Don. *Forging the Alliance.* New York, Arbor House. 1989.
De Porte, A. W. *Europe Between the Superpowers.** New Haven: Yale University Press, 1985.
Flanagan, Stephen J., and Fen O. Hampton, eds. *Securing Europe's Future.* Dover, Mass.: Auburn House, 1986.
Gelb, Norman. *The Berlin Wall.* New York: Times Books, 1987.
Goldsmith, Walter, ed. *Reagan's Leadership and the Atlantic Alliance.* New York: Pergamon-Brassey's, 1987.
Grosser, Alfred. *The Western Alliance.* New York: Vintage Books, 1982.
Hanreider, Wolfram E. *Germany, America, Europe.* New Haven: Yale University Press, 1989.
Hoffmann, Stanley. *Gulliver's Troubles, or the Setting of American Foreign Policy.** New York: McGraw-Hill, 1968.
Holborn, Hajo. *The Political Collapse of Europe.* New York: Alfred A. Knopf, 1951.
Joffe, Josef. *The Limited Partnership.* Cambridge, Mass.: Ballinger, 1987.
Jones, Joseph. *The Fifteen Weeks.* New York: Viking Press, 1955.
Kleiman, Robert. *Atlantic Crisis.** New York: W. W. Norton, 1964.
Krauss, Melvyn. *How NATO Weakens the West.* New York: Simon & Schuster, 1986.
Mally, Gerhard. *Interdependence.* Lexington, Mass.: Lexington Books, 1976.
Mander, John. *Berlin, Hostage for the West.** Baltimore: Penguin Books, 1962.
Newhouse, John, ed. *U.S. Troops in Europe.** Washington, D.C.: Brookings Institution, 1971.
Osgood, Robert E. *NATO.* Chicago: University of Chicago Press, 1962.
Pierre, Andrew J., ed. *Nuclear Weapons in Europe.** New York: Council on Foreign Relations, 1984.
Pipes, Richard, ed. *Soviet Strategy in Europe.* New York: Crane, Russak, 1976.
Speier, Hans. *Divided Berlin.* New York: Praeger Publishers, 1961.
Steel, Ronald. *The End of Alliance.** New York: Delta Books, 1966.
Talbott, Strobe. *Deadly Gambits.** New York: Alfred A. Knopf, 1984.
Treverton, Gregory F. *Making the Alliance Work.* Ithaca: Cornell University Press, 1986.
Tucker, Robert W., and Linda Wrigley. *The Atlantic Alliance and Its Critics.** New York: Praeger Publishers, 1983.
Wyden, Peter. *The Wall.* New York: Simon and Schuster, 1989.

American Policy in Asia

Barnett, A. Doak. *China Policy.** Washington, D.C.: Brookings Institution, 1977.
_____. *China and the Major Powers in East Asia.** Washington, D.C.: Brookings Institution, 1977.
Berman, Larry. *Lyndon Johnson's War.* New York: W. W. Norton, 1989.
Clough, Ralph N. *East Asia and U.S. Security.** Washington, D.C.: Brookings Institution, 1975.
Clubb, O. Edmund. *China and Russia.** New York: Columbia University Press, 1971.

Cohen, Warren I. *America's Response to China.* 3d ed.* New York: Columbia University Press, 1989.

Cumings, Bruce. *The Origins of the Korean War.* Princeton: Princeton University Press, 1981.

Dulles, Foster R. *American Foreign Policy Toward Communist China.** New York: Crowell, 1972.

Fall, Bernard B. *The Two Viet-Nams.* 2d rev. ed. New York: Praeger Publishers, 1967.

Feis, Herbert. *China Tangle.** Princeton: Princeton University Press, 1953.

Gelb, Leslie, et al. *The Pentagon Papers.** New York: Bantam Books, 1971.

Gelb, Leslie, and Richard K. Betts. *The Irony of Vietnam.** Washington, D.C.: Brookings Institution, 1979.

Gurtov, Melvin. *The First Vietnam Crisis.** New York: Columbia University Press, 1967.

Halberstam, David. *The Best and the Brightest.** New York: Random House, 1969.

Hammer, Ellen J. *The Struggle for Indochina, 1940-1955.** Stanford: Stanford University Press, 1966.

Herring, George C. *America's Longest War.* 2d ed.* New York, John Wiley & Sons, 1988.

Hinton, Harold C. *Three and a Half Powers.** Bloomington: Indiana University Press, 1975.

Hoopes, Townsend. *The Limits of Intervention.** New York: McKay, 1969.

Karnow, Stanley C. *Vietnam.* New York: Viking Press, 1983.

Kim, Samuel S., ed. *China and the World.* Boulder: Westview Press, 1984.

Lake, Anthony, ed. *The Vietnam Legacy.* New York: New York University Press, 1976.

Lewy, Guenter. *America in Vietnam.** New York: Oxford University Press, 1978.

Lomperis, Timothy J. *The War Everybody Lost—and Won.** Washington, D.C.: CQ Press, 1987.

Meisner, Maurice. *Mao's China.* New York: Free Press, 1977.

Merrill, John. *Korea.* Newark, N.J.: University of Delaware Press, 1989.

Oksenberg, Michel, and Robert Oxnam, eds. *Dragon and Eagle.* New York: Basic Books, 1978.

Schell, Orville. *To Get Rich Is Glorious.* New York: Pantheon, 1984.

Sheehan, Neil. *A Bright Shining Lie.* New York: Random House, 1988.

Spanier, John W. *The Truman-MacArthur Controversy and the Korean War.* Rev. ed.* New York: W. W. Norton, 1965.

Sutter, Robert. *Chinese Foreign Policy After the Cultural Revolution.* Boulder: Westview Press, 1978.

Thompson, Sir Robert. *No Exit from Vietnam.* New York: McKay, 1969.

Thompson, W. Scott, ed. *The Third World.* Rev. ed. San Francisco: Institute for Contemporary Studies, 1983.

Tsou, Tang. *America's Failure in China, 1941-1950,* 2 vols.* Chicago: Phoenix Books, 1963.

American Policy in the Middle East-Persian Gulf

"America in Captivity: Points of Decision in the Hostage Crisis," *New York Times Magazine,* May 17, 1981.

Bill, James A. *The Eagle and the Lion.** New Haven: Yale University Press, 1988.

Cohen, Roger, and Claudio Gati. *In The Eyes of the Storm.* New York: Farrar, Straus and Giroux, 1991.

Cottam, Richard W. *Iran and the United States.** Pittsburgh: University of Pittsburgh Press, 1988.
Doran, Charles, *Myth, Oil and Politics.* New York: Free Press, 1977.
Golan, Galia. *Yom Kippur and After.* New York: Cambridge University Press, 1977.
Miller, Judith, and Lauria Mylroie. *Saddam Hussein and the Crisis in the Gulf.* New York: Times Books, 1990.
Quandt, William. *Saudi Arabia in the 1980s.** Washington, D.C.: Brookings Institution, 1981.
_____. *Camp David.* Washington, D.C.: Brookings Institution, 1986.
_____, ed. *The Middle East.* Washington, D.C.: Brookings Institution, 1988.
Roger, Louis, and Owen Roger, eds. *Suez 1956.* New York: Oxford, 1989.
Sadat, Anwar. *In Search of Identity.* New York: Harper & Row, 1978.
Safran, Nadav. *Israel: The Embattled Ally.** Cambridge: Harvard University Press, 1978.
_____. *Saudi Arabia: The Ceaseless Quest for Security.* Cambridge: Harvard University Press, 1985.
Schiff, Ze'ev, and Ehud Ya'ari (ed. and trans. Ina Friedman). *Israel's Lebanon War.* New York: Simon & Schuster, 1984.
_____. (ed. and trans. Ina Friedman). *Intifada.* New York: Simon & Schuster, 1989.
Shipler, David K. *Arab and Jew.* New York: Times Books, 1986.
Sick, Gary. *All Fall Down.* New York: Penguin Books, 1986.
Spiegel, Steven L. *The Other Arab-Israeli Conflict.* Chicago: University of Chicago Press, 1985.
Woodward, Bob. *The Commanders.* New York: Simon & Schuster, 1991.
Wright, Robin. *Sacred Rage: The Crusade of Modern Islam.* New York: Touchstone, 1986.

American Policy in Africa and Latin America

Bender, Gerald, James Coleman, and Richard Sklar, eds. *African Crisis Areas and U.S. Foreign Policy.* Berkeley and Los Angeles: University of California Press, 1985.
Blasier, Cole. *The Giant's Rival: The U.S.S.R. and Latin America.** Rev. ed. Pittsburgh: University of Pittsburgh Press, 1988.
_____. *The Hovering Giant.** Rev. ed. Pittsburgh: University of Pittsburgh Press, 1985.
Christian, Shirley. *Nicaragua: Revolution in the Family.* New York: Random House, 1985.
Dinges, John. *Our Man in Panama.* New York: Random House, 1990.
Domínguez, Jorge I. *To Make a World Safe for Revolution.* Cambridge, Mass.: Harvard University Press, 1989.
Duncan, W. Raymond. *The Soviet Union and Cuba.* New York: Praeger Publishers, 1985.
Erisman, H. Michael. *Cuba's International Relations.* Boulder: Westview Press, 1985.
La Feber, Walter. *The Panama Canal: The Crisis in Historical Perspective.** New York: Oxford University Press, 1978.
_____. *Inevitable Revolutions: The United States in Central America.* New York: W. W. Norton, 1983.
Lake, Anthony. *The "Tar Baby" Option.* New York: Columbia University Press, 1976.
_____. *Somoza Falling.* Boston: Houghton Mifflin, 1989.

426   Selected Bibliography

Leiken, Robert S., ed. *Central America*. New York: Pergamon Press, 1984.
Lemarchand, René, ed. *American Policy in Southern Africa*. Washington, D.C.: University Press of America, 1978.
Lowenthal, Abraham F. *Partners in Conflict.** Baltimore: Johns Hopkins University Press, 1987.
Pastor, Robert A. *Condemned to Repetition.** Princeton: Princeton University Press, 1987.
Rabe, Stephen G. *Eisenhower and Latin America.** Chapel Hill: University of North Carolina Press, 1988.
Schraeder, Peter J. *Intervention in the 1980s.** Boulder: Lynne Rienner Publishers, 1989.
Shafer, Michael D. *Deadly Paradigms*. Princeton: Princeton University Press, 1988.
Sigmund, Paul. *The Overthrow of Allende and the Politics of Chile*. Pittsburgh: University of Pittsburgh, 1977.
Suchliki, Jaime. *Cuba*. New York: Brassey's, 1990.

The International Political Economy, Trade and Interdependence

Atlantic Council Working Group on the U.S. and the Developing Countries. *The United States and the Developing Countries*. Boulder: Westview Press, 1977.
Baldwin, David A. *Economic Statecraft*. Princeton: Princeton University Press, 1985.
Bhagwati, Jagdish, ed. *The New International Economic Order*. Cambridge: MIT Press, 1977.
Blake, David, and Robert Walters. *The Politics of Economic Relations*. 3d ed.* Englewood Cliffs, N.J.: Prentice-Hall, 1987.
Brown, Harrison. *The Human Future Revisited*. New York: W. W. Norton, 1978.
Cohen, Benjamin J. *In Whose Interest?: International Banking and American Foreign Policy*. New Haven: Yale University Press, 1986.
Fishlow, Albert, Carlos Diaz-Alejandro, Richard Fagen, and Roger Hansen. *Rich and Poor Nations in the World Economy*. New York: McGraw-Hill (for the Council on Foreign Relations, 1980s Project), 1978.
Friedberg, Aaron L. *The Weary Titan.** Princeton: Princeton University Press, 1988.
Gilpin, Robert. *The Political Economy of International Relations.** Princeton: Princeton University Press, 1987.
Kennedy, Paul. *The Rise and Fall of the Great Powers.** New York: Random House, 1987.
Keohane, Robert O. *After Hegemony.** Princeton: Princeton University Press, 1984.
Keohane, Robert O., and Joseph Nye. *Power and Interdependence.** Boston: Little, Brown, 1977.
Krasner, Stephen D. *Structural Conflict*. Berkeley and Los Angeles: University of California Press, 1985.
Lewis, Arthur. *The Evolution of the International Economic Order.** Princeton: Princeton University Press, 1978.
Lewis, John P., and Valeriana Kallab, eds. *Development Strategies Reconsidered*. New Brunswick, N.J.: Transaction Books, 1986.
Morse, Edward. *Modernization and the Transformation of International Relations*. New York: Free Press, 1976.
Nye, Joseph S., Jr. *Bound to Lead*. New York: Basic Books, 1990.
Prestowitz, Clyde. *Trading Places.** New York: Basic Books, 1988.
Report of the Independent Commission on International Development Issues under the Chairmanship of Willy Brandt, *North-South: A Programme for Survival*.

Cambridge: MIT Press, 1980.
Rothstein, Robert. *The Weak in the World of the Strong.* New York: Columbia University Press, 1977.
Spero, Joan. *The Politics of International Economic Relations.* 4th ed.* New York: St. Martin's, 1990.
Thurow, Lester C. *The Zero-Sum Solution.* New York: Simon & Schuster, 1985.
Tucker, Robert. *Inequality of Nations.* New York: Basic Books, 1977.
Tulchin, Martin, and Susan Tulchin. *Buying into America.* New York: Times Books, 1988.
Vernon, Raymond, ed. *The Oil Crisis.** New York: W. W. Norton, 1976.
Vogel, Ezra. *Japan as Number One.* New York: Harper and Row, 1979.
Wriggins, Howard, and Gunnar Adler-Karlsson. *Reducing Global Inequities.* New York: McGraw-Hill (for the Council on Foreign Relations, 1980s Project), 1978.

Memoirs, Biographies, and Histories of American Statesmen, Soldiers and Administrations

Acheson, Dean. *Present at the Creation.* New York: W. W. Norton, 1969.
Ambrose, Stephen E. *Eisenhower.* 2 vols. New York: Simon & Schuster, 1983 and 1984.
Bell, Coral. *The Reagan Paradox.** New Brunswick, N.J.: Rutgers University Press, 1989.
Brown, Harold. *Thinking About National Security.* Boulder: Westview Press, 1983.
Brzezinski, Zbigniew. *Power and Principle.** New York: Farrar, Strauss & Giroux, 1983.
Bundy, McGeorge, ed. *The Pattern of Responsibility.* Boston: Houghton Mifflin, 1952.
_____. *Danger and Survival.* New York: Random House, 1988.
Burns, James MacGregor. *Roosevelt.* New York: Harcourt Brace Jovanovich, 1970.
Byrnes, James F. *Speaking Frankly.* New York: Harper & Brothers, 1947.
Cannon, Lou. *Reagan.* New York: Random House, 1981.
Carter, Jimmy. *Keeping Faith.* New York: Bantam Books, 1982.
Churchill, Winston S. *The Second World War.* 6 vols. Boston: Houghton Mifflin, 1948-1953.
Dallek, Robert. *Franklin D. Roosevelt and American Foreign Policy, 1932-1945.* New York: Oxford University Press, 1979.
Eisenhower, David. *Eisenhower at War.* New York: Random House, 1986.
Eisenhower, Dwight D. *Mandate for Change.** New York: New American Library, 1965.
_____. *Waging Peace.* New York: Doubleday, 1965.
Feis, Herbert. *Churchill, Roosevelt, Stalin.* Princeton: Princeton University Press, 1957.
Ferrell, Robert H. *George C. Marshall.* New York: Cooper Square Publishers, 1966.
Gerson, Louis. *John Foster Dulles.* New York: Cooper Square Publishers, 1967.
Guhin, Michael. *John Foster Dulles.* New York: Columbia University Press, 1972.
Haig, Alexander. *Caveat.* New York: Macmillan, 1984.
Harriman, W. Averell. *Special Envoy to Churchill and Stalin, 1941-1946.* New York: Random House, 1975.
Hoopes, Townsend. *The Devil and John Foster Dulles.** Boston: Atlantic/Little, Brown, 1975.
Isaacson, Walter, and Evan Thomas. *The Wise Men.* New York: Simon & Schuster, 1986.

Johnson, Lyndon B. *The Vantage Point.** New York: Popular Library, 1971.
Kalb, Marvin, and Bernard Kalb. *Kissinger.** Boston: Little, Brown, 1974.
Kearns, Doris. *Lyndon Johnson and the American Dream.** New York: Harper & Row, 1976.
Kennedy, Robert S. *Thirteen Days.** New York: W. W. Norton, 1971.
Kissinger, Henry A. *The White House Years.* Boston: Little, Brown, 1979.
———. *Years of Upheaval.* Boston: Little, Brown, 1982.
Manchester, William. *American Caesar.* Boston: Little, Brown, 1978.
Melanson, Richard A., ed. *Reevaluating Eisenhower.* Urbana-Champaign: University of Illinois Press, 1987.
McLellan, David S. *Cyrus Vance.* Totowa, N.J.: Rowman & Allanheld, 1985.
Nixon, Richard. *RN.* New York: Grosset & Dunlap, 1978.
———. *Seize the Moment.* New York: Simon & Schuster, 1992.
Parmet, Herbert S. *Eisenhower and the American Crusades.* New York: Macmillan, 1972.
Pogue, Forrest C. *George C. Marshall.* New York: Viking Press, 1987.
Rusk, Dean, as told to Richard Rusk. *As I Saw It.* New York: W. W. Norton, 1990.
Schlesinger, Arthur M., Jr. *A Thousand Days.** New York: Crest Books, 1967.
Schulzinger, Robert D. *Henry Kissinger.* New York: Columbia University Press, 1989.
Sherwood, Robert E. *Roosevelt and Hopkins.** New York: Harper, 1948.
Smith, Gaddis. *Dean Acheson.* New York: Cooper Square Publishers, 1972.
Sorensen, Theodore C. *Kennedy.** New York: Bantam Books, 1966.
Stoessinger, John. *Henry Kissinger.** New York: W. W. Norton, 1976.
Truman, Harry S. *Memoirs.* 2 vols.* New York: New American Library, 1965.
Vance, Cyrus. *Hard Choices.* New York: Simon & Schuster, 1982.

Soviet Foreign Policy

Adomeit, Hannes. *Soviet Risk-Taking and Crisis Behavior.** Boston: Allen & Unwin, 1982.
Bialer, Seweryn. *The Soviet Paradox.* New York: Alfred A. Knopf, 1986.
Bialer, Seweryn, and Michael Mandelbaum. *Gorbachev's Russia and American Foreign Policy.* Boulder: Westview Press, 1988.
———. *The Global Rivals.** New York: Knopf, 1988.
Brzezinski, Zbigniew. *The Grand Failure.* New York: Scribner's, 1989.
Byrnes, Robert F., ed. *After Brezhnev.** Bloomington: Indiana University Press, 1983.
Caldwell, Dan, ed. *Soviet International Behavior and U.S. Policy Options.* Lexington, Mass.: Lexington Books, 1985.
Colton, Timothy J. *The Dilemma of Reform in the Soviet Union.* New York: Council of Foreign Relations, 1986.
Dallin, Alexander. *Black Box.* Berkeley and Los Angeles: University of California Press, 1985.
Daniels, Robert V. *Russia, The Roots of Confrontation.* Cambridge: Harvard University Press, 1985.
Dibb, Paul. *The Soviet Union.* Urbana-Champaign: University of Illinois Press, 1986.
Dinerstein, Herbert S. *The Making of a Missile Crisis.* Baltimore: Johns Hopkins University Press, 1976.
Donaldson, Robert H., ed. *The Soviet Union in the Third World.* 2d ed. Boulder: Westview Press, 1984.
Duncan, W. Raymond, ed. *Soviet Policy in the Third World.* New York: Pergamon

Press, 1980.

Garthoff, Raymond L. *Détente and Confrontation.* Washington, D.C.: Brookings Institution, 1985.

Gati, Charles. *Hungary and the Soviet Bloc.* Durham, N.C.: Duke University Press, 1986.

———. *The Bloc That Failed.* Bloomington: Indiana University Press, 1990.

Goldman, Marshall I. *U.S.S.R. in Crisis.* New York: W. W. Norton, 1983.

———. *Economic Reform in the Age of High Technology.* New York: W. W. Norton, 1987.

———. *Gorbachev's Challenge.* New York: W. W. Norton, 1987.

Gorbachev, Mikhail. *Perestroika.* New York: Bessie/Harper & Row, 1987.

Gwertzman, Bernard, and Michael T. Kaufman, eds. *The Collapse of Communism.* New York: Times Books, 1990.

Hammond, Thomas T. *Red Flag Over Afghanistan.** Boulder: Westview Press, 1984.

Hough, Jerry. *The Struggle for the Third World.* Washington, D.C.: Brookings Institution, 1986.

Krickus, Richard J. *The Superpowers in Crisis.** New York: Pergamon-Brassey's, 1987.

Luttwak, Edward. *The Grand Strategy of the Soviet Union.** New York: St. Martin's, 1984.

MacFarlane, S. Neil. *Superpower Rivalry and Third World Radicalism.* Baltimore: Johns Hopkins University Press, 1985.

Mastny, Vojtech. *Russia's Road to the Cold War.* New York: Columbia University Press, 1979.

Nogee, Joseph L., and Robert H. Donaldson. *Soviet Foreign Policy since World War II.* 4th ed. New York: Pergamon Press, 1992.

Nye, Joseph S., Jr., ed. *The Making of America's Soviet Policy.* New Haven: Yale University Press, 1984.

Papp, Daniel S. *Soviet Policies Toward the Developing World During the 1980s.* Maxwell Air Force Base, Ala.: Air University Press, 1986.

Pipes, Richard. *Survival Is Not Enough.* New York: Simon & Schuster, 1984.

Rubinstein, Alvin Z. *Soviet Foreign Policy Since World War II.** 2d ed. Boston: Little, Brown, 1985.

———. *Moscow's Third World Strategy.* Princeton: Princeton University Press, 1988.

Rush, Myron. *Strategic Power and Soviet Foreign Policy.* Chicago: University of Chicago, 1966.

Saivetz, Carol R., and Sylvia Woodby. *Soviet-Third World Relations.* Boulder, Colo.: Westview Press, 1985.

Shelton, Judy. *The Coming Soviet Crash.* New York: Free Press, 1989.

Sherr, Alan B. *The Other Side of Arms Control.** Boston: Unwin Hyman, 1988.

Taubman, William. *Stalin's American Policy.* New York: W. W. Norton, 1982.

Valkenier, Elizabeth K. *The Soviet Union and the Third World.* New York: Praeger Publishers, 1984.

Index